Excel

PRELIMINARY

MATHEMATICS

LYN BAKER

PASCAL
PRESS

Reprinted 2003, 2004, 2006, 2008, 2009, 2010, 2012

ISBN 978 1 74020 255 8

Pascal Press
PO Box 250
Glebe NSW 2037
(02) 8585 4044
www.pascalpress.com.au

Publisher: Vivienne Joannou
Edited by May McCool
Typeset by Precision Typesetting (Barbara Nilsson)
Cover and page design by DiZign Pty Ltd
Printed by Green Giant Press

Students
All care has been taken in the preparation of this study guide, but please check with your teacher or the Board of Studies about the exact requirements of the course you are studying as they can change from year to year.

Contents

Introduction

This book covers all the topics from the **Preliminary (Year 11)** part of the Mathematics course. This preliminary work is important not only for study in Year 11 but many of the skills included here are essential knowledge for what follows in the HSC (Year 12) course. Some preliminary work will also be **tested in the HSC exa**m.

The chapters can be studied in any order, as each topic is a distinct unit. However, sometimes the skills in one topic may call upon those from another topic (eg the distance formula from the linear functions topic is used in locus problems in the real functions topic). You may, of course, study parts of a topic rather than complete the chapter as a complete unit.

- At the front of each unit a **checklist** of the skills required in order for you to have a thorough understanding of the topic is provided.
- Throughout the book certain **symbols** have been used.

  This indicates a hint or idea. It may be an easier way of doing something, or a suggestion to make it easier to remember a rule.

  This indicates something with which to be careful. It may explain a common mistake or highlight a trap that should be avoided.

  15 This number which appears beside an example is the question number of a corresponding exercise that is located at the end of the chapter.
- How to use the cross-referenced exercises and examples:
  - Using the question numbers for each example you can, if you wish, complete each question immediately after reading the example. The page reference to the relevant exercises is located at the bottom of every page for your convenience.
  - Alternatively, you can do all the exercises at once as a test of all the skills needed for a topic. If you have difficulty with a question, go back to the cross-referenced example in the chapter and work through it before you consult the worked solution at the back of the book.
- For each of the **seven topics** each required skill is outlined and any rule given. An explanation or proof is often provided as to why the rule is used. This is followed by examples of the types of questions which involve that particular skill. Each example is followed by a worked solution.

- After the units, **sample topic tests** are supplied to further test your knowledge. These are different from the exercises because they are mixed, often involve several parts and may require a little more thought. Each one can be completed as a test or simply used for extra revision. Again worked solutions and separate answers have been supplied at the back of the book.
- After the topic tests there are **three sample examination papers** covering all of the topics. These can be used at the end of Year 11 and throughout Year 12.
- **Worked solutions are provided for every question** in the study guide.
- The **answers are found in a separate Quick Answer section** at the back of the book.
- **Page numbers of the Quick Answers and Worked Solutions** to every question in the Exercises, Topic Tests and Sample Examination Papers are found at the bottom of the pages.

Tips for Success in Preliminary Mathematics

- The biggest help to you will be a thorough knowledge of the content of the course. Work through every topic several times until you feel that you genuinely understand all the concepts. Wherever possible, try to understand why a rule exists, rather than just remember it. Practice lots and lots of questions.
- Always know what to expect in any assessment task. Find out all the information that you can before the test begins. Exactly what will be tested? How much time will there be? How will marks be allocated? Will any special equipment be needed?
- Approved calculators, including graphics calculators, can be used. Any calculator will only be useful if you know how to use it. Make sure you know how to use *your* calculator.
- Whether doing a test, an assignment, classwork or just revision, always read questions carefully. Be sure that you are answering the question that has been asked. If you are not sure what is required, read the question again and again. It may become clear.
- Take care copying the question and between lines of working. A wrong sign, for example, might make an answer not only wrong but much more difficult. Always work neatly and set work out correctly. Only use '=' when the two parts are equal.
- Draw diagrams. In geometry and trigonometry particularly, always draw a diagram and put on all data. Draw clear diagrams of a reasonable size. In other instances, a quick sketch might make the solution to a question much clearer and quicker.
- Verify answers wherever possible. Check that the solution to an equation does satisfy the original equation. Always think about the relevance of an answer. Can an angle of a right-angled triangle be 106°? Can a salesperson earn more in commission than the total sales?
- Don't falsify work in an attempt to get the right answer. Marks are awarded for working and correct working is often more important that the answer.
- When doing a test always do the easy questions first. If there is something you cannot do, leave it and come back to it at the end. If you cannot do the first part of a question, you might still be able to do subsequent parts. If you can't "show that $x = y$" you may still use the fact that $x = y$ in answering the rest of the question.

If you work hard and are well-prepared you can feel confident that you will be able to do your best.

Good Luck!

Lyn Baker

B.A. Dip.Ed

1 Basic Arithmetic and Algebra

Your Checklist

For a complete understanding of this topic you must be able to:	✓
■ Understand what is meant by a rational number	
■ Add, subtract, multiply and divide fractions and decimals	
■ Convert between fractions, decimals and percentages	
■ Change repeating decimals to fractions	
■ Determine powers and roots of rational numbers	
■ Understand scientific notation	
■ Round off to a certain number of decimal places	
■ Understand significant figures	
■ Round off to a certain number of significant figures	
■ Evaluate expressions involving grouping symbols, powers, roots, fractions etc	
■ Add, subtract, multiply and simplify surds	
■ Divide surds by rationalising denominators	
■ Understand inequalities	
■ Understand absolute values	
■ Simplify algebraic expressions	
■ Remove grouping symbols and collect like terms	
■ Add, subtract, multiply and simplify algebraic expressions	
■ Substitute into an algebraic expression	
■ Solve problems arising from substitution	
■ Factorise (common factors, difference of two squares, factorising by grouping, trinomials, sum and difference of two cubes)	
■ Reduce, add and subtract, multiply and divide algebraic fractions	
■ Solve linear equations	
■ Solve inequalities [know when to reverse an inequality sign]	
■ Solve absolute value equations	
■ Graph solutions on a number line	
■ Solve quadratic equations	
■ Solve simultaneous equations	

1.1 Numbers

- An **integer** is a whole number (positive, negative or zero).
- A **rational number** is any number that can be expressed in the form $\frac{p}{q}$, where p and q are integers. All integers, fractions, and terminating or repeating decimals are rational.
- An **irrational number** cannot be expressed in the form $\frac{p}{q}$.

Examples of irrational numbers are any non-repeating, non-terminating decimals, π, and surds like $\sqrt{2}$ and $\sqrt{3}$.

> Many questions require an exact answer. This may be in the form of a fraction, surd, terminating or repeating decimal, or in terms of an irrational number (like 2π). It must not be a decimal approximation (as given by a calculator).

1.2 Fractions

> All of the questions shown in this section can easily be answered by simply using a calculator. However, it is important to understand the principles involved. You will need to be able to perform similar calculations with surds and with algebraic terms.

- The **numerator** is the top part of the fraction and the **denominator** is the bottom part.
- **Multiplying** both the numerator and denominator by the same number, or **dividing** both numerator and denominator by the same number, will produce an equivalent fraction. (i.e. the value of the fraction does not change.)
- **Adding to** (or **subtracting from**) both numerator and denominator, or raising both numerator and denominator to a power, will **not** produce an **equivalent fraction**.
- Answers should be given in **simplest form**. Simplify fractions by dividing both numerator and denominator by their highest common factor.

Q Express each fraction in simplest form: **1**

a $\frac{9}{15}$ b $\frac{20}{120}$

A a $\frac{9}{15}=\frac{3}{5}$ [dividing both numerator and denominator by 3]

b $\frac{20}{120}=\frac{1}{6}$ [dividing by 20, the largest common factor]

- A **mixed number** consists of a whole number part and a fractional part (e.g. $3\frac{4}{5}$).
- An **improper fraction** has its numerator greater than its denominator (e.g. $\frac{19}{5}$).
- To **add (or subtract) fractions**, we must have a common denominator. (Always look for the lowest common denominator.) If the denominators are the same, simply add (or subtract) the numerators.

Q Find: **2**

a $\frac{3}{8}+\frac{1}{8}$ b $\frac{4}{5}-\frac{1}{4}$

A a $\frac{3}{8}+\frac{1}{8}=\frac{4}{8}$
$=\frac{1}{2}$

b $\frac{4}{5}-\frac{1}{4}=\frac{16}{20}-\frac{5}{20}$
$=\frac{11}{20}$

- To **multiply fractions**, multiply the numerators and multiply the denominators. Cancelling can be done either before or after multiplying but only cancel a number in the numerator with one in the denominator.

Q Find: **3**

a $\frac{2}{3}\times\frac{4}{5}$ b $\frac{2}{3}\times\frac{9}{10}$

A a $\frac{2}{3}\times\frac{4}{5}=\frac{8}{15}$

b $\frac{2}{3}\times\frac{9}{10}=\frac{18}{30}$ or $\frac{\cancel{2}^1}{\cancel{3}_1}\times\frac{\cancel{9}^3}{\cancel{10}_5}=\frac{3}{5}$
$=\frac{3}{5}$

- The **reciprocal of a fraction** is the number (fraction) by which it can be multiplied to give 1.

Q Find the reciprocal of: **4**

a $\frac{3}{11}$ b $2\frac{5}{6}$

Go to page 25 for Exercises

A a The reciprocal of $\frac{3}{11} = \frac{11}{3}$

$= 3\frac{2}{3}$

b $2\frac{5}{6} = \frac{17}{6}$

The reciprocal of $\frac{17}{6} = \frac{6}{17}$

- To **divide by a fraction**, multiply by the reciprocal.

Q Find: 5

a $\frac{3}{5} \div \frac{4}{7}$ b $8 \div \frac{1}{4}$

A a $\frac{3}{5} \div \frac{4}{7} = \frac{3}{5} \times \frac{7}{4}$

$= \frac{21}{20}$

$= 1\frac{1}{20}$

b $8 \div \frac{1}{4} = 8 \times 4$ $\left[\frac{4}{1} = 4\right]$

$= 32$

1.3 Decimals

- While **operations with decimals** can be quickly and easily done with a calculator, you should also be able to do simple additions, subtractions, multiplications and divisions without a calculator.

Q Find: 6

a 12.67 + 23.87 b 56.8 − 9.125
c 1.2 × 1.1 d 84.2 ÷ 0.2

A a 12.67 + 23.87 = 36.54
b 56.8 − 9.125 = 47.675
c 1.2 × 1.1 = 1.32
d 84.2 ÷ 0.2 = 421

- Decimals may be either **terminating** (e.g. 0.7) or **non-terminating** (e.g. 0.783965034...). Non-terminating decimals may be either repeating or non-repeating.
- **Repeating** decimals may sometimes appear not to repeat when displayed on a calculator because the last digit in the display may have been rounded up.
- **Terminating decimals** can easily be converted to fractions, using place value to determine the denominator of the fraction.

Q Change to fractions in simplest form: 7

a 0.65 b 0.575
c 0.036 d 3.4168

A a $0.65 = \frac{65}{100}$

$= \frac{13}{20}$

b $0.575 = \frac{575}{1000}$

$= \frac{23}{40}$

c $0.036 = \frac{36}{1000}$

$= \frac{9}{250}$

d $3.4168 = 3\frac{4168}{10000}$

$= 3\frac{521}{1250}$

- To **convert a fraction to a decimal**, divide the numerator by the denominator.

Q Express as decimals: 8

a $\frac{3}{8}$ b $\frac{5}{12}$ c $\frac{6}{11}$ d $\frac{4}{7}$

A a $\frac{3}{8} = 0.375$ $[3 \div 8 = 0.375]$

b $\frac{5}{12} = 0.416\,666\,666\ldots$

$= 0.41\dot{6}$

c $\frac{6}{11} = 0.545\,454\,545\ldots$

$= 0.\dot{5}\dot{4}$

d $\frac{4}{7} = 0.571\,428\,571\,42\ldots$

$= 0.\overline{571\,428}$ $[\text{or } 0.\dot{5}71\,42\dot{8}]$

1.4 Changing repeating decimals to fractions

- **Repeating decimals** can be converted to fractions by multiplying by a particular power of ten and then subtracting to eliminate the repeating part.
- The **power of ten** by which we multiply must be such that the repeating digits line up underneath one another so that when we subtract they all disappear.
  - If there is **1 repeating digit** (e.g. $0.\dot{4}$, $12.5\dot{6}$) we multiply by 10.
  - If there are **2 repeating digits** (e.g. $0.\dot{3}\dot{9}$, $6.7\dot{8}\dot{1}$) we multiply by 100.
  - If there are **3 repeating digits** (e.g. $0.\dot{4}5\dot{3}$, $2.\dot{3}4\dot{5}$) we multiply by 1000.
  - If there are ***n*** **repeating digits, multiply by 10^n.**

Q Change these repeating decimals to fractions: 9

a $0.\dot{4}$ b $0.\dot{3}\dot{9}$ c $6.7\dot{8}\dot{1}$ d $2.\dot{3}4\dot{5}$

Go to page 25 for Exercises

A a
$$\begin{aligned} 0.\dot{4} &= 0.444\,444\,444\ldots \\ \text{Let } x &= 0.444\,444\,444\ldots \\ 10x &= 4.444\,444\,444\ldots \\ 9x &= 4 \quad \text{[subtract]} \\ x &= \frac{4}{9} \\ 0.\dot{4} &= \frac{4}{9} \end{aligned}$$

b
$$\begin{aligned} 0.\dot{3}\dot{9} &= 0.393\,939\,393\ldots \\ \text{Let } x &= 0.393\,939\,393\ldots \\ 100x &= 39.393\,939\,393\ldots \\ 99x &= 39 \\ x &= \frac{39}{99} \\ &= \frac{13}{33} \\ 0.\dot{3}\dot{9} &= \frac{13}{33} \end{aligned}$$

c
$$\begin{aligned} 6.7\dot{8}\dot{1} &= 6.781\,818\,181\ldots \\ \text{Let } x &= 0.781\,818\,181\ldots \\ 100x &= 78.181\,818\,181\ldots \\ 99x &= 77.4 \\ x &= \frac{77.4}{99} \\ &= \frac{774}{990} \\ &= \frac{43}{55} \\ 6.7\dot{8}\dot{1} &= 6\frac{43}{55} \end{aligned}$$

d
$$\begin{aligned} 2.\dot{3}4\dot{5} &= 2.345\,345\,345\ldots \\ \text{Let } x &= 0.345\,345\,345\ldots \\ 1000x &= 345.345\,345\,345\ldots \\ 999x &= 345 \\ x &= \frac{345}{999} \\ &= \frac{115}{333} \\ 2.\dot{3}4\dot{5} &= 2\frac{115}{333} \end{aligned}$$

1.5 Percentages

- **Per cent** means out of 100.
- To **convert percentages to fractions** express them out of 100 and simplify if possible.

Q Convert each percentage to a fraction in its simplest form: 10

a 57% b 36% c 90% d $5\frac{1}{4}\%$

Go to page 25 for Exercises

A a $57\% = \frac{57}{100}$

b $36\% = \frac{36}{100} = \frac{9}{25}$

c $90\% = \frac{90}{100} = \frac{9}{10}$

d $5\frac{1}{4}\% = \frac{5\frac{1}{4}}{100} = \frac{21}{400}$

- To **convert a percentage to a decimal** simply divide by 100.

Q Convert to decimals: 11

a 39% b 7% c 600% d $12\frac{1}{2}\%$

A a 39% = 0.39 b 7% = 0.07

c 600% = 6 d $12\frac{1}{2}\% = 0.125$

- To **change any amount to a percentage**, multiply by 100%.
  Remember that 100% = 1. Multiplying by 100% is just multiplying by 1, so the actual value of the number will not change.

Q Change to percentages:

a $\frac{17}{25}$ b $\frac{5}{8}$ c $\frac{4}{9}$ 12

d 0.08 e 1.15 f 0.075 13

A a $\frac{17}{25} = \frac{17}{25} \times 100\% = 68\%$

b $\frac{5}{8} = \frac{5}{8} \times 100\% = 62\frac{1}{2}\%$

c $\frac{4}{9} = \frac{4}{9} \times 100\% = 44\frac{4}{9}\%$

d $0.08 = 0.08 \times 100\% = 8\%$

e $1.15 = 1.15 \times 100\% = 115\%$

f $0.075 = 0.075 \times 100\% = 7.5\%$

1.6 Applications of percentages

Many applications of percentages fall into one of three basic types. Read the question carefully to identify exactly what is required.

- **Finding a percentage of an amount**
  To find a certain percentage of an amount, simply multiply. Remember: 'per cent' means 'out of a hundred'.

Q A real estate company charges a comission of 3% on the first \$100 000 of a sale and 4% on the remainder. Find the total commission when a house is sold for \$240 000. 14

A Commission $= 3\% \times \$100\,000 + 4\% \times \$140\,000$
$= \$8600$

- **Expressing as a percentage**
The required answer is a percentage, so multiply by 100% to convert to a percentage.

Q A survey was taken of 120 boys and 150 girls from a particular school. The survey found that 81 boys and 108 girls have seen a certain movie. Is the percentage of boys who have seen the movie more or less than the percentage of girls? Justify your answer. 15

A % of girls who have seen the movie $= \frac{108}{150} \times 100\%$
$= 72\%$

% of boys who have seen the movie $= \frac{81}{120} \times 100\%$
$= 67.5\%$

∴ The percentage of girls who have seen the movie is greater than the percentage of boys.

- **Finding 100%**
The whole of an amount is 100%. If we know the value of a given percentage, we can easily find the whole amount by the unitary method. First find 1%, then find 100%.

Q The price of a suit has been discounted by 15%. If it sold for \$467.50, what was the original price? 16

A Discount = 15%
Price paid = 100% − 15%
= 85%
85% is \$467.50
1% is $\frac{\$467.50}{85}$
100% is $\frac{\$467.50}{85} \times 100 = \$550.00$
The original price of the suit was \$550.

1.7 Powers and roots

- Powers and roots can be easily found **using a calculator.**

Q Find: 17

a $(0.7)^5$ b 3^{12} c 5^{-6} d $8^{-\frac{2}{3}}$

A a $(0.7)^5 = 0.16807$ b $3^{12} = 531\,441$
c $5^{-6} = 0.000\,064$ d $8^{-\frac{2}{3}} = 0.25$

Q Find: 18

a $\sqrt{42.7716}$ b $\sqrt[7]{16384}$

A a $\sqrt{42.7716} = 6.54$ b $\sqrt[7]{16384} = 4$

- Some powers and roots can easily be found **without using a calculator.**

Change mixed numbers to improper fractions first.

Q Find: 19

a $(0.06)^2$ b $\left(4\frac{1}{3}\right)^2$ c $\left(2\frac{1}{2}\right)^3$
d $\sqrt{1.21}$ e $\sqrt{12\frac{1}{4}}$

A a $(0.06)^2 = 0.06 \times 0.06$
$= 0.0036$

b $\left(4\frac{1}{3}\right)^2 = \left(\frac{13}{3}\right)^2 = \frac{13^2}{3^2} = \frac{169}{9} = 18\frac{7}{9}$

c $\left(2\frac{1}{2}\right)^3 = \left(\frac{5}{2}\right)^3 = \frac{5^3}{2^3} = \frac{125}{8} = 15\frac{5}{8}$

d $\sqrt{1.21} = \sqrt{\frac{121}{100}} = \frac{\sqrt{121}}{\sqrt{100}} = \frac{11}{10} = 1.1$

e $\sqrt{12\frac{1}{4}} = \sqrt{\frac{49}{4}} = \frac{\sqrt{49}}{\sqrt{4}} = \frac{7}{2} = 3\frac{1}{2}$

It is important to understand these techniques as you will be required to use similar techniques with pronumerals and functions later in the course.

1.8 Scientific (or Standard) Notation

- In **scientific notation**, every number can be expressed as the product of a number between 1 and 10, and a power of ten.

The power of ten tells us the number of places the decimal point has moved, not the number of zeroes.

- If the **power is positive**, the decimal point moves to the right.

$3.1 \times 10^4 = 31\,000$ [31 000]

- If the **power is negative**, the decimal point moves to the left.

$3.1 \times 10^{-4} = 0.000\,31$ [0.000 31]

Go to page 25 for Exercises

- When using a **calculator** with scientific notation, make sure you **understand the output**.

Don't use both 'exp' and '× 10'

If using scientific mode, be careful to return the caclulator to normal mode afterwards!

Q Express in scientific notation: 20

a	200 000 000	b	4 560 000
c	780	d	0.0009
e	0.000 000 57	f	0.035

A
- a $200\,000\,000 = 2 \times 10^8$
- b $4\,560\,000 = 4.56 \times 10^6$
- c $780 = 7.8 \times 10^2$
- d $0.0009 = 9 \times 10^{-4}$
- e $0.000\,000\,57 = 5.7 \times 10^{-7}$
- f $0.035 = 3.5 \times 10^{-2}$

Q Write as normal numbers: 21

a	4×10^5	b	3.27×10^3
c	9.134×10^7	d	5.1×10^{-6}
e	2×10^{-1}	f	7.213×10^{-9}

A
- a $4 \times 10^5 = 400\,000$ $[4 \times 100\,000]$
- b $3.27 \times 10^3 = 3270$
- c $9.134 \times 10^7 = 91\,340\,000$
- d $5.1 \times 10^{-6} = 0.000\,0051$
- e $2 \times 10^{-1} = 0.2$
- f $7.213 \times 10^{-9} = 0.000\,000\,007\,213$

Q Find the answer, in scientific notation, when the sum of 3.64×10^6 and 9.26×10^5 is divided by the product of 7.61×10^8 and 5×10^{-2}. 22

A
$$\left(3.64 \times 10^6 + 9.26 \times 10^5\right) \div \left(7.61 \times 10^8 \times 5 \times 10^{-2}\right) = 0.12$$
$$= 1.2 \times 10^{-1}$$

1.9 Rounding off

- **Rounding off** correct to n decimal places means we require n digits after the decimal point.
- When rounding off, if the **next digit is less than 5** the number is not changed. If the **next digit is 5 or larger**, the number is rounded up.

You can use a calculator to round off, using the **fix mode.**

Take care to return your calculator to normal mode when the question is finished!

Go to page 25 for Exercises

Q Round off correct to two decimal places: 23

a 34.571 b 0.1768 c 9.435 d 3.998

A
- a 34.571 = 34.57 correct to 2 decimal places [the 3rd digit after the decimal point, 1, is less than 5]
- b 0.1768 = 0.18 correct to 2 decimal places [the 3rd digit after the decimal point, 6, is greater than 5]
- c 9.435 = 9.44 correct to 2 decimal places [the 3rd digit after the decimal point is 5]
- d 3.998 = 4.00 correct to 2 decimal places [the zeroes must remain in the answer]

Q Round off correct to three decimal places: 24

a 12.8778 b 0.003 45 c 198.2995

A
- a 12.8778 = 12.878 correct to 3 decimal places
- b 0.003 45 = 0.003 correct to 3 decimal places
- c 198.2995 = 198.300 correct to 3 decimal places

Q Round off correct to one decimal place: 24

a 0.25 b 6.5289 c 19.99

A
- a 0.25 = 0.3 correct to 1 decimal place
- b 6.5289 = 6.5 correct to 1 decimal place
- c 19.99 = 20.0 correct to 1 decimal place

1.10 Significant figures

- The **first significant figure** is the first non-zero digit. For example, in 297 650, 2 is the first significant figure. In 0.005 821, 5 is the first significant figure.

Don't leave out any zeroes before the first significant figure. They are necessary to give the correct place value!

- The **rounding off** is done in the same way as rounding off to a certain number of decimal points. If the following digit after the required number of significant figures is 5 or higher we round up.

Q Round off correct to three significant figures: 25

a 9 876 543 b 0.009 6095 c 50 201

A
- a 9 876 543 = 9 880 000 correct to 3 significant figures
- b 0.009 6095 = 0.009 61 correct to 3 significant figures
- c 50 201 = 50 200 correct to 3 significant figures

Q Write each of these numbers correct to two significant figures: 25

a 0.040 875 b 0.000 000 535
c 743 821.7864

A a $0.040\,875 = 0.041$ correct to 2 significant figures

b $0.000\,000\,535 = 0.000\,000\,54$ correct to 2 significant figures

c $743\,821.7864 = 740\,000$ correct to 2 significant figures

Q Express in scientific notation, correct to four significant figures: 26

a $23\,687\,149$ b $0.000\,827\,361$

A a $23\,687\,149 = 2.369 \times 10^7$ correct to 4 significant figures

b $0.000\,827\,361 = 8.274 \times 10^{-4}$ correct to 4 significant figures

- **Zeroes** may or may not be significant. If 80 400 000 is given as being correct to four significant figures then the first four digits (8, 0, 4 and 0) are significant but the remaining zeroes are not.

1.11 Combinations of operations

- When a mathematical calculation involves a combination of different operations, these **must be performed in a certain order**.
  1. First, remove any grouping symbols, beginning with the innermost set of brackets.
  2. Then perform any multiplications or divisions, working from left to right.
  3. Finally perform any additions or subtractions, again working from left to right.
- Most **scientific calculators** follow this order of operations and care must be taken when a different order is required.

Q Evaluate $\left[(3.4)^2 + 17 \times (7.5 - 6.8)\right] \div (11.1 - 8 \times 1.1)$ 27

A $\left[(3.4)^2 + 17 \times (7.5 - 6.8)\right] \div (11.1 - 8 \times 1.1) = 10.2$

Enter it into your calculator exactly as it appears here.

- Care must be taken with **fractions**. The whole of the numerator must be divided by the whole of the denominator. Use bracket keys or the memory.

Q Find $\dfrac{17.94 - 2.37}{5.16 \times 3.96}$, giving the answer correct to two decimal places. 28

A $\dfrac{17.94 - 2.37}{5.16 \times 3.96} = 0.761\,980\,267\ldots$ [by calculator $(17.94 - 2.37) \div (5.16 \times 3.96)$]

$= 0.76$ correct to 2 decimal places

- A **square root symbol** works like a bracket.

Q Find $\sqrt{9^2 + 11^2}$, giving the answer correct to three decimal places. 28

A $\sqrt{9^2 + 11^2} = 14.212\,670\,4\ldots$ [by calculator]

$= 14.213$ correct to 3 decimal places

Q Find $\sqrt[5]{\dfrac{3.75}{2.4}}$, correct to 2 significant figures. 28

A $\sqrt[5]{\dfrac{3.75}{2.4}} = 1.093\,362\,074\ldots$ [by calculator]

$= 1.1$ to 2 significant figures

Q Find the exact value of $\dfrac{\left(2\frac{1}{2}\right)^2}{1\frac{1}{4} + 3\frac{3}{4}}$ 29

A $\dfrac{\left(2\frac{1}{2}\right)^2}{1\frac{1}{4} + 3\frac{3}{4}} = 1\frac{1}{4}$

Basic Algebra

1.12 Addition and subtraction

- **Like terms** have exactly the same pronumeral part.
- Only like terms can be **added together** or **subtracted from** each other.
- **Unlike terms** cannot be simplified.

Q Simplify: 30

a $7x^2 + 5x - 8x - x^2$ b $3a - 5b - 2a + 9b$

c $4k + 3 - k^2 + 6k - 5$ d $8pq - 7p + q - 3q + 2q$

A a $7x^2 + 5x - 8x - x^2 = 6x^2 - 3x$

b $3a - 5b - 2a + 9b = a + 4b$

c $4k + 3 - k^2 + 6k - 5 = -k^2 + 10k - 2$

d $8pq - 7p + q - 3q + 2q = 8pq - 7p$

1.13 Multiplying and dividing

- When **multiplying** we multiply any numbers and multiply any pronumerals.

Go to pages 25 and 26 for Exercises

- When multiplying, **if the base is the same**, add the indices.

Q Simplify: 31

a $2x \times 3y \times 4z$ b $5a^4 \times 3$

c $6e^3 \times 5e^2$ d $p^5q^3r \times 2pq^2r^4$

A a $2x \times 3y \times 4z = 24xyz$

b $5a^4 \times 3 = 15a^4$

c $6e^3 \times 5e^2 = 30e^5$

d $p^5q^3r \times 2pq^2r^4 = 2p^6q^5r^5$

- When **dividing** we divide any numbers and divide any pronumerals.

- When **dividing**, if the **base is the same**, subtract the indices.

Q Simplify: 32

a $12n \div 6$ b $8x^8 \div 2x^2$

c $15a^4b^7 \div 3ab^6$ d $\dfrac{3x^4y^3z}{9x^2y^5z^3}$

A a $12n \div 6 = 2n$ b $8x^8 \div 2x^2 = 4x^6$

c $15a^4b^7 \div 3ab^6 = 5a^3b$ d $\dfrac{3x^4y^3z}{9x^2y^5z^3} = \dfrac{x^2}{3y^2z^2}$

- When **raising a power to a power**, multiply the indices.

Q Simplify: 33

a $(3x^3)^2$ b $(p^5q^2)^4$ c $4(a^3bc^2)^3$ d $(2e^4f^3)^5$

A a $(3x^3)^2 = 9x^6$ b $(p^5q^2)^4 = p^{20}q^8$

c $4(a^3bc^2)^3 = 4a^9b^3c^6$ d $(2e^4f^3)^5 = 32e^{20}f^{15}$

1.14 Expanding grouping symbols

- When **expanding** grouping symbols, every term inside the bracket must be multiplied by the term outside.

Q Expand: 34

a $5(4p-3q)$ b $a(7a^2+3a-6)$

c $6e(e^2-1)$ d $-3(8-5y)$

e $4ab^3(a^2b^2+3ab^4)$ f $-(5t-3u+v)$

A a $5(4p-3q) = 20p-15q$

b $a(7a^2+3a-6) = 7a^3+3a^2-6a$

c $6e(e^2-1) = 6e^3-6e$

d $-3(8-5y) = -24+15y$

e $4ab^3(a^2b^2+3ab^4) = 4a^3b^5+12a^2b^7$

f $-(5t-3u+v) = -5t+3u-v$

- Algebraic expressions can be **simplified** by first removing any grouping symbols and then collecting like terms.

Take extra care with the signs!

Q Expand and simplify: 35

a $7n-3(n-5)$ b $a(a+8)+5(2a-7)$

c $3k(2k-5)-4(k^2-2k+3)$

d $4(7m-3n)-(5m+9n)$

A a $7n-3(n-5) = 7n-3n+15$
$= 4n+15$

b $a(a+8)+5(2a-7) = a^2+8a+10a-35$
$= a^2+18a-35$

c $3k(2k-5)-4(k^2-2k+3)$
$= 6k^2-15k-4k^2+8k-12$
$= 2k^2-7k-12$

d $4(7m-3n)-(5m+9n) = 28m-12n-5m-9n$
$= 23m-21n$

1.15 Binomial products

- $(a+b)(x+y) = ax+ay+bx+by$

Q Expand: 36

a $(x+5)(x+2)$ b $(t-6)(t+4)$

c $(5a+3b)(2a-3b)$ d $(6x-5y)(y-3z)$

A a $(x+5)(x+2) = x^2+2x+5x+10$
$= x^2+7x+10$

b $(t-6)(t+4) = t^2+4t-6t-24$
$= t^2-2t-24$

c $(5a+3b)(2a-3b) = 10a^2-15ab+6ab-9b^2$
$= 10a^2-9ab-9b^2$

d $(6x-5y)(y-3z) = 6xy-18xz-5y^2+15yz$

Go to page 26 for Exercises

Q Expand and simplify: **37**

a $8e^2 - (2e-5)(4e-1)$

b $(7n-2)(2n-7)-(5n+1)(n+2)$

A a $8e^2 - (2e-5)(4e-1) = 8e^2 - (8e^2 - 2e - 20e + 5)$
$= 8e^2 - (8e^2 - 22e + 5)$
$= 8e^2 - 8e^2 + 22e - 5$
$= 22e - 5$

b $(7n-2)(2n-7)-(5n+1)(n+2)$
$= (14n^2 - 49n - 4n + 14) - (5n^2 + 10n + n + 2)$
$= 14n^2 - 53n + 14 - 5n^2 - 10n - n - 2$
$= 9n^2 - 64n + 12$

Q Subtract $4mn - 2$ from the product of $3m + 5n$ and $m^2 - n$ **38**

A $(3m+5n)(m^2-n)-(4mn-2)$
$= 3m^3 - 3mn + 5m^2n - 5n^2 - 4mn + 2$
$= 3m^3 - 7mn + 5m^2n - 5n^2 + 2$

- In a **binomial product**, every term in the second bracket must be multiplied by every term in the first bracket. We can extend this rule to other products.

Q Expand and simplify: **39**

a $(3n-1)(n^2-5n+4)$ b $(a+b+c)(a+b-2)$

A a $(3n-1)(n^2-5n+4)$
$= 3n^3 - 15n^2 + 12n - n^2 + 5n - 4$
$= 3n^3 - 16n^2 + 17n - 4$

b $(a+b+c)(a+b-2)$
$= a^2 + ab - 2a + ab + b^2 - 2b + ac + bc - 2c$
$= a^2 + 2ab - 2a + b^2 - 2b + ac + bc - 2c$

1.16 The square of a binomial

- Finding the **square of a binomial** is just a special application of a binomial product.

$(a+b)^2 = (a+b)(a+b)$
$= a^2 + ab + ab + b^2$
$= a^2 + 2ab + b^2$

$(a-b)^2 = (a-b)(a-b)$
$= a^2 - ab - ab + b^2$
$= a^2 - 2ab + b^2$

- We simply remember the **rules**:

$$(a+b)^2 = a^2 + 2ab + b^2$$
$$(a-b)^2 = a^2 - 2ab + b^2$$

Q Expand: **40**

a $(x+7)^2$ b $(y-3)^2$

c $(2a-9)^2$ d $(3m^2+4pq^3)^2$

A a $(x+7)^2 = x^2 + 2 \times x \times 7 + 7^2$
$= x^2 + 14x + 49$

b $(y-3)^2 = y^2 - 2 \times y \times 3 + 3^2$
$= y^2 - 6y + 9$

c $(2a-9)^2 = (2a)^2 - 2 \times 2a \times 9 + 9^2$
$= 4a^2 - 36a + 81$

d $(3m^2+4pq^3)^2$
$= (3m^2)^2 + 2 \times 3m^2 \times 4pq^3 + (4pq^3)^2$
$= 9m^4 + 24m^2pq^3 + 16p^2q^6$

Q Expand and simplify: **40**

a $(4p-5)^2 - (4p+5)^2$

b $(3x+y)(2x-3y)-(x-2y)^2$

A a $(4p-5)^2 - (4p+5)^2$
$= 16p^2 - 40p + 25 - (16p^2 + 40p + 25)$
$= 16p^2 - 40p + 25 - 16p^2 - 40p - 25$
$= -80p$

b $(3x+y)(2x-3y)-(x-2y)^2$
$= 6x^2 - 9xy + 2xy - 3y^2 - (x^2 - 4xy + 4y^2)$
$= 6x^2 - 7xy - 3y^2 - x^2 + 4xy - 4y^2$
$= 5x^2 - 3xy - 7y^2$

- When **completing the square** we add a term to an expression in order to form a perfect square.

Q Add a term to each expression to complete the square: **41**

a $x^2 + 12x$ b $p^2 - 18p$

c $4a^2 - 4a$ d $9x^2 + 12xy$

A a $x^2 + 12x \rightarrow x^2 + 12x + 36$ $[x^2 + 2 \times x \times 6 + 6^2]$

b $p^2 - 18p \rightarrow p^2 - 18p + 81$ $[p^2 - 2 \times p \times 9 + 9^2]$

c $4a^2 - 4a \rightarrow 4a^2 - 4a + 1$ $[(2a)^2 - 2 \times 2a \times 1 + 1^2]$

d $9x^2 + 12xy \rightarrow 9x^2 + 12xy + 4y^2$
$[(3x)^2 + 2 \times 3x \times 2y + (2y)^2]$

Go to page 26 for Exercises

1.17 Sum by difference

- Whenever the sum of two terms is multiplied by their difference the result is the difference of the squares of each of the terms.

$$(a+b)(a-b) = a^2 - ab + ab - b^2$$
$$= a^2 - b^2$$

This gives us the rule:

$$(a+b)(a-b) = a^2 - b^2$$

Q Expand: 42

a $(t+6)(t-6)$ b $(3n-2)(3n+2)$

c $(4a+5b)(4a-5b)$ d $(p^2-qr)(p^2+qr)$

A a $(t+6)(t-6) = t^2 - 6^2$
$= t^2 - 36$

b $(3n-2)(3n+2) = (3n)^2 - 2^2$
$= 9n^2 - 4$

c $(4a+5b)(4a-5b) = (4a)^2 - (5b)^2$
$= 16a^2 - 25b^2$

d $(p^2-qr)(p^2+qr) = (p^2)^2 - (qr)^2$
$= p^4 - q^2r^2$

Q Expand and simplify: 43

a $(x+8)^2 - (x+3)(x-3)$

b $(1-4p)(1+4p) - p(4p-11)$

A a $(x+8)^2 - (x+3)(x-3)$
$= x^2 + 16x + 64 - (x^2 - 9)$
$= x^2 + 16x + 64 - x^2 + 9$
$= 16x + 73$

b $(1-4p)(1+4p) - p(4p-11)$
$= 1 - 16p^2 - 4p^2 + 11p$
$= 1 - 20p^2 + 11p$

1.18 Substitution

- In algebraic expressions, pronumerals stand in the place of numbers. When substituting, we **replace the pronumerals** with the numbers they represent.
- The **same pronumeral** in the same expression can have different values at different times (but not at the same time).

☞ Go to page 26 for Exercises

- Always include these **three steps**:
  1. Write down the expression or formula.
  2. Show the substitution.
  3. Write down the answer.

Q $y = x^2 - 5x + 7$. Find y when: 44

a $x = 0$ b $x = 3$ c $x = -1$

A a $y = x^2 - 5x + 7$
When $x = 0$
$y = 0^2 - 5 \times 0 + 7$
$y = 7$

b $y = x^2 - 5x + 7$
When $x = 3$
$y = 3^2 - 5 \times 3 + 7$
$y = 1$

c $y = x^2 - 5x + 7$
When $x = -1$
$y = (-1)^2 - 5 \times -1 + 7$
$y = 13$

Q If $m = Bh^2$, find m when $B = 20$ and $h = 1.75$ 45

A $m = Bh^2$
When $B = 20, h = 1.75$
$m = 20 \times (1.75)^2$
$m = 61.25$

[Bh^2 means $B \times h^2$
Only h is squared]

Q $x = \dfrac{1-t^2}{t}$. Find x when $t = \dfrac{1}{4}$ 46

A $x = \dfrac{1-t^2}{t}$
When $t = \dfrac{1}{4}$
$$x = \frac{1-\left(\frac{1}{4}\right)^2}{\frac{1}{4}}$$
$x = 3\dfrac{3}{4}$

Q Given $r = \sqrt[3]{\dfrac{3V}{4\pi}}$, find the value of r, to one decimal place, when $V = 9$ 47

A $r = \sqrt[3]{\dfrac{3V}{4\pi}}$
When $V = 9$
$r = \sqrt[3]{\dfrac{3 \times 9}{4\pi}}$
$r = 1.290\ 381\ 021$ [by calculator]
$r = 1.3$ correct to 1 decimal place

Q Find the value of $4a^2 + 1$ when $a = 2\sqrt{3}$ 48

A When $a = 2\sqrt{3}$

$$4a^2 + 1 = 4\left(2\sqrt{3}\right)^2 + 1$$
$$= 4 \times 12 + 1$$
$$= 49$$

- It may be necessary to **solve an equation** resulting from a substitution.

Q In the formula $A = \frac{h}{2}\left(a + b\right)$, find b given $h = 18$, $a = 3$ and $A = 72$. **49**

A $h = 18, a = 3, A = 72$

$$A = \frac{h}{2}\left(a + b\right)$$
$$72 = \frac{18}{2}\left(3 + b\right)$$
$$72 = 9\left(3 + b\right)$$
$$8 = 3 + b$$
$$b = 5$$

1.19 Factorisation

When factorising, we rewrite an expression as a product of its factors. There are several different types of factorising.

- **Finding common factors**
  If each term of an expression has the same factor, then the expression has a common factor.

$$ab + ac = a(b + c)$$

Q Factorise: **50**

a $5a - 35$ b $a^2 + 6a$
c $12 - 16b$ d $2c^2 - 8cd$
e $7x - 7y + 14$ f $p^4q^8 - pq^6$

A a $5e - 35 = 5\left(e - 7\right)$ b $a^2 + 6a = a\left(a + 6\right)$

c $12 - 16b = 4\left(3 - 4b\right)$

d $2c^2 - 8cd = 2c\left(c - 4d\right)$

e $7x - 7y + 14 = 7\left(x - y + 2\right)$

f $p^4q^8 - pq^6 = pq^6\left(p^3q^2 - 1\right)$

- **A difference of two squares**

$$x^2 - y^2 = (x - y)(x + y)$$

Q Factorise: **51**

a $h^2 - 25$ b $36e^2 - 1$
c $49m^2 - 81n^2$ d $a^4 - b^2c^2$

A a $h^2 - 25 = \left(h - 5\right)\left(h + 5\right)$

b $36e^2 - 1 = \left(6e\right)^2 - 1^2$
$= \left(6e - 1\right)\left(6e + 1\right)$

c $49m^2 - 81n^2 = \left(7m\right)^2 - \left(9n\right)^2$
$= \left(7m - 9n\right)\left(7m + 9n\right)$

d $a^4 - b^2c^2 = \left(a^2\right)^2 - \left(bc\right)^2$
$= \left(a^2 - bc\right)\left(a^2 + bc\right)$

- **Factorising by grouping**
  An expression involving four or more terms might not have a common factor but some of the terms, grouped together, may have a common factor.

$$ax + ay + bx + by = a(x + y) + b(x + y)$$
$$= (x + y)(a + b)$$

Q Factorise: **52**

a $ab + 9a + bc + 9c$ b $x^2 - 7x + xy - 7y$
c $p^2 - pq + p - q$ d $e^2 + 5e + 3ef + 15f$

A a $ab + 9a + bc + 9c = a\left(b + 9\right) + c\left(b + 9\right)$
$= \left(b + 9\right)\left(a + c\right)$

b $x^2 - 7x + xy - 7y = x\left(x - 7\right) + y\left(x - 7\right)$
$= \left(x - 7\right)\left(x + y\right)$

c $p^2 - pq + p - q = p\left(p - q\right) + 1\left(p - q\right)$
$= \left(p - q\right)\left(p + 1\right)$

d $e^2 + 5e + 3ef + 15f = e\left(e + 5\right) + 3f\left(e + 5\right)$
$= \left(e + 5\right)\left(e + 3f\right)$

Take care with the signs. Check by expanding that the answer is correct.

Q Factorise: **53**

a $m^2 - mn - 6m + 6n$
b $kt + 4t - 3k - 12$

A a $m^2 - mn - 6m + 6n = m\left(m - n\right) - 6\left(m - n\right)$
$= \left(m - n\right)\left(m - 6\right)$

b $kt + 4t - 3k - 12 = t\left(k + 4\right) - 3\left(k + 4\right)$
$= \left(k + 4\right)\left(t - 3\right)$

Go to page 26 for Exercises

- **Factorising trinomials**
  We factorise trinomials by looking for two numbers (or terms) whose sum is the coefficient of the middle term and whose product is the end term.

$$x^2 + (a+b)x + ab = (x+a)(x+b)$$

Q Factorise: 54

a $n^2 + 8n + 15$ b $e^2 - 6e - 16$
c $g^2 - 6g + 5$ d $a^2 + 5ab - 24b^2$

A
a $n^2 + 8n + 15 = (n+5)(n+3)$

b $e^2 - 6e - 16 = (e-8)(e+2)$

c $g^2 - 6g + 5 = (g-5)(g-1)$

d $a^2 + 5ab - 24b^2 = (a+8b)(a-3b)$

If the coefficient of the first term is not 1, the trinomial may still be able to be factorised. We can use inspection, the cross method, or a grouping method to find the correct factorisation.

Q Factorise: 55

a $2x^2 + 11x + 12$ b $3x^2 - 4x + 1$
c $8a^2 - 2a - 15$ d $6p^2 + 7p - 49$

A
a $$\begin{aligned} 2x^2 + 11x + 12 &= 2x^2 + 8x + 3x + 12 \\ &= 2x(x+4) + 3(x+4) \\ &= (x+4)(2x+3) \end{aligned}$$

b $$\begin{aligned} 3x^2 - 4x + 1 &= 3x^2 - 3x - x + 1 \\ &= 3x(x-1) - 1(x-1) \\ &= (x-1)(3x-1) \end{aligned}$$

c $$\begin{aligned} 8a^2 - 2a - 15 &= 8a^2 - 12a + 10a - 15 \\ &= 4a(2a-3) + 5(2a-3) \\ &= (2a-3)(4a+5) \end{aligned}$$

d $$\begin{aligned} 6p^2 + 7p - 49 &= 6p^2 + 21p - 14p - 49 \\ &= 3p(2p+7) - 7(2p+7) \\ &= (2p+7)(3p-7) \end{aligned}$$

1.20 Sum and difference of two cubes

- An expression which is the sum or difference of two cubes can be factorised.
- **Sum of two cubes:**

$$x^3 + y^3 = (x+y)\left(x^2 - xy + y^2\right)$$

Go to pages 26 and 27 for Exercises

- **Difference of two cubes:**

$$x^3 - y^3 = (x-y)\left(x^2 + xy + y^2\right)$$

Q Factorise: 56

a $n^3 + 8$ b $27p^3 - 125$
c $1 - y^3$ d $8a^3 + 27b^3$

A
a $$\begin{aligned} n^3 + 8 &= n^3 + 2^3 \\ &= (n+2)(n^2 - 2n + 4) \end{aligned}$$

b $$\begin{aligned} 27p^3 - 125 &= (3p)^3 - 5^3 \\ &= (3p-5)(9p^2 + 15p + 25) \end{aligned}$$

c $$\begin{aligned} 1 - y^3 &= 1^3 - y^3 \\ &= (1-y)(1 + y + y^2) \end{aligned}$$

d $$\begin{aligned} 8a^3 + 27b^3 &= (2a)^3 + (3b)^3 \\ &= (2a+3b)(4a^2 - 6ab + 9b^2) \end{aligned}$$

1.21 Mixed factorisation

When deciding how to factorise a particular expression there are steps which you should follow:

Step 1 Is there a **common factor**?

If there is no common factor (or if the common factor has already been removed), consider the following:

Step 2 If there are **2 terms**, is the expression a difference of 2 squares, or the sum or difference of 2 cubes?

Step 3 If there are **3 terms**, is the expression a trinomial that can be factorised?

Step 4 If there are **4 or more terms**, can the expression be factorised by grouping?

Q Factorise: 57

a $p^2 - 4p$ b $p^2 - 4$
c $p^2 - 4p + 4$ d $p^2 - 4p + 4pq - 16q$
e $p^3 - 64$ f $p^3 + 4p$

A
a $p^2 - 4p = p(p-4)$

b $p^2 - 4 = (p-2)(p+2)$

c $p^2 - 4p + 4 = (p-2)^2 \quad [(p-2)(p-2)]$

d $$\begin{aligned} p^2 - 4p + 4pq - 16q &= p(p-4) + 4q(p-4) \\ &= (p-4)(p+4q) \end{aligned}$$

e $p^3 - 64 = p^3 - 4^3$
$= (p-4)(p^2 + 4p + 16)$

f $p^3 + 4p = p(p^2 + 4)$ $[p^2 + 4$ cannot be factorised$]$

- We should always **factorise as fully as possible**. This might require a combination of different types of factorisation.

Always look for a common factor first!

Q Factorise fully: **58**

a $2x^2 - 50$ b $3e^2 - 24e + 36$
c $2 + 16y^3$ d $x^2 - 49 + xy + 7y$
e $n^4 - 81$ f $abc - abd + 2ac^2 - 2acd$

A a $2x^2 - 50 = 2(x^2 - 25)$
$= 2(x-5)(x+5)$

b $3e^2 - 24e + 36 = 3(e^2 - 8e + 12)$
$= 3(e-6)(e-2)$

c $2 + 16y^3 = 2(1 + 8y^3)$
$= 2(1+2y)(1 - 2y + 4y^2)$

d $x^2 - 49 + xy + 7y = (x-7)(x+7) + y(x+7)$
$= (x+7)(x-7+y)$

e $n^4 - 81 = (n^2 - 9)(n^2 + 9)$
$= (n-3)(n+3)(n^2+9)$

f $abc - abd + 2ac^2 - 2acd = a(bc - bd + 2c^2 - 2cd)$
$= a[b(c-d) + 2c(c-d)]$
$= a(c-d)(b+2c)$

Surds

- Numbers such as $\sqrt{2}$, $\sqrt{5}$, $7\sqrt{3}$... are called **surds**.
- Surds are **irrational numbers** (i.e. they cannot be expressed in the form $\frac{p}{q}$, where p and q are integers).
- **Square roots of perfect squares** are not surds (e.g. $\sqrt{4}$ is not a surd because $\sqrt{4} = 2$).
- Putting $\sqrt{2}$ **into a calculator** gives a decimal approximation ($\sqrt{2} \approx 1.414213562...$)

If asked for an exact answer, do not give a decimal approximation.

1.22 Adding and subtracting surds

- **Only like surds** can be added together or subtracted.

$$a\sqrt{c} + b\sqrt{c} = (a+b)\sqrt{c}$$

Q Simplify: **59**

a $5\sqrt{3} + 3\sqrt{3}$
b $9\sqrt{7} - \sqrt{7}$
c $2\sqrt{5} + \sqrt{2} + 4\sqrt{5} - 2\sqrt{2}$
d $\sqrt{6} + 4 - 2\sqrt{3} + 7 + 5\sqrt{6}$

A a $5\sqrt{3} + 3\sqrt{3} = 8\sqrt{3}$
b $9\sqrt{7} - \sqrt{7} = 8\sqrt{7}$
c $2\sqrt{5} + \sqrt{2} + 4\sqrt{5} - 2\sqrt{2} = 6\sqrt{5} - \sqrt{2}$
d $\sqrt{6} + 4 - 2\sqrt{3} + 7 + 5\sqrt{6} = 6\sqrt{6} - 2\sqrt{3} + 11$

1.23 Multiplying and dividing surds

- We use these rules:

$$\sqrt{a} \times \sqrt{b} = \sqrt{ab} \qquad (\sqrt{a})^2 = \sqrt{a^2} = a$$

$$a\sqrt{b} \times c\sqrt{d} = ac\sqrt{bd} \qquad \sqrt{a} \div \sqrt{b} = \frac{\sqrt{a}}{\sqrt{b}} = \sqrt{\frac{a}{b}}$$

Q Find: **60**

a $\sqrt{3} \times \sqrt{7}$ b $3\sqrt{5} \times 2\sqrt{6}$
c $(\sqrt{3})^2$ d $5\sqrt{2} \times 3\sqrt{2}$
e $\sqrt{10} \div \sqrt{2}$ f $\sqrt{20} \div \sqrt{5}$
g $9\sqrt{6} \div 3\sqrt{3}$ h $(2\sqrt{7})^2$

A a $\sqrt{3} \times \sqrt{7} = \sqrt{21}$ b $3\sqrt{5} \times 2\sqrt{6} = 6\sqrt{30}$

c $(\sqrt{3})^2 = 3$ d $5\sqrt{2} \times 3\sqrt{2} = 15\sqrt{4}$
$= 15 \times 2$
$= 30$

Go to page 27 for Exercises

e $\sqrt{10} \div \sqrt{2} = \sqrt{5}$

f $\sqrt{20} \div \sqrt{5} = \sqrt{4}$
$= 2$

g $9\sqrt{6} \div 3\sqrt{3} = 3\sqrt{2}$

h $(2\sqrt{7})^2 = 4 \times 7$
$= 28$

1.24 Simplifying surds

- When simplifying surds, look to see if a surd has a **perfect square as a factor**. Then use the rule:

$$\sqrt{a^2b} = \sqrt{a^2} \times \sqrt{b} = a\sqrt{b}$$

Q Simplify: 61

a $\sqrt{18}$ b $\sqrt{600}$ c $\sqrt{63}$
d $\sqrt{72}$ e $7\sqrt{8}$

A a $\sqrt{18} = \sqrt{9} \times \sqrt{2} = 3\sqrt{2}$

b $\sqrt{600} = \sqrt{100} \times \sqrt{6} = 10\sqrt{6}$

c $\sqrt{63} = \sqrt{9} \times \sqrt{7} = 3\sqrt{7}$

d $\sqrt{72} = \sqrt{36} \times \sqrt{2} = 6\sqrt{2}$

e $7\sqrt{8} = 7 \times \sqrt{4} \times \sqrt{2} = 14\sqrt{2}$

Q Express as complete (single) surds: 62

a $7\sqrt{2}$ b $5\sqrt{3}$

A a $7\sqrt{2} = \sqrt{49} \times \sqrt{2} = \sqrt{98}$

b $5\sqrt{3} = \sqrt{25} \times \sqrt{3} = \sqrt{75}$

Q Simplify: 63

a $\sqrt{2} \times \sqrt{14}$ b $\sqrt{30} \times \sqrt{70}$

A a $\sqrt{2} \times \sqrt{14} = \sqrt{28} = \sqrt{4} \times \sqrt{7} = 2\sqrt{7}$

b $\sqrt{30} \times \sqrt{70} = \sqrt{2100} = \sqrt{100} \times \sqrt{21} = 10\sqrt{21}$

- We should always simplify surds before adding or subtracting.

✔ Surds that may not seem to be like surds may be when they are simplified!

Q Simplify: 64

a $\sqrt{50} + \sqrt{32}$ b $2\sqrt{12} + 3\sqrt{108}$
c $\sqrt{54} - \sqrt{45} - \sqrt{24}$

Go to page 27 for Exercises

A a $\sqrt{50} + \sqrt{32} = \sqrt{25} \times \sqrt{2} + \sqrt{16} \times \sqrt{2}$
$= 5\sqrt{2} + 4\sqrt{2}$
$= 9\sqrt{2}$

b $2\sqrt{12} + 3\sqrt{108} = 2 \times \sqrt{4} \times \sqrt{3} + 3 \times \sqrt{36} \times \sqrt{3}$
$= 4\sqrt{3} + 18\sqrt{3}$
$= 22\sqrt{3}$

c $\sqrt{54} - \sqrt{45} - \sqrt{24} = \sqrt{9} \times \sqrt{6} - \sqrt{9} \times \sqrt{5} - \sqrt{4} \times \sqrt{6}$
$= 3\sqrt{6} - 3\sqrt{5} - 2\sqrt{6}$
$= \sqrt{6} - 3\sqrt{5}$

1.25 Binomial products with surds

- Binomial products involving surds are **expanded** in exactly the same way as any other binomial product.

$$(a+b)(c+d) = ac + ad + bc + bd$$

Q Expand and simplify: 65

a $(\sqrt{2} + \sqrt{5})(\sqrt{7} + \sqrt{3})$ b $(2 - 3\sqrt{5})(\sqrt{5} - 2)$
c $(4 - 3\sqrt{2})(2\sqrt{6} + 3\sqrt{3})$

A a $(\sqrt{2} + \sqrt{5})(\sqrt{7} + \sqrt{3}) = \sqrt{14} + \sqrt{6} + \sqrt{35} + \sqrt{15}$

b $(2 - 3\sqrt{5})(\sqrt{5} - 2) = 2\sqrt{5} - 4 - 3\sqrt{25} + 6\sqrt{5}$
$= 8\sqrt{5} - 4 - 15$
$= 8\sqrt{5} - 19$

c $(4 - 3\sqrt{2})(2\sqrt{6} + 3\sqrt{3}) = 8\sqrt{6} + 12\sqrt{3} - 6\sqrt{12} - 9\sqrt{6}$
$= -\sqrt{6} + 12\sqrt{3} - 6 \times \sqrt{4} \times \sqrt{3}$
$= -\sqrt{6} + 12\sqrt{3} - 12\sqrt{3}$
$= -\sqrt{6}$

1.26 The square of a binomial with surds

- The rules are:

$$(a+b)^2 = a^2 + 2ab + b^2 \qquad (a-b)^2 = a^2 - 2ab + b^2$$

Q Expand and simplify: 66

a $(\sqrt{5} + \sqrt{3})^2$ b $(6 - \sqrt{2})^2$ c $(4\sqrt{3} - 2\sqrt{2})^2$

A a $(\sqrt{5} + \sqrt{3})^2 = (\sqrt{5})^2 + 2 \times \sqrt{5} \times \sqrt{3} + (\sqrt{3})^2$
$= 5 + 2\sqrt{15} + 3$
$= 8 + 2\sqrt{15}$

b $\left(6-\sqrt{2}\right)^2 = 6^2 - 2\times 6\times\sqrt{2} + \left(\sqrt{2}\right)^2$
$= 36 - 12\sqrt{2} + 2$
$= 38 - 12\sqrt{2}$

c $\left(4\sqrt{3}-2\sqrt{2}\right)^2 = \left(4\sqrt{3}\right)^2 - 2\times 4\sqrt{3}\times 2\sqrt{2} + \left(2\sqrt{2}\right)^2$
$= 48 - 16\sqrt{6} + 8$
$= 56 - 16\sqrt{6}$

1.27 Sum by difference with surds

- When the **sum of two terms** is **multiplied** by the **difference of the same two terms** the result is the difference of two squares.

$$(a+b)(a-b)=a^2-b^2$$

Q Expand and simplify: **67**

a $\left(\sqrt{7}-\sqrt{3}\right)\left(\sqrt{7}+\sqrt{3}\right)$ b $\left(5\sqrt{2}+3\right)\left(5\sqrt{2}-3\right)$

c $\left(4\sqrt{10}+7\sqrt{5}\right)\left(4\sqrt{10}-7\sqrt{5}\right)$

A a $\left(\sqrt{7}-\sqrt{3}\right)\left(\sqrt{7}+\sqrt{3}\right) = \left(\sqrt{7}\right)^2 - \left(\sqrt{3}\right)^2$
$= 7 - 3$
$= 4$

b $\left(5\sqrt{2}+3\right)\left(5\sqrt{2}-3\right) = \left(5\sqrt{2}\right)^2 - 3^2$
$= 50 - 9$
$= 41$

c $\left(4\sqrt{10}+7\sqrt{5}\right)\left(4\sqrt{10}-7\sqrt{5}\right) = \left(4\sqrt{10}\right)^2 - \left(7\sqrt{5}\right)^2$
$= 16\times 10 - 49\times 5$
$= 160 - 245$
$= -85$

- Surds such as these where we have the sum and the difference of the same two surds are called conjugates.
- The **conjugate** of $\sqrt{a}+\sqrt{b}$ **is** $\sqrt{a}-\sqrt{b}$

Q Write down the conjugate of $3\sqrt{5}-2\sqrt{3}$ **68**

A The conjugate of $3\sqrt{5}-2\sqrt{3}$ is $3\sqrt{5}+2\sqrt{3}$.

- **Multiplying a binomial surd by its conjugate** always gives a rational number.

Q Show that if $4\sqrt{3}+7$ is multiplied by its conjugate the result is rational. **69**

A The conjugate of $4\sqrt{3}+7$ is $4\sqrt{3}-7$

$\left(4\sqrt{3}+7\right)\left(4\sqrt{3}-7\right) = \left(4\sqrt{3}\right)^2 - 7^2$
$= 16\times 3 - 49$
$= 48 - 49$
$= -1$

$\therefore$ the product of $4\sqrt{3}+7$ with its conjugate is rational

1.28 Rationalising the denominator

- By **multiplying by an appropriate term**, any surd can be expressed with a rational denominator.
- If the **denominator is a single surd** we use the rule:

$$\left(\sqrt{a}\right)^2 = a \qquad \frac{1}{\sqrt{a}} = \frac{1}{\sqrt{a}}\times\frac{\sqrt{a}}{\sqrt{a}} = \frac{\sqrt{a}}{a}$$

We are only multiplying by one, so the surd is not changing in value $\left(\frac{\sqrt{a}}{\sqrt{a}}=1\right)$.

Q Rationalise the denominator of: **70**

a $\frac{1}{\sqrt{5}}$ b $\frac{2}{\sqrt{7}}$ c $\frac{3}{\sqrt{3}}$ d $\frac{5}{3\sqrt{6}}$

A a $\frac{1}{\sqrt{5}} = \frac{1}{\sqrt{5}}\times\frac{\sqrt{5}}{\sqrt{5}} = \frac{\sqrt{5}}{5}$

b $\frac{2}{\sqrt{7}} = \frac{2}{\sqrt{7}}\times\frac{\sqrt{7}}{\sqrt{7}} = \frac{2\sqrt{7}}{7}$

c $\frac{3}{\sqrt{3}} = \frac{3}{\sqrt{3}}\times\frac{\sqrt{3}}{\sqrt{3}} = \frac{3\sqrt{3}}{3} = \sqrt{3}$

d $\frac{5}{3\sqrt{6}} = \frac{5}{3\sqrt{6}}\times\frac{\sqrt{6}}{\sqrt{6}} = \frac{5\sqrt{6}}{18}$

- If the **denominator is a binomial surd**, we use the fact that multiplying any surd by its conjugate always gives a rational number. We multiply both the numerator and denominator by the conjugate of the denominator.

Q Rationalise the denominator of: **71**

a $\frac{3}{5-\sqrt{3}}$ b $\frac{\sqrt{5}+\sqrt{6}}{\sqrt{5}-\sqrt{6}}$

c $\frac{10}{\sqrt{7}+\sqrt{2}}$ d $\frac{\sqrt{2}}{2\sqrt{3}+1}$

Go to page 27 for Exercises

A a $\dfrac{3}{5-\sqrt{3}}=\dfrac{3}{5-\sqrt{3}}\times\dfrac{5+\sqrt{3}}{5+\sqrt{3}}$

$=\dfrac{3\left(5+\sqrt{3}\right)}{25-3}$

$=\dfrac{15+3\sqrt{3}}{22}$

b $\dfrac{\sqrt{5}+\sqrt{6}}{\sqrt{5}-\sqrt{6}}=\dfrac{\sqrt{5}+\sqrt{6}}{\sqrt{5}-\sqrt{6}}\times\dfrac{\sqrt{5}+\sqrt{6}}{\sqrt{5}+\sqrt{6}}$

$=\dfrac{5+2\sqrt{30}+6}{5-6}$

$=\dfrac{11+2\sqrt{30}}{-1}$

$=-11-2\sqrt{30}$

c $\dfrac{10}{\sqrt{7}+\sqrt{2}}=\dfrac{10}{\sqrt{7}+\sqrt{2}}\times\dfrac{\sqrt{7}-\sqrt{2}}{\sqrt{7}-\sqrt{2}}$

$=\dfrac{10\left(\sqrt{7}-\sqrt{2}\right)}{7-2}$

$=\dfrac{10\left(\sqrt{7}-\sqrt{2}\right)}{5}$

$=2\left(\sqrt{7}-\sqrt{2}\right)$

d $\dfrac{\sqrt{2}}{2\sqrt{3}+1}=\dfrac{\sqrt{2}}{2\sqrt{3}+1}\times\dfrac{2\sqrt{3}-1}{2\sqrt{3}-1}$

$=\dfrac{2\sqrt{6}-\sqrt{2}}{12-1}$

$=\dfrac{2\sqrt{6}-\sqrt{2}}{11}$

Q Show that $\dfrac{4}{2-\sqrt{3}}+\dfrac{1}{4\sqrt{3}+7}$ is rational. 72

A $\dfrac{4}{2-\sqrt{3}}+\dfrac{1}{4\sqrt{3}+7}$

$=\dfrac{4}{2-\sqrt{3}}\times\dfrac{2+\sqrt{3}}{2+\sqrt{3}}+\dfrac{1}{4\sqrt{3}+7}\times\dfrac{4\sqrt{3}-7}{4\sqrt{3}-7}$

$=\dfrac{4\left(2+\sqrt{3}\right)}{4-3}+\dfrac{4\sqrt{3}-7}{48-49}$

$=\dfrac{8+4\sqrt{3}}{1}+\dfrac{4\sqrt{3}-7}{-1}$

$=8+4\sqrt{3}-4\sqrt{3}+7$

$=15$

$\therefore\ \dfrac{4}{2-\sqrt{3}}+\dfrac{1}{4\sqrt{3}+7}$ is rational

Q Find the value of the integers a and b such that $\dfrac{7}{5-3\sqrt{2}}=a+\sqrt{b}$ 73

A $\dfrac{7}{5-3\sqrt{2}}=a+\sqrt{b}$

$\dfrac{7}{5-3\sqrt{2}}=\dfrac{7}{5-3\sqrt{2}}\times\dfrac{5+3\sqrt{2}}{5+3\sqrt{2}}$

$=\dfrac{7\left(5+3\sqrt{2}\right)}{25-18}$

$=\dfrac{7\left(5+3\sqrt{2}\right)}{7}$

$=5+3\sqrt{2}$

$=5+\sqrt{9}\times\sqrt{2}$

$=5+\sqrt{18}$

$\therefore\ a=5$ and $b=18$

Algebra

1.29 Algebraic fractions

- **Reducing algebraic fractions**

  Algebraic fractions can be reduced by first factorising and then cancelling.

Only cancel a factor which is common to the numerator and denominator.

Q Simplify: 74

a $\dfrac{5x-15}{5}$ **b** $\dfrac{9x+12y}{9}$

c $\dfrac{x^2-5x+6}{x^2+3x-10}$ **d** $\dfrac{e^2-e}{e^2-1}$

Go to page 27 for Exercises

A a $\dfrac{5x-15}{5}=\dfrac{5(x-3)}{5}$

$=x-3$

b $\dfrac{9x+12y}{9}=\dfrac{3(3x+4y)}{9}$

$=\dfrac{3x+4y}{3}$

c $\dfrac{x^2-5x+6}{x^2+3x-10}=\dfrac{(x-3)(x-2)}{(x+5)(x-2)}$

$=\dfrac{x-3}{x+5}$

d $\dfrac{e^2 - e}{e^2 - 1} = \dfrac{e(e-1)}{(e-1)(e+1)}$

$= \dfrac{e}{e+1}$

Be extra careful if every term in either the numerator or the denominator cancels out.

Q Simplify: 74

a $\dfrac{a}{a^2 - 3a}$ b $\dfrac{4m - 7}{14 - 8m}$

c $\dfrac{n^2 - 4n - 5}{n - 5}$ d $\dfrac{a^2 - 4a + 4}{a^2 - 4}$

A a $\dfrac{a}{a^2 - 3a} = \dfrac{a}{a(a-3)}$

$= \dfrac{1}{a-3}$

[We divide both the numerator and denominator by a. $a \div a = 1$ so the numerator is 1.]

b $\dfrac{4m-7}{14-8m} = \dfrac{4m-7}{2(7-4m)}$ $[4m - 7 = -(7 - 4m)]$

$= -\dfrac{1}{2}$

c $\dfrac{n^2 - 4n - 5}{n - 5} = \dfrac{(n-5)(n+1)}{n-5}$

$= \dfrac{n+1}{1}$

$= n + 1$

d $\dfrac{a^2 - 4a + 4}{a^2 - 4} = \dfrac{(a-2)^2}{(a-2)(a+2)}$

$= \dfrac{a-2}{a+2}$

Adding and subtracting algebraic fractions

Addition or subtraction of algebraic fractions requires a common denominator.

Q Express as a single fraction: 75

a $\dfrac{3a}{5} + \dfrac{a}{3}$ b $\dfrac{5t+1}{3} + \dfrac{t-5}{9}$

A a $\dfrac{3a}{5} + \dfrac{a}{3} = \dfrac{9a}{15} + \dfrac{5a}{15}$

$= \dfrac{14a}{15}$

b $\dfrac{5t+1}{3} + \dfrac{t-5}{9} = \dfrac{15t+3}{9} + \dfrac{t-5}{9}$

$= \dfrac{16t-2}{9}$

When subtracting, take care with the signs. The vinculum (fraction line) works like a bracket.

Q Find: 76

a $\dfrac{8k}{9} - \dfrac{2k}{5}$ b $1 - \dfrac{y}{x+y}$

c $\dfrac{2m+3}{12} - \dfrac{3m-7}{8}$

A a $\dfrac{8k}{9} - \dfrac{2k}{5} = \dfrac{40k}{45} - \dfrac{18k}{45}$

$= \dfrac{22k}{45}$

b $1 - \dfrac{y}{x+y} = \dfrac{x+y}{x+y} - \dfrac{y}{x+y}$

$= \dfrac{x}{x+y}$

c $\dfrac{2m+3}{12} - \dfrac{3m-7}{8} = \dfrac{2(2m+3)}{24} - \dfrac{3(3m-7)}{24}$

$= \dfrac{4m + 6 - 9m + 21}{24}$

$= \dfrac{27 - 5m}{24}$

It may be necessary to factorise each denominator in order to find the lowest common denominator. Both the numerator and denominator can be left in factorised form.

Q Find: 77

a $\dfrac{x+2}{x^2 - x} + \dfrac{x+3}{x^2 + x}$ b $\dfrac{n+2}{n^2 - 5n + 6} - \dfrac{n+5}{n^2 + n - 12}$

A a $\dfrac{x+2}{x^2 - x} + \dfrac{x+3}{x^2 + x} = \dfrac{x+2}{x(x-1)} + \dfrac{x+3}{x(x+1)}$

$= \dfrac{(x+1)(x+2)}{x(x-1)(x+1)} + \dfrac{(x-1)(x+3)}{x(x-1)(x+1)}$

$= \dfrac{x^2 + 3x + 2}{x(x-1)(x+1)} + \dfrac{x^2 + 2x - 3}{x(x-1)(x+1)}$

$= \dfrac{2x^2 + 5x - 1}{x(x-1)(x+1)}$

b $\dfrac{n+2}{n^2 - 5n + 6} - \dfrac{n+5}{n^2 + n - 12}$

$= \dfrac{n+2}{(n-3)(n-2)} - \dfrac{n+5}{(n-3)(n+4)}$

$= \dfrac{(n+2)(n+4)}{(n-3)(n-2)(n+4)} - \dfrac{(n+5)(n-2)}{(n-3)(n-2)(n+4)}$

continued ...

Go to page 27 for Exercises

$$= \frac{n^2+6n+8}{(n-3)(n-2)(n+4)} - \frac{n^2+3n-10}{(n-3)(n-2)(n+4)}$$
$$= \frac{(n^2+6n+8)-(n^2+3n-10)}{(n-3)(n-2)(n+4)}$$
$$= \frac{3n+18}{(n-3)(n-2)(n+4)}$$
$$= \frac{3(n+6)}{(n-3)(n-2)(n+4)}$$

- **Multiplying algebraic fractions**
  We **multiply** fractions by multiplying the numerators together and multiplying the denominators together.

✔ Before multiplying, factorise and cancel if possible.

Q Simplify: 78

a $\frac{e^2-5e}{e+3} \times \frac{e^2+3e}{e^2-3e-10}$

b $\frac{x^2+5x-14}{x^2+2x-8} \times \frac{x^2-x-20}{x^2+2x-35}$

A a $\frac{e^2-5e}{e+3} \times \frac{e^2+3e}{e^2-3e-10} = \frac{e(e-5)}{e+3} \times \frac{e(e+3)}{(e-5)(e+2)}$
$$= \frac{e^2}{e+2}$$

b $\frac{x^2+5x-14}{x^2+2x-8} \times \frac{x^2-x-20}{x^2+2x-35}$
$$= \frac{(x+7)(x-2)}{(x+4)(x-2)} \times \frac{(x+4)(x-5)}{(x+7)(x-5)}$$
$$= 1$$

- **Dividing algebraic fractions**
  To **divide** by any fraction, multiply by the reciprocal.

Q Simplify: 79

a $\frac{n+4}{n^2+5n} \div \frac{n+3}{n^2+4n-5}$

b $\frac{1}{x^2+4x-12} \div \frac{1}{x^2-5x+6}$

A a $\frac{n+4}{n^2+5n} \div \frac{n+3}{n^2+4n-5} = \frac{n+4}{n^2+5n} \times \frac{n^2+4n-5}{n+3}$
$$= \frac{n+4}{n(n+5)} \times \frac{(n+5)(n-1)}{n+3}$$
$$= \frac{(n+4)(n-1)}{n(n+3)}$$

Go to page 28 for Exercises

b $\frac{1}{x^2+4x-12} \div \frac{1}{x^2-5x+6}$
$$= \frac{1}{x^2+4x-12} \times \frac{x^2-5x+6}{1}$$
$$= \frac{1}{(x+6)(x-2)} \times \frac{(x-3)(x-2)}{1}$$
$$= \frac{x-3}{x+6}$$

1.30 Linear equations

- Linear equations can be **solved** by:
  - adding the same term to both sides
  - subtracting the same term from both sides
  - multiplying both sides by the same term
  - dividing both sides by the same term.

✔ Remember: The solution to an equation can always be checked by substituting the answer into the original equation.

Q Solve: 80

a $7x-19=72$

b $\frac{t}{5}+93=-65$

c $57-8y=123$

d $6p-15=32-7p$

A a $7x-19=72$
$7x=91$
$x=13$

b $\frac{t}{5}+93=-65$
$\frac{t}{5}=-158$
$t=-790$

c $57-8y=123$
$-8y=66$
$y=-8.25$

d $6p-15=32-7p$
$13p=47$
$p=3\frac{8}{13}$

✔ When the solution to an equation is not a whole number, the answer may be given as either a fraction or a decimal. It is better to give the answer as a fraction, rather than round off a decimal.

- It may be necessary to **remove grouping symbols** or collect like terms before solving an equation.

Q Solve: 81

a $4(6t+5)=10$

b $9m-17+3m=18+6m+m$

c $3(7n-10)=5(9n+1)$

d $5(3x-1)-2(3x+4)=7x$

A a $4(6t+5)=10$
$24t+20=10$
$24t=-10$
$t=-\frac{5}{12}$

b $9m - 17 + 3m = 18 + 6m + m$

$$12m - 17 = 18 + 7m$$
$$5m = 35$$
$$m = 7$$

c $3(7n - 10) = 5(9n + 1)$

$$21n - 30 = 45n + 5$$
$$-24n = 35$$
$$n = -1\frac{11}{24}$$

d $5(3x - 1) - 2(3x + 4) = 7x$

$$15x - 5 - 6x - 8 = 7x$$
$$9x - 13 = 7x$$
$$2x = 13$$
$$x = 6.5$$

- When solving equations involving fractions, first multiply both sides of the equation by the lowest common denominator.

Take care to multiply every term in the equation!

Q Solve: 82

a $\frac{7x - 4}{9} = -2$ b $\frac{5a}{a - 4} = \frac{3}{7}$

c $\frac{3k - 3}{2k + 7} = \frac{9k + 1}{6k - 5}$ d $\frac{2d}{3} - \frac{d - 1}{5} = 3d + 8$

A a
$$\frac{7x - 4}{9} = -2$$
$$\left(\frac{7x - 4}{9}\right) \times 9 = -2 \times 9$$
$$7x - 4 = -18$$
$$7x = -14$$
$$x = -2$$

b
$$\frac{5a}{a - 4} = \frac{3}{7}$$
$$7(5a) = 3(a - 4)$$
$$35a = 3a - 12$$
$$32a = -12$$
$$a = -\frac{3}{8}$$

c
$$\frac{3k - 3}{2k + 7} = \frac{9k + 1}{6k - 5}$$
$$(3k - 3)(6k - 5) = (9k + 1)(2k + 7)$$
$$18k^2 - 33k + 15 = 18k^2 + 65k + 7$$
$$-98k = -8$$
$$k = \frac{4}{49}$$

d
$$\frac{2d}{3} - \frac{d - 1}{5} = 3d + 8$$
$$15\left(\frac{2d}{3}\right) - 15\left(\frac{d - 1}{5}\right) = 15(3d + 8)$$
$$5(2d) - 3(d - 1) = 45d + 120$$
$$10d - 3d + 3 = 45d + 120$$
$$7d + 3 = 45d + 120$$
$$-38d = 117$$
$$d = -3\frac{3}{38}$$

Inequalities and Absolute Values

1.31 Linear inequalities

Inequalities are solved in a similar way to linear equations. However, care must be taken to obey the following rules:

- The **inequality sign remains the same** if a number is added to, or subtracted from, both sides of an inequality, or if the inequality is multiplied or divided by a positive number.

Q Solve: 83

a $2x - 7 \le -3$ b $\frac{x}{4} + 3 > 9$

c $\frac{x + 2}{3} \ge -2$ d $7x - 4 < 5 - 2x$

A a
$$2x - 7 \le -3$$
$$2x \le 4$$
$$x \le 2$$

b
$$\frac{x}{4} + 3 > 9$$
$$\frac{x}{4} > 6$$
$$x > 24$$

c
$$\frac{x + 2}{3} \ge -2$$
$$x + 2 \ge -6$$
$$x \ge -8$$

d
$$7x - 4 < 5 - 2x$$
$$9x < 9$$
$$x < 1$$

- The inequality sign is **reversed** if an inequality is multiplied or divided by a **negative** number.

Q Solve: 84

a $9 - 5x < 1$ b $8 - \frac{x}{3} \ge 6$

c $2x - 5 \le 11 + 7x$ d $\frac{4 - 3x}{11} > -7$

A a
$$9 - 5x < 1$$
$$-5x < -8$$
$$x > 1.6$$

b
$$8 - \frac{x}{3} \ge 6$$
$$-\frac{x}{3} \ge -2$$
$$x \le 6$$

Go to page 28 for Exercises

c $2x - 5 \le 11 + 7x$
$-5x \le 16$
$x \ge -3.2$

d $\frac{4 - 3x}{11} > -7$
$4 - 3x > -77$
$-3x > -81$
$x < 27$

If $4 < x$, we can reverse the whole inequality (not just the inequality sign), to get $x > 4$.

1.32 Graphing on the number line

- **Circle the boundary position** (3 if $x < 3$, -2 if $x \ge -2$ and so on), then **draw a line** in the direction indicated by the inequality sign. The circle marking the **boundary is shaded** if the boundary is included ($\ge$ and $\le$), but **unshaded** if the boundary is not included ($>$ or $<$).

Q Graph on a number line: 85

a $x < 3$ b $x \ge -2$

A a $x < 3$

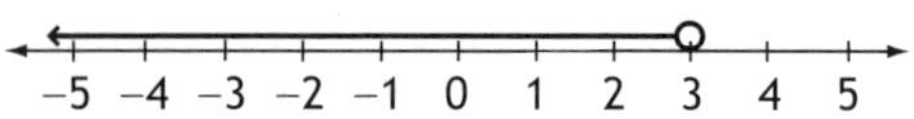

b $x \ge -2$

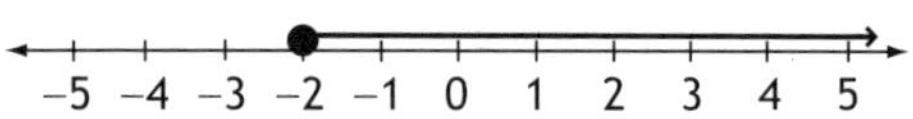

Q Solve, graphing each solution on a number line: 86

a $8 + 3x \le -1$ b $-4x + 9 > 1$

A a $8 + 3x \le -1$
$3x \le -9$
$x \le -3$

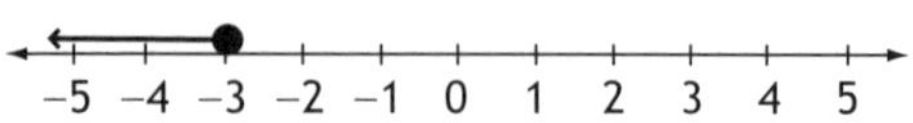

b $-4x + 9 > 1$
$-4x > -8$
$x < 2$

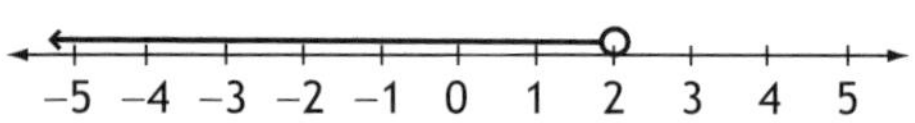

1.33 Absolute values

- $|x|$ means '**the absolute value of x**'. The absolute value of a number is its magnitude regardless of its sign. (i.e. the size of the number without considering whether it is positive or negative.) So $|2| = 2$ and $|-2| = 2$.

- We have the **definition**: $|a| = a$ if $a \ge 0$
$= -a$ if $a < 0$

This definition can be confusing because of the negative sign in the bottom part of the definition and we know that an absolute value of a number is never negative. But:

$|2| = 2$ (because $2 > 0$ we use the top part of the definition)

$|-2| = -(-2) = 2$ (because $-2 < 0$ we use the bottom part of the definition)

Taking the negative of a negative number will always be positive.

- Other **important results**: $|ab| = |a| \times |b|$
$|a + b| \le |a| + |b|$

Q Simplify: 87

a $|-3| \times |2|$ b $|-6|$ c $|-4| \times |-2|$
d $|8|$ e $|2 + 6|$ f $|2| + |6|$
g $|-3| + |5|$ h $|-3 + 5|$

A a $|-3| \times |2| = 3 \times 2 = 6$
b $|-6| = 6$
c $|-4| \times |-2| = 4 \times 2 = 8$
d $|8| = 8$
e $|2 + 6| = |8| = 8$
f $|2| + |6| = 2 + 6 = 8$
g $|-3| + |5| = 3 + 5 = 8$
h $|-3 + 5| = |2| = 2$

- The **answer** to a calculation involving an absolute value may be negative.

Q Simplify: 88

a $|9 - 5|$ b $|5 - 9|$ c $|5| - |9|$
d $|-5| - |-9|$ e $4|-6|$ f $3|4| - 7|-2|$

A a $|9 - 5| = |4| = 4$
b $|5 - 9| = |-4| = 4$
c $|5| - |9| = 5 - 9 = -4$
d $|-5| - |-9| = 5 - 9 = -4$
e $4|-6| = 4 \times 6 = 24$
f $3|4| - 7|-2| = 3 \times 4 - 7 \times 2 = 12 - 14 = -2$

- **Geometrically**:
$|x|$ is the **distance of x from the origin** on the number line and $|x - y|$ is the **distance of x from y** on the number line.

Go to page 28 for Exercises

Q Graph on a number line: 89

a $|x| = 3$ **b** $|x| < 4$ **c** $|x| \geq 2$

d $|x-1| = 3$ **e** $|x+2| > 1$

A a $|x| = 3$ [x is 3 units from the origin]

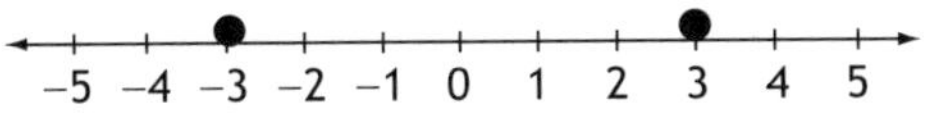

b $|x| < 4$ [x is less than 4 units from the origin]

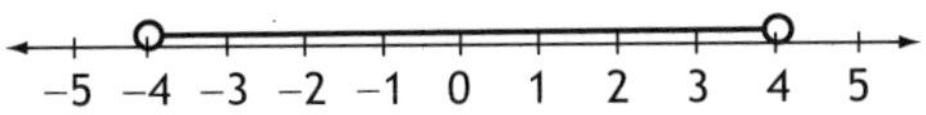

c $|x| \geq 2$ [x is 2 units or more from the origin]

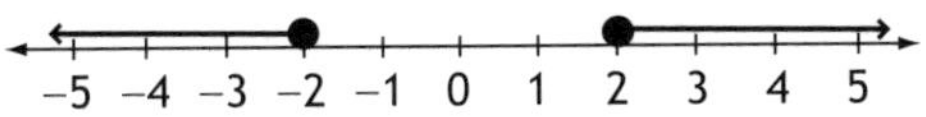

d $|x-1| = 3$ [x is 3 units from 1 on the number plane]

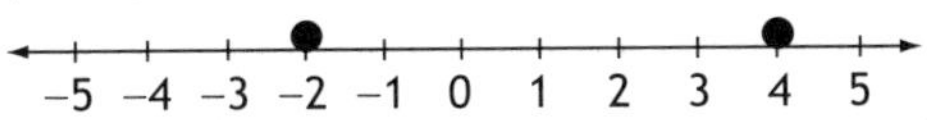

e $|x+2| > 1$ [x is more than 1 unit from -2]

$$\left[|x+2| = |x-(-2)|\right]$$

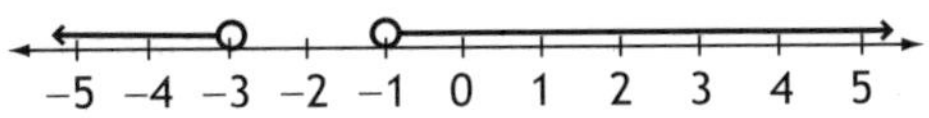

- Absolute values can also be graphed on the number plane.

Q Graph on the number plane: 90

a $|x| = 3$ **b** $|y| = 5$ **c** $y = |x|$

A a $|x| = 3$

$\therefore x = 3$ or $x = -3$

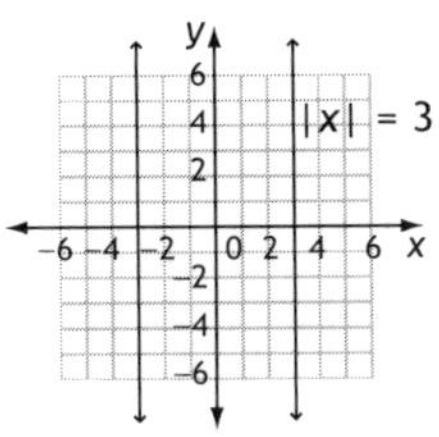

b $|y| = 5$

$\therefore y = 5$ or $y = -5$

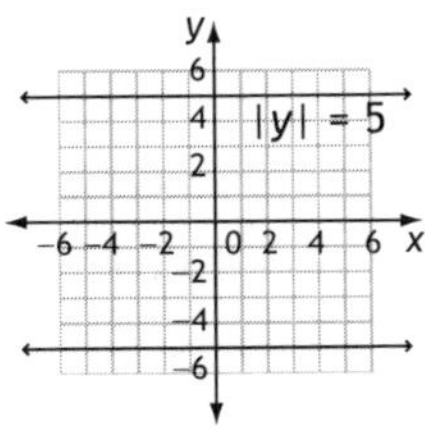

c $y = |x|$

$\therefore y = x$ if $x \geq 0$ and

$y = -x$ if $x < 0$

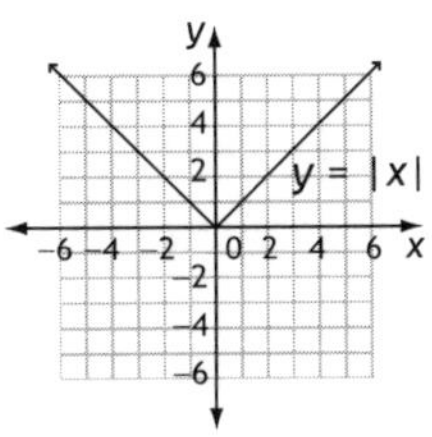

1.34 Equations and inequalities with absolute values

- Equations and inequations involving absolute values can be solved either **algebraically or geometrically**.

Q Solve: 91

a $|x| = 1$ **b** $|x+2| = 3$ **c** $|2x-3| = 5$

A a $|x| = 1$ [x is 1 unit from the origin]

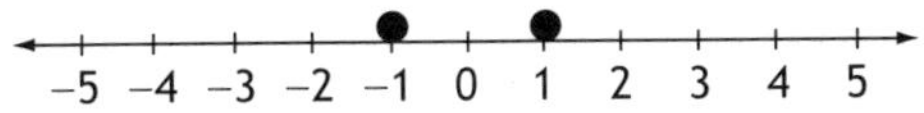

$\therefore x = -1$ or $x = 1$

or: $|x| = 1$

$x = -1$ or $x = 1$

b $|x+2| = 3$ [x is 3 units from -2]

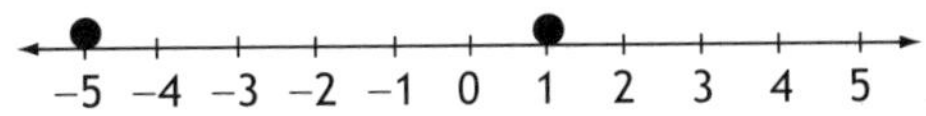

$\therefore x = -5$ or $x = 1$

or: $|x+2| = 3$

$x+2 = -3$ or $x+2 = 3$

$x = -5$ or $x = 1$

c $|2x-3| = 5$ [$2x$ is 5 units from 3]

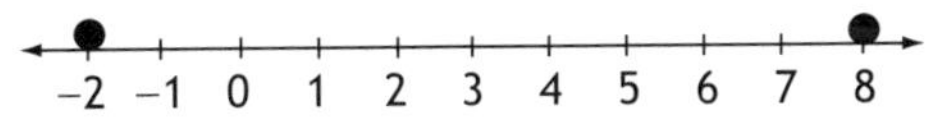

$\therefore 2x = -2$ or $2x = 8$

$x = -1$ or $x = 4$

or: $|2x-3| = 5$

$2x - 3 = -5$ or $2x - 3 = 5$

$2x = -2$ $2x = 8$

$x = -1$ $x = 4$

- Take care when solving inequalities with absolute values that the inequality signs are correct.

Q Solve: 92

a $|x-1| < 4$ **b** $|x+3| \leq 5$ **c** $|3x-2| > 2$

A a $|x-1| < 4$ [x is less than 4 units from 1]

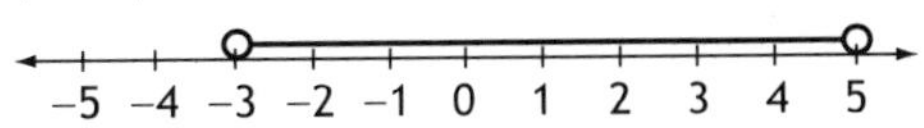

$\therefore -3 < x < 5$

or: $|x-1| < 4$

$-4 < x - 1 < 4$

$-3 < x < 5$

Go to page 28 for Exercises

b $\left|x+3\right| \le 5$ [x is 5 units or less from -3]

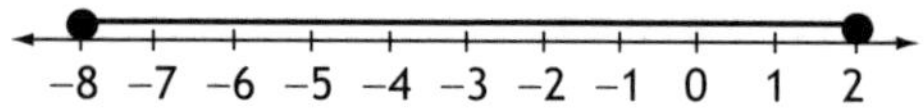

$\therefore -8 \le x \le 2$

or: $\left|x+3\right| \le 5$

$-5 \le x+3 \le 5$

$-8 \le x \le 2$

c $\left|3x-2\right| > 2$ [$3x$ is more than 2 units from 2]

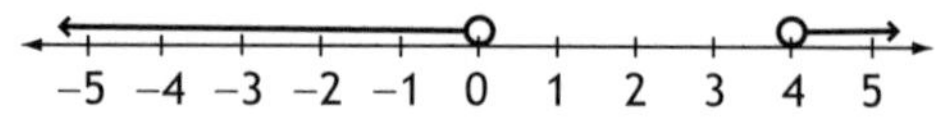

$3x < 0$ or $3x > 4$

$\therefore$ $x < 0$ or $x > 1\frac{1}{3}$

or: $\left|3x-2\right| > 2$

$3x-2 < -2$ or $3x-2 > 2$

$3x < 0$ or $3x > 4$

$x < 0$ or $x > 1\frac{1}{3}$

Quadratic Equations and Simultaneous Equations

1.35 Quadratic equations

- A quadratic equation is one with a term that is squared (x^2), and has no other terms with higher powers.

Solving quadratic equations by factorising

- We first factorise the quadratic expression and then use the rule:

  If the product of two numbers is zero then at least one of the numbers must be zero.

Q Solve: 93

a $x^2 - 6x - 27 = 0$ b $m^2 - 11m + 28 = 0$

c $2x^2 + 9x + 10 = 0$ d $6a^2 - a - 1 = 0$

A a

$x^2 - 6x - 27 = 0$

$(x-9)(x+3) = 0$

$x - 9 = 0$ or $x + 3 = 0$

$x = 9$ $x = -3$

b

$m^2 - 11m + 28 = 0$

$(m-4)(m-7) = 0$

$m - 4 = 0$ or $m - 7 = 0$

$m = 4$ $m = 7$

c

$2x^2 + 9x + 10 = 0$

$(2x+5)(x+2) = 0$

$2x + 5 = 0$ or $x + 2 = 0$

$2x = -5$ $x = -2$

$x = -2.5$ $x = -2$

d

$6a^2 - a - 1 = 0$

$(3a+1)(2a-1) = 0$

$3a + 1 = 0$ or $2a - 1 = 0$

$3a = -1$ $2a = 1$

$a = -\frac{1}{3}$ $a = \frac{1}{2}$

Go to page 28 for Exercises

The rule only applies when the product is zero.

- If a quadratic expression is equal to a **non-zero number** we rearrange the question so that it is equal to zero.

Q Solve: 94

a $4x^2 = x$ b $n^2 = 8n + 20$

c $5x^2 = 6 - 13x$ d $(x+8)(x+2) = 16$

A a

$4x^2 = x$

$4x^2 - x = 0$

$x(4x-1) = 0$

$x = 0$ or $4x - 1 = 0$

$x = 0$ $4x = 1$

$x = 0$ $x = \frac{1}{4}$

b

$n^2 = 8n + 20$

$n^2 - 8n - 20 = 0$

$(n-10)(n+2) = 0$

$n - 10 = 0$ or $n + 2 = 0$

$n = 10$ $n = -2$

c

$5x^2 = 6 - 13x$

$5x^2 + 13x - 6 = 0$

$(5x-2)(x+3) = 0$

$5x - 2 = 0$ or $x + 3 = 0$

$5x = 2$ $x = -3$

$x = \frac{2}{5}$ $x = -3$

d

$(x+8)(x+2) = 16$

$x^2 + 10x + 16 = 16$

$x^2 + 10x = 0$

$x(x+10) = 0$

$x = 0$ or $x + 10 = 0$

$x = 0$ $x = -10$

- If the quadratic expression is a **perfect square**, we can solve the equation by taking square roots.

Don't forget, there will be two possible answers (the positive and negative square root).

Q Solve: **95**

a $(x+4)^2 = 9$ b $(2p-3)^2 = 7$

A a $(x+4)^2 = 9$

$x + 4 = 3$ or $x + 4 = -3$

$x = -1$ $x = -7$

b $(2p-3)^2 = 7$

$2p - 3 = \sqrt{7}$ or $2p - 3 = -\sqrt{7}$

$2p = 3 + \sqrt{7}$ $2p = 3 - \sqrt{7}$

$p = \dfrac{3+\sqrt{7}}{2}$ $p = \dfrac{3-\sqrt{7}}{2}$

The quadratic formula

- The solution of the quadratic equation $ax^2 + bx + c = 0$ is given by:

$$x = \frac{-b \pm \sqrt{b^2 - 4ac}}{2a}$$

Q Solve each equation giving the solutions correct to three decimal places: **96**

a $3x^2 - 9x + 4 = 0$ b $2x^2 + 7x - 3 = 0$

A a $3x^2 - 9x + 4 = 0$

$a = 3, b = -9, c = 4$

$x = \dfrac{-b \pm \sqrt{b^2 - 4ac}}{2a}$

$x = \dfrac{-(-9) \pm \sqrt{(-9)^2 - 4 \times 3 \times 4}}{2 \times 3}$

$x = \dfrac{9 \pm \sqrt{33}}{6}$

$x = \dfrac{9+\sqrt{33}}{6}$ or $x = \dfrac{9-\sqrt{33}}{6}$

$x = 2.457\,427\,108\ldots$ $x = 0.542\,572\,892\ldots$

$x = 2.457$ $x = 0.543$

to 3 decimal places

b $2x^2 + 7x - 3 = 0$

$a = 2, b = 7, c = -3$

$x = \dfrac{-b \pm \sqrt{b^2 - 4ac}}{2a}$

$x = \dfrac{-7 \pm \sqrt{7^2 - 4 \times 2 \times -3}}{2 \times 2}$

$x = \dfrac{-7 \pm \sqrt{73}}{4}$

continued ...

$x = \dfrac{-7+\sqrt{73}}{4}$ or $x = \dfrac{-7-\sqrt{73}}{4}$

$x = 0.386\,000\,936\ldots$ $x = -3.886\,000\,936\ldots$

$x = 0.386$ $x = -3.886$

to 3 decimal places

Q Solve each equation, leaving the answers in simplest surd form: **97**

a $4x^2 + 7x + 2 = 0$ b $x^2 - 8x + 13 = 0$

A a $4x^2 + 7x + 2 = 0$

$a = 4, b = 7, c = 2$

$x = \dfrac{-b \pm \sqrt{b^2 - 4ac}}{2a}$

$x = \dfrac{-7 \pm \sqrt{7^2 - 4 \times 4 \times 2}}{2 \times 4}$

$x = \dfrac{-7 \pm \sqrt{17}}{8}$

b $x^2 - 8x + 13 = 0$

$a = 1, b = -8, c = 13$

$x = \dfrac{-b \pm \sqrt{b^2 - 4ac}}{2a}$

$x = \dfrac{-(-8) \pm \sqrt{(-8)^2 - 4 \times 1 \times 13}}{2 \times 1}$

$x = \dfrac{8 \pm \sqrt{12}}{2}$

$x = \dfrac{8 \pm 2\sqrt{3}}{2}$

$x = \dfrac{2(4 \pm \sqrt{3})}{2}$

$x = 4 \pm \sqrt{3}$

- Quadratic equations are studied in more detail in Chapter 6 (see page 88).

1.36 Simultaneous equations

- When **two equations, with two unknowns**, are satisfied by the same solution they are said to be simultaneous equations. Simultaneous equations can be solved algebraically or graphically.
- The **graphical solution** is dealt with in Chapter 3: Linear Functions and Lines.
- **Algebraically**, simultaneous equations can be solved by substitution or elimination.

The substitution method

- In the substitution method, an expression is formed for one of the unknowns from one equation and this expression is substituted into the second equation.

Go to page 28 for Exercises

The solution should always be checked by substitution into one of the original equations (the one not used to find the second value in the answer). Although shown here, this check does not need to be written.

Q Solve the following pairs of equations simultaneously: 98

a $y = 9x - 5$
$y = -7x + 11$

b $3x + 5y = 8$
$2x + y = 10$

A **a**

$y = 9x - 5$ **i**

$y = -7x + 11$ **ii**

$\therefore\ 9x - 5 = -7x + 11$

$16x = 16$

$x = 1$

Substitute in **i** $y = 9x - 5$

$y = 9 \times 1 - 5$

$y = 4$

$\therefore x = 1$ and $y = 4$

Check in **ii** $4 = -7 \times 1 + 11$

$4 = 4$

b

$3x + 5y = 8$ **i**

$2x + y = 10$ **ii**

From **ii** $y = 10 - 2x$ **iii**

Substitute **iii** into **i** $3x + 5(10 - 2x) = 8$

$3x + 50 - 10x = 8$

$-7x + 50 = 8$

$-7x = -42$

$x = 6$

Substitute in **iii** $y = 10 - 2x$

$y = 10 - 2 \times 6$

$y = -2$

$\therefore x = 6$ and $y = -2$

Check in **i** $3 \times 6 + 5 \times -2 = 8$

$8 = 8$

The elimination method

- In the elimination method, the two equations are either added or subtracted so that one of the unknowns is eliminated.

Q Solve these pairs of simultaneous equations: 99

a $8x + y = 15$
$3x + y = 5$

b $6m - 5n = 4$
$2m + 5n = -12$

A **a**

$8x + y = 15$ **i**

$3x + y = 5$ **ii**

Subtract **i** – **ii** $5x = 10$

$x = 2$

Substitute in **i** $8x + y = 15$

continued ...

$8 \times 2 + y = 15$

$16 + y = 15$

$y = -1$

$\therefore x = 2$ and $y = -1$

Check in **ii** $3 \times 2 - 1 = 5$

b

$6m - 5n = 4$ **i**

$2m + 5n = -12$ **ii**

Add **i** + **ii** $8m = -8$

$m = -1$

Substitute in **i** $6m - 5n = 4$

$6 \times -1 - 5n = 4$

$-6 - 5n = 4$

$-5n = 10$

$n = -2$

$\therefore m = -1$ and $n = -2$

Check in **ii** $2 \times -1 + 5 \times -2 = -12$

It may be necessary to first multiply each equation so that the coefficients of one of the unknowns are the same.

Make sure that you multiply every term in the equation.

Q Solve these pairs of simultaneous equations: 100

a $3p + q = 7$
$5p - 3q = 21$

b $7a + 2b - 8 = 0$
$3a + 5b - 20 = 0$

A **a**

$3p + q = 7$ **i**

$5p - 3q = 21$ **ii**

i $\times 3$ $9p + 3q = 21$ **iii**

iii + **ii** $14p = 42$

$p = 3$

Substitute in **i** $3p + q = 7$

$3 \times 3 + q = 7$

$9 + q = 7$

$q = -2$

$\therefore p = 3$ and $q = -2$

Check in **ii** $5 \times 3 - 3 \times -2 = 21$

b

$7a + 2b - 8 = 0$ **i**

$3a + 5b - 20 = 0$ **ii**

i $\times 5$ $35a + 10b - 40 = 0$ **iii**

ii $\times 2$ $6a + 10b - 40 = 0$ **iv**

iii – **iv** $29a = 0$

$a = 0$

Substitute in **i** $7a + 2b - 8 = 0$

$7 \times 0 + 2b - 8 = 0$

$2b = 8$

$b = 4$

$\therefore a = 0$ and $b = 4$

Check in **ii** $3 \times 0 + 5 \times 4 - 20 = 0$

Go to page 28 for Exercises

Exercises Basic Arithmetic and Algebra

1 Express each fraction in simplest form:

a $\frac{21}{49}$ b $\frac{32}{72}$

2 Find:

a $\frac{2}{9}+\frac{5}{9}$ b $\frac{1}{12}+\frac{2}{3}$

c $\frac{7}{10}-\frac{3}{10}$ d $\frac{5}{6}-\frac{1}{3}$

3 Find:

a $\frac{1}{4}\times\frac{5}{8}$ b $\frac{3}{5}\times\frac{10}{11}$ c $\frac{4}{9}\times\frac{3}{8}$

4 Find the reciprocal of:

a $\frac{5}{7}$ b $4\frac{1}{3}$

5 Find:

a $\frac{2}{3}\div\frac{3}{4}$ b $\frac{5}{6}\div\frac{2}{3}$ c $3\div\frac{2}{5}$

6 Find:

a $0.5 + 0.6$ b $7 - 1.64$
c 0.03×0.02 d $0.8 \div 0.008$

7 Change to fractions in simplest form:

a 0.48 b 0.214
c 0.0008 d 5.45

8 Express as decimals:

a $\frac{7}{8}$ b $\frac{11}{12}$ c $\frac{5}{6}$ d $\frac{1}{11}$

9 Change to fractions in simplest form:

a $0.\dot{8}$ b $0.\dot{4}\dot{2}$ c $7.\dot{2}\dot{3}\dot{7}$ d $0.05\dot{1}$

10 Convert to fractions in simplest form:

a 63% b 20% c 8% d $87\frac{1}{2}\%$

11 Convert to decimals:

a 16% b 4% c 900% d $3\frac{3}{4}\%$

12 Change to percentages:

a $\frac{19}{25}$ b $\frac{3}{8}$ c $\frac{1}{6}$

13 Change to percentages:

a 0.56 b 1.07 c 0.0125

14 A tradesman offers a 15% discount to return customers. How much would a return customer save on a job that should normally cost $1350?

15 A shop increases the price of a shirt from $48 to $60. Express the increase as a percentage of the old price.

16 In the 1996 census it was found that 33.75% of Australians lived in Sydney. If Sydney's population was 6 037 875, find Australia's population in 1996.

17 Find:

a 5^8 b $(0.3)^6$ c 2^{-4} d $16^{-1.5}$

18 Find:

a $\sqrt{76.7376}$ b $\sqrt[5]{161051}$

19 Find (without a calculator):

a $(0.05)^2$ b $\left(2\frac{2}{5}\right)^2$ c $\left(1\frac{1}{2}\right)^4$

d $\sqrt{1.44}$ e $\sqrt{11\frac{1}{9}}$

20 Express in scientific notation:

a 50 000 b 46 700 000 c 3120
d 0.000 007 e 0.000 061 839

21 Express as normal numbers:

a 3×10^4 b 5.18×10^9
c 6.25×10^{-5} d 1×10^{-3}

22 Find the answer, in scientific notation, when the product of 3.8×10^3 and 9.1×10^5 is divided by the sum of 6.3×10^{-3} and 7×10^{-4}

23 Round off correct to two decimal places:

a 5.2398 b 19.215 c 0.683 47

24 Write correct to three decimal places:

a 2.4175 b 345.219 45 c 9.999 85

25 Write correct to four significant figures:

a 251 576 328 b 13.2376
c 0.030 847 6 d 0.009 817 526

26 Express in scientific notation, correct to three significant figures:

a 8 567 283 956 b 0.000 148 137 285

27 Evaluate $\left\{\left[(5.2+9.7)\times(7.1-2.35)\right]\div 12.5+8.2\right\}\times 9.1$

28 Find:

a $\frac{7.11\times 1.6}{15.8\div 2.5}$ b $\sqrt{6^2+13^2}$ (to 1 decimal place)

c $\sqrt[4]{\frac{250.216\,32}{1.2}}$

Go to page 219 for Quick Answers & pages 148 and 149 for Worked Solutions

29 Find the exact value of $\dfrac{3\frac{2}{3}-1\frac{5}{6}}{5\frac{3}{7}+5\frac{4}{7}}$.

30 Simplify:

a $9p^2 - p^2 + 7p - 10p$

b $7k^2 + k^3 - 6k + 5 - 9k^3 + 8k - 7$

31 Simplify:

a $4a \times 5b \times 6c$ b $3x^3 \times 9x$

c $8t^3 \times 4t^4$ d $3x^5y^3 \times 2xy^4$

32 Simplify:

a $10d \div 2d$ b $6t^6 \div 2t^2$

c $14a^3b^2c \div 2abc$ d $\dfrac{8m^8n^6}{12m^5n^9}$

33 Simplify:

a $\left(4a^5\right)^2$ b $\left(x^3y^4\right)^3$

c $7\left(c^3d^7\right)^2$ d $\left(3a^2b^3c^4\right)^4$

34 Expand:

a $3(8x - y)$ b $e\left(3e^2 - 5e + 7\right)$

c $-5(2x - 11y + z)$ d $4x\left(x^2 - 3\right)$

e $2p^4q^3\left(pq^7 + 5p^2q^3\right)$ f $-(7 - 8u)$

35 Expand and simplify:

a $9m - (3m + 4)$ b $7e(5e - 7) + 2\left(9e^2 - 8\right)$

c $5n(3n + 2) - 3\left(n^2 - 3n + 1\right)$

36 Expand:

a $(a + 4)(a - 5)$ b $(b - 6)(b - 1)$

c $(8p + 3q)(2p + 5q)$ d $(7x - y)(y + 2z)$

37 Expand and simplify:

a $9t^2 - (3t + 7)(t - 8)$ b $(4 - 3n)(2 + n) - n(5n + 1)$

38 Subtract $3p - 11$ from the product of $2p + 8$ and $p + 7$

39 Expand and simplify:

a $(2k + 3)\left(k^2 + 9k + 1\right)$ b $(a + b + 3)(a - b + 5)$

40 Expand:

a $(e - 8)^2$ b $(5m + 2n)^2$ c $\left(a^2 - 7b\right)^2$

41 Add a term to each expression to complete the square:

a $a^2 + 10a$ b $b^2 - 16b$

c $25c^2 + 20c$ d $16d^2 - 24de$

42 Expand:

a $(y + 7)(y - 7)$ b $(3k - 8)(3k + 8)$

c $\left(x^2 - 5y\right)\left(x^2 + 5y\right)$

43 Expand and simplify:

a $(u + 4)^2 + (u + 3)(u - 3)$

b $(3k + 5)(3k - 5) - (2k - 3)^2$

44 $y = x^2 + 3x - 2$. Find y when:

a $x = 0$ b $x = 1$ c $x = -2$

45 If $r = kt^2$, find r when $k = 9.5$ and $t = 10$.

46 $y = \dfrac{x + 1}{1 - 2x}$. Find the value of y when $x = \dfrac{1}{3}$

47 Given $A = \pi\left(R^2 - r^2\right)$, find A, correct to 3 decimal places, when $R = 14$ and $r = 9$.

48 Find the value of $7 - 2n^2$ when $n = 3\sqrt{2}$

49 In the formula $S = \dfrac{n}{2}\left[2a + (n - 1)d\right]$, find a when $n = 38$, $d = -3$ and $S = -1083$.

50 Factorise:

a $7k + 28$ b $h^2 - 8h$

c $16x + 12y - 36z$ d $5n^2 + 25mn$

e $a^3b^7 - a^4b^6$

51 Factorise:

a $e^2 - 100$ b $1 - r^2$

c $64p^2 - 121q^2$ d $g^4 - 9h^2k^2$

52 Factorise:

a $pq + 6p + qr + 6r$ b $z^2 + 7z + yz + 7y$

c $m^2 - 3m + 2mn - 6n$ d $x^2 + xy + x + y$

53 Factorise:

a $ab - 9a - 7b + 63$ b $p^2 + pq - mp - mq$

54 Factorise:

a $x^2 + 7x + 12$ b $g^2 + 3g - 88$

c $k^2 - 9k + 20$ d $c^2 - 2cd - 35d^2$

55 Factorise:

a $2x^2 + 9x + 10$ b $3x^2 + 23x - 8$

c $4a^2 - 23a + 15$ d $6n^2 - 5n - 6$

☞ Go to pages 219 and 220 for Quick Answers & pages 149–151 for Worked Solutions

56 Factorise:

a $a^3 - 27$ b $h^3 + 1000$

c $8 - 125k^3$ d $64p^3 + 343q^3$

57 Factorise:

a $x^2 - 9$ b $x^2 - 9x$

c $x^2 + 8x - 9$ d $x^3 + 8x^2$

e $x^3 - 8$ f $x^3 + x^2 + x + 1$

58 Factorise fully:

a $3c^2 - 300$ b $7y^3 + 7$

c $5h^2 - 20h - 25$ d $m^4 - 16$

e $k^2 - 9 + 7km - 21m$ f $pqr + 3pr - 5pq - 15p$

59 Simplify:

a $4\sqrt{6} + 3\sqrt{6}$ b $3\sqrt{3} + 2\sqrt{3} - 8\sqrt{2}$

c $6\sqrt{11} + \sqrt{11}$ d $9\sqrt{5} - 4\sqrt{5} - 5\sqrt{5}$

e $8 - 3\sqrt{7} + 7\sqrt{2} - 2 + \sqrt{7}$

60 Find:

a $\sqrt{6} \times \sqrt{5}$ b $2\sqrt{3} \times 4\sqrt{10}$

c $\left(\sqrt{7}\right)^2$ d $\left(5\sqrt{2}\right)^2$

e $3\sqrt{6} \times 7\sqrt{6}$ f $\sqrt{15} \div \sqrt{5}$

g $\sqrt{63} \div \sqrt{7}$ h $12\sqrt{10} \div 4\sqrt{5}$

61 Simplify:

a $\sqrt{28}$ b $\sqrt{45}$ c $\sqrt{300}$

d $\sqrt{75}$ e $3\sqrt{40}$

62 Express as complete (single) surds:

a $5\sqrt{7}$ b $9\sqrt{6}$

63 Simplify:

a $\sqrt{3} \times \sqrt{12}$ b $\sqrt{10} \times \sqrt{15}$ c $2\sqrt{6} \times 3\sqrt{2}$

64 Simplify:

a $\sqrt{98} + \sqrt{72}$ b $\sqrt{24} + \sqrt{6} - \sqrt{20}$

c $5\sqrt{8} + 2\sqrt{18}$

65 Expand and simplify:

a $\left(\sqrt{7} + \sqrt{5}\right)\left(\sqrt{3} + \sqrt{2}\right)$ b $\left(\sqrt{11} - 9\right)\left(\sqrt{2} - 7\right)$

c $\left(3\sqrt{3} + 8\right)\left(3 - 2\sqrt{5}\right)$ d $\left(4\sqrt{6} - 5\sqrt{3}\right)\left(3\sqrt{6} + 2\right)$

66 Expand and simplify:

a $\left(\sqrt{10} + \sqrt{3}\right)^2$ b $\left(\sqrt{13} - 4\right)^2$ c $\left(2\sqrt{6} + 3\sqrt{2}\right)^2$

67 Expand and simplify:

a $\left(\sqrt{3} - \sqrt{2}\right)\left(\sqrt{3} + \sqrt{2}\right)$ b $\left(1 - \sqrt{5}\right)\left(1 + \sqrt{5}\right)$

c $\left(5\sqrt{10} + 2\sqrt{7}\right)\left(5\sqrt{10} - 2\sqrt{7}\right)$

d $\left(4\sqrt{6} - 7\right)\left(4\sqrt{6} + 7\right)$

68 Write down the conjugate of $8 - 6\sqrt{7}$.

69 Show that if $\sqrt{11} + 2\sqrt{3}$ is multiplied by its conjugate the answer is rational.

70 Rationalise the denominator of:

a $\dfrac{1}{\sqrt{2}}$ b $\dfrac{11}{\sqrt{11}}$ c $\dfrac{\sqrt{2}}{\sqrt{3}}$ d $\dfrac{3}{2\sqrt{5}}$

71 Rationalise the denominator of:

a $\dfrac{1}{\sqrt{3} - \sqrt{2}}$ b $\dfrac{\sqrt{7} - \sqrt{3}}{\sqrt{7} + \sqrt{3}}$

c $\dfrac{7}{\sqrt{5} + 2}$ d $\dfrac{\sqrt{5} + 1}{3\sqrt{6} - \sqrt{2}}$

72 Show that $\dfrac{6}{2\sqrt{7} + 5} - \dfrac{8}{3 - \sqrt{7}}$ is rational.

73 Find the value of the integers a and b such that $\dfrac{33}{2\sqrt{3} + 1} = a + b\sqrt{3}$.

74 Simplify:

a $\dfrac{7a - 14b}{7}$ b $\dfrac{10}{2 - 4m}$ c $\dfrac{8x + 6}{12x + 9}$

d $\dfrac{h^2 - 5h}{h}$ e $\dfrac{n^2 - 1}{n^2 - n}$ f $\dfrac{d + 6}{d^2 - 2d - 48}$

g $\dfrac{e^2 - 9}{e^2 + 6e + 9}$ h $\dfrac{x^2 + 4x + 3}{x^2 - 4x - 21}$

75 Express as a single fraction:

a $\dfrac{7e}{11} + \dfrac{2e}{11}$ b $\dfrac{3h}{8} + \dfrac{h}{8}$

c $\dfrac{5d}{9} + \dfrac{3d}{7}$ d $\dfrac{4u - 3}{v} + \dfrac{7 - u}{v}$

e $\dfrac{3m - 4}{5} + \dfrac{2m - 3}{3}$

76 Find:

a $\dfrac{5z}{12} - \dfrac{z}{3}$ b $1 - \dfrac{b}{a}$

c $\dfrac{2k + 5}{7} - \dfrac{k - 8}{9}$ d $\dfrac{8m - 7}{15} - \dfrac{3m + 7}{10}$

77 Find:

a $\dfrac{1}{x^2 + 7x + 12} - \dfrac{1}{x^2 + 9x + 20}$ b $\dfrac{2a + 3}{a^2 + a} + \dfrac{a - 4}{a^2 - 1}$

☞ Go to page 220 for Quick Answers & pages 151–154 for Worked Solutions

78 Simplify:

a $\dfrac{x^2+4x}{3x+7}\times\dfrac{5x+10}{x^2+6x+8}$

b $\dfrac{a^2-a-6}{a^2+2a-15}\times\dfrac{a^2+12a+35}{a^2+9a+14}$

79 Simplify:

a $\dfrac{u^2+6u}{u^2+5u-6}\div\dfrac{u^2+9u+8}{u^2-1}$

b $\dfrac{z^2+13z+36}{z^2-9}\div\dfrac{z^2+18z+81}{z^2+7z+12}$

80 Solve:

a $9m+15=78$ b $\dfrac{k}{4}-17=63$

c $123-6j=145$ d $12e+43=7e-67$

81 Solve:

a $7(12w-5)=91$

b $11n+23-6n-14=3n+19-n$

c $8(3b+7)=5(2b-9)$

d $3(6v+1)-4(v-7)=5(2v+5)$

82 Solve:

a $\dfrac{3k+5}{7}=7$ b $\dfrac{a+1}{2a-1}=\dfrac{2}{3}$

c $\dfrac{5u+3}{2u-7}=\dfrac{5u+8}{2u+9}$ d $\dfrac{4n}{5}+\dfrac{2n-5}{8}=n+1$

83 Solve:

a $5a+6>-4$ b $\dfrac{m}{5}-6\geq-1$

c $\dfrac{3k+4}{5}<7$ d $9p+2\leq 3p-10$

84 Solve:

a $7-3x>4$ b $11-\dfrac{w}{6}\leq-8$

c $\dfrac{9-x}{4}<-2$ d $6e+8\geq 29+13e$

85 Graph on a number line:

a $x\leq 1$ b $x>-3$

86 Solve, graphing the solution on a number line:

a $2-9x\geq 11$ b $8x+1<33$

87 Simplify:

a $|-12|$ b $|4|\times|-3|$ c $|-5|\times|-2|$

d $|10|$ e $|4+1|$ f $|4|+|1|$

g $|-9|+|7|$ h $|-9+7|$

88 Simplify:

a $|8-3|$ b $|3-8|$ c $|3|-|8|$

d $3|-8|$ e $2|-4|-3|-3|$

89 Graph on a number line:

a $|x|=2$ b $|x|<1$ c $|x|\geq 3$

d $|x-2|=3$ e $|x+3|>2$

90 Graph on a number plane:

a $|x|=2$ b $|y|=4$ c $y=|x|$

91 Solve:

a $|x|=4$ b $|x-1|=5$ c $|3x-2|=1$

92 Solve:

a $|x|\leq 3$ b $|x-2|>2$

c $|x+1|<3$ d $|4x-3|\geq 1$

93 Solve:

a $x^2-10x+16=0$ b $u^2+13u+40=0$

c $2n^2+7n-15=0$ d $4a^2-24a+35=0$

94 Solve:

a $x^2=7x$ b $g^2=12g-32$

c $(k+9)(k+1)=33$ d $7x^2=25x+12$

95 Solve:

a $(m+5)^2=25$ b $(3e-4)^2=2$

96 Solve each equation giving the solutions correct to 4 decimal places:

a $x^2-9x+11=0$ b $5x^2+8x-6=0$

97 Solve each equation, leaving the answers in simplest surd form:

a $x^2+11x+12=0$ b $2x^2-8x-3=0$

98 Solve the following pairs of equations simultaneously (using the substitution method):

a $y=2x+7$, $y=4x+13$ b $4x-7y=-1$, $3x+y=18$

99 Solve these pairs of simultaneous equations (using the elimination method):

a $5p-q=13$, $2p-q=7$ b $11a+9b=34$, $5a-9b=-50$

100 Solve these pairs of simultaneous equations (using the elimination method):

a $12y+7z-13=0$, $6y+z+11=0$ b $7g-3h=9$, $5g+2h=23$

Go to pages 220 and 221 for Quick Answers & pages 154–158 for Worked Solutions. See pages 124 and 125 for Topic Tests

2 Plane Geometry

Your Checklist

For a complete understanding of this topic you must be able to: ✓

- Understand the terms and symbols used in geometry
- Understand and use diagrams and draw diagrams from given data
- Understand the definitions of special triangles and quadrilaterals
- Find angles on a straight line
- Find vertically opposite angles
- Find angles at a point
- Understand what is meant by parallel lines and transversals
- Understand and find alternate, corresponding and co-interior angles
- Test for parallel lines
- Find the angle sum of a triangle
- Find the exterior angle of a triangle
- Find the angle sum of a quadrilateral
- Know the names of special polygons
- Find the angle sum of a polygon
- Know what is meant by a regular polygon
- Find each angle of a regular polygon
- Find the sum of the exterior angles of a polygon
- Understand what is meant by congruence
- Know and use the four tests for congruent triangles
- Understand the properties of isosceles and equilateral triangles
- Understand the properties of a parallelogram, rhombus, rectangle and square
- Understand the intercept properties of transversals to parallel lines
- Understand what is meant by similarity
- Know and use the three tests for similar triangles
- Understand Pythagoras' theorem
- Find areas of triangles and quadrilaterals
- Solve problems involving the application of any of the above properties

2.1 Notation, symbols, terms and definitions

- In plane geometry we deal with **points**, **lines** and **plane** (two-dimensional) **figures**.
- A capital letter is used to denote a **point**. An **angle** is usually named by three points, the centre letter being the vertex of the angle. If there is no possibility of confusion a single point may be used. The notation $\angle BAC$ or $B\hat{A}C$ or $\hat{A}$ or $\angle A$ is used for angle BAC.

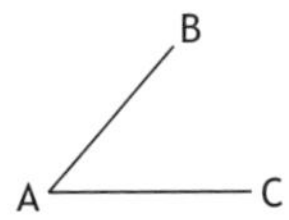

- Two points are used to name a **line**. PQ may refer to the line PQ, the interval from P to Q or the length from P to Q. The meaning is usually obvious.

Symbols

$\parallel$	is parallel to
$\perp$	is perpendicular to (at right angles)
$\equiv$	is congruent to
$\vert\vert\vert$	is similar to
ΔABC	triangle ABC
$\therefore$	therefore
$\because$	because (or since)

Terms

A **right angle** measures 90°.

Perpendicular means at right angles. A perpendicular is a line at right angles to another. The **foot of a perpendicular** is the point where it makes the right angle.

Bisect means cut in half.

A **line** means a straight line. It has infinite length.

An **interval**, or **line segment**, is part of the line between two points.

A **ray** is part of a line, from a point onward.

Collinear points are points on the same straight line.

Concurrent lines pass through the same point.

Parallel lines are lines in the same plane which never meet.

Produced means continued. P is a point on AB produced means that the interval AB is extended beyond B to a point P.

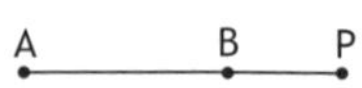

An **altitude** is a perpendicular line from the base of a figure to its highest point.

Go to page 45 for Exercises

Definitions

- A **triangle** is a three sided figure. The triangle is:
  - **scalene** if all three sides (and all three angles) are unequal;
  - **isosceles** if two sides (and two angles) are equal;
  - **equilateral** if all three sides (and all three angles) are equal.
- A **quadrilateral** is a four-sided figure.
  - A **parallelogram** is a quadrilateral with both pairs of opposite sides parallel.
  - A **rectangle** is a parallelogram with one angle 90°.
  - A **rhombus** is a parallelogram with one pair of adjacent sides equal.
  - A **square** is a rectangle with two adjacent sides equal.
  - A **trapezium** is a quadrilateral with one pair of opposite sides parallel.
- A **polygon** is a many-sided figure. A regular polygon has all sides equal and all angles equal.

2.2 Angles in a right angle

- A right angle measures 90°.

∟ ... means the angle is 90°. It is a right angle. The lines are perpendicular.

Q Find the value of x. 1

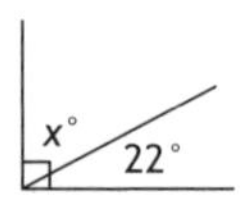

A $x + 22 = 90$ [angles in a right angle]

$x = 68$

2.3 Angles on a straight line

- The angles on a straight line total 180°.

$a° + b° + c° = 180°$

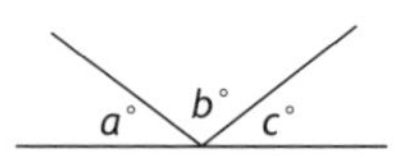

This rule only refers to angles that share a common vertex on a straight line.

Q Find the value of x. 2

a

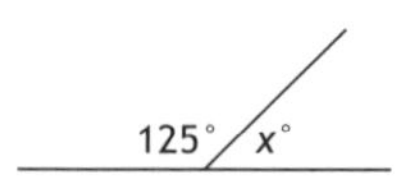

b

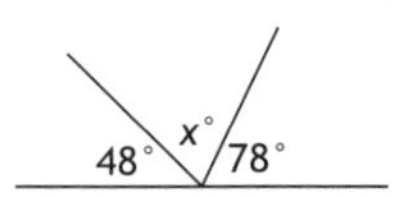

c

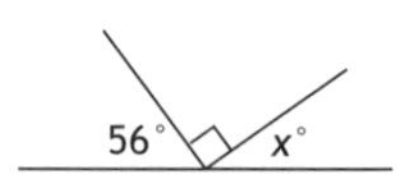

A a $x + 125 = 180$ [angles on a straight line]

$x = 55$

b $48 + x + 78 = 180$ [angles on a straight line]

$x + 126 = 180$

$x = 54$

c $56 + 90 + x = 180$ [angles on a straight line]

$x = 34$

Q AB is a straight line. CO ⊥ DO. ∠BOD = 37°. 3
Find the size of ∠AOC.

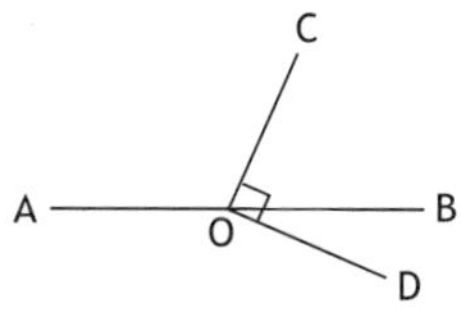

A $\angle COB = 90° - 37°$ [angles in a right angle]

$= 53°$

$\angle AOC + \angle COB = 180°$ [angles on a straight line]

$\angle AOC + 53° = 180°$

$\angle AOC = 127°$

Q The angles on a straight line are in the ratio 1 : 2 : 3. Find the size of each angle. 4

A Let the three angles measure $x°, 2x°$ and $3x°$.

$x + 2x + 3x = 180$ [angles on a straight line]

$6x = 180$

$x = 30$

∴ the angles are 30°, 60° and 90°.

2.4 Vertically opposite angles

- When two straight lines intersect, two pairs of vertically opposite angles are formed.
- Vertically opposite angles are equal.

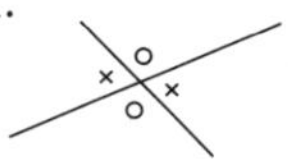

Proof:

Let AC and BD be two straight lines intersecting at E.

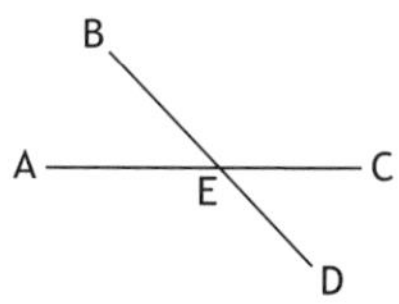

$\angle AEB + \angle BEC = 180°$ [angles on a straight line, AC]

$\angle DEC + \angle BEC = 180°$ [angles on a straight line, BD]

$\therefore \angle AEB = \angle DEC$

Similarly $\angle BEC = \angle AED$

Q Find the value of x. 5

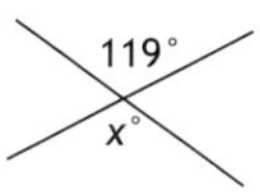

A $x = 119$ [vertically opposite angles]

Q AB and CD are two straight lines, intersecting at O. 6
∠AOC = 51°.
Find ∠AOD, ∠BOD and ∠COB.

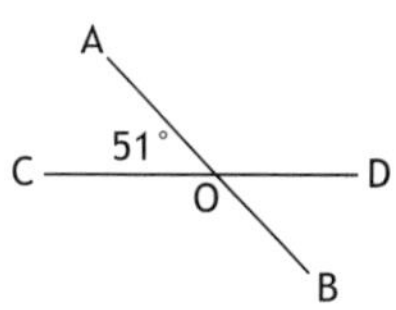

A $\angle AOD = 180° - \angle AOC$ [angles on a straight line]

$\angle AOD = 129°$

$\angle BOD = 51°$ [vertically opposite ∠AOC]

$\angle COB = 129°$ [vertically opposite ∠AOD]

Q PR and QS are two straight lines intersecting at T. 5

a Find the value of x.

b Find the size of ∠PTS.

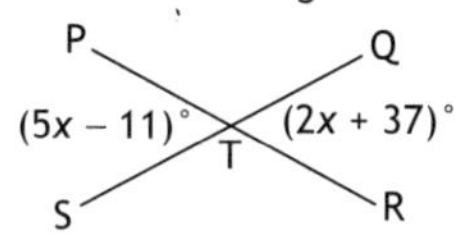

A a $\angle PTS = \angle QTR$ [vertically opposite angles]

$\therefore 5x - 11 = 2x + 37$

$3x = 48$

$x = 16$

b When $x = 16$

$5x - 11 = 5 \times 16 - 11$

$= 69$

$\therefore \angle PTS = 69°$

Q AB and CD are two straight lines intersecting at E. 6
FE bisects ∠AED.
∠BEC = 136°.
Find ∠DEF.

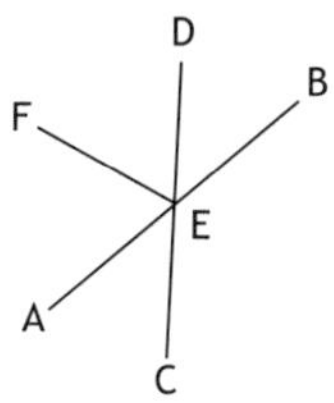

A $\angle AED = 136°$ [vertically opposite ∠BEC]

$\angle DEF = 136° \div 2$ [FE bisects ∠AED]

$\therefore \angle DEF = 68°$

2.5 Angles at a point

- A complete revolution measures 360°.

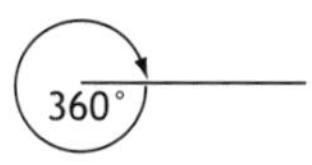

- Angles which meet at a point total 360°.

Q Find the value of x. 7

a

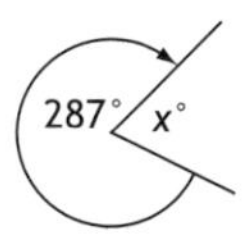

b

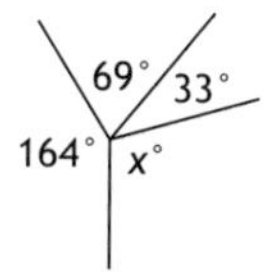

c

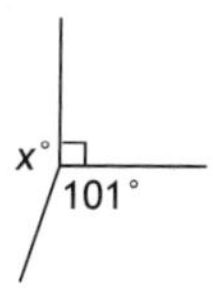

d

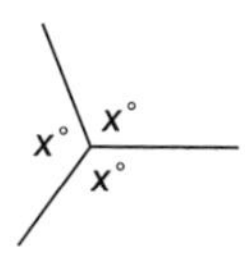

A a $x° + 287° = 360°$ [angles at a point]

$x° = 73°$

b $x° + 33° + 69° + 164° = 360°$ [angles at a point]

$x° + 266° = 360°$

$x° = 94°$

Go to page 45 for Exercises

c $x + 90 + 101 = 360$ [angles at a point]

$x + 191 = 360$

$x = 169$

d $x + x + x = 360$ [angles at a point]

$3x = 360$

$x = 120$

When giving the size of an angle, the units (degrees) should always be given (e.g. $\angle ABC = 65°43'$). When working with pronumerals, the '°' sign may be included as in **a** and **b** above or omitted as in **c** and **d**.

Be consistent. In **a** above, put either $x° = 73°$ or $x = 73$, but not $x = 73°$.

Q $\angle AOB = \angle COD = \angle DOE$ 8

$\angle BOC = 124°$

$\angle AOD = 90°$

Find the size of $\angle AOE$.

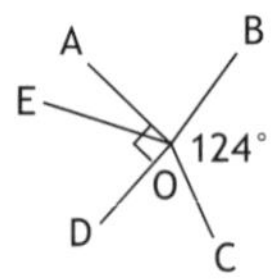

A Let $\angle AOB = x°$

$\therefore$ $COD = x°$

$\angle AOB + \angle BOC + \angle COD + \angle DOA = 360°$ [angles at a point]

$x + 124 + x + 90 = 360$

$2x + 214 = 360$

$2x = 146$

$x = 73$

$\therefore \angle DOE = 73°$ [$\angle DOE = \angle AOB$]

$\angle AOE + \angle DOE = 90°$ [angles in a right angle]

$\angle AOE = 17°$

2.6 Parallel lines

- If a pair of lines are in the same plane but never meet, they are parallel. On a diagram we show lines are parallel by the use of arrows (e.g. lines with two arrows are parallel to other lines shown with the same number of arrows).

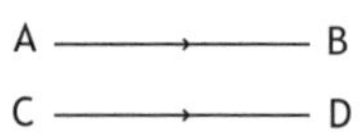

means AB is parallel to CD.
AB || CD

- A **transversal** is a line drawn across a pair (or more) of straight lines.

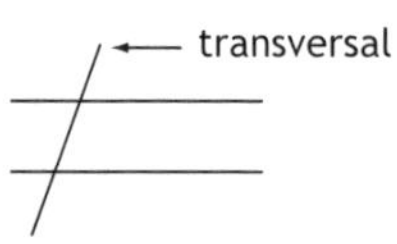

- When straight lines are cut by a transversal some special types of angles are formed.
  - Corresponding angles are found in the corresponding (or same) position on each of the lines. **If the lines are parallel the corresponding angles are equal.**

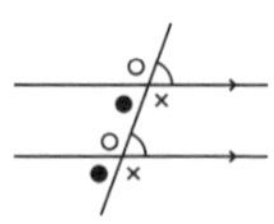

  - Alternate angles are found inside the lines on alternate sides of the transversal. **When the lines are parallel the alternate angles are equal.**

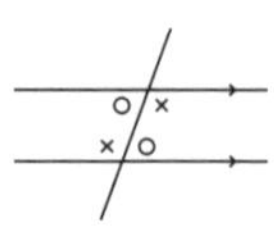

  - Co-interior (or allied) angles are found inside the lines on the same side of the transversal. **If the lines are parallel the co-interior angles are supplementary.** This means they add to 180°.

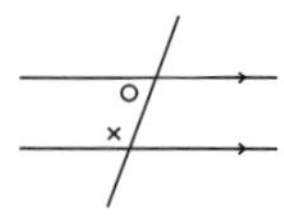

Q Find the value of x. 9

a

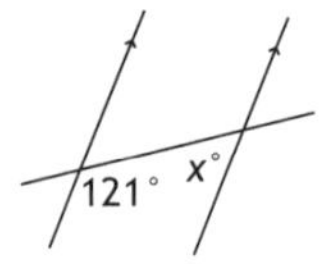

b

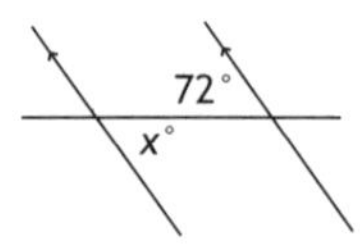

c

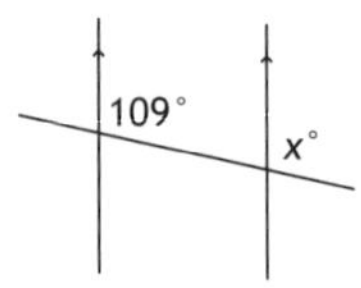

A a $x + 121 = 180$ [co-interior angles, || lines]

$x = 59$

b $x = 72$ [alternate angles, || lines]

c $x = 109$ [corresponding angles, || lines]

Q $\angle ADC = 111°$ 10

Find $\angle JIL$.

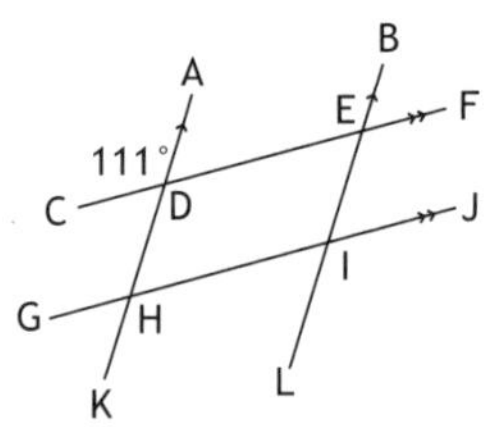

A $\angle ADC = 111°$

$\angle BED = 111°$ [corresponding to $\angle ADC$, AK || BL]

$\angle FEL = 111°$ [vertically opposite $\angle BED$]

$\angle JIL = 111°$ [corresponding to $\angle FEL$, CF || GJ]

- If two lines are **parallel to a third line**, they are parallel to each other.

Q AC || FG. DE || FG. 11

$\angle DEB = 145°$

$\angle BFG = 70°$

Show that $\angle ABE = \angle EBF$.

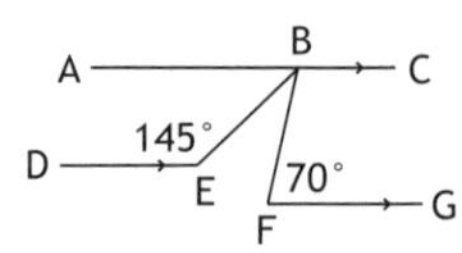

A $\angle ABF = 70°$ [alternate to $\angle BFG$, AC || FG]

AC || DE [both parallel to FG]

$\therefore \angle ABE = 35°$ [co-interior to $\angle DEB$, AC || DE]

$\angle EBF = \angle ABF - \angle ABE$

$= 70° - 35°$

$= 35°$

$\therefore \angle ABE = \angle EBF$

Q PQ is parallel to TS. 12

$\angle PQR = 67°$

$\angle TSR = 58°$

Find the size of $\angle QRS$.

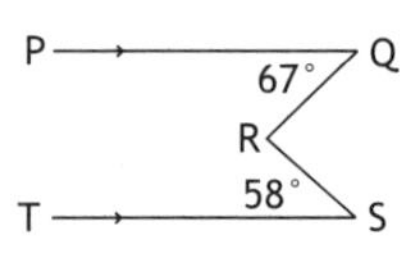

Go to page 45 for Exercises

A

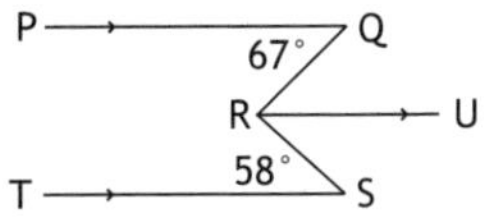

Construct RU, parallel to PQ.

$\angle QRU = 67°$ [alternate to $\angle PQR$, RU || PQ]

TS || RU [both parallel to PQ]

$\therefore \angle SRU = 58°$ [alternate to $\angle TSR$, RU || TS]

$\therefore \angle QRS = 67° + 58°$

$= 125°$

- A pair of straight lines are parallel if:
  - the corresponding angles are equal, or
  - the alternate angles are equal, or
  - the co-interior angles are supplementary.

Q In each diagram, determine whether AB is parallel to CD. **13**

a

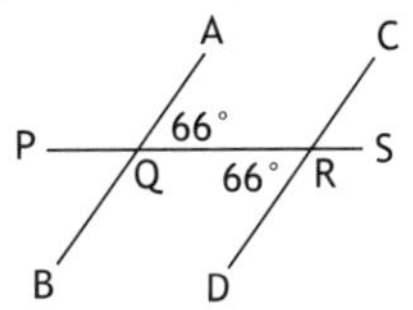

b

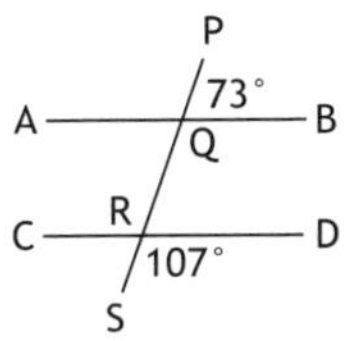

c

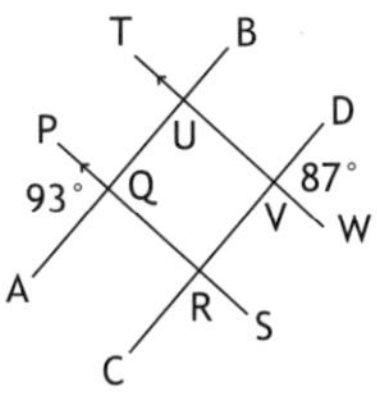

A **a** $\angle AQR = \angle QRD$

$\therefore$ AB || CD [alternate angles are equal]

b $\angle BQS = 180° - 73°$ [angles on a straight line]

$= 107°$

$\therefore \angle BQS = \angle DRS$

$\therefore$ AB || CD [corresponding angles are equal]

c $\angle TUA = 93°$ [corresponding to $\angle PQA$, PS || TW]

$\therefore \angle BUW = 93°$ [vertically opposite to $\angle TUA$]

$\angle BUW \neq \angle DVW$

$\therefore$ AB is not parallel to CD

[corresponding angles are not equal]

2.7 The angle sum of a triangle

- The angle sum of a triangle is 180°.

Proof:

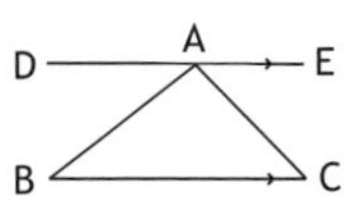

Draw DE through A, parallel to BC.

$\angle DAB = \angle ABC$ [alternate angles, DE || BC]

$\angle CAE = \angle ACB$ [alternate angles, DE || BC]

$\angle DAB + \angle BAC + \angle CAE = 180°$

[angles on a straight line]

$\therefore \angle ABC + \angle BAC + \angle ACB = 180°$

Q Find the value of x. **14**

a

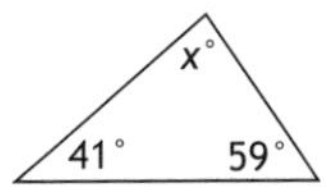

b

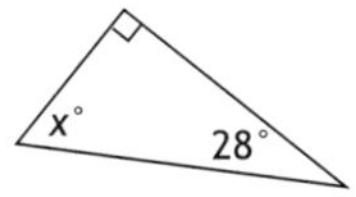

c

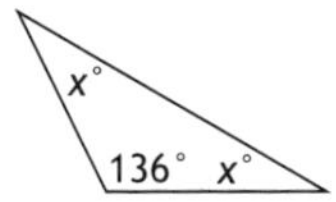

A **a** $x + 41 + 59 = 180$ [angle sum of a triangle]

$x + 100 = 180$

$x = 80$

b $x + 28 + 90 = 180$ [angle sum of a triangle]

$x + 118 = 180$

$x = 62$

c $x + x + 136 = 180$ [angle sum of a triangle]

$2x + 136 = 180$

$2x = 44$

$x = 22$

Q The sizes of the three angles of a triangle are in the ratio 4 : 5 : 6. Find the size of each angle. **15**

A Let the angle sizes be $4x°$, $5x°$ and $6x°$.

$4x + 5x + 6x = 180$ [angle sum of a triangle]

$15x = 180$

$x = 12$

$\therefore 4x = 4 \times 12$

$= 48$

$5x = 60$

$6x = 72$

$\therefore$ the angles of the triangle measure 48°, 60° and 72°

Check: $48° + 60° + 72° = 180°$

2.8 The exterior angle of a triangle

- If a side of a triangle is extended, the angle formed on the outside of the triangle is called an exterior angle.
- **The exterior angle of a triangle is equal to the sum of the interior opposite angles.**

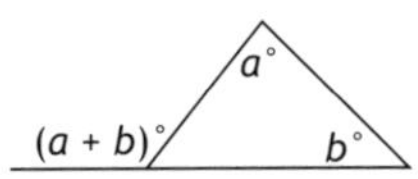

Proof:

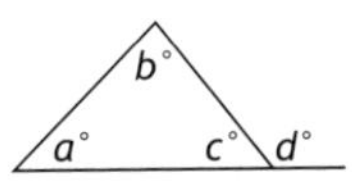

$a° + b° + c° = 180°$ [angle sum of a triangle]

but $d° + c° = 180°$ [angles on a straight line]

$\therefore d° = a° + b°$

Go to page 45 for Exercises

Q Find the value of x. 16

a

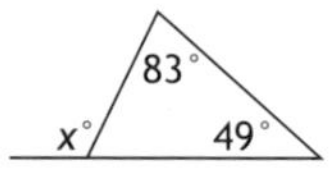

b

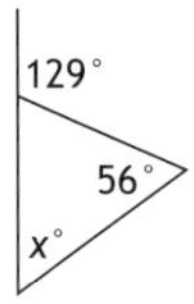

c

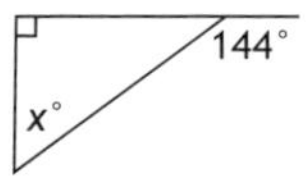

d

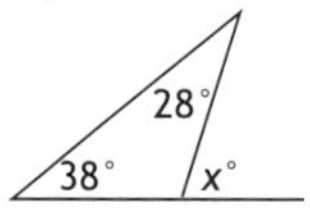

A a $x = 83 + 49$ [exterior angle of a triangle]
$= 132$

b $x + 56 = 129$ [exterior angle of a triangle]
$x = 73$

c $x + 90 = 144$ [exterior angle of a triangle]
$x = 54$

d $x = 28 + 38$ [exterior angle of a triangle]
$= 66$

Q In the diagram, $\angle PQS = 147°$ and $\angle QST = 129°$. Find the size of $\angle QRS$. 17

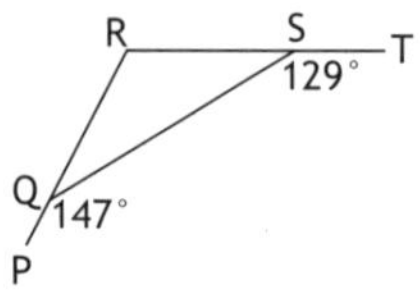

A $\angle PQS + \angle SQR = 180°$ [angles on a straight line]
$\angle SQR = 180° - 147°$
$= 33°$
$\angle QST = \angle SQR + \angle QRS$ [exterior angle of ΔRQS]
$\therefore \angle QRS = 129° - 33°$
$= 96°$

2.9 The angle sum of a quadrilateral

- Any quadrilateral can be divided into two triangles by the drawing of a diagonal. Since the angle sum of a triangle is 180°, the angle sum of a quadrilateral is 2 × 180° = 360°.

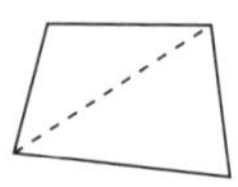

The angle sum of any quadrilateral is 360°.

Q Find the value of x. 18

a

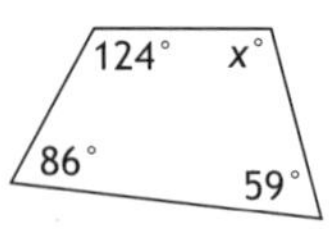

b

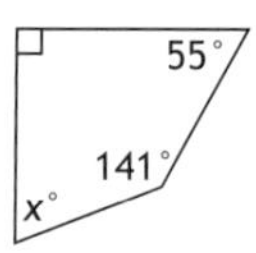

c

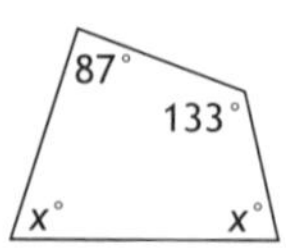

d

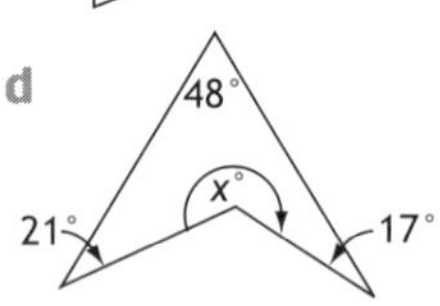

A a $x + 124 + 86 + 59 = 360$ [angle sum of a quad.]
$x + 269 = 360$
$x = 91$

b $x + 141 + 55 + 90 = 360$ [angle sum of a quad.]
$x + 286 = 360$
$x = 74$

c $x + x + 87 + 133 = 360$ [angle sum of a quad.]
$2x + 220 = 360$
$2x = 140$
$x = 70$

d $x + 17 + 48 + 21 = 360$ [angle sum of a quad.]
$x + 86 = 360$
$x = 274$

Go to pages 45 and 46 for Exercises

Q The angles of a quadrilateral are in the ratio 3 : 4 : 5 : 6. Find the size of the largest angle. 19

A Let the angles measure $3x°$, $4x°$, $5x°$ and $6x°$.
$3x + 4x + 5x + 6x = 360$ [angle sum of a quad.]
$18x = 360$
$x = 20$
$\therefore 6x = 6 \times 20$
$= 120$
$\therefore$ the largest angle measures 120°

2.10 The angle sum of a polygon

- A polygon is a many-sided plane figure. There are special names given to polygons with certain numbers of sides:

Number of sides	Name
5	pentagon
6	hexagon
7	heptagon
8	octagon
9	nonagon (or enneagon)
10	decagon
12	dodecagon

- A polygon with n sides can be divided into $(n-2)$ triangles by drawing straight lines from one vertex to all other vertices (except adjacent ones).

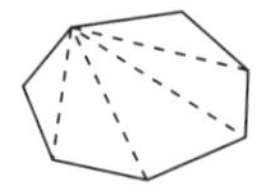

- Angle sum of the polygon $= (n-2) \times 180°$
$= (2n-4) \times 90°$

The angle sum of any polygon is $(2n - 4)$ right angles, where n is the number of sides.

Q Find the angle sum of: 20

a a hexagon

b a decagon

A a A hexagon has 6 sides.
Angle sum $= (2n - 4)$ right angles
$= (2 \times 6 - 4) \times 90°$
$= 720°$

b A decagon has 10 sides.
Angle sum $= (2n - 4)$ right angles
$= (2 \times 10 - 4) \times 90°$
$= 1440°$

Q If the angle sum of a polygon is 2880°, find the number of sides. 21

A Angle sum $= (2n - 4)$ right angles

$2880° = (2n - 4) \times 90°$

$\therefore\ 2n - 4 = 2880° \div 90°$

$2n - 4 = 32$

$2n = 36$

$n = 18$

$\therefore$ the polygon has 18 sides

Q Find the value of x. 22

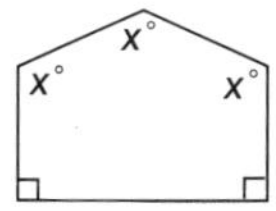

A The polygon has 5 sides (pentagon).

Angle sum $= (2n - 4)$ right angles

$= (2 \times 5 - 4) \times 90°$

$= 540°$

$x + x + x + 90 + 90 = 540$

$3x + 180 = 540$

$3x = 360$

$x = 120$

2.11 Regular polygons

- A regular polygon is one in which all the sides are equal and all the angles are equal.

Q Find the size of each angle of a regular octagon. 23

A An octagon has 8 sides.

Angle sum $= (2n - 4)$ right angles

$= (2 \times 8 - 4) \times 90°$

$= 1080°$

A regular octagon has 8 equal angles.

Each angle $= 1080° \div 8$

$= 135°$

$\therefore$ each angle of a regular octagon measures 135°

Q A 20-sided polygon has all its sides equal. Find the size of each of its angles. 24

A Polygon has 20 equal angles.

Angle sum $= (2n - 4)$ right angles

$= (2 \times 20 - 4) \times 90°$

$= 3240°$

Each angle $= 3240° \div 20$

$= 162°$

Q Each angle of a regular polygon measures 156°. How many sides has the polygon? 25

A Let the number of sides be n.

Each angle $= 156°$

$\therefore$ angle sum $= 156n°$

but angle sum $= (2n - 4)$ right angles

continued ...

$\therefore\ (2n - 4) \times 90° = 156n°$

$180n° - 360° = 156n°$

$24n° = 360°$

$n = 15$

$\therefore$ the polygon has 15 sides

2.12 The exterior angles of a polygon

- **The sum of the exterior angles of any polygon is 360°.**

$v° + w° + x° + y° + z° = 360°$

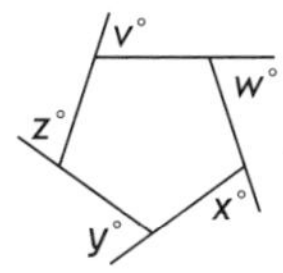

Proof:

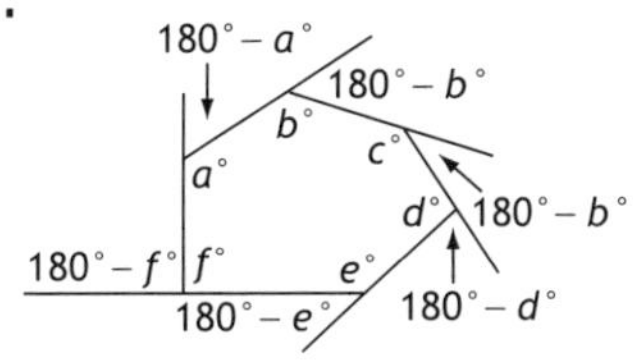

If $a°, b°, c°, d°, e°, \ldots$ are the interior angles of a polygon, the exterior angles are $180° - a°$, $180° - b°$, $180° - c°$, $180° - d°, \ldots$

Now $a° + b° + c° + d° + e° + \ldots = (2n - 4) \times 90°$

$= 180° \times n - 360°$

Exterior angle sum

$= 180° - a° + 180° - b° + 180° - c° + 180° - d° + \ldots$

$= 180° \times n - (a° + b° + c° + d° + e° + \ldots)$

$= 180° \times n - (180° \times n - 360°)$

$= 360°$

Q Find the value of x. 26

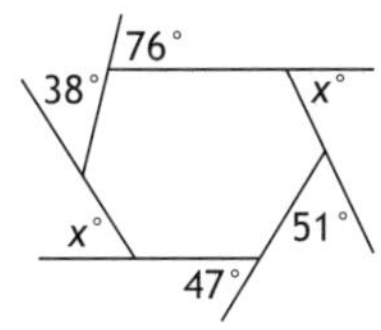

A $76 + x + 51 + 47 + x + 38 = 360$

[angle sum of exterior angles]

$2x + 212 = 360$

$2x = 148$

$x = 74$

Q Find the size of each exterior angle of a regular dodecagon. 27

A Angle sum of exterior angles = 360°

A dodecagon has 12 sides.

Each exterior angle = 360° ÷ 12

= 30°

$\therefore$ each exterior angle of a regular dodecagon is 30°

Q Find the size of each: 28

a exterior angle **b** interior angle

of a regular heptagon.

A **a** Angle sum of exterior angles = 360°

A heptagon has 7 sides.

Each exterior angle = 360° ÷ 7

= 51°26′ [nearest minute]

Go to page 46 for Exercises

b Each exterior angle = 51°26'

∴ each interior angle = 180° − 51°26'

= 128°34' [nearest minute]

2.13 Congruent triangles

- Triangles are congruent if they are exactly the same shape and the same size.
- There are **four tests** for congruent triangles. Two triangles are congruent if:
  - three sides of one are respectively equal to three sides of the other (**SSS**), or

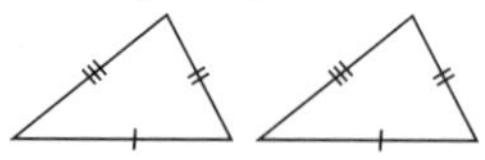

  - two sides and the included angle of one are respectively equal to two sides and the **included angle** of the other (**SAS**), or

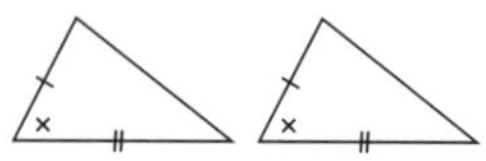

  - two angles and a side of one are respectively equal to two angles and the **corresponding side** of the other (**AAS**), or

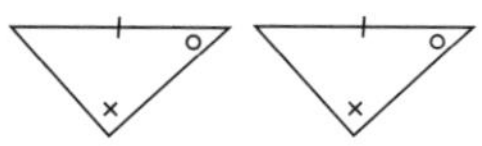

  - the hypotenuse and one side of a right-angled triangle are respectively equal to the hypotenuse and one side of another right-angled triangle (**RHS**).

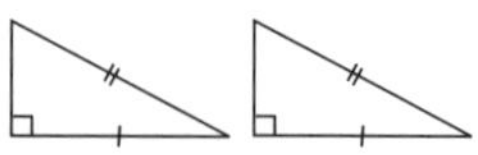

In the SAS test, the angle must be the *included* angle (the angle between the two sides).

In the AAS test, the side must be the *corresponding* side (the side must be in the same corresponding position in both triangles).

Q Prove that each pair of triangles are congruent. **29**

a

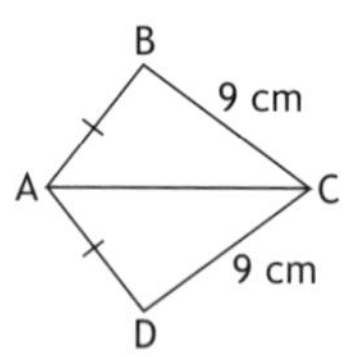

ΔABC, ΔADC

b

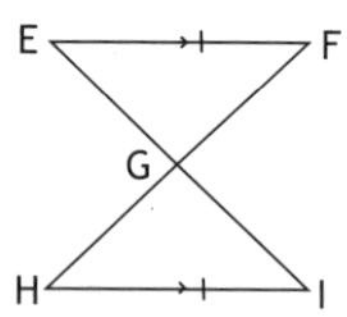

ΔEFG, ΔIHG

c

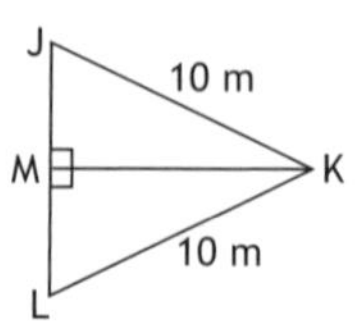

ΔJKM, ΔLKM

d

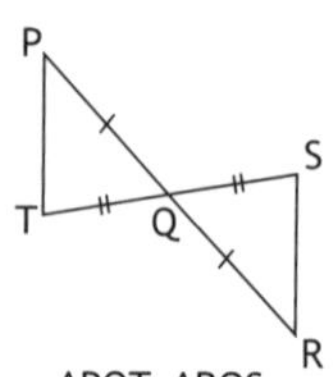

ΔPQT, ΔRQS
(PR, TS straight lines)

Go to page 46 for Exercises

A **a** In ΔABC, ΔADC

AB = AD	[given]
BC = DC	[both 9 cm]
AC = AC	[common side]
∴ ΔABC ≡ ΔADC	[SSS]

b In ΔEFG, ΔIHG

∠EFG = ∠IHG	[alternate, EF ‖ HI]
∠FEG = ∠HIG	[alternate, EF ‖ HI]
EF = IH	[given]
∴ ΔEFG ≡ ΔIHG	[AAS]

c In ΔJKM, ΔLKM

∠JMK = ∠LMK	[both 90°]
JK = LK	[both 10 cm]
MK = MK	[common side]
∴ ΔJKM ≡ ΔLKM	[RHS]

d In ΔPQT, ΔRQS

PQ = RQ	[given]
∠PQT = ∠RQS	[vertically opposite]
TQ = SQ	[given]
∴ ΔPQT ≡ ΔRQS	[SAS]

2.14 Results from congruent triangles

- If two triangles are congruent, then the corresponding sides are equal and the corresponding angles are equal.
- By proving two triangles congruent we can then prove other properties.

Q In the diagram, AB = ED and BE = DA. **30**

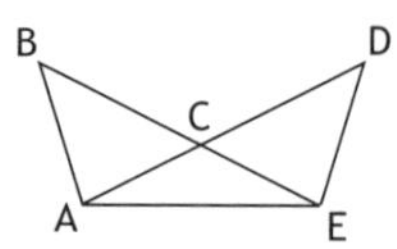

a Prove that ΔABE is congruent to ΔEDA.

b Hence show that ∠BAD = ∠DEB.

A **a** In ΔABE, ΔEDA

AB = ED	[given]
BE = DA	[given]
AE = EA	[common side]
∴ ΔABE ≡ ΔEDA	[SSS]

b ∠BAE = ∠DEA

[corresponding angles of congruent triangles]

and ∠DAE = ∠BEA

[corresponding angles of congruent triangles]

∴ ∠BAD = ∠DEB

Q In ΔACB, AC = CB. D is a point on AB such that DC bisects ∠ACB. Find the size of ∠ADC. **31**

A In ΔACD, ΔBCD

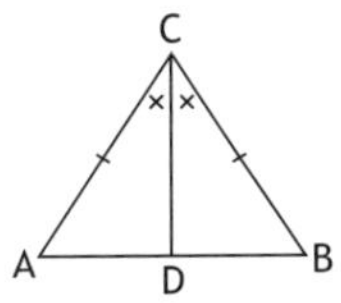

$AC = BC$ [given]
$\angle ACD = \angle BCD$ [DC bisects $\angle ACB$]
$CD = CD$ [common side]
$\therefore \Delta ACD \equiv \Delta BCD$ [SAS]
$\therefore \angle ADC = \angle BDC$
[corresponding angles of congruent triangles]
but $\angle ADC + \angle BDC = 180°$ [angles on a straight line]
$\therefore \angle ADC = 90°$

Q X is a point on PQ such that $RX \perp PQ$ and XR bisects $\angle PRQ$. Show that PR = QR. **32**

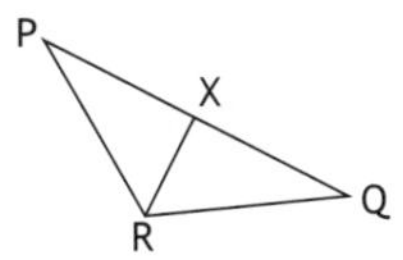

A In ΔPXR, ΔQXR

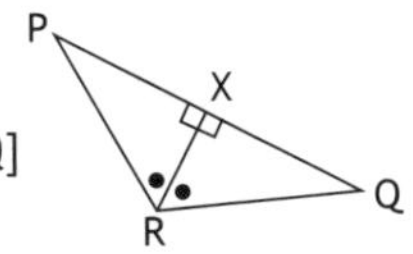

$\angle PXR = \angle QXR$ [$RX \perp PQ$]
$\angle PRX = \angle QRX$ [XR bisects $\angle PRQ$]
$RX = RX$ [common side]
$\therefore \Delta PXR \equiv \Delta QXR$ [AAS]
$\therefore PR = QR$
[corresponding sides of congruent triangles]

2.15 Special triangles

- An **isosceles triangle** has two equal sides and two equal angles. The angles opposite the equal sides are equal. The angles opposite the equal sides are often referred to as the base angles of the triangle, even though they may not be at the bottom of the diagram.
- **Equilateral triangles** have three equal sides and three equal angles. Each angle of an equilateral triangle measures 60°.

Q Find the value of x. **33**

a

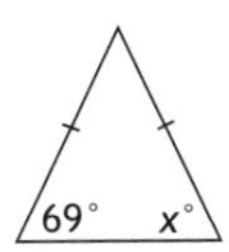

b

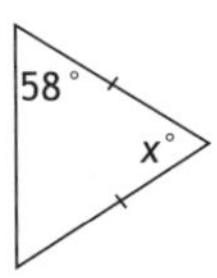

c

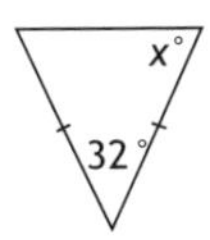

d

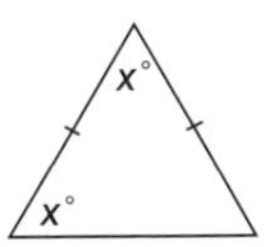

e

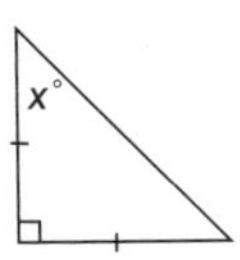

A **a** $x = 69$ [base angles of isosceles triangle]

b Both base angles of the isosceles triangle measure 58°.
$x + 2 \times 58 = 180$ [angle sum of a triangle]
$x = 180 - 116$
$= 64$

c Base angles of isosceles triangle = $x°$
$2x + 32 = 180$ [angle sum of a triangle]
$2x = 148$
$x = 74$

d Base angles of isosceles triangle = $x°$
$\therefore$ the triangle is equilateral [all angles are equal]
$\therefore x = 60$

e Base angles of isosceles triangle = $x°$
$2x + 90 = 180$ [angle sum of a triangle]
$2x = 90$
$x = 45$

Q $\angle ABC = 90°$ **34**
$\angle BAD = 73°$
AB = DB
BC = DC
Find $\angle BCD$.

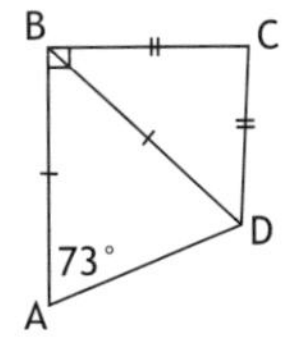

A $\angle BAD = 73°$
$\therefore \angle ADB = 73°$ [base angles of isosceles triangle]
$\angle ABD = 180° - 2 \times 73°$ [angle sum of a triangle]
$\angle ABD = 34°$
$\therefore \angle DBC = 56°$ [$\angle ABC = 90°$, given]
$\angle BDC = 56°$ [base angles of isosceles triangle]
$\angle BCD = 180° - 2 \times 56°$ [angle sum of a triangle]
$\angle BCD = 68°$

2.16 Properties of quadrilaterals

- A **parallelogram** is defined as a quadrilateral with both pairs of opposite sides parallel. A parallelogram has the following properties:
  - the opposite sides are equal
  - the opposite angles are equal
  - the diagonals bisect each other

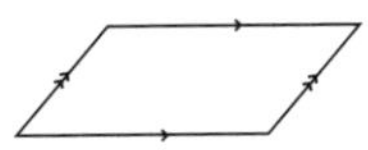

- A **rhombus** is defined as a parallelogram with a pair of adjacent sides equal. A rhombus has the following properties:
  - all the properties of a parallelogram
  - the diagonals bisect each other at right angles
  - the diagonals bisect the angles through which they pass

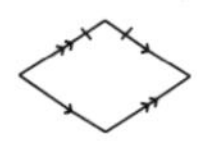

- A **rectangle** is defined as a parallelogram with one right-angle. A rectangle has the following properties:
  - all the properties of a parallelogram
  - the diagonals are equal

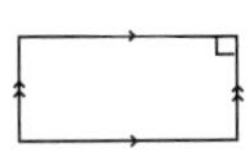

- A **square** is defined as a rectangle with a pair of adjacent sides equal. A square has all the above properties.

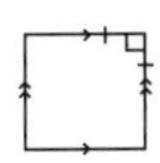

Go to page 46 for Exercises

Q Find the values of x and y. 35

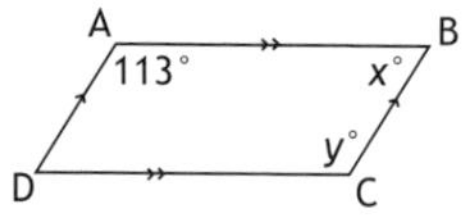

A ABCD is a parallelogram.

$x + 113 = 180$ [co-interior angles, AD || BC]

$x = 67$

$y = 113$ [opposite angles of a parallelogram]

Q PQ || SR. QR || PS. 36

PQ = QR. ∠SPR = 57°.

Find ∠PQR.

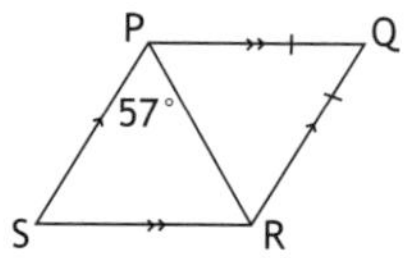

A PQRS is a rhombus.

∠SPQ = 2∠SPR [diagonals bisect the angles]

∴ ∠SPQ = 114°

∠SPQ + ∠PQR = 180° [co-interior angles, SP || RQ]

∠PQR = 180° − 114°

= 66°

Q 37

a Find x.

b Find the length of the diagonals.

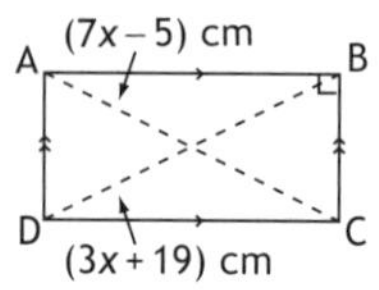

A **a** ABCD is a rectangle.

∴ the diagonals are equal

$7x - 5 = 3x + 19$

$4x = 24$

$x = 6$

b When $x = 6$

$7x - 5 = 7 \times 6 - 5$

$= 37$

Check: $3x + 19 = 3 \times 6 + 19 = 37$

∴ the diagonals are both 37 cm long

Q ABCD is a parallelogram. 38

a Find the value of x.

b Find the length of each side of the parallelogram.

c What conclusions can be drawn about the parallelogram? Justify the answer.

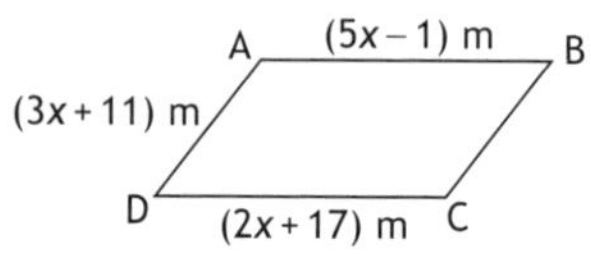

A **a** ABCD is a parallelogram.

∴ the opposite sides are equal

$5x - 1 = 2x + 17$

$3x = 18$

$x = 6$

b When $x = 6$

$5x - 1 = 5 \times 6 - 1$

$= 29$

∴ AB = CD = 29 m

$3x + 11 = 3 \times 6 + 11$

$= 29$

∴ AD = BC = 29 m

c ABCD is a rhombus because it is a parallelogram with a pair of adjacent sides equal.

Go to pages 46 and 47 for Exercises

Q AB || DC 38

BC || AD

Prove that AB = CD.

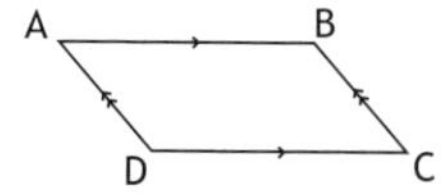

A Draw in diagonal AC.

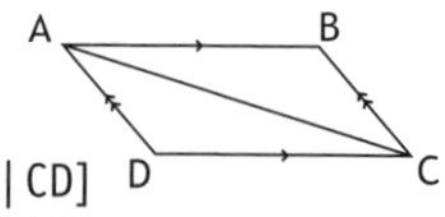

In ΔABC, ΔCDA

∠BAC = ∠DCA [alternate, AB || CD]

∠ACB = ∠CAD [alternate, BC || AD]

AC = CA [common side]

∴ ΔABC ≡ ΔCDA [AAS]

∴ AB = CD

[corresponding sides of congruent triangles]

2.17 Tests for special quadrilaterals

- A **quadrilateral is**:
  - a **parallelogram** if:
    - both pairs of opposite sides are equal, or
    - both pairs of opposite angles are equal, or
    - one pair of opposite sides are parallel and equal, or
    - the diagonals bisect each other.
  - a **rhombus** if:
    - all the sides are equal, or
    - the diagonals bisect each other at right angles.
- A **parallelogram** is a rectangle if the diagonals are equal.

Q What special type of quadrilateral are each of these. Justify the answer. 39

a

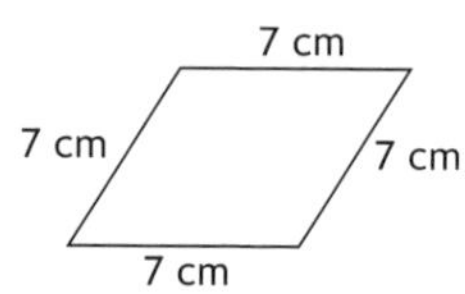

b

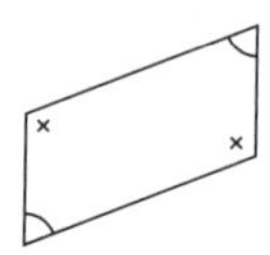

c

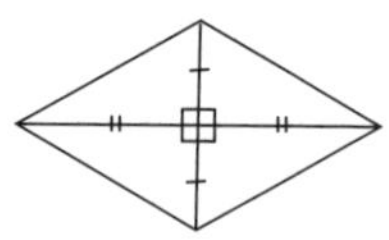

d

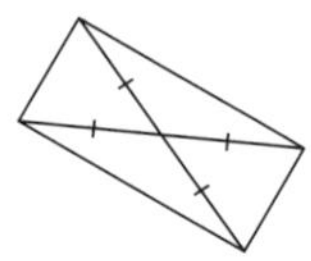

A **a** A rhombus because all the sides are equal.

b A parallelogram because both pairs of opposite angles are equal.

c A rhombus because the diagonals bisect each other at right-angles.

d A rectangle because it is a parallelogram (the diagonals bisect each other) and the diagonals are equal.

Q ΔABC is isosceles with AB = BC. 40

D is the midpoint of AC.

BD is produced to E, so that BD = DE.

Show that ABCE is a rhombus.

A AD = DC [D is the midpoint of AC]
BD = DE [given]
∴ the diagonals bisect each other
∴ ABCE is a parallelogram
but AB = BC [given]
∴ ABCE is a rhombus
[a parallelogram with a pair of adjacent sides equal]

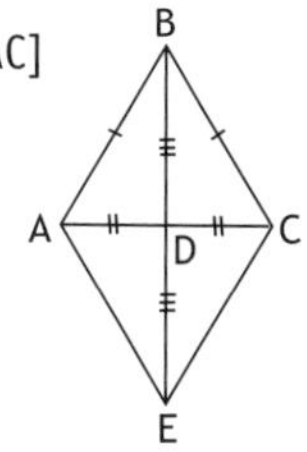

Q A quadrilateral has both pairs of opposite angles equal. Prove that the quadrilateral is a parallelogram. 40

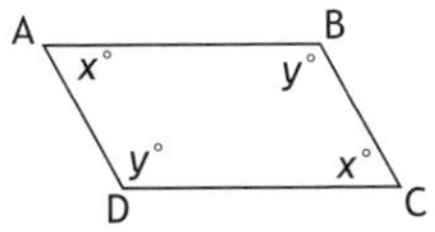

A Let ∠DAB = ∠BCD = $x°$
and ∠ABC = ∠CDA = $y°$
$2x + 2y = 360$ [angle sum of a quadrilateral]
∴ $x + y = 180$
∴ AB || CD and AD || BC
[co-interior angles are supplementary]
∴ ABCD is a parallelogram

2.18 Similar triangles

- Similar figures are exactly the same shape, but not necessarily the same size.
- Two **triangles are similar** if:
  - the corresponding angles are equal, or two pairs of corresponding angles are equal, or
  - the corresponding sides are proportional, or
  - two pairs of corresponding sides are proportional and the included angles are equal.

Q Show that each pair of triangles are similar. 41

a

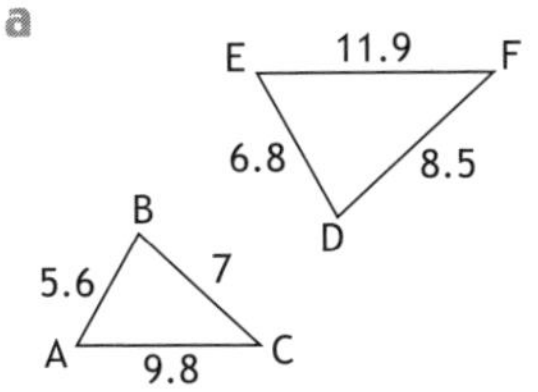

ΔABC, ΔEDF

b

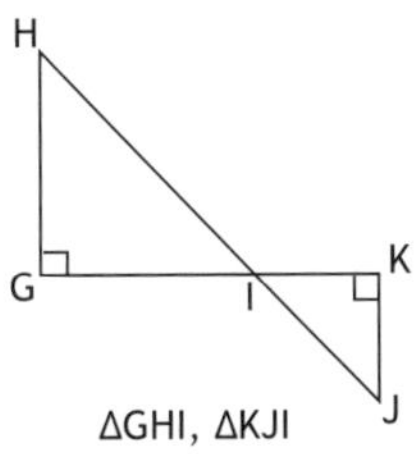

ΔGHI, ΔKJI
(HJ, GK straight lines)

c

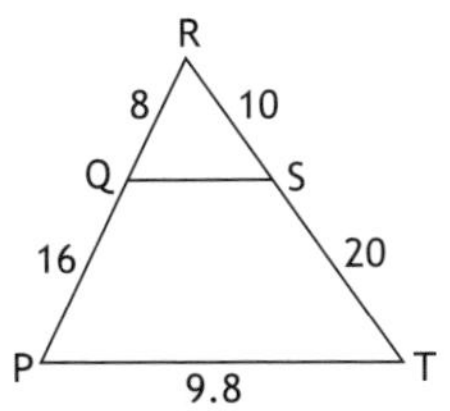

ΔPRT, ΔQRS

A **a** In ΔABC, ΔEDF

$\frac{AB}{ED} = \frac{5.6}{6.8} = \frac{14}{17}$ $\frac{BC}{DF} = \frac{7}{8.5} = \frac{14}{17}$

continued ...

$\frac{AC}{EF} = \frac{9.8}{11.9} = \frac{14}{17}$

∴ $\frac{AB}{ED} = \frac{BC}{DF} = \frac{AC}{EF}$

∴ ΔABC ||| ΔEDF

b In ΔGHI, ΔKJI
∠HGI = ∠JKI [both 90°, given]
∠GIH = ∠KIJ [vertically opposite]
∴ ΔGHI ||| ΔKJI

c In ΔPRT, ΔQRS
∠PRT = ∠QRS [common angle]

$\frac{PR}{QR} = \frac{24}{8} = 3$ $\frac{TR}{SR} = \frac{30}{10} = 3$

∴ $\frac{PR}{QR} = \frac{TR}{SR}$

∴ ΔPRT ||| ΔQRS

In the answer to part **a**, the corresponding sides can easily be matched; the two smallest sides, the two largest sides, and the other two sides.

In the answer to part **b**, it is only necessary to show that two pairs of corresponding angles are equal because the third pair must then also be equal.

- If two triangles are similar, then the corresponding angles are equal and the corresponding sides are in proportion.

Q **a** In the diagram, BE is parallel to CD. Show that ΔABE is similar to ΔACD. 42

b If AB = 28 m, BC = 8 m, CD = 18 m and ED = 5 m, find BE and AD.

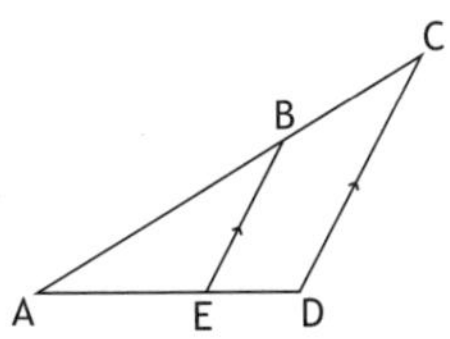

A **a** In ΔABE, ΔACD
∠BAE = ∠CAD [common angle]
∠ABE = ∠ACD [corresponding angles, BE || CD]
∴ ΔABE ||| ΔACD

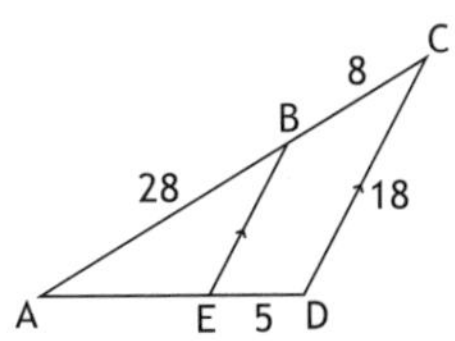

b AC = 28 + 8
= 36 m

$\frac{BE}{CD} = \frac{AB}{AC}$

[corresponding sides of similar triangles]

$\frac{BE}{18} = \frac{28}{36}$

$BE = \frac{28 \times 18}{36}$
= 14 m

continued ...

Go to page 47 for Exercises

Let AE $= x$ m

$\therefore \quad AD = (x+5)$ m

$\dfrac{AE}{AD} = \dfrac{AB}{AC}$

[corresponding sides of similar triangles]

$$\frac{x}{x+5} = \frac{28}{36}$$

$$36x = 28(x+5)$$
$$36x = 28x + 140$$
$$8x = 140$$
$$x = 17.5$$

$\therefore AD = 17.5 + 5$

$= 22.5$ m

$\therefore$ BE = 14 m and AD = 22.5 m

Q AB and CD are two straight lines, intersecting at E. AC || DB. AC = 91 mm, AE = 63 mm, CE = 56 mm and BD = 52 mm. Find the length of DE. **43**

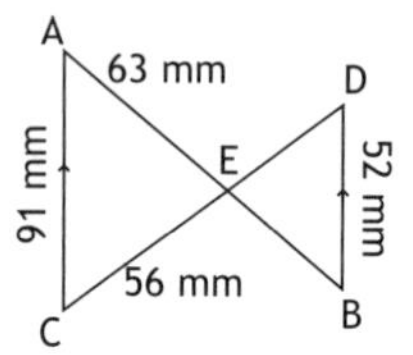

A In ΔACE, ΔBDE

$\angle ACE = \angle BDE$ [alternate angles, AC || DB]

$\angle AEC = \angle BED$ [vertically opposite angles]

$\therefore \Delta ACE \;|||\; \Delta BDE$

$\dfrac{AC}{BD} = \dfrac{CE}{DE}$ [corresponding sides of similar triangles]

$$\frac{91}{52} = \frac{56}{DE}$$
$$DE = \frac{56 \times 52}{91}$$
$$= 32 \text{ mm}$$

2.19 Properties from similar triangles

These properties are simple results derivable from similar triangles.

- A line parallel to one side of a triangle divides the other two sides in proportion.

Q In ΔPQR, S is a point on PQ and T a point on PR such that ST is parallel to QR. **44**

Show that $\dfrac{PS}{PQ} = \dfrac{PT}{PR}$.

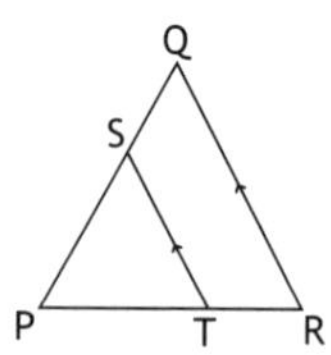

A In ΔPST, ΔPQR

$\angle SPT = \angle QPR$ [common angle]

$\angle PST = \angle PQR$ [corresponding angles, ST || QR]

$\therefore \Delta PST \;|||\; \Delta PQR$

$\therefore \quad \dfrac{PS}{PQ} = \dfrac{PT}{PR}$ [corresponding sides of similar triangles]

Go to page 47 for Exercises

- A line joining the midpoints of two sides of a triangle is parallel to the third side and half its length.

Q D and E are the midpoints respectively of sides AB and CB of a triangle. Show that: **45**

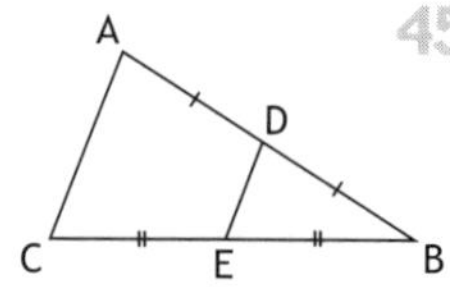

a ΔABC and ΔDBE are similar.

b AC is parallel to DE.

c $DE = \dfrac{1}{2}AC$

A a In ΔABC, ΔDBE

$\dfrac{DB}{AB} = \dfrac{1}{2}$ [D is the midpoint of AB]

$\dfrac{EB}{CB} = \dfrac{1}{2}$ [E is the midpoint of CB]

$\angle ABC = \angle DBE$ [common angle]

$\therefore \Delta ABC \;|||\; \Delta DBE$

b $\angle BAC = \angle BDE$

[corresponding angles of similar triangles]

$\therefore$ AC || DE [corresponding angles are equal]

c $\dfrac{DE}{AC} = \dfrac{DB}{AB}$ [corresponding sides of similar triangles are proportional]

$\therefore \dfrac{DE}{AC} = \dfrac{1}{2}$

$\therefore DE = \dfrac{1}{2}AC$

2.20 Intercept properties of transversals to parallel lines

- Parallel lines preserve the ratios of intercepts on transversals.

This result follows from similar triangles.

$\Delta PQT \;|||\; \Delta PRS$

[corresponding angles are equal]

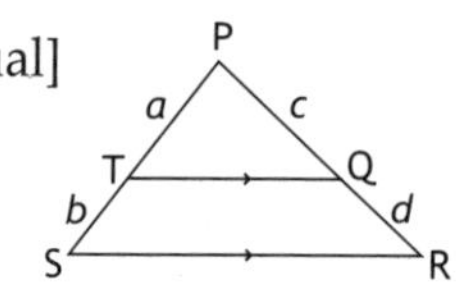

$$\therefore \quad \frac{PT}{PS} = \frac{PQ}{PR}$$
$$\frac{a}{a+b} = \frac{c}{c+d}$$
$$a(c+d) = c(a+b)$$
$$ac + ad = ac + bc$$
$$ad = bc$$

$\therefore \quad \dfrac{a}{b} = \dfrac{c}{d}$ [on dividing by bd]

Q Find the value of x. **46**

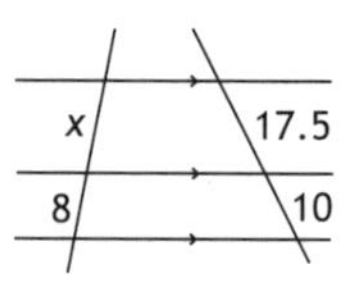

A Parallel lines preserve ratios.

$$\frac{x}{8} = \frac{17.5}{10}$$
$$10x = 140$$
$$x = 14$$

Q AC = 36 mm. Find BC. 47

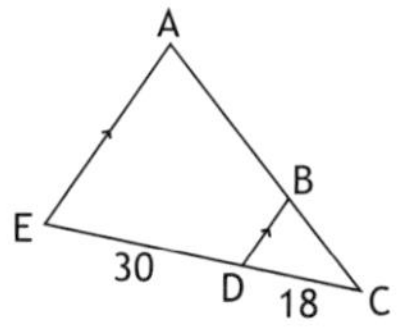

A Let BC = x mm

$AB = 36 - x$

Parallel lines preserve ratios

$\therefore \dfrac{x}{36 - x} = \dfrac{18}{30}$

$30x = 18(36 - x)$

$30x = 648 - 18x$

$48x = 648$

$x = 13.5$

$\therefore$ BC = 13.5 mm

- If a family of parallel lines cuts equal intercepts on one transversal, it does so on all transversals. This is just a special case of the rule that parallel lines preserve ratios.

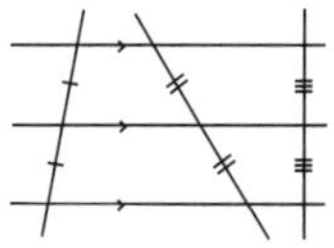

Q AB = BC = 15 cm 46

DE = 19 cm

GI = 27 cm

Find:

a EF **b** HI

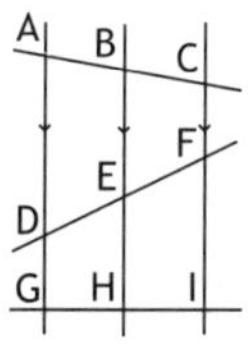

A Parallel lines cut equal intercepts on all transversals.

a EF = DE

$\therefore$ EF = 19 cm

b $HI = \dfrac{1}{2}GI$

$\therefore$ HI = 13.5 cm

2.21 Pythagoras' theorem

- In any right-angled triangle, the square of the hypotenuse is equal to the sum of the squares of the other two sides.

$$c^2 = a^2 + b^2$$

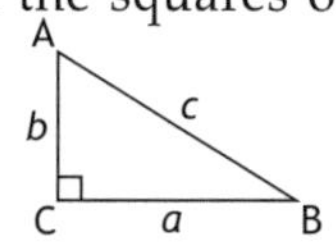

Proof:

Construct the perpendicular from C to AB, meeting AB in D.

Let AD = x

$\therefore$ BD = $c - x$

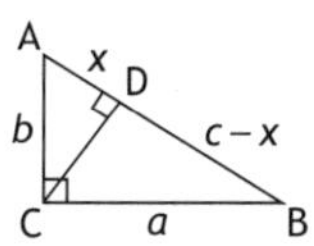

In ΔADC, ΔACB

∠ADC = ∠ACB [both 90°]

∠DAC = ∠CAB [common angle]

∴ ΔADC ||| ΔACB

$\therefore \dfrac{AC}{AD} = \dfrac{AB}{AC}$

$\dfrac{b}{x} = \dfrac{c}{b}$

$\therefore b^2 = cx$ **i**

continued ...

In ΔBCD, ΔBAC

∠BDC = ∠BCA [both 90°]

∠DBC = ∠CBA [common angle]

∴ ΔBCD ||| ΔBAC

$\therefore \dfrac{BC}{BD} = \dfrac{BA}{BC}$

$\dfrac{a}{c-x} = \dfrac{c}{a}$

$\therefore a^2 = c(c-x)$

$a^2 = c^2 - cx$

$a^2 = c^2 - b^2$ [from **i**]

$a^2 + b^2 = c^2$

Q Find x: 48

a

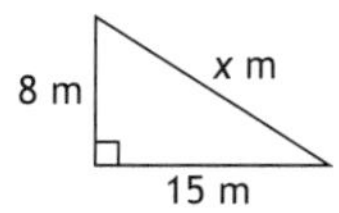

b

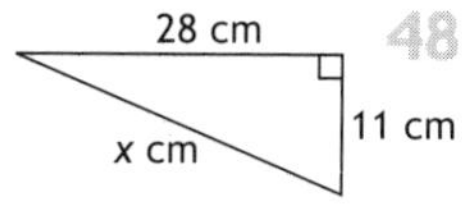

A

a $x^2 = 8^2 + 15^2$

$= 289$

$x = \sqrt{289}$ $[x > 0]$

$= 17$

b $x^2 = 28^2 + 11^2$

$= 905$

$x = \sqrt{905}$ $[x > 0]$

$= 30.08321791\ldots$

$= 30.1$ [1 d.p.]

Q Find x: 49

a

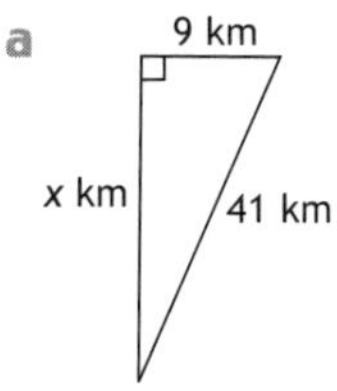

b

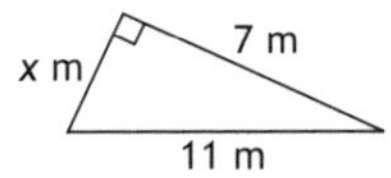

A

a $x^2 = 41^2 - 9^2$

$= 1600$

$x = \sqrt{1600}$ $[x > 0]$

$= 40$

b $x^2 = 11^2 - 7^2$

$= 72$

$x = \sqrt{72}$ $[x > 0]$

$= 8.485281374\ldots$

$= 8.5$ [1 d.p.]

Be careful not to confuse finding the hypotenuse with finding one of the other sides of the right-angled triangle.

Q Find x: 50

a

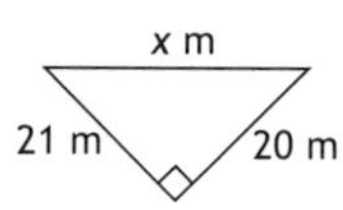

b

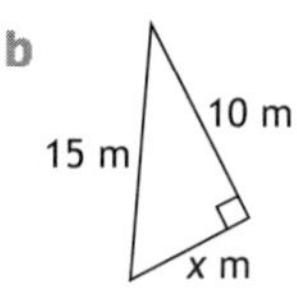

c

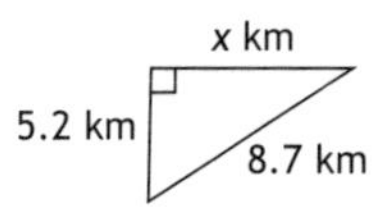

d

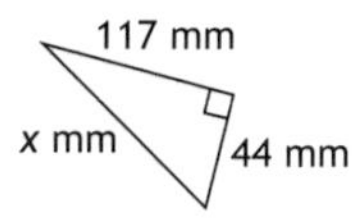

Go to page 47 for Exercises

A a $x^2 = 20^2 + 21^2$
$= 841$
$x = \sqrt{841} \quad [x > 0]$
$= 29$

b $x^2 = 15^2 - 10^2$
$= 125$
$x = \sqrt{125} \quad [x > 0]$
$= 11.18033989\ldots$
$= 11.2 \quad [1 \text{ d.p.}]$

c $x^2 = 8.7^2 - 5.2^2$
$= 48.65$
$x = \sqrt{48.65} \quad [x > 0]$
$= 6.974955197\ldots$
$= 7.0 \quad [1 \text{ d.p.}]$

d $x^2 = 44^2 + 117^2$
$= 15\,625$
$x = \sqrt{15\,625} \quad [x > 0]$
$= 125$

Q Find the exact value of x of each triangle: **51**

a

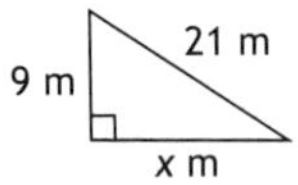

b

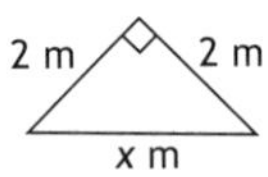

A a $x^2 = 21^2 - 9^2$
$= 360$
$x = \sqrt{360} \quad [x > 0]$
$= 6\sqrt{10}$

b $x^2 = 2^2 + 2^2$
$= 8$
$x = \sqrt{8} \quad [x > 0]$
$= 2\sqrt{2}$

- If the sides of a triangle a, b and c are such that $c^2 = a^2 + b^2$, then the triangle is right-angled.

Q Decide whether the triangles are right-angled: **52**

a

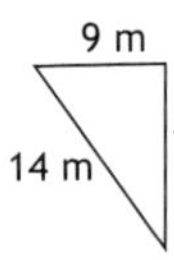

b

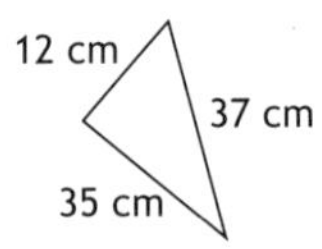

c

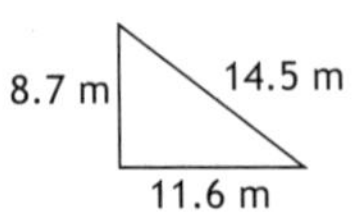

d

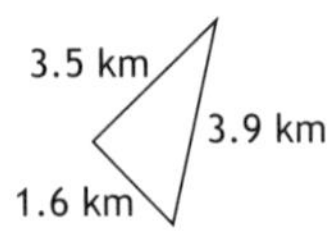

A a $9^2 + 11^2 = 202$
$14^2 = 196$
$\therefore 9^2 + 11^2 \neq 14^2$
$\therefore$ the triangle is not right-angled

b $12^2 + 35^2 = 1369$
$37^2 = 1369$
$\therefore 12^2 + 35^2 = 37^2$
$\therefore$ the triangle is right-angled

c $8.7^2 + 11.6^2 = 210.25$
$14.5^2 = 210.25$
$\therefore 8.7^2 + 11.6^2 = 14.5^2$
$\therefore$ the triangle is right-angled

d $1.6^2 + 3.5^2 = 14.81$
$3.9^2 = 15.21$
$\therefore 1.6^2 + 3.5^2 \neq 3.9^2$
$\therefore$ the triangle is not right-angled

Go to page 47 for Exercises

2.22 Area

- The formula for finding each of these areas should be known.

Rectangle length × breadth
$A = lb$

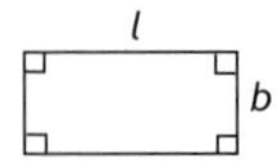

Triangle $\frac{1}{2}$ × base × perpendicular height
$A = \frac{1}{2}bh$

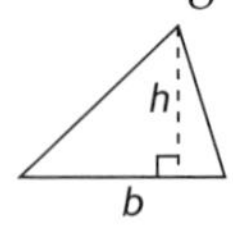

Parallelogram base × perpendicular height
$A = bh$

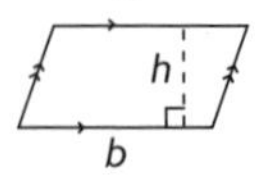

Rhombus half the product of the diagonals
$A = \frac{1}{2}xy$

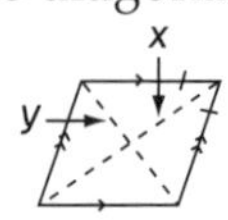

Trapezium half the sum of the parallel sides × perpendicular height
$A = \frac{h}{2}(a+b)$

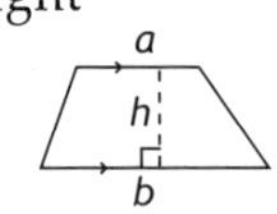

Area is always measured in units²

Q Find the area of each of the following figures: **53**

a

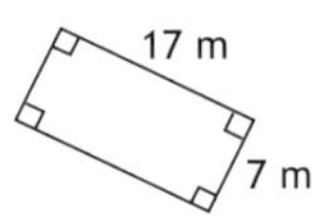

b

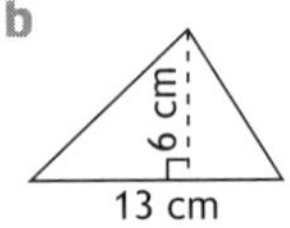

c

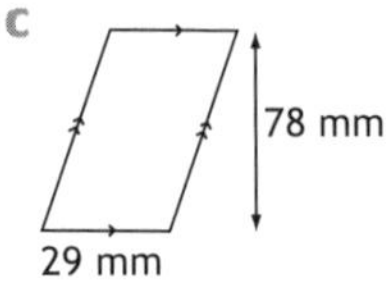

A a $A = lb$
$= 17 \times 7$
$\therefore \text{area} = 119 \text{ m}^2$

b $A = \frac{1}{2}bh$
$= \frac{1}{2} \times 13 \times 6$
$\therefore \text{area} = 39 \text{ cm}^2$

c $A = bh$
$= 29 \times 78$
$\therefore \text{area} = 2262 \text{ mm}^2$

Not all measurements given on a diagram will be used in finding the area. Care must be taken to use the correct measurements, especially the perpendicular height.

Q Find the area of these figures: **54**

a

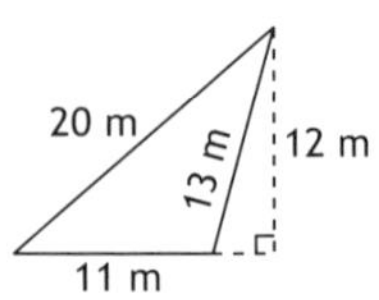

b

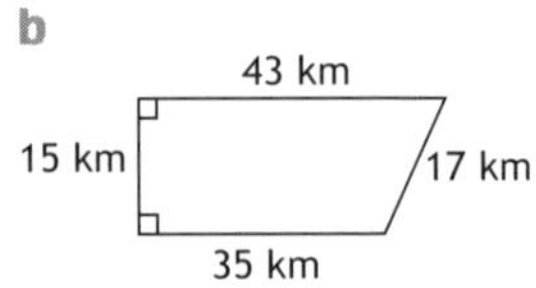

A a

$$A = \tfrac{1}{2}bh$$
$$= \tfrac{1}{2} \times 11 \times 12$$
$$\therefore \text{area} = 66 \text{ m}^2$$

b

$$A = \frac{h}{2}(a + b)$$
$$= \frac{15}{2} \times (43 + 35)$$
$$\therefore \text{area} = 585 \text{ km}^2$$

Don't forget that a rhombus is a parallelogram. In finding the area of a rhombus it may be easier to use the formula for a parallelogram rather than the formula for a rhombus.

Q Find the area of each rhombus: **55**

a

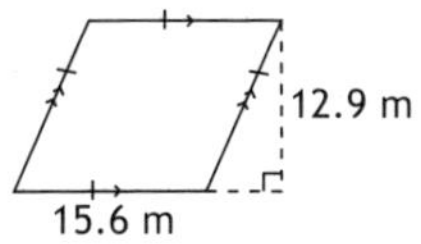

b

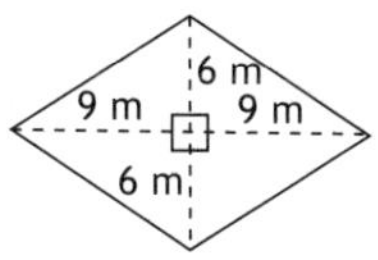

A a

$$A = bh$$
$$= 15.6 \times 12.9$$
$$\therefore \text{area} = 201.24 \text{ m}^2$$

b

$$A = \tfrac{1}{2}xy$$
$$= \tfrac{1}{2} \times 12 \times 18$$
$$\therefore \text{area} = 108 \text{ m}^2$$

- It may be necessary to use a combination of the different formulas. If the area involves two of the same shapes we often use capital letters to show the formula for the larger shape.

Q Find the shaded area: **56**

a

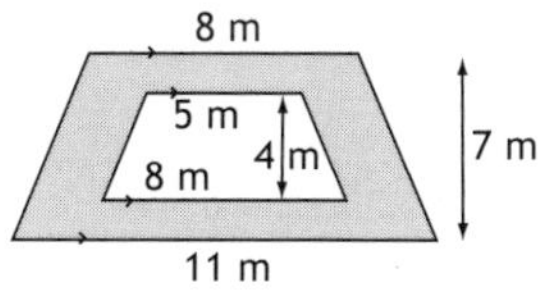

b

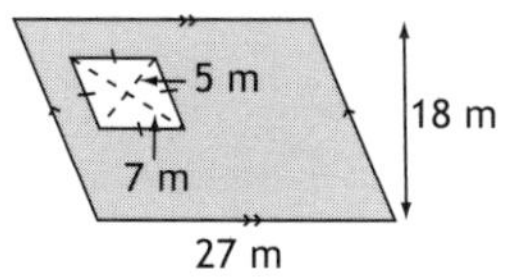

A a

$$A = \frac{H}{2}(A + B) - \frac{h}{2}(a + b)$$
$$= \frac{7}{2} \times (8 + 11) - \frac{4}{2} \times (5 + 8)$$
$$\therefore \text{area} = 40.5 \text{ m}^2$$

b

$$A = bh - \tfrac{1}{2}xy$$
$$= 27 \times 18 - \tfrac{1}{2} \times 7 \times 5$$
$$\therefore \text{area} = 468.5 \text{ m}^2$$

- The area of any quadrilateral can be found by dividing it into triangles.

Q Find the area: **57**

a

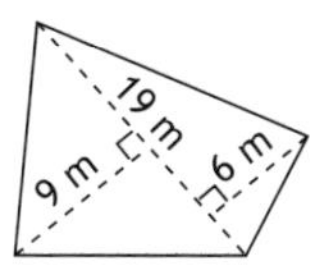

b

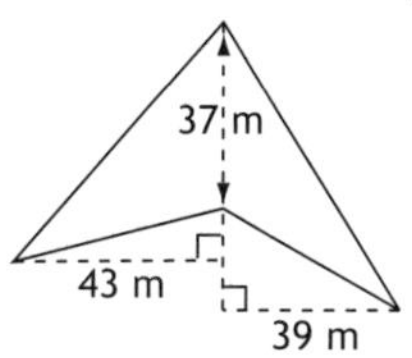

A a

$$A = \tfrac{1}{2}bh + \tfrac{1}{2}BH$$
$$= \tfrac{1}{2} \times 19 \times 6 + \tfrac{1}{2} \times 19 \times 9$$
$$\therefore \text{area} = 142.5 \text{ m}^2$$

b

$$A = \tfrac{1}{2}BH + \tfrac{1}{2}bh$$
$$= \tfrac{1}{2} \times 37 \times 43 + \tfrac{1}{2} \times 37 \times 39$$
$$\therefore \text{area} = 1517 \text{ m}^2$$

In both cases we could just find the area of one triangle with common base and combined height.

2.23 Solving geometrical problems

- In solving geometrical problems always draw a clear diagram and mark on all the given information. Reasons should be given for every step.

Q ΔXYZ is equilateral. **58**

ZY is produced to W so that ZY = YW.

Find $\angle ZXW$.

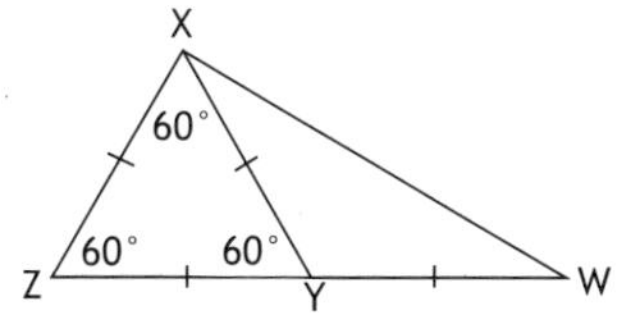

A ΔXYZ is equilateral.

$\therefore\ \angle XYZ = \angle YZX = \angle ZXY = 60°$

and $XY = YZ = XZ$

but $ZY = YW$ [given]

$\therefore\ XY = YW$

$\angle XWY = \angle YXW$

[base angles of isosceles ΔXWY]

$\angle XWY + \angle YXW = \angle XYZ$ [exterior angle of ΔXWY]

$\therefore\ 2\angle YXW = 60°$

$\angle YXW = 30°$

$\angle ZXW = 60° + 30°$

$= 90°$

Q KL || MN. KL = MN. **59**

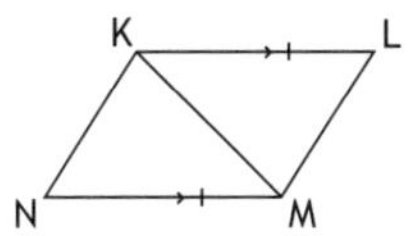

a Show that $\Delta LKM \equiv \Delta NMK$.

b Hence show that LM || KN.

A a In ΔLKM, ΔNMK

KL = MN	[given]
$\angle LKM = \angle NMK$	[alternate, KL || MN]
KM = MK	[common side]
$\therefore \Delta LKM \equiv \Delta NMK$	[SAS]

b $\angle LMK = \angle NKM$

[corresponding angles of congruent triangles]

$\therefore$ LM || KN [alternate angles are equal]

Go to pages 47 and 48 for Exercises

Q Find the area of this wall. **60**

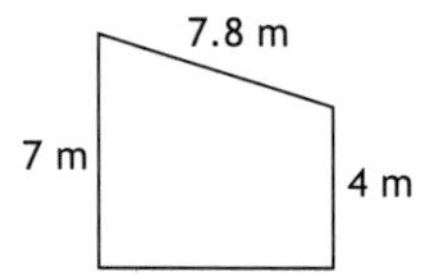

A Divide the figure into a rectangle and right-angled triangle.

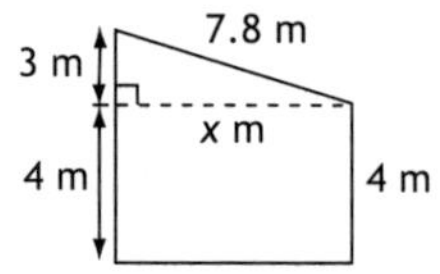

The height of the triangle is 3 m.
Let x m be the base of the triangle.

By Pythagoras' theorem

$$\begin{aligned} x^2 &= 7.8^2 - 3^2 \\ &= 51.84 \\ x &= \sqrt{51.84} \quad [x > 0] \\ &= 7.2 \end{aligned}$$

$$\begin{aligned} A &= \frac{h}{2}(a + b) \\ &= \frac{7.2}{2}(7 + 4) \\ &= 39.6 \end{aligned}$$

$\therefore$ the area of the wall is 39.6 m^2

☞ Go to page 48 for Exercises

Exercises Plane Geometry

1 Find the value of x.

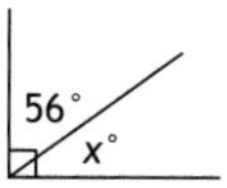

2 Find the value of x.

a

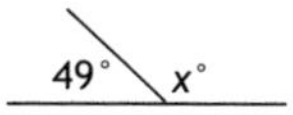

b

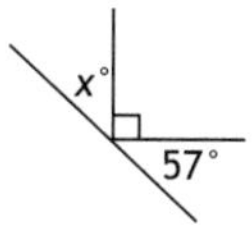

3 EC is a straight line.
∠ABD = 90°
∠ABC = 138°
Find ∠EBD.

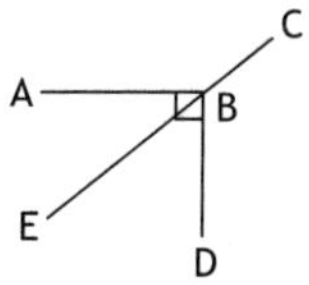

4 The three angles on a straight line are in the ratio 2 : 3 : 4. Find the size of each angle.

5 Find the value of x.

a

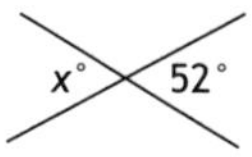

b

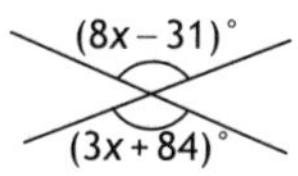

6 ∠PTQ = 76°
Find ∠QTR, ∠RTS and ∠STP.

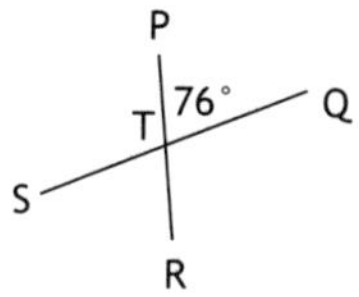

7 Find the value of x.

a

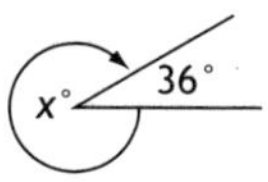

b

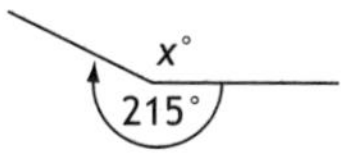

c

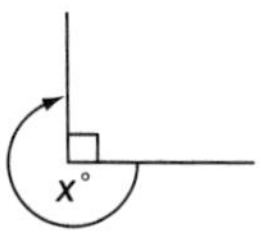

d

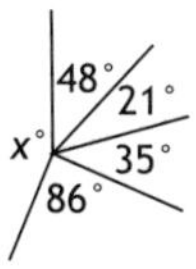

8 OB bisects ∠AOC.
Find ∠AOB.

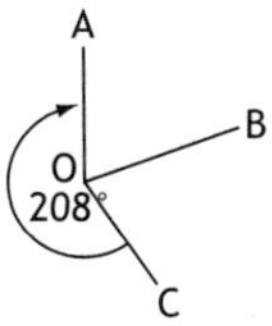

9 Find the value of x.

a

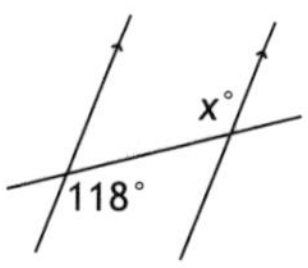

b

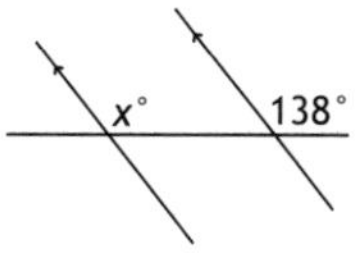

c

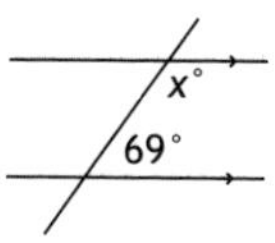

10 ∠YCD = 94°
Find ∠BFE (giving reasons).

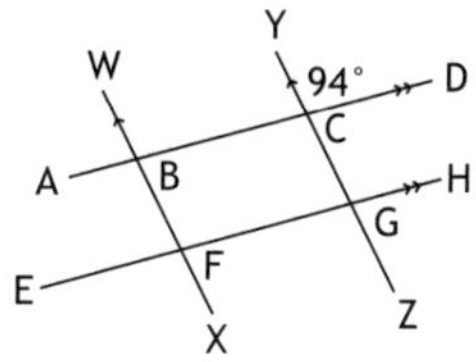

11 ∠ACD = 131°
∠AEF = 105°
Find the size of ∠EAC.

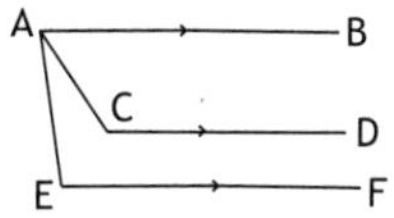

12 AB is parallel to DE.
∠BCD = 90°
∠ABC = 152°
Find ∠CDE.

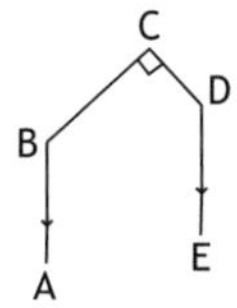

13 In each diagram determine whether AB is parallel to CD.

a

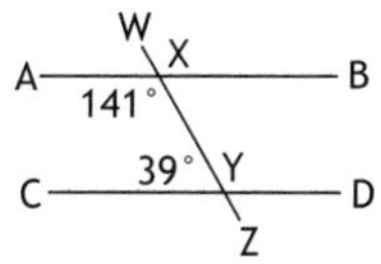

b

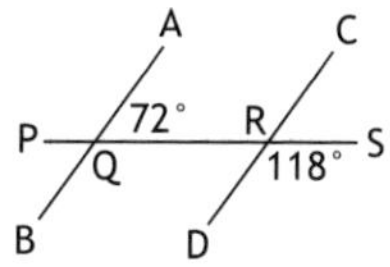

c

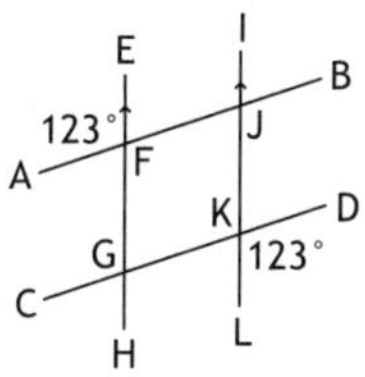

14 Find the value of x.

a

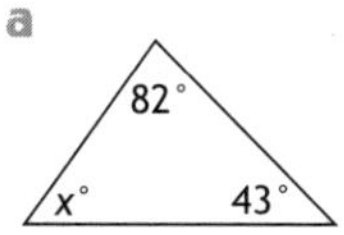

b

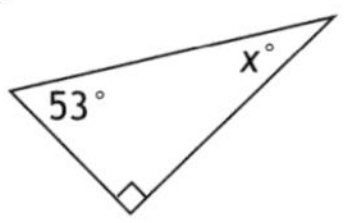

c

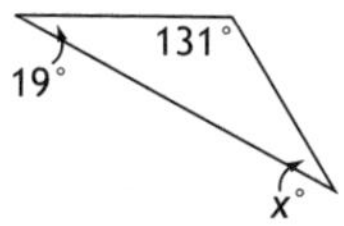

15 The sizes of the three angles of a triangle are in the ratio 1 : 2 : 3. Find the size of each angle.

16 Find the value of x.

a

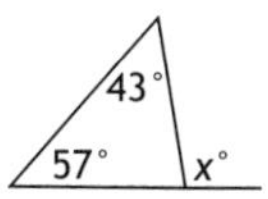

b

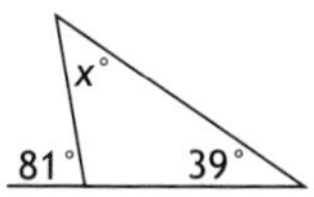

c

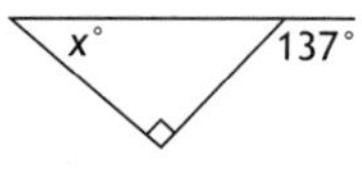

d

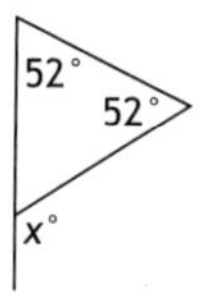

17 ∠ACE = 49°
∠BDE = 97°
Find the size of ∠ABD.

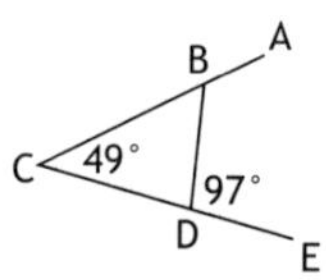

Go to page 221 for Quick Answers & pages 158 and 159 for Worked Solutions

18 Find the value of x.

a

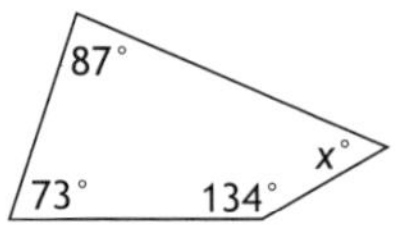

b

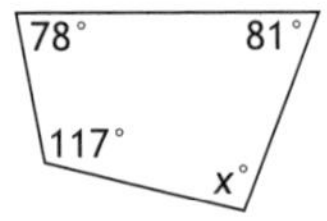

c

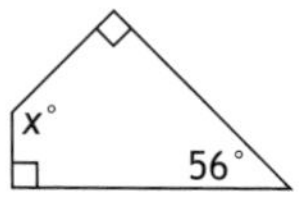

d

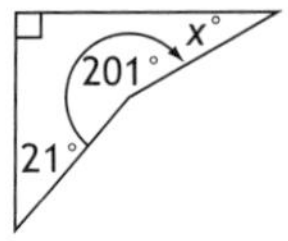

19 The angles of a quadrilateral are in the ratio 2 : 3 : 4 : 6. Find the size of the smallest angle.

20 Find the angle sum of:

a an octagon **b** a dodecagon

21 If the angle sum of a polygon is 3780°, find the number of sides.

22 Find the value of x.

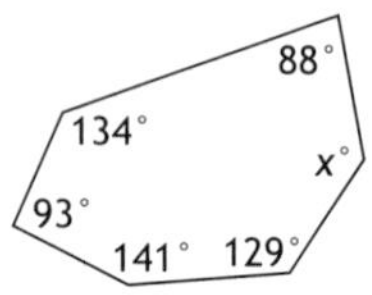

23 Find the size of each angle of a regular:

a pentagon **b** decagon

24 A 24-sided polygon has all its angles equal. Find the size of each of its angles.

25 Each angle of a regular polygon measures 160°. How many sides has the polygon?

26 Find the value of x.

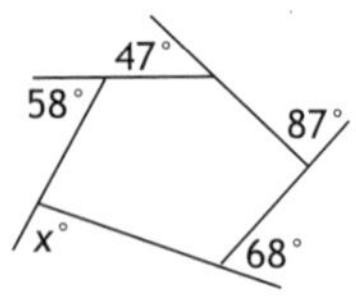

27 Find the size of each exterior angle of a regular pentagon.

28 Find the size of each:

a exterior angle **b** interior angle

of a regular hexagon.

29 Prove that each pair of triangles are congruent.

a

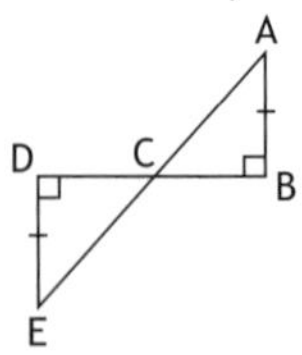

ΔABC, ΔEDC
(AE, DB straight lines)

b

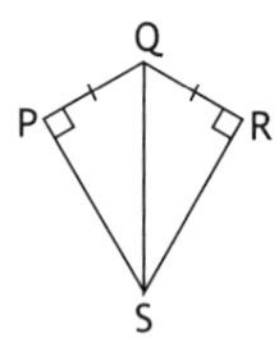

ΔPQS, ΔRQS

c

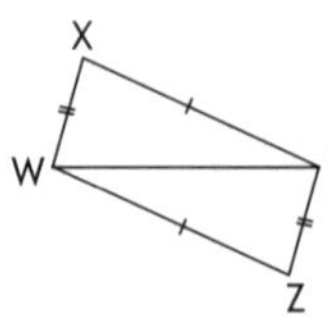

ΔWXY, ΔYZW

d

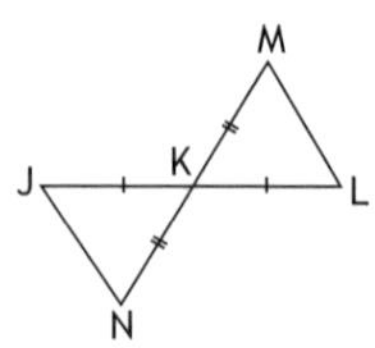

ΔJKN, ΔLKM
(JL, MN straight lines)

30 B is a point on line AC such that BC = BE.
D is a point on BE such that BD = AB.
AE = CD
Use congruent triangles to find the size of ∠ABE.

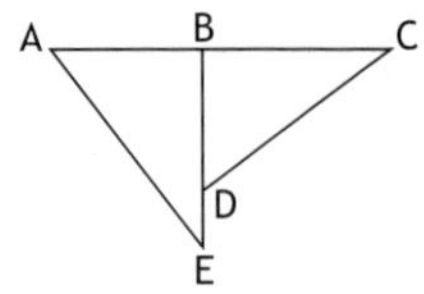

31 ST is parallel to QR.
P is the midpoint of SR.
Show that P is the midpoint of TQ.

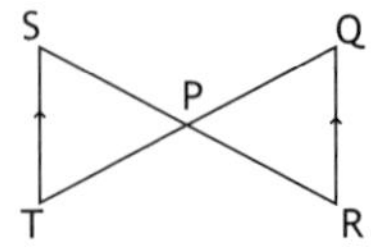

32 ABCD is a quadrilateral with all four sides equal.
Show that diagonal CA bisects ∠DAB.

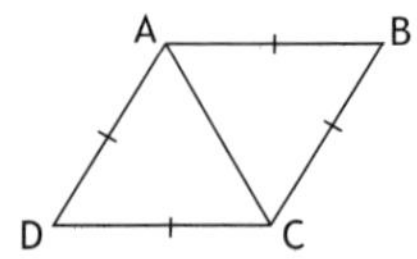

33 Find the value of x.

a

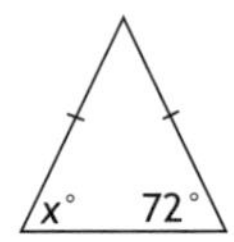

b

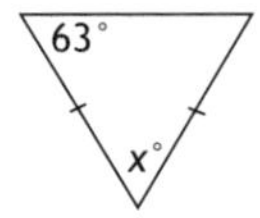

c

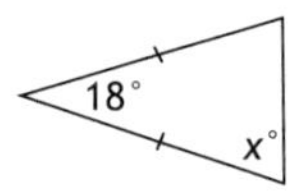

d

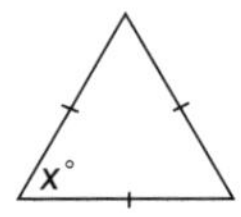

34 AB = BC
AC = DC
∠ABC = 26°
∠BCD = 133°
Find the size of ∠ADC.

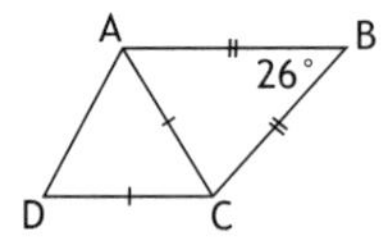

35 Find the values of a and b.

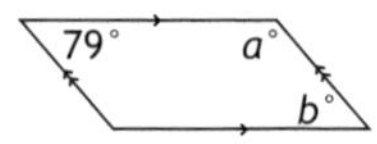

36 ABCD is a rhombus.
∠DAB = 126°
Find ∠BDC.

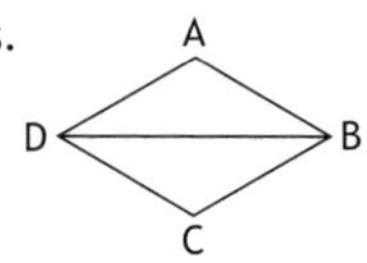

37 The diagonals of a rectangle measure $(5x + 27)$ cm and $(2x + 45)$ cm.

a Find the value of x.

b Find the length of each diagonal.

38 PQRS is a parallelogram.

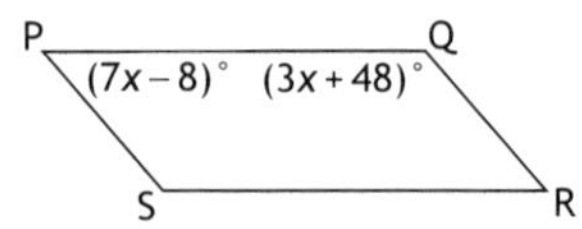

a Find x.

b Find ∠PQR.

c What conclusion can be drawn about the parallelogram? Justify the answer.

39 What special type of quadrilateral are each of these? Justify the answer.

a

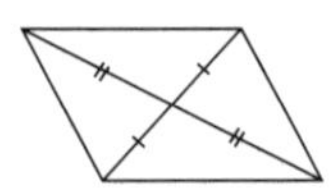

b

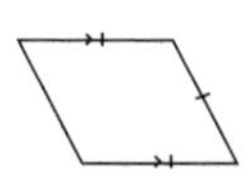

c

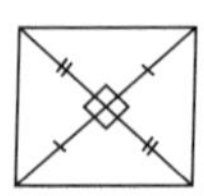

d

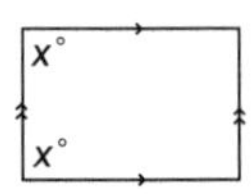

Go to page 221 for Quick Answers & pages 159–162 for Worked Solutions

40 ABCD is a quadrilateral in which AB = DC and AB || DC.

a Prove that $\Delta BAC \equiv \Delta DCA$.

b Hence prove that BC || AD.

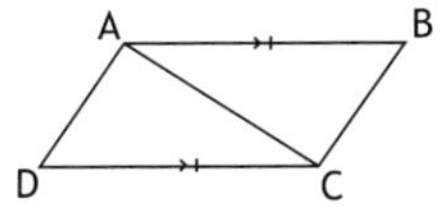

41 Show that the given pairs of triangles are similar.

a

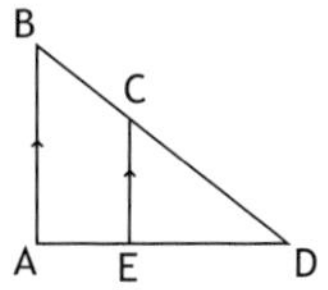

ΔABD, ΔECD

b

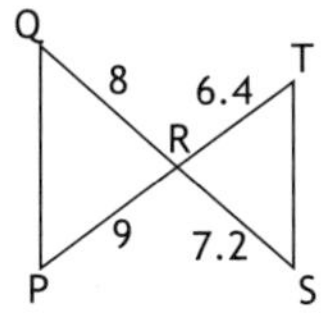

ΔPQR, ΔSTR
[PT, QS are straight lines]

c

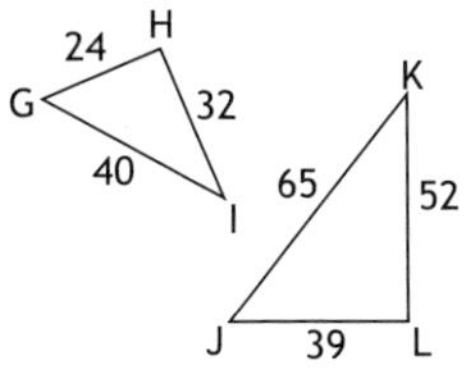

ΔGHI, ΔJLK

42 $\angle AEB = \angle BDC$
AC = 43.2 units

a Show that ΔAEB and ΔBDC are similar.

b Find the length of AB.

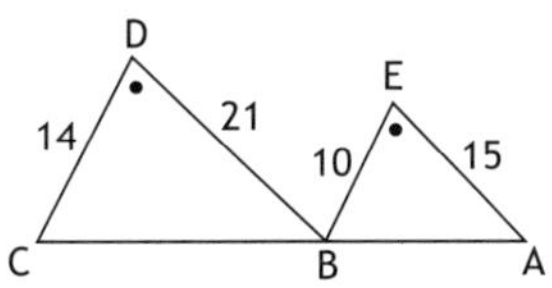

43 BE is parallel to CD.

a Show that $\Delta ABE \,|||\, \Delta ACD$.

b Show that $\Delta EBF \,|||\, \Delta CDF$.

c AB = 4 cm. BC = 6 cm. EF = 2 cm. Find EC.

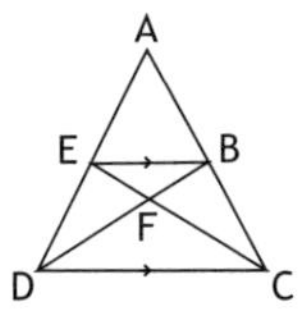

44 DE is parallel to AB.
Use similar triangles to show that $\frac{CD}{CA} = \frac{CE}{CB}$.

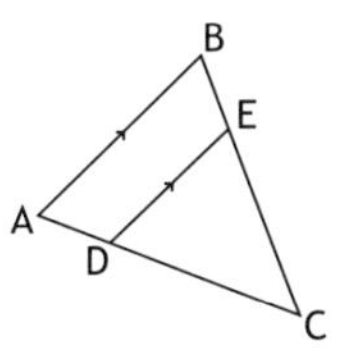

45 PT = TS = 6 m. QR = RS = 11 m. TR = 7 m

a Show that triangles PQS and TRS are similar.

b Show that PQ || TR.

c Find the length of PQ.

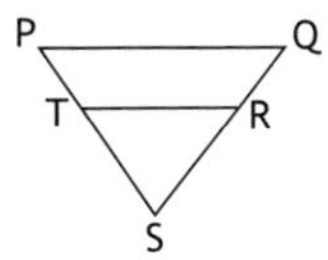

46 Find the value of x.

a

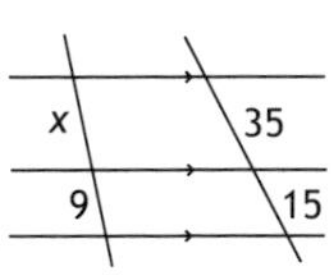

b

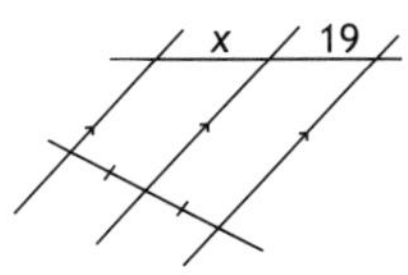

47 AC = 28 m. AE = 12 m. ED = 8 m. Find BC.

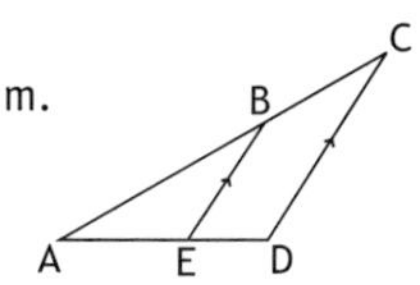

48 Find the length of the hypotenuse:

a

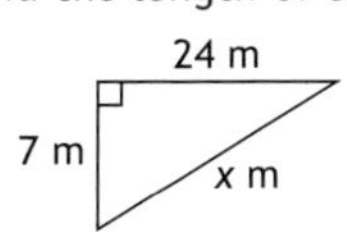

b

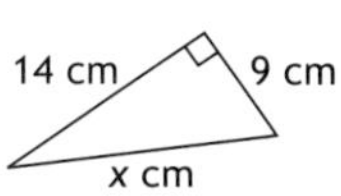

49 Find the length of the side:

a

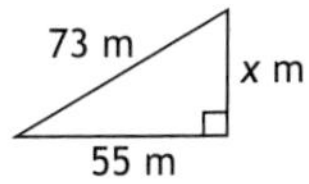

b

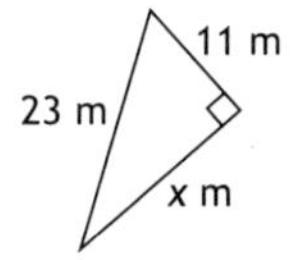

50 Find the length of the side marked x.

a

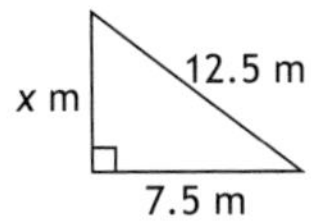

b

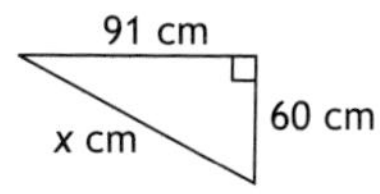

c

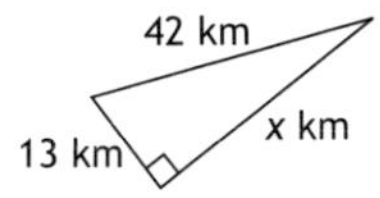

d

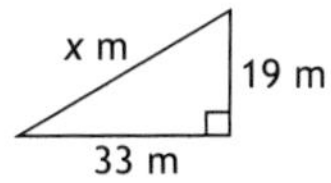

51 Find the exact length of the side marked x.

a

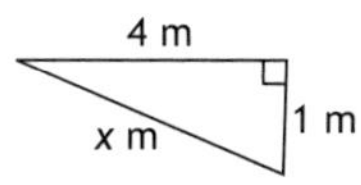

b

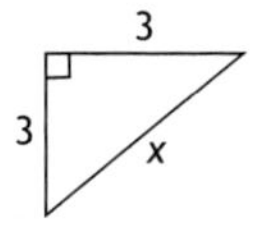

c

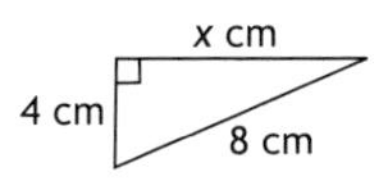

52 Determine whether the following triangles are right-angled.

a

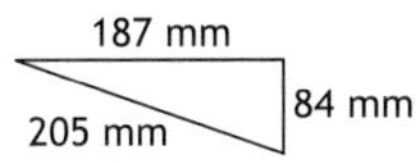

b

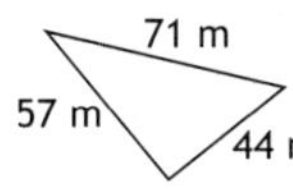

c

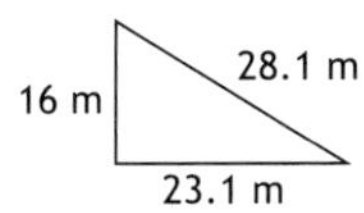

d

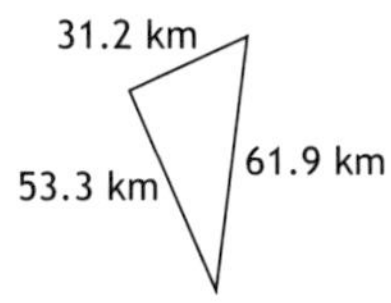

53 Find the area of each of the following figures:

a

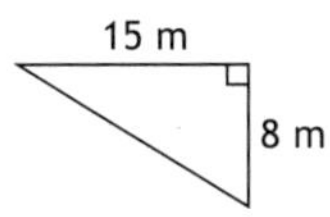

b

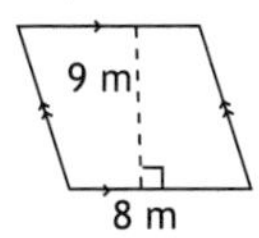

c

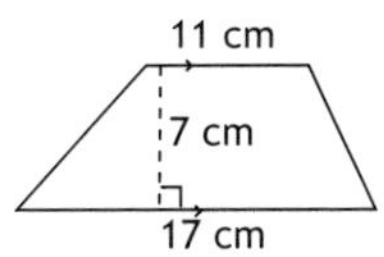

54 Find the area:

a

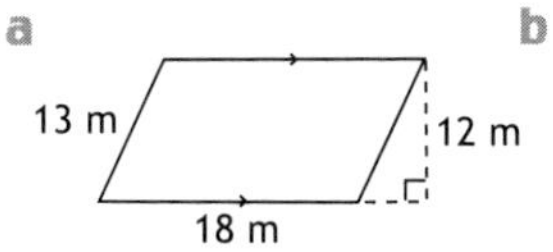

b

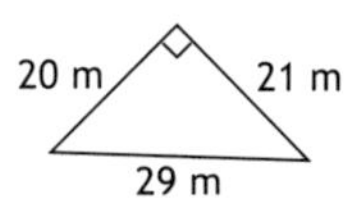

55 Find the area of each rhombus:

a

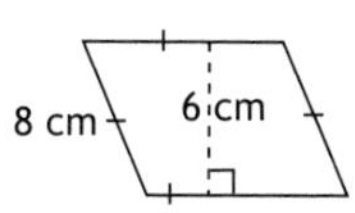

b

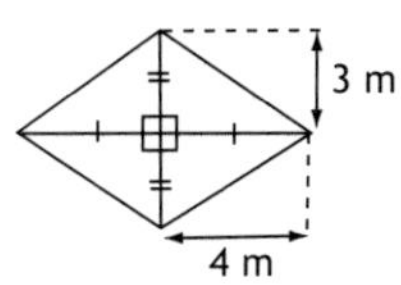

Go to page 221 for Quick Answers & pages 162–164 for Worked Solutions

56 Find the shaded area:

a 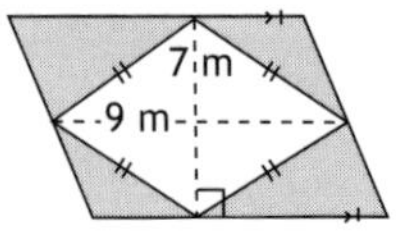

b 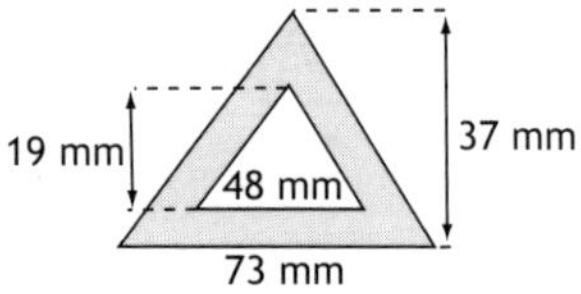

57 Find the area:

a 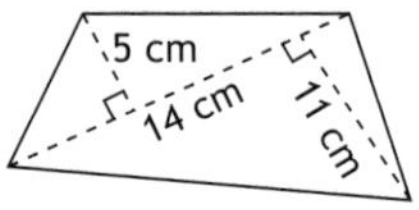

b 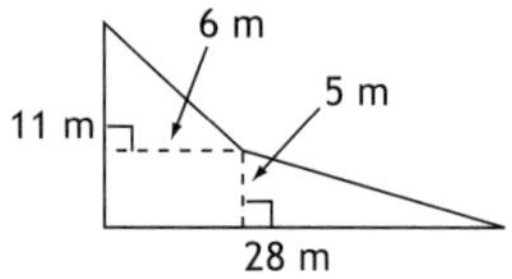

58 BC = CD.
AB || CD.
$\angle BCD = 38°$
Find $\angle DBA$, giving reasons.

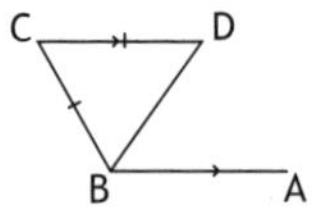

59 T is the point of intersection of PR and QS.
PT = ST.
$\angle TQR = \angle TRQ$.

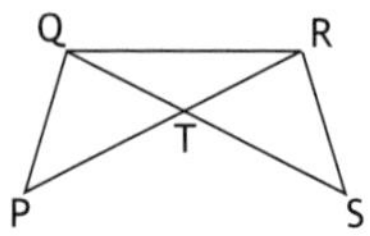

a Show that $\Delta QTP \equiv \Delta RTS$.

b Hence show that $\Delta PQR \equiv \Delta SRQ$.

60 ΔABC is right-angled at B.
D is a point on side AC such that $BD \perp AC$.

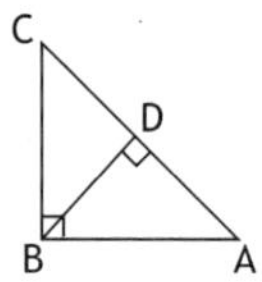

a Show that triangles ABD and ACB are similar.

b If AB = 15 m and AC = 25 m, find:
   i BC
   ii BD

c Hence find the area of ΔABD.

Go to page 221 for Quick Answers & pages 164 and 165 for Worked Solutions. See pages 126 and 127 for Topic Tests

3 Linear Functions and Lines

Your Checklist

For a complete understanding of this topic you must be able to:	✓
■ Understand that the linear function $y = mx + b$ is represented by a straight line	
■ Understand the geometrical significance of m and b	
■ Graph points and lines on a number plane	
■ Find the gradient of a line joining two points	
■ Find the equation of a straight line passing through a given point with given gradient	
■ Find the equation of a straight line passing through two given points	
■ Verify that a point satisfies the equation of a line	
■ Understand that the equation $ax + by + c = 0$ represents a straight line	
■ Express equations of lines in either gradient-intercept form, $y = mx + b$, or general form, $ax + by + c = 0$, and convert either form to the other	
■ Find the gradient and y-intercept of a line expressed in general form	
■ Know that parallel lines have the same gradient	
■ Understand the condition for two lines to be perpendicular, $m_1m_2 = -1$	
■ Find the equation of a line, through a particular point, parallel or perpendicular to a given line	
■ Solve two equations simultaneously to find the point of intersection of two straight lines	
■ Find the equation of any line passing through the point of intersection of two other lines	
■ Understand that straight lines divide the number plane into different regions	
■ Understand that linear inequalities can be used to describe regions in the number plane	
■ Understand and use the distance formula	
■ Understand and use the perpendicular distance formula	
■ Understand and use the midpoint formula	

3.1 Linear functions and lines

- The **linear function** $y = mx + b$ represents a straight line.
- We can **find the points** to draw a straight line by using tables of values.

✔ Two points determine a line. Using three values in the table of values gives us a check. If the points don't form a straight line you know you have done something wrong.

Always draw the line right across the grid. Don't just 'join the dots'.

Q Graph each of the straight lines: **1**

a $y = x + 3$ **b** $y = 3x - 4$ **c** $y = -2x$

d $y = \frac{3}{2}x + 1$ **e** $x = -1$ **f** $y = 2$

A **a** $y = x + 3$

x	−1	0	1
y	2	3	4

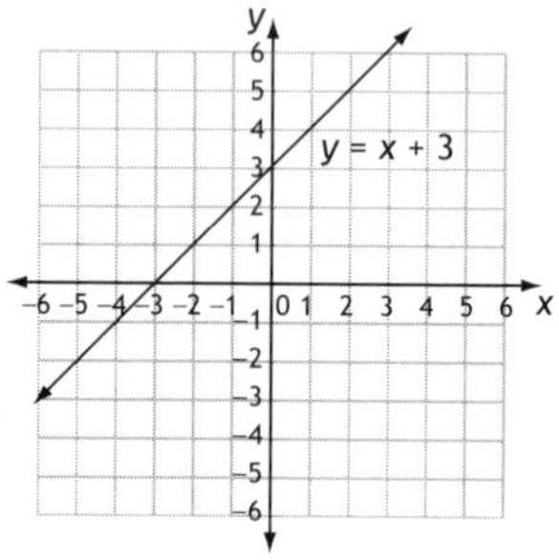

b $y = 3x - 4$

x	−1	0	1
y	−7	−4	−1

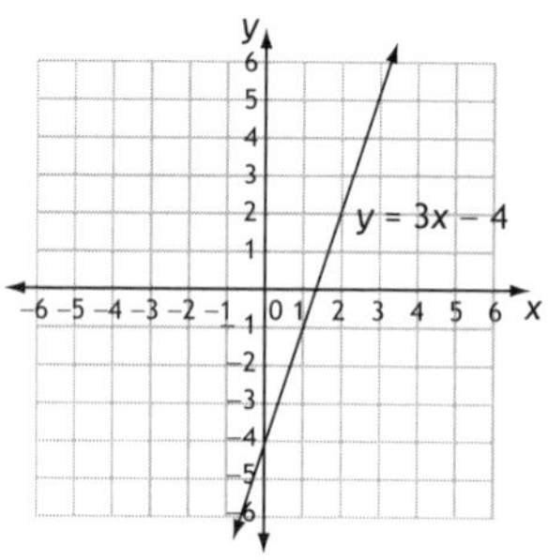

c $y = -2x$

x	−1	0	1
y	2	0	−2

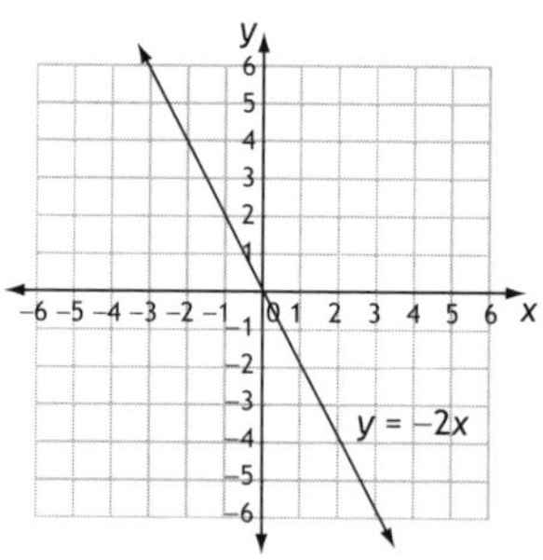

d $y = \frac{3}{2}x + 1$

x	−1	0	1
y	$-\frac{1}{2}$	1	$2\frac{1}{2}$

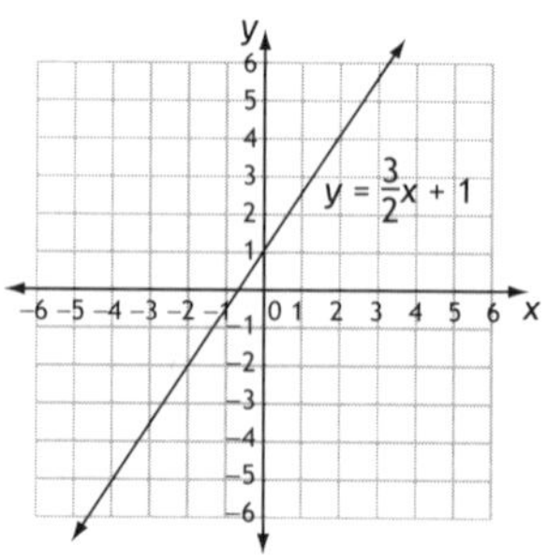

e $x = -1$
For every value of y,
$x = -1$

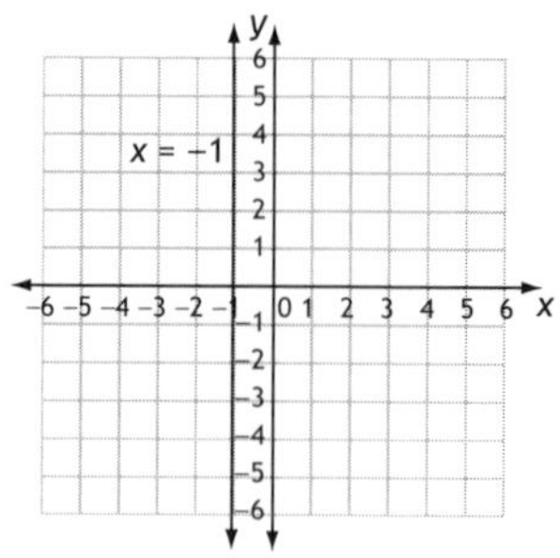

f $y = 2$
For every value of x,
$y = 2$

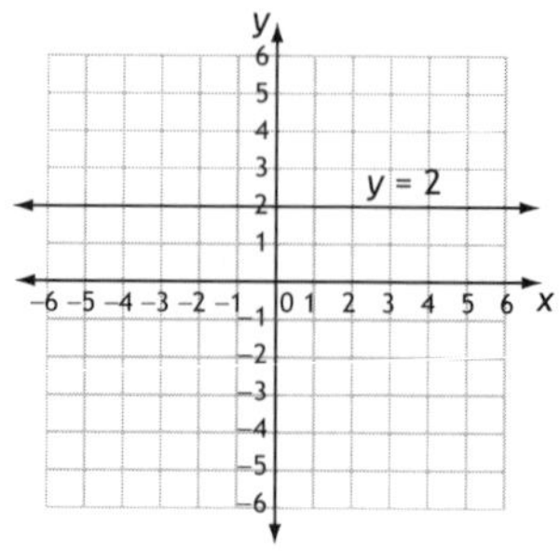

Go to page 60 for Exercises

3.2 The gradient of a line

- The **gradient** of a line is its slope. It is the measure of how steep a line is.
- The **symbol** m is used to represent the gradient of a line.

$$\text{gradient} = \frac{\text{change in vertical position (rise)}}{\text{change in horizontal position (run)}}$$

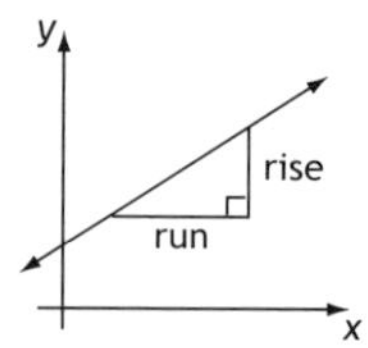

- If a line leans to the right the **gradient is positive**.
  e.g. / /
- If the line leans to the left the **gradient is negative**.
  e.g. \ \

Examples:

A gradient of $\frac{2}{3}$ means that from any point on the line, running across 3 units to the right and rising up 2 units will give another point on the line.

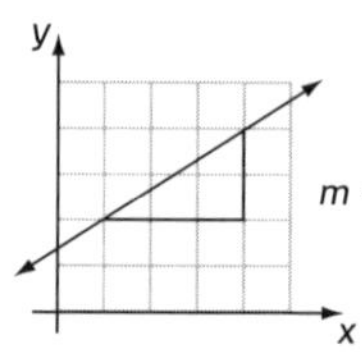

A gradient of 3 $\left(\frac{3}{1}\right)$ means that from any point on the line, moving across 1 unit and up 3 units will give another point.

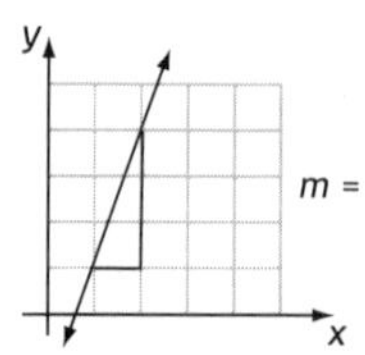

A gradient of $-\frac{3}{4}$ means from any point on the line, moving across 4 units to the right and down 3 units will give another point.

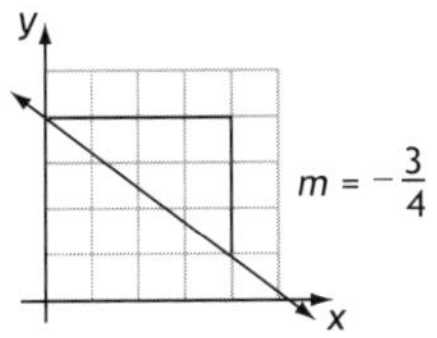

$\left(-\frac{3}{4} = \frac{-3}{4} \text{ so the rise is negative}\right)$

- A line **parallel to the x-axis** has zero gradient.
  $m = 0$
- A line **parallel to the y-axis** has infinite slope.
  m is undefined

3.3 The y-intercept

- The y-intercept, or intercept on the y-axis, is where the line cuts the y-axis.

3.4 The gradient-intercept form of a line

- The line $y = mx + b$ has gradient m and y-intercept b.

Q Write down the gradient and y-intercept for each line: **2**

a $y = 4x + 3$ b $y = x - 3$

c $y = \frac{2}{5}x$ d $y = 2 - x$

e $y = 4$

A a $y = 4x + 3$
gradient $m = 4$
y-intercept $= 3$

b $y = x - 3$
gradient $m = 1$
y-intercept $= -3$

c $y = \frac{2}{5}x$
gradient $m = \frac{2}{5}$
y-intercept $= 0$

d $y = 2 - x$
gradient $m = -1$
y-intercept $= 2$

e $y = 4$
gradient $m = 0$
y-intercept $= 4$

Q Write down the equation of the line with: **3**

a gradient 3 and y-intercept -2

b gradient $-\frac{3}{4}$ and y-intercept 1

A a $m = 3$, y-intercept $= -2$
$y = 3x - 2$

b $m = -\frac{3}{4}$, y-intercept $= 1$
$y = -\frac{3}{4}x + 1$

- The gradient and y-intercept can be used to easily graph a straight line.

First use the y-intercept as one point on the line. Then use the gradient to find the second point.

Q Write down the gradient and y-intercept and graph each line: **4**

a $y = 2x - 1$ b $y = -\frac{4}{3}x$

A a $y = 2x - 1$
$m = 2$
y-intercept $= -1$
First plot (0, −1). Then from this point move across 1 unit to the right and up 2 units to the second point.

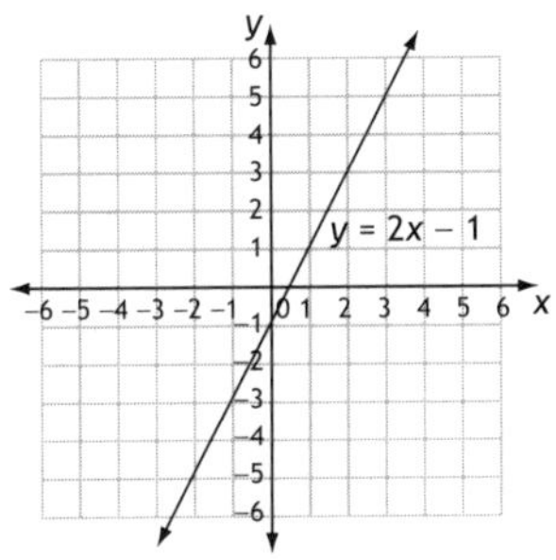

b $y = -\frac{4}{3}x$
$m = -\frac{4}{3}$
y-intercept $= 0$

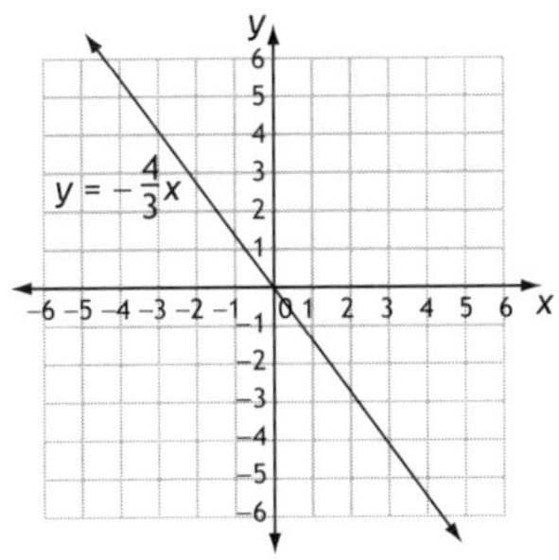

3.5 The angle a line makes with the positive x-axis

- If a line makes an angle of θ with the positive x-axis then:

$$\tan\theta = \frac{\text{opposite}}{\text{adjacent}} = \frac{\text{rise}}{\text{run}} = m$$

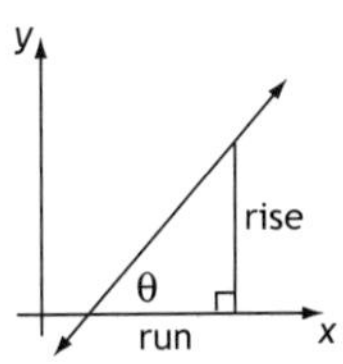

- If θ is the angle the line makes with the positive direction of the x-axis, then $m = \tan\theta$.

$$m = \tan\theta$$

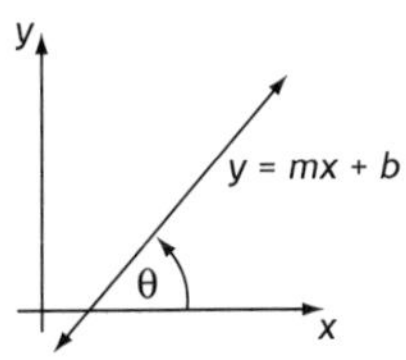

Go to page 60 for Exercises

Q The gradient of a line is $\frac{3}{5}$. Find, to the nearest whole degree, the angle the line makes with the positive direction of the x-axis.

A $\tan\theta = m$

$$= \frac{3}{5}$$

$$\theta = 30.96375653\ldots°$$

$$= 31° \text{ [nearest degree]}$$

Q Find the size of the angle the line $y = 2x - 3$ makes with the positive x-axis. 5

A $y = 2x - 3$

gradient: $m = 2$

$$\tan\theta = 2$$

$$\theta = 63.43494882\ldots° \text{ [by calculator]}$$

$$= 63° \text{ [nearest degree]}$$

$\therefore$ the line $y = 2x - 3$ makes an angle of $63°$ with the x-axis

Q A line crosses the y-axis at $y = -1$ and makes an angle of $45°$ with the positive direction of the x-axis. What is the equation of the line? 6

A y-intercept is -1

$$m = \tan\theta$$

$$= \tan 45°$$

$\therefore\ m = 1$

The equation of the line is $y = x - 1$

3.6 The gradient formula

To **find the gradient of the line joining two points,** we note that the change in vertical position will be the difference between the y coordinates and the change in horizontal position will be the difference in x coordinates.

$$\therefore m = \frac{y_2 - y_1}{x_2 - x_1}$$

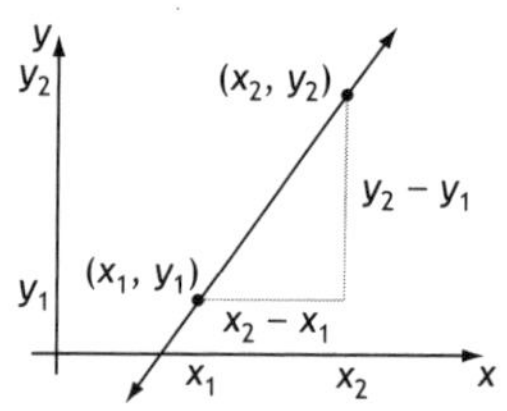

- The **gradient of the line** joining the points (x_1, y_1) and (x_2, y_2) is given by:

$$m = \frac{y_2 - y_1}{x_2 - x_1}$$

Q Find the gradient of the line joining: 7

a (2, 9) to (7, −1) **b** (−3, −2) to (1, 8)
c (4, 7) to (7, 7) **d** (−6, 0) to (0, −6)

Go to page 60 for Exercises

A **a** $(2,9),\ (7,-1)$

$$m = \frac{y_2 - y_1}{x_2 - x_1} = \frac{-1-9}{7-2} = -2$$

b $(-3,-2),\ (1,8)$

$$m = \frac{y_2 - y_1}{x_2 - x_1} = \frac{8-(-2)}{1-(-3)} = \frac{5}{2}$$

c $(4,7),\ (7,7)$

$$m = \frac{y_2 - y_1}{x_2 - x_1} = \frac{7-7}{7-4} = 0$$

d $(-6,0),\ (0,-6)$

$$m = \frac{y_2 - y_1}{x_2 - x_1} = \frac{-6-0}{0-(-6)} = -1$$

Q The gradient of the line joining P(−7, 1) to Q(2, y) is $\frac{1}{3}$. Find y. 8

A **a** $P(-7,1),\ Q(2,y),\ m = \frac{1}{3}$

$$m = \frac{y_2 - y_1}{x_2 - x_1}$$

$$\frac{1}{3} = \frac{y-1}{2-(-7)}$$

$$\frac{1}{3} = \frac{y-1}{9}$$

$$9 = 3(y-1)$$

$$9 = 3y - 3$$

$$3y = 12$$

$$y = 4$$

3.7 The equation of a straight line

Only one line will pass through a particular point (x_1, y_1) with a specific gradient m. Every other point on that line must satisfy the gradient formula.

For any point (x, y): $m = \frac{y - y_1}{x - x_1}$

$$\therefore y - y_1 = m(x - x_1)$$

- The **equation of the straight line** passing through the point (x_1, y_1) with gradient m is given by:

$$y - y_1 = m(x - x_1)$$

Q Find the equation of the straight line passing through the point: 9

a (3, 4) with gradient $m = 2$
b (−2, 6) with gradient $m = -3$
c (−1, −5) with gradient $m = -\frac{4}{5}$

A a $(3,4),\ m=2$

$$y-y_1=m(x-x_1)$$
$$y-4=2(x-3)$$
$$y-4=2x-6$$
$$y=2x-2$$

b $(-2,6),\ m=-3$

$$y-y_1=m(x-x_1)$$
$$y-6=-3(x-(-2))$$
$$y-6=-3(x+2)$$
$$y-6=-3x-6$$
$$y=-3x$$

c $(-1,-5),\ m=-\frac{4}{5}$

$$y-y_1=m(x-x_1)$$
$$y-(-5)=-\frac{4}{5}(x-(-1))$$
$$y+5=-\frac{4}{5}(x+1)$$
$$y+5=-\frac{4}{5}x-\frac{4}{5}$$
$$y=-\frac{4}{5}x-5\frac{4}{5}$$

Q A line has gradient $\frac{1}{2}$ and passes through the point (5, –1). Find the coordinates of the point where the line cuts the y-axis. 10

A $(5,-1),\ m=\frac{1}{2}$

$$y-y_1=m(x-x_1)$$
$$y-(-1)=\frac{1}{2}(x-5)$$
$$y+1=\frac{1}{2}x-2\frac{1}{2}$$
$$y=\frac{1}{2}x-3\frac{1}{2}$$

y-intercept $=-3\frac{1}{2}$

$\therefore$ the line cuts the y-axis at $P\left(0,-3\frac{1}{2}\right)$

3.8 The equation of a line in general form

- **In general form**, the equation of a line is expressed equal to zero.
- **Any fractions are eliminated** by multiplying the whole equation by the lowest common denominator.
- The **general equation of a line** is $ax + by + c = 0$. a is usually a positive number. If a is a negative number, multiply the whole equation by –1.

Q Express in general form: 11

a $y=4x-1$

b $y=-\frac{3}{2}x+\frac{1}{3}$

A a

$$y=4x-1$$
$$4x-y-1=0$$

b

$$y=-\frac{3}{2}x+\frac{1}{3}$$
$$6y=-9x+2$$
$$9x+6y-2=0$$

Q Write the equations of these lines in gradient-intercept form: 12

a $3x-y+7=0$

b $2x+5y-10=0$

A a

$$3x-y+7=0$$
$$3x+7=y$$
$$y=3x+7$$

b

$$2x+5y-10=0$$
$$5y=-2x+10$$
$$y=\frac{-2}{5}x+\frac{10}{5}$$
$$y=-\frac{2}{5}x+2$$

Q Find the equation of the line through the point (8, –3) with gradient $\frac{1}{4}$. Express the answer in general form. 13

A $(8,-3),\ m=\frac{1}{4}$

$$y-y_1=m(x-x_1)$$
$$y-(-3)=\frac{1}{4}(x-8)$$
$$y+3=\frac{1}{4}(x-8)$$
$$4y+12=x-8$$
$$x-4y-20=0$$

$\therefore$ the required equation is $x-4y-20=0$

Q Write down the gradient and y-intercept of the line $5x + 2y - 8 = 0$. Graph the line. 14

A

$$5x+2y-8=0$$
$$2y=-5x+8$$
$$y=-\frac{5}{2}x+4$$

$\therefore$ gradient $m=-\frac{5}{2}$

y-intercept is 4

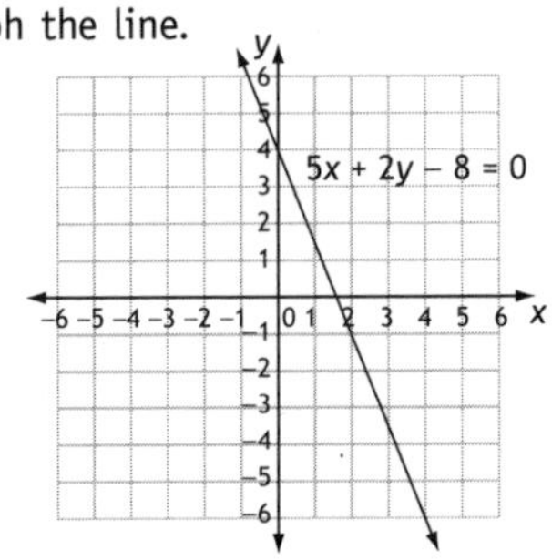

3.9 The equation of a line through two points

- The **equation of the line** through two points (x_1, y_1) and (x_2, y_2) is given by:

$$\frac{y-y_1}{x-x_1}=\frac{y_2-y_1}{x_2-x_1}$$

Go to page 60 for Exercises

- The equation of a line through two points can simply be found by first finding the gradient, $m = \frac{y_2 - y_1}{x_2 - x_1}$, and then using $y - y_1 = m(x - x_1)$.

Replacing m gives an alternative form of the two-point formula:

$$y - y_1 = \frac{y_2 - y_1}{x_2 - x_1}(x - x_1)$$

Q 15 Find the equation of the line passing through:

a (3, 6) and (−1, 9) **b** (−2, −4) and (3, −1)

c (0, 5) and (−2, −1)

A **a** $(3, 6), (-1, 9)$

$$\frac{y - y_1}{x - x_1} = \frac{y_2 - y_1}{x_2 - x_1}$$

$$\frac{y - 6}{x - 3} = \frac{9 - 6}{-1 - 3}$$

$$\frac{y - 6}{x - 3} = -\frac{3}{4}$$

$$y - 6 = -\frac{3}{4}(x - 3) \quad \text{or} \quad 4(y - 6) = -3(x - 3)$$

$$y - 6 = -\frac{3}{4}x + 2\frac{1}{4} \qquad 4y - 24 = -3x + 9$$

$$y = -\frac{3}{4}x + 8\frac{1}{4} \qquad 3x + 4y - 33 = 0$$

Check that both points satisfy the equation. If they do, the answer MUST be right!

b $(-2, -4), (3, -1)$

$$\frac{y - y_1}{x - x_1} = \frac{y_2 - y_1}{x_2 - x_1}$$

$$\frac{y - (-4)}{x - (-2)} = \frac{-1 - (-4)}{3 - (-2)}$$

$$\frac{y + 4}{x + 2} = \frac{3}{5}$$

$$5(y + 4) = 3(x + 2)$$

$$5y + 20 = 3x + 6$$

$$3x - 5y - 14 = 0$$

c $(0, 5), (-2 - 1)$

$$\frac{y - y_1}{x - x_1} = \frac{y_2 - y_1}{x_2 - x_1}$$

$$\frac{y - 5}{x - 0} = \frac{-1 - 5}{-2 - 0}$$

$$\frac{y - 5}{x} = 3$$

$$y - 5 = 3x$$

$$3x - y + 5 = 0$$

Go to page 60 for Exercises

3.10 The gradient and y-intercept of a line in general form

- The line $ax + by + c = 0$ has gradient $m = -\frac{a}{b}$ and y-intercept $= -\frac{c}{b}$.

Rearranging the equation $ax + by + c = 0$ gives $by = -ax - c$

$$y = -\frac{a}{b}x - \frac{c}{b}$$

So the gradient is $-\frac{a}{b}$ and the y-interept is $-\frac{c}{b}$.

Q 16 Find the gradient and y-intercept of the lines:

a $4x - 2y + 7 = 0$ **b** $5x + y - 3 = 0$

A **a** $4x - 2y + 7 = 0$

$$m = -\frac{a}{b} \qquad y\text{-intercept} = -\frac{c}{b}$$

$$m = -\frac{4}{-2} \qquad y\text{-intercept} = -\frac{7}{-2}$$

$$m = 2 \qquad y\text{-intercept} = 3\frac{1}{2}$$

b $5x + y - 3 = 0$

$$m = -\frac{a}{b} \qquad y\text{-intercept} = -\frac{c}{b}$$

$$m = -\frac{5}{1} \qquad y\text{-intercept} = -\frac{-3}{1}$$

$$m = -5 \qquad y\text{-intercept} = 3$$

or $5x + y - 3 = 0$

$$y = -5x + 3$$

∴ the gradient is -5 and the y-intercept is 3

Q 17 Find the size of the angle, correct to the nearest whole degree, that the line $2x - 4y - 5 = 0$ makes with the positive x-axis.

A $2x - 4y - 5 = 0$

$$m = -\frac{a}{b} = -\frac{2}{-4} = \frac{1}{2}$$

Now $m = \tan\theta$

$$\therefore \tan\theta = \frac{1}{2}$$

$$\theta = 26.56505118\ldots^\circ = 27^\circ \text{ [nearest degree]}$$

∴ the line $2x - 4y - 5 = 0$ makes an angle of 27° with the positive x-axis

3.11 Parallel lines

- Parallel lines have the same gradient.

Q Show that the line joining the point (2, −1) to the point (−3, −8) is parallel to the line $7x - 5y + 1 = 0$. **18**

A The line joining (2, −1) to (−3, −8) has gradient

$$m = \frac{y_2 - y_1}{x_2 - x_1}$$
$$= \frac{-8-(-1)}{-3-2}$$
$$= \frac{-7}{-5}$$
$$= \frac{7}{5}$$

The line $7x - 5y + 1 = 0$ has gradient $m = -\frac{a}{b}$

$$= -\frac{7}{-5}$$
$$= \frac{7}{5}$$

∴ both lines have the same gradient so they are parallel

- Any line parallel to the line $ax + by + c = 0$ has equation of the form $ax + by + k = 0$.

Q Find the equation of the line passing through the point (5, −3) parallel to the line $x - 4y + 11 = 0$. **19**

A (5, −3) parallel to $x - 4y + 11 = 0$.

Parallel line has equation $x - 4y + k = 0$

The point (5, −3) lies on the line

$$5 - 4 \times (-3) + k = 0$$
$$17 + k = 0$$
$$k = -17$$

∴ the required equation is $x - 4y - 17 = 0$

Alternatively: $x - 4y + 11 = 0$

gradient $m = -\frac{a}{b}$

$$= -\frac{1}{-4}$$
$$= \frac{1}{4}$$

$(5, -3)$, $m = \frac{1}{4}$

$$y - y_1 = m(x - x_1)$$
$$y - (-3) = \frac{1}{4}(x - 5)$$
$$y + 3 = \frac{1}{4}(x - 5)$$
$$4y + 12 = x - 5$$
$$x - 4y - 17 = 0$$

3.12 Perpendicular lines

- Two lines, with gradients m_1 and m_2 respectively, are perpendicular if $m_1 m_2 = -1$.

Q Write down the gradient of any line perpendicular to $y = -3x + 6$. **20**

A $y = -3x + 6$ has gradient $m_1 = -3$

Let gradient of any perpendicular lines be m_2.

$$m_1 m_2 = -1$$
$$-3 \times m_2 = -1$$
$$m_2 = \frac{1}{3}$$

In practice, we simply note that perpendicular gradients are negative reciprocals.

Q Show that the lines $y = 4x + 7$ and $2x + 8y - 1 = 0$ are perpendicular. **21**

A $y = 4x + 7$ has gradient $m_1 = 4$

$2x + 8y - 1 = 0$ has gradient

$$m_2 = -\frac{a}{b}$$
$$= -\frac{2}{8}$$
$$= -\frac{1}{4}$$
$$m_1 m_2 = 4 \times -\frac{1}{4}$$
$$= -1$$

∴ the lines are perpendicular

- Any line perpendicular to the line $ax + by + c = 0$ has equation $bx - ay + k = 0$.

Q Find the equation of the line passing through (−1, 3) and perpendicular to the line $3x - 2y + 7 = 0$. **22**

A $3x - 2y + 7 = 0$

Perpendicular line is in the form

$$-2x - 3y + k = 0$$

This line passes through $(-1, 3)$

$$-2 \times -1 - 3 \times 3 + k = 0$$
$$-7 + k = 0$$
$$k = 7$$

∴ $-2x - 3y + 7 = 0$

∴ the required line is $2x + 3y - 7 = 0$

or gradient $m_1 = \frac{3}{2}$ ∴ perpendicular line has $m_2 = -\frac{2}{3}$

$(-1, 3)$, $m = -\frac{2}{3}$

$$y - y_1 = m(x - x_1)$$
$$y - 3 = -\frac{2}{3}[x - (-1)]$$
$$y - 3 = -\frac{2}{3}(x + 1)$$
$$3(y - 3) = -2(x + 1)$$
$$3y - 9 = -2x - 2$$
$$2x + 3y - 7 = 0$$

☞ Go to page 60 for Exercises

Intersection of two lines

- The point of intersection of two lines can be found graphically, or by solving the two simultaneous equations.
- There might not always be a single point of intersection. If the two lines are parallel they will not intersect. The two equations may be in different forms but still be equations of the same straight line $\left(\text{e.g. } y = \frac{1}{2}x - \frac{3}{4},\ 2x - 4y - 3 = 0\right)$. They will coincide at every point.

Q Graph the lines $y = 2x - 5$ and $y = -x + 4$. Write down the coordinates of the point of intersection. 23

A

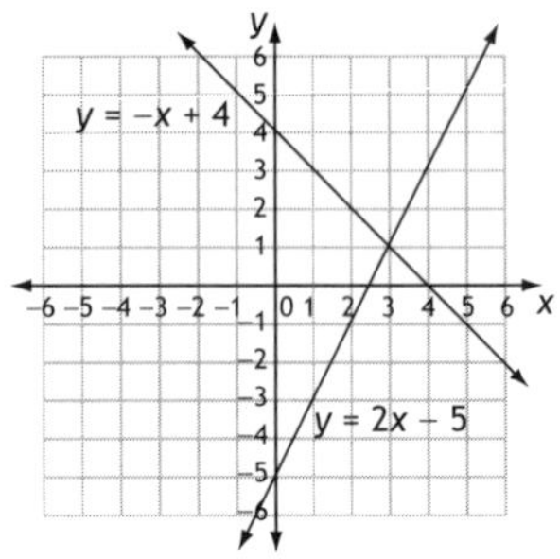

The point of intersection is (3, 1).

Check:

$$y = 2x - 5 \qquad y = -x + 4$$
$$1 = 2 \times 3 - 5 \qquad 1 = -3 + 4$$
$$1 = 1 \qquad 1 = 1$$

✔ Always check to see if the point of intersection found satisfies both equations.

Q Find the point of intersection of the lines $y = -5x + 8$ and $y = 6 - x$. 24

A At the point of intersection, the y values are equal.

$$-5x + 8 = 6 - x$$
$$-4x = -2$$
$$x = \frac{1}{2}$$

Now

$$y = 6 - x$$
$$= 6 - \frac{1}{2}$$
$$= 5\frac{1}{2}$$

$\therefore$ the point of intersection is $\left(\frac{1}{2}, 5\frac{1}{2}\right)$

Check:

$$y = -5x + 8$$
$$5\frac{1}{2} = -5 \times \frac{1}{2} + 8$$
$$5\frac{1}{2} = 5\frac{1}{2}$$

Q Find the point at which the lines $2x + 5y - 31 = 0$ and $3x + 4y - 15 = 0$ intersect. 25

A

$$2x + 5y - 31 = 0 \quad \textbf{i}$$
$$3x + 4y - 15 = 0 \quad \textbf{ii}$$
$$\textbf{i} \times 4 \quad 8x + 20y - 124 = 0 \quad \textbf{iii}$$
$$\textbf{ii} \times 5 \quad 15x + 20y - 75 = 0 \quad \textbf{iv}$$
$$\textbf{iv} - \textbf{iii} \quad 7x + 49 = 0$$
$$7x = -49$$
$$x = -7$$

Substitute in **i**

$$2 \times -7 + 5y - 31 = 0$$
$$5y - 45 = 0$$
$$y = 9$$

$\therefore$ the point of intersection is $(-7, 9)$

3.14 Lines through a point of intersection

Q Find the point of intersection of the lines k: $6x + 5y - 19 = 0$ and l: $x - 5y - 9 = 0$. Show that the line p: $2x + 3y - 5 = 0$ passes through the point of intersection of lines k and l. 26

A

$$6x + 5y - 19 = 0 \quad \textbf{i}$$
$$x - 5y - 9 = 0 \quad \textbf{ii}$$
$$\textbf{i} + \textbf{ii} \quad 7x - 28 = 0$$
$$7x = 28$$
$$x = 4$$

Substitute in **ii**

$$4 - 5y - 9 = 0$$
$$-5y - 5 = 0$$
$$-5y = 5$$
$$y = -1$$

$\therefore$ the point of intersection is $(4, -1)$

If p passes through (4, −1), these coordinates must satisfy the equation of the line.

$$2x + 3y - 5 = 0$$
$$2 \times 4 + 3 \times -1 - 5 = 0$$
$$0 = 0$$

$\therefore$ the line p passes through the point of intersection of lines k and l

- Any line passing through the point of intersection of $a_1x + b_1y + c_1 = 0$ and $a_2x + b_2y + c_2 = 0$ has the equation:

$$a_1x + b_1y + c_1 + k(a_2x + b_2y + c_2) = 0$$

Q Find the equation of the line through the point of intersection of $8x + 3y = 0$ and $7x + 2y - 5 = 0$ and also through the point (−1, −2). 27

A The equation is in the form:

$$(8x + 3y) + k(7x + 2y - 5) = 0$$

(−1, −2) must satisfy this equation.

continued ...

Go to pages 60 and 61 for Exercises

$$\therefore (8 \times -1 + 3 \times -2) + k(7 \times -1 + 2 \times -2 - 5) = 0$$
$$-14 - 16k = 0$$
$$-16k = 14$$
$$k = -\frac{7}{8}$$

$$\therefore (8x + 3y) - \frac{7}{8}(7x + 2y - 5) = 0$$
$$8(8x + 3y) - 7(7x + 2y - 5) = 0$$
$$64x + 24y - 49x - 14y + 35 = 0$$
$$15x + 10y + 35 = 0$$
[divide by 5] $\quad 3x + 2y + 7 = 0$

$\therefore$ the required equation is $3x + 2y + 7 = 0$

3.15 Regions determined by lines

- Any straight line divides the number plane into two regions. Each region is defined by a linear inequality.
- An **unbroken line** indicates the line is included in the region.
- A **broken line** indicates the line forms the boundary of, but is not included in, the region.
- **To determine on which side of the line the required region lies**, choose any point not on the line. Substitute the coordinates of this point into the inequality. If the result is true, the region is that side of the line containing the point. If the result is false, the region is on the other side.

Q 28 Indicate by shading the regions where:

a $y < x + 1$

b $3x + y - 5 \le 0$

A a $y < x + 1$

Take (0, 0)

Test in $y < x + 1$

$0 < 0 + 1$

[true]

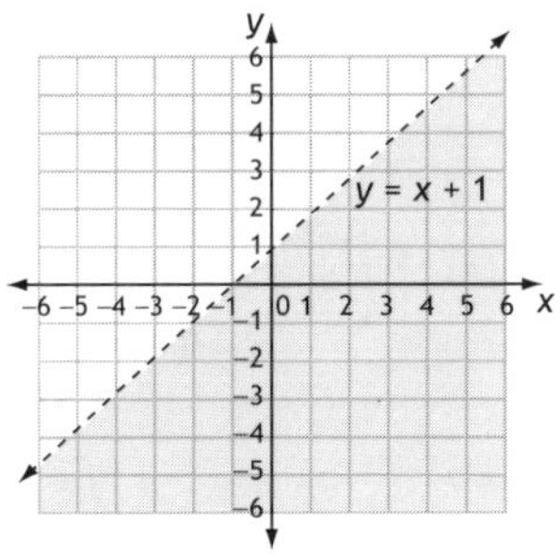

b $3x + y - 5 \le 0$

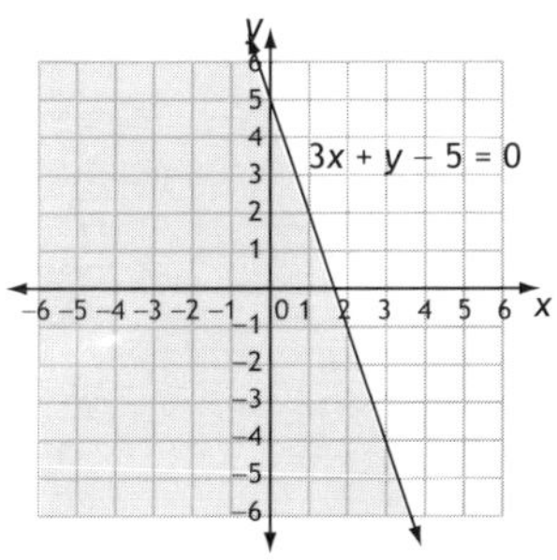

Q 29 Illustrate on a number plane the regions where both equations hold:

a $y > 4 - x$ and $y < 2x - 3$

b $2x - y + 4 > 0$ and $5x + 3y - 8 \le 0$

A a $y > 4 - x$ and $y < 2x - 3$

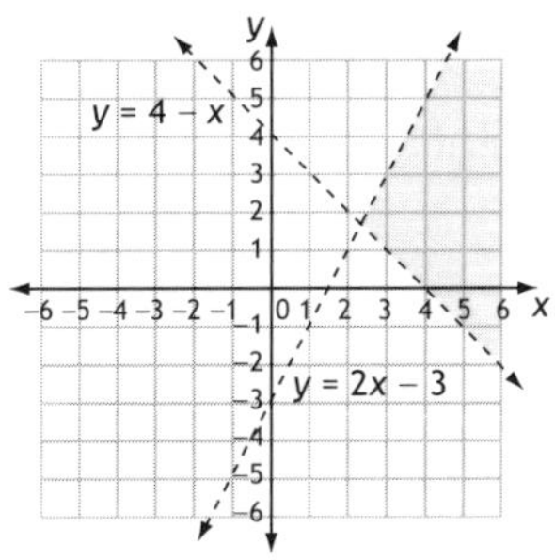

b $2x - y + 4 > 0$ and $5x + 3y - 8 \le 0$

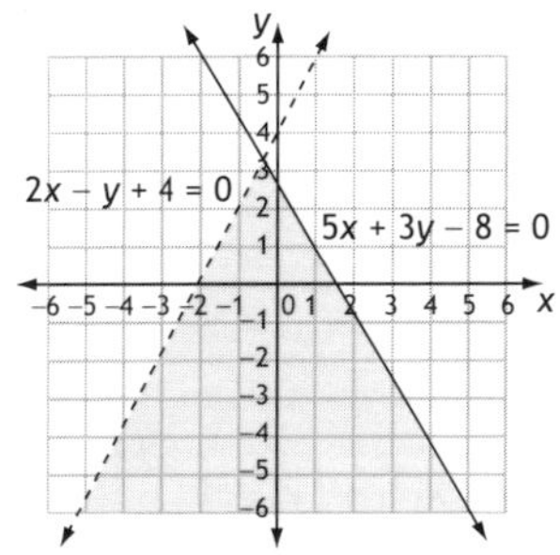

Q 30 Write down a set of three inequalities which define the triangle shaded in the diagram.

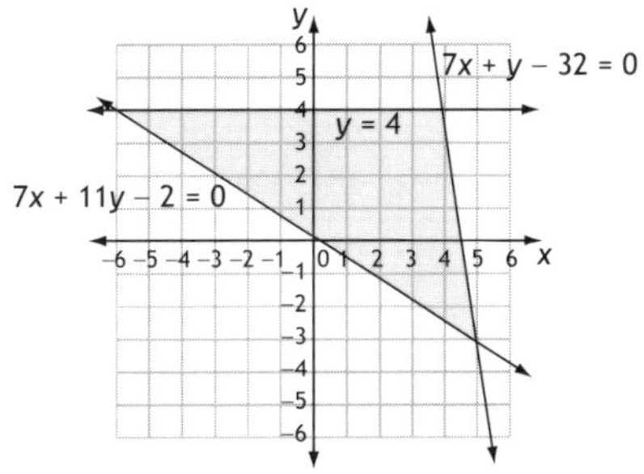

A Choose any point inside the triangle.

Take (0, 2)

Test in $7x + 11y - 2$

$7 \times 0 + 11 \times 2 - 2 = 20 \quad [> 0]$

$\therefore \quad 7x + 11y - 2 \ge 0$

Test in $7x + y - 32$

$7 \times 0 + 2 - 32 = -30 \quad [< 0]$

$\therefore \quad 7x + y - 32 \le 0$

Test in $y = 4$

$2 < 4$

$\therefore \quad y \le 4$

$\therefore$ the required inequalities are

$7x + 11y - 2 \ge 0$, $7x + y - 32 \le 0$ and $y \le 4$

Go to page 61 for Exercises

3.16 The distance between two points

- To find the distance between two points, Pythagoras' theorem gives us a formula:

$$d^2 = (x_2 - x_1)^2 + (y_2 - y_1)^2$$

$$\therefore d = \sqrt{(x_2 - x_1)^2 + (y_2 - y_1)^2}$$

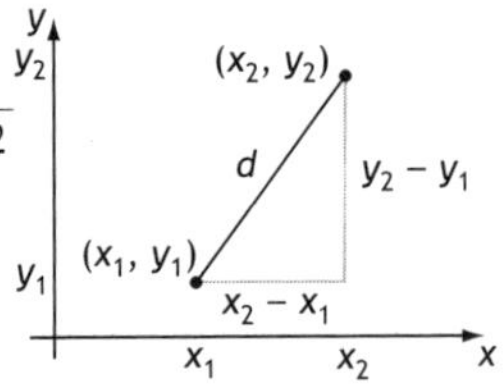

- The **distance** between the points (x_1, y_1) and (x_2, y_2) is given by:

$$d = \sqrt{(x_2 - x_1)^2 + (y_2 - y_1)^2}$$

Distances are always given in simplest surd form rather than decimal approximations.

Q Find the distance between each pair of points: 31

a (1, −7) and (9, 8)
b (−3, −2) and (−1, −6)

A a $(1, -7)$ and $(9, 8)$

$$d = \sqrt{(x_2 - x_1)^2 + (y_2 - y_1)^2}$$
$$= \sqrt{(9 - 1)^2 + (8 - (-7))^2}$$
$$= \sqrt{289}$$

$\therefore$ distance = 17 units

b $(-3, -2)$ and $(-1, -6)$

$$d = \sqrt{(x_2 - x_1)^2 + (y_2 - y_1)^2}$$
$$= \sqrt{(-1 - (-3))^2 + (-6 - (-2))^2}$$
$$= \sqrt{20}$$

$\therefore$ distance = $2\sqrt{5}$ units

Although the distance formula can be used when two points have either the same x coordinate or the same y coordinate, it is easier to simply find the distance along the line.

Q Show that the point A(3, −1) is equidistant from B(6, 3) and C(−2, −1). 32

A $A(3, -1)$, $B(6, 3)$

$$d = \sqrt{(x_2 - x_1)^2 + (y_2 - y_1)^2}$$
$$= \sqrt{(6 - 3)^2 + (3 - (-1))^2}$$
$$= \sqrt{25}$$

$\therefore$ AB = 5 units

$A(3, -1)$, $C(-2, -1)$

AC is the distance from $x = 3$ to $x = -2$ along the line $y = -1$.

$\therefore$ AC = 5 units

$\therefore$ AB = AC

$\therefore$ A is equidistant from B and C

3.17 Perpendicular distance from a point to a line

- The **perpendicular distance** from the point (x_1, y_1) to the line $ax + by + c = 0$ is given by:

$$d = \left| \frac{ax_1 + by_1 + c}{\sqrt{a^2 + b^2}} \right|$$

Q Find the perpendicular distance from the point: 33

a $(1, 3)$ to the line $6x - 8y + 3 = 0$

b $(2, -4)$ to the line $3x - 2y - 1 = 0$

expressing the answer in simplest surd form

A a $(1, 3)$, $6x - 8y + 3 = 0$

$a = 6, b = -8, c = 3$

$$d = \left| \frac{ax_1 + by_1 + c}{\sqrt{a^2 + b^2}} \right|$$
$$= \left| \frac{6 \times 1 + (-8) \times 3 + 3}{\sqrt{6^2 + (-8)^2}} \right|$$
$$= \left| \frac{-15}{10} \right|$$

$\therefore$ distance = 1.5 units

b $(2, -4)$, $3x - 2y - 1 = 0$

$a = 3, b = -2, c = -1$

$$d = \left| \frac{ax_1 + by_1 + c}{\sqrt{a^2 + b^2}} \right|$$
$$= \left| \frac{3 \times 2 + (-2) \times (-4) + (-1)}{\sqrt{3^2 + (-2)^2}} \right|$$
$$= \left| \frac{13}{\sqrt{13}} \right|$$
$$= \frac{13}{\sqrt{13}} \times \frac{\sqrt{13}}{\sqrt{13}}$$
$$= \frac{13\sqrt{13}}{13}$$

$\therefore$ distance = $\sqrt{13}$ units

Go to page 61 for Exercises

Q B and C are two points on the line $4x + 3y + 2 = 0$, such that BC = 10 units. A is the point (3, −2). Find the area of the triangle ABC. 34

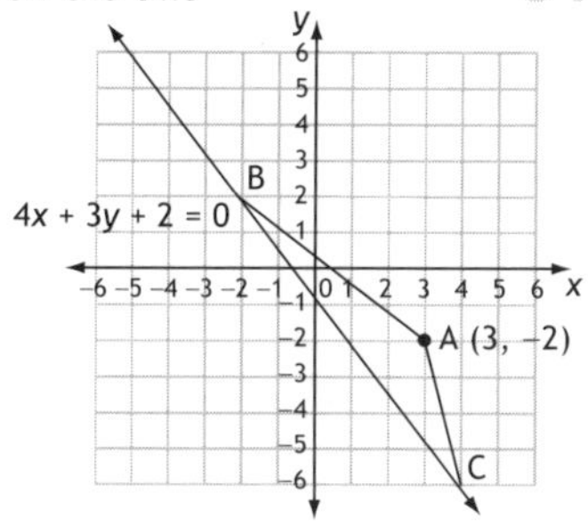

A The perpendicular distance from the line BC to A will give the height of the triangle.

$A(3, -2)$, $4x + 3y + 2 = 0$

$a = 4, b = 3, c = 2$

$$d = \left|\frac{ax_1 + by_1 + c}{\sqrt{a^2 + b^2}}\right|$$

$$= \left|\frac{4 \times 3 + 3 \times (-2) + 2}{\sqrt{4^2 + 3^2}}\right|$$

$$= \frac{8}{5}$$

$$A = \frac{1}{2}bh$$
$$= \frac{1}{2} \times 10 \times \frac{8}{5}$$
$$= 8$$

∴ the area of the triangle is 8 units^2

3.18 The mid-point formula

Let M be the mid-point of $P(x_1, y_1)$ and $Q(x_2, y_2)$. Draw MA and QB parallel to the y-axis and PB parallel to the x-axis.

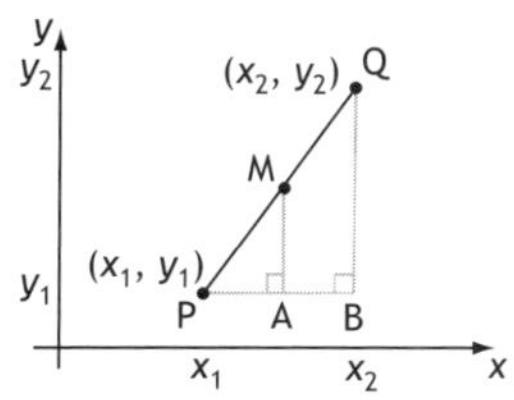

As triangles PMA and PQB are similar (the corresponding angles are equal) A will be the mid-point of PB.

∴ the x coordinate of M is midway between the x coordinates of P and Q. Similarly, the y coordinate of M will be midway between the y coordinates of P and Q.

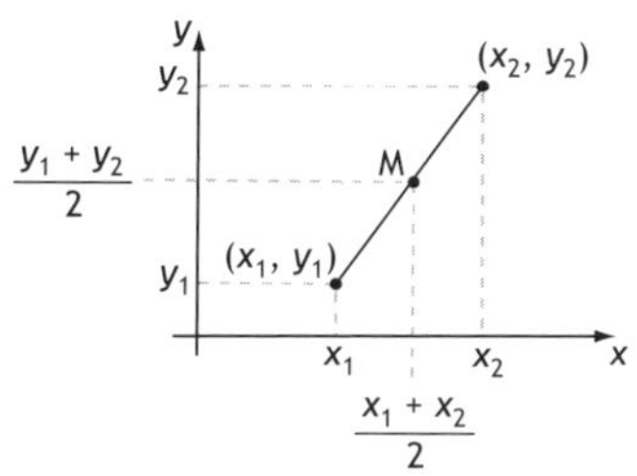

- The mid-point of the interval joining (x_1, y_1) to (x_2, y_2) is given by:

$$M(x, y) = \left(\frac{x_1 + x_2}{2}, \frac{y_1 + y_2}{2}\right)$$

Q Find the mid-point of the interval joining: 35

a $(8, -3)$ to $(12, -7)$

b $(-3, -1)$ to $(5, 6)$

A a $(8, -3), (12, -7)$

$$M(x, y) = \left(\frac{x_1 + x_2}{2}, \frac{y_1 + y_2}{2}\right)$$
$$= \left(\frac{8 + 12}{2}, \frac{-3 + (-7)}{2}\right)$$
$$= (10, -5)$$

b $(-3, -1), (5, 6)$

$$M(x, y) = \left(\frac{x_1 + x_2}{2}, \frac{y_1 + y_2}{2}\right)$$
$$= \left(\frac{-3 + 5}{2}, \frac{-1 + 6}{2}\right)$$
$$= \left(1, 2\frac{1}{2}\right)$$

Q (−5, 3) is the mid-point of P and Q(2, −5). Find the coordinates of P. 36

A $(x_1, y_1), (2, -5)$

$$M(x, y) = \left(\frac{x_1 + x_2}{2}, \frac{y_1 + y_2}{2}\right)$$
$$(-5, 3) = \left(\frac{x_1 + 2}{2}, \frac{y_1 + (-5)}{2}\right)$$

$$\therefore \frac{x_1 + 2}{2} = -5 \quad \text{and} \quad \frac{y_1 - 5}{2} = 3$$
$$x_1 + 2 = -10 \qquad y_1 - 5 = 6$$
$$x_1 = -12 \qquad y_1 = 11$$

∴ P is the point $(-12, 11)$

Go to page 61 for Exercises

Exercises Linear Functions and Lines

1 Graph each of these straight lines:

a $y = x - 5$ b $y = 2x + 1$

c $y = 2 - 3x$ d $y = \frac{3}{4}x - \frac{1}{4}$

e $x = 3$ f $y = -4$

2 Write down the gradient and y-intercept for each of these lines:

a $y = 7x + 3$ b $y = -4x - 2$

c $y = 6 - 5x$ d $y = \frac{2}{3}x - \frac{3}{5}$

e $y = -2$ f $y = -x$

3 Write down the equation of the line with:

a gradient 8, y-intercept -1

b gradient 1, y-intercept 0

c gradient $\frac{1}{4}$, y-intercept 9

4 Write down the gradient and y-intercept and graph each line:

a $y = x + 2$

b $y = -2x - 1$

5 Find the size of the angle, to the nearest degree, that the line $y = 3x - 11$ makes with the positive direction of the x-axis.

6 A line makes an angle of 135° with the positive x-axis. It crosses the y-axis at $y = 7$. What is the equation of the line?

7 Find the gradient of the line joining:

a (3, 7) to (4, 11)

b (−2, 5) to (7, −1)

8 The gradient of the line joining P(x, −3) and Q(6, 9) is 3. Find the value of x.

9 Find the equation of the straight line passing through:

a (2, 5) with gradient 3

b (−3, −1) with gradient 2

c (4, 0) with gradient −5

d (−1, 2) with gradient $\frac{3}{2}$

10 A line with gradient $m = -2$ cuts the x-axis at (7, 0). Where does it cut the y-axis?

11 Express in general form:

a $y = 3x + 2$

b $y = -2x - 5$

c $y = \frac{2}{5}x - \frac{1}{5}$

12 Write the equations of these lines in gradient-intercept form:

a $2x + y - 7 = 0$

b $3x - 2y + 6 = 0$

c $x + 4y - 2 = 0$

13 Find the equation of the line, in general form, which passes through the point:

a (1, 8) with gradient −4

b (−2, −5) with gradient $\frac{4}{3}$

14 Write down the gradient and y-intercept, and graph the line $3x + 4y - 4 = 0$.

15 Find the equation of the straight line joining:

a (3, 1) to (5, 2)

b (−2, 4) to (2, 10)

c (−6, −7) to (−3, 8)

16 Find the gradient and y-intercept of the lines:

a $3x - 2y + 8 = 0$

b $x + 5y + 2 = 0$

c $4x + 3y = 0$

17 Find the size of the angle, to the nearest whole degree, that the line $7x - 3y + 5 = 0$ makes with the positive x-axis.

18 Show that the line joining (5, 1) and (−3, 4) is parallel to the line $3x + 8y = 1$.

19 Find the equation of the line through (7, 1) parallel to the line $2x + 4y - 7 = 0$.

20 Find the gradient of any line perpendicular to the line $2x + 5y - 5 = 0$.

21 Show that the lines $y = 2 - 3x$ and $3x - 9y + 5 = 0$ are perpendicular.

22 Find the equation of the line passing through (4, −2) perpendicular to the line $6x + 5y + 1 = 0$.

23 Graph the lines $y = 3x - 3$ and $x + 2y - 1 = 0$ and hence write down the point of intersection.

24 Find the point of intersection of the pairs of lines:

a $y = 5x - 1$ and $y = -x + 5$

b $x + y - 6 = 0$ and $2x - y + 12 = 0$

25 Find the point at which the lines $5x - 3y - 19 = 0$ and $7x + 2y - 8 = 0$ intersect.

26 Show that the line $x + 3y - 25 = 0$ passes through the point of intersection of the lines $2x - y + 6 = 0$ and $3x + y - 11 = 0$.

Go to pages 221 and 222 for Quick Answers & pages 165–168 for Worked Solutions

27 Find the equation of the line passing through the point of intersection of the lines $6x + 5y - 8 = 0$ and $4x + 7y + 2 = 0$, and also through the point $(-1, 6)$.

28 On separate diagrams indicate by shading the region where:

a $y < 2x + 2$

b $5x + 2y - 4 \geq 0$

29 Indicate on a diagram the region where both equations hold simultaneously:

a $y \geq x$ and $y \leq 3x - 1$

b $5x + y > 0$ and $3x - 4y - 5 > 0$

30 Write down a set of three inequalities which describe the triangular region shaded in the diagram.

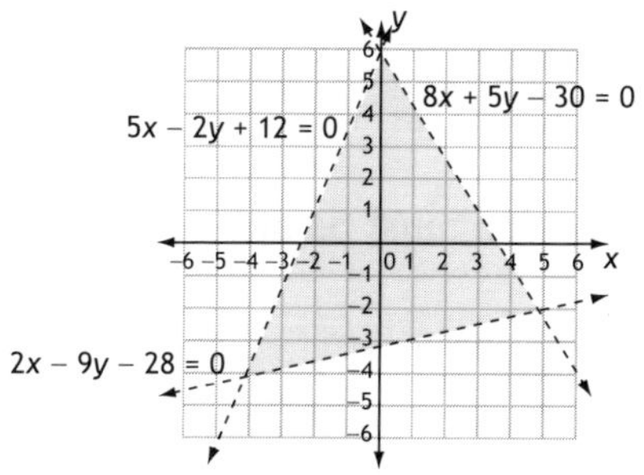

31 Find the distance between each pair of points:

a (4, 7) and (−3, 7)

b (3, 12) and (8, 0)

c (−4, 8) and (5, −2)

32 Show that the point P(1, −7) is equidistant from Q(9, −1) and R(−5, 1).

33 Find the perpendicular distance from the point:

a (6, 2) to the line $8x - 6y + 3 = 0$

b (−3, −2) to the line $2x - 3y = 9$

34 The line $4x + 3y - 9 = 0$ just touches a circle with centre (−3, 2). Find the length of the radius of the circle.

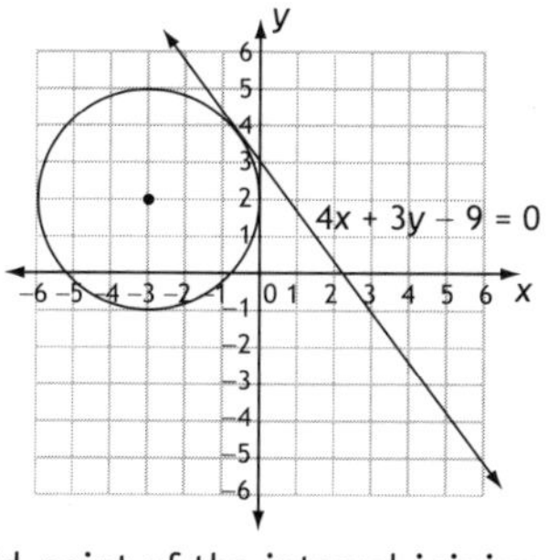

35 Find the mid-point of the interval joining:

a (9, 1) and (3, 7) b (−4, −6) and (−1, 0)

36 (−2, 5) is the mid-point of P(8, −2) and Q. Find the coordinates of Q.

Go to page 222 for Quick Answers & pages 168 and 169 for Worked Solutions. See pages 128 and 129 for Topic Tests

4 Real Functions of a Real Variable

Your Checklist

For a complete understanding of this topic you must be able to:	✓
Understand what is meant by a function	
Use function notation	
Understand the difference between dependent and independent variables	
Understand the terms domain and range	
Find the domain and range of given functions	
Draw graphs of functions	
Understand what is meant by an asymptote	
Investigate the behaviour of a function (Is it symmetrical? When is it increasing? Are there asymptotes? etc)	
Understand odd and even functions and their symmetry properties	
Recognise the equation of a circle and find its centre and radius	
Understand that a circle is not a function (but that if it is divided in half by a line parallel to the *x*-axis, the two resulting semi-circles are functions)	
Understand that an algebraic representation, an equation, can be found for a set of points which satisfy a given geometrical condition	
Solve locus problems	
Show regions on a diagram	
Understand the significance of a solid or broken boundary	
Write down inequalities to describe a region	
Describe regions in words	

4.1 Functional notation

- A **function** $y = f(x)$ is such that for each real value of x for which the function is defined, there is one, and only one, real value of y.
- The **value of** y will vary, depending on the value of x and so y is called the dependent variable. x can take any value (for which the function is defined), and so is called the independent variable.

Q Find the value of the function $y = x^3 - 7$, when $x = 2$. 1

A

$$y = x^3 - 7$$

When $x = 2$, $y = 2^3 - 7 = 1$

- The **notation** $f(x)$ means the value of the function f, at x. A function may be referred to as $y = f(x)$, the function $f(x)$, or the function f.

Q If $f(x) = 3x^2 - x + 1$, find: 2

a $f(4)$ **b** $f(0)$

c $f(-1)$ **d** $f\left(\frac{1}{2}\right)$

A **a**

$$f(x) = 3x^2 - x + 1$$
$$f(4) = 3 \times 4^2 - 4 + 1 = 45$$

b

$$f(x) = 3x^2 - x + 1$$
$$f(0) = 3 \times 0^2 - 0 + 1 = 1$$

c

$$f(x) = 3x^2 - x + 1$$
$$f(-1) = 3 \times (-1)^2 - (-1) + 1 = 5$$

d

$$f(x) = 3x^2 - x + 1$$
$$f\left(\frac{1}{2}\right) = 3 \times \left(\frac{1}{2}\right)^2 - \left(\frac{1}{2}\right) + 1 = 1\frac{1}{4}$$

- A **function** may have a different definition for different values of x.

Q If $f(x) = \begin{cases} 5 - x^2, & x \geq 1 \\ (x-3)^2, & x < 1 \end{cases}$, find: 3

a $f(3)$ **b** $f(-6)$

A **a**

$$f(x) = \begin{cases} 5 - x^2, & x \geq 1 \\ (x-3)^2, & x < 1 \end{cases}$$

$f(3) = 5 - 3^2$ [3 > 1, use top definition]

$= -4$

b

$$f(x) = \begin{cases} 5 - x^2, & x \geq 1 \\ (x-3)^2, & x < 1 \end{cases}$$

$f(-6) = (-6-3)^2$ [−6 < 1, use bottom definition]

$= 81$

4.2 Working with functions

- Some questions with functions may involve the **substitution of an algebraic expression**. For example, $f(-x)$ is the value of the function when x is replaced by $-x$.

Q $f(x) = x^2 - x$. Find $f(x) - f(-x)$. 4

A

$$f(x) = x^2 - x$$
$$f(-x) = (-x)^2 - (-x) = x^2 + x$$
$$f(x) - f(-x) = x^2 - x - (x^2 + x) = x^2 - x - x^2 - x = -2x$$

Q Find the value of $\frac{f(x+h) - f(x)}{h}$ when $f(x) = x^2 - 2x$. 5

A

$$f(x) = x^2 - 2x$$
$$\frac{f(x+h) - f(x)}{h} = \frac{(x+h)^2 - 2(x+h) - (x^2 - 2x)}{h}$$
$$= \frac{x^2 + 2xh + h^2 - 2x - 2h - x^2 + 2x}{h}$$
$$= \frac{2xh + h^2 - 2h}{h}$$
$$= \frac{h(2x + h - 2)}{h}$$
$$= 2x + h - 2$$

- Although many functions use the notation $y = f(x)$, functions can use **any variables**.

Q **a** If $h(t) = 1 - 2t^2$, find $h(-2)$. 6, 7

b $g(y) = \sqrt{100 - y^2}$. Find $g(8)$.

Go to page 71 for Exercises

A a $h(t) = 1 - 2t^2$

$h(-2) = 1 - 2(-2)^2$
$= -7$

b $g(y) = \sqrt{100 - y^2}$

$g(8) = \sqrt{100 - 8^2}$
$= 6$

Q If $f(u) = \dfrac{u-1}{u+1}$, show that $f\left(\dfrac{1}{u}\right) = -f(u)$. 8

A
$$f(u) = \frac{u-1}{u+1}$$
$$f\left(\frac{1}{u}\right) = \frac{\frac{1}{u} - 1}{\frac{1}{u} + 1} = \frac{\frac{1-u}{u}}{\frac{1+u}{u}} = \frac{1-u}{u} \times \frac{u}{1+u} = \frac{1-u}{1+u} = -\frac{u-1}{u+1} = -f(u)$$

4.3 Domain and range

- If $y = f(x)$, the **domain** is the set of all possible values of the independent variable x, and the **range** is the set of possible values of the dependent variable y.
- In many cases the domain of a particular function is specified in the **definition of that function**, e.g. $y = 2x^2 - 3$, for $-1 \le x \le 5$.
- At other times no domain will be specified. The domain in these cases is the set of real numbers for which f(x) is a real number, and is called the **natural domain**.

Q Find the natural domain for each function: 9

a $y = x^2 + 9$ b $y = \sqrt{25 - x^2}$

c $y = \dfrac{1}{2-x}$

A a $y = x^2 + 9$

Domain: all real x

[Every value of x will give a value of y.]

b $y = \sqrt{25 - x^2}$

Domain: $25 - x^2 \ge 0$

$25 \ge x^2$

$\therefore -5 \le x \le 5$

[The square root of a negative number is not a real number, so the expression beneath the square root sign cannot be negative.]

c $y = \dfrac{1}{2-x}$

Domain: $2 - x \ne 0$

$x \ne 2$

Domain is all real numbers except $x = 2$

[Division by zero does not produce a real number, so the denominator cannot be zero.]

- When **finding the range** (or image), we must consider the values at the ends of the domain, any maximum or minimum values, and any values for which y is undefined.

Q Find the range of possible values of the function $y = 7 - 3x$, $-4 \le x \le 5$. 10

A $y = 7 - 3x, \ -4 \le x \le 5$

When $x = -4$ $y = 7 - 3 \times (-4)$
$= 19$

When $x = 5$ $y = 7 - 3 \times 5$
$= -8$

$\therefore -8 \le y \le 19$

[$y = 7 - 3x$ is a straight line so we only need consider the values at the ends of the domain.]

Q Find the natural domain and range for the function $y = 4 - x^2$. 11

A $y = 4 - x^2$

Domain: all real x $x^2 \ge 0$ for all real x

$\therefore -x^2 \le 0$

$4 - x^2 \le 4$

Range: $y \le 4$

If the function is graphed, the domain and range can easily be read.

4.4 Graphs of functions

- You should be able to easily graph the common functions: straight line, parabola, hyperbola etc. The graph of a function must clearly show all essential features.

Go to page 71 for Exercises

In particular you should distinguish that particular graph from all others of the same type.

Q Draw separate sketches of the following functions: **12**

a $y = 3 - x$ b $xy = 1$

c $y = x^2 - 4$ d $y = |x|$

e $y = x^3$ f $y = \sqrt{9 - x^2}$

A a straight line

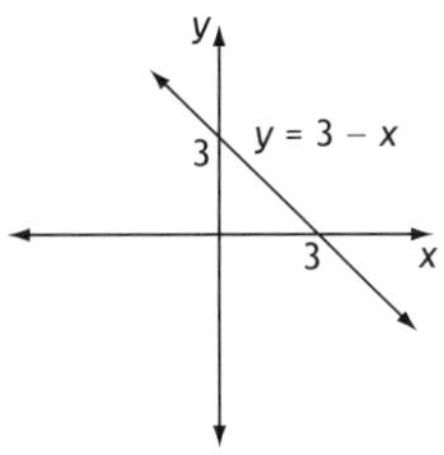

b hyperbola

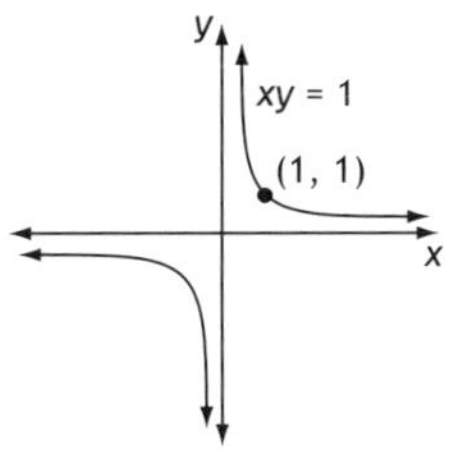

c parabola

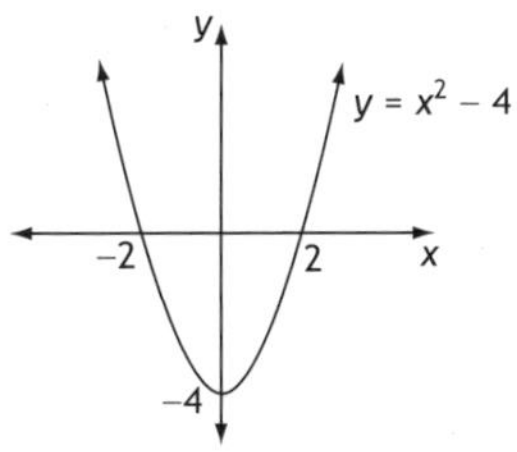

d absolute value

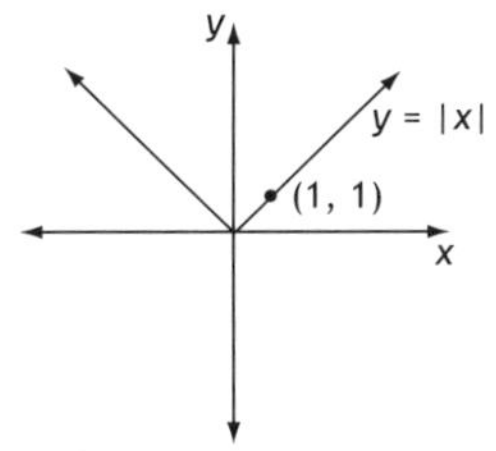

e cubic curve

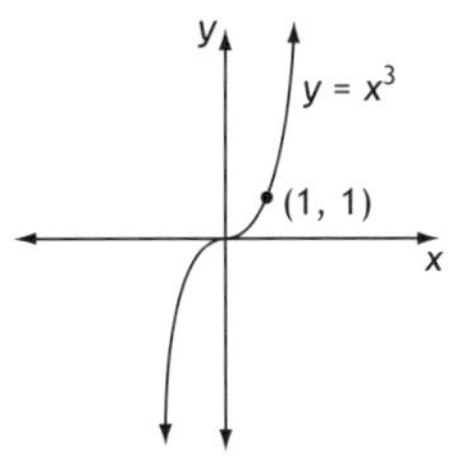

f semi-circle

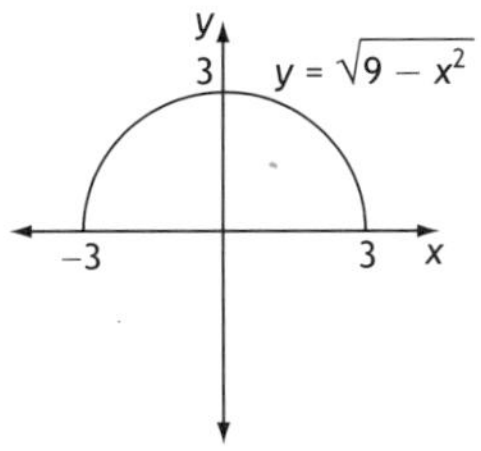

For more information on graphing straight lines see Chapter 3: Linear Functions and Lines, and on graphing parabolas see Chapter 6: The Quadratic Polynomial and the Parabola.

- **Arrows at the end** of a sketch indicate that the graph continues.
- When a graph has a restricted domain, or when there is a jump in the graph, we use **circles to show the endpoints**.
- A **solid circle** indicates that the point is a part of the graph.
- An **empty circle** shows that the graph begins from that point but does not include the point.

Because a function can only have one y value for every x value, there cannot be more than one solid circle for any x value.

Q Sketch: **13**

a $y = 2^x, \ -1 \le x \le 3$

b $f(x) = \begin{cases} 5 - x^2, & x \le 1 \\ x^2 - 3, & x > 1 \end{cases}$

A a

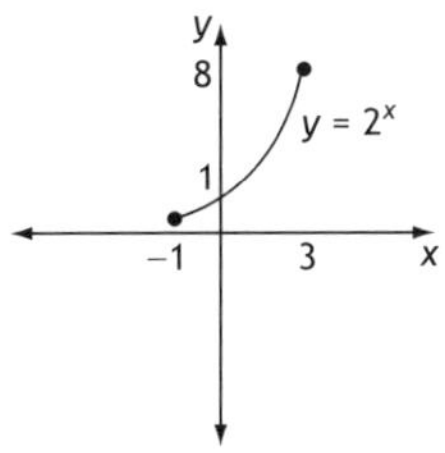

b

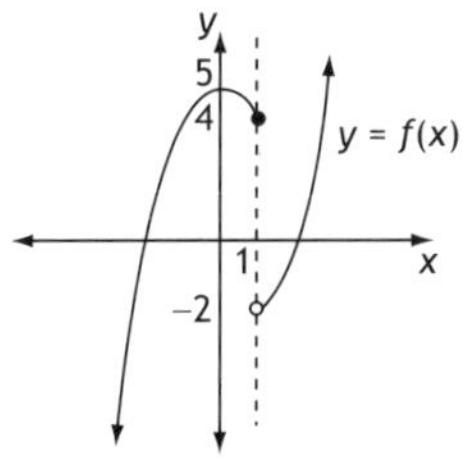

Care must be taken to restrict the graph to the given domain.

4.5 Even and odd functions

- **A function is even** if $f(-x) = f(x)$ for all values of x. The graph of an even function is symmetrical about the y-axis. Fold along the y-axis and the function will map onto itself.

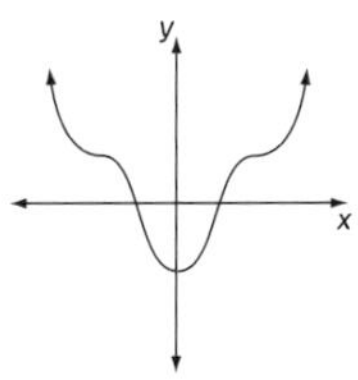

- **A function is odd** if $f(-x) = -f(x)$ for all values of x. The graph of an odd function has point symmetry about the origin. Place a pin at the origin and turn through 180°.

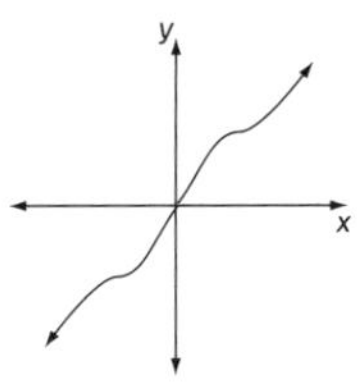

Q Determine whether the function is even, odd or neither: **14**

a $f(x) = x^3$ b $f(x) = x^2 - 3x$

c $f(x) = x^4 - 9x^2 + 7$ d $f(x) = \dfrac{x}{x^2 - 1}$

A a

$$f(x) = x^3$$
$$f(-x) = (-x)^3$$
$$= -x^3$$
$$\therefore f(-x) = -f(x)$$

$\therefore$ the function is odd

Go to page 71 for Exercises

b $f(x) = x^2 - 3x$

$$f(-x) = (-x)^2 - 3(-x)$$
$$= x^2 + 3x$$

$\therefore$ the function is neither even nor odd

c $f(x) = x^4 - 9x^2 + 7$

$$f(-x) = (-x)^4 - 9(-x)^2 + 7$$
$$= x^4 - 9x^2 + 7$$

$\therefore$ the function is even

d $f(x) = \dfrac{x}{x^2 - 1}$

$$f(-x) = \frac{-x}{(-x)^2 - 1}$$
$$= \frac{-x}{x^2 - 1}$$
$$\therefore f(-x) = -f(x)$$

$\therefore$ the function is odd

Q Sketch the functions and state whether they are even or odd: 15

a $y = x^2 - 5$ **b** $y = -3x$

A a

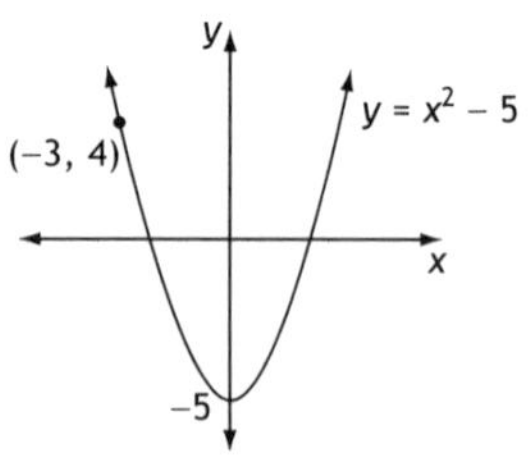

Even function (symmetrical about the y-axis)

b

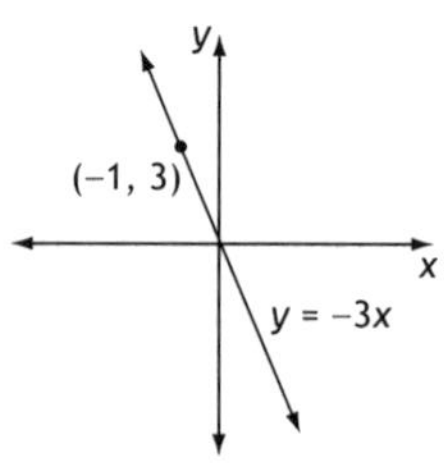

Odd function (point symmetry about the origin)

4.6 Further graphs

- An **asymptote** is a straight line which a curve begins to imitate. Some common curves which have asymptotes are hyperbolas and exponential curves.

Q Sketch: 16

a $y = \dfrac{-4}{x}$ **b** $y = 2^{-x}$

c $y = \dfrac{1}{x+2}$

A a

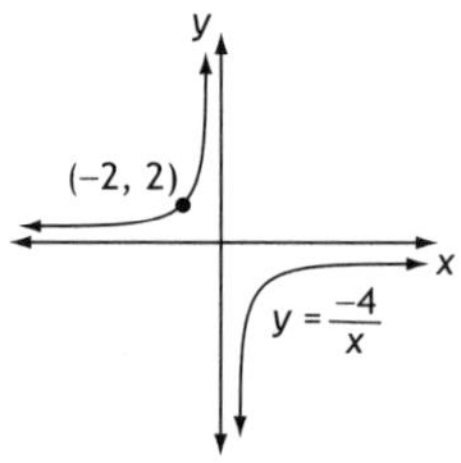

The axes are asymptotes.

b

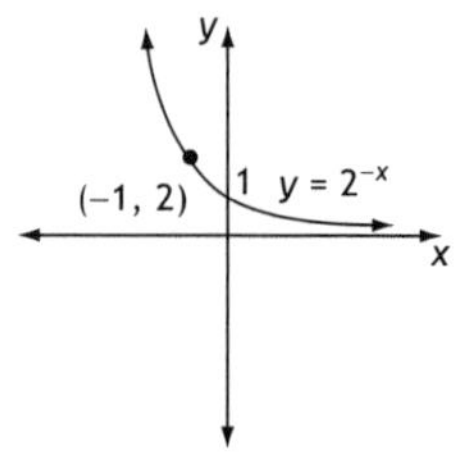

The x-axis is an asymptote.

c

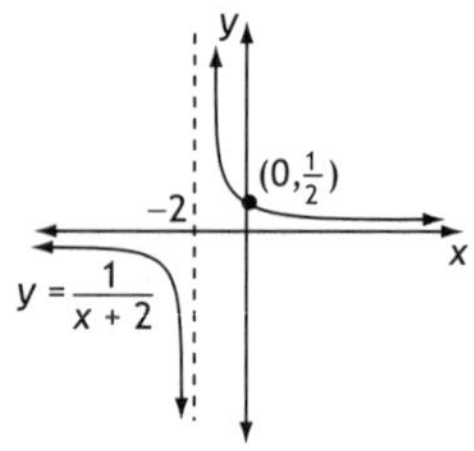

The lines $x = -2$ and $y = 0$ are asymptotes.

- When attempting to **sketch any graph** the following checklist might be considered:
  - is it a basic shape: parabola, circle, hyperbola etc?
  - what is the domain and range?
  - where does the curve cross the coordinate axes?
  - when is it positive or negative?
  - when does it increase or decrease?
  - is it an even or odd function, or does it have some other symmetry properties?
  - is it a smooth curve or are there any holes or sharp corners?
  - are there any asymptotes?

Q Sketch the function $y = \dfrac{1}{x^2 - 1}$. 17

A $f(x) = \dfrac{1}{x^2 - 1}$

$$f(-x) = \frac{1}{(-x)^2 - 1}$$
$$= \frac{1}{x^2 - 1}$$

$\therefore$ the function is even and will be symmetrical about the y-axis.

Domain: $x^2 \neq 1$

$x \neq \pm 1$

When $x = 0$, $y = -1$

If $0 < x < 1$, $y < 0$

As x gets closer to 1, y has larger negative values.

If $x > 1$, $y > 0$

When x is close to 1, y is large.
As the values of x get larger, y gets closer to 0.

continued ...

Go to page 71 for Exercises

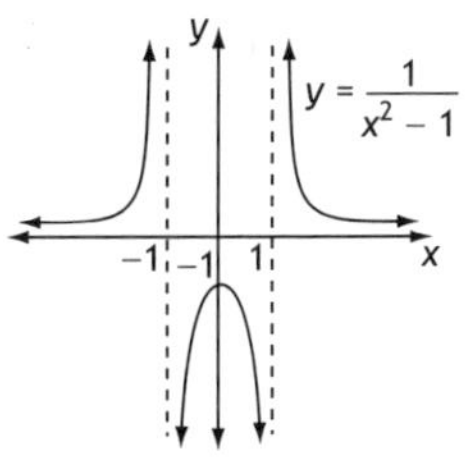

4.7 The equation of a circle

- A circle is defined as the set of points in the plane which are equidistant from a fixed point (the centre).
- The equation of a circle with **centre** (a, b) and **radius** r units is given by:

$$(x-a)^2 + (y-b)^2 = r^2$$

This equation comes directly from using the distance formula to find the distance between the points (x, y) and (a, b) and letting the distance be r.

- The equation of a circle with centre (0, 0) and radius r units is given by:

$$x^2 + y^2 = r^2$$

Q Find the equation of the circle, centre (4, −1) and radius 6 units. 18

A

$$(x-a)^2 + (y-b)^2 = r^2$$
$$(x-4)^2 + (y-(-1))^2 = 6^2$$
$\therefore\ (x-4)^2 + (y+1)^2 = 36$ is the required equation

Q Find the centre and radius of the circle: 19

a $(x-3)^2 + (y-1)^2 = 64$

b $(x+5)^2 + (y-2)^2 = 8$

A a $(x-3)^2 + (y-1)^2 = 64$

Centre $(3, 1)$, radius $= 8$ units

b $(x+5)^2 + (y-2)^2 = 8$

Centre $(-5, 2)$, radius $= \sqrt{8}$ units $= 2\sqrt{2}$ units

It may be necessary to complete squares in order to find the centre and radius of a circle.

Q Find the centre and radius of the circle: 20

a $x^2 + y^2 - 6y + 5 = 0$

b $x^2 + y^2 - 4x + 10y + 20 = 0$

A a

$$x^2 + y^2 - 6y + 5 = 0$$
$$x^2 + y^2 - 6y + 9 = 4$$
$$x^2 + (y-3)^2 = 2^2$$
$\therefore$ centre $(0, 3)$, radius 2 units

b

$$x^2 + y^2 - 4x + 10y + 20 = 0$$
$$x^2 - 4x + y^2 + 10y = -20$$
$$x^2 - 4x + 4 + y^2 + 10y + 25 = 9$$
$$(x-2)^2 + (y+5)^2 = 3^2$$
$\therefore$ centre $(2, -5)$, radius 3 units

If we know the centre and any point on a circle we can find the radius by either finding the equation of the circle and substituting the given point, or by using the distance formula.

Q The circle, centre (−7, 5), passes through the point (8, −3). Find the radius. 21

A Centre $(-7, 5)$

$$(x-(-7))^2 + (y-5)^2 = r^2$$
$$(x+7)^2 + (y-5)^2 = r^2$$

The coordinates of the point $(8, -3)$ must satisfy the equation of the circle.

$$(8+7)^2 + (-3-5)^2 = r^2$$
$$289 = r^2$$

$\therefore$ the radius of the circle will be 17 units

or $(-7, 5)$, $(8, -3)$

$$d = \sqrt{(x_2 - x_1)^2 + (y_2 - y_1)^2}$$
$$= \sqrt{(8-(-7))^2 + (-3-5)^2}$$
$$= \sqrt{289}$$
$$= 17$$

$\therefore$ the radius of the circle is 17 units

4.8 Semi-circular functions

- The **equation** $x^2 + y^2 = r^2$ is not a function because for most values of x there are two values of y. We can **rearrange this equation** and divide it into **two parts**, where each part will be a function.

Go to page 71 for Exercises

i.e. $x^2 + y^2 = r^2$

$$y^2 = r^2 - x^2$$

$$y = \pm\sqrt{r^2 - x^2}$$

$\therefore$ The two parts are $y = \sqrt{r^2 - x^2}$ and $y = -\sqrt{r^2 - x^2}$, both of which are functions.

- The **graphs** of these two functions are **semi-circles**.

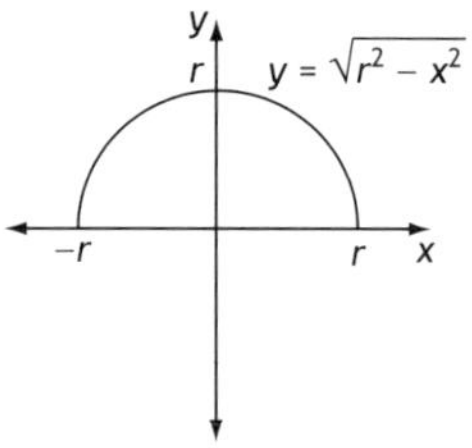

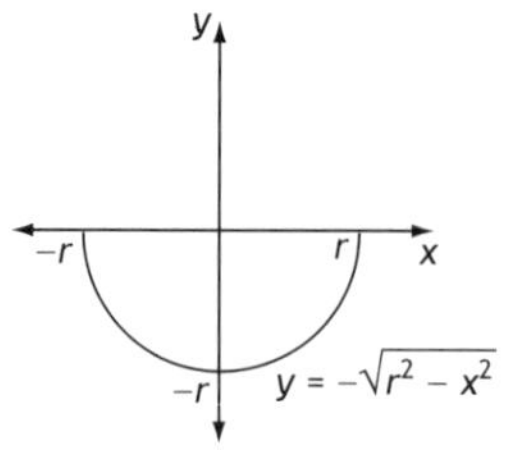

Q Graph the functions: **22**

a $y = -\sqrt{16 - x^2}$ **b** $y = \sqrt{9 - x^2}$

A **a** $y = -\sqrt{16 - x^2}$
Semi-circle:
centre $(0, 0)$
radius 4 units

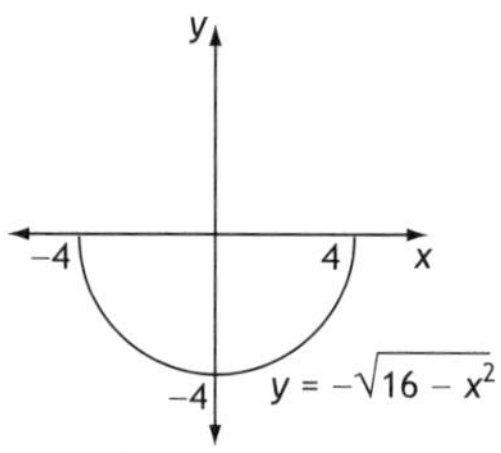

b $y = \sqrt{9 - x^2}$
Semi-circle:
centre $(0, 0)$
radius 3 units

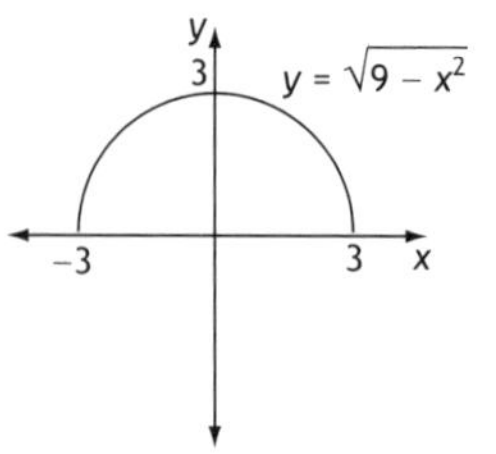

- From $(x - a)^2 + (y - b)^2 = r^2$ we get $y = b + \sqrt{r^2 - (x - a)^2}$ and $y = b - \sqrt{r^2 - (x - a)^2}$.

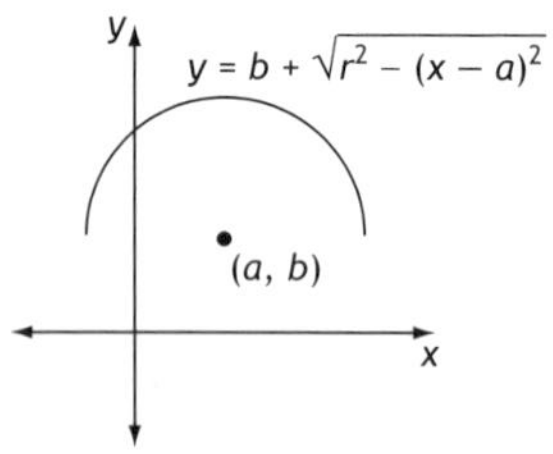

Domain: $a - r \le x \le a + r$
Range: $b \le y \le b + r$

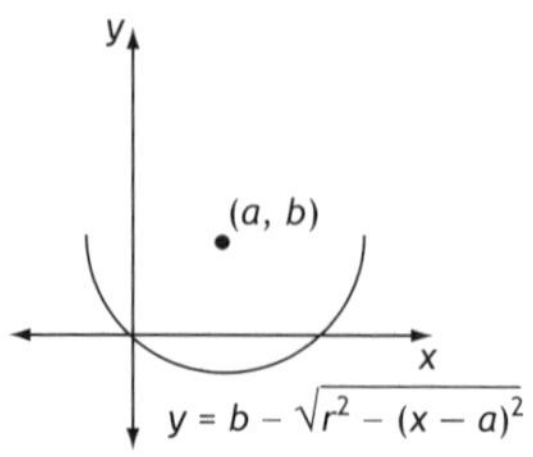

Domain: $a - r \le x \le a + r$
Range: $b - r \le y \le b$

Go to page 72 for Exercises

Q Write down the coordinates of the centre, the radius, the domain and the range, and sketch each function: **23**

a $y = 1 + \sqrt{25 - (x + 2)^2}$

b $y = 8 - \sqrt{4 - (x - 3)^2}$

A **a** $y = 1 + \sqrt{25 - (x + 2)^2}$

Centre: $(-2, 1)$
Radius: 5 units
Domain: $-7 \le x \le 3$
Range: $1 \le y \le 6$

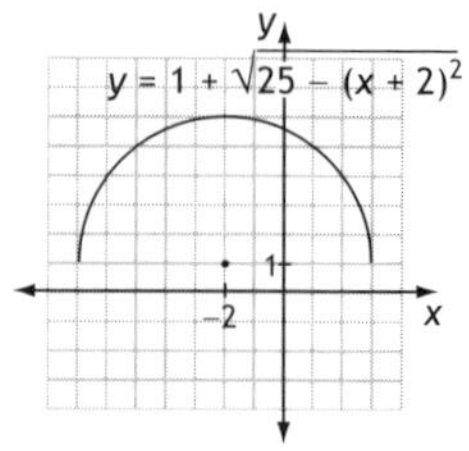

b $y = 8 - \sqrt{4 - (x - 3)^2}$

Centre: $(3, 8)$
Radius: 2 units
Domain: $1 \le x \le 5$
Range: $6 \le y \le 8$

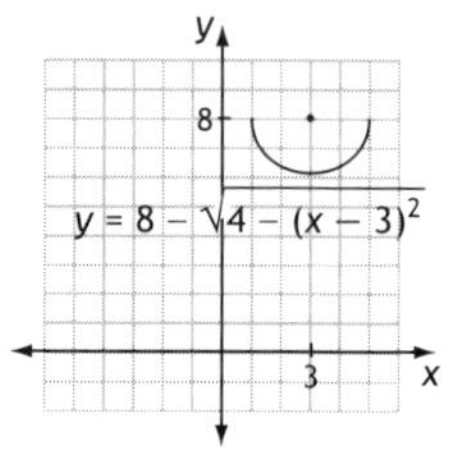

4.9 Locus problems

- A **locus** is a set of points obeying a given condition, or conditions. When finding a locus we are simply finding a geometric description or an algebraic equation that defines those conditions.

Q A point moves so that its distance from the point (–6, 4) is equal to 3 units. **24**

a Give a geometrical description of the locus.

b Find the equation of the locus.

A **a** The locus is a circle with centre (–6, 4) and radius 3 units.

b Equation is given by:

$(x - (-6))^2 + (y - 4)^2 = 3^2$

$\therefore\ (x + 6)^2 + (y - 4)^2 = 9$ is the equation of the locus

Q Give a geometrical description of the locus whose equation is $x^2 - y^2 = 0$. Graph the locus. **25**

A

$$x^2 - y^2 = 0$$

$$(x + y)(x - y) = 0$$

$x + y = 0$ or $x - y = 0$

$y = -x$ $y = x$

$\therefore$ the locus is the pair of straight lines $y = -x$ and $y = x$

continued ...

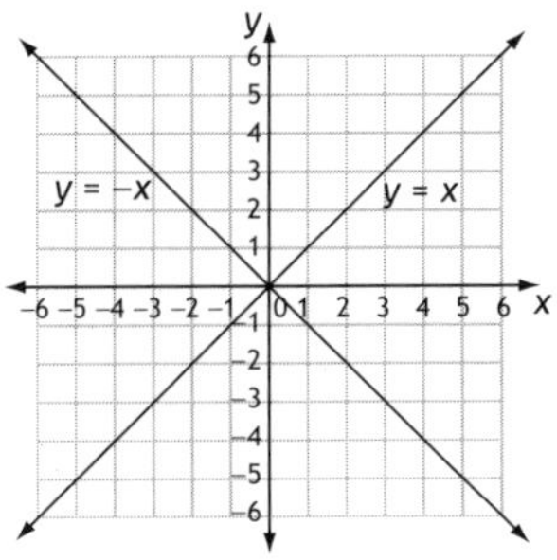

Q Find the equation of the locus of points P(*x*, *y*), which are equidistant from A(–4, 1) and B(7, –2). 26

A

$$PA = PB$$
$$PA^2 = PB^2$$
$$(x+4)^2 + (y-1)^2 = (x-7)^2 + (y+2)^2$$
$$x^2 + 8x + 16 + y^2 - 2y + 1$$
$$= x^2 - 14x + 49 + y^2 + 4y + 4$$
$$22x - 6y - 36 = 0$$
$$11x - 3y - 18 = 0$$

$\therefore$ the equation of the locus is $11x - 3y - 18 = 0$

The locus of points P which are equidistant from two other fixed points, A and B, will be the perpendicular bisector of AB.

Q Find the equation of the locus of points P(*x*, *y*) whose distance from the point Q(11, –11) is twice their distance from R(2, 1). 27
Give a geometrical description of the locus.

A

$$PQ = 2PR$$
$$PQ^2 = 4PR^2$$
$$(x-11)^2 + (y+11)^2 = 4\left[(x-2)^2 + (y-1)^2\right]$$
$$x^2 - 22x + 121 + y^2 + 22y + 121$$
$$= 4\left[x^2 - 4x + 4 + y^2 - 2y + 1\right]$$
$$x^2 - 22x + y^2 + 22y + 242 = 4x^2 - 16x + 4y^2 - 8y + 20$$
$$3x^2 + 6x + 3y^2 - 30y = 222$$
$$x^2 + 2x + y^2 - 10y = 74$$
$$x^2 + 2x + 1 + y^2 - 10y + 25 = 100$$
$$(x+1)^2 + (y-5)^2 = 10^2$$

$\therefore$ the locus is a circle, centre $(-1, 5)$, radius 10 units

4.10 Locus and the parabola

- The locus of a point whose distance from a fixed point is equal to its distance from a fixed line is a **parabola**.

Q Find the equation of the locus of points P whose distance from the point S(6, –7) is equal to their distance from the line *y* = –9. 28

A $S(6, -7)$, $P(x, y)$

$$d = \sqrt{(x_2 - x_1)^2 + (y_2 - y_1)^2}$$
$$= \sqrt{(x-6)^2 + (y+7)^2}$$

$P(x, y)$, $y + 9 = 0$

$$d = \left|\frac{ax_1 + by_1 + c}{\sqrt{a^2 + b^2}}\right|$$
$$= \left|\frac{0 \times x + 1 \times y + 9}{\sqrt{0^2 + 1^2}}\right|$$
$$= |y + 9|$$

Now these two distances are equal.
$\therefore$ the square of their distances will also be equal

$$(x-6)^2 + (y+7)^2 = (y+9)^2$$
$$x^2 - 12x + 36 + y^2 + 14y + 49 = y^2 + 18y + 81$$
$$x^2 - 12x + 4 = 4y$$
$$y = \frac{1}{4}x^2 - 3x + 1$$

- It is not actually necessary to **use** the **perpendicular distance formula**. The perpendicular distance from a point to a line parallel to the *x*-axis is just the absolute value of the difference between the *y* values.
- A **parabola** can be **defined** as the locus of a point whose distance from a fixed point, called the focus, is equal to its distance from a fixed line, the directrix.

Q Find the locus of a point P(*x*, *y*) which moves so that its distance from S(0, *A*) is equal to its distance from the line *y* = –*A*. 29

A $P(x, y)$, $S(0, A)$

$$PS^2 = (x-0)^2 + (y-A)^2$$
$$= x^2 + (y-A)^2$$

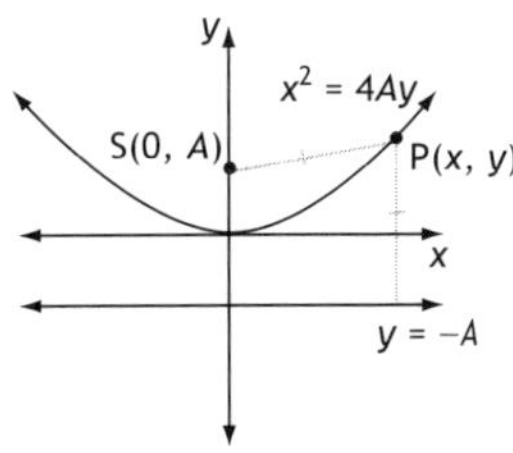

$P(x, y)$, $y + A = 0$

$$d = |y + A|$$
$$d^2 = (y + A)^2$$

$$\therefore\ x^2 + (y-A)^2 = (y+A)^2$$
$$x^2 + y^2 - 2Ay + A^2 = y^2 + 2Ay + A^2$$
$$x^2 = 4Ay$$

The parabola is dealt with in more detail in Chapter 6.

Go to page 72 for Exercises

4.11 Regions and inequalities

- An **inequality in x and y** can be represented as a region of the Cartesian plane.
- If the **inequality is $\le$ or $\ge$**, the boundary forms part of the region, shown by a solid curve or line on a diagram.
  If the **inequality is $<$ or $>$**, the boundary does not form part of the region. This is shown by a broken line.
- To determine on which side of the boundary the required region lies, test a point in the inequality. If the inequality is true for the point, then the required region contains that point. If the inequality is not true, then the required region does not contain the point.

Q Indicate clearly on a diagram the region determined by the inequality: 30

a $y < 2x - 3$ **b** $x^2 + y^2 \ge 9$

A a

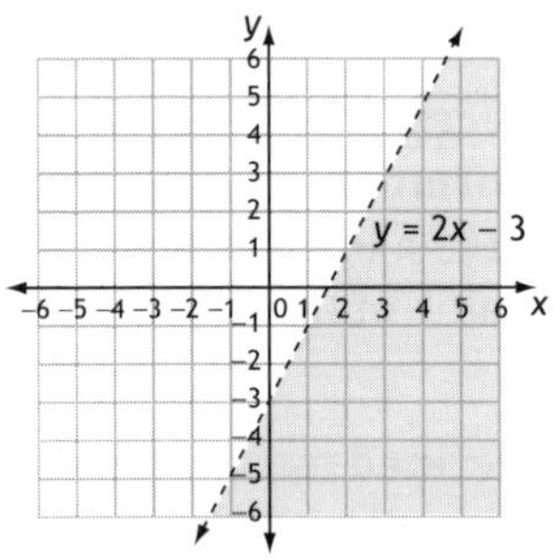

Test (0, 0)
$0 < 2(0) - 3$ [false]
$\therefore$ (0, 0) is not in the region

b

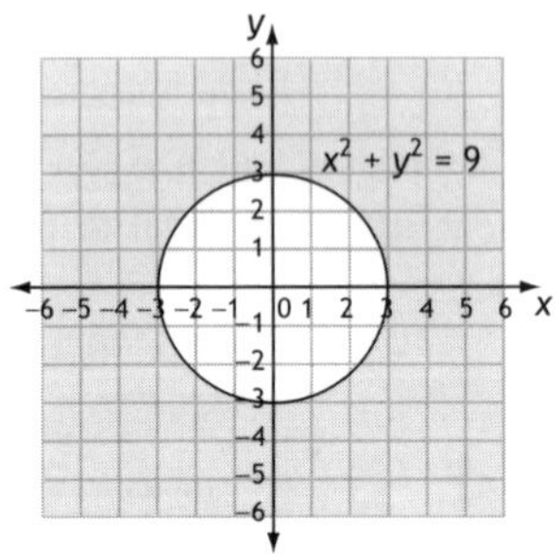

- When **two or more inequalities** are used to define a region, the required region is the part that is common to all inequalities.

Q Draw a clear sketch of the region which satisfies the inequalities $y > x^2$ and $x + y < 1$. 31

A

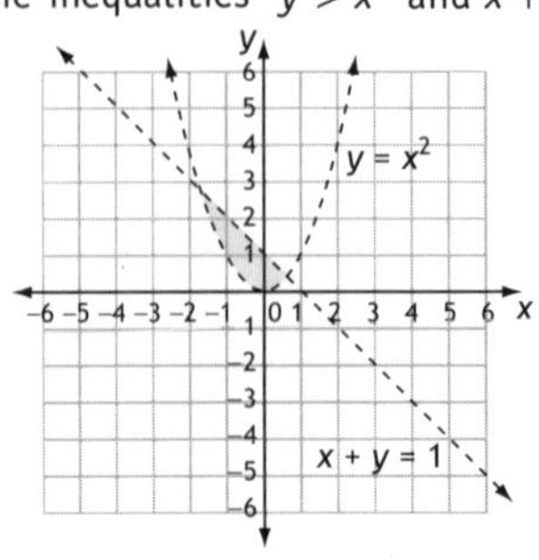

Go to page 72 for Exercises

Q Give a geometrical description of the region determined by the inequalities: 32

$y \le \sqrt{4 - x^2}$, $x \le 0$, $y \ge 0$. Sketch the region.

A The region is the upper left quadrant of a circle, centre (0, 0), radius 2 units.

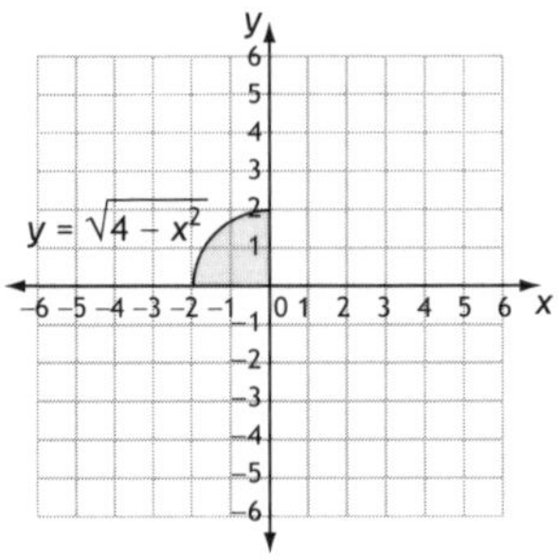

Q Find a system of inequalities in x and y which exactly define the region of the Cartesian plane which lies inside a circle, centre (1, −2), radius 4 units, below the line $y = 1$, and to the right of the y-axis. Sketch the region. 33

A $(x-1)^2 + (y+2)^2 < 16,\ \ y < 1,\ \ x > 0$

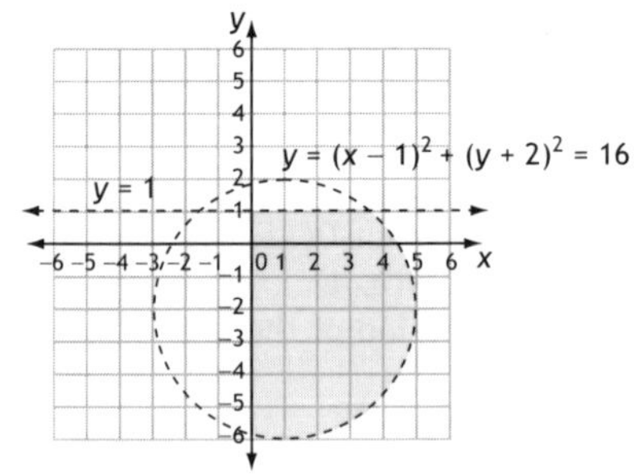

Exercises Real Functions of a Real Variable

1 Find the value of the function:

a $y = 9 - 2x$ when $x = 4$

b $y = x^2 - 5x$ when $x = 3$

2 If $f(x) = x^3 - x^2 + x - 4$, find:

a $f(1)$ b $f(2)$ c $f(0)$

d $f(-3)$ e $f\left(\frac{1}{2}\right)$

3 If $f(x) = \begin{cases} 3x - 4 & \text{for } x < 2 \\ x & \text{for } 2 \le x \le 3 \\ x^2 - 6 & \text{for } x > 3 \end{cases}$, find:

a $f(5)$ b $f(-1)$ c $f(2.5)$

4 $f(x) = x^3 + x$. Find $f(x) + f(-x)$.

5 Find the value of $\dfrac{f(x+h) - f(x)}{h}$ when $f(x) = x^2 + 4x$.

6 If $p(x) = 3x^2 - 5x$, find:

a $p(2)$ b $p(-2)$

7 If $h(z) = \dfrac{z+2}{z+7}$, find $h(3)$.

8 If $g(n) = n^2 + \dfrac{1}{n^2}$, show that $g(4) = g\left(\dfrac{1}{4}\right)$.

9 Find the natural domain for each function:

a $y = 3x^2$ b $y = \dfrac{x+3}{x+4}$

c $y = \sqrt{x^2 - 16}$ d $y = \dfrac{1}{x^3 + 1}$

10 Find the range of possible values for each function:

a $y = 2x + 7, \ -2 \le x \le 3$

b $y = x^2, \ -4 \le x \le 4$

11 Find the natural domain and range for the function:

a $y = x^2 + 3$ b $y = \dfrac{1}{x}$

12 Draw separate graphs of the following functions:

a $y = 2x + 1$ b $y = 3 - x^2$

c $y = \dfrac{4}{x}$ d $y = |x| + 1$

e $y = \sqrt{25 - x^2}$ f $y = 3^x$

13 Graph:

a $y = -x^3, \ -2 \le x \le 2$

b $f(x) = \begin{cases} x^2 - 2, & x \le 2 \\ x, & x > 2 \end{cases}$

14 Determine whether each function is odd, even or neither:

a $y = -x^2$ b $y = x^3 + 2$

c $f(x) = x + \dfrac{1}{x}$ d $f(x) = x^4 - 2x^2$

15 Sketch the function and state whether it is odd, even or neither:

a $y = |x|$ b $y = 1 - 2x$

c $xy = -2$

16 Sketch:

a $y = 10^x$ b $y = \dfrac{3}{x}$

17 Sketch the function $y = \dfrac{1}{x+1}$.

18 Find the equations of the circles:

a centre (0, 0), radius 7 units

b centre (−2, −5), radius 1 unit

19 Find the centre and radius of each circle:

a $(x-2)^2 + (y+4)^2 = 16$

b $(x+3)^2 + (y-1)^2 = 12$

20 Find the centre and radius of each circle:

a $x^2 + y^2 - 16x - 8y - 20 = 0$

b $x^2 + y^2 + 22x - 2y + 41 = 0$

21 The circle with centre (−2, 4) passes through the point (13, 12). Find the equation of the circle.

☞ Go to pages 222 and 223 for Quick Answers & pages 169–171 for Worked Solutions

22 Graph the functions:

a $y = \sqrt{36 - x^2}$

b $y = -\sqrt{25 - x^2}$

23 Write down the centre, radius, domain and range, and sketch each function:

a $f(x) = 7 + \sqrt{4 - (x+1)^2}$

b $y = 2 - \sqrt{16 - (x-3)^2}$

24 A point P(x, y) moves so that its distance from the point (1, −5) is equal to 4 units.

a Give a geometrical description of the locus.

b Find the equation of the locus.

25 Give a geometrical description of the locus whose equation is $x^2 = 4 - y^2$. Graph the locus.

26 Find the equation of the locus of points which are equidistant from (3, 8) and (7, −2).

27 a Find the gradient of the line joining P(x, y) and Q(1, 5).

b Find the gradient of the line joining P(x, y) to R(9, −1).

c Find the equation that satisfies the condition that PQ is perpendicular to PR.

d Write a geometrical description of the locus of points P.

28 Find the equation of the locus of points P(x, y) whose distance from the point (5, 0) is equal to their distance from the line $x + 5 = 0$.

29 Find the equation of the locus of points P(x, y) whose distance from the point (1, 4) is equal to their distance from the x-axis.

30 Indicate clearly on a diagram the region defined by the inequality:

a $y \geq 4 - 3x$

b $y < 3 - x^2$

31 Draw a clear sketch of the region which satisfies the inequalities:

$$x^2 + (y-1)^2 \leq 16, \quad y \geq x, \quad x < 1$$

32 Give a geometrical description of the region determined by the inequalities:

$$x^2 + y^2 \leq 12\frac{1}{4}, \quad x > 0, \quad y < 2$$

33 Find a system of inequalities in x and y which exactly define the region of the Cartesian plane which lies inside the circle, centre the origin, radius 2 units, above the x-axis and to the right of the line $x = -1$. Sketch the region.

Go to pages 223 & 224 for Quick Answers & pages 171 & 172 for Worked Solutions. See pages 130 & 131 for Topic Tests

5 Trigonometric Ratios

Your Checklist

For a complete understanding of this topic you must be able to:	✓
Use the trigonometric ratios in right-angled triangles	
Understand and use the reciprocal ratios (sec θ, cosec θ and cot θ)	
Understand angles of any magnitude (with reference to the unit circle)	
Know the definitions of sine and cosine for any angle	
Know the definitions of the other ratios in terms of sine and cosine	
Draw graphs of the trigonometric ratios	
Know and use the Pythagorean relations ($\sin^2\theta + \cos^2\theta = 1$, etc)	
Find ratios of obtuse, reflex and negative angles, and those greater than 360°, in terms of the ratios of acute angles	
Know the exact ratios of some special angles	
Solve equations involving the trigonometric ratios	
Understand and use angles of elevation and depression	
Understand and use compass directions and bearings	
Understand and use the sine rule to find both sides and angles	
Understand and use the cosine rule to find both sides and angles	
Know when to use the sine rule and when to use the cosine rule	
Understand and use the formula for finding the area of a triangle (given two sides and the included angle)	

5.1 Review

- The **hypotenuse** is always the longest side of a right-angled triangle, the side opposite the right angle. The **opposite** and **adjacent** sides depend on the angle being used.

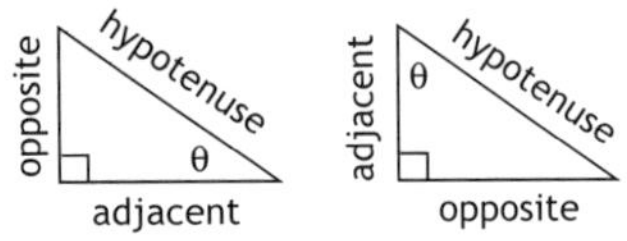

$$\sin\theta = \frac{\text{opposite}}{\text{hypotenuse}} \qquad \cos\theta = \frac{\text{adjacent}}{\text{hypotenuse}}$$

$$\tan\theta = \frac{\text{opposite}}{\text{adjacent}}$$

Q Find x, giving the answer correct to one decimal place. 1

a

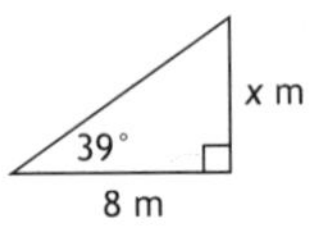

b

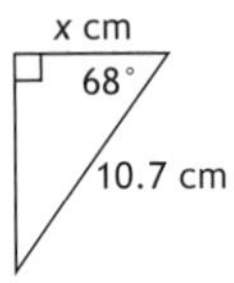

A **a** $\tan 39° = \dfrac{x}{8}$

$\therefore \quad x = 8 \times \tan 39°$

$= 6.478272266\ldots$

$= 6.5$ [1 decimal place]

b $\cos 68° = \dfrac{x}{10.7}$

$\therefore \quad x = 10.7 \times \cos 68°$

$= 4.00829055\ldots$

$= 4.0$ [1 decimal place]

Q Find the length of the side BC, giving the answer correct to two decimal places. 2

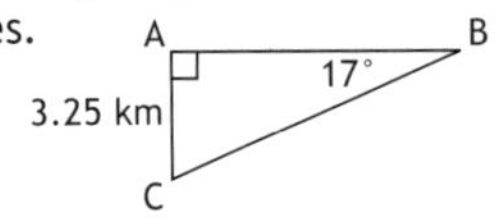

A $\sin 17° = \dfrac{3.25}{BC}$

$\therefore \quad BC = \dfrac{3.25}{\sin 17°}$

$= 11.11598676\ldots$

$= 11.12$ km [2 decimal places]

Q Find θ correct to the nearest minute. 3

a

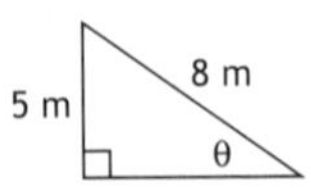

b

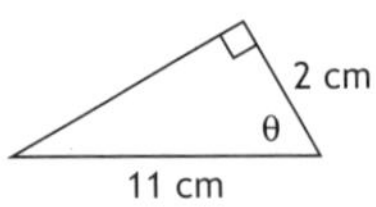

A **a** $\sin\theta = \dfrac{5}{8}$

$\theta = 38°41'$

[by calculator, to the nearest minute]

b $\cos\theta = \dfrac{2}{11}$

$\theta = 79°31'$

[by calculator, to the nearest minute]

Go to page 86 for Exercises

5.2 The reciprocal trigonometric ratios

- Each of the trigonometric ratios, sine, cosine and tangent, has a **reciprocal**.
  - The **reciprocal of sine** is **cosecant**. This is abbreviated to cosec.

$$\mathbf{cosec}\,\theta = \frac{1}{\sin\theta}$$

  - The **reciprocal of cos** is **secant**. This is abbreviated to sec.

$$\mathbf{sec}\,\theta = \frac{1}{\cos\theta}$$

  - The **reciprocal of tangent** is **cotangent**. This is abbreviated to cot.

$$\mathbf{cot}\,\theta = \frac{1}{\tan\theta}$$

- When **evaluating the cosec, sec or cot of an angle** we find the sin, cos or tan of the same angle and then take the reciprocal.

Q Find, correct to three decimal places: 4

a cosec 49° **b** sec 78°

c cot 19° **d** sec 67°35′

A **a** $\text{cosec } 49° = \dfrac{1}{\sin 49°}$

$= 1.325012993\ldots$

$= 1.325$ [3 decimal places]

b $\sec 78° = \dfrac{1}{\cos 78°}$

$= 4.809734345\ldots$

$= 4.810$ [3 decimal places]

c $\cot 19° = \dfrac{1}{\tan 19°}$

$= 2.904210878\ldots$

$= 2.904$ [3 decimal places]

d $\sec 67°35' = \dfrac{1}{\cos 67°35'}$

$= 2.622336593\ldots$

$= 2.622$ [3 decimal places]

- To **find the size of an angle** for which we know the corresponding cosec, sec or cot ratio, first take the reciprocal of both sides.

Q Find θ, to the nearest minute, if: 5

a $\cot\theta = 0.7659$ **b** $\operatorname{cosec}\theta = 1.473$
c $\sec\theta = 3.676$ **d** $\cot\theta = 5.108$

A **a**
$$\cot\theta = 0.7659$$
$$\tan\theta = \frac{1}{0.7659} = 1.30565348\ldots$$
$$\theta = 52.55149624\ldots° = 52°33'$$

b
$$\operatorname{cosec}\theta = 1.473$$
$$\sin\theta = \frac{1}{1.473} = 0.678886625\ldots$$
$$\theta = 42.75670121\ldots° = 42°45'$$

c
$$\sec\theta = 3.676$$
$$\cos\theta = \frac{1}{3.676} = 0.27203482\ldots$$
$$\theta = 74.21461353\ldots° = 74°13'$$

d
$$\cot\theta = 5.108$$
$$\tan\theta = \frac{1}{5.108} = 0.195771339\ldots$$
$$\theta = 11.07677837\ldots° = 11°5'$$

It is not necessary to show all this working. It is done here so that you can better understand what is required.

5.3 The unit circle

- The **unit circle** is a circle of radius 1 unit. This circle has equation $x^2 + y^2 = 1$.
- If θ is the angle of rotation, in an anticlockwise direction, from the positive x-axis, then:

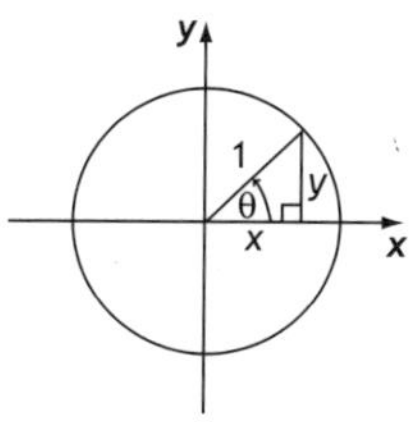

$$\textbf{sin}\ \theta = \frac{\text{opposite}}{\text{hypotenuse}} = \frac{y}{1} = y \qquad \textbf{cosec}\ \theta = \frac{1}{\sin\theta} = \frac{1}{y}$$

$$\textbf{cos}\ \theta = \frac{\text{adjacent}}{\text{hypotenuse}} = \frac{x}{1} = x \qquad \textbf{sec}\ \theta = \frac{1}{\cos\theta} = \frac{1}{x}$$

$$\textbf{tan}\ \theta = \frac{\text{opposite}}{\text{adjacent}} = \frac{y}{x} = \frac{\sin\theta}{\cos\theta} \qquad \textbf{cot}\ \theta = \frac{1}{\tan\theta} = \frac{x}{y} = \frac{\cos\theta}{\sin\theta}$$

Q If θ is an acute angle and $\sin\theta = 0.6$, find: 6

a $\cos\theta$ **b** $\tan\theta$ **c** $\sec\theta$

A **a**
$$\sin\theta = 0.6$$
$$\therefore\ y = 0.6$$
$$\text{Now } x^2 + y^2 = 1$$
$$x^2 + (0.6)^2 = 1$$
$$x^2 + 0.36 = 1$$
$$x^2 = 0.64$$
$$\therefore\ x = 0.8 \quad [\text{as } \theta \text{ is acute, } x > 0]$$
$$\therefore\ \cos\theta = 0.8$$

b
$$\tan\theta = \frac{\sin\theta}{\cos\theta} = \frac{0.6}{0.8} = 0.75$$

c
$$\sec\theta = \frac{1}{\cos\theta} = \frac{1}{0.8} = 1.25$$

5.4 Angles of any magnitude

- The **coordinate axes** divide the unit circle into 4 quarters or quadrants. These are numbered from 1 to 4.

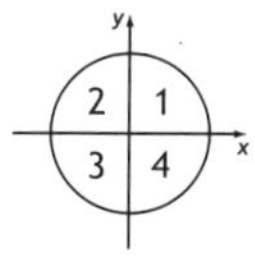

- The **definitions of the trigonometric ratios** can be extended to angles of any size:

$$\sin\theta = y \qquad \cos\theta = x \qquad \tan\theta = \frac{y}{x}$$

$$\operatorname{cosec}\theta = \frac{1}{y} \qquad \sec\theta = \frac{1}{x} \qquad \cot\theta = \frac{x}{y}$$

where θ is the angle of rotation (anticlockwise) from the positive x-axis.

- In the **2nd quadrant**, $x < 0$ and $y > 0$.
$\therefore$ if $90° < \theta < 180°$, sin θ is positive but cos θ and tan θ are both negative.

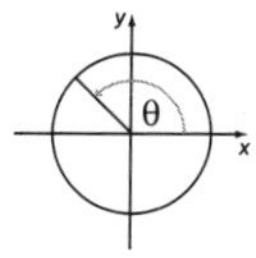

Go to page 86 for Exercises

- In the **3rd quadrant**, $x < 0$ and $y < 0$.
  $\therefore$ if $180° < \theta < 270°$, $\tan\theta$ is positive but $\sin\theta$ and $\cos\theta$ are both negative.

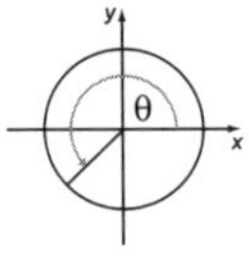

- In the **4th quadrant**, $x > 0$ and $y < 0$.
  $\therefore$ if $270° < \theta < 360°$, $\cos\theta$ is positive but $\sin\theta$ and $\tan\theta$ are both negative.

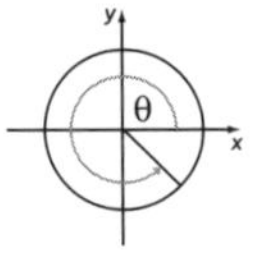

- **Summary**:
  - In the 1st quadrant, **A**ll of the ratios are positive.
  - In the 2nd quadrant, only **S**ine is positive.
  - In the 3rd quadrant, only **T**angent is positive.
  - In the 4th quadrant, only **C**osine is positive.

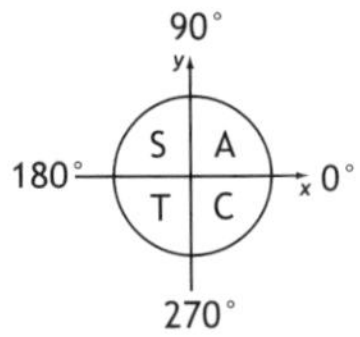

You might use the mnemonic 'All Stations To Central' to remember the order.

Q Determine whether the ratio will be positive or negative: 7

a	sin 110°	**b**	cos 200°
c	tan 300°	**d**	cos 65°
e	sin 285°	**f**	cot 195°

A
- a sin 110° is positive (2nd quadrant)
- b cos 200° is negative (3rd quadrant)
- c tan 300° is negative (4th quadrant)
- d cos 65° is positive (1st quadrant)
- e sin 285° is negative (4th quadrant)
- f cot 195° is positive (3rd quadrant)

Cosec, sec and cot will have the same signs as their reciprocals.

- We can define the size of an **angle of any magnitude** in terms of an acute angle.

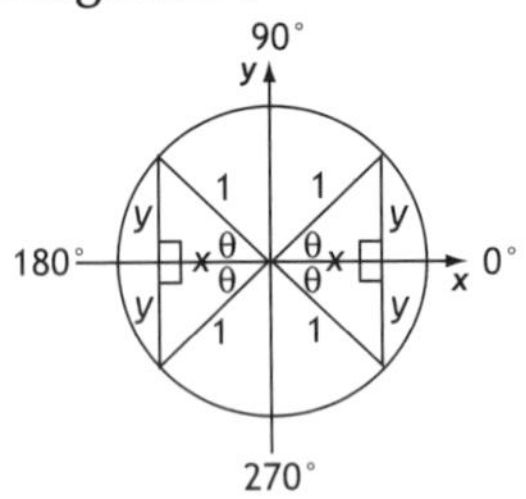

The triangles in each of the four quadrants are congruent.

- In the **2nd quadrant** the obtuse angle of rotation from the positive x-axis is equal to $(180° - \theta)$.

So $\sin(180° - \theta) = y = \sin\theta$ [y is positive]

$\cos(180° - \theta) = x = -\cos\theta$ [x is negative]

$\tan(180° - \theta) = \dfrac{y}{x} = -\tan\theta$

- In the **3rd quadrant** the reflex angle of rotation from the positive x-axis is equal to $(180° + \theta)$.

So $\sin(180° + \theta) = y = -\sin\theta$ [y is negative]

$\cos(180° + \theta) = x = -\cos\theta$ [x is negative]

$\tan(180° + \theta) = \dfrac{y}{x} = \tan\theta$

- In the **4th quadrant** the reflex angle of rotation from the positive x-axis is equal to $(360° - \theta)$.

So $\sin(360° - \theta) = y = -\sin\theta$ [y is negative]

$\cos(360° - \theta) = x = \cos\theta$ [x is positive]

$\tan(360° - \theta) = \dfrac{y}{x} = -\tan\theta$

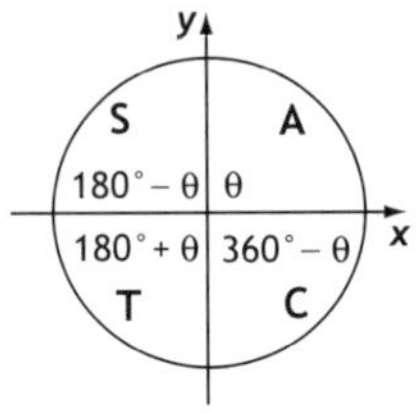

θ is acute

- Any **angle greater than 360°** has completed more than one revolution.
- A **negative angle** has rotated in a clockwise direction from the positive x-axis.

Q If $\cos\theta = 0.781$, write down the value of: 8

a	$\cos(180° - \theta)$	**b**	$\cos(180° + \theta)$
c	$\cos(360° - \theta)$	**d**	$\cos(-\theta)$

A

a $\cos(180° - \theta) = -\cos\theta$
$= -0.781$

b $\cos(180° + \theta) = -\cos\theta$
$= -0.781$

c $\cos(360° - \theta) = \cos\theta$
$= 0.781$

d $\cos(-\theta) = \cos(360° - \theta)$
$= 0.781$

Q Given that sin 30° = 0.5, find: 9

a sin 150° **b** sin 330°

A

a $\sin 150° = \sin(180° - 30°)$
$= \sin 30°$
$= 0.5$

b $\sin 330° = \sin(360° - 30°)$
$= -\sin 30°$
$= -0.5$

Go to page 86 for Exercises

- When **finding the size of an angle with a given trigonometric ratio**, we need to consider all the possible values in the given domain.

Q Find all the values of θ, $0° \le \theta \le 360°$, for which $\tan\theta = 1.2349$. 10

A $\tan 51° = 1.2349$

tan is positive in the 1st and 3rd quadrants

$\therefore\ \theta = 51°$ or $\theta = 180° + 51°$

$\theta = 51°$ $\theta = 231°$

Q Find all the values of θ, $0° \le \theta \le 360°$, for which $\sin\theta = -0.5592$. 10

A $\sin 34° = 0.5592$

sin is negative in the 3rd and 4th quadrants

$\therefore\ \theta = 180° + 34°$ or $\theta = 360° - 34°$

$\theta = 214°$ $\theta = 326°$

5.5 Co-ratios

- **Sine and cosine are co-ratios**. The sine of any acute angle is equal to the cosine of the complementary angle.
- Tangent and cotangent are co-ratios.
- Secant and cosecant are also co-ratios.

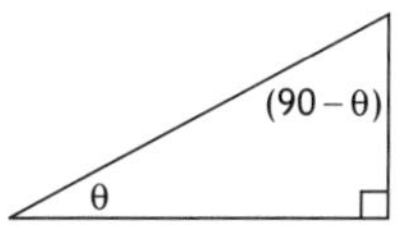

$$\sin(90° - \theta) = \cos\theta \qquad \cos(90° - \theta) = \sin\theta$$
$$\tan(90° - \theta) = \cot\theta \qquad \cot(90° - \theta) = \tan\theta$$
$$\sec(90° - \theta) = \operatorname{cosec}\theta \qquad \operatorname{cosec}(90° - \theta) = \sec\theta$$

Q If $\sin 73° = 0.9563$, write down the value of: 11

a $\cos 17°$ **b** $\cos 163°$

A **a** $\cos 17° = \sin(90° - 17°)$
$= \sin 73°$
$= 0.9563$

b $\cos 163° = \cos(180° - 17°)$
$= -\cos 17°$
$= -0.9563$

The pairs of complementary ratios, the co-ratios, can be easily remembered: sine and <u>co</u>sine, tangent and <u>co</u>tangent, secant and <u>co</u>secant.

5.6 The graphs of sin *x*°, cos *x*° and tan *x*°

- The graphs of the trigonometric ratios are **periodic** (they repeat after a given interval).

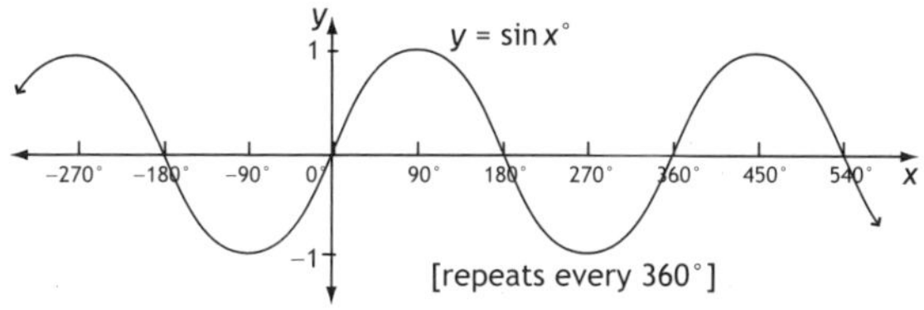

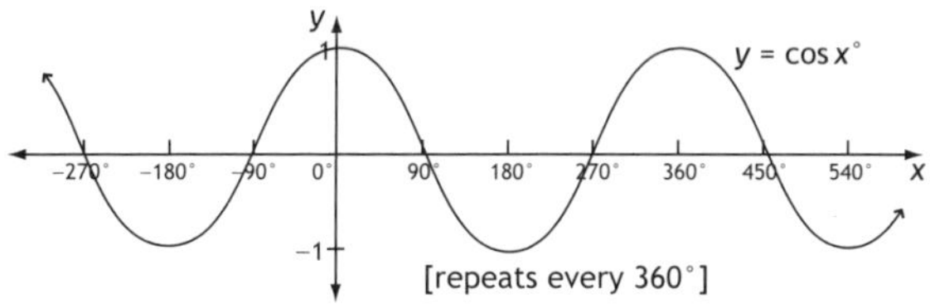

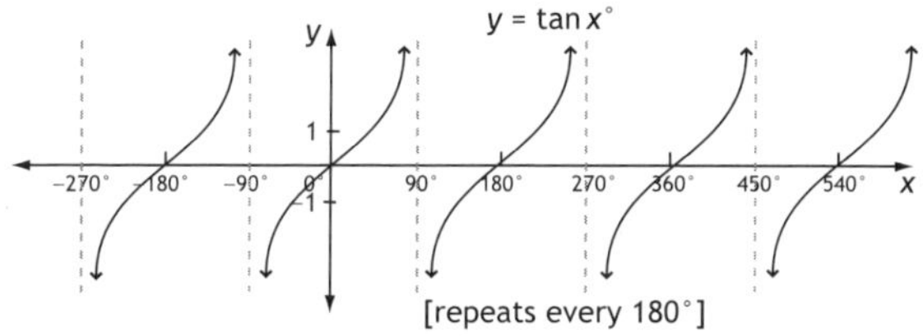

Care must be taken to draw the graph over the specified domain.

Q Graph $y = \sin x°$, $0° < x° < 360°$. 12

A

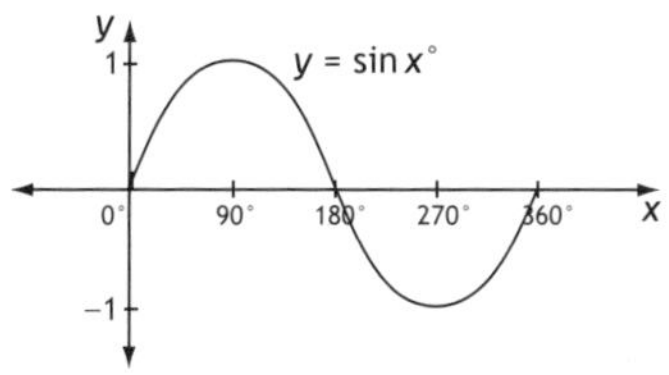

5.7 Pythagorean identities

- Remember that $\cos^2\theta$ means $(\cos\theta)^2$. The ^{2} is written after the 'cos' so that we don't confuse $(\cos\theta)^2$ with $\cos(\theta^2)$.
- Some identities involving the trig ratios can easily be derived.
  From the unit circle we have $x^2 + y^2 = 1$.
  - Substituting $\cos\theta = x$ and $\sin\theta = y$ into the equation gives:
  $$\cos^2\theta + \sin^2\theta = 1$$
  - $$\cos^2\theta + \sin^2\theta = 1$$
  Dividing by $\cos^2\theta$: $$\frac{\cos^2\theta}{\cos^2\theta} + \frac{\sin^2\theta}{\cos^2\theta} = \frac{1}{\cos^2\theta}$$
  $$1 + \tan^2\theta = \sec^2\theta$$

Go to page 86 for Exercises

- $$\cos^2\theta + \sin^2\theta = 1$$

Dividing by $\sin^2\theta$: $$\frac{\cos^2\theta}{\sin^2\theta} + \frac{\sin^2\theta}{\sin^2\theta} = \frac{1}{\sin^2\theta}$$
$$\cot^2\theta + 1 = \operatorname{cosec}^2\theta$$

These results are called the **Pythagorean identities**:

i.e. $$\cos^2\theta + \sin^2\theta = 1$$
$$1 + \tan^2\theta = \sec^2\theta$$
$$\cot^2\theta + 1 = \operatorname{cosec}^2\theta$$

Q Show that $(\sin\theta + \cos\theta)(\sin\theta - \cos\theta) = 2\sin^2\theta - 1$. 13

A $$(\sin\theta + \cos\theta)(\sin\theta - \cos\theta) = \sin^2\theta - \cos^2\theta$$
$$= \sin^2\theta - (1 - \sin^2\theta)$$
$$= \sin^2\theta - 1 + \sin^2\theta$$
$$= 2\sin^2\theta - 1$$

Q Simplify $\dfrac{1}{\operatorname{cosec}\theta + \cot\theta} - \dfrac{1}{\operatorname{cosec}\theta - \cot\theta}$. 14

A $$\frac{1}{\operatorname{cosec}\theta + \cot\theta} - \frac{1}{\operatorname{cosec}\theta - \cot\theta}$$
$$= \frac{\operatorname{cosec}\theta - \cot\theta - (\operatorname{cosec}\theta + \cot\theta)}{(\operatorname{cosec}\theta + \cot\theta)(\operatorname{cosec}\theta - \cot\theta)}$$
$$= \frac{\operatorname{cosec}\theta - \cot\theta - \operatorname{cosec}\theta - \cot\theta}{\operatorname{cosec}^2\theta - \cot^2\theta}$$
$$= \frac{-2\cot\theta}{1}$$
$$= -2\cot\theta$$

5.8 The exact ratios

- From an isosceles right-angled triangle and from an equilateral triangle we derive the exact values of the **trigonometric ratios of 30°, 45° and 60°**.

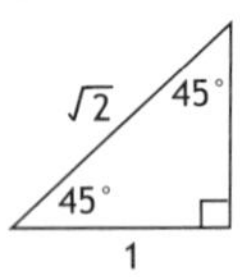

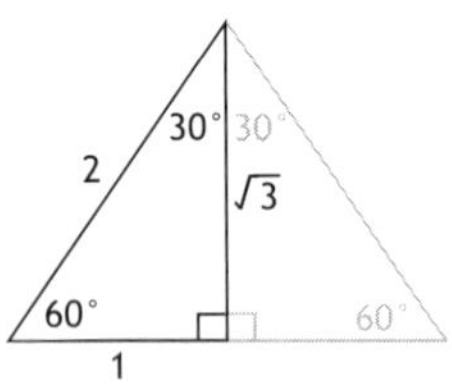

$$\sin 45° = \frac{1}{\sqrt{2}} \qquad \sin 30° = \frac{1}{2} \qquad \sin 60° = \frac{\sqrt{3}}{2}$$
$$\cos 45° = \frac{1}{\sqrt{2}} \qquad \cos 30° = \frac{\sqrt{3}}{2} \qquad \cos 60° = \frac{1}{2}$$
$$\tan 45° = 1 \qquad \tan 30° = \frac{1}{\sqrt{3}} \qquad \tan 60° = \sqrt{3}$$

Go to page 86 for Exercises

- The **exact values for 0° and 90°** should also be known:

$\sin 0° = 0$ $\sin 90° = 1$

$\cos 0° = 1$ $\cos 90° = 0$

$\tan 0° = 0$ $\tan 90°$ is undefined

Q Find the exact value of: 15

a sin 135° **b** tan 300°
c cos 150° **d** tan 225°
e sec 315° **f** cosec 240°

A **a** $$\sin 135° = \sin(180 - 45)°$$
$$= \sin 45°$$
$$= \frac{1}{\sqrt{2}}$$

b $$\tan 300° = \tan(360 - 60)°$$
$$= -\tan 60°$$
$$= -\sqrt{3}$$

c $$\cos 150° = \cos(180 - 30)°$$
$$= -\cos 30°$$
$$= -\frac{\sqrt{3}}{2}$$

d $$\tan 225° = \tan(180 + 45)°$$
$$= \tan 45°$$
$$= 1$$

e $$\sec 315° = \sec(360 - 45)°$$
$$= \sec 45°$$
$$= \sqrt{2}$$

f $$\operatorname{cosec} 240° = \operatorname{cosec}(180 + 60)°$$
$$= -\operatorname{cosec} 60°$$
$$= -\frac{2}{\sqrt{3}}$$

Q $\angle ABC = 105°$ 16
$\angle BDC = 45°$
$\angle ADB = \angle BCD = 90°$
DC = 6 cm
Find the exact length of AD.

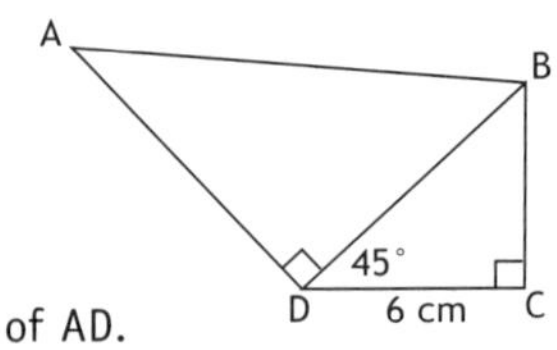

A $$\cos 45° = \frac{DC}{BD}$$
$$\frac{1}{\sqrt{2}} = \frac{6}{BD}$$
$$\therefore\ BD = 6\sqrt{2} \text{ cm}$$
$$\angle DBC = 180° - (90 + 45)° \quad [\text{angle sum of } \Delta DBC]$$
$$= 45°$$

continued ...

$$\angle ABD = 105° - 45°$$
$$= 60°$$
$$\tan 60° = \frac{AD}{BD}$$
$$AD = BD \times \tan 60°$$
$$= 6\sqrt{2} \times \sqrt{3}$$
$$= 6\sqrt{6} \text{ cm}$$

5.9 Further applications of exact ratios

- The **exact ratios** can be used to find the trigonometric ratios of other angles.

Q In the diagram, $\angle ACB = 30°$ and AC = CD. **17**

a Show that $\angle BAD = 75°$.

b If AB = 1 unit, show that $\tan 75° = 2 + \sqrt{3}$.

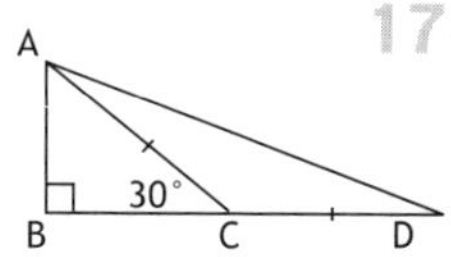

A **a**

$$\angle BAC = 180° - (90 + 30)° \quad [\text{angle sum of } \Delta ABC]$$
$$= 60°$$
$$\angle BCA = \angle CAD + \angle ADC \quad [\text{exterior angle of } \Delta ACD]$$
$$\text{but } \angle CAD = \angle ADC \quad [\text{base angles of isosceles triangle}]$$
$$2\angle CAD = 30°$$
$$\angle CAD = 15°$$
$$\angle BAD = \angle BAC + \angle CAD$$
$$= 60° + 15°$$
$$\therefore \angle BAD = 75°$$

b In ΔABC:

$$\tan 60° = \frac{BC}{AB}$$
$$\sqrt{3} = \frac{BC}{1}$$
$$\therefore BC = \sqrt{3} \text{ units}$$
$$\cos 60° = \frac{AB}{AC}$$
$$\frac{1}{2} = \frac{1}{AC}$$
$$\therefore AC = 2 \text{ units}$$
$$\text{but } CD = AC \quad [\text{given}]$$
$$\therefore CD = 2 \text{ units}$$
$$BD = BC + CD$$
$$= (\sqrt{3} + 2) \text{ units}$$
$$\tan 75° = \frac{BD}{AB}$$
$$= \frac{2 + \sqrt{3}}{1}$$
$$= 2 + \sqrt{3}$$

5.10 Trigonometric equations

- The **rules and ratios can be used** to solve simple equations. Care must be taken to find all the solutions in the specified domain.

Q Find a value of θ for which $4\tan 2\theta = 5\tan 29°$. **18**

A

$$4\tan 2\theta = 5\tan 29°$$
$$\tan 2\theta = \frac{5\tan 29°}{4}$$
$$= 0.692886314\ldots \quad [\text{by calculator}]$$
$$\therefore 2\theta = 34.71755862\ldots°$$
$$\theta = 17.35877931\ldots°$$
$$= 17°22' \quad [\text{nearest minute}]$$

- The question says '**find a value**', so we only need to give one answer. There are other possible solutions.

Q Find all values of x, $0° \le x \le 360°$, for which: **19**

a $9\cos x - 3 = 4\cos x$

b $\sin x = \cos x$

A **a**

$$9\cos x - 3 = 4\cos x$$
$$5\cos x = 3$$
$$\cos x = 0.6$$
$$x = 53°8' \quad \text{or} \quad x = 360° - 53°8'$$
$$x = 53°8' \quad \quad x = 306°52'$$

b $\sin x = \cos x$

Now $\cos x \ne 0$ $[\cos x = 0 \text{ is not a solution}]$, so we can divide by $\cos x$.

$$\frac{\sin x}{\cos x} = \frac{\cos x}{\cos x}$$
$$\tan x = 1$$
$$x = 45° \quad \text{or} \quad x = 180° + 45°$$
$$x = 45° \quad \quad x = 225°$$

Q If $3\operatorname{cosec}^2 x = 4$, find all possible values of x, $-180° \le x \le 180°$. **20**

A

$$3\operatorname{cosec}^2 x = 4$$
$$\operatorname{cosec}^2 x = \frac{4}{3}$$
$$\operatorname{cosec} x = \pm\frac{2}{\sqrt{3}}$$
$$\therefore \sin x = \pm\frac{\sqrt{3}}{2}$$
$$\text{Now } \sin 60° = \frac{\sqrt{3}}{2}$$

continued ...

Go to page 86 for Exercises

sin is positive in the 1st and 2nd quadrants

$\therefore\ x = 60^\circ \quad \text{or} \quad x = (180 - 60)^\circ$

$x = 60^\circ \quad\quad x = 120^\circ$

sin is negative in the 3rd and 4th quadrants

$\therefore\ x = -60^\circ \quad \text{or} \quad x = -(180 - 60)^\circ$

$x = -60^\circ \quad\quad x = -120^\circ$

5.11 Compass bearings

- **True bearings are measured** in a clockwise direction from north. They are always given using three digits. A bearing of 050° means 50° from north in a clockwise direction.

When working with compass bearings always draw a diagram, using the correct directions.

Q M is due west of L. 21
What is the bearing of M from K?

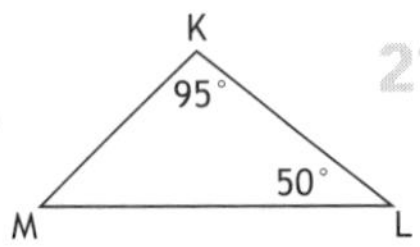

A Let A be a point due north of K and B be a point due north of L.

$\angle BLM = 90^\circ$ [M is due west of L]

$\angle BLK = 90^\circ - 50^\circ$

$= 40^\circ$

$\therefore\ \angle AKL = 180^\circ - 40^\circ$

$= 140^\circ$

Reflex $\angle AKM = 140^\circ + 95^\circ$

$= 235^\circ$

$\therefore$ the bearing of M from K is 235°

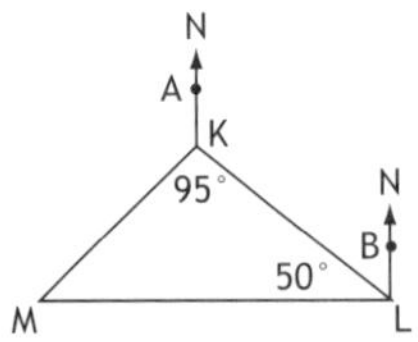

Q Gorton (G) is due east of Fraser (F) and due north of Hawke (H). The bearing of Hawke from Fraser is 128°. If the distance from Gorton to Hawke is 17.5 km, find the distance from Fraser to Hawke. 22

A $\angle GFH = 128^\circ - 90^\circ$

$= 38^\circ$

$\sin 38^\circ = \frac{17.5}{FH}$

$\therefore\ FH = \frac{17.5}{\sin 38^\circ}$

$= 28.4247118\ldots$ [calculator]

$= 28.4$ km [1 decimal place]

$\therefore$ the distance from Fraser to Hawke is 28.4 km

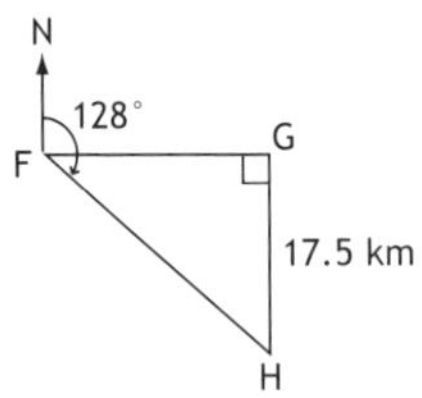

Q C is 9.4 km from B on a bearing of 222°. 23
How far south of B is C?

Go to pages 86 and 87 for Exercises

A Let D be the point due south of B and due east of C.

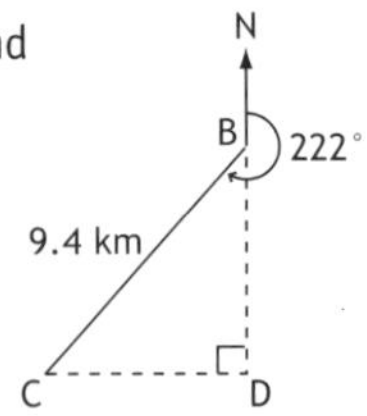

$\angle CBD = 222^\circ - 180^\circ$

$= 42^\circ$

$\cos 42^\circ = \frac{BD}{9.4}$

$\therefore\ BD = 9.4 \times \cos 42^\circ$

$= 6.985561359\ldots$

$= 7$ km [nearest kilometre]

$\therefore$ C is 7 km south of B

5.12 Angles of elevation and depression

- **Angles of elevation** and **depression** are measured from the horizontal.

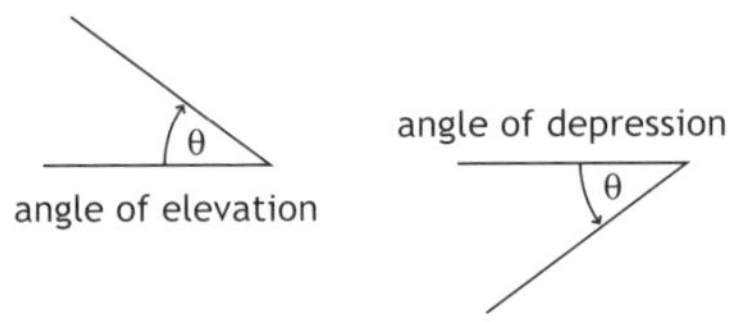

Q Find the height of a tree which casts a shadow 19 metres long when the angle of elevation of the sun is 39°. 24

A Let the height of the tree be h metres.

$\tan 39^\circ = \frac{h}{19}$

$h = 19 \times \tan 39^\circ$

$= 15.38589663\ldots$

$= 15.4$ [1 decimal place]

$\therefore$ the tree is 15.4 m high

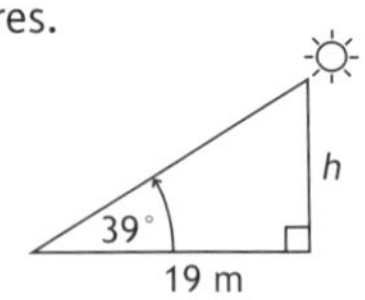

Q A 9 metre cable, attached to the top of a pole, reaches the ground at a point 5.2 metres from the base of the pole. What is the angle of elevation of the top of the pole from the point where the cable reaches the ground? 25

A Let θ be the angle of elevation.

$\cos\theta = \frac{5.2}{9}$

$\therefore\ \theta = 54.70560532\ldots$

$= 55^\circ$ [nearest degree]

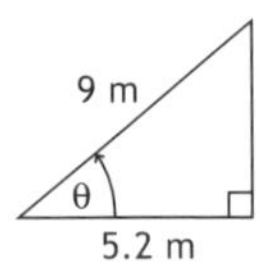

When working with angles of depression, we often make use of the fact that alternate angles, formed when a transversal cuts a pair of parallel lines, are equal.

Q An office building and a house are 28 metres apart. From the top of the office building the angle of depression of the base of the house is 21°. 26
How high is the office building?

A Let the height of the office building be x metres.

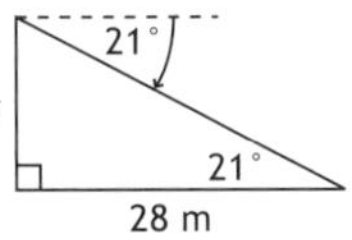

$$\tan 21° = \frac{x}{28}$$
$$\therefore \quad x = 28 \times \tan 21°$$
$$= 10.74819298\ldots$$
$$= 10.7 \quad [1 \text{ decimal place}]$$

$\therefore$ the office building is 10.7 metres high

5.13 The sine rule

- The **sine rule** states:

$$\frac{a}{\sin A} = \frac{b}{\sin B} = \frac{c}{\sin C}$$

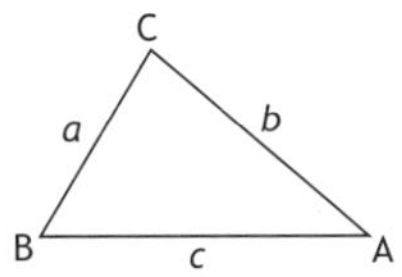

where a, b and c are the sides opposite, respectively, angles A, B and C.

Proof:

Draw in the perpendicular from C to AB.
Let CD = x.

In ΔBCD,

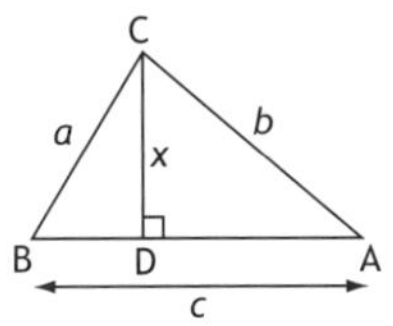

$$\sin B = \frac{x}{a}$$
$$\therefore \quad x = a \sin B$$

In ΔADC,

$$\sin A = \frac{x}{b}$$
$$\therefore \quad x = b \sin A$$
$$\therefore \quad a \sin B = b \sin A$$
$$\therefore \quad \frac{a}{\sin A} = \frac{b}{\sin B} \quad [\text{on dividing by } \sin A \sin B]$$

Similarly we can prove that:

$$\frac{a}{\sin A} = \frac{c}{\sin C} \text{ and } \frac{b}{\sin B} = \frac{c}{\sin C}$$

When using the sine rule we only use two of the three equal expressions at one time. That is, we work with pairs of opposite sides and angles.

Q Find the length of side AB, giving the answer correct to 1 decimal place. 27

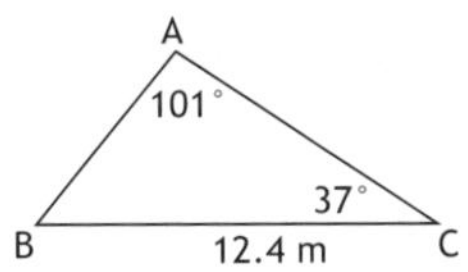

A

$$\frac{c}{\sin C} = \frac{a}{\sin A}$$
$$\frac{c}{\sin 37°} = \frac{12.4}{\sin 101°}$$
$$c = \frac{12.4 \sin 37°}{\sin 101°}$$
$$= 7.602179741\ldots \quad [\text{calculator}]$$
$$\therefore \quad AB = 7.6 \text{ m} \quad [1 \text{ decimal place}]$$

It may be necessary to first find the third angle of the triangle, using the angle sum of a triangle is 180°.

We often quote the sine rule using the letters that name the vertices of the triangle.

Q Find the length of the side RQ. 28

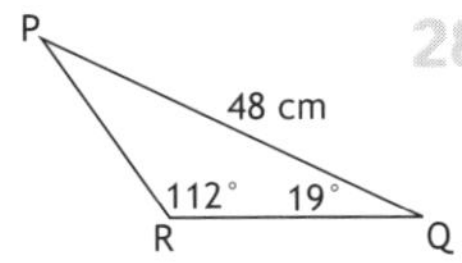

A

$$\angle P = 180° - (112 + 19)°$$
$$= 49°$$
$$\frac{p}{\sin P} = \frac{r}{\sin R}$$
$$\frac{p}{\sin 49°} = \frac{48}{\sin 112°}$$
$$p = \frac{48 \sin 49°}{\sin 112°}$$
$$= 39.07106414\ldots \quad [\text{calculator}]$$
$$\therefore \quad RQ = 39.1 \text{ cm} \quad [1 \text{ decimal place}]$$

5.14 Using the sine rule to find an angle

- When using the sine rule to **find the size of angles**, we usually use it in the inverted form:

$$\frac{\sin A}{a} = \frac{\sin B}{b} = \frac{\sin C}{c}$$

- Using the sine rule to find an angle gives **two possible results**, an acute angle and an obtuse angle. The second (obtuse) answer may not always be valid because it might mean that the angle sum of the triangle would have to exceed 180°. You must always consider whether both answers are possible.

Do not use the shape of a triangle to determine whether an angle would be acute or obtuse, as it may not be drawn to scale.

Q Find the size of angle A. 29

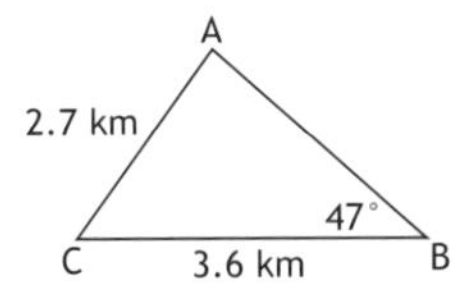

A

$$\frac{\sin A}{a} = \frac{\sin B}{b}$$
$$\frac{\sin A}{3.6} = \frac{\sin 47°}{2.7}$$
$$\sin A = \frac{3.6 \sin 47°}{2.7}$$
$$= 0.975138268\ldots$$
$$\therefore \quad \angle A = 77° \text{ or } 103°$$

[by calculator, to the nearest degree]

Go to page 87 for Exercises

Q Find the size of angle KLM. Give the answer correct to the nearest minute. **29**

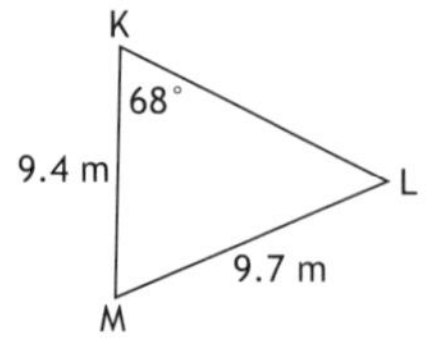

A
$$\frac{\sin L}{l} = \frac{\sin K}{k}$$
$$\frac{\sin L}{9.4} = \frac{\sin 68^\circ}{9.7}$$
$$\sin L = \frac{9.4 \sin 68^\circ}{9.7}$$
$$= 0.898508065\ldots$$
$\therefore \angle KLM = 63°58'$ or $116°2'$

[by calculator, to the nearest degree]

but if $\angle KLM = 116°2'$ the angle sum of $\Delta KLM > 180°$

$\therefore \angle KLM = 63°58'$

It may be necessary to use the sine rule to find a different angle, and then use the angle sum of a triangle to find the required angle.

Q Find the size of $\angle DEF$. **30**

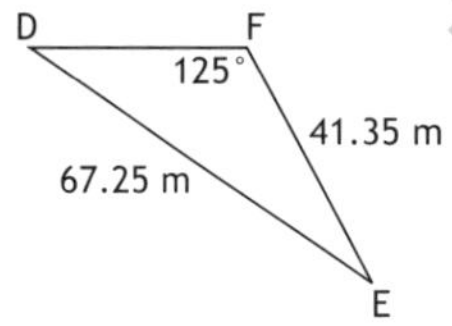

A
$$\frac{\sin D}{d} = \frac{\sin F}{f}$$
$$\frac{\sin D}{41.35} = \frac{\sin 125^\circ}{67.25}$$
$$\sin D = \frac{41.35 \sin 125^\circ}{67.25}$$
$$= 0.503671926\ldots$$
$\therefore \quad \angle D = 30°$

[by calculator, to the nearest degree]

[$\angle EDF$ cannot be obtuse]

$\therefore \angle DEF = 180° - (125 + 30)°$

$= 25°$

5.15 The cosine rule

- The cosine rule is **used to find the third side of a triangle**, given two sides and the included angle. The cosine rule states:

$$a^2 = b^2 + c^2 - 2bc \cos A$$

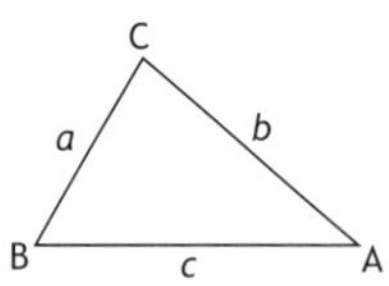

where a, b and c are the sides opposite, respectively, angles A, B and C.

Proof:

Draw the perpendicular from C to AB.
Let AD = x
$\therefore$ BD = $c - x$
Let CD = y

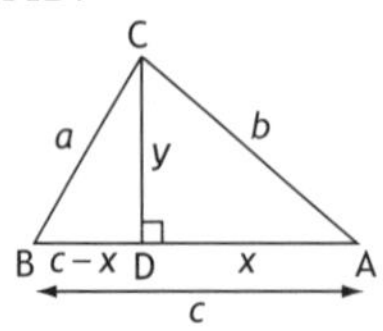

In ΔADC, $\cos A = \dfrac{x}{b}$

$\therefore \quad x = b \cos A$ **i**

Also, $b^2 = x^2 + y^2$ **ii**

In ΔBCD, $a^2 = (c - x)^2 + y^2$

$= c^2 - 2cx + x^2 + y^2$

$\therefore \quad a^2 = c^2 - 2cx + b^2$ from **ii**

$= b^2 + c^2 - 2cb \cos A$ from **i**

$\therefore \quad a^2 = b^2 + c^2 - 2bc \cos A$

Q Find the length of BC. **31**

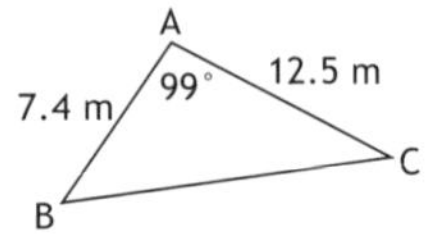

A $a^2 = b^2 + c^2 - 2bc \cos A$

$= (12.5)^2 + (7.4)^2 - 2 \times 12.5 \times 7.4 \times \cos 99°$

$= 239.950376\ldots$

$a = 15.4903317\ldots \quad [a > 0]$

$= 15.5 \quad$ [1 decimal place]

$\therefore$ the length of BC is 15.5 metres

Great care must be taken when entering the cosine rule into a calculator. The order of operations is important and must be done correctly. Don't forget to take the square root.

Many mistakes are made with the cosine rule. Practise lots of questions.

Q Use the cosine rule to find the length of the side XY. **32**

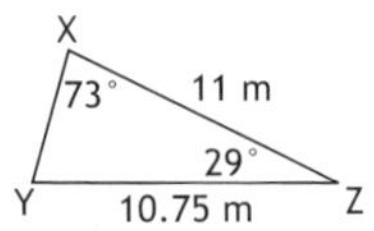

A $z^2 = x^2 + y^2 - 2xy \cos Z$

$= (10.75)^2 + (11)^2 - 2 \times 10.75 \times 11 \times \cos 29°$

$= 29.71493926\ldots$

$z = 5.451141097\ldots \quad [z > 0]$

$= 5.5 \quad$ [1 decimal place]

$\therefore$ the length of XY is 5.5 metres

We must use the angle which is included between the two known sides. We don't need to know that $\angle X = 73°$.

5.16 Using the cosine rule to find an angle

- The cosine rule is also used to **find any angle** given three sides of a triangle. We use the rule:

$$\cos A = \frac{b^2 + c^2 - a^2}{2bc}$$

Go to page 87 for Exercises

- This rule is just a rearrangement of the previous rule:

$$a^2 = b^2 + c^2 - 2bc\cos A$$
$$2bc\cos A = b^2 + c^2 - a^2$$
$$\cos A = \frac{b^2 + c^2 - a^2}{2bc}$$

Take care to use the measurements in the right order. The side opposite to the required angle is the one that is subtracted.

Be careful when using your calculator. You must divide the whole numerator by the whole denominator. Use the memory or bracket keys.

Q Find the size of θ to the nearest whole degree. 33

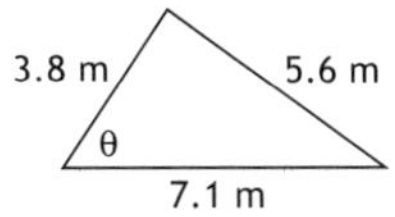

A

$$\cos A = \frac{b^2 + c^2 - a^2}{2bc}$$
$$\cos\theta = \frac{(3.8)^2 + (7.1)^2 - (5.6)^2}{2 \times 3.8 \times 7.1}$$
$$= 0.620644922\ldots$$
$$\therefore\ \theta = 51.63675458\ldots^\circ$$
$$= 52^\circ\ \left[\text{nearest whole degree}\right]$$

- If the **value of cos A is negative**, the required angle will be obtuse.

Q Find the size of ∠PQR. Give the answer correct to the nearest minute. 34

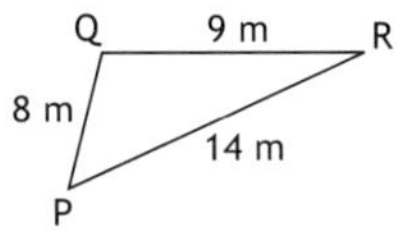

A

$$\cos Q = \frac{p^2 + r^2 - q^2}{2pr}$$
$$= \frac{9^2 + 8^2 - 14^2}{2 \times 9 \times 8}$$
$$= -0.354166666\ldots$$
$$\therefore \angle Q = 110.74238\ldots^\circ$$
$$= 110^\circ 45'\ \left[\text{nearest minute}\right]$$

5.17 The area of a triangle

- The area of any triangle can be found by using the formula:

$$\mathbf{A = \frac{1}{2}ab\sin C}$$

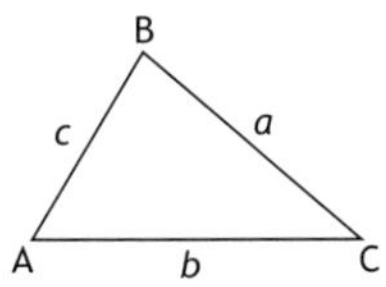

where C is the angle **included** between sides a and b.

Proof:

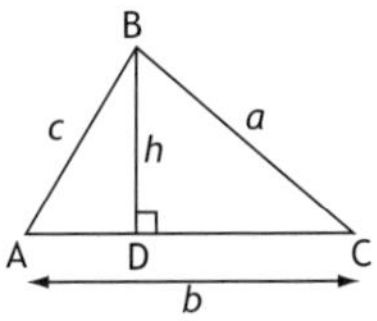

Draw BD perpendicular to AC.
Let BD = h
Area of ΔABC is given by :

$$A = \frac{1}{2}bh \qquad \textbf{i}$$

In ΔBCD, $\sin C = \dfrac{h}{a}$

$$\therefore\ h = a\sin C$$

Substituting into **i**

$$A = \frac{1}{2}b \times a\sin C$$
$$\therefore\ A = \frac{1}{2}ab\sin C$$

Q Find the area of ΔABC. 35

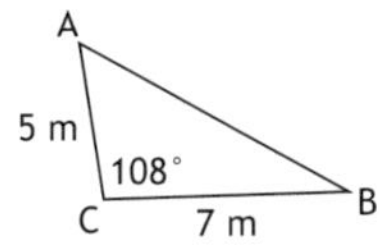

A

$$A = \frac{1}{2}ab\sin C$$
$$= \frac{1}{2} \times 7 \times 5 \times \sin 108^\circ$$
$$= 16.64348904\ldots\ \left[\text{calculator}\right]$$
$$\text{Area} = 16.6\ \text{m}^2\ \left[1\ \text{decimal place}\right]$$

Q Find the area of ΔPQR. 35

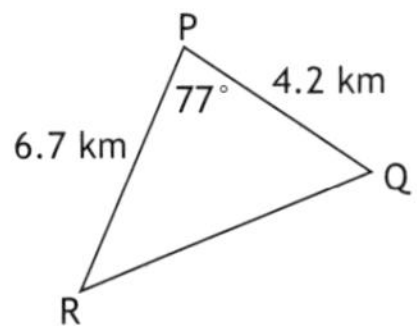

A

$$A = \frac{1}{2}qr\sin P$$
$$= \frac{1}{2} \times 6.7 \times 4.2 \times \sin 77^\circ$$
$$= 13.70938681\ldots\ \left[\text{calculator}\right]$$
$$\text{Area} = 13.7\ \text{km}^2\ \left[1\ \text{decimal place}\right]$$

- The area of any parallelogram can also be found.

Q ABCD is a parallelogram. 36
AB = 17 m
BC = 10 m
∠ABC = 63°
Find the area of ABCD.

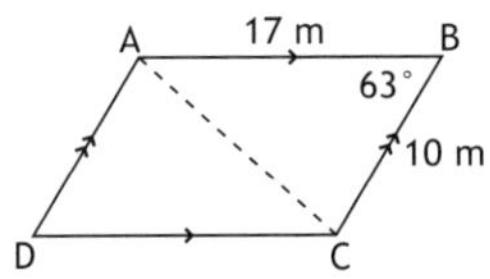

A

$$A = 2 \times \frac{1}{2}ac\sin B$$
$$= 10 \times 17 \times \sin 63^\circ$$
$$= 151.4711091\ldots\ \left[\text{calculator}\right]$$
$$\text{Area} = 151.5\ \text{m}^2\ \left[1\ \text{decimal place}\right]$$

Go to page 87 for Exercises

5.18 Combinations of the rules

- Use the **sine rule** to find:
  - a side, given two angles and a side, or
  - an angle, given two sides and an angle.
- Use the **cosine rule** to find:
  - a side, given two sides and the included angle, or
  - an angle, given three sides.

✔ You need to be able to quickly decide which rule to use, and be able to use it competently. A question could require a combination of these rules.

Q A person standing at A finds the angle of elevation of the top of a tree is 13°. She then walks 200 metres towards the tree, on level ground, and finds that the angle of elevation of the top of the tree is now 35°. 37

a Find the size of $\angle ADB$.
b Find the length of BD.
c Find the height of the tree.

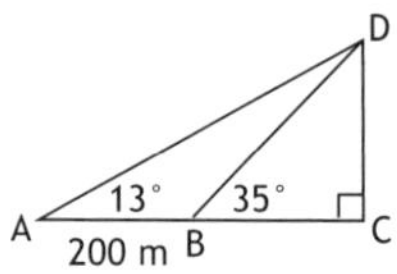

A **a** $\angle DBC = \angle ADB + \angle BAD$ [exterior angle of ΔADB]

$\therefore \angle ADB = 35° - 13°$

$= 22°$

b
$$\frac{a}{\sin A} = \frac{d}{\sin D}$$
$$\frac{a}{\sin 13°} = \frac{200}{\sin 22°}$$
$$a = \frac{200 \sin 13°}{\sin 22°}$$
$$= 120.0998906\ldots$$
$\therefore$ BD = 120 m [nearest metre]

c In ΔDCB, $\sin 35° = \dfrac{DC}{DB}$

$\therefore$ $DC = DB \sin 35°$

$= 68.88646723\ldots$

$= 69$ m [nearest metre]

$\therefore$ the tree is 69 metres high

✔ When using the answer to a previous part in a subsequent question, always use the exact value from the calculator's memory.

Q The diagram represents a triangular parcel of land with dimensions as shown. 38

a Find the size of the angle at B.
b Find the area of the land in hectares correct to two decimal places.

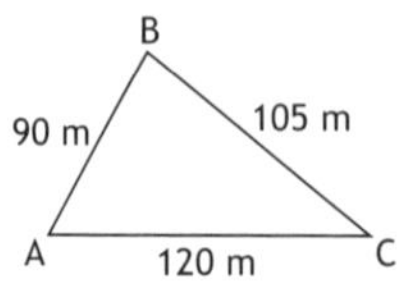

☞ Go to page 87 for Exercises

A **a**
$$\cos B = \frac{a^2 + c^2 - b^2}{2ac}$$
$$= \frac{105^2 + 90^2 - 120^2}{2 \times 105 \times 90}$$
$$= 0.25$$
$\therefore \angle B = 75.52248781\ldots$

$= 75°31'$ [nearest minute]

b
$$A = \frac{1}{2} ac \sin B$$
$$= \frac{1}{2} \times 105 \times 90 \times \sin B$$
$$= 4574.961578\ldots$$
$\therefore$ Area $= 4575$ m^2

$= 0.46$ ha [2 decimal places]

5.19 Using expressions in further calculations

- It is not always necessary to find the **actual size of an angle or a side** which is needed to find another angle or side. Unless you are asked for its size, you may just find an expression for the intermediate step.

Q $\angle QPS = 123°$ 39

a Use the sine rule in ΔPQR to find an expression for the length of PR.
b Hence show that the length of PS is given by $\dfrac{12 \sin 84° \cos 71°}{\sin 52°}$.
c Find the length of PS to the nearest centimetre.

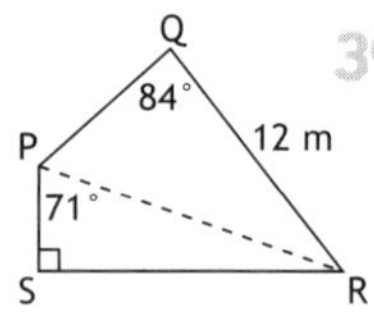

A **a** $\angle QPS = 123°$

$\therefore \angle QPR = 123° - 71°$

$= 52°$

In ΔPQR, $\dfrac{q}{\sin Q} = \dfrac{p}{\sin P}$
$$\frac{q}{\sin 84°} = \frac{12}{\sin 52°}$$
$$q = \frac{12 \sin 84°}{\sin 52°}$$
$$\therefore \quad PR = \frac{12 \sin 84°}{\sin 52°}$$

b In ΔPRS, $\cos 71° = \dfrac{PS}{PR}$

$\therefore$ $PS = PR \cos 71°$
$$= \frac{12 \sin 84° \cos 71°}{\sin 52°}$$

c $\quad PS = \dfrac{12\sin 84° \cos 71°}{\sin 52°}$

$= 4.930663546\ldots$

$= 4.93$ m [nearest centimetre]

Q **a** Use the cosine rule in $\triangle ABC$ to find a simple expression for AC^2.

40

b Find the size of $\angle ADC$.

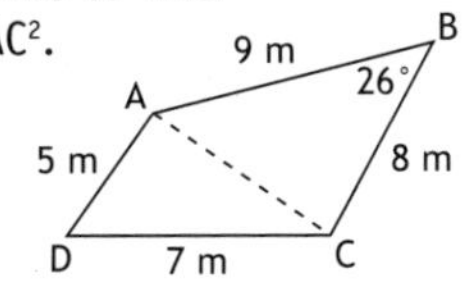

A **a** In $\triangle ABC$, $b^2 = a^2 + c^2 - 2ac \cos B$

$= 8^2 + 9^2 - 2 \times 8 \times 9 \times \cos 26°$

$\therefore \; AC^2 = 145 - 144 \cos 26°$

b In $\triangle ADC$, $\cos D = \dfrac{a^2 + c^2 - d^2}{2ac}$

$= \dfrac{7^2 + 5^2 - AC^2}{2 \times 7 \times 5}$

$= 0.834662038\ldots$

$\angle D = 33.41933632\ldots°$

$\therefore \; \angle ADC = 33°$ [nearest whole degree]

Go to page 87 for Exercises

Exercises Trigonometric Ratios

1 Find the value of x, giving the answer correct to two decimal places:

a 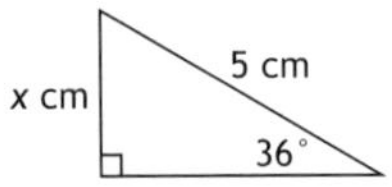

b 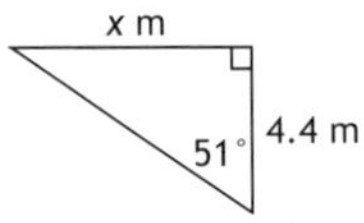

c 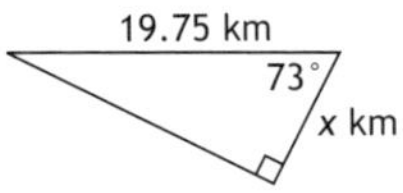

2 Find the length of side QR, giving the answer correct to one decimal place:

a 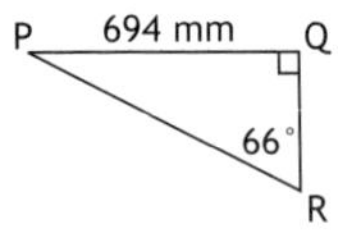

b 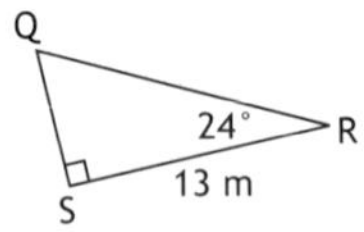

3 Find the value of θ, giving the answer correct to the nearest minute:

a 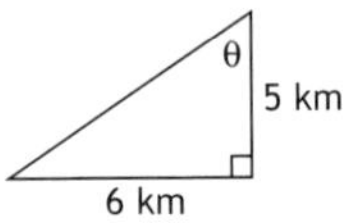

b 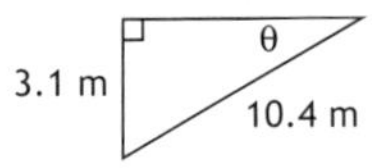

c 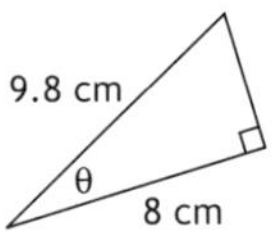

4 Find, correct to four decimal places, the value of:
- a cosec 25°
- b sec 13°
- c cot 20°
- d sec 28° 15′
- e cosec 48° 45′
- f cot 87° 26′

5 Find the value of θ to the nearest minute if:
- a sec θ = 4.5976
- b cot θ = 0.2376
- c cosec θ = 10.4334

6 If cos θ = 0.6 and 0° ≤ θ ≤ 90° find:
- a sin θ
- b tan θ
- c cosec θ

7 Determine whether the ratio will be positive or negative:
- a sin 97°
- b tan 176°
- c cos 321°
- d sec 205°
- e cosec 289°

8 If sin θ = 0.549 write down the value of:
- a $\sin(180° - \theta)$
- b $\sin(180° + \theta)$
- c $\sin(-\theta)$
- d $\sin(360° - \theta)$

9 Given that tan 45° = 1 find:
- a tan 315°
- b tan (−45°)
- c tan 225°
- d tan 135°
- e tan 405°

10 Find all values of θ, 0° ≤ θ ≤ 360°, for which:
- a sin θ = 0.8953
- b cos θ = −0.2126
- c tan θ = −2.1357

11 If cos 60° = 0.5 find:
- a sin 30°
- b cos 240°
- c sin 330°

12 Graph:
- a $y = \cos x°$ for $0° \le x \le 360°$
- b $y = \sin x°$ for $-180° \le x \le 180°$
- c $y = \tan x°$ for $-90° \le x \le 90°$

13 Show that $\cot^2\theta - \cos^2\theta = \cos^2\theta \cot^2\theta$.

14 Show that $\tan\theta + \cot\theta = \dfrac{1}{\sin\theta\cos\theta}$.

15 Find the exact value of:
- a sin 30°
- b tan 45°
- c cos 120°
- d tan 315°
- e sin 180°
- f tan 150°
- g cos 330°
- h tan (−60°)
- i sin 270°
- j cot 30°
- k cosec 300°

16 DC = 1 unit
∠ABD = ∠DBC = 30°
Fnd the exact length of AB.

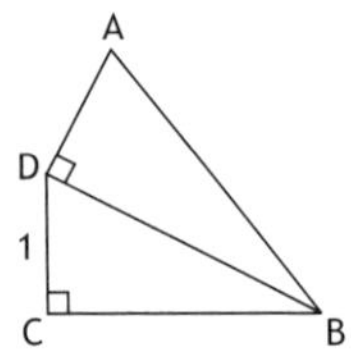

17 BD = AD
BC = 1 unit

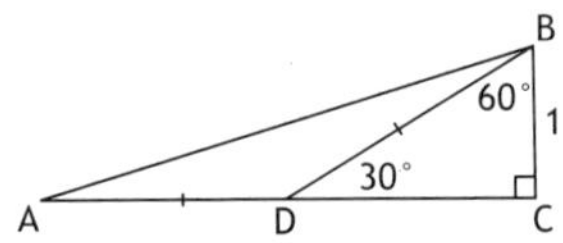

- a Find the exact length of AC.
- b Hence show that $\tan 15° = 2 - \sqrt{3}$.

18 Find a value of θ for which $8\cos 3\theta = 5 - 2\cos 75°$.

19 Find all values of x, 0° ≤ x ≤ 360°, for which:
- a $9\sin x = 4\sin x + 3$
- b $\sin x - \tan x = 0$
- c $2\cos^2 x - 1 = 0$

20 If $\cot^2 x = 3$ find all possible values of x in the domain −180° ≤ x ≤ 180°.

21 J is a point due north of L.
What is the bearing of L from K?

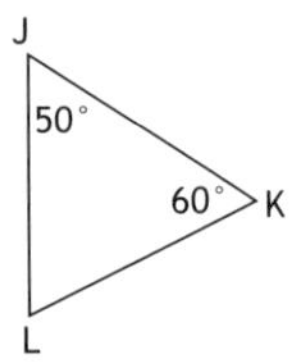

Go to page 224 for Quick Answers & pages 173–176 for Worked Solutions

22 Timms (T) is 16 kilometres due east of Saxby (S) and due north of Upton (U). The bearing of Upton from Saxby is 108°. Find the distance between Upton and Saxby.

23 Jackson (J) is 5.7 kilometres from Kendall (K) on a bearing of 294°. How far north of Kendall is Jackson?

24 From a boat, 80 metres from the base of a cliff, the angle of elevation of a point at the top of the cliff is 32°. How high is the cliff?

25 Find the angle of elevation of the sun when a 7 m high pole casts a shadow 11 m long.

26 From the observation deck of a tower, a boy notes that the angle of depression of his brother on the ground is 15°. If the observation deck is 38 m above the ground, how far apart are the brothers?

27 Find the length of side YZ correct to 1 decimal place:

a

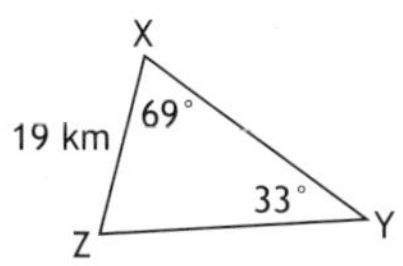

b

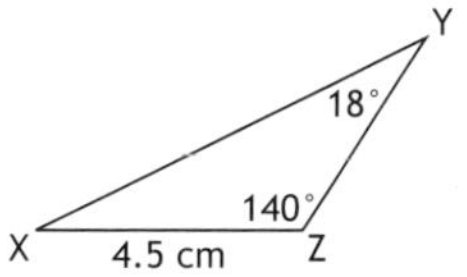

28 Find the length of the side YZ.

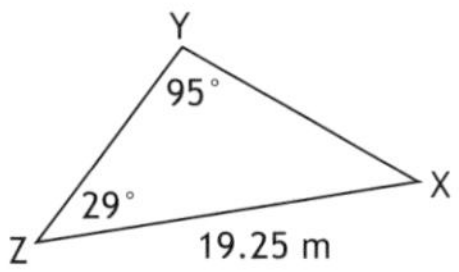

29 Find the size of angle P to the nearest whole degree.

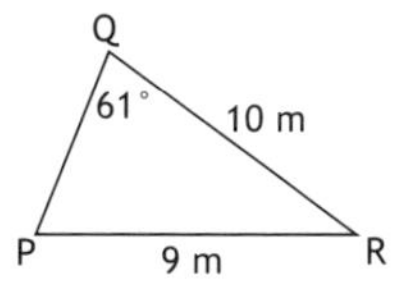

30 Find the size of angle H to the nearest minute.

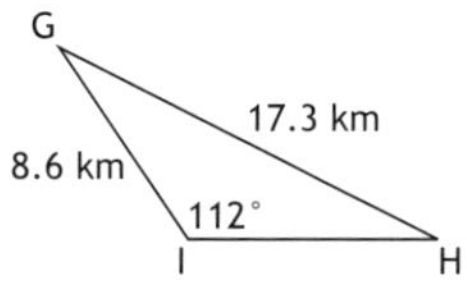

31 Find the length of AB.

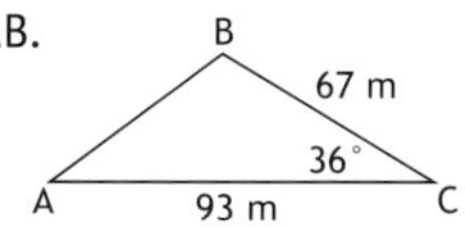

32 Use the cosine rule to find the length of LM. Give the answer to the nearest metre.

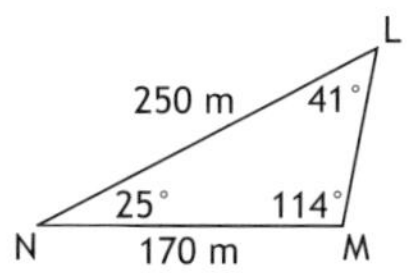

33 Find the size of ∠CAB to the nearest whole degree.

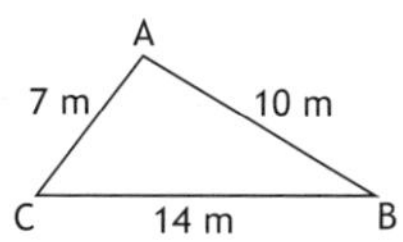

34 Find the value of θ to the nearest minute.

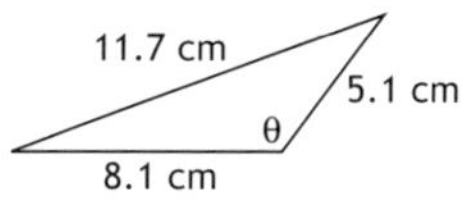

35 Find the area of each triangle:

a

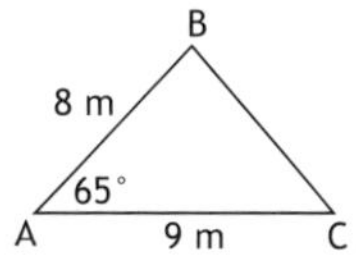

b

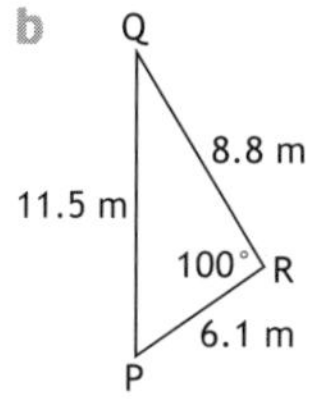

36 Find the area of the parallelogram.

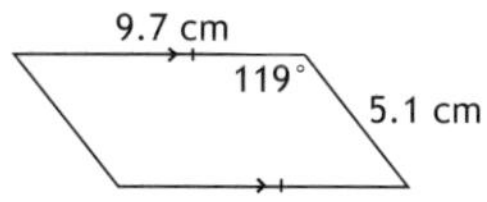

37 DC = 18 m

a Find AC.

b Find AB.

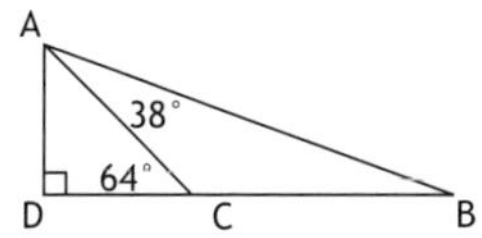

38 LM = MN

a Use the cosine rule in ΔLMN to find length LN.

b Hence find KN.

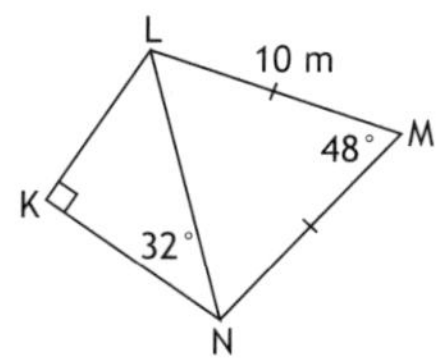

39 **a** Show that

$$BD = \frac{9.4 \sin 43°}{\sin 70°}.$$

b Hence find AB.

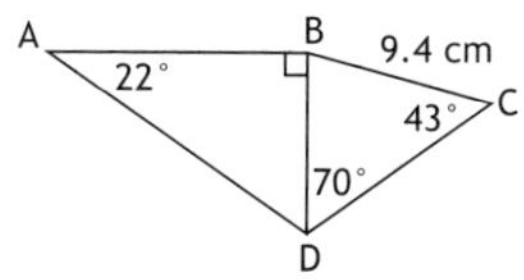

40 ∠SPQ = 147°
Let ∠QPR = θ.

a Show that $\cos\theta = \frac{1}{2}$.

b Find the area of ΔPRS.

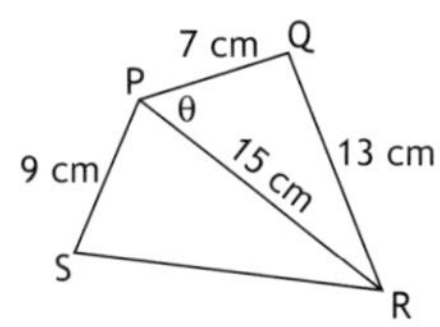

Go to page 224 for Quick Answers & pages 176–178 for Worked Solutions. See pages 132 and 133 for Topic Tests.

6 The Quadratic Polynomial and the Parabola

Your Checklist

For a complete understanding of this topic you must be able to:	✓
■ Understand what is meant by the quadratic polynomial $ax^2 + bx + c$	
■ Understand what is meant by the quadratic function $y = ax^2 + bx + c$	
■ Draw graphs of quadratic functions	
■ Understand what is meant by a root of a quadratic equation	
■ Solve quadratic equations by factorisation	
■ Solve quadratic equations by completing the square	
■ Understand and use the quadratic formula	
■ Solve quadratic inequalities	
■ Find the axis of symmetry for the parabola $y = ax^2 + bx + c$	
■ Find the greatest value, or the least value of $y = ax^2 + bx + c$	
■ Understand what is meant by the discriminant	
■ Use the discriminant to determine the nature of the roots of a quadratic equation (real, rational etc)	
■ Understand that a quadratic equation may have no roots, one or two real roots but cannot have more than two real roots (unless $a = b = c = 0$)	
■ Use the relations between the roots (α and β) of a quadratic equation and the coefficients (a, b and c)	
■ Understand the significance of a quadratic expression being positive definite, negative definite or indefinite	
■ Determine which of the above conditions applies to a quadratic expression	
■ Understand and solve problems involving the identity of two quadratic expressions	
■ Solve equations which reduce to quadratic equations	
■ Understand the definition of a parabola as a locus	
■ Understand the significance of the equation $x^2 = 4Ay$	
■ Understand the significance of the equation $(x - x_0)^2 = 4A(y - y_0)$	
■ Understand the terms vertex, focus, focal length, directrix, and axis	
■ Find each of these features of a parabola given its equation	
■ Find the equation of a parabola from information about its features	
■ Draw the graph of a parabola showing its essential features	

- A **quadratic polynomial** is an expression of the form $ax^2 + bx + c$.
- In this course a, b and c will always be rational numbers, usually integers.
- The **quadratic function** is $y = ax^2 + bx + c$. The domain of x is the set of all real numbers.

6.1 Solving quadratic equations by factorising

Quadratic equations are also found in the algebra chapter at the beginning of this book.

- We know that:

$$(x + p)(x + q) = x^2 + (p + q)x + pq$$

When factorising a quadratic expression, we look for two terms (p and q) whose sum is the co-efficient of x and whose product is the constant term.

$$x^2 + (p + q)x + pq = (x + p)(x + q)$$

- In **solving a quadratic equation**, we use the result that if the product of two numbers is zero, then one or both of the numbers must be zero.

Q Solve: 1

a $x^2 + 10x + 21 = 0$ b $a^2 - 7a - 18 = 0$
c $e^2 + 5e - 24 = 0$ d $m^2 - 3m + 2 = 0$
e $12 + 4p - p^2 = 0$ f $3u^2 - 6u - 72 = 0$

A a
$$x^2 + 10x + 21 = 0$$
$$(x+7)(x+3) = 0$$
$$x + 7 = 0 \quad \text{or} \quad x + 3 = 0$$
$$x = -7 \qquad\qquad x = -3$$

b
$$a^2 - 7a - 18 = 0$$
$$(a-9)(a+2) = 0$$
$$a - 9 = 0 \quad \text{or} \quad a + 2 = 0$$
$$a = 9 \qquad\qquad a = -2$$

c
$$e^2 + 5e - 24 = 0$$
$$(e+8)(e-3) = 0$$
$$e + 8 = 0 \quad \text{or} \quad e - 3 = 0$$
$$e = -8 \qquad\qquad e = 3$$

d
$$m^2 - 3m + 2 = 0$$
$$(m-2)(m-1) = 0$$
$$m - 2 = 0 \quad \text{or} \quad m - 1 = 0$$
$$m = 2 \qquad\qquad m = 1$$

e
$$12 + 4p - p^2 = 0$$
$$(6-p)(2+p) = 0$$
$$6 - p = 0 \quad \text{or} \quad 2 + p = 0$$
$$p = 6 \qquad\qquad p = -2$$

f
$$3u^2 - 6u - 72 = 0$$
$$3(u^2 - 2u - 24) = 0$$
$$3(u-6)(u+4) = 0$$
$$u - 6 = 0 \quad \text{or} \quad u + 4 = 0$$
$$u = 6 \qquad\qquad u = -4$$

If the coefficient of x^2 is greater than 1, there are several methods of finding the correct factorisation. Whatever method is used, check by expanding that the factorisation is correct.

Q Solve: 2

a $7n^2 - 19n - 6 = 0$
b $4h^2 + 16h + 15 = 0$

A a
$$7n^2 - 19n - 6 = 0$$
$$(7n+2)(n-3) = 0$$
$$7n + 2 = 0 \quad \text{or} \quad n - 3 = 0$$
$$7n = -2 \qquad\qquad n = 3$$
$$n = -\frac{2}{7} \qquad\qquad n = 3$$

b
$$4h^2 + 16h + 15 = 0$$
$$(2h+5)(2h+3) = 0$$
$$2h + 5 = 0 \quad \text{or} \quad 2h + 3 = 0$$
$$2h = -5 \qquad\qquad 2h = -3$$
$$h = -2.5 \qquad\qquad h = -1.5$$

6.2 Completing the square

- One method of solving quadratic equations involves expressing the equation in terms of a **perfect square**. We use the results:

$$\mathbf{(a + b)^2 = a^2 + 2ab + b^2} \text{ and } \mathbf{(a - b)^2 = a^2 - 2ab + b^2}$$

Q Solve by completing the square: 3

a $x^2 - 14x = 15$ b $x^2 + 18x + 70 = 0$
c $4x^2 - 12x + 5 = 0$ d $9x^2 + 6x = 4$

A a
$$x^2 - 14x = 15$$
$$x^2 - 14x + 49 = 15 + 49$$
$$(x-7)^2 = 64$$
$$x - 7 = -8 \quad \text{or} \quad x - 7 = 8$$
$$x = -1 \qquad\qquad x = 15$$

Go to page 103 for Exercises

b $x^2 + 18x + 70 = 0$

$x^2 + 18x + 81 = 11$

$(x+9)^2 = 11$

$x + 9 = \pm\sqrt{11}$

$x = -9 \pm \sqrt{11}$

c $4x^2 - 12x + 5 = 0$

$4x^2 - 12x + 9 = 4$

$(2x-3)^2 = 4$

$2x - 3 = -2$ or $2x - 3 = 2$

$2x = 1$ $\quad$ $2x = 5$

$x = \frac{1}{2}$ $\quad$ $x = 2\frac{1}{2}$

d $9x^2 + 6x = 4$

$9x^2 + 6x + 1 = 5$

$(3x+1)^2 = 5$

$3x + 1 = \pm\sqrt{5}$

$3x = -1 \pm \sqrt{5}$

$x = \frac{-1 \pm \sqrt{5}}{3}$

Q Express $x^2 - 4x + 11 = 0$ in the form $(x-p)^2 + q = 0$, and hence find the minimum value of $y = x^2 - 4x + 11$. 4

A $x^2 - 4x + 11 = 0$

$x^2 - 4x + 4 + 7 = 0$

$\therefore\ (x-2)^2 + 7 = 0$

Now $(x-2)^2 \geq 0$ for all real values of x

$\therefore\ (x-2)^2 + 7 \geq 7$

$\therefore$ the minimum value of y is 7

[This value occurs when $(x-2)^2 = 0$, i.e. when $x = 2$]

Q Use the method of completing the square to solve $ax^2 + bx + c = 0$. 4

A $ax^2 + bx + c = 0$

$x^2 + \frac{b}{a}x = -\frac{c}{a}$

$x^2 + \frac{b}{a}x + \left(\frac{b}{2a}\right)^2 = \left(\frac{b}{2a}\right)^2 - \frac{c}{a}$

continued ...

$\left(x + \frac{b}{2a}\right)^2 = \frac{b^2}{4a^2} - \frac{c}{a}$

$= \frac{b^2 - 4ac}{4a^2}$

$x + \frac{b}{2a} = \pm\sqrt{\frac{b^2 - 4ac}{4a^2}}$

$= \pm\frac{\sqrt{b^2 - 4ac}}{2a}$

$x = -\frac{b}{2a} \pm \frac{\sqrt{b^2 - 4ac}}{2a}$

$= \frac{-b \pm \sqrt{b^2 - 4ac}}{2a}$

6.3 The quadratic formula

- We use the result found by solving the quadratic equation $ax^2 + bx + c = 0$ by the method of completing the square as a formula.
If $ax^2 + bx + c = 0$ then:

$$x = \frac{-b \pm \sqrt{b^2 - 4ac}}{2a}$$

This is called the **quadratic formula**. It can be used to solve any quadratic equation for which a solution exists.

Q Use the quadratic formula to solve these equations, leaving the answers in simplest surd form where necessary: 5

a $3x^2 + 5x - 2 = 0$ $\quad$ **b** $x^2 - x - 1 = 0$

c $2x^2 + 8x + 3 = 0$ $\quad$ **d** $9x^2 - 3x - 8 = 0$

A **a** $3x^2 + 5x - 2 = 0$

$a = 3, b = 5, c = -2$

$x = \frac{-b \pm \sqrt{b^2 - 4ac}}{2a}$

$= \frac{-5 \pm \sqrt{5^2 - 4 \times 3 \times -2}}{2 \times 3}$

$= \frac{-5 \pm \sqrt{49}}{6}$

$x = \frac{-5+7}{6}$ or $x = \frac{-5-7}{6}$

$x = \frac{1}{3}$ $\quad$ $x = -2$

b $x^2 - x - 1 = 0$

$a = 1, b = -1, c = -1$

$x = \frac{-b \pm \sqrt{b^2 - 4ac}}{2a}$

$= \frac{-(-1) \pm \sqrt{(-1)^2 - 4 \times 1 \times -1}}{2 \times 1}$

$= \frac{1 \pm \sqrt{5}}{2}$

Go to page 103 for Exercises

c $2x^2 + 8x + 3 = 0$

$a = 2, b = 8, c = 3$

$$x = \frac{-b \pm \sqrt{b^2 - 4ac}}{2a}$$
$$= \frac{-8 \pm \sqrt{8^2 - 4 \times 2 \times 3}}{2 \times 2}$$
$$= \frac{-8 \pm \sqrt{40}}{4}$$
$$= \frac{-8 \pm 2\sqrt{10}}{4}$$
$$= \frac{2\left(-4 \pm \sqrt{10}\right)}{4}$$
$$= \frac{-4 \pm \sqrt{10}}{2}$$

d $9x^2 - 3x - 8 = 0$

$a = 9, b = -3, c = -8$

$$x = \frac{-b \pm \sqrt{b^2 - 4ac}}{2a}$$
$$= \frac{-(-3) \pm \sqrt{(-3)^2 - 4 \times 9 \times -8}}{2 \times 9}$$
$$= \frac{3 \pm \sqrt{297}}{18}$$
$$= \frac{3 \pm 3\sqrt{33}}{18}$$
$$= \frac{3\left(1 \pm \sqrt{33}\right)}{18}$$
$$= \frac{1 \pm \sqrt{33}}{6}$$

6.4 Roots of quadratic equations

- If $y = ax^2 + bx + c$, a value of x for which $y = 0$ is called **a root** of the quadratic equation $ax^2 + bx + c = 0$.

Q Show that 0.8 is a root of the quadratic equation $10x^2 + 7x - 12 = 0$. 6

A $y = 10x^2 + 7x - 12$

When $x = 0.8$

$y = 10(0.8)^2 + 7(0.8) - 12$

$= 0$

$\therefore x = 0.8$ is a root of the equation $10x^2 + 7x - 12 = 0$

- We can **find the roots** of a quadratic equation by solving the equation, using factorisation, completing the square or the quadratic formula.

Q Find the roots of: 7

a $3x^2 - 25x + 8 = 0$

b $5x^2 - 7x + 1 = 0$

A a $3x^2 - 25x + 8 = 0$

$(3x - 1)(x - 8) = 0$

$3x - 1 = 0$ or $x - 8 = 0$

$3x = 1$ $\quad x = 8$

$x = \frac{1}{3}$ $\quad x = 8$

$\therefore$ the roots are $\frac{1}{3}$ and 8

b $5x^2 - 7x + 1 = 0$

$a = 5, b = -7, c = 1$

$$x = \frac{-b \pm \sqrt{b^2 - 4ac}}{2a}$$
$$= \frac{-(-7) \pm \sqrt{(-7)^2 - 4 \times 5 \times 1}}{2 \times 5}$$
$$= \frac{7 \pm \sqrt{29}}{10}$$

$\therefore$ the roots are $\frac{7 + \sqrt{29}}{10}$ and $\frac{7 - \sqrt{29}}{10}$

Q By completing the square, show that: 8

a $x^2 - 6x + 13 = 0$ has no real roots

b $25x^2 - 20x + 4 = 0$ has only one root

A a $x^2 - 6x + 13 = 0$

$x^2 - 6x = -13$

$x^2 - 6x + 9 = -4$

$(x - 3)^2 = -4$

but $(x - 3)^2 \geq 0$ for all real values of x

$\therefore x^2 - 6x + 13 = 0$ has no real roots

b $25x^2 - 20x + 4 = 0$

$(5x - 2)^2 = 0$

$5x - 2 = 0$

$5x = 2$

$x = 0.4$

$\therefore 25x^2 - 20x + 4 = 0$ has only one root 0.4

- A root of the quadratic equation $ax^2 + bx + c = 0$ may also be referred to as a zero of the quadratic polynomial $P(x) = ax^2 + bx + c$.

Go to page 103 for Exercises

6.5 The graph of a quadratic function

- The graph of $y = ax^2 + bx + c$ will be a **parabola**.
- The coefficient of x^2 (a) will determine the concavity of the parabola.
    - If $a > 0$, the curve is concave up. ∪
    - If $a < 0$, the curve is concave down. ∩
    - The **value of a** also determines how wide or narrow the curve will be. The larger the absolute value of a, the narrower the curve.

Q Graph:

a $y = x^2$ b $y = 3x^2$

c $y = -x^2$ d $y = \frac{1}{2}x^2$

A a

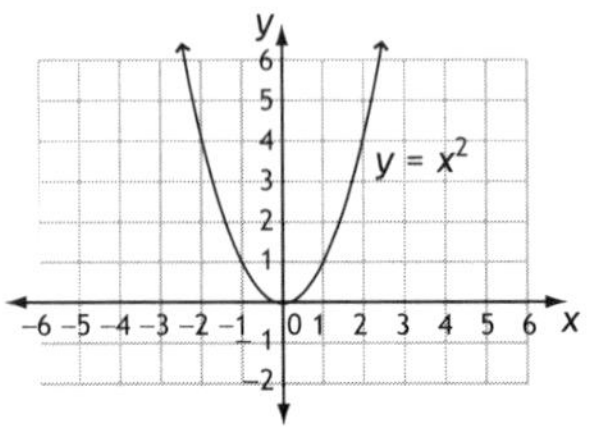

b

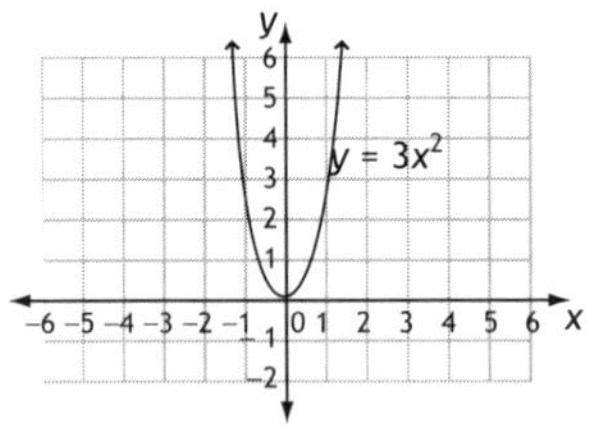

c

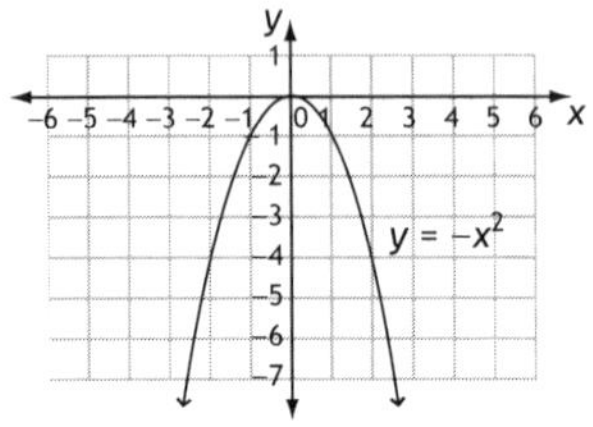

d

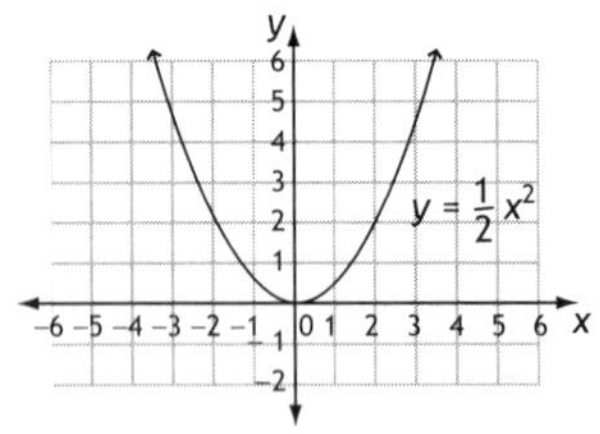

- The **value of c**, the constant term, has the effect of moving the curve up or down.

Q Graph:

a $y = x^2 + 4$ b $y = 2x^2 - 1$

c $y = 3 - x^2$ d $y = -3x^2 - 2$

A a

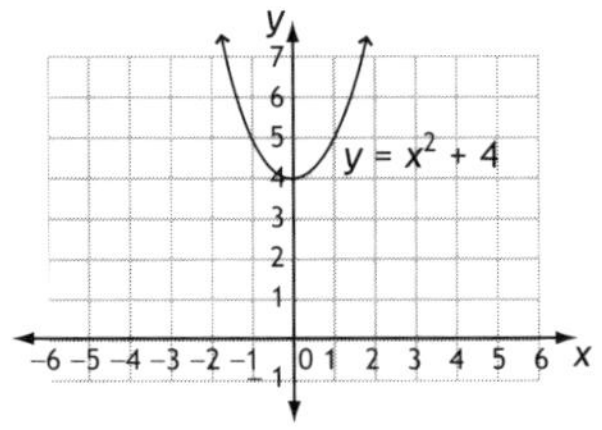

b

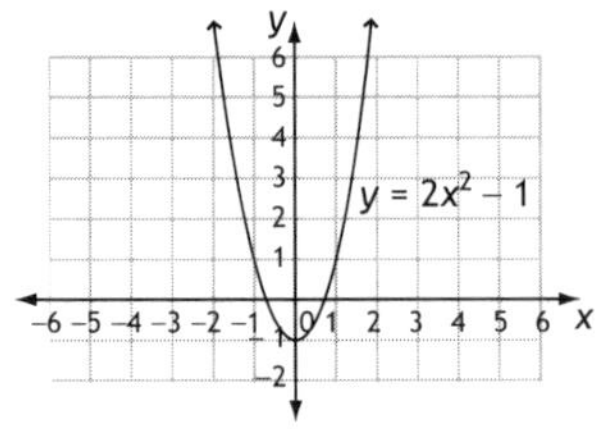

c

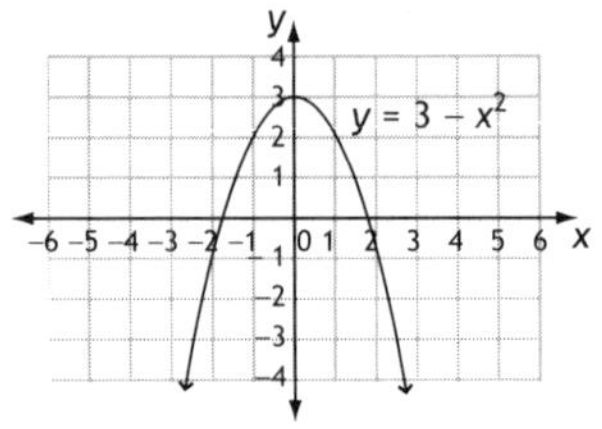

d

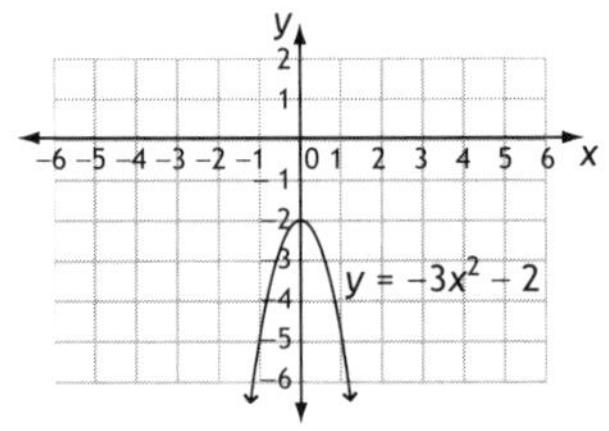

- If $y = (x - p)^2$, p has the effect of moving the curve to the right or to the left.

Q Graph:

a $y = (x-1)^2$ b $y = (x+5)^2$ c $y = -(x-3)^2$

A a

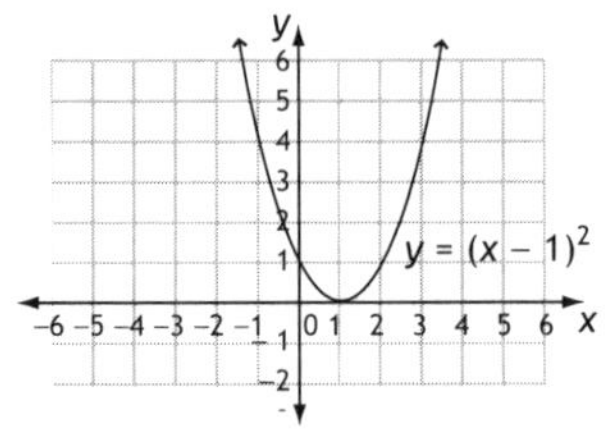

b

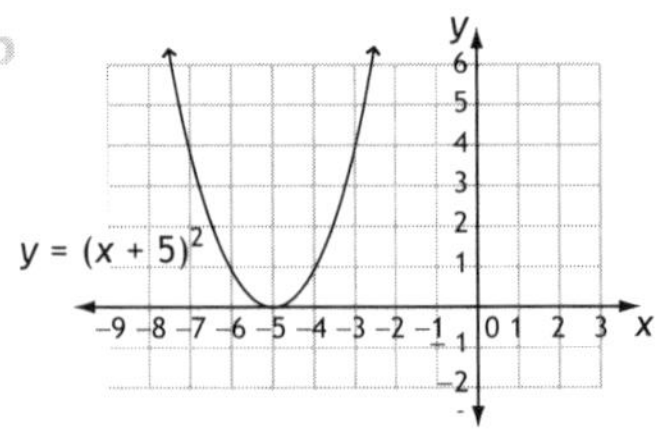

c

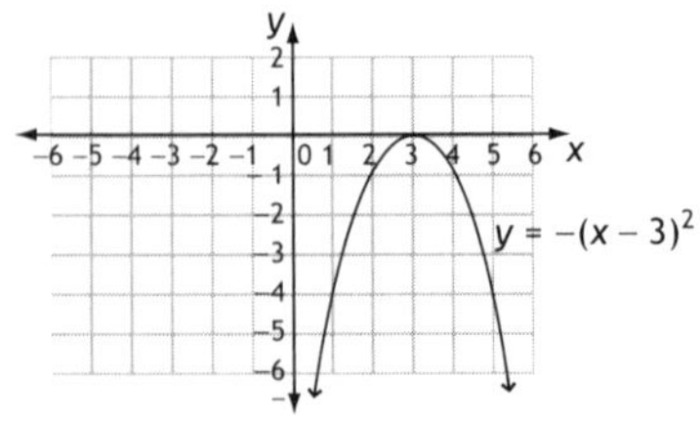

Go to page 103 for Exercises

- In graphing $y = ax^2 + bx + c$ the following points may be considered.
  - a will determine the concavity of the parabola and c will be the y-intercept.
  - The **roots** of the equation , if they exist, will determine where the curve cuts the x-axis.
  - The curve will be **symmetrical**.
  - The **vertex** and **axis of symmetry** could be found.
  - A **table of values** can be drawn up.
  - The expression may be able to be **rearranged** into the form $(x - p)^2 + q$.
  - For **large values** of x, $ax^2 + bx + c \approx ax^2$.

The x-coordinate of the vertex will always be midway between the roots. The y-coordinate can be found by substituting the x-coordinate into the equation.

Q Sketch: **10**

a $y = x^2 - 3x$ b $y = x^2 + 2x - 8$

c $y = -x^2 + 6x - 5$ d $y = x^2 - 4x + 7$

e $y = 3x^2 + 5x - 2$ f $y = 3 + 10x - 8x^2$

A a $y = x^2 - 3x$

When $y = 0$,

$x^2 - 3x = 0$

$x(x - 3) = 0$

$x = 0$ or $x = 3$

vertex $(1.5, -2.25)$

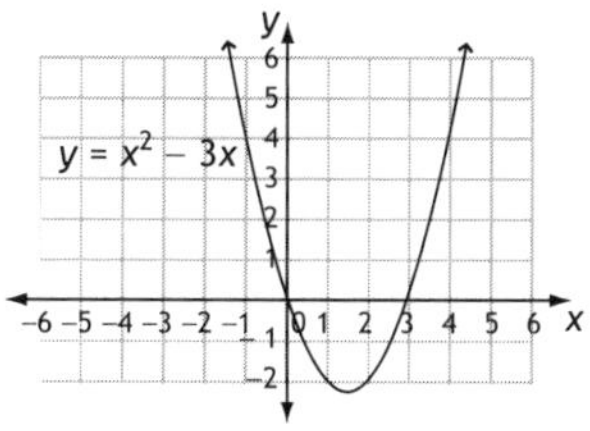

b $y = x^2 + 2x - 8$

When $y = 0$,

$x^2 + 2x - 8 = 0$

$(x + 4)(x - 2) = 0$

$x = -4$ or $x = 2$

vertex $(-1, -9)$

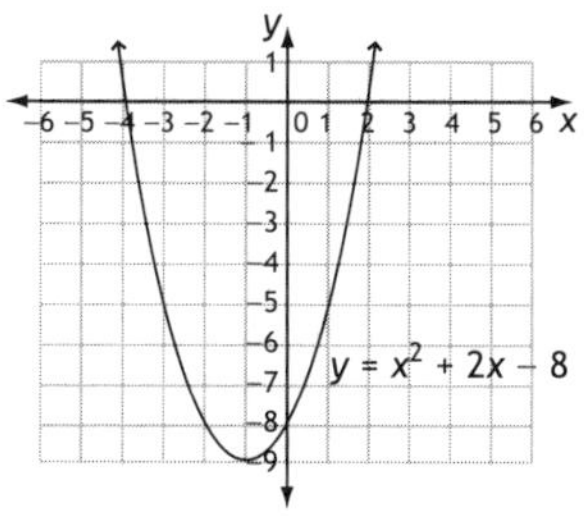

c $y = -x^2 + 6x - 5$

When $y = 0$,

$-x^2 + 6x - 5 = 0$

$-(x - 1)(x - 5) = 0$

$x = 1$ or $x = 5$

vertex $(3, 4)$

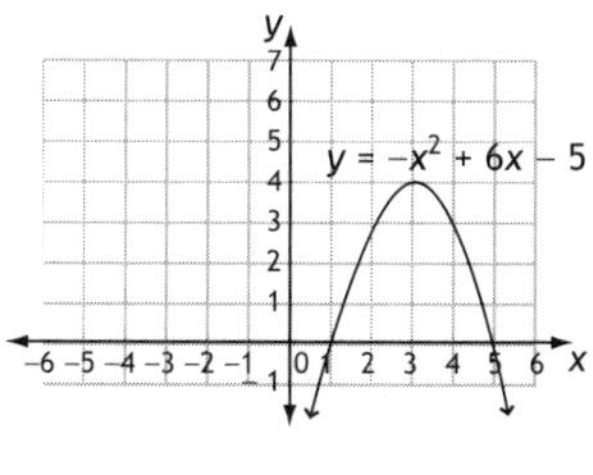

d $y = x^2 - 4x + 7$

When $y = 0$,

$x^2 - 4x + 7 = 0$

has no real roots

$x^2 - 4x + 7 = (x - 2)^2 + 3$

vertex $(2, 3)$

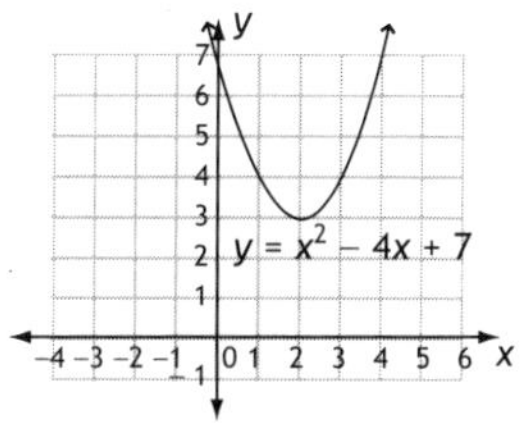

e $y = 3x^2 + 5x - 2$

When $y = 0$,

$3x^2 + 5x - 2 = 0$

$(3x - 1)(x + 2) = 0$

$x = \frac{1}{3}$ or $x = -2$

vertex $\left(-\frac{5}{6}, -4\frac{1}{12}\right)$

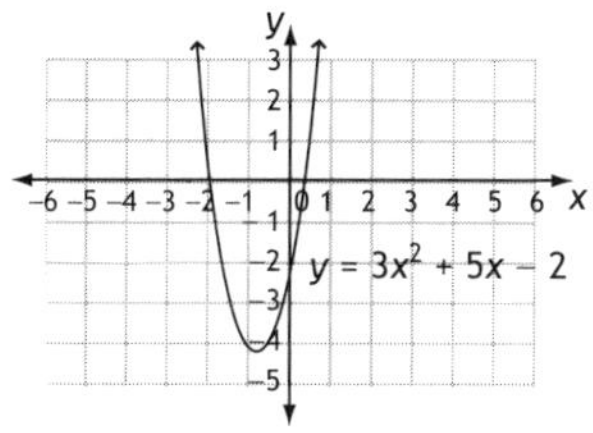

f $y = 3 + 10x - 8x^2$

When $y = 0$,

$3 + 10x - 8x^2 = 0$

$(3 - 2x)(1 + 4x) = 0$

$x = 1\frac{1}{2}$ or $x = -\frac{1}{4}$

vertex $\left(\frac{5}{8}, 6\frac{1}{8}\right)$

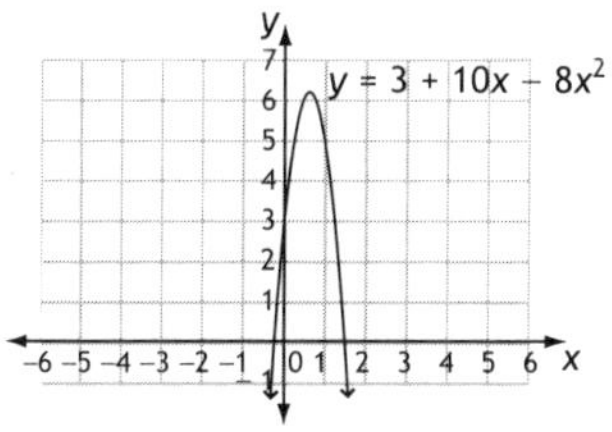

6.6 Quadratic inequalities

When solving a quadratic inequality, great care must be taken to find the whole solution and to have the inequality signs correct.

- The sketch of a quadratic function can be used to help solve quadratic inequalitites.

When solving quadratic inequalities you are not expected to perfectly graph the function. Just use the concavity of the graph and its roots to see where the expression is positive and where it is negative.

Q Solve: **11**

a $x^2 + 5x > 0$ b $x^2 - 4x - 5 \le 0$

c $6 - x - x^2 < 0$ d $4x^2 - 16x + 15 \ge 0$

A a $x^2 + 5x > 0$

Let $y = x^2 + 5x$

$= x(x + 5)$

From the graph,

$y > 0$ when $x < -5$ or $x > 0$

$\therefore x^2 + 5x > 0$ when $x < -5$ or $x > 0$

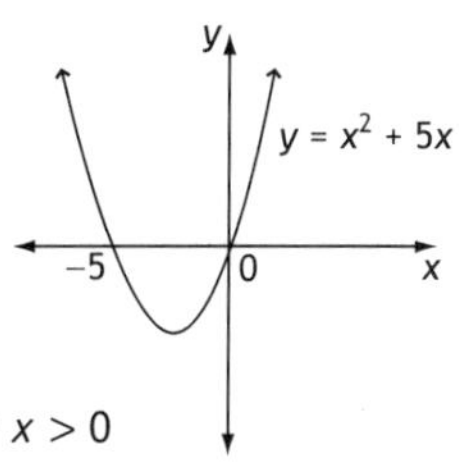

Go to page 103 for Exercises

b $x^2 - 4x - 5 \leq 0$

Let $y = x^2 - 4x - 5$

$= (x-5)(x+1)$

From the graph,

$y \leq 0$ when $-1 \leq x \leq 5$

$\therefore x^2 - 4x - 5 \leq 0$ when $-1 \leq x \leq 5$

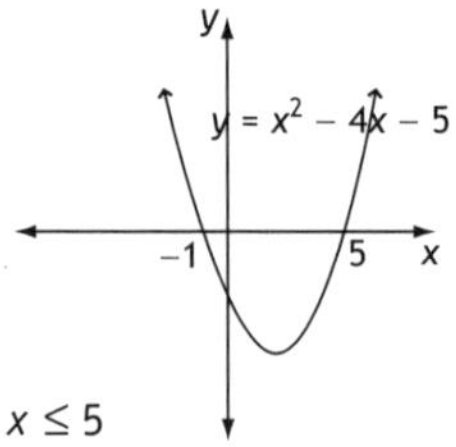

c $6 - x - x^2 < 0$

Let $y = 6 - x - x^2$

$= (3+x)(2-x)$

From the graph,

$y < 0$ when $x < -3$ or $x > 2$

$\therefore 6 - x - x^2 < 0$ when $x < -3$ or $x > 2$

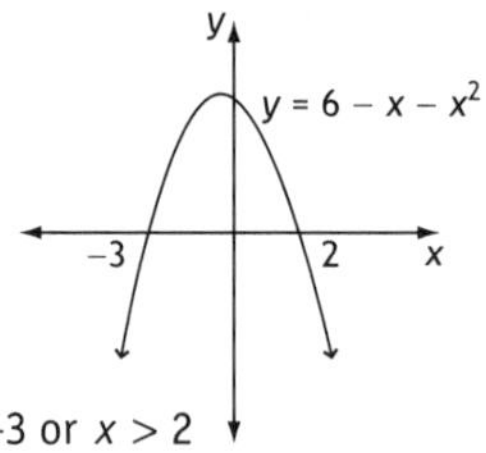

d $4x^2 - 16x + 15 \geq 0$

Let $y = 4x^2 - 16x + 15$

$= (2x-5)(2x-3)$

From the graph,

$y \geq 0$ when $x \leq 1.5$ or $x \geq 2.5$

$\therefore 4x^2 - 16x + 15 \geq 0$ when $x \leq 1.5$ or $x \geq 2.5$

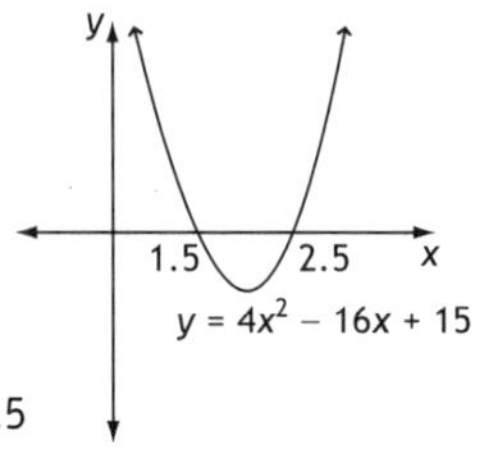

6.7 Sum and product of roots

- If α and β are the roots of $ax^2 + bx + c = 0$ then:

$$ax^2 + bx + c = a(x-\alpha)(x-\beta)$$
$$= a\left[x^2 - (\alpha+\beta)x + \alpha\beta\right]$$
$$= ax^2 - a(\alpha+\beta)x + a\alpha\beta$$
$$\therefore\ b = -a(\alpha+\beta) \quad \text{and} \quad c = a\alpha\beta$$
$$\therefore\ \alpha+\beta = -\frac{b}{a} \quad \text{and} \quad \alpha\beta = \frac{c}{a}$$

If α and β are the roots of $ax^2 + bx + c = 0$ then:

$$\alpha+\beta = -\frac{b}{a} \quad \text{and} \quad \alpha\beta = \frac{c}{a}$$

We can use these results to find out information about a quadratic expression without needing to solve an equation.

Q If α and β are roots of $2x^2 + 7x - 4 = 0$, find: 12

a $\alpha + \beta$ **b** $\alpha\beta$

c $\frac{1}{\alpha} + \frac{1}{\beta}$ **d** $\alpha^2 + \beta^2$

A $2x^2 + 7x - 4 = 0$

$a = 2, b = 7, c = -4$

continued ...

a $\alpha + \beta = -\frac{b}{a}$

$= -\frac{7}{2}$

$= -3\frac{1}{2}$

b $\alpha\beta = \frac{c}{a}$

$= \frac{-4}{2}$

$= -2$

c $\frac{1}{\alpha} + \frac{1}{\beta} = \frac{\alpha+\beta}{\alpha\beta}$

$= \frac{-3\frac{1}{2}}{-2}$

$= 1\frac{3}{4}$

d $\alpha^2 + \beta^2 = (\alpha+\beta)^2 - 2\alpha\beta$

$= \left(-\frac{7}{2}\right)^2 - 2(-2)$

$= 16\frac{1}{4}$

Q If $4x^2 + px + q = 0$ has one root twice the other, show that $p^2 = 18q$. 13

A $4x^2 + px + q = 0$

$a = 4, b = p, c = q$

Let the roots be α and 2α

$\alpha + 2\alpha = -\frac{b}{a}$

$3\alpha = -\frac{p}{4}$

$\therefore\ \alpha = -\frac{p}{12}$ **i**

and $\alpha \times 2\alpha = \frac{c}{a}$

$2\alpha^2 = \frac{q}{4}$ **ii**

Substitute **i** into **ii**

$2\left(-\frac{p}{12}\right)^2 = \frac{q}{4}$

$\frac{2p^2}{144} = \frac{q}{4}$

$\therefore\ p^2 = 18q$

6.8 Axis of symmetry

- The axis of symmetry of the parabola $y = ax^2 + bx + c$ will be a straight line parallel to the y-axis, midway between the roots (α and β).

$$\text{Axis: } x = \frac{\alpha+\beta}{2}$$
$$= \frac{1}{2}\left(-\frac{b}{a}\right)$$
$$= -\frac{b}{2a}$$

Go to page 103 for Exercises

When $x = -\dfrac{b}{2a}$,

$$y = a\left(-\frac{b}{2a}\right)^2 + b\left(-\frac{b}{2a}\right) + c$$
$$= \frac{b^2}{4a} - \frac{b^2}{2a} + c$$
$$= \frac{4ac - b^2}{4a}$$

The parabola $y = ax^2 + bx + c$ has **axis of symmetry**:

$$x = -\frac{b}{2a}$$

The **greatest or least value of y** on the parabola occurs on this line and is given by:

$$\frac{4ac - b^2}{4a}$$

It may sometimes be easier to substitute to find the value of y than to use the formula.

- If $a > 0$, the parabola is concave up, ∪, so there will be a least value.
  If $a < 0$, the parabola is concave down, ∩, so there will be a greatest value.

Q Find the equation of the axis of symmetry and the greatest or least value of y on the parabola: 14

a $y = x^2 + 4x - 7$ **b** $y = -3x^2 + 6x + 4$

A **a** $y = x^2 + 4x - 7$

$a = 1, b = 4, c = -7$

Axis: $x = -\dfrac{b}{2a}$

$= -\dfrac{4}{2 \times 1}$

$= -2$

The least (since $a > 0$) value is:

$\dfrac{4ac - b^2}{4a} = \dfrac{4 \times 1 \times -7 - 4^2}{4 \times 1}$

$= -11$

$\therefore$ the parabola has axis $x = -2$ and the least value of y is -11

b $y = -3x^2 + 6x + 4$

$a = -3, b = 6, c = 4$

Axis: $x = -\dfrac{b}{2a}$

$= -\dfrac{6}{2 \times -3}$

$= 1$

continued ...

The greatest (since $a < 0$) value is:

$\dfrac{4ac - b^2}{4a} = \dfrac{4 \times -3 \times 4 - 6^2}{4 \times -3}$

$= 7$

$\therefore$ the parabola has axis $x = 1$ and the least value of y is 7

Q Find the vertex of the parabola $y = 3x^2 - 15x + 11$. 15

A $y = 3x^2 - 15x + 11$

$a = 3, b = -15, c = 11$

Axis: $x = -\dfrac{b}{2a}$

$= -\dfrac{-15}{2 \times 3}$

$= 2\dfrac{1}{2}$

Least value $= \dfrac{4ac - b^2}{4a}$

$= \dfrac{4 \times 3 \times 11 - (-15)^2}{4 \times 3}$

$= -7\dfrac{3}{4}$

$\therefore$ the vertex is $\left(2\frac{1}{2}, -7\frac{3}{4}\right)$

6.9 The discriminant

- $\Delta = b^2 - 4ac$ is called the discriminant. It is used to discriminate between the types of roots.
- $b^2 - 4ac$ is just that part of the quadratic formula that is under the square root sign so $y = ax^2 + bx + c$ only has real roots when $b^2 - 4ac \geq 0$.
- If $b^2 - 4ac = 0$, the formula gives just one value for x, so the equation has just one distinct root (we say the two roots are equal).
- If $b^2 - 4ac$ is a perfect square, $\sqrt{b^2 - 4ac}$ will be a rational number, so the roots will also be rational.
- If $\Delta \geq 0$, the roots are real.
  If $\Delta < 0$, the roots are not real.
  If $\Delta = 0$, the roots are equal.
  If **Δ is a perfect square**, the roots are rational.

Q Determine whether or not the roots are real, rational and equal: 16

a $3x^2 - 5x - 1 = 0$

b $4x^2 + 7x + 3 = 0$

c $x^2 + 3x + 5 = 0$

d $9x^2 - 12x + 4 = 0$

Go to page 103 for Exercises

A a $3x^2 - 5x - 1 = 0$

$a = 3, b = -5, c = -1$

$\Delta = b^2 - 4ac$

$= (-5)^2 - 4 \times 3 \times -1$

$= 37$

$\therefore$ the roots are real, irrational and unequal

b $4x^2 + 7x + 3 = 0$

$a = 4, b = 7, c = 3$

$\Delta = b^2 - 4ac$

$= 7^2 - 4 \times 4 \times 3$

$= 1$

$\therefore$ the roots are real, rational and unequal

c $x^2 + 3x + 5 = 0$

$a = 1, b = 3, c = 5$

$\Delta = b^2 - 4ac$

$= 3^2 - 4 \times 1 \times 5$

$= -11$

$\therefore$ the roots are not real

d $9x^2 - 12x + 4 = 0$

$a = 9, b = -12, c = 4$

$\Delta = b^2 - 4ac$

$= (-12)^2 - 4 \times 9 \times 4$

$= 0$

$\therefore$ the roots are real, rational and equal

Q Find the values of m for which $3x^2 - mx + m = 0$ has: **17**

a equal roots

b roots that are not real

A $3x^2 - mx + m = 0$

$a = 3, b = -m, c = m$

$\Delta = b^2 - 4ac$

$= (-m)^2 - 4 \times 3 \times m$

$= m^2 - 12m$

a The roots are equal when:

$\Delta = 0$

$m^2 - 12m = 0$

$m(m - 12) = 0$

$m = 0$ or $m - 12 = 0$

$m = 0$ $\quad$ $m = 12$

b The roots are not real when:

$\Delta < 0$

$m^2 - 12m < 0$

Let $y = m^2 - 12m$

From the graph

$y < 0$ when $0 < m < 12$

$\therefore$ the roots are not real when $0 < m < 12$

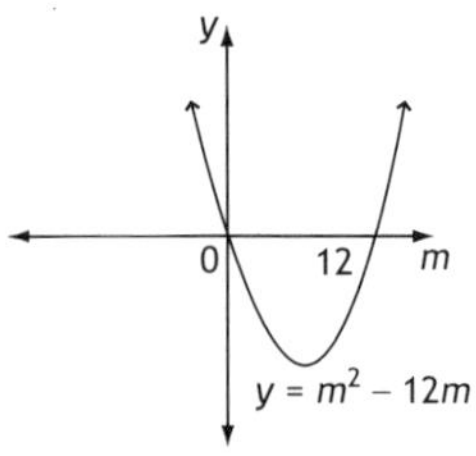

6.10 Positive definite, negative definite and indefinite expressions

- If $\Delta > 0$, $ax^2 + bx + c = 0$ has **real roots** and the graph of $y = ax^2 + bx + c$ crosses the x-axis. y is sometimes positive and sometimes negative.
- If $\Delta < 0$, $ax^2 + bx + c = 0$ has **no real roots** and the graph of $y = ax^2 + bx + c$ will not cross the x-axis. y will always be positive or always be negative. If $a > 0$, the curve is concave up and y will always be positive. If $a < 0$, the curve is concave down and y will always be negative.
- If $\Delta = 0$, $ax^2 + bx + c = 0$ has **equal roots** and the graph of $y = ax^2 + bx + c$ will meet but not cross the x-axis. If $a > 0$ then $y \geq 0$ for all values of x and if $a < 0$ then $y \leq 0$ for all x.
- These results give us the following definitions:
  - If a quadratic function is positive for all values of x, it is **positive definite**. $\Delta < 0, a > 0$
  - If a quadratic function is negative for all values of x, it is **negative definite**. $\Delta < 0, a < 0$
  - If a quadratic function is not positive definite or negative definite, it is **indefinite**. $\Delta \geq 0$

Q Determine whether the following expressions are positive definite, negative definite or indefinite: **18**

a $x^2 + 9x - 2$

b $-5x^2 + 8x - 7$

c $7x^2 - 10x + 4$

d $11 - 6x - x^2$

A a $x^2 + 9x - 2$

$a = 1, b = 9, c = -2$

$\Delta = b^2 - 4ac$

$= 9^2 - 4 \times 1 \times -2$

$= 89$

$\Delta > 0$ $\therefore$ the expression is indefinite

b $-5x^2 + 8x - 7$

$a = -5, b = 8, c = -7$

$\Delta = b^2 - 4ac$

$= 8^2 - 4 \times -5 \times -7$

$= -76$

$\Delta < 0, a < 0$

$\therefore$ the expression is negative definite

Go to page 103 for Exercises

c $7x^2 - 10x + 4$

$a = 7, b = -10, c = 4$

$\Delta = b^2 - 4ac$

$= (-10)^2 - 4 \times 7 \times 4$

$= -12$

$\Delta < 0, a > 0$

$\therefore$ the expression is positive definite

d $11 - 6x - x^2$

$a = -1, b = -6, c = 11$

$\Delta = b^2 - 4ac$

$= (-6)^2 - 4 \times -1 \times 11$

$= 80$

$\Delta > 0$

$\therefore$ the expression is indefinite

Q For what values of p will the expression $5x^2 - 4x + p$ always be positive? **19**

A $5x^2 - 4x + p$

$a = 5, b = -4, c = p$

$a > 0$, the expression will be positive definite when $\Delta < 0$

i.e. $b^2 - 4ac < 0$

$(-4)^2 - 4 \times 5 \times p < 0$

$16 - 20p < 0$

$-20p < -16$

$p > 0.8$

The expression will always be positive when $p > 0.8$

6.11 Equations reducible to quadratics

- Some equations require expanding and simplifying or rearranging to form a standard quadratic equation.

Remember, when solving a quadratic equation by factorising, the equation must first be equal to zero.

Q Solve: **20**

a $(x-5)(x+2) = 78$ b $9x^2 = (x-8)^2$

A a $(x-5)(x+2) = 78$

$x^2 - 3x - 10 = 78$

$x^2 - 3x - 88 = 0$

$(x+8)(x-11) = 0$

$x + 8 = 0$ or $x - 11 = 0$

$x = -8$ $x = 11$

b $9x^2 = (x-8)^2$

$9x^2 = x^2 - 16x + 64$

$8x^2 + 16x - 64 = 0$

$8(x^2 + 2x - 8) = 0$

$x^2 + 2x - 8 = 0$

$(x+4)(x-2) = 0$

$x + 4 = 0$ or $x - 2 = 0$

$x = -4$ $x = 2$

- An equation may be able to be **reduced to a quadratic equation** by use of a simple substitution.

Q Solve: **21**

a $x^4 - 13x^2 + 36 = 0$

b $4x^4 + 11x^2 - 3 = 0$

c $9^x - 10(3^x) + 9 = 0$

d $(n^2 + 4n)^2 - 9(n^2 + 4n) = 36$

A a $x^4 - 13x^2 + 36 = 0$

Let $u = x^2$

$\therefore u^2 - 13u + 36 = 0$

$(u-4)(u-9) = 0$

$u - 4 = 0$ or $u - 9 = 0$

$u = 4$ $u = 9$

$\therefore x^2 = 4$ $x^2 = 9$

$x = \pm 2$ $x = \pm 3$

$\therefore x = -3, -2, 2$ or 3

b $4x^4 + 11x^2 - 3 = 0$

Let $u = x^2$

$\therefore 4u^2 + 11u - 3 = 0$

$(4u - 1)(u + 3) = 0$

$4u - 1 = 0$ or $u + 3 = 0$

$4u = 1$ $u = -3$

$u = 0.25$ $u = -3$

$\therefore x^2 = 0.25$ $x^2 = -3$

$x = \pm 0.5$ no real solution

$\therefore x = -0.5$ or 0.5

c $9^x - 10(3^x) + 9 = 0$

$(3^2)^x - 10(3^x) + 9 = 0$

$(3^x)^2 - 10(3^x) + 9 = 0$

Let $u = 3^x$

$\therefore u^2 - 10u + 9 = 0$

continued ...

Go to page 103 for Exercises

$(u-9)(u-1)=0$

$u-9=0$ or $u-1=0$

$u=9$ $\quad u=1$

$\therefore\ 3^x=9$ $\quad 3^x=1$

$x=2$ $\quad x=0$

$\therefore x=0$ or 2

d $(n^2+4n)^2-9(n^2+4n)=36$

Let $u=n^2+4n$

$\therefore u^2-9u=36$

$u^2-9u-36=0$

$(u-12)(u+3)=0$

$u-12=0$ or $u+3=0$

$\therefore n^2+4n-12=0$ $\quad n^2+4n+3=0$

$(n-2)(n+6)=0$ $\quad (n+3)(n+1)=0$

$n-2=0$ or $n+6=0$ $\quad n+3=0$ or $n+1=0$

$n=2$ $\quad n=-6$ $\quad n=-3$ $\quad n=-1$

$\therefore n=-6,-3,-1$ or 2

6.12 Identities of quadratic expressions

- If $ax^2+bx+c=dx^2+ex+f$ for more than two values of x, then the equality is true for all values of x, and $a=d$, $b=e$ and $c=f$. We say:

$$ax^2+bx+c\equiv dx^2+ex+f$$

$\equiv$ means 'identically equal to'

Q 22 Express $5x^2+7x-3$ in the form $Ax(x-1)+Bx+C$.

A

$Ax(x-1)+Bx+C=Ax^2-Ax+Bx+C$

$=Ax^2-x(A-B)+C$

$5x^2+7x-3\equiv Ax^2-x(A-B)+C$

$\therefore A=5$ $\quad A-B=-7$ $\quad C=-3$

$5-B=-7$

$B=12$

$\therefore A=5$, $B=12$ and $C=-3$

$\therefore 5x^2+7x-3=5x(x-1)+12x-3$

- An **alternative method** of solution is to substitute different values for x. If the expression is an identity then it must be true for any value of x we choose to substitute.

Choose values of x which simplify the working.

Go to page 104 for Exercises

Q 23 Express $4x^2-3x+1$ in the form $Ax(x+1)+B(x+1)+C$.

A

$4x^2-3x+1\equiv Ax(x+1)+B(x+1)+C$

Let $x=-1$,

$4(-1)^2-3(-1)+1=A(-1)(-1+1)+B(-1+1)+C$

$8=C$

Let $x=0$,

$4(0)^2-3(0)+1=A(0)(0+1)+B(0+1)+C$

$1=B+8$

$B=-7$

Let $x=1$,

$4(1)^2-3(1)+1=A(1)(1+1)+B(1+1)+C$

$2=2A-14+8$

$2A=8$

$A=4$

$\therefore 4x^2-3x+1=4x(x+1)-7(x+1)+8$

Q 24 $P(x)=ax^2+bx+c$, $P(0)=8$, $P(1)=3$ and $P(-1)=25$. Find $P(x)$.

A

$P(x)=ax^2+bx+c$

$P(0)=8$

$\therefore\ 8=a\times 0^2+b\times 0+c$

$c=8$

$P(x)=ax^2+bx+8$

$P(1)=3$

$\therefore\ 3=a\times 1^2+b\times 1+8$

$3=a+b+8$

$-5=a+b$ **i**

$P(-1)=25$

$\therefore\ 25=a\times(-1)^2+b\times -1+8$

$25=a-b+8$

$17=a-b$ **ii**

i + ii $\quad 2a=12$

$a=6$

Substitute in **i** $\quad 6+b=-5$

$b=-11$

$\therefore a=6$, $b=-11$, $c=8$ and $P(x)=6x^2-11x+8$

- If a, b and c are all zero, then $ax^2+bx+c=0$ for all values of x. If $ax^2+bx+c=0$ for more than two values of x, then $a=0$, $b=0$ and $c=0$.

6.13 The parabola $x^2 = 4Ay$

- A parabola is defined as the locus of a point which moves so that its distance from a fixed point (the focus) is equal to its distance from a fixed line (the directrix). If we choose any point on the parabola, the distance from that point to the focus will be equal to the perpendicular distance from that point to the directrix.

SP = PQ

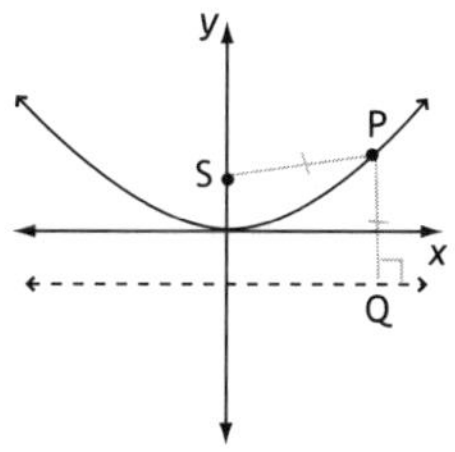

- The parabola $x^2 = 4Ay$ has its **vertex** at the origin (0, 0).
- The **focal length**, A units, is the distance from the vertex to the focus.
- The **axis** (axis of symmetry) of the parabola is the y-axis ($x = 0$).
- The **focus** has coordinates $(0, A)$.
- The **directrix** has equation $y = -A$.

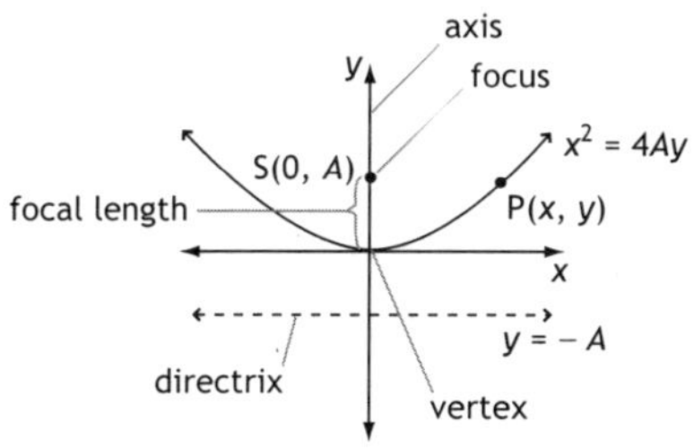

See 'Locus and Parabola' in Chapter 4 (page 69) for a derivation of the equation $x^2 = 4Ay$.

Q For the parabola $x^2 = 12y$, find the focal length. Write down the coordinates of the vertex and the focus, and the equations of the axis and the directrix. Sketch the curve. 25

A

$$x^2 = 12y$$
$$4A = 12$$
$$A = 3$$

$\therefore$ the focal length is 3 units

vertex	$(0, 0)$
focus	$(0, 3)$
axis	$x = 0$
directrix	$y = -3$

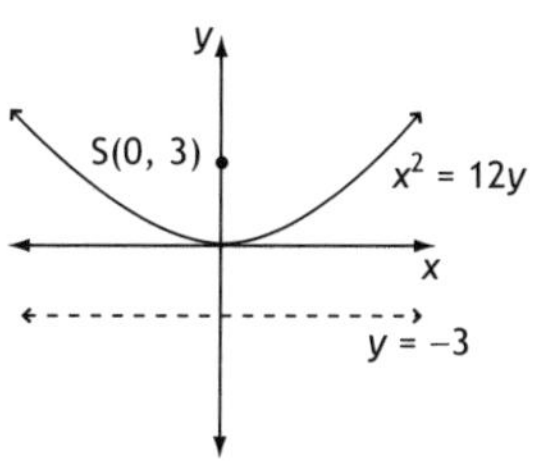

6.14 The parabolas $x^2 = -4Ay$ and $y^2 = \pm 4Ax$

- The parabola $x^2 = -4Ay$ has its vertex at the origin and the axis is the y-axis, but it is 'upside down'. The focal length is A units but the focus is at $(0, -A)$ and the directrix has equation $y = A$.
- The parabola $y^2 = 4Ax$ has its vertex at the origin and its axis is the x-axis. The parabola is 'sideways', opening to the right. The focal length is A units but the focus is at $(A, 0)$ and the directrix has equation $x = -A$.
- The parabola $y^2 = -4Ax$ has its vertex at the origin and its axis is the x-axis. The parabola is 'sideways', opening to the left. The focal length is A units but the focus is at $(-A, 0)$ and the directrix has equation $x = A$.

Q Graph each of the following parabolas, showing clearly the focus and directrix: 25

a $x^2 = -4y$ **b** $y^2 = x$

c $y^2 = -8x$

A **a**

$$x^2 = -4y$$
$$4A = 4$$
$$A = 1$$

$\therefore$ the focal length is 1 unit

vertex	$(0, 0)$
focus	$(0, -1)$
axis	$x = 0$
directrix	$y = 1$

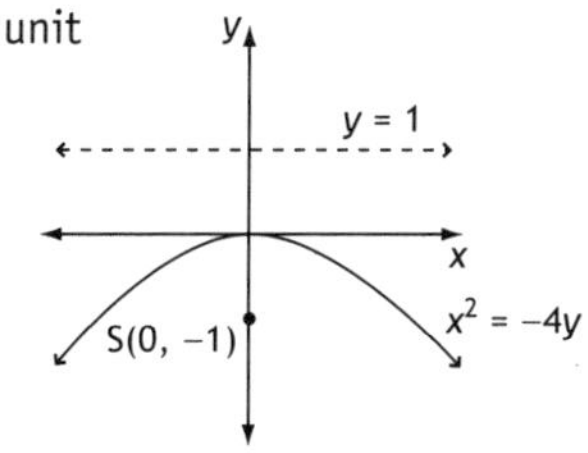

b

$$y^2 = x$$
$$4A = 1$$
$$A = \frac{1}{4}$$

$\therefore$ the focal length is $\frac{1}{4}$ unit

vertex	$(0, 0)$
focus	$\left(\frac{1}{4}, 0\right)$
axis	$y = 0$
directrix	$x = -\frac{1}{4}$

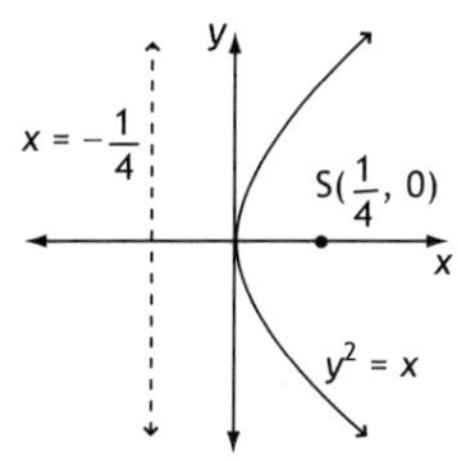

Go to page 104 for Exercises

c $y^2 = -8x$

$4A = 8$

$A = 2$

$\therefore$ the focal length is 2 units

vertex $(0, 0)$

focus $(-2, 0)$

axis $y = 0$

directrix $x = 2$

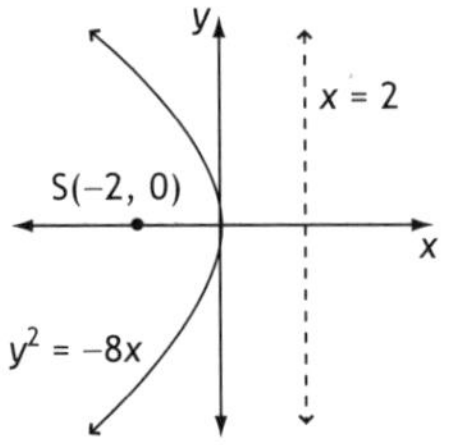

6.15 When the vertex is not the origin

- Not all parabolas have their vertex at the origin.

$(x - x_0)^2 = 4A(y - y_0)$ is a parabola with vertex at (x_0, y_0) and focal length A units. The equation of the axis of the parabola is $x = x_0$, the focus is at $S(x_0, y_0 + A)$ and the equation of the directrix is $y = y_0 - A$.

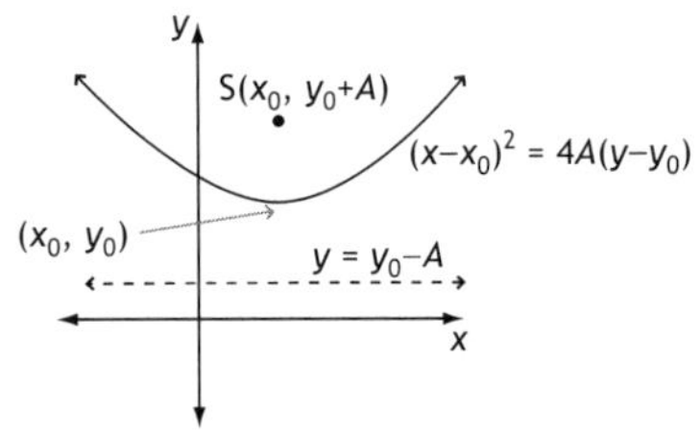

Q For each parabola, find the coordinates of the focus and vertex, the equation of the axis and directrix and sketch their graphs: 26

a $(x-2)^2 = 4(y-5)$ **b** $(x-3)^2 = 8(y+1)$

A **a** $(x-2)^2 = 4(y-5)$

vertex $(2, 5)$

axis $x = 2$

$4A = 4$

$A = 1$

$\therefore$ the focal length is 1 unit

The focus is 1 unit above the vertex.

focus $(2, 6)$

The directrix is 1 unit below the vertex.

directrix $y = 4$

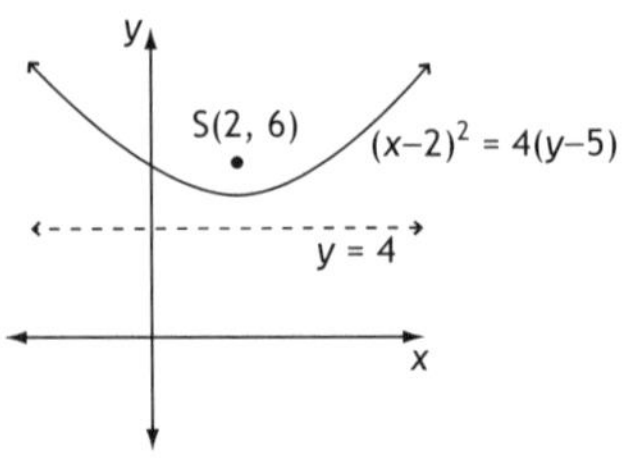

b $(x-3)^2 = 8(y+1)$

vertex $(3, -1)$

axis $x = 3$

$4A = 8$

$A = 2$

$\therefore$ the focal length is 2 units

The focus is 2 units above the vertex.

focus $(3, 1)$

The directrix is 2 units below the vertex.

directrix $y = -3$

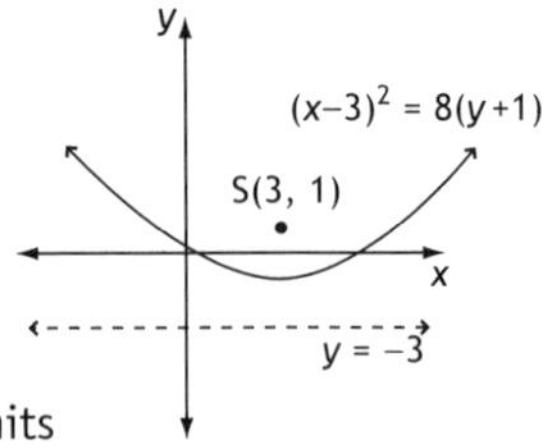

Q For each parabola, find the coordinates of the focus and vertex, the equations of the axis and directrix and sketch their graphs: 26

a $(x+2)^2 = -12(y+3)$ **b** $(y-1)^2 = 6(x-4)$

c $(y+2)^2 = -20x$

A **a** $(x+2)^2 = -12(y+3)$

vertex $(-2, -3)$

axis $x = -2$

$4A = 12$

$A = 3$

$\therefore$ the focal length is 3 units

The negative sign means the parabola is upside down. The focus is 3 units below the vertex and the directrix is 3 units above the vertex.

focus $(-2, -6)$

directrix $y = 0$

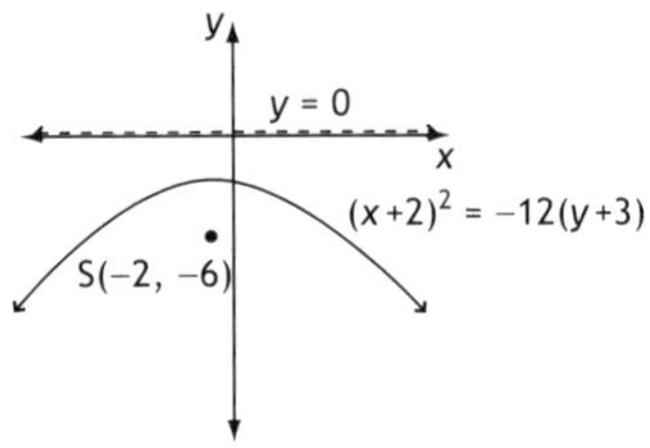

b $(y-1)^2 = 6(x-4)$

[Because the x and y values have 'swapped around', the parabola is sideways. The axis will be parallel to the x-axis. The x-coordinate of the vertex is found on the right hand side of the equation.]

vertex $(4, 1)$

axis $y = 1$

$4A = 6$

$A = 1.5$

$\therefore$ the focal length is 1.5 units

[The focus is 1.5 units to the right of the vertex and the directrix is 1.5 units to the left.]

focus $(5.5, 1)$

directrix $x = 2.5$

continued ...

Go to page 104 for Exercises

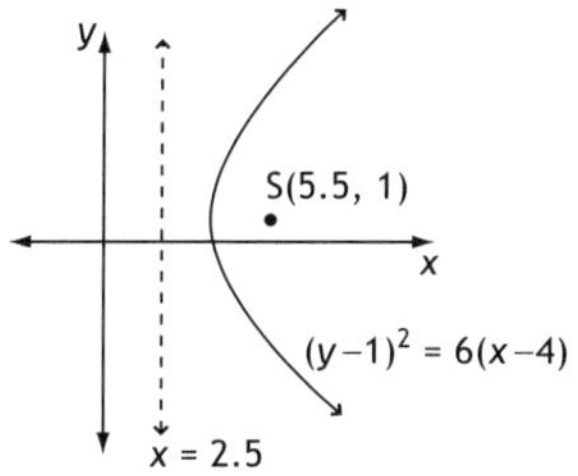

c $(y+2)^2 = -20x$

The parabola is sideways opening to the left.

vertex $(0, -2)$

axis $y = -2$

$4A = 20$

$A = 5$

$\therefore$ the focal length is 5 units

The focus is 5 units to the left of the vertex and the directrix is 5 units to the right of the vertex.

focus $(-5, -2)$

directrix $x = 5$

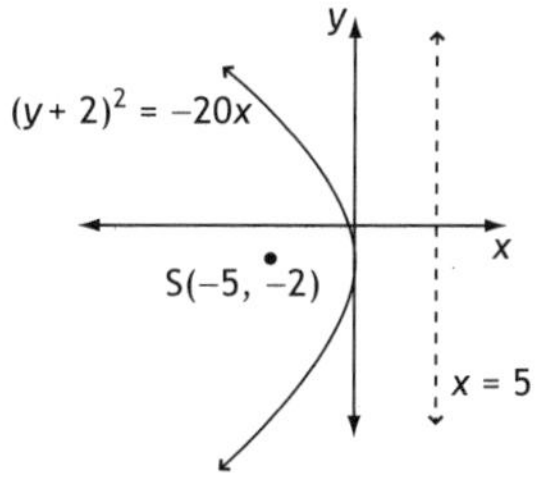

6.16 Finding the focus and directrix of $y = ax^2 + bx + c$ or $x = ay^2 + by + c$

- The equation $y = ax^2 + bx + c$ can be changed into the form $(x - x_0)^2 = 4A(y - y_0)$ by completing the square.

Q Express each equation in the form $(x - x_0)^2 = 4A(y - y_0)$: **27**

a $y = x^2 - 8x + 2$ b $y = \frac{1}{4}x^2 - 3x + 7$

c $y = 3x^2 + 6x - 8$ d $y = 4 - x - x^2$

A a

$$\begin{aligned} y &= x^2 - 8x + 2 \\ x^2 - 8x &= y - 2 \\ x^2 - 8x + 16 &= y - 2 + 16 \\ (x-4)^2 &= y + 14 \end{aligned}$$

b

$$\begin{aligned} y &= \frac{1}{4}x^2 - 3x + 7 \\ 4y &= x^2 - 12x + 28 \\ x^2 - 12x &= 4y - 28 \\ x^2 - 12x + 36 &= 4y - 28 + 36 \\ (x-6)^2 &= 4y + 8 \\ (x-6)^2 &= 4(y+2) \end{aligned}$$

c

$$\begin{aligned} y &= 3x^2 + 6x - 8 \\ 3x^2 + 6x &= y + 8 \\ x^2 + 2x &= \frac{y}{3} + 2\frac{2}{3} \\ x^2 + 2x + 1 &= \frac{y}{3} + 3\frac{2}{3} \\ (x+1)^2 &= \frac{y}{3} + \frac{11}{3} \\ (x+1)^2 &= \frac{1}{3}(y + 11) \end{aligned}$$

d

$$\begin{aligned} y &= 4 - x - x^2 \\ x^2 + x &= -y + 4 \\ x^2 + x + \frac{1}{4} &= -y + 4\frac{1}{4} \\ \left(x + \frac{1}{2}\right)^2 &= -\left(y - 4\frac{1}{4}\right) \end{aligned}$$

- Expressing a function $y = ax^2 + bx + c$ in the form $(x - x_0)^2 = 4A(y - y_0)$ allows us to easily find the coordinates of the **focus**, the equation of the **directrix** and other features of the parabola.

Q Find the coordinates of the focus and the equation of the directrix of each parabola:. **28**

a $y = \frac{1}{8}x^2 - x + 1$

b $x = y^2 + 4y - 10$

A a

$$\begin{aligned} y &= \frac{1}{8}x^2 - x + 1 \\ 8y &= x^2 - 8x + 8 \\ x^2 - 8x &= 8y - 8 \\ x^2 - 8x + 16 &= 8y + 8 \\ (x-4)^2 &= 8(y+1) \end{aligned}$$

vertex $(4, -1)$

axis $x = 4$

$4A = 8$

$A = 2$

$\therefore$ focal length is 2 units

focus $(4, 1)$

directrix $y = -3$

b

$$\begin{aligned} x &= y^2 + 4y - 10 \\ y^2 + 4y &= x + 10 \\ y^2 + 4y + 4 &= x + 14 \\ (y+2)^2 &= x + 14 \end{aligned}$$

vertex $(-14, -2)$

axis $y = -2$

continued ...

Go to page 104 for Exercises

$$4A = 1$$
$$A = \frac{1}{4}$$
$\therefore$ focal length is $\frac{1}{4}$ unit

focus $\left(-13\frac{3}{4}, -2\right)$

directrix $x = -14\frac{1}{4}$

6.17 Finding the equation of a parabola

- Using information about the features of the parabola (focus, vertex, focal length, axis or directrix), it is possible to write down its equation.

A rough sketch may help to determine the orientation of the parabola and hence which form of the equation should be used.

Q Find the equation of the parabola with: 29

a vertex (3, −2), focus (3, 7)
b vertex (−1, 5), directrix $y = 8$
c focus (2, 4), directrix $x = -2$

A a vertex $(3, -2)$, focus $(3, 7)$ $\therefore$ axis $x = 3$

focal length $= 7 - (-2)$
$= 9$ units
$\therefore A = 9$
$$(x - x_0)^2 = 4A(y - y_0)$$
$$(x - 3)^2 = 4 \times 9(y - (-2))$$
$$(x - 3)^2 = 36(y + 2)$$

b vertex $(-1, 5)$, directrix $y = 8$ $\therefore$ axis $x = -1$

focal length $= 8 - 5$
$= 3$ units
$\therefore A = 3$
$$(x - x_0)^2 = -4A(y - y_0)$$
$$(x - (-1))^2 = -4 \times 3(y - 5)$$
$$(x + 1)^2 = -12(y - 5)$$

c focus $(2, 4)$, directrix $x = -2$ $\therefore$ axis $y = 4$

focal length $= \frac{1}{2}[2 - (-2)]$
$= 2$ units
$\therefore A = 2$
vertex $(0, 4)$

continued ...

$$(y - y_0)^2 = 4A(x - x_0)$$
$$(y - 4)^2 = 4 \times 2(x - 0)$$
$$(y - 4)^2 = 8x$$

- There may be insufficient information to determine the exact equation of a parabola, but we may be able to find the **equation of the family of parabolas** that share the particular features.

Q Find the equation of the family of parabolas with: 30

a vertex (−2, 0), axis $x = -2$
b vertex (1, −3), focal length 2 units
c axis $x = 5$, focal length 1 unit, directrix the x-axis

A a vertex $(-2, 0)$, axis $x = -2$
$$(x - x_0)^2 = \pm 4A(y - y_0)$$
$$(x - (-2))^2 = \pm 4A(y - 0)$$
$$(x + 2)^2 = \pm 4Ay$$

b vertex $(1, -3)$, focal length 2 units $\therefore A = 2$

Either: axis: $x = 1$
$$(x - x_0)^2 = \pm 4A(y - y_0)$$
$$(x - 1)^2 = \pm 4 \times 2 \times (y - (-3))$$
$$(x - 1)^2 = \pm 8(y + 3)$$
or : axis: $y = -3$
$$(y - y_0)^2 = \pm 4A(x - x_0)$$
$$(y - (-3))^2 = \pm 4 \times 2 \times (x - 1)$$
$$(y + 3)^2 = \pm 8(x - 1)$$

c axis $x = 5$, focal length 1 unit, $\therefore A = 1$

directrix x-axis $(y = 0)$

Either: vertex $(5, 1)$
$$(x - x_0)^2 = 4A(y - y_0)$$
$$(x - 5)^2 = 4 \times 1 \times (y - 1)$$
$$(x - 5)^2 = 4(y - 1)$$
or : vertex $(5, -1)$
$$(x - x_0)^2 = -4A(y - y_0)$$
$$(x - 5)^2 = -4 \times 1 \times (y - (-1))$$
$$(x - 5)^2 = -4(y + 1)$$

Go to page 104 for Exercises

Exercises Quadratic Polynomial and the Parabola

1 Solve:

a $x^2 - 11x + 30 = 0$ b $y^2 + 7y + 10 = 0$

c $h^2 - 6h - 16 = 0$ d $6 - 5a - a^2 = 0$

e $2w^2 + 20w - 48 = 0$

2 Solve:

a $3x^2 - 17x - 6 = 0$ b $6z^2 + 13z - 28 = 0$

3 Solve by completing the square:

a $x^2 + 10x = 24$ b $x^2 - 24x + 137 = 0$

c $25x^2 - 20x = 12$ d $4x^2 + 28x + 47 = 0$

4 Express $x^2 + 8x + 25 = 0$ in the form $(x + p)^2 + q = 0$ and hence find the minimum value of $y = x^2 + 8x + 25$.

5 Use the quadratic formula to solve, leaving answers in simplest surd form where necessary:

a $45 + 2x - 8x^2 = 0$ b $3x^2 + 11x + 7 = 0$

c $x^2 - 6x + 2 = 0$

6 Show that $x = -1.5$ is a root of the quadratic equation $6x^2 - 31x - 60 = 0$.

7 Find the roots of:

a $2x^2 - 11x + 5 = 0$ b $x^2 + 7x + 2 = 0$

8 By completing the square show that:

a $x^2 + 8x + 17 = 0$ has no real roots

b $9x^2 + 12x + 4 = 0$ has only one root

9 Sketch:

a $y = 2x^2$ b $y = x^2 + 3$

c $y = 2 - x^2$ d $y = (x + 2)^2$

10 Sketch:

a $y = x^2 + 2x$ b $y = x^2 - 6x + 8$

c $y = 4 - 3x - x^2$ d $y = 2x^2 - 13x + 15$

11 Solve:

a $x^2 - 3x \le 0$ b $x^2 + 2x - 8 > 0$

c $3 + 2x - x^2 < 0$ d $3x^2 + 11x + 6 \ge 0$

12 If α and β are the roots of $2x^2 + 11x + 6 = 0$, find:

a $\alpha + \beta$ b $\alpha\beta$

c $\alpha^2 + \beta^2$ d $\dfrac{1}{\alpha} + \dfrac{1}{\beta}$

e $\alpha^2\beta + \alpha\beta^2$

13 The roots of $3x^2 + kx + 4 = 0$ are such that one root is three times the other. Find the two possible values of k.

14 Find the equation of the axis of symmetry and the greatest or least value of y on the following parabolas:

a $y = x^2 - 10x + 9$ b $y = -x^2 + 2x - 9$

c $y = 5x^2 - 4x + 11$

15 Find the vertex of each parabola:

a $y = 2x^2 + 8x - 5$ b $y = 10 - 2x - 3x^2$

16 Find the discriminant and hence determine whether or not the roots are real. If the roots are real, determine whether they are rational or irrational, and equal or unequal:

a $4x^2 - 3x - 2 = 0$ b $2x^2 + x + 7 = 0$

c $16x^2 - 8x + 1 = 0$ d $9x^2 - 36x + 20 = 0$

17 Find the value of m for which:

a $x^2 - 6x + m = 0$ has real roots

b $3x^2 + mx + 12 = 0$ has equal roots

18 Determine whether the following expressions are positive definite, negative definite or indefinite:

a $2x^2 + x - 5$ b $-x^2 + 5x - 8$

c $-3x^2 + 6x + 8$ d $7x^2 + 4x + 1$

19 For what values of k will the expression $9x^2 + kx + 4$ always be positive?

20 Solve:

a $(x + 3)(x + 2) = 20$ b $16x^2 = (x + 6)^2$

21 Solve:

a $x^4 - 26x^2 + 25 = 0$

b $3x^4 - 10x^2 - 8 = 0$

c $4^x - 10(2^x) + 16 = 0$

d $(x^2 - 8x)^2 + 3(x^2 - 8x) - 108 = 0$

Go to pages 224 and 225 for Quick Answers & pages 178–182 for Worked Solutions

22 Express $3x^2 - 2x + 3$ in the form $Ax(x+1) + Bx + C$.

23 Express $5x^2 - 4x - 7$ in the form $Ax(x-1) + B(x-1) + C$.

24 $Q(x) = ax^2 + bx + c$. $Q(0) = 5$, $Q(1) = 3$ and $Q(-1) = 13$. Find $Q(x)$.

25 Sketch each parabola showing the focus and directrix:

a $x^2 = 16y$ b $y^2 = 20x$

c $x^2 = -8y$ d $y^2 = -2x$

26 For each parabola find the coordinates of the vertex and focus, the equations of the axis and the directrix, and sketch:

a $(x-4)^2 = 12(y-2)$ b $(y+6)^2 = -4(x-4)$

c $y^2 = 16(x-1)$ d $(x+3)^2 = -8(y+3)$

27 Express each equation in the form $(x - x_0)^2 = 4A(y - y_0)$:

a $y = x^2 - 4x + 7$ b $y = -\frac{1}{2}x^2 - x + \frac{1}{2}$

c $y = 4x^2 - 40x + 97$ d $y = 9 - 8x - 2x^2$

28 Find the coordinates of the focus and equation of the directrix for each parabola:

a $y = x^2 + 10x + 25$ b $x = \frac{1}{2}y^2 - 3y + 5$

29 Find the equation of the parabola with:

a vertex (2, 5), focus (2, 9)
b vertex (6, 4), focus (6, −3)
c vertex (1, −2), directrix $x = 3$
d focus (1, 5), directrix $y = -5$

30 Find the equation of the family of parabolas with:

a vertex (−1, 3), axis $x = -1$, focal length 2.25 units
b focus (3, 0), axis the x-axis, focal length 3 units

☞ Go to pages 225 & 226 for Quick Answers & pages 182–184 for Worked Solutions. See pages 134 & 135 for Topic Tests

7 The Tangent to a Curve and the Derivative of a Function

Your Checklist

For a complete understanding of this topic you must be able to: ✓

- Understand what is meant for a curve to be continuous
- Understand the concept of a limit of a function
- Use the notation $\lim\limits_{x \to c} f(x)$ and evaluate limits
- Understand the formal definition of continuity
- Determine whether a function is continuous at a given point
- Understand what is meant by a continuous function
- Know what a secant is and find the gradient of a secant to a curve
- Understand that a tangent is the limiting position of a secant
- Find the gradient of a tangent to a curve at a point (the limiting value of the gradient of the secant)
- Find the equation of the tangent to a curve at a given point on the curve
- Find the equation of the normal to a curve at a given point on the curve
- Draw graphs of curves showing the tangent at a point
- Understand the terms derivative and differential coefficient
- Understand the notations $f'(c)$ and $\frac{dy}{dx}$ at $x = c$
- Use alternative forms of finding the derivative $\lim\limits_{h \to 0} \frac{f(c+h) - f(c)}{h}$
- Find the gradient function or derivative $y = f'(x)$
- Understand the notations $f'(x)$, $\frac{dy}{dx}$, $\frac{d}{dx}(f(x))$ and y'
- Understand and use the rule to differentiate x^n
- Know that the derivative of a constant is zero
- Find the derivative of a term multiplied by a constant
- Understand that the derivative of a sum of terms is equal to the sum of the derivatives of each of the terms
- Find derivatives using different variables
- Use the composite function rule (chain rule)
- Use the product rule
- Use the quotient rule

7.1 Limits

- The notation $\lim_{x \to c} f(x)$, [the limit of $f(x)$ as x approaches c], is used to show the value the function approaches as x gets closer and closer to c. For example, $\lim_{x \to 4}\left(2x^2 + 5\right) = 37$ means that as x gets closer and closer to 4, $2x^2 + 5$ gets closer and closer to 37.

  In many cases, the limit as x approaches a value is just the value of the function at that point.

Q Find: 1

a $\lim_{x \to 1}\left(3x + 7\right)$ b $\lim_{x \to 3}\left(x^2 - 8\right)$

A a $\lim_{x \to 1}\left(3x + 7\right) = 3 \times 1 + 7$
$= 10$

b $\lim_{x \to 3}\left(x^2 - 8\right) = 3^2 - 8$
$= 1$

- **If $f(x)$ is undefined at $x = c$**, the limit as x approaches c can still exist.

Q Find: 2

a $\lim_{x \to 2} \frac{x^2 - 4}{x - 2}$ b $\lim_{h \to 0} \frac{3h^2 - 5h}{h}$

c $\lim_{x \to 5} \frac{x^2 - 8x + 15}{x^2 - 3x - 10}$

A a
$$\begin{aligned}\lim_{x \to 2} \frac{x^2 - 4}{x - 2} &= \lim_{x \to 2} \frac{(x-2)(x+2)}{x - 2} \\ &= \lim_{x \to 2}(x + 2) \\ &= 2 + 2 \\ &= 4\end{aligned}$$

We are considering the function when x approaches 2. x is not equal to 2 so we can divide by $x - 2$.

b
$$\begin{aligned}\lim_{h \to 0} \frac{3h^2 - 5h}{h} &= \lim_{h \to 0} \frac{h(3h - 5)}{h} \\ &= \lim_{h \to 0}(3h - 5) \\ &= 3 \times 0 - 5 \\ &= -5\end{aligned}$$

c
$$\begin{aligned}\lim_{x \to 5} \frac{x^2 - 8x + 15}{x^2 - 3x - 10} &= \lim_{x \to 5} \frac{(x-5)(x-3)}{(x-5)(x+2)} \\ &= \lim_{x \to 5} \frac{x - 3}{x + 2} \\ &= \frac{5 - 3}{5 + 2} \\ &= \frac{2}{7}\end{aligned}$$

Go to page 120 for Exercises

You can use your calculator to get the idea of a limit. Substitute values closer and closer to 2 in example **a** and you should see that the values get closer and closer to 4.

- $\lim_{x \to \infty} f(x)$ [the limit of $f(x)$ as x tends to infinity] shows the value the function approaches as x becomes very large.

Q Find: 3

a $\lim_{x \to \infty} \frac{1}{x}$ b $\lim_{x \to -\infty} \frac{x + 1}{x}$

A a $\lim_{x \to \infty} \frac{1}{x} = 0$
[as x gets larger, $\frac{1}{x}$ gets closer and closer to 0]

b $\lim_{x \to -\infty} \frac{x + 1}{x} = \lim_{x \to -\infty}\left(1 + \frac{1}{x}\right)$ $\left[\frac{x+1}{x} = \frac{x}{x} + \frac{1}{x}\right]$
$= 1$

7.2 Continuity

- Informally, a curve is **continuous** if it is unbroken. If there are gaps or jumps in the curve it is **discontinuous**.

Q State whether the following curves are continuous or discontinuous. 4

a
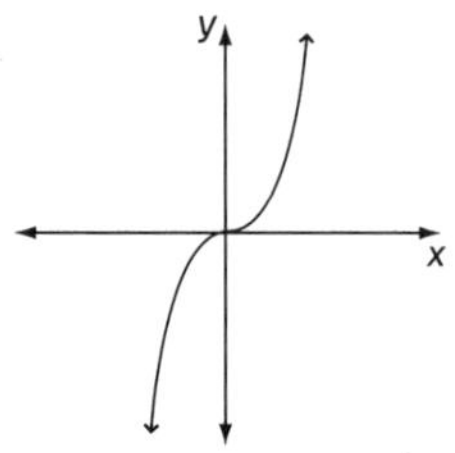

b
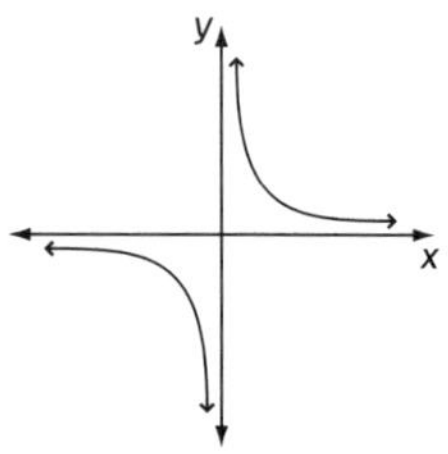

c
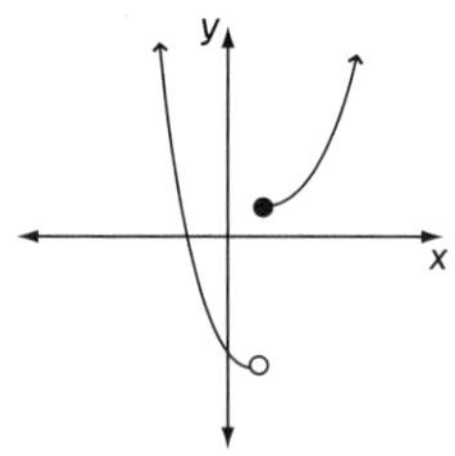

d
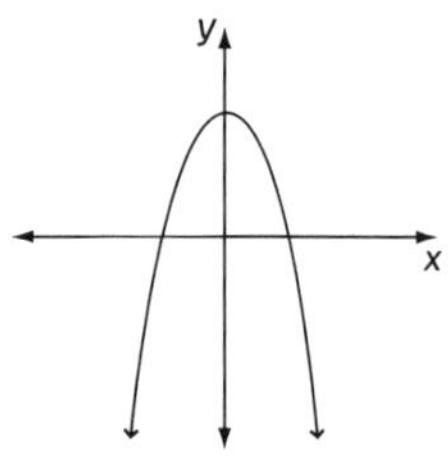

A a continuous b discontinuous
c discontinuous d continuous

- A function is **continuous** at a given point $x = c$ if $f(c)$ exists and if, as x gets closer and closer to c, $f(x)$ gets closer and closer to $f(c)$.

- The formal definition of continuity is:

  A function is **continuous at $x = c$** if:
  - $f(x)$ is defined at c, and
  - $\lim_{x \to c} f(x)$ exists, and
  - $f(c)$ is equal to this limit.

Q Determine whether the following functions are continuous at $x = 2$: 5

a $f(x) = x^3 - 8$ b $f(x) = \dfrac{x+3}{x^2 - 2x}$

c $f(x) = \begin{cases} \dfrac{x^2 - 8x + 12}{x - 2} & \text{if } x \neq 2 \\ 4 & \text{if } x = 2 \end{cases}$

A a

$$\begin{aligned} f(x) &= x^3 - 8 \\ f(2) &= 2^3 - 8 \\ &= 0 \\ \lim_{x \to 2}(x^3 - 8) &= 2^3 - 8 \\ &= 0 \end{aligned}$$

$\therefore f(2) = \lim_{x \to 2} f(x)$

$\therefore$ the curve is continuous at $x = 2$

b

$$\begin{aligned} f(x) &= \frac{x+3}{x^2 - 2x} \\ f(2) &= \frac{2+3}{2^2 - 2 \times 2} \\ &= \frac{5}{0} \end{aligned}$$

$\therefore f(2)$ is undefined

$\therefore$ the curve is not continuous at $x = 2$

c

$$f(x) = \begin{cases} \dfrac{x^2 - 8x + 12}{x - 2} & \text{if } x \neq 2 \\ 4 & \text{if } x = 2 \end{cases}$$

$f(2) = 4$

$$\begin{aligned} \lim_{x \to 2} f(x) &= \lim_{x \to 2} \frac{x^2 - 8x + 12}{x - 2} \\ &= \lim_{x \to 2} \frac{(x-6)(x-2)}{x-2} \\ &= \lim_{x \to 2}(x - 6) \\ &= 2 - 6 \\ &= -4 \end{aligned}$$

$\therefore f(2) \neq \lim_{x \to 2} f(x)$

$\therefore$ the curve is not continuous at $x = 2$

- A function $f(x)$ is said to be continuous, or to be a continuous function, if it is continuous at every point.

7.3 The gradient of a secant

- A **secant** is a straight line passing through two points on a curve.

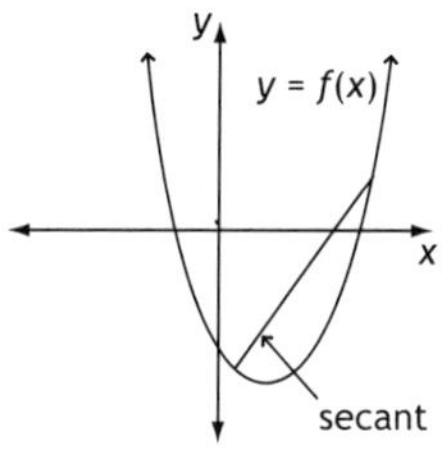

- The **gradient of a secant** to the curve $y = f(x)$, through $[c, f(c)]$ and $[x, f(x)]$ is given by:

$$m = \frac{f(x) - f(c)}{x - c}$$

- This formula comes directly from the formula for the gradient of a line:

$$m = \frac{y_2 - y_1}{x_2 - x_1}$$

Q Find the gradient of the secant to the curve: 6

a $y = f(x)$ through the points (1, 2) and (2, 16)

b $y = x^2$ passing through the points where $x = 0$ and $x = 5$

c $y = 2x^4 - 3x^2 + 5$ through $x = 3$ and $x = 4$

d $y = \dfrac{1}{x}$ passing through the points where $x = 2$ and $x = 6$

A a $y = f(x)$, $(1, 2)$, $(2, 16)$

$$\begin{aligned} m &= \frac{f(x) - f(c)}{x - c} \\ &= \frac{16 - 2}{2 - 1} \\ &= 14 \end{aligned}$$

$\therefore$ the gradient of the secant is 14

b $y = x^2$, $x = 0$, $x = 5$

$$\begin{aligned} m &= \frac{f(x) - f(c)}{x - c} \\ &= \frac{5^2 - 0^2}{5 - 0} \\ &= 5 \end{aligned}$$

$\therefore$ the gradient of the secant is 5

c $y = 2x^4 - 3x^2 + 5$, $x = 3$, $x = 4$

$$\begin{aligned} m &= \frac{f(x) - f(c)}{x - c} \\ &= \frac{(2 \times 4^4 - 3 \times 4^2 + 5) - (2 \times 3^4 - 3 \times 3^2 + 5)}{4 - 3} \\ &= 329 \end{aligned}$$

$\therefore$ the gradient of the secant is 329

Go to page 120 for Exercises

d $y = \frac{1}{x}, \quad x = 2, \quad x = 6$

$$m = \frac{f(x) - f(c)}{x - c}$$
$$= \frac{\frac{1}{6} - \frac{1}{2}}{6 - 2}$$
$$= -\frac{1}{12}$$

$\therefore$ the gradient of the secant is $-\frac{1}{12}$

7.4 The gradient of a tangent

- A **tangent to a curve** is a line which touches the curve in just one point.
- The **gradient of a secant** to a curve $y = f(x)$, through $(c, f(c))$ and $(x, f(x))$ is:

$$m = \frac{f(x) - f(c)}{x - c}.$$

As x gets closer and closer to c (from either side), the gradient of the secant becomes closer and closer to the gradient of the tangent at $(c, f(c))$.

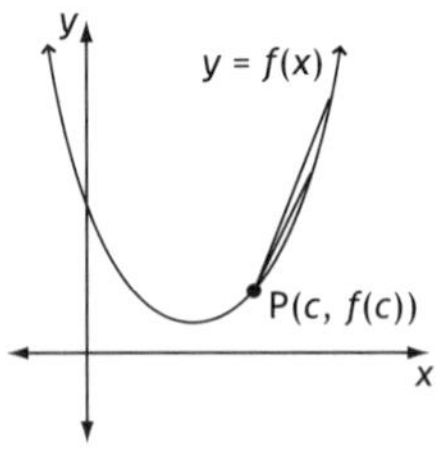

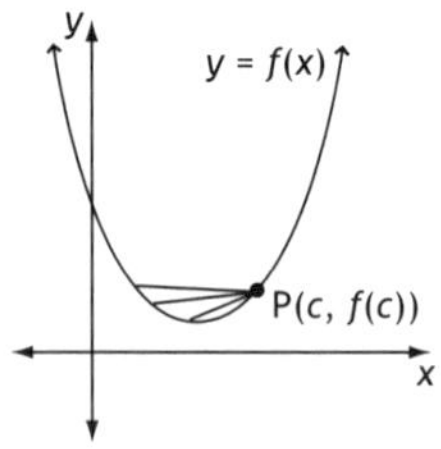

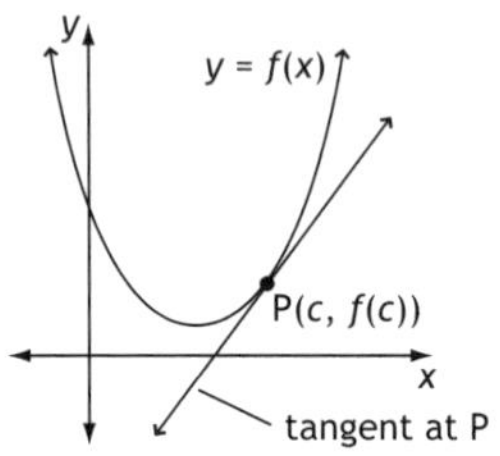

- The **tangent line** is the limiting position of the secant. The limiting value of the gradient of the secant at P is defined to be the gradient of the tangent at P, or simply the gradient of the curve at P.
- The **notation** $f'(c)$ is used to mean the gradient of the tangent to the curve $y = f(x)$ at $x = c$.

$$f'(c) = \lim_{x \to c} \frac{f(x) - f(c)}{x - c}$$

Q Find the gradient of the tangent to $y = x^2$ at the point where $x = 1$. Verify the answer with a sketch. 7

A
$$f'(c) = \lim_{x \to c} \frac{f(x) - f(c)}{x - c}$$
$$f'(1) = \lim_{x \to 1} \frac{f(x) - f(1)}{x - 1}$$
$$= \lim_{x \to 1} \frac{x^2 - 1^2}{x - 1}$$
$$= \lim_{x \to 1} \frac{(x-1)(x+1)}{x - 1}$$
$$= \lim_{x \to 1} (x + 1)$$
$$= 1 + 1$$
$$= 2$$

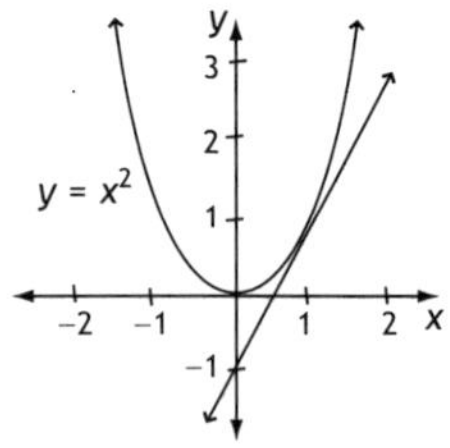

Q Find the gradient of the tangent to the curve $y = x^3$ at the point where $x = 2$. 8

A
$$f'(c) = \lim_{x \to c} \frac{f(x) - f(c)}{x - c}$$
$$f'(2) = \lim_{x \to 2} \frac{f(x) - f(2)}{x - 2}$$
$$= \lim_{x \to 2} \frac{x^3 - 2^3}{x - 2}$$
$$= \lim_{x \to 2} \frac{(x-2)(x^2 + 2x + 4)}{x - 2}$$
$$= \lim_{x \to 2} (x^2 + 2x + 4)$$
$$= 2^2 + 2 \times 2 + 4$$
$$= 12$$

7.5 The equation of the tangent

- Using $f'(c) = \lim_{x \to c} \frac{f(x) - f(c)}{x - c}$ we can find the **gradient** of a tangent to a curve at any point, provided it exists.
- To find the **equation of the tangent** we must simply find the equation of a straight line. We use the formula:

$$y - y_1 = m(x - x_1)$$

Q Find the equation of the tangent to the curve: 9

a $y = x^2 + 3x$ at $(1, 4)$ b $y = 1 - x^2$ when $x = 2$

A a $y = x^2 + 3x, \quad (1, 4)$

$$f'(c) = \lim_{x \to c} \frac{f(x) - f(c)}{x - c}$$
$$f'(1) = \lim_{x \to 1} \frac{f(x) - f(1)}{x - 1}$$

continued ...

Go to page 120 for Exercises

$$= \lim_{x \to 1} \frac{x^2 + 3x - 4}{x - 1}$$
$$= \lim_{x \to 1} \frac{(x-1)(x+4)}{x-1}$$
$$= \lim_{x \to 1}(x+4)$$
$$= 1 + 4$$
$$= 5$$

$m = 5,\ (1, 4)$

$$y - y_1 = m(x - x_1)$$
$$y - 4 = 5(x - 1)$$
$$y - 4 = 5x - 5$$
$$y = 5x - 1$$

$\therefore$ the equation of the tangent is $y = 5x - 1$

b $y = 1 - x^2$ when $x = 2$

$$f'(c) = \lim_{x \to c} \frac{f(x) - f(c)}{x - c}$$
$$f'(2) = \lim_{x \to 2} \frac{f(x) - f(2)}{x - 2}$$
$$= \lim_{x \to 2} \frac{1 - x^2 - (1 - 2^2)}{x - 2}$$
$$= \lim_{x \to 2} \frac{4 - x^2}{x - 2}$$
$$= \lim_{x \to 2} \frac{(2-x)(2+x)}{x-2}$$
$$= \lim_{x \to 2} -(2 + x)$$
$$= -(2 + 2)$$
$$= -4$$

When $x = 2$, $y = 1 - 2^2$
$$= -3$$

$m = -4,\ (2, -3)$

$$y - y_1 = m(x - x_1)$$
$$y - (-3) = -4(x - 2)$$
$$y + 3 = -4x + 8$$
$$y = -4x + 5$$

$\therefore$ the equation of the tangent is $y = -4x + 5$

- A **sketch of the curve** can verify the equation of the tangent.

Q Sketch each curve, showing the tangent at the given point: 10

a $y = x^2 + 3x$ at (1, 4)

b $y = 1 - x^2$ when $x = 2$

A a $y = x^2 + 3x$

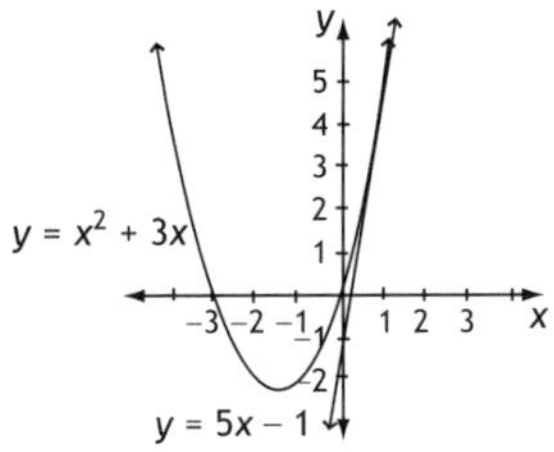

b $y = 1 - x^2$

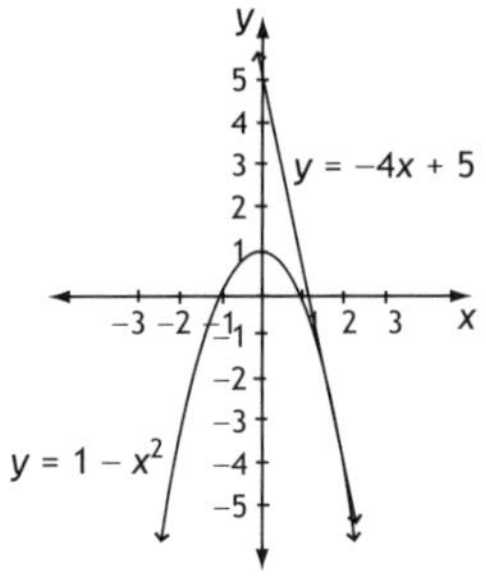

7.6 The derivative

- The **gradient** $f'(c)$ of the curve $y = f(x)$ at the point $P(c, f(c))$ is defined as:

$$\lim_{x \to c} \frac{f(x) - f(c)}{x - c} \text{ provided this limit exists.}$$

- $f'(c)$ is also known as the **derivative**, or differential coefficient, of $f(x)$ at $x = c$.
- The **derivative** $f'(c)$ can also be written in different forms:
  - If $x = c + h$, then $f(x) = f(c + h)$ and $x - c = h$ giving $f'(c) = \lim_{h \to 0} \frac{f(c+h) - f(c)}{h}$.
  - If $\Delta x = h$ and $\Delta y = f(c + h) - f(c)$ then $f'(c) = \lim_{\Delta x \to 0} \frac{\Delta y}{\Delta x}$.

You need to be familiar with the different expressions for $f'(c)$.

Q Find the derivative of the function: 11

a $f(x) = 2x^2 - 3x$ when $x = 4$

b $f(x) = x - x^2$ at $x = 3$

A a $f(x) = 2x^2 - 3x,\ x = 4$

$$f'(c) = \lim_{h \to 0} \frac{f(c+h) - f(c)}{h}$$
$$f'(4) = \lim_{h \to 0} \frac{f(4+h) - f(4)}{h}$$
$$= \lim_{h \to 0} \frac{2(4+h)^2 - 3(4+h) - (2 \times 4^2 - 3 \times 4)}{h}$$
$$= \lim_{h \to 0} \frac{32 + 16h + 2h^2 - 12 - 3h - 20}{h}$$

continued ...

Go to page 120 for Exercises

$$= \lim_{h \to 0} \frac{13h + 2h^2}{h}$$
$$= \lim_{h \to 0} (13 + 2h)$$
$$= 13$$

$\therefore$ the derivative of $f(x) = 2x^2 - 3x$ at $x = 4$ is 13

b $f(x) = x - x^2$ at $x = 3$

$$f'(c) = \lim_{h \to 0} \frac{f(c+h) - f(c)}{h}$$
$$f'(3) = \lim_{h \to 0} \frac{f(3+h) - f(3)}{h}$$
$$= \lim_{h \to 0} \frac{(3+h) - (3+h)^2 - (3 - 3^2)}{h}$$
$$= \lim_{h \to 0} \frac{3 + h - 9 - 6h - h^2 + 6}{h}$$
$$= \lim_{h \to 0} \frac{-5h - h^2}{h}$$
$$= \lim_{h \to 0} (-5 - h)$$
$$= -5$$

$\therefore$ the derivative of $f(x) = x - x^2$ at $x = 3$ is -5

- When **finding the derivative at a point**, we are finding the **gradient of the curve** at that point.

Q Find the derivative of $f(x) = 5x - 8$ at: 12

a $x = 1$ b $x = -3$ c $x = 9$

A a
$$f'(c) = \lim_{h \to 0} \frac{f(c+h) - f(c)}{h}$$
$$f'(1) = \lim_{h \to 0} \frac{f(1+h) - f(1)}{h}$$
$$= \lim_{h \to 0} \frac{5(1+h) - 8 - (5 \times 1 - 8)}{h}$$
$$= \lim_{h \to 0} \frac{5 + 5h - 8 + 3}{h}$$
$$= \lim_{h \to 0} \frac{5h}{h}$$
$$= 5$$

b
$$f'(c) = \lim_{h \to 0} \frac{f(c+h) - f(c)}{h}$$
$$f'(-3) = \lim_{h \to 0} \frac{f(-3+h) - f(-3)}{h}$$
$$= \lim_{h \to 0} \frac{5(-3+h) - 8 - (5 \times -3 - 8)}{h}$$
$$= \lim_{h \to 0} \frac{-15 + 5h - 8 + 23}{h}$$
$$= \lim_{h \to 0} \frac{5h}{h}$$
$$= 5$$

c
$$f'(c) = \lim_{h \to 0} \frac{f(c+h) - f(c)}{h}$$
$$f'(9) = \lim_{h \to 0} \frac{f(9+h) - f(9)}{h}$$
$$= \lim_{h \to 0} \frac{5(9+h) - 8 - (5 \times 9 - 8)}{h}$$
$$= \lim_{h \to 0} \frac{45 + 5h - 8 - 37}{h}$$
$$= \lim_{h \to 0} \frac{5h}{h}$$
$$= 5$$

$y = 5x - 8$ is a straight line with gradient 5 and y-intercept -8. The derivative of this fuction at any point will always be 5.

Go to page 120 for Exercises

7.7 The gradient function

- Most common curves have a tangent at every point in their domain. The derivative therefore exists at all of these points. We can use the definition of the gradient at a point to find an expression for the gradient at any point, the gradient function or derivative.
- We use the notations $f'(x)$ or $\frac{dy}{dx}$ for the gradient function.

Q Find the gradient function $f'(x)$ for the function $f(x) = x^2 + x$. 13

A
$$f(x) = x^2 + x$$
$$f'(c) = \lim_{x \to c} \frac{f(x) - f(c)}{x - c}$$
$$= \lim_{x \to c} \frac{x^2 + x - (c^2 + c)}{x - c}$$
$$= \lim_{x \to c} \frac{x^2 + x - c^2 - c}{x - c}$$
$$= \lim_{x \to c} \frac{x^2 - c^2 + x - c}{x - c}$$
$$= \lim_{x \to c} \frac{(x+c)(x-c) + x - c}{x - c}$$
$$= \lim_{x \to c} \frac{(x-c)(x+c+1)}{x - c}$$
$$= \lim_{x \to c} (x + c + 1)$$
$$= 2c + 1$$
$$\therefore f'(x) = 2x + 1$$

Q 14

a Find the gradient function for the curve $y = x^3 - 5$.

b Hence find the gradient of the tangent to the curve at the point where:

i $x = -1$ ii $x = 4$

A a $y = x^3 - 5$

$$f'(c) = \lim_{x \to c} \frac{f(x) - f(c)}{x - c}$$

$$= \lim_{x \to c} \frac{x^3 - 5 - (c^3 - 5)}{x - c}$$

$$= \lim_{x \to c} \frac{x^3 - c^3}{x - c}$$

$$= \lim_{x \to c} \frac{(x - c)(x^2 + cx + c^2)}{x - c}$$

$$= \lim_{x \to c} (x^2 + cx + c^2)$$

$$= c^2 + c^2 + c^2$$

$$= 3c^2$$

$$\therefore \frac{dy}{dx} = 3x^2$$

b i $\frac{dy}{dx} = 3x^2$

When $x = -1$, $\frac{dy}{dx} = 3(-1)^2$

$= 3$

When $x = -1$, the gradient of the tangent to the curve is 3.

ii $\frac{dy}{dx} = 3x^2$

When $x = 4$, $\frac{dy}{dx} = 3(4)^2$

$= 48$

When $x = 4$, the gradient of the tangent to the curve is 48.

Q 15

a Find the gradient function for the function $f(x) = x^2 + 1$.

b Draw sketches, on separate diagrams, of $y = f(x)$ and $y = f'(x)$.

c Explain the geometrical significance of these results.

A a $f(x) = x^2 + 1$

$$f'(c) = \lim_{x \to c} \frac{f(x) - f(c)}{x - c}$$

$$= \lim_{x \to c} \frac{x^2 + 1 - (c^2 + 1)}{x - c}$$

continued ...

$$= \lim_{x \to c} \frac{x^2 - c^2}{x - c}$$

$$= \lim_{x \to c} \frac{(x + c)(x - c)}{x - c}$$

$$= \lim_{x \to c} (x + c)$$

$$= c + c$$

$$= 2c$$

$$\therefore f'(x) = 2x$$

b

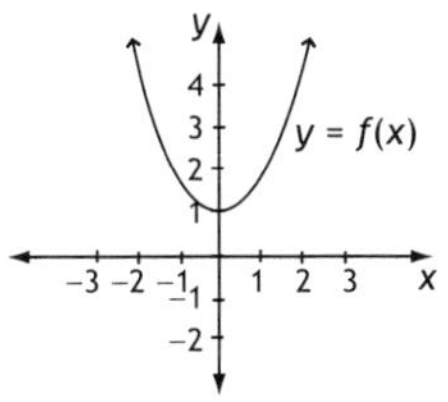

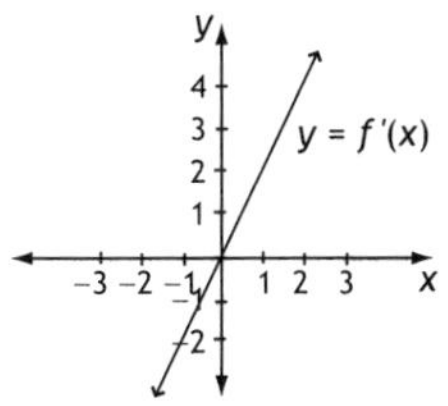

c The graph of $y = f'(x)$ shows the gradient of the curve at every point. From the graph of $y = f'(x)$ we can immediately see certain things about the relationship between the curve $y = x^2 + 1$ and its gradient at any point. For example, the gradient is positive when $x > 0$, where the graph is increasing. The gradient is negative when $x < 0$, when the curve is decreasing and is zero at $x = 0$, when the curve reaches its minimum value.

- If $f(x)$ has a derivative for every point in its domain, it is said to be a differentiable function. If $f(x)$ is said to be differentiable, it has a derivative for each point in its domain. **Differentiating from first principles** means finding the gradient function by using either:

$$f'(c) = \lim_{x \to c} \frac{f(x) - f(c)}{x - c}$$

or

$$f'(c) = \lim_{h \to 0} \frac{f(c + h) - f(c)}{h}$$

Q 16

Find, from first principles, the derivative of $f(x) = 7x - 2x^2$.

A $f(x) = 7x - 2x^2$

$$f'(c) = \lim_{h \to 0} \frac{f(c + h) - f(c)}{h}$$

$$= \lim_{h \to 0} \frac{7(c + h) - 2(c + h)^2 - (7c - 2c^2)}{h}$$

$$= \lim_{h \to 0} \frac{7c + 7h - 2(c^2 + 2ch + h^2) - 7c + 2c^2}{h}$$

continued ...

Go to page 120 for Exercises

$$= \lim_{h \to 0} \frac{7c + 7h - 2c^2 - 4ch - 2h^2 - 7c + 2c^2}{h}$$
$$= \lim_{h \to 0} \frac{7h - 4ch - 2h^2}{h}$$
$$= \lim_{h \to 0} \frac{h(7 - 4c - 2h)}{h}$$
$$= \lim_{h \to 0} (7 - 4c - 2h)$$
$$= 7 - 4c$$
$$\therefore f'(x) = 7 - 4x$$

7.8 The derivative of x^n

- From the **derivative from first principles**, we find that:

$$\text{if } y = x^2, \ \frac{dy}{dx} = 2x \qquad \text{if } y = x^3, \ \frac{dy}{dx} = 3x^2$$
$$\text{if } y = x^4, \ \frac{dy}{dx} = 4x^3 \qquad \text{if } y = x^5, \ \frac{dy}{dx} = 5x^4$$

From these results you might be able to see that a pattern is forming. We have a **rule** which we can use whenever n is a positive integer:

$$\text{If } y = x^n, \ \frac{dy}{dx} = nx^{n-1}$$

Q Differentiate: 17

a $y = x^6$ b $y = x^9$

c $y = x^{13}$ d $f(x) = x^{25}$

A a $y = x^6$, $\frac{dy}{dx} = 6x^5$ b $y = x^9$, $\frac{dy}{dx} = 9x^8$

c $y = x^{13}$, $\frac{dy}{dx} = 13x^{12}$ d $f(x) = x^{25}$, $f'(x) = 25x^{24}$

- We can use this rule for obtaining the derivative when **finding the gradient or equation of a tangent** to a curve.

Q Find the gradient of the tangent to the curve $y = x^3$ at the point where $x = 1$. 18

A $y = x^3$

$\frac{dy}{dx} = 3x^2$

When $x = 1$, $\frac{dy}{dx} = 3 \times 1^2$

$= 3$

$\therefore$ the gradient of the tangent is 3

Q Find the equation of the tangent to the curve $y = x^2$ at the point (2, 4). 19

A $y = x^2$

$\frac{dy}{dx} = 2x$

When $x = 2$, $\frac{dy}{dx} = 2 \times 2$

$= 4$

$\therefore$ the gradient of the tangent is 4 (i.e. $m = 4$)

$(2, 4)$, $m = 4$

$y - y_1 = m(x - x_1)$

$y - 4 = 4(x - 2)$

$y - 4 = 4x - 8$

$y = 4x - 4$

$\therefore$ the equation of the tangent is $y = 4x - 4$

- These results can be verified by **drawing the graphs** of the functions showing the tangent at the given points:

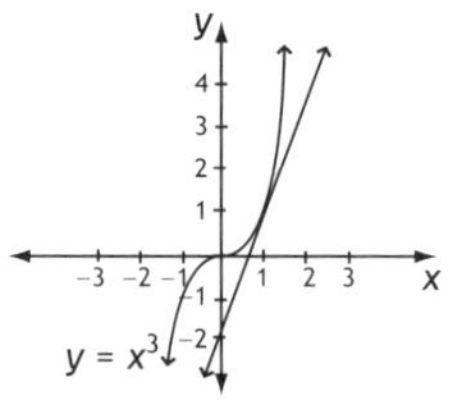

Gradient of tangent is 3

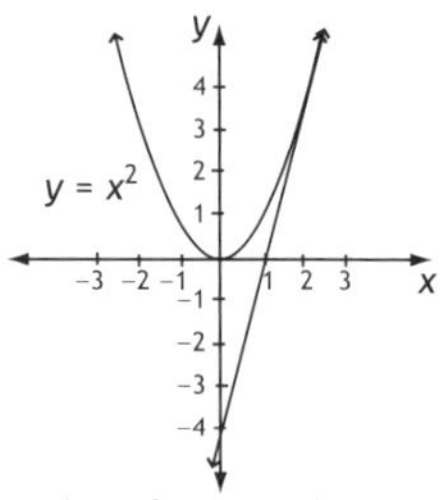

Equation of tangent is $y = 4x - 4$

7.9 Some rules for working with differentiation

- The **derivative of any constant** is 0. If c is a constant, $y = c$ is a straight line parallel to the x-axis. The gradient at any point on the line is 0.

Q Differentiate: 20

a $y = 6$ b $f(x) = 17$

c $f(x) = -3$ d $y = 0$

A a $y = 6$, $\frac{dy}{dx} = 0$ b $f(x) = 17$, $f'(x) = 0$

c $f(x) = -3$, $f'(x) = 0$ d $y = 0$, $\frac{dy}{dx} = 0$

- The **derivative of a sum** (or difference) is the sum (or difference) of the derivatives.

Go to page 121 for Exercises

Q Differentiate: 21

a $y = x^3 + x^2$

b $f(x) = 9 - x^4$

c $y = x^5 - x^2 - x$

d $f(x) = x^8 + x^7 + x^5 - x^2 - 1$

A a $y = x^3 + x^2$

$\frac{dy}{dx} = 3x^2 + 2x$

b $f(x) = 9 - x^4$

$f'(x) = 0 - 4x^3$

$= -4x^3$

c $y = x^5 - x^2 - x$

$\frac{dy}{dx} = 5x^4 - 2x - 1$

d $f(x) = x^8 + x^7 + x^5 - x^2 - 1$

$f'(x) = 8x^7 + 7x^6 + 5x^4 - 2x$

- If a **term is multiplied by a constant**, the derivative will also be multiplied by that constant.

Q Find the derivative of: 22

a $y = 5x$ b $y = 7x^2$

c $y = -x^8$ d $f(x) = 72x^{37}$

A a $y = 5x$

$\frac{dy}{dx} = 5 \times 1$

$= 5$

b $y = 7x^2$

$\frac{dy}{dx} = 7 \times 2x$

$= 14x$

c $y = -x^8$

$\frac{dy}{dx} = -1 \times 8x^7$

$= -8x^7$

d $f(x) = 72x^{37}$

$f'(x) = 72 \times 37x^{36}$

$= 2664x^{36}$

It is not necessary to show the middle step.

Q Differentiate: 23

a $f(x) = 3x^2 - 7x + 2$

b $f(x) = -4x^5 - 3x^4 + 6x^3 - 9x^2$

c $y = 5 - 6x - 3x^3$

d $y = x^7 - 7x^6$

A a $f(x) = 3x^2 - 7x + 2$

$f'(x) = 6x - 7$

b $f(x) = -4x^5 - 3x^4 + 6x^3 - 9x^2$

$f'(x) = -20x^4 - 12x^3 + 18x^2 - 18x$

c $y = 5 - 6x - 3x^3$

$\frac{dy}{dx} = -6 - 9x^2$

d $y = x^7 - 7x^6$

$\frac{dy}{dx} = 7x^6 - 42x^5$

7.10 A normal to a curve

- A **normal** to a curve at a point is perpendicular to the tangent at that point.

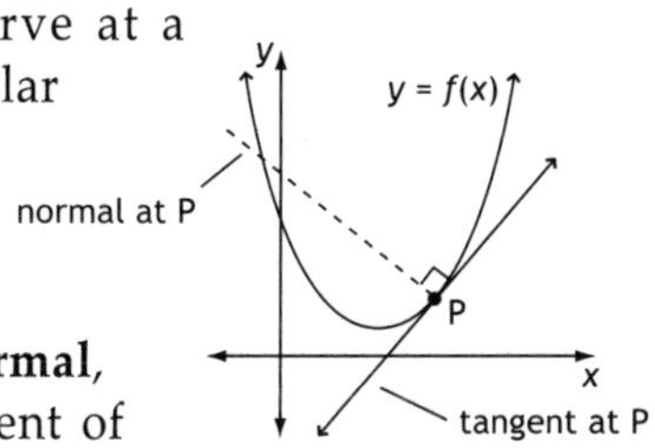

- To find the **gradient of the normal**, first find the gradient of the tangent, and use the fact that if two lines are perpendicular, then their gradients, m_1 and m_2, are such that $\boldsymbol{m_1 m_2 = -1}$.

Q Find the equation of the normal to the curve: 24

a $y = x^3 + 1$ at the point (1, 2)

b $y = 4x^2 - x$ at the point where $x = -1$

A a $y = x^3 + 1$

$\frac{dy}{dx} = 3x^2$

When $x = 1$, $\frac{dy}{dx} = 3 \times 1^2$

$= 3$

$\therefore$ the gradient of the tangent is 3

$\therefore$ the gradient of the normal is $-\frac{1}{3}$

$m = -\frac{1}{3}$, $(1, 2)$

$y - y_1 = m(x - x_1)$

$y - 2 = -\frac{1}{3}(x - 1)$

$3(y - 2) = -(x - 1)$

$3y - 6 = -x + 1$

$x + 3y - 7 = 0$

$\therefore$ the equation of the normal at $(1, 2)$ is $x + 3y - 7 = 0$

b $y = 4x^2 - x$

$\frac{dy}{dx} = 8x - 1$

When $x = -1$, $\frac{dy}{dx} = (8 \times -1) - 1$

$= -9$

$\therefore$ the gradient of the tangent is -9

continued ...

Go to page 121 for Exercises

$\therefore$ the gradient of the normal is $\frac{1}{9}$

$y = 4x^2 - x$

When $x = -1$, $y = 4 \times (-1)^2 - (-1)$
$= 5$

$m = \frac{1}{9}$, $(-1, 5)$

$$y - y_1 = m(x - x_1)$$
$$y - 5 = \frac{1}{9}(x - (-1))$$
$$9(y - 5) = (x + 1)$$
$$9y - 45 = x + 1$$
$$x - 9y + 46 = 0$$

$\therefore$ the equation of the normal is $x - 9y + 46 = 0$

7.11 Notations

- The notations $\frac{dy}{dx}$, y', $f'(x)$ and $\frac{d}{dx}(f(x))$ are all used for the derivative.

Q Differentiate: **25**

a $y = 3x^4 - 9x^3 + 7x^2 + 5$

b $f(x) = 2x^8 + 5x^5 - 4x$

c $1 - x - x^2$

A a $y = 3x^4 - 9x^3 + 7x^2 + 5$
$y' = 12x^3 - 27x^2 + 14x$

b $f(x) = 2x^8 + 5x^5 - 4x$
$f'(x) = 16x^7 + 25x^4 - 4$

c $\frac{d}{dx}(1 - x - x^2) = -1 - 2x$

- $\frac{dy}{dx}$ means 'the derivative of y with respect to x'. This notation will change with functions involving different variables.

Q Differentiate with respect to t: **26**

a $y = t^3 - 3t^2$ b $x = -5t^6 + 2t - 8$

A a $y = t^3 - 3t^2$
$\frac{dy}{dt} = 3t^2 - 6t$

b $x = -5t^6 + 2t - 8$
$\frac{dx}{dt} = -30t^5 + 2$

Q Differentiate: **27**

a $u = x^9 - 4$ with respect to x

b $a = y^3 - y^2 + y - 1$ with respect to y

c $m = n^4 - 4n^3 + 6n^2 - 4n + 1$ with respect to n

A a $u = x^9 - 4$
$\frac{du}{dx} = 9x^8$

b $a = y^3 - y^2 + y - 1$
$\frac{da}{dy} = 3y^2 - 2y + 1$

c $m = n^4 - 4n^3 + 6n^2 - 4n + 1$
$\frac{dm}{dn} = 4n^3 - 12n^2 + 12n - 4$

- $\frac{d}{dx}(f(x))$ means 'the derivative, with respect to x, of the function'.

Q Find: **28**

a $\frac{d}{dt}(2t^2 - 5t)$ b $\frac{d}{dv}(-v^6 - 5v^4)$

A a $\frac{d}{dt}(2t^2 - 5t) = 4t - 5$

b $\frac{d}{dv}(-v^6 - 5v^4) = -6v^5 - 20v^3$

Q If: **29**

a $g(x) = 9x^2 + 17$, find $g'(x)$

b $h(t) = 1 - t - 2t^2$, find $h'(t)$

c $p(q) = -7q^6 + 18q^3 - 56q^2$, find $p'(q)$

A a $g(x) = 9x^2 + 17$
$g'(x) = 18x$

b $h(t) = 1 - t - 2t^2$
$h'(t) = -1 - 4t$

c $p(q) = -7q^6 + 18q^3 - 56q^2$
$p'(q) = -42q^5 + 54q^2 - 112q$

✔ Take care with the setting out. A function is not generally equal to its derivative. If $y = x^2$, $\frac{dy}{dx} = 2x$. Don't write $x^2 = 2x$.

7.12 The derivative of x^{-n}

- The derivative of $\frac{1}{x}$ can be found from **first principles**.

$$f(x) = \frac{1}{x}$$

$$f'(c) = \lim_{h \to 0} \frac{f(c+h) - f(c)}{h}$$

continued ...

Go to page 121 for Exercises

$$= \lim_{h\to 0} \frac{\frac{1}{c+h} - \frac{1}{c}}{h}$$

$$= \lim_{h\to 0} \frac{\frac{c-(c+h)}{c(c+h)}}{h}$$

$$= \lim_{h\to 0} \left[\frac{-h}{c(c+h)} \times \frac{1}{h}\right]$$

$$= \lim_{h\to 0} \frac{-1}{c(c+h)}$$

$$= \frac{-1}{c^2}$$

$$\therefore f'(x) = \frac{-1}{x^2}$$

But $\frac{1}{x} = x^{-1}$ and $\frac{d}{dx}\left(x^{-1}\right) = -x^{-2}$

This obeys the general law that we use when n is a positive integer:

$$\frac{d}{dx}\left(x^n\right) = nx^{n-1}$$

This law also works when n is a negative integer.

Q Differentiate: **30**

a x^{-5} b $x^{-4} + x$

c $2x^{-9}$ d $1 - x^{-6}$

A a $y = x^{-5}$

$y' = -5x^{-6}$

b $y = x^{-4} + x$

$y' = -4x^{-5} + 1$

c $y = 2x^{-9}$

$y' = -18x^{-10}$

d $y = 1 - x^{-6}$

$y' = -\left(-6x^{-7}\right)$

$= 6x^{-7}$

In general, when differentiating we should give the answer in the same form as the question. If the question was in index form leave the answer in index form. If the question is in fractional form, change the answer back to fractional form.

Q Differentiate: **31**

a $\frac{1}{x^2}$ b $f(x) = \frac{4}{x} - \frac{1}{x^3}$

A a $f(x) = \frac{1}{x^2}$

$= x^{-2}$

$f'(x) = -2x^{-3}$

$= \frac{-2}{x^3}$

b $f(x) = \frac{4}{x} - \frac{1}{x^3}$

$= 4x^{-1} - x^{-3}$

$f'(x) = 4 \times -x^{-2} - \left(-3x^{-4}\right)$

$= -4x^{-2} + 3x^{-4}$

$= -\frac{4}{x^2} + \frac{3}{x^4} \quad \left[= \frac{3 - 4x^2}{x^4}\right]$

7.13 The derivative of $x^{\frac{1}{2}}$

- When finding a derivative from first principles we often need to use 'tricks' in order to find the required limit. In **using first principles** to find the derivative of $x^{\frac{1}{2}}$ we use the result of a difference of two squares:

$a^2 - b^2 = (a-b)(a+b)$ and apply it to $x - c$.

$$x - c = \left(x^{\frac{1}{2}} - c^{\frac{1}{2}}\right)\left(x^{\frac{1}{2}} + c^{\frac{1}{2}}\right)$$

$$f(x) = x^{\frac{1}{2}}$$

$$f'(x) = \lim_{x\to c} \frac{f(x) - f(c)}{x - c}$$

$$= \lim_{x\to c} \frac{x^{\frac{1}{2}} - c^{\frac{1}{2}}}{x - c}$$

$$= \lim_{x\to c} \frac{x^{\frac{1}{2}} - c^{\frac{1}{2}}}{\left(x^{\frac{1}{2}} - c^{\frac{1}{2}}\right)\left(x^{\frac{1}{2}} + c^{\frac{1}{2}}\right)}$$

$$= \lim_{x\to c} \frac{1}{x^{\frac{1}{2}} + c^{\frac{1}{2}}}$$

$$= \frac{1}{2c^{\frac{1}{2}}}$$

$$\therefore f'(x) = \frac{1}{2x^{\frac{1}{2}}}$$

But $\frac{1}{2x^{\frac{1}{2}}} = \frac{1}{2}x^{-\frac{1}{2}}$

- The rule $\frac{d}{dx}\left(x^n\right) = nx^{n-1}$ can be extended to include all rational values of n.

Q Differentiate: **32**

a $y = x^{2.9}$ b $y = 6\sqrt{x}$ c $y = \sqrt[3]{x^2}$

A a $y = x^{2.9}$

$\frac{dy}{dx} = 2.9x^{1.9}$

Go to page 121 for Exercises

b
$$y = 6\sqrt{x} = 6x^{\frac{1}{2}}$$
$$\frac{dy}{dx} = 6 \times \frac{1}{2}x^{-\frac{1}{2}} = 3x^{-\frac{1}{2}} = \frac{3}{\sqrt{x}}$$

c
$$y = \sqrt[3]{x^2} = x^{\frac{2}{3}}$$
$$\frac{dy}{dx} = \frac{2}{3}x^{\frac{2}{3}-1} = \frac{2}{3}x^{-\frac{1}{3}} = \frac{2}{3\sqrt[3]{x}}$$

Write the function in simplest index form before differentiating.

Q Differentiate: 33

a $f(x) = \dfrac{1}{\sqrt[5]{x}}$ b $f(x) = x\sqrt{x}$

A a
$$f(x) = \frac{1}{\sqrt[5]{x}} = x^{-\frac{1}{5}}$$
$$f'(x) = -\frac{1}{5}x^{-\frac{6}{5}} = -\frac{1}{5\sqrt[5]{x^6}}$$

b
$$f(x) = x\sqrt{x} = x^1 \times x^{\frac{1}{2}} = x^{\frac{3}{2}}$$
$$f'(x) = \frac{3}{2}x^{\frac{1}{2}} = \frac{3\sqrt{x}}{2}$$

7.14 The composite function rule

This is also known as the **chain rule** or as finding the derivative of a **function of a function**.

- If $y = f(u)$ where $u = f(x)$ then:

$$\frac{dy}{dx} = \frac{dy}{du} \times \frac{du}{dx}$$

Q Differentiate $y = (3x+2)^2$. 34

A
$y = u^2$ where $u = 3x + 2$

$\dfrac{dy}{du} = 2u$ $\dfrac{du}{dx} = 3$

$$\frac{dy}{dx} = 2u \times 3 = 6u = 6(3x+2)$$

In practice we don't usually write down all those steps!

Q Differentiate $y = (x^2 - 2)^2$ 35

a by expanding
b by the chain rule

A a
$$y = (x^2-2)^2 = x^4 - 4x^2 + 4$$
$$\frac{dy}{dx} = 4x^3 - 8x$$

b
$$y = (x^2-2)^2$$
$$\frac{dy}{dx} = 2(x^2-2) \times \frac{d}{dx}(x^2-2) = 2(x^2-2) \times 2x = 4x(x^2-2) = 4x^3 - 8x$$

Q Differentiate: 36

a $y = (2x-1)^5$ b $y = (x^2 - 2x + 3)^9$

A a
$$y = (2x-1)^5$$
$$\frac{dy}{dx} = 5(2x-1)^4 \times \frac{d}{dx}(2x-1) = 5(2x-1)^4 \times 2 = 10(2x-1)^4$$

b
$$y = (x^2-2x+3)^9$$
$$\frac{dy}{dx} = 9(x^2-2x+3)^8 \times \frac{d}{dx}(x^2-2x+3) = 9(x^2-2x+3)^8 \times (2x-2) = 18(x-1)(x^2-2x+3)^8$$

- We make use of the index rules when differentiating **square roots and reciprocals**.

Q Differentiate: 37

a $y = \sqrt{x^2-9}$ b $y = \dfrac{1}{7-3x}$

A a
$$y = \sqrt{x^2-9} = (x^2-9)^{\frac{1}{2}}$$
$$\frac{dy}{dx} = \frac{1}{2}(x^2-9)^{-\frac{1}{2}} \times \frac{d}{dx}(x^2-9) = \frac{1}{2} \times \frac{1}{\sqrt{x^2-9}} \times 2x = \frac{x}{\sqrt{x^2-9}}$$

Go to pages 121 and 122 for Exercises

b $y = \frac{1}{7-3x}$

$= (7-3x)^{-1}$

$\frac{dy}{dx} = -(7-3x)^{-2} \times \frac{d}{dx}(7-3x)$

$= -(7-3x)^{-2} \times -3$

$= \frac{3}{(7-3x)^2}$

Many mistakes in differentiating result from failure to properly use the composite function rule. Take care whenever you are differentiating a function of a function.

7.15 The product rule

- When differentiating a function which is the **product of two other functions**, the result is not the same as the product of the derivatives.

If $y = x^3$ $\quad$ If $y = x$ $\quad$ If $y = x^2$

$\frac{dy}{dx} = 3x^2$ $\quad$ $\frac{dy}{dx} = 1$ $\quad$ $\frac{dy}{dx} = 2x$

Now $\quad x^3 = x \times x^2$

but $\quad 3x^2 \neq 1 \times 2x$

- One way to differentiate products is to expand, where possible.

Q Differentiate by first expanding: **38**

a $y = x(x^2+3)$ $\quad$ **b** $y = (x+4)(x+3)$

A **a** $y = x(x^2+3)$

$= x^3 + 3x$

$\frac{dy}{dx} = 3x^2 + 3$

b $y = (x+4)(x+3)$

$= x^2 + 7x + 12$

$\frac{dy}{dx} = 2x + 7$

Notice that the results were not the product of the derivatives of the separate parts.

- There is a **rule** for differentiating products. If $y = uv$ then:

$$\frac{dy}{dx} = u\frac{dv}{dx} + v\frac{du}{dx}$$

Q Differentiate by the product rule: **39**

a $y = x(x^2+3)$ $\quad$ **b** $y = (x+4)(x+3)$

A **a** $y = x(x^2+3)$

Let $u = x,\ v = x^2+3$

$\frac{dy}{dx} = u\frac{dv}{dx} + v\frac{du}{dx}$

$= x \times \frac{d}{dx}(x^2+3) + (x^2+3) \times \frac{d}{dx}(x)$

$= x \times 2x + (x^2+3) \times 1$

$= 2x^2 + x^2 + 3$

$= 3x^2 + 3$

b $y = (x+4)(x+3)$

Let $u = x+4,\ v = x+3$

$\frac{dy}{dx} = u\frac{dv}{dx} + v\frac{du}{dx}$

$= (x+4) \times \frac{d}{dx}(x+3) + (x+3) \times \frac{d}{dx}(x+4)$

$= (x+4) \times 1 + (x+3) \times 1$

$= x + 4 + x + 3$

$= 2x + 7$

For very simple products, the product rule is more cumbersome than first expanding then differentiating. When the products are complex, however, the product rule should be used.

Q Differentiate:

a $y = (3x^2+7x-5)(8x-1)$

b $y = (x^2+x-1)(x^2+1)$

A **a** $y = (3x^2+7x-5)(8x-1)$

$\frac{dy}{dx} = u\frac{dv}{dx} + v\frac{du}{dx}$

$= (3x^2+7x-5) \times \frac{d}{dx}(8x-1)$

$+ (8x-1) \times \frac{d}{dx}(3x^2+7x-5)$

$= (3x^2+7x-5) \times 8 + (8x-1) \times (6x+7)$

$= 24x^2 + 56x - 40 + 48x^2 + 50x - 7$

$= 72x^2 + 106x - 47$

b $y = (x^2+x-1)(x^2+1)$

$\frac{dy}{dx} = u\frac{dv}{dx} + v\frac{du}{dx}$

$= (x^2+x-1) \times \frac{d}{dx}(x^2+1)$

$+ (x^2+1) \times \frac{d}{dx}(x^2+x-1)$

continued ...

Go to page 122 for Exercises

$$= (x^2 + x - 1) \times 2x + (x^2 + 1) \times (2x + 1)$$
$$= 2x^3 + 2x^2 - 2x + 2x^3 + x^2 + 2x + 1$$
$$= 4x^3 + 3x^2 + 1$$

- The product rule only needs to be used where the expression to be differentiated is the product of two or more functions. It is not necessary to use the product rule when the product involves a constant and a function. The product rule will give the correct answer but is longer and more involved than straight differentiation.

7.16 Combinations of the product rule and the composite function rule

- Many expressions that need to be differentiated involve **products of composite functions**.

Q Differentiate: 41

a $y = x(x^2 + 5)^4$

b $y = x^2(3x - 1)^7$

c $y = 2x\sqrt{x + 1}$

A a
$$y = x(x^2 + 5)^4$$
$$\frac{dy}{dx} = u\frac{dv}{dx} + v\frac{du}{dx}$$
$$= x \times \frac{d}{dx}(x^2 + 5)^4 + (x^2 + 5)^4 \times \frac{d}{dx}(x)$$
$$= x \times 4(x^2 + 5)^3 \times 2x + (x^2 + 5)^4 \times 1$$
$$= 8x^2(x^2 + 5)^3 + (x^2 + 5)^4$$
$$= (x^2 + 5)^3[8x^2 + (x^2 + 5)]$$
$$= (x^2 + 5)^3(9x^2 + 5)$$

b
$$y = x^2(3x - 1)^7$$
$$\frac{dy}{dx} = u\frac{dv}{dx} + v\frac{du}{dx}$$
$$= x^2 \times \frac{d}{dx}(3x - 1)^7 + (3x - 1)^7 \times \frac{d}{dx}(x^2)$$
$$= x^2 \times 7(3x - 1)^6 \times 3 + (3x - 1)^7 \times 2x$$
$$= 21x^2(3x - 1)^6 + 2x(3x - 1)^7$$
$$= x(3x - 1)^6[21x + 2(3x - 1)]$$
$$= x(3x - 1)^6(27x - 2)$$

c
$$y = 2x\sqrt{x + 1}$$
$$= 2x(x + 1)^{\frac{1}{2}}$$
$$\frac{dy}{dx} = u\frac{dv}{dx} + v\frac{du}{dx}$$
$$= 2x \times \frac{d}{dx}(x + 1)^{\frac{1}{2}} + (x + 1)^{\frac{1}{2}} \times \frac{d}{dx}(2x)$$
$$= 2x \times \frac{1}{2}(x + 1)^{-\frac{1}{2}} \times 1 + (x + 1)^{\frac{1}{2}} \times 2$$
$$= \frac{x}{\sqrt{x + 1}} + 2\sqrt{x + 1}$$
$$= \frac{x}{\sqrt{x + 1}} + \frac{2(x + 1)}{\sqrt{x + 1}}$$
$$= \frac{3x + 2}{\sqrt{x + 1}}$$

7.17 The quotient rule

- Whenever **one function is divided by another**, we use the quotient rule to find the derivative.

If $y = \frac{u}{v}$ (where u and v are functions of x) then:

$$\frac{dy}{dx} = \frac{v\frac{du}{dx} - u\frac{dv}{dx}}{v^2}$$

Q Use the quotient rule to differentiate: 42

a $y = \frac{1}{2x}$

b $y = \frac{x + 1}{x + 2}$

A a
$$y = \frac{1}{2x}$$
$$u = 1, \; v = 2x$$
$$\frac{dy}{dx} = \frac{v\frac{du}{dx} - u\frac{dv}{dx}}{v^2}$$
$$= \frac{2x \times 0 - 1 \times 2}{(2x)^2}$$
$$= \frac{-2}{4x^2}$$
$$= \frac{-1}{2x^2}$$

This function can be easily differentiated if written as $\frac{1}{2}x^{-1}$ or differentiated by the composite function rule writing $y = (2x)^{-1}$.

Go to page 122 for Exercises

b $y = \frac{x+1}{x+2}$

$u = x+1,\ v = x+2$

$$\frac{dy}{dx} = \frac{v\frac{du}{dx} - u\frac{dv}{dx}}{v^2}$$

$$= \frac{(x+2)\times 1 - (x+1)\times 1}{(x+2)^2}$$

$$= \frac{x+2-x-1}{(x+2)^2}$$

$$= \frac{1}{(x+2)^2}$$

Q Differentiate: 43

a $y = \frac{x}{x^2+1}$ b $y = \frac{x^3+2}{3x}$

A a $y = \frac{x}{x^2+1}$

$$\frac{dy}{dx} = \frac{v\frac{du}{dx} - u\frac{dv}{dx}}{v^2}$$

$$= \frac{(x^2+1)\times 1 - x\times 2x}{(x^2+1)^2}$$

$$= \frac{x^2+1-2x^2}{(x^2+1)^2}$$

$$= \frac{1-x^2}{(x^2+1)^2}$$

b $y = \frac{x^3+2}{3x}$

$$\frac{dy}{dx} = \frac{v\frac{du}{dx} - u\frac{dv}{dx}}{v^2}$$

$$= \frac{3x\times 3x^2 - (x^3+2)\times 3}{(3x)^2}$$

$$= \frac{9x^3-3x^3-6}{9x^2}$$

$$= \frac{6(x^3-1)}{9x^2}$$

$$= \frac{2(x^3-1)}{3x^2}$$

7.18 Combinations of the quotient rule and the composite function rule

- Some expressions that we need to differentiate involve **quotients of composite functions**.

Q Differentiate: 44

a $y = \frac{(2x+3)^4}{x}$ b $y = \frac{x-1}{(3x-1)^2}$

A a $y = \frac{(2x+3)^4}{x}$

$$\frac{dy}{dx} = \frac{v\frac{du}{dx} - u\frac{dv}{dx}}{v^2}$$

$$= \frac{x\times 4(2x+3)^3\times 2 - (2x+3)^4\times 1}{x^2}$$

$$= \frac{8x(2x+3)^3 - (2x+3)^4}{x^2}$$

$$= \frac{(2x+3)^3[8x-(2x+3)]}{x^2}$$

$$= \frac{(2x+3)^3(6x-3)}{x^2}$$

$$= \frac{3(2x+3)^3(2x-1)}{x^2}$$

b $y = \frac{x-1}{(3x-1)^2}$

$$\frac{dy}{dx} = \frac{v\frac{du}{dx} - u\frac{dv}{dx}}{v^2}$$

$$= \frac{(3x-1)^2\times 1 - (x-1)\times 2(3x-1)\times 3}{\left[(3x-1)^2\right]^2}$$

$$= \frac{(3x-1)^2 - 6(x-1)(3x-1)}{(3x-1)^4}$$

$$= \frac{(3x-1)[3x-1-6(x-1)]}{(3x-1)^4}$$

$$= \frac{3x-1-6x+6}{(3x-1)^3}$$

$$= \frac{-3x+5}{(3x-1)^3}$$

Go to page 122 for Exercises

Exercises The Tangent to a Curve and the Derivative of a Function

Note: Questions 7 to 16 are intended to be answered using first principles.

1 Find:

a $\lim_{x \to 2}(4x - 1)$ b $\lim_{x \to 3}(1 - x^2)$

c $\lim_{x \to -1}(3 + 5x)$

2 Find:

a $\lim_{x \to 4} \frac{x^2 - 16}{x - 4}$ b $\lim_{h \to 0} \frac{h^2 - 16h}{h}$

c $\lim_{x \to 10} \frac{x^2 - 16x + 60}{x^2 - 6x - 40}$

3 Find:

a $\lim_{x \to -\infty} \frac{3}{x}$ b $\lim_{x \to \infty} \frac{1 - x^2}{x^2}$

4 State whether the following curves are continuous or discontinuous:

a
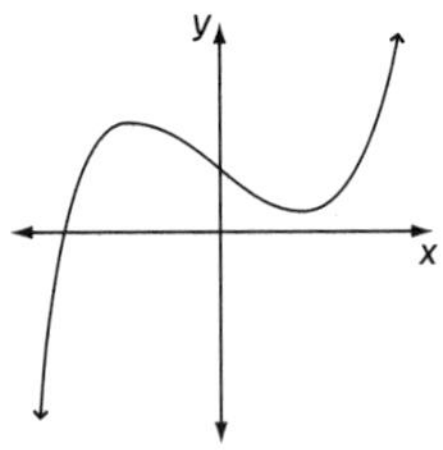

b
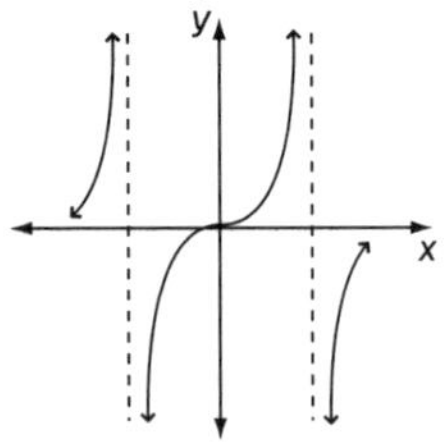

c
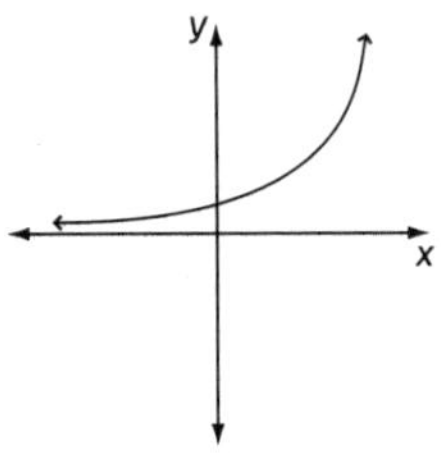

d
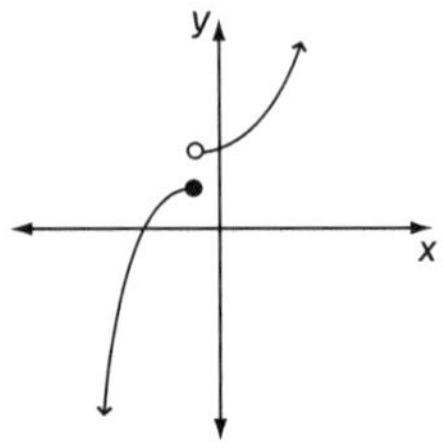

5 Determine whether the following functions are continuous at $x = 3$:

a $f(x) = \frac{x^2 - 9}{x - 3}$ b $f(x) = 2x^2 + 7$

c $f(x) = \begin{cases} x^2 - 8 & \text{if } x > 3 \\ 1 & \text{if } x = 3 \\ 2x - 5 & \text{if } x < 3 \end{cases}$

d $f(x) = \frac{x^2 + 2x - 15}{x + 5}$

6 Find the gradient of the secant to the curve:

a $y = f(x)$ through (2, 5) and (5, 11)

b $y = x^3$ through the points where $x = 1$ and $x = 2$

c $y = x^2 - x$ through the points where $x = -1$ and $x = 3$

7 Find the gradient of the tangent to the curve $y = x^2$ at the point where $x = -1$. Show the curve and tangent on a sketch.

8 Find the gradient of the tangent to the curve $y = 3 - x^2$ at the point where $x = 1$.

9 Find the equation of the tangent to the curve:

a $y = x^3$ at $(-1, -1)$ b $y = 2x^2$ at $x = 1$

10 Sketch both of the curves in Question 9, showing the tangent.

11 Find the derivative of the function:

a $f(x) = 4x^2$ when $x = 2$

b $f(x) = x^2 + 2x$ at $x = 5$

c $f(x) = 1 - x^3$ when $x = 0$

12 Find the derivative of $f(x) = 7 - 2x$ at:

a $x = 1$ b $x = 4$

c $x = -2$

13 Find the gradient function $f'(x)$ for the function:

a $f(x) = x^2$ b $f(x) = x - x^2$

c $f(x) = x^3 + x$

14 a Find the gradient function for the curve $y = x^2 + 3x$.

b Hence find the gradient of the tangent to the curve at the point where $x = 3$.

15 For the function $f(x) = 2 - \frac{1}{2}x^2$:

a find the gradient function $f'(x)$

b draw sketches, on separate diagrams, of $y = f(x)$ and $y = f'(x)$

c describe some features of the relationship between $y = f(x)$ and $y = f'(x)$

16 Find, from first principles, the derivative of:

a $3x - 7$ b $7x^2 + 1$

Go to page 226 for Quick Answers & pages 184–188 for Worked Solutions

17 Differentiate:

a $y = x^4$　　b $y = x^8$

c $y = x^{11}$　　d $y = x^{47}$

18 Find the gradient of the tangent to the curve $y = x^5$ at the point where $x = 3$.

19 a Find the equation of the tangent to the curve $y = x^2$ at the point (1, 1).
b Draw a sketch showing the curve and tangent.

20 Differentiate:

a $y = 5$　　b $y = 12$

c $f(x) = -7$　　d $f(x) = 0$

21 Differentiate:

a $y = x^6 + x^4$　　b $y = x^7 - x^5$

c $f(x) = x^3 + 8$　　d $f(x) = x^8 - x^2 + x - 4$

e $f(x) = x^4 - x^3 + 6$

22 Find the derivative of:

a $y = 3x$　　b $f(x) = 2x^2$

c $y = -3x^4$　　d $y = -x^6$

e $f(x) = 12x^9$

23 Differentiate:

a $y = 4x^2 + 5x$

b $y = 3x^3 - 2x^2 + x + 1$

c $f(x) = -x^5 + 7x^4 - 2x^3$

d $f(x) = 2x^8 - 3x^{10}$

e $y = 3x^6 - 2x^5 - 3x^4 + 5x^3 - 9x^2 - 3$

24 Find the equation of the normal to the curve:

a $y = x^2$ at $x = \dfrac{1}{2}$　　b $y = x - x^2$ at $(1, 0)$

25 Differentiate:

a $y = 2x^{10} - 3x$　　b $f(x) = 1 - 3x - 2x^2$

c $3x^9 - 2x^8 + 7x^7$

26 Differentiate with respect to t:

a $y = 3t^4 - 5t^2$　　b $s = 9t^3 + 6t^2 - t$

27 Differentiate:

a $p = 4q^2 - 9$, with respect to q

b $u = 3v^2 + 8v - 7$, with respect to v

c $h = -m^4 + 5m^3 - 2m - 3$, with respect to m

28 Find:

a $\dfrac{d}{dx}\left(7x^2 - x\right)$　　b $\dfrac{d}{dt}\left(t - 6t^2\right)$

c $\dfrac{d}{du}\left(u^3 + 5u^2 - 7u\right)$

29 If:

a $f(y) = y^3 + y^2$, find $f'(y)$

b $p(x) = 2x^4 - x^3 + 5x^2 + 5x - 11$, find $p'(x)$

c $g(a) = -4a^5 - 7a^3 + 9a - 1$, find $g'(a)$

30 Differentiate:

a x^{-3}　　b $x^2 + x^{-2}$

c $-3x^{-4}$　　d $x^{-8} - 7x + 3$

31 Differentiate:

a $\dfrac{1}{x^7}$　　b $\dfrac{2}{x^6}$　　c $\dfrac{1}{x} - \dfrac{3}{x^2}$

32 Differentiate:

a $y = x^{1.3}$　　b $y = 2x^{2.5}$

c $y = 4\sqrt{x}$　　d $y = \sqrt[4]{x}$

e $y = \sqrt{x^7}$

33 Differentiate:

a $y = x^{-0.7}$　　b $f(x) = \dfrac{1}{\sqrt{x}}$

c $y = \dfrac{4}{\sqrt[3]{x}}$　　d $f(x) = x^2\sqrt{x}$

34 If $y = u^3$ where $u = 5x - 1$, find $\dfrac{dy}{dx}$.

35 Differentiate $\left(x^2 + 5\right)^2$:

a by expanding
b by the composite function rule

36 Differentiate:

a $y = \left(4x + 3\right)^3$　　b $f(x) = \left(x^3 - 5\right)^7$

c $\left(x^2 + 7x - 6\right)^4$

☞ Go to pages 226 and 227 for Quick Answers & pages 188–190 for Worked Solutions

37 Differentiate:

a $y=\sqrt{16-x^2}$ b $\frac{1}{4x}$

c $y=\frac{1}{(2x+3)^5}$

38 Differentiate, by first expanding:

a $y=x(x^2-3x+4)$

b $y=(x-2)(x+7)$

39 Differentiate using the product rule:

a $y=x(x^2-3x+4)$

b $y=(x-2)(x+7)$

40 Use the product rule to differentiate:

a $y=(x-3)(x^2+x-3)$

b $y=(x^4-2)(5-3x-x^2)$

41 Differentiate:

a $y=x(x^2-1)^5$ b $y=x^3(5-4x)^4$

c $(x-1)^2(x+2)^3$ d $\sqrt{x}(4x-1)^6$

e $x\sqrt{1-x}$

42 Use the quotient rule to differentiate:

a $\frac{1}{3x}$

b $\frac{x-1}{x+3}$

43 Differentiate:

a $y=\frac{2x}{x^3-5}$

b $y=\frac{x^2-3x-1}{x}$

44 Differentiate:

a $y=\frac{(5x+3)^5}{x}$

b $f(x)=\frac{2x-1}{(x+1)^3}$

☞ Go to page 227 for Quick Answers & pages 190–192 for Worked Solutions. See pages 136 and 137 for Topic Tests

8 Topic Tests and Sample Examination Papers

Contents

Topic Test 1 Basic Arithmetic and Algebra

Time Allowed: 30 minutes

Total Marks: 20

Directions:

- Attempt all questions.
- The marks allocated for each question are shown at the right of the page.
- All necessary working should be shown.
- Approved calculators may be used.

		Marks
1	Simplify $\lvert -6\rvert - 2\lvert -5\rvert$	1
2	Find the value of $\dfrac{3.6 + 4.25}{\sqrt{5.1^2 + 2.3^2}}$ correct to one decimal place.	1
3	Simplify $1 - 4(2m - 1)$	1
4	A car is insured for an 'agreed value' of \$21 400. When the policy is renewed the new 'agreed value' is \$17 120. Find the percentage decrease in the value of the car.	1
5	Express $0.91\dot{6}$ as a fraction in simplest terms.	2
6	By rationalising the denominator, express $\dfrac{15}{4 - \sqrt{11}}$ in the form $a + b\sqrt{11}$	2
7	Solve $\dfrac{3a - 1}{3} - \dfrac{2a - 3}{4} = 7$	2
8	Simplify $\dfrac{\left(a^2b^3\right)^4 \div ab^2}{\left(a^3b\right)^2 \times a^2b^3}$	2
9	Given that $r = \sqrt{\dfrac{3V}{\pi h}}$, find r if $V = 10\ 000$ and $h = 2.5$ Give the answer to two significnt figures.	2
10	Simplify $\dfrac{m^2 - 25}{m^2 - 7m + 10} \div \dfrac{m^2 + 9m + 20}{m^2 + m - 6}$	2
11	Find the values of x which satisfy the inequality $9 - \dfrac{x}{3} \geq 12$	2
12	Solve $2x^2 - 6x + 1 = 0$, giving the answers in simplest surd form.	2

Go to page 227 for Quick Answers & page 193 for Worked Solutions

Topic Test 2 — Basic Arithmetic and Algebra

Time Allowed: 30 minutes

Total Marks: 20

Directions:

- Attempt all questions.
- The marks allocated for each question are shown at the right of the page.
- All necessary working should be shown.
- Approved calculators may be used.

		Marks
1	Simplify $\sqrt{2\frac{7}{9}}$	1
2	Expand and simplify $(2x-1)^2-(x+1)(x-1)$	2
3	Evaluate $(0.0535)^3 \div 45\,500$, giving the answer in scientific notation, correct to three significant figures.	1
4	A real-estate agent earns a commission of 4% on all sales of land. If a total of \$91 000 is paid for a block of land, including commission, how much is the commission?	1
5	Factorise fully: x^3-x^2-9x+9	2
6	Solve $5(3x-2)=7-2(3-x)$	2
7	If $s=ut+\frac{1}{2}at^2$, find the value of a when $s=130$, $u=1$ and $t=5$	2
8	Express $\frac{1}{11}$ as a recurring decimal.	1
9	Find the integers x and y such that $(6-\sqrt{3})^2=x+y\sqrt{3}$	2
10	Solve the simultaneous equations: $5p-2q=20$, $3p+4q=38$	2
11	Solve $\frac{x-4}{5}\le 1+\frac{x}{3}$	2
12	Express $\frac{2}{e^2+2e}-\frac{3}{e^2+3e}$ as a single fraction in simplest form.	2

Go to page 227 for Quick Answers & page 194 for Worked Solutions

Topic Test 3 Plane Geometry

Time Allowed: 30 minutes

Total Marks: 20

Directions:

- Attempt all questions.
- The marks allocated for each question are shown at the right of the page.
- All necessary working should be shown.
- Approved calculators may be used.

Marks

1 ΔABC is right-angled at B

a Find the only possible value of x.

b Find the area of the triangle. 4

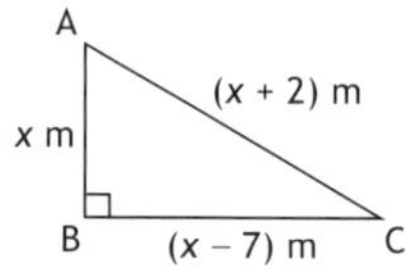

2 ΔADB is right-angled at D.
AC bisects $\angle DAB$.
AC = CB.
Find the size of $\angle ACB$. 3

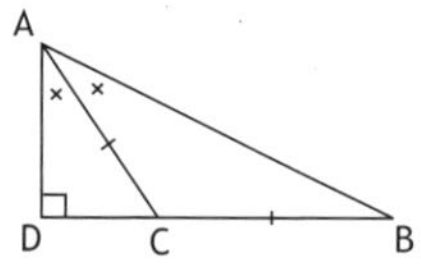

3 AE is parallel to BD.
F is the point of intersection of BE and AD.

a Show that triangles BCD and ACE are similar.

b Show that triangles BFD and EFA are similar.

c If AB = 24 cm, BC = 16 cm and FD = 8 cm, find the length of AF. 7

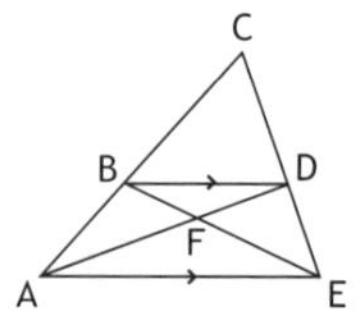

4 PQ is perpendicular to QR.
PS is perpendicular to SR.
QR = SR.

a By proving triangles PQR and PSR congruent, show that $\angle PRQ = \angle PRS$.

b If T is the point of intersection of PR and QS, show that $\angle QTR = 90°$. 6

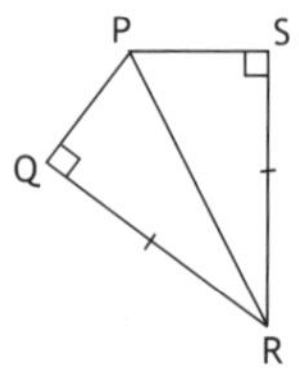

Go to page 227 for Quick Answers & pages 194 and 195 for Worked Solutions

Topic Test 4 Plane Geometry

Time Allowed: 30 minutes

Total Marks: 20

Directions:

- Attempt all questions.
- The marks allocated for each question are shown at the right of the page.
- All necessary working should be shown.
- Approved calculators may be used.

Marks

1 $\angle PQR = 158°$
$\angle RST = 132°$
Find the size of $\angle QRS$. 2

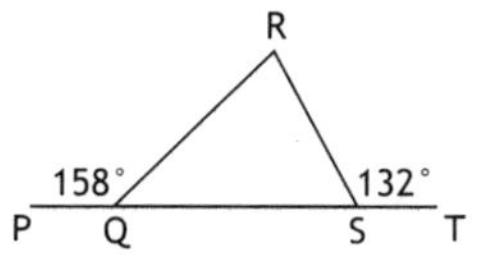

2 Find:

a the angle sum of an octagon.

b the size of each angle of a regular octagon. 3

3 AC = BC. BD = DC
DB bisects $\angle ABC$
Let $\angle ABD = x°$

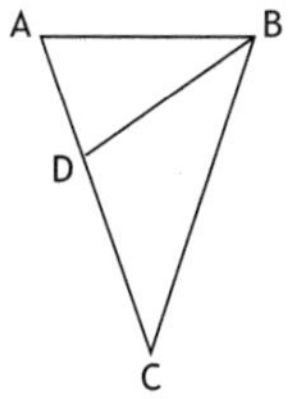

a Show that $\angle BAC = 2x°$.

b Find the size of $\angle ACB$. 3

4 ABCD is a rhombus.
E is the midpoint of AB.
F is the midpoint of AD.
G is the point of intersection of EF and AC.

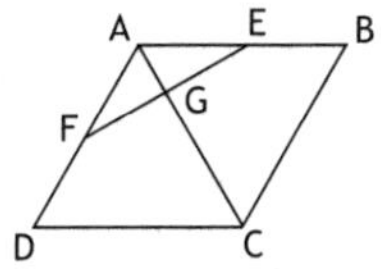

a Prove that triangles AEG and AFG are congruent.

b Show that EF is perpendicular to AC. 5

5 ABCD is a rectangle.
AB is produced to E and AD is produced to F so that E, C and F are collinear.
AB = 8 cm, BC = 18 cm and AF = 24 cm.

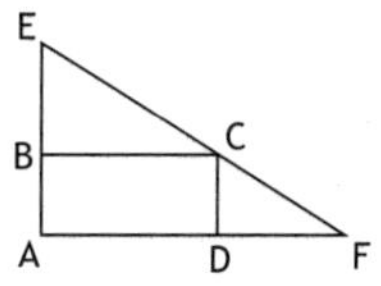

a Show that ΔEBC and ΔCDF are similar.

b Find the length of EB.

c Find the length of EF. 7

Go to page 227 for Quick Answers & pages 195 and 196 for Worked Solutions

Topic Test 5 Linear Functions and Lines

Time Allowed: 30 minutes

Total Marks: 20

Directions:

- Attempt all questions.
- The marks allocated for each question are shown at the right of the page.
- All necessary working should be shown.
- Approved calculators may be used.

Marks

1 a Find P, the point where the line l_1: $2x - 5y + 15 = 0$ cuts the y-axis.

b Find the equation of the line l_2 through Q(0, –2), parallel to l_1.

c Find the coordinates of R, the point where l_2 cuts the x-axis.

d On a diagram shade the region between the two lines l_1 and l_2.

e Write down a pair of inequalities to describe the region between l_1 and l_2. 8

2 The lines k: $2x - 3y + 39 = 0$ and l: $ax + 2y + 13 = 0$ are perpendicular.

a Find the value of a.

b Find the coordinates of P, the point of intersection of k and l.

c Find the equation of the line through Q(5, –1), parallel to k.

d This line meets line l in R. Find the coordinates of R.

e Find M, the midpoint of PQ.

f If M is the midpoint of SR, find the coordinates of S.

g Show that S lies on line k.

h Show that QS is parallel to RP. 12

Go to page 227 for Quick Answers & pages 196 and 197 for Worked Solutions

Topic Test 6 Linear Functions and Lines

Time Allowed: 30 minutes

Total Marks: 20

Directions:

- Attempt all questions.
- The marks allocated for each question are shown at the right of the page.
- All necessary working should be shown.
- Approved calculators may be used.

Marks

1 The points P, Q and R have coordinates (3, 5), (10, –1) and (1, –3) respectively.

a Find the equation of the line l_1 that passes through P, parallel to QR.

b Find M, the midpoint of PR.

c Find the equation of the line l_2 that passes through Q and M.

d Find S, the point of intersection of l_1 and l_2.

e Show that SR is parallel to PQ.

f Show that PQ = PS. **12**

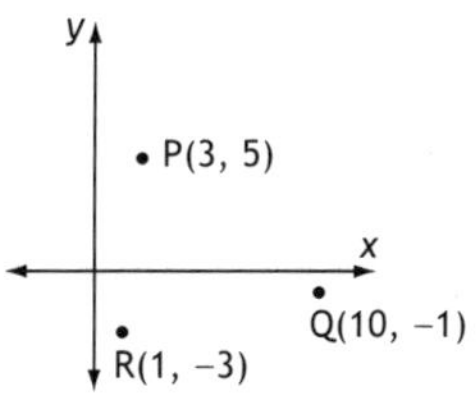

2 **a** Find the equation of the straight line l_2 which passes through the point (–2, 2) and is perpendicular to $l_1 : 2x - y - 4 = 0$.

b Show that l_1 and l_2 intersect on the x-axis.

c Find the equation of the line through (–2, 2) that meets l_1 on the y-axis.

d Draw a diagram and write down a set of inequalities that define the region inside the triangle created by these lines. **8**

Go to page 227 for Quick Answers & pages 197 and 198 for Worked Solutions

Topic Test 7 Real Functions of a Real Variable

Time Allowed: 30 minutes

Total Marks: 20

Directions:

- Attempt all questions.
- The marks allocated for each question are shown at the right of the page.
- All necessary working should be shown.
- Approved calculators may be used.

Marks

1 For the function $y = \dfrac{1}{2x-1}$ state:

a the natural domain

b the range. 2

2 A function is defined by the following rule: $f(x) = \begin{cases} 1-x & \text{if} \quad x < -1 \\ 2 & \text{if} \quad -1 \le x \le 1 \\ x+1 & \text{if} \quad x > 1 \end{cases}$

Sketch $y = f(x)$. 3

3 Given $f(x) = x^2 + x$:

a find $f(x+h) - f(x)$

b simplify $\dfrac{f(x+h) - f(x)}{h}$ 2

4 a If $f(x) = a + bx - cx^2$, find $f(x) + f(-x)$.

b Is $f(x) + f(-x)$ an even or odd function? 3

5 a On the same set of axes, carefully sketch the graphs of: $y = x^2 + 4$ and $y = x^3$.

b Hence find the solution of the equation $x^3 = x^2 + 4$ 4

6 The point P(x, y) is equidistant from the lines $y = 4x$ and $x - 4y = 0$. Show that the locus is a pair of straight lines. 6

Go to page 228 for Quick Answers & pages 198 and 199 for Worked Solutions

Topic Test 8 Real Functions of a Real Variable

Time Allowed: 30 minutes
Total Marks: 20

Directions:

- Attempt all questions.
- The marks allocated for each question are shown at the right of the page.
- All necessary working should be shown.
- Approved calculators may be used.

Marks

1 Given $f(x) = x^2 - 6x + 11$:

a determine the domain and range of the function

b find $f(x - 2)$. 2

2 A function is defined as $f(x) = \begin{cases} x+1 & \text{for } x < 0 \\ 1 & \text{for } 0 \le x < 1 \\ x & \text{for } x \ge 1 \end{cases}$

a Evaluate $f(-2) + f(2)$.

b Sketch $y = f(x)$. 4

3 Sketch the region where both of the following inequalities hold simultaneously:
$x^2 + y^2 \le 16$ and $y > | x |$ 4

4 A is the point (0, 2). P is the point (x, y) and l is the line $x + 1 = 0$.

a Find the distance PA.

b Find the perpendicular distance from P to l.

c Find the equation of the locus of points P such that the distance PA is twice the perpendicular distance from P *to l*. 6

5 **a** On the same set of axes graph $y = \sqrt{25 - x^2}$ and $y = 2x - 2$.

b Hence write down any solutions of the equation $2x - 2 = \sqrt{25 - x^2}$. 4

Go to page 228 for Quick Answers & page 199 for Worked Solutions

Topic Test 9 Trigonometric Ratios

Time Allowed: 30 minutes

Total Marks: 20

Directions:

- Attempt all questions.
- The marks allocated for each question are shown at the right of the page.
- All necessary working should be shown.
- Approved calculators may be used.

Marks

1 A kite is flying on a 25 m long string. A person lying on the ground holding the string notes that the angle of elevation of the kite is 39°.
How high is the kite above the ground? **2**

2 A triangle has sides which are 6 cm, 7 cm and 9 cm in length.
Find the size of the largest angle. **3**

3 **a** Express $\operatorname{cosec}\theta$ and $\cot\theta$ in terms of $\sin\theta$ and $\cos\theta$.

b Hence show that $\operatorname{cosec}^2\theta - \cot^2\theta = 1$, given that $1 - \cos^2\theta = \sin^2\theta$. **2**

4 ABCD is a parallelogram.
AB = 5 m, BC = 3 m and $\angle ABC = 60°$.

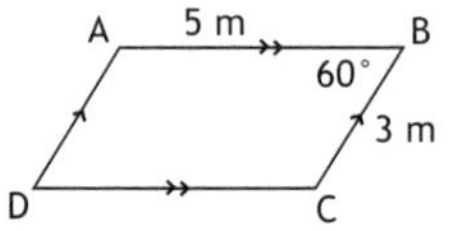

a Find the exact length of the diagonal BD.

b Find the exact area of the parallelogram. **4**

5 A and B are two points 800 metres apart on a straight road.
A monument (M) is located to one side of the road so that $\angle MAB = 64°$ amd $\angle MBA = 71°$ as shown in the diagram.

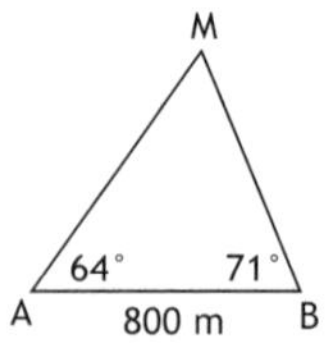

a Find an expression for MB.

b How far is the monument from the road?
Give the answer correct to the nearest ten metres. **5**

6 Solve, for $0° \le \theta \le 360°$, $2\sin^2\theta + \sin\theta - 1 = 0$ **4**

Go to page 228 for Quick Answers & pages 199 and 200 for Worked Solutions

Topic Test 10 Trigonometric Ratios

Time Allowed: 30 minutes

Total Marks: 20

Directions:

- Attempt all questions.
- The marks allocated for each question are shown at the right of the page.
- All necessary working should be shown.
- Approved calculators may be used.

Marks

1 The diagram shows part of a verandah of a house. The railing at one end of the verandah is 2.5 m long and meets the house at an angle of 70°. How wide is the verandah between the house and the front railing? **2**

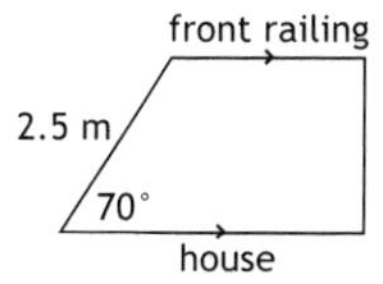

2 Show that $\tan\alpha + \cot\alpha = \dfrac{1}{\sin\alpha\ \cos\alpha}$ **2**

3 Three points, A, B and C, are such that C is 94 metres from A and 57 metres from B. The bearing of A from C is 312° and of B from C is 286°. Find the distance from A to B. **4**

4 In ΔABC, ∠A = 45° and ∠C = 75°. D is a point on AC such that AD = 2 cm. If DB bisects ∠ABC, find the exact length of DB. **4**

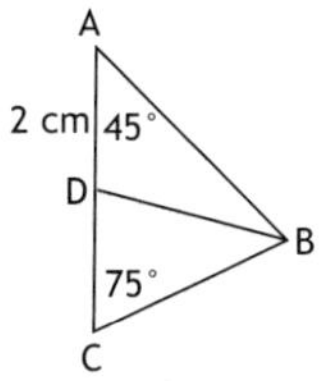

5 If $\tan\theta = -1$ and $0° \le \theta \le 180°$, find θ. **2**

6 If $\cos\theta = -0.6$ and $\sin\theta < 0$, find the exact value of $\tan\theta$. **2**

7 AB = 301 m, ∠ACD = 147°, ∠BAD = 22° and ∠CBD = 29°.

a Find an expression for BD.

b Use this expression to find BC. **4**

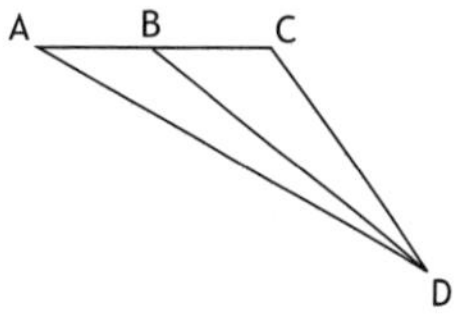

Go to page 228 for Quick Answers & pages 200 and 201 for Worked Solutions

Topic Test 11 The Quadratic Polynomial and the Parabola

Time Allowed: 30 minutes

Total Marks: 20

Directions:

- Attempt all questions.
- The marks allocated for each question are shown at the right of the page.
- All necessary working should be shown.
- Approved calculators may be used.

		Marks
1	Find the minimum value of $3x^2 - 7x + 4$.	2
2	The parabola $x^2 = 4Ay$ passes through the point $(-12, 6)$. What is the focal length of this parabola?	2
3	Find the values of m for which $9x^2 + 6x + m^2$ is always positive.	3
4	Find the values of the constants a and b such that $x^2 - x = ax(x + 1) + bx$ for all values of x.	2
5	$P(x) = (m - 2)x^2 + (m + 1)x + 3$ For what range of values of m does the equation $P(x) = 0$ have real roots?	3
6	S is the point $(2, 0)$. P is the point (x, y) and l is the line $y = 4$. **a** Write down the equation of the locus of points P such that the distance of P from S is equal to the perpendicular distance of P from l. **b** Sketch the locus.	4
7	The quadratic equation $kx^2 - (3k + 1)x - 15 = 0$ has 5 as one of its roots. Find the other root.	4

Go to page 228 for Quick Answers & pages 201 and 202 for Worked Solutions

Topic Test 12 — The Quadratic Polynomial and the Parabola

Time Allowed: 30 minutes

Total Marks: 20

Directions:

- Attempt all questions.
- The marks allocated for each question are shown at the right of the page.
- All necessary working should be shown.
- Approved calculators may be used.

		Marks
1	The equation of a parabola is $(x - 1)^2 = 12y$.	
	a Find the coordinates of the vertex.	
	b Find the coordinates of the focus.	2
2	Find all values of x for which $(x^2 + 7x)^2 + 2(x^2 + 7x) = 80$.	4
3	Without sketching, determine whether the curve $y = 3x^2 - 8x + 5$ will cross the x-axis.	3
4	The quadratic equation $x^2 + qx + r = 0$ has roots which are in the ratio 3 : 2. Show that $6q^2 = 25r$.	3
5	Find the points of intersection of the line $y = 2x + 3$ with the parabola $x^2 = -4y$.	2
6	**a** Sketch the parabola $x^2 = 16y$, showing the coordinates of the focus S.	
	b A second parabola also has its focus at S. The vertex of this second parabola is at (–2, 4). Find the equation of this parabola.	
	c P is the point where the directrix of the second parabola intersects with the directrix of the parabola $x^2 = 16y$. Find the coordinates of the point P.	6

Go to page 228 for Quick Answers & pages 202 and 203 for Worked Solutions

Topic Test 13 The Tangent to a Curve and the Derivative of a Function

Time Allowed: 30 minutes

Total Marks: 20

Directions:

- Attempt all questions.
- The marks allocated for each question are shown at the right of the page.
- All necessary working should be shown.
- Approved calculators may be used.

Marks

1 If $f(x) = x^6 - 2x^3 + 7x$, find $f'(2)$. 2

2 Find $\lim\limits_{x \to -2} \dfrac{4 - x^2}{x + 2}$ 2

3 **a** Differentiate $f(x) = x^2 - 6x + 5$.

b Hence find the point on the curve where the gradient of the tangent is 0. 3

4 Find the equation of the normal to the curve $y = 3x - 2x^2$ at $x = 1$. 3

5 Use the quotient rule to differentiate $\dfrac{5x}{x^2 - 2}$ 2

6 **a** Express $\dfrac{1}{1-x}$ in index form.

b Hence differentiate $\dfrac{1}{1-x}$ by use of the composite function rule. 3

7 Differentiate $2x^3$ from first principles. 5

Go to page 228 for Quick Answers & pages 203 and 204 for Worked Solutions

Topic Test 14 The Tangent to a Curve and the Derivative of a Function

Time Allowed: 30 minutes

Total Marks: 20

Directions:

- Attempt all questions.
- The marks allocated for each question are shown at the right of the page.
- All necessary working should be shown.
- Approved calculators may be used.

Marks

1 Differentiate:

a $\frac{3}{x^5}$ b $x(7-4x)^9$ c $\frac{2x+1}{2x-1}$ 6

2 Find the gradient of the secant to the curve $y = x^2 + 1$ which passes through the points where $x = -1$ and $x = 3$. 2

3 $f(x)=\begin{cases}\frac{x^2-3x+2}{x-2} & \text{for } x \neq 2\\ 1 & \text{for } x = 2\end{cases}$

Determine whether $f(x)$ is continuous at $x = 2$. 2

4 a Find the equation of the tangent to the curve $y = (x-2)^2$ at the point where $x = 3$.

b Draw a graph showing the curve and tangent. 4

5 a Write down the derivative of $x^2 + 8x$.

b Verify this result from first principles. 6

Go to page 229 for Quick Answers & pages 204 and 205 for Worked Solutions

Sample Examination Paper One

Time Allowed: 3 hours

Total Marks: 120

Directions:

- Attempt all questions.
- All questions are of equal value.
  The marks allocated for each part of a question are shown at the right of the page.
- All necessary working should be shown.
- Approved calculators may be used.

Marks

Question 1

a Write 275 596 240 in scientific notation, correct to four significant figures. 2

b Solve $| x + 1 | = 3$. 2

c Factorise fully $7m^2 - 28$. 2

d **i** Express $\frac{x-5}{3} - \frac{2x+1}{4}$ as a single fraction.

ii Hence solve $\frac{x-5}{3} - \frac{2x+1}{4} < 1$. 2

e Find the value of the integers a and b if $a - \sqrt{b} = \frac{8}{1-\sqrt{5}}$. 2

f Express $0.\dot{6}\dot{3}$ as a fraction in its simplest form. 2

Question 2

Line l has equation $y = 2x + 2$.

Line k has equation $x + 2y - 14 = 0$.

a Show that l is perpendicular to k. 2

b Find P, the point of intersection of l and k. 2

c Find Q and R, the points where l and k, respectively, cut the x-axis. 2

d Graph the lines on a diagram and shade the region inside the triangle PQR. 2

e Write down three inequalities which define the inside of the triangle. 2

f Find the area of the shaded triangle. 2

Go to page 229 for Quick Answers & page 205 for Worked Solutions

Question 3

a Solve the equation $5(2x - 3) - 4(2 - x) = 19$. 2

b AB = BC. BE = BD.
$\angle EDA = 21°$. $\angle DAE = 58°$.
Find the size of:
i $\angle BDE$
ii $\angle CBD$ 4

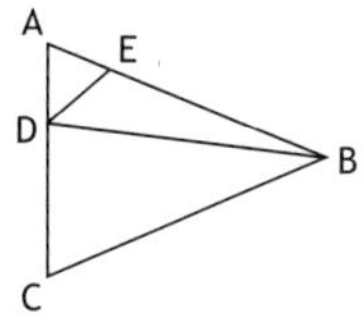

c For the parabola $x^2 = -12y$, find:
i the focal length
ii the coordinates of the vertex
iii the coordinates of the focus
iv the equation of the directrix 4

d i Given $g(t) = t^2 - 4t - 2$, evaluate $g(1)$.
ii For what values of t does $g(t) = 3$? 2

Question 4

a Prior to the release of a new model, cars are being sold at a discount of 6% off the normal price. If the normal price is \$21 600, find:
i The amount of the discount.
ii The discounted price.
iii The new model when released is priced at \$22 800. What is the percentage increase in price? 3

b i Find an expression for $\dfrac{f(x+h) - f(x)}{h}$ when $f(x) = 6x - x^2$.
ii Hence find the gradient function $f'(x)$ from first principles.
iii Find the gradient of the curve $y = f(x)$ when $x = 3$. 5

c i Given $x^2 + 12x = p$, use the method of completing the square to find an expression for x in terms of p.
ii If $p = 253$, find all possible values of x. 2

d Find the exact area of triangle ABC. 2

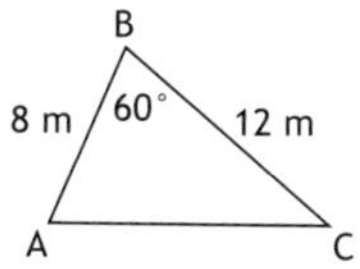

Question 5

a Differentiate:

i $(x^2 - 2)^5$ ii $\dfrac{2x - 3}{3x + 4}$ iii $x(3x + 1)^8$ 6

b Solve for $0° \le x \le 360°$, $4\cos^2 x - 3 = 0$. 3

c On a number plane, shade the region satisfied by the following conditions:
$x^2 + y^2 \le 9, \quad y > x, \quad x < -1$ 3

Go to page 229 for Quick Answers & pages 205–207 for Worked Solutions

Question 6

a i The perimeter of this right triangle is 8.4 metres. Find an expression for the hypotenuse, x, in terms of the height, h.

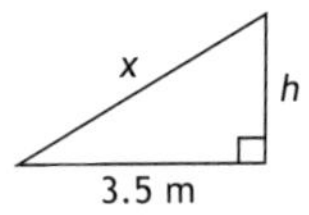

ii Find h.

iii Find the length of the hypotenuse. 3

b Determine whether $f(x) = \begin{cases} \dfrac{x^2 + x}{x+1} & \text{if } x \neq -1 \\ 1 & \text{if } x = -1 \end{cases}$ is continuous at $x = -1$. 4

c PQRS is a rhombus of side 2 m.

T is a point on diagonal PR such that TR = TS.

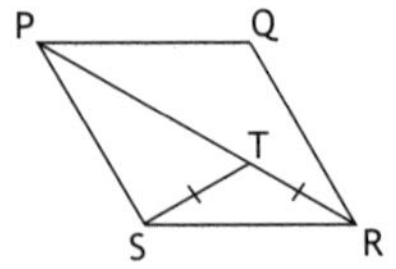

i Show that triangles TRS and SPR are similar.

If TR = $(\sqrt{5} - 1)$ m:

ii find the exact length of PR

iii show that PT = PS 5

Question 7

a If $h(t) = -t^5 + 4t^4 + 5t^2 - 9t + 7$, find $h'(4)$. 2

b A function is defined as $f(x) = \begin{cases} x + a & \text{for } x < 0 \\ a - bx & \text{for } x \geq 0 \end{cases}$

i If $f(3) = 4$ and $f(-3) = 7$, find a and b.

ii Sketch $y = f(x)$.

iii What is the natural domain and range? 5

c DE is the perpendicular bisector of the hypotenuse, AC, of a right-angled triangle. EA bisects ∠BAC.

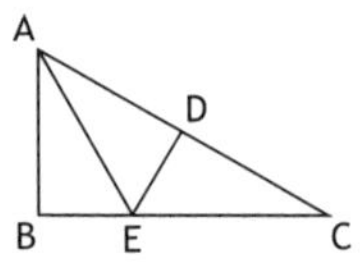

i Show that triangles AED and CED are congruent.

ii Find the size of angle ECD. 5

Question 8

a Calculate the discriminant of the equation $9x^2 - 42x + 49 = 0$.

What conclusions can be drawn about the nature of the roots of this equation? 2

b S is a point on QR such that QS = PS = RS = 7 m. PR = 12 m.

i Show that $\cos R = \dfrac{6}{7}$.

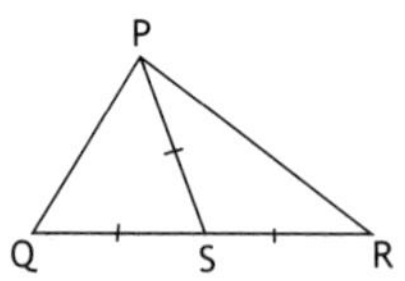

ii Find the exact length of PQ.

iii Find the size of ∠QPR. 5

c A is the point (–2, 3) and B is the point (6, –3). P is the point (x, y).

i Write down expressions for the gradients of PA and PB.

ii Show that the equation of the locus of all points such that PA is perpendicular to PB is given by $x^2 - 4x + y^2 - 21 = 0$.

iii Describe the locus in words. 5

Go to page 229 for Quick Answers & pages 207 and 208 for Worked Solutions

Question 9

a Solve the pair of simultaneous equations: $3a + 4b - 5 = 0$

$$5a - b - 16 = 0$$ 3

b Find the equation of the normal to the curve $y = \sqrt{x}$ at (1, 1). 4

c A, B and C have coordinates (5, 8), (4, 1) and (0, 3) respectively.

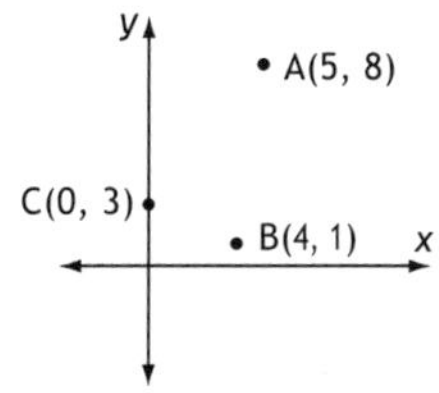

- **i** Find the coordinates of D, the midpoint of BC.
- **ii** Find the equation of the line joining A to D.
- **iii** If AD (produced) meets the y-axis at E, show that CE = BE. 5

Question 10

a Simplify $5 - 5\cos^2\theta - 4\sin^2\theta$. 1

b
- **i** Write down the coordinates of the focus S of the parabola $x^2 = 4y$.
- **ii** Find the two points of intersection of the parabolas $x^2 = 4y$ and $y = 13 - 3x^2$.
- **iii** Show that the straight line joining those two points also passes through S. 5

c ΔABC is right-angled at B.
D is a point on AC so that BD is perpendicular to AC. BC = 1 unit.
DA = CD + 1. $\angle$BCA = θ.

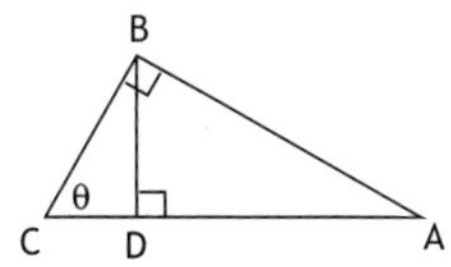

- **i** Show that $2\cos\theta + 1 = \sec\theta$.
- **ii** Deduce that $2\cos^2\theta + \cos\theta - 1 = 0$.
- **iii** Hence find θ. 6

Go to page 229 for Quick Answers & pages 208 and 209 for Worked Solutions

Sample Examination Paper Two

Time Allowed: 3 hours

Total Marks: 120

Directions:

- Attempt all questions.
- All questions are of equal value.
  The marks allocated for each part of a question are shown at the right of the page.
- All necessary working should be shown.
- Approved calculators may be used.

Marks

Question 1

a When buying tiles a purchaser orders an extra 15% in case of breakages.
If she buys 345 tiles, how many were actually needed? 2

b If $S = \dfrac{a\left(1 - r^n\right)}{1 - r}$, find S when $a = 64$, $n = 5$ and $r = \dfrac{1}{2}$ 2

c Graph the solution of $|\, x - 3 \,| \geq 4$ on a number line. 2

d Find, correct to two decimal places, $\dfrac{3.2 + 4.7}{3.2 \times 4.7}$ 2

e Simplify $\left(2a^2b^3\right)^3 \div \left(ab^2\right)^4$ 2

f Simplify $\dfrac{\sqrt{75} - \sqrt{3}}{\sqrt{12}}$ 2

Question 2

a PR, ST and UV are parallel lines. QV = 18 cm, QS = 12 cm and SU = 3 cm.
Find the length of TV. 2

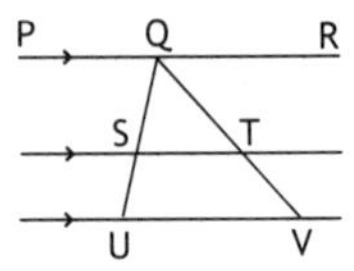

b A circle of radius 13 units has its centre at (2, –5). Find the coordinates of the points where the circle cuts the x-axis. 3

c **i** The line l has equation $y = 2x - 2$. Find, to the nearest degree, the angle the line makes with the x-axis.
ii Show that A(4, 6) lies on l.
iii Find the equation of the line through B(–3, 2), parallel to l.
iv Find the shortest distance between the two lines. 7

Go to page 229 for Quick Answers & pages 209 and 210 for Worked Solutions

Question 3

a Use the product rule to differentiate $y = x(2 - 3x)^4$. 2

b Solve $9 - 4x > 3$. 2

c Express $5x^2 - x + 4$ in the form $A + B(1 + x) + Cx(1 + x)$. 3

d **i** Sketch the function $y = x^2 - 2x$ for $0 \leq x \leq 4$. Write down the range.
ii If the function in i is part of an even function, $f(x)$, defined for $-4 \leq x \leq 4$, sketch $y = f(x)$ on a second diagram.
iii If the function in i was part of an odd function, $g(x)$, sketch $y = g(x)$ on another diagram. 5

Question 4

a Factorise and simplify $\dfrac{x^2 - 4x - 12}{x^2 - 4}$ 2

b $q^7 = 1.2765$. Find the value of q correct to four significant figures. 2

c Find the equation of the tangent to the curve $y = x^5 - 2x^4$ at the point where $x = 2$. 3

d P and Q are two positions on the coast, 2500 metres apart. Q is due south of P. From P, a ship bears 074°T and from Q it bears 047°T. Find the distance of the ship from Q. Give the answer to the nearest 100 metres. 5

Question 5

a Find the value of the derivative of $\dfrac{x+4}{x+1}$ when $x = 2$. 3

b PQRS is a square.
X is a point on diagonal PR such that XR = XS.
Find the size of $\angle$PXS. 3

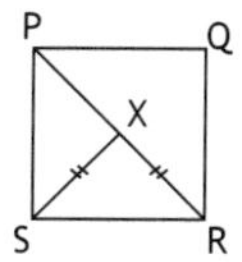

c A, B and P are the points (1, –3), (7, 5) and (x, y) respectively.
i Find expressions for PA^2 and PB^2.
ii The point P moves so that $PA^2 + PB^2 = 100$.
Show that the path traced out by this point is a circle and write down its centre and radius. 6

Question 6

a Simplify $\dfrac{1}{u} - \dfrac{2}{u(3-u)}$ 2

b Find the perimeter of a triangular paddock which has two sides 400 m and 600 m long, and the angle between the two sides is 75°. 3

c For the parabola $x^2 - 4x - 4 = 8y$, find:
i the coordinates of the vertex.
ii the focal length. 3

d **i** For what values of m will the equation $x^2 + (m + 7)x + (m + 6) = 0$ have equal roots?
ii Are the roots of this equation rational for all rational values of m? Justify your answer. 4

Go to pages 229 and 230 for Quick Answers & pages 210 and 211 for Worked Solutions

Question 7

a i If $f(x) = x^2 - x^3$, show that $f(x) - f(c) = (x - c)[(x + c) - (x^2 + cx + c^2)]$.
ii Hence find from first principles the gradient $f'(x)$. 4

b A(2, 3), B(4, −1) and C(−6, 1) are vertices of a triangle.
i Find P and Q, the midpoints of AC and CB respectively.
ii Show that PQ is parallel to AB.
iii Find the length of AB in simplest surd form.
iv Show that AB is twice the length of PQ. 8

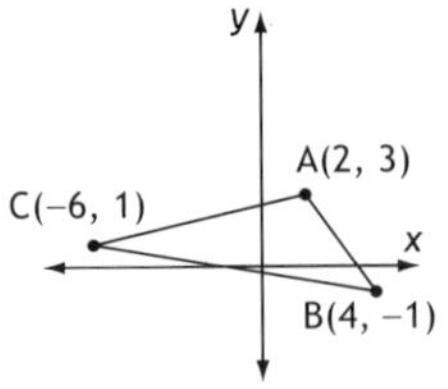

Question 8

a Find $\lim_{x \to 3} \dfrac{x^2 - 9}{x^2 - 7x + 12}$ 3

b i Find the equation of the axis of symmetry of the parabola $y = 2x^2 - 8x + 11$.
ii Find the coordinates of the vertex.
iii What conclusions can be drawn about the roots of the equation $2x^2 - 8x + 11 = 0$? 4

c ABCD is a rectangle.
E is a point on DC such that AE is perpendicular to EB.
i Prove that triangles ADE and ECB are similar.
ii If AD = 12 cm and DE = 9 cm, find the area of the rectangle. 5

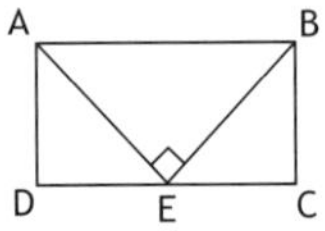

Question 9

a P is a point on the unit circle $x^2 + y^2 = 1$.
i Find x.
ii Find $\tan\angle POA$. 2

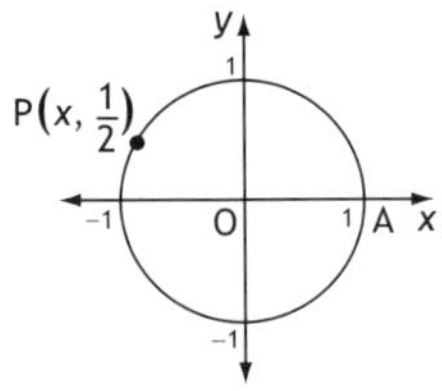

b DC is perpendicular to AC.
DE is perpendicular to AE.
AE = DC = 15 cm. BC = 8 cm.
i Show that ΔDCB and ΔAEB are congruent.
ii Find DE. 5

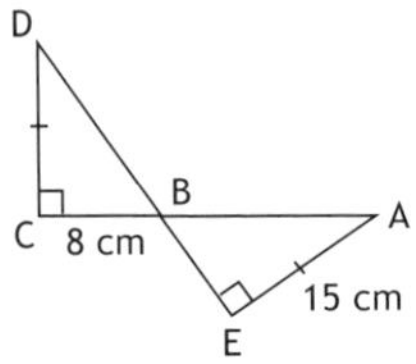

c Given $f(x) = \begin{cases} ax + b & \text{for } x < 2 \\ bx - a & \text{for } 2 \le x \le 4 \\ x^2 - 4x & \text{for } x > 4 \end{cases}$

i Find a and b if $f(-3) = f(2) = f(5)$.
ii Sketch $y = f(x)$. 5

Question 10

a Find all possible values of x. 3

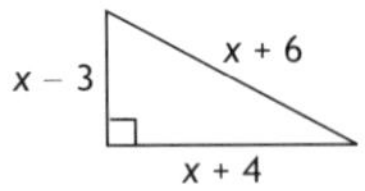

b Find all values of x such that $x(x + 3) \le 4$. 4

c i Show that $\cos^2\theta - \sin^2\theta = 1 - 2\sin^2\theta$.

ii Hence solve $\cos^2\theta - \sin^2\theta = \dfrac{1}{2}$, $0° \le \theta \le 360°$. 5

Go to page 230 for Quick Answers & pages 212–214 for Worked Solutions

Sample Examination Paper Three

Time Allowed: 3 hours

Total Marks: 120

Directions:

- Attempt all questions.
- All questions are of equal value.
  The marks allocated for each part of a question are shown at the right of the page.
- All necessary working should be shown.
- Approved calculators may be used.

Marks

Question 1

a Jupiter is approximately 780 million kilometres from the Sun.
Write this distance in scientitifc notation. 1

b Simplify $(7x - 1) - (3x - 8)$. 2

c After a $12\frac{1}{2}\%$ staff discount has been allowed, an employee of a furniture store pays \$1484 for a lounge suite. What is the full price? 2

d If $m = \dfrac{2k}{3-t}$, find k when $m = 9$ and $t = 2\frac{3}{4}$ 3

e Evaluate $2|-2| - 4|7|$ 1

f Show that $\sqrt{3} - 2 + \dfrac{1}{\sqrt{3} - 2}$ is a rational number. 3

Question 2

a Differentiate $p = 3q^7 - q^9$ with respect to q. 1

b The equation $ax^2 + bx + c = 0$ has solutions for $x = 0$, $x = 1$ and $x = 2$.
What conclusions can be drawn about the values of a, b and c? 2

c Simplify $\dfrac{7x - 21}{x^2 - 9} \times \dfrac{x^2 - 9x}{x^2 - 7x - 18}$ 3

d **i** Find the equation of the line l_1 with angle of inclination of 135° and y-intercept 5.

ii Find the equation of the line l_2 which passes through the point (15, 2) and which is parallel to $7x + y + 8 = 0$.

iii Show that P(7, 8) is equidistant from l_1 and l_2. 6

Go to page 230 for Quick Answers & page 214 for Worked Solutions

Question 3

a AB is parallel to DC. AB = BD = BC.
$\angle BCD = 68°$. Find the size of $\angle BAD$. 2

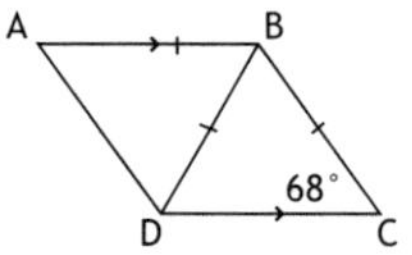

b A is 8 kilometres due north of B and 16 kilometres due west of C.
  i Show this information on a diagram.
  ii Find the bearing of B from C. 3

c i Sketch the graphs of $y = 3 - x$ and $y = |x|$ on the same set of axes.
  ii Write down the coordinates of all, if any, points of intersection of $y = 3 - x$ and $y = |x|$. 3

d A parabola has focus at (–4, 3) and vertex at (–1, 3).
Find the equation of the parabola and draw a sketch showing all essential features. 4

Question 4

a Express $0.2\dot{1}\dot{3}$ as a single fraction. 3

b If α and β are the roots of the equation $9x^2 - 6x + 2 = 0$, show that $\alpha^2 + \beta^2 = 0$. 3

c SV is perpendicular to VQ and SU is perpendicular to UQ.
  i Prove that triangles STV and QTU are similar.
  ii If SV = 70 m, VT = 24 m and SU = 110 m, find VQ. 6

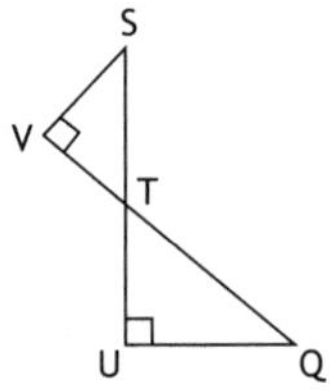

Question 5

a If $f(x) = \dfrac{x^2+1}{x}$, show that $f\left(\dfrac{1}{x}\right) = f(x)$. 2

b AB = 1 m. $\angle ACB = 45°$ and $\angle ADC = 30°$.
  i Show that $DC = \left(\sqrt{3} - 1\right)$ m.
  ii Hence show that $\sin 15° = \dfrac{\sqrt{3}-1}{2\sqrt{2}}$ 5

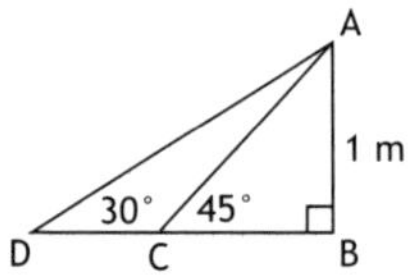

c i Show that if $f(x) = x^4$, then $f(x) - f(c) = (x^2 + c^2)(x + c)(x - c)$.
  ii Hence find from first principles the gradient function $f'(x)$. 5

Question 6

a Find the value of $13^{-1.5}$ correct to three decimal places. 2

b i $f(x) = x^3$ find $f'(x)$.
  ii On separate diagrams, graph $y = f(x)$ and $y = f'(x)$.
  iii Discuss the relationship between the two graphs. 5

c i On the same set of axes graph $y = \cos x°$ for $0° \le x° \le 720°$, and $y = \dfrac{1}{2}$.
  ii Hence find all solutions, $0° \le x° \le 720°$, of the equation $\cos x° = \dfrac{1}{2}$. 5

Go to page 230 for Quick Answers & pages 215 and 216 for Worked Solutions

Question 7

a Solve $5x^2 = 2x + 3$. 3

b **i** For the function $f(x) = \sqrt{4 - x^2}$ write down the natural domain and range.
ii Sketch the curve $y = f(x)$. 3

c Show that the equation $x^2 + (p + 2)x + p = 0$ has real roots for all values of p. 3

d The gradient of a tangent to the curve $y = x^2 - 5x$ is -3. Find the point of contact. 3

Question 8

a The locus of points which are equidistant from a fixed point and a fixed line is given by $y = \frac{1}{2}x^2 - 2x - 1$.
i What are the coordinates of the fixed point?
ii What is the equation of the line? 5

b ABCD is a square. BEC is an equilateral triangle.
i Show that $\angle ABE = \angle DCE$.
ii Show that ΔABE and ΔDCE are congruent.
iii Show that ΔAED is isosceles.
iv Find the size of $\angle AED$. 7

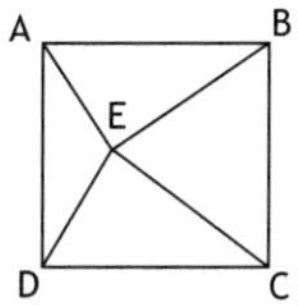

Question 9

a Find all values of x between 0° and 360° for which $\tan x + \sqrt{3} = 0$. 4

b P(–1, 8), Q(5, 5) and R(2, –2) are all vertices of a triangle.
i Find the length of QR.
ii Find the equation of QR.
iii Find the perpendicular distance from P to QR.
iv Find the area of ΔPQR. 8

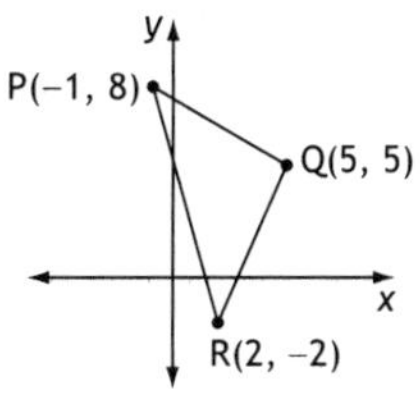

Question 10

a Differentiate: **i** $y = \dfrac{1}{x}$ **ii** $y = x\sqrt{x}$ 4

b P is the point (x, y).
Q is the point (1, –2) and R is the point (7, 4).
i Find expressions for PQ^2 and PR^2.
ii Find the equation of the locus of points P which are equidistant from Q and R. Describe this locus in words.
iii Show that the equation of the locus of points for which the distance between P and Q is equal to twice the distance between P and R is a circle and determine its centre and radius. 8

Go to page 230 for Quick Answers & pages 216–218 for Worked Solutions

Worked Solutions to Exercises

Basic Arithmetic and Algebra

1 a $\frac{21}{49}=\frac{3}{7}$ b $\frac{32}{72}=\frac{4}{9}$

2 a $\frac{2}{9}+\frac{5}{9}=\frac{7}{9}$

b $\frac{1}{12}+\frac{2}{3}=\frac{1}{12}+\frac{8}{12}=\frac{9}{12}=\frac{3}{4}$

c $\frac{7}{10}-\frac{3}{10}=\frac{4}{10}=\frac{2}{5}$

d $\frac{5}{6}-\frac{1}{3}=\frac{5}{6}-\frac{2}{6}=\frac{3}{6}=\frac{1}{2}$

3 a $\frac{1}{4}\times\frac{5}{8}=\frac{5}{32}$

b $\frac{3}{5}\times\frac{10}{11}=\frac{30}{55}=\frac{6}{11}$

c $\frac{4}{9}\times\frac{3}{8}=\frac{12}{72}=\frac{1}{6}$

4 a The reciprocal of $\frac{5}{7}=\frac{7}{5}=1\frac{2}{5}$

b $4\frac{1}{3}=\frac{13}{3}$

The reciprocal of $4\frac{1}{3}=\frac{3}{13}$

5 a $\frac{2}{3}\div\frac{3}{4}=\frac{2}{3}\times\frac{4}{3}=\frac{8}{9}$

b $\frac{5}{6}\div\frac{2}{3}=\frac{5}{6}\times\frac{3}{2}=\frac{15}{12}=1\frac{1}{4}$

c $3\div\frac{2}{5}=\frac{3}{1}\times\frac{5}{2}=\frac{15}{2}=7\frac{1}{2}$

6 a $0.5+0.6=1.1$ b $7-1.64=5.36$
c $0.03\times0.02=0.0006$ d $0.8\div0.008=100$

7 a $0.48=\frac{48}{100}=\frac{12}{25}$

b $0.214=\frac{214}{1000}=\frac{107}{500}$

c $0.0008=\frac{8}{10\,000}=\frac{1}{1250}$

d $5.45=5\frac{45}{100}=5\frac{9}{20}$

8 a $\frac{7}{8}=0.875$

b $\frac{11}{12}=0.916\,666\,666\ldots=0.91\dot{6}$

c $\frac{5}{6}=0.833\,333\,333\ldots=0.8\dot{3}$

d $\frac{1}{11}=0.090\,909\,090\ldots=0.\dot{0}\dot{9}$

9 a

$$\begin{aligned}0.\dot{8}&=0.888\,888\,888\ldots\\ \text{Let } x&=0.888\,888\,888\ldots\\ 10x&=8.888\,888\,888\ldots\\ 9x&=8\\ x&=\frac{8}{9}\\ \therefore 0.\dot{8}&=\frac{8}{9}\end{aligned}$$

b

$$\begin{aligned}0.\dot{4}\dot{2}&=0.424\,242\,424\ldots\\ \text{Let } x&=0.424\,242\,424\ldots\\ 100x&=42.424\,242\,424\ldots\\ 99x&=42\\ x&=\frac{42}{99}\\ &=\frac{14}{33}\\ \therefore 0.\dot{4}\dot{2}&=\frac{14}{33}\end{aligned}$$

c

$$\begin{aligned}7.\dot{2}3\dot{7}&=7.237\,237\,237\ldots\\ \text{Let } x&=0.237\,237\,237\ldots\\ 1000x&=237.237\,237\,237\ldots\\ 999x&=237\\ x&=\frac{237}{999}\\ &=\frac{79}{333}\\ \therefore 7.\dot{2}\dot{3}\dot{7}&=7\frac{79}{333}\end{aligned}$$

d

$$\begin{aligned}0.05\dot{1}&=0.051\,111\,111\ldots\\ \text{Let } x&=0.051\,111\,111\ldots\\ 10x&=0.511\,111\,111\ldots\\ 9x&=0.46\\ x&=\frac{0.46}{9}\quad\left[=\frac{46}{900}\right]\\ &=\frac{23}{450}\\ \therefore 0.05\dot{1}&=\frac{23}{450}\end{aligned}$$

10 a $63\% = \frac{63}{100}$

b $20\% = \frac{20}{100} = \frac{1}{5}$

c $8\% = \frac{8}{100} = \frac{2}{25}$

d $87\frac{1}{2}\% = \frac{87\frac{1}{2}}{100} = \frac{175}{200} = \frac{7}{8}$

11 a $16\% = 0.16$

b $4\% = 0.04$

c $900\% = 9$ [or 9.0]

d $3\frac{3}{4}\% = 0.0375$

12 a $\frac{19}{25} = \frac{19}{25} \times 100\% = 76\%$

b $\frac{3}{8} = \frac{3}{8} \times 100\% = 37.5\%$

c $\frac{1}{6} = \frac{1}{6} \times 100\% = 16\frac{2}{3}\%$

13 a $0.56 = 0.56 \times 100\% = 56\%$

b $1.07 = 107\%$

c $0.0125 = 1.25\%$

14 Savings = 15% of \$1350
= \$202.50

The customer would save \$202.50

15 Price increase = \$60 − \$48
= \$12

Percentage increase $= \frac{12}{48} \times 100\% = 25\%$

16 33.75% of the population = 6 037 875

1% of the population $= \frac{6\,037\,875}{33.75}$

100% of the population $= \frac{6\,037\,875}{33.75} \times 100\% = 17\,890\,000$

Australia's population was 17 890 000 in 1996

17 a $5^8 = 390\,625$

b $(0.3)^6 = 0.000\,729$

c $2^{-4} = 0.0625$

d $16^{-1.5} = 0.015\,625$

18 a $\sqrt{76.7376} = 8.76$

b $\sqrt[5]{161\,051} = 11$

19 a $(0.05)^2 = 0.05 \times 0.05 = 0.0025$

b $\left(2\frac{2}{5}\right)^2 = \left(\frac{12}{5}\right)^2 = \frac{144}{25} = 5\frac{19}{25}$

c $\left(1\frac{1}{2}\right)^4 = \left(\frac{3}{2}\right)^4 = \frac{3^4}{2^4} = \frac{81}{16} = 5\frac{1}{16}$

d $\sqrt{1.44} = \sqrt{\frac{144}{100}} = \frac{12}{10} = 1.2$

e $\sqrt{11\frac{1}{9}} = \sqrt{\frac{100}{9}} = \frac{10}{3} = 3\frac{1}{3}$

20 a $50\,000 = 5 \times 10^4$

b $46\,700\,000 = 4.67 \times 10^7$

c $3120 = 3.12 \times 10^3$

d $0.000\,007 = 7 \times 10^{-6}$

e $0.000\,061\,839 = 6.1839 \times 10^{-5}$

21 a $3 \times 10^4 = 30\,000$

b $5.18 \times 10^9 = 5\,180\,000\,000$

c $6.25 \times 10^{-5} = 0.000\,062\,5$

d $1 \times 10^{-3} = 0.001$

22 $\left(3.8 \times 10^3 \times 9.1 \times 10^5\right) \div \left(6.3 \times 10^{-3} + 7 \times 10^{-4}\right) = 4.94 \times 10^{11}$

23 a 5.2398 = 5.24 to 2 decimal places
b 19.215 = 19.22 to 2 decimal places
c 0.683 47 = 0.68 to 2 decimal places

24 a 2.4175 = 2.418 to 3 decimal places
b 345.219 45 = 345.219 to 3 decimal places
c 9.999 85 = 10.000 to 3 decimal places

25 a 251 576 328 = 251 600 000 to 4 significant figures
b 13.2376 = 13.24 to 4 significant figures
c 0.030 847 6 = 0.030 85 to 4 significant figures
d 0.009 817 526 = 0.009 818 to 4 significant figures

26 a $8\,567\,283\,956 = 8.57 \times 10^9$ [to 3 sig figs]

b $0.000\,148\,137\,285 = 1.48 \times 10^{-4}$ [to 3 sig figs]

27 $\{[(5.2 + 9.7) \times (7.1 - 2.35)] \div 12.5 + 8.2\} \times 9.1 = 126.1442$

28 a $\frac{7.11 \times 1.6}{15.8 \div 2.5} = 1.8$

b $\sqrt{6^2 + 13^2} = 14.317\,821\,06\ldots$
$= 14.3$ [to 1 decimal place]

c $\sqrt[4]{\frac{250.21632}{1.2}} = 3.8$

29 $\frac{3\frac{2}{3} - 1\frac{5}{6}}{5\frac{3}{7} + 5\frac{4}{7}} = \frac{1}{6}$

30 a $9p^2 - p^2 + 7p - 10p = 8p^2 - 3p$

b $7k^2 + k^3 - 6k + 5 - 9k^3 + 8k - 7$
$= 7k^2 - 8k^3 + 2k - 2$

31 a $4a \times 5b \times 6c = 120abc$ b $3x^3 \times 9x = 27x^4$

c $8t^8 \times 4t^4 = 32t^{12}$ d $3x^5y^3 \times 2xy^4 = 6x^6y^7$

32 a $10d \div 2d = 5$ b $6t^6 \div 2t^2 = 3t^4$

c $14a^3b^2c \div 2abc = 7a^2b$ d $\dfrac{8m^8n^6}{12m^5n^9} = \dfrac{2m^3}{3n^3}$

33 a $\left(4a^5\right)^2 = 16a^{10}$ b $\left(x^3y^4\right)^3 = x^9y^{12}$

c $7\left(c^3d^7\right)^2 = 7c^6d^{14}$ d $\left(3a^2b^3c^4\right)^4 = 81a^8b^{12}c^{16}$

34 a $3(8x - y) = 24x - 3y$

b $e\left(3e^2 - 5e + 7\right) = 3e^3 - 5e^2 + 7e$

c $-5(2x - 11y + z) = -10x + 55y - 5z$

d $4x\left(x^2 - 3\right) = 4x^3 - 12x$

e $2p^4q^3\left(pq^7 + 5p^2q^3\right) = 2p^5q^{10} + 10p^6q^6$

f $-(7 - 8u) = -7 + 8u$

35 a $9m - (3m + 4) = 9m - 3m - 4$
$= 6m - 4$

b $7e(5e - 7) + 2\left(9e^2 - 8\right) = 35e^2 - 49e + 18e^2 - 16$
$= 53e^2 - 49e - 16$

c $5n(3n + 2) - 3\left(n^2 - 3n + 1\right)$
$= 15n^2 + 10n - 3n^2 + 9n - 3$
$= 12n^2 + 19n - 3$

36 a $(a + 4)(a - 5) = a^2 - 5a + 4a - 20$
$= a^2 - a - 20$

b $(b - 6)(b - 1) = b^2 - b - 6b + 6$
$= b^2 - 7b + 6$

c $(8p + 3q)(2p + 5q) = 16p^2 + 40pq + 6pq + 15q^2$
$= 16p^2 + 46pq + 15q^2$

d $(7x - y)(y + 2z) = 7xy + 14xz - y^2 - 2yz$

37 a $9t^2 - (3t + 7)(t - 8) = 9t^2 - \left(3t^2 - 17t - 56\right)$
$= 9t^2 - 3t^2 + 17t + 56$
$= 6t^2 + 17t + 56$

b $(4 - 3n)(2 + n) - n(5n + 1) = 8 - 2n - 3n^2 - 5n^2 - n$
$= 8 - 3n - 8n^2$

38 $(2p + 8)(p + 7) - (3p - 11) = 2p^2 + 22p + 56 - 3p + 11$
$= 2p^2 + 19p + 67$

39 a $(2k + 3)\left(k^2 + 9k + 1\right)$
$= 2k^3 + 18k^2 + 2k + 3k^2 + 27k + 3$
$= 2k^3 + 21k^2 + 29k + 3$

b $(a + b + 3)(a - b + 5)$
$= a^2 - ab + 5a + ab - b^2 + 5b + 3a - 3b + 15$
$= a^2 + 8a - b^2 + 2b + 15$

40 a $(e - 8)^2 = e^2 - 2 \times e \times 8 + 8^2$
$= e^2 - 16e + 64$

b $(5m + 2n)^2 = (5m)^2 + 2 \times 5m \times 2n + (2n)^2$
$= 25m^2 + 20mn + 4n^2$

c $\left(a^2 - 7b\right)^2 = \left(a^2\right)^2 - 2 \times a^2 \times 7b + (7b)^2$
$= a^4 - 14a^2b + 49b^2$

41 a $a^2 + 10a \rightarrow a^2 + 2 \times a \times 5 + 5^2$
$= a^2 + 10a + 25$

b $b^2 - 16b \rightarrow b^2 - 2 \times b \times 8 + 8^2$
$= b^2 - 16b + 64$

c $25c^2 + 20c \rightarrow (5c)^2 + 2 \times 5c \times 2 + 2^2$
$= 25c^2 + 20c + 4$

d $16d^2 - 24de \rightarrow (4d)^2 - 2 \times 4d \times 3e + (3e)^2$
$= 16d^2 - 24de + 9e^2$

42 a $(y + 7)(y - 7) = y^2 - 7^2$
$= y^2 - 49$

b $(3k - 8)(3k + 8) = (3k)^2 - 8^2$
$= 9k^2 - 64$

c $\left(x^2 - 5y\right)\left(x^2 + 5y\right) = \left(x^2\right)^2 - (5y)^2$
$= x^4 - 25y^2$

43 a $(u + 4)^2 + (u + 3)(u - 3) = u^2 + 8u + 16 + u^2 - 9$
$= 2u^2 + 8u + 7$

b $(3k + 5)(3k - 5) - (2k - 3)^2$
$= 9k^2 - 25 - \left(4k^2 - 12k + 9\right)$
$= 9k^2 - 25 - 4k^2 + 12k - 9$
$= 5k^2 + 12k - 34$

44 a $y = x^2 + 3x - 2$
When $x = 0$, $y = 0^2 + 3 \times 0 - 2$
$= -2$

b $y = x^2 + 3x - 2$
When $x = 1$, $y = 1^2 + 3 \times 1 - 2$
$= 2$

c $y = x^2 + 3x - 2$

When $x = -2$, $y = (-2)^2 + 3 \times (-2) - 2$
$= -4$

45 $r = kt^2$

When $k = 9.5$ and $t = 10$, $r = 9.5 \times 10^2$
$= 950$

46 $y = \dfrac{x+1}{1-2x}$

When $x = \dfrac{1}{3}$, $y = \dfrac{\frac{1}{3}+1}{1-2\times\frac{1}{3}}$
$= 4$

47 $A = \pi\left(R^2 - r^2\right)$

When $R = 14$ and $r = 9$,
$A = \pi\left(14^2 - 9^2\right)$
$= 361.283\,155\,2\ldots$ [calculator]
$= 361.283$ [3 decimal places]

48 When $n = 3\sqrt{2}$,
$7 - 2n^2 = 7 - 2 \times \left(3\sqrt{2}\right)^2$
$= 7 - 36$
$= -29$

49 $S = \dfrac{n}{2}\left[2a + (n-1)d\right]$

When $n = 38$, $d = -3$ and $S = -1083$,
$-1083 = \dfrac{38}{2}\left[2a + (38-1)\times -3\right]$
$-1083 = 19\left[2a - 111\right]$
$-1083 = 38a - 2109$
$38a = 1026$
$a = 27$

50 **a** $7k + 28 = 7(k+4)$ **b** $h^2 - 8h = h(h-8)$

c $16x + 12y - 36z = 4(4x + 3y - 9z)$

d $5n^2 + 25mn = 5n(n + 5m)$

e $a^3b^7 - a^4b^6 = a^3b^6(b - a)$

51 **a** $e^2 - 100 = (e-10)(e+10)$

b $1 - r^2 = (1-r)(1+r)$

c $64p^2 - 121q^2 = (8p - 11q)(8p + 11q)$

d $g^4 - 9h^2k^2 = \left(g^2 - 3hk\right)\left(g^2 + 3hk\right)$

52 **a** $pq + 6p + qr + 6r = p(q+6) + r(q+6)$
$= (q+6)(p+r)$

b $z^2 + 7z + yz + 7y = z(z+7) + y(z+7)$
$= (z+7)(z+y)$

c $m^2 - 3m + 2mn - 6n = m(m-3) + 2n(m-3)$
$= (m-3)(m+2n)$

d $x^2 + xy + x + y = x(x+y) + 1(x+y)$
$= (x+y)(x+1)$

53 **a** $ab - 9a - 7b + 63 = a(b-9) - 7(b-9)$
$= (b-9)(a-7)$

b $p^2 + pq - mp - mq = p(p+q) - m(p+q)$
$= (p+q)(p-m)$

54 **a** $x^2 + 7x + 12 = (x+4)(x+3)$

b $g^2 + 3g - 88 = (g+11)(g-8)$

c $k^2 - 9k + 20 = (k-5)(k-4)$

d $c^2 - 2cd - 35d^2 = (c - 7d)(c + 5d)$

55 **a** $2x^2 + 9x + 10 = 2x^2 + 4x + 5x + 10$
$= 2x(x+2) + 5(x+2)$
$= (x+2)(2x+5)$

b $3x^2 + 23x - 8 = 3x^2 + 24x - x - 8$
$= 3x(x+8) - 1(x+8)$
$= (x+8)(3x-1)$

c $4a^2 - 23a + 15 = 4a^2 - 20a - 3a + 15$
$= 4a(a-5) - 3(a-5)$
$= (a-5)(4a-3)$

d $6n^2 - 5n - 6 = 6n^2 - 9n + 4n - 6$
$= 3n(2n-3) + 2(2n-3)$
$= (2n-3)(3n+2)$

56 **a** $a^3 - 27 = (a-3)\left(a^2 + 3a + 9\right)$

b $h^3 + 1000 = (h+10)\left(h^2 - 10h + 100\right)$

c $8 - 125k^3 = (2 - 5k)\left(4 + 10k + 25k^2\right)$

d $64p^3 + 343q^3 = (4p + 7q)\left(16p^2 - 28pq + 49q^2\right)$

57 **a** $x^2 - 9 = (x-3)(x+3)$

b $x^2 - 9x = x(x-9)$

c $x^2 + 8x - 9 = (x+9)(x-1)$

d $x^3 + 8x^2 = x^2(x+8)$

e $x^3 - 8 = (x-2)\left(x^2 + 2x + 4\right)$

f $x^3 + x^2 + x + 1 = x^2(x+1) + 1(x+1)$
$= (x+1)(x^2+1)$

58 a $3c^2 - 300 = 3(c^2 - 100)$
$= 3(c-10)(c+10)$

b $7y^3 + 7 = 7(y^3+1)$
$= 7(y+1)(y^2 - y + 1)$

c $5h^2 - 20h - 25 = 5(h^2 - 4h - 5)$
$= 5(h-5)(h+1)$

d $m^4 - 16 = (m^2-4)(m^2+4)$
$= (m-2)(m+2)(m^2+4)$

e $k^2 - 9 + 7km - 21m = (k-3)(k+3) + 7m(k-3)$
$= (k-3)(k+3+7m)$

f $pqr + 3pr - 5pq - 15p = p(qr + 3r - 5q - 15)$
$= p[r(q+3) - 5(q+3)]$
$= p(q+3)(r-5)$

59 a $4\sqrt{6} + 3\sqrt{6} = 7\sqrt{6}$
b $3\sqrt{3} + 2\sqrt{3} - 8\sqrt{2} = 5\sqrt{3} - 8\sqrt{2}$
c $6\sqrt{11} + \sqrt{11} = 7\sqrt{11}$
d $9\sqrt{5} - 4\sqrt{5} - 5\sqrt{5} = 0$
e $8 - 3\sqrt{7} + 7\sqrt{2} - 2 + \sqrt{7} = 6 - 2\sqrt{7} + 7\sqrt{2}$

60 a $\sqrt{6} \times \sqrt{5} = \sqrt{30}$
b $2\sqrt{3} \times 4\sqrt{10} = 8\sqrt{30}$
c $(\sqrt{7})^2 = 7$
d $(5\sqrt{2})^2 = 25 \times 2$
$= 50$
e $3\sqrt{6} \times 7\sqrt{6} = 21 \times 6$
$= 126$
f $\sqrt{15} \div \sqrt{5} = \sqrt{3}$
g $\sqrt{63} \div \sqrt{7} = \sqrt{9}$
$= 3$
h $12\sqrt{10} \div 4\sqrt{5} = 3\sqrt{2}$

61 a $\sqrt{28} = \sqrt{4} \times \sqrt{7}$
$= 2\sqrt{7}$
b $\sqrt{45} = \sqrt{9} \times \sqrt{5}$
$= 3\sqrt{5}$
c $\sqrt{300} = \sqrt{100} \times \sqrt{3}$
$= 10\sqrt{3}$
d $\sqrt{75} = \sqrt{25} \times \sqrt{3}$
$= 5\sqrt{3}$
e $3\sqrt{40} = 3 \times \sqrt{4} \times \sqrt{10}$
$= 6\sqrt{10}$

62 a $5\sqrt{7} = \sqrt{25} \times \sqrt{7}$
$= \sqrt{175}$
b $9\sqrt{6} = \sqrt{81} \times \sqrt{6}$
$= \sqrt{486}$

63 a $\sqrt{3} \times \sqrt{12} = \sqrt{36}$
$= 6$
b $\sqrt{10} \times \sqrt{15} = \sqrt{150}$
$= \sqrt{25} \times \sqrt{6}$
$= 5\sqrt{6}$
c $2\sqrt{6} \times 3\sqrt{2} = 6\sqrt{12}$
$= 6 \times \sqrt{4} \times \sqrt{3}$
$= 12\sqrt{3}$

64 a $\sqrt{98} + \sqrt{72} = \sqrt{49} \times \sqrt{2} + \sqrt{36} \times \sqrt{2}$
$= 7\sqrt{2} + 6\sqrt{2}$
$= 13\sqrt{2}$

b $\sqrt{24} + \sqrt{6} - \sqrt{20} = \sqrt{4} \times \sqrt{6} + \sqrt{6} - \sqrt{4} \times \sqrt{5}$
$= 2\sqrt{6} + \sqrt{6} - 2\sqrt{5}$
$= 3\sqrt{6} - 2\sqrt{5}$

c $5\sqrt{8} + 2\sqrt{18} = 5 \times \sqrt{4} \times \sqrt{2} + 2 \times \sqrt{9} \times \sqrt{2}$
$= 10\sqrt{2} + 6\sqrt{2}$
$= 16\sqrt{2}$

65 a $(\sqrt{7} + \sqrt{5})(\sqrt{3} + \sqrt{2}) = \sqrt{21} + \sqrt{14} + \sqrt{15} + \sqrt{10}$

b $(\sqrt{11} - 9)(\sqrt{2} - 7) = \sqrt{22} - 7\sqrt{11} - 9\sqrt{2} + 63$

c $(3\sqrt{3} + 8)(3 - 2\sqrt{5}) = 9\sqrt{3} - 6\sqrt{15} + 24 - 16\sqrt{5}$

d $(4\sqrt{6} - 5\sqrt{3})(3\sqrt{6} + 2)$
$= 12\sqrt{36} + 8\sqrt{6} - 15\sqrt{18} - 10\sqrt{3}$
$= 12 \times 6 + 8\sqrt{6} - 15 \times \sqrt{9} \times \sqrt{2} - 10\sqrt{3}$
$= 72 + 8\sqrt{6} - 45\sqrt{2} - 10\sqrt{3}$

66 a $(\sqrt{10} + \sqrt{3})^2 = (\sqrt{10})^2 + 2 \times \sqrt{10} \times \sqrt{3} + (\sqrt{3})^2$
$= 10 + 2\sqrt{30} + 3$
$= 13 + 2\sqrt{30}$

b $(\sqrt{13} - 4)^2 = (\sqrt{13})^2 - 2 \times \sqrt{13} \times 4 + 4^2$
$= 13 - 8\sqrt{13} + 16$
$= 29 - 8\sqrt{13}$

c $(2\sqrt{6} + 3\sqrt{2})^2 = (2\sqrt{6})^2 + 2 \times 2\sqrt{6} \times 3\sqrt{2} + (3\sqrt{2})^2$
$= 24 + 12\sqrt{12} + 18$
$= 42 + 12 \times \sqrt{4} \times \sqrt{3}$
$= 42 + 24\sqrt{3}$

67 a $(\sqrt{3} - \sqrt{2})(\sqrt{3} + \sqrt{2}) = (\sqrt{3})^2 - (\sqrt{2})^2$
$= 3 - 2$
$= 1$

b $(1 - \sqrt{5})(1 + \sqrt{5}) = 1^2 - (\sqrt{5})^2$
$= 1 - 5$
$= -4$

c $(5\sqrt{10} + 2\sqrt{7})(5\sqrt{10} - 2\sqrt{7}) = (5\sqrt{10})^2 - (2\sqrt{7})^2$
$= 250 - 28$
$= 222$

d $(4\sqrt{6}-7)(4\sqrt{6}+7)=(4\sqrt{6})^2-7^2$
$=96-49$
$=47$

68 The conjugate of $8-6\sqrt{7}$ is $8+6\sqrt{7}$.

69 The conjugate of $\sqrt{11}+2\sqrt{3}$ is $\sqrt{11}-2\sqrt{3}$

$(\sqrt{11}+2\sqrt{3})(\sqrt{11}-2\sqrt{3})=(\sqrt{11})^2-(2\sqrt{3})^2$
$=11-12$
$=-1$

$\therefore$ the product is rational

70 **a** $\frac{1}{\sqrt{2}}=\frac{1}{\sqrt{2}}\times\frac{\sqrt{2}}{\sqrt{2}}$
$=\frac{\sqrt{2}}{2}$

b $\frac{11}{\sqrt{11}}=\frac{11}{\sqrt{11}}\times\frac{\sqrt{11}}{\sqrt{11}}$
$=\frac{11\sqrt{11}}{11}$
$=\sqrt{11}$

c $\frac{\sqrt{2}}{\sqrt{3}}=\frac{\sqrt{2}}{\sqrt{3}}\times\frac{\sqrt{3}}{\sqrt{3}}$
$=\frac{\sqrt{6}}{3}$

d $\frac{3}{2\sqrt{5}}=\frac{3}{2\sqrt{5}}\times\frac{\sqrt{5}}{\sqrt{5}}$
$=\frac{3\sqrt{5}}{10}$

71 **a** $\frac{1}{\sqrt{3}-\sqrt{2}}=\frac{1}{\sqrt{3}-\sqrt{2}}\times\frac{\sqrt{3}+\sqrt{2}}{\sqrt{3}+\sqrt{2}}$
$=\frac{\sqrt{3}+\sqrt{2}}{3-2}$
$=\sqrt{3}+\sqrt{2}$

b $\frac{\sqrt{7}-\sqrt{3}}{\sqrt{7}+\sqrt{3}}=\frac{\sqrt{7}-\sqrt{3}}{\sqrt{7}+\sqrt{3}}\times\frac{\sqrt{7}-\sqrt{3}}{\sqrt{7}-\sqrt{3}}$
$=\frac{7-2\sqrt{21}+3}{7-3}$
$=\frac{10-2\sqrt{21}}{4}$
$=\frac{2(5-\sqrt{21})}{4}$
$=\frac{5-\sqrt{21}}{2}$

c $\frac{7}{\sqrt{5}+2}=\frac{7}{\sqrt{5}+2}\times\frac{\sqrt{5}-2}{\sqrt{5}-2}$
$=\frac{7(\sqrt{5}-2)}{5-4}$
$=7(\sqrt{5}-2)$

d $\frac{\sqrt{5}+1}{3\sqrt{6}-\sqrt{2}}=\frac{\sqrt{5}+1}{3\sqrt{6}-\sqrt{2}}\times\frac{3\sqrt{6}+\sqrt{2}}{3\sqrt{6}+\sqrt{2}}$
$=\frac{3\sqrt{30}+\sqrt{10}+3\sqrt{6}+\sqrt{2}}{54-2}$
$=\frac{3\sqrt{30}+\sqrt{10}+3\sqrt{6}+\sqrt{2}}{52}$

72 $\frac{6}{2\sqrt{7}+5}-\frac{8}{3-\sqrt{7}}$
$=\frac{6}{2\sqrt{7}+5}\times\frac{2\sqrt{7}-5}{2\sqrt{7}-5}-\frac{8}{3-\sqrt{7}}\times\frac{3+\sqrt{7}}{3+\sqrt{7}}$
$=\frac{6(2\sqrt{7}-5)}{28-25}-\frac{8(3+\sqrt{7})}{9-7}$
$=\frac{6(2\sqrt{7}-5)}{3}-\frac{8(3+\sqrt{7})}{2}$
$=2(2\sqrt{7}-5)-4(3+\sqrt{7})$
$=4\sqrt{7}-10-12-4\sqrt{7}$
$=-22$

$\therefore \frac{6}{2\sqrt{7}+5}-\frac{8}{3-\sqrt{7}}$ is rational

73 $\frac{33}{2\sqrt{3}+1}=a+b\sqrt{3}$

$\frac{33}{2\sqrt{3}+1}=\frac{33}{2\sqrt{3}+1}\times\frac{2\sqrt{3}-1}{2\sqrt{3}-1}$
$=\frac{33(2\sqrt{3}-1)}{12-1}$
$=\frac{33(2\sqrt{3}-1)}{11}$
$=3(2\sqrt{3}-1)$
$=6\sqrt{3}-3$
$=-3+6\sqrt{3}$
$\therefore a=-3$ and $b=6$

74 **a** $\frac{7a-14b}{7}=\frac{7(a-2b)}{7}$
$=a-2b$

b $\frac{10}{2-4m}=\frac{10}{2(1-2m)}$
$=\frac{5}{1-2m}$

c $\frac{8x+6}{12x+9}=\frac{2(4x+3)}{3(4x+3)}$
$=\frac{2}{3}$

d $\frac{h^2-5h}{h}=\frac{h(h-5)}{h}$
$=h-5$

e $\frac{n^2-1}{n^2-n}=\frac{(n-1)(n+1)}{n(n-1)}$
$=\frac{n+1}{n}$

f $\frac{d+6}{d^2-2d-48}=\frac{d+6}{(d-8)(d+6)}$
$=\frac{1}{d-8}$

g $\frac{e^2-9}{e^2+6e+9}=\frac{(e-3)(e+3)}{(e+3)^2}$
$=\frac{e-3}{e+3}$

h $\dfrac{x^2+4x+3}{x^2-4x-21}=\dfrac{(x+3)(x+1)}{(x-7)(x+3)}$

$=\dfrac{x+1}{x-7}$

75 **a** $\dfrac{7e}{11}+\dfrac{2e}{11}=\dfrac{9e}{11}$

b $\dfrac{3h}{8}+\dfrac{h}{8}=\dfrac{4h}{8}$

$=\dfrac{h}{2}$

c $\dfrac{5d}{9}+\dfrac{3d}{7}=\dfrac{35d}{63}+\dfrac{27d}{63}$

$=\dfrac{62d}{63}$

d $\dfrac{4u-3}{v}+\dfrac{7-u}{v}=\dfrac{3u+4}{v}$

e $\dfrac{3m-4}{5}+\dfrac{2m-3}{3}=\dfrac{3(3m-4)+5(2m-3)}{15}$

$=\dfrac{9m-12+10m-15}{15}$

$=\dfrac{19m-27}{15}$

76 **a** $\dfrac{5z}{12}-\dfrac{z}{3}=\dfrac{5z}{12}-\dfrac{4z}{12}$

$=\dfrac{z}{12}$

b $1-\dfrac{b}{a}=\dfrac{a}{a}-\dfrac{b}{a}$

$=\dfrac{a-b}{a}$

c $\dfrac{2k+5}{7}-\dfrac{k-8}{9}=\dfrac{9(2k+5)-7(k-8)}{63}$

$=\dfrac{18k+45-7k+56}{63}$

$=\dfrac{11k+101}{63}$

d $\dfrac{8m-7}{15}-\dfrac{3m+7}{10}=\dfrac{2(8m-7)-3(3m+7)}{30}$

$=\dfrac{16m-14-9m-21}{30}$

$=\dfrac{7m-35}{30}\quad\left[=\dfrac{7(m-5)}{30}\right]$

77 **a** $\dfrac{1}{x^2+7x+12}-\dfrac{1}{x^2+9x+20}$

$=\dfrac{1}{(x+3)(x+4)}-\dfrac{1}{(x+5)(x+4)}$

$=\dfrac{(x+5)-(x+3)}{(x+3)(x+4)(x+5)}$

$=\dfrac{x+5-x-3}{(x+3)(x+4)(x+5)}$

$=\dfrac{2}{(x+3)(x+4)(x+5)}$

b $\dfrac{2a+3}{a^2+a}+\dfrac{a-4}{a^2-1}$

$=\dfrac{2a+3}{a(a+1)}+\dfrac{a-4}{(a-1)(a+1)}$

$=\dfrac{(2a+3)(a-1)+a(a-4)}{a(a+1)(a-1)}$

$=\dfrac{2a^2+a-3+a^2-4a}{a(a+1)(a-1)}$

$=\dfrac{3a^2-3a-3}{a(a+1)(a-1)}$

$=\dfrac{3(a^2-a-1)}{a(a+1)(a-1)}$

78 **a** $\dfrac{x^2+4x}{3x+7}\times\dfrac{5x+10}{x^2+6x+8}$

$=\dfrac{x(x+4)}{3x+7}\times\dfrac{5(x+2)}{(x+4)(x+2)}$

$=\dfrac{5x}{3x+7}$

b $\dfrac{a^2-a-6}{a^2+2a-15}\times\dfrac{a^2+12a+35}{a^2+9a+14}$

$=\dfrac{(a-3)(a+2)}{(a-3)(a+5)}\times\dfrac{(a+7)(a+5)}{(a+7)(a+2)}$

$=1$

79 **a** $\dfrac{u^2+6u}{u^2+5u-6}\div\dfrac{u^2+9u+8}{u^2-1}$

$=\dfrac{u(u+6)}{(u+6)(u-1)}\div\dfrac{(u+8)(u+1)}{(u-1)(u+1)}$

$=\dfrac{u(u+6)}{(u+6)(u-1)}\times\dfrac{(u-1)(u+1)}{(u+8)(u+1)}$

$=\dfrac{u}{u+8}$

b $\dfrac{z^2+13z+36}{z^2-9}\div\dfrac{z^2+18z+81}{z^2+7z+12}$

$=\dfrac{(z+9)(z+4)}{(z-3)(z+3)}\div\dfrac{(z+9)^2}{(z+4)(z+3)}$

$=\dfrac{(z+9)(z+4)}{(z-3)(z+3)}\times\dfrac{(z+4)(z+3)}{(z+9)^2}$

$=\dfrac{(z+4)^2}{(z-3)(z+9)}$

80 **a** $9m+15=78$

$9m=63$

$m=7$

b $\dfrac{k}{4}-17=63$

$\dfrac{k}{4}=80$

$k=320$

c $123 - 6j = 145$
$-6j = 22$
$j = -3\frac{2}{3}$

d $12e + 43 = 7e - 67$
$12e = 7e - 110$
$5e = -110$
$e = -22$

81 **a** $7(12w - 5) = 91$
$84w - 35 = 91$
$84w = 126$
$w = 1.5$

b $11n + 23 - 6n - 14 = 3n + 19 - n$
$5n + 9 = 2n + 19$
$3n = 10$
$n = 3\frac{1}{3}$

c $8(3b + 7) = 5(2b - 9)$
$24b + 56 = 10b - 45$
$14b = -101$
$b = -7\frac{3}{14}$

d $3(6v + 1) - 4(v - 7) = 5(2v + 5)$
$18v + 3 - 4v + 28 = 10v + 25$
$14v + 31 = 10v + 25$
$4v = -6$
$v = -1.5$

82 **a** $\frac{3k + 5}{7} = 7$
$3k + 5 = 49$
$3k = 44$
$k = 14\frac{2}{3}$

b $\frac{a + 1}{2a - 1} = \frac{2}{3}$
$3(a + 1) = 2(2a - 1)$
$3a + 3 = 4a - 2$
$-a = -5$
$a = 5$

c $\frac{5u + 3}{2u - 7} = \frac{5u + 8}{2u + 9}$
$(5u + 3)(2u + 9) = (5u + 8)(2u - 7)$
$10u^2 + 51u + 27 = 10u^2 - 19u - 56$
$70u = -83$
$u = -1\frac{13}{70}$

d $\frac{4n}{5} + \frac{2n - 5}{8} = n + 1$
$40 \times \left(\frac{4n}{5}\right) + 40 \times \left(\frac{2n - 5}{8}\right) = 40(n + 1)$
$8(4n) + 5(2n - 5) = 40n + 40$
$32n + 10n - 25 = 40n + 40$
$42n - 25 = 40n + 40$
$2n = 65$
$n = 32.5$

83 **a** $5a + 6 > -4$
$5a > -10$
$a > -2$

b $\frac{m}{5} - 6 \geq -1$
$\frac{m}{5} \geq 5$
$m \geq 25$

c $\frac{3k + 4}{5} < 7$
$3k + 4 < 35$
$3k < 31$
$k < 10\frac{1}{3}$

d $9p + 2 \leq 3p - 10$
$6p \leq -12$
$p \leq -2$

84 **a** $7 - 3x > 4$
$-3x > -3$
$x < 1$

b $11 - \frac{w}{6} \leq -8$
$-\frac{w}{6} \leq -19$
$w \geq 114$

c $\frac{9 - x}{4} < -2$
$9 - x < -8$
$-x < -17$
$x > 17$

d $6e + 8 \geq 29 + 13e$
$-7e \geq 21$
$e \leq -3$

85 **a** $x \leq 1$

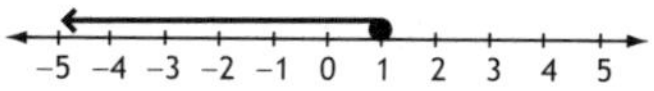

b $x > -3$

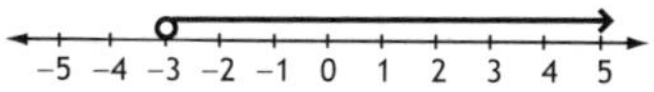

86 **a** $2 - 9x \geq 11$
$-9x \geq 9$
$x \leq -1$

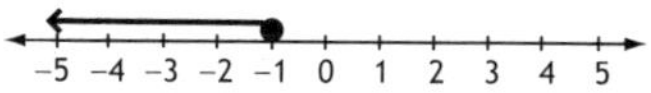

b $8x + 1 < 33$
$8x < 32$
$x < 4$

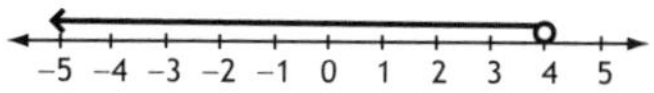

87 **a** $|-12| = 12$

b $|4| \times |-3| = 4 \times 3$
$= 12$

c $|-5| \times |-2| = 5 \times 2$
$= 10$

d $|10| = 10$

e $|4 + 1| = |5|$
$= 5$

f $|4| + |1| = 4 + 1$
$= 5$

g $|-9| + |7| = 9 + 7$
$= 16$

h $|-9 + 7| = |-2|$
$= 2$

88 **a** $|8 - 3| = |5|$
$= 5$

b $|3 - 8| = |-5|$
$= 5$

c $|3| - |8| = 3 - 8$
$= -5$

d $3|-8| = 3 \times 8$
$= 24$

e $2|-4| - 3|-3| = 2 \times 4 - 3 \times 3$
$= -1$

89 **a** $|x| = 2$

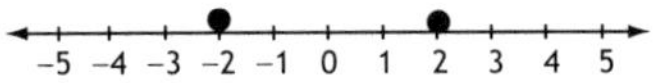

b $|x| < 1$

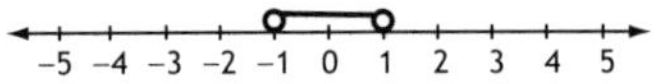

c $|x| \geq 3$

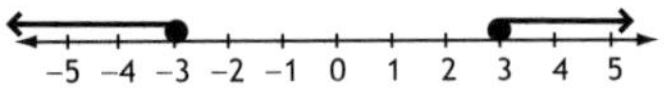

d $|x - 2| = 3$

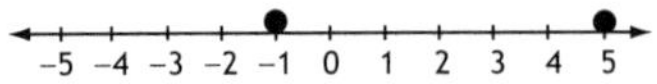

e $|x + 3| > 2$

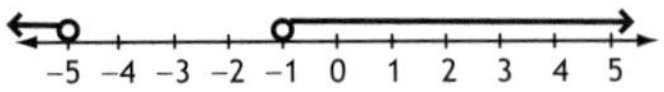

90 **a** $|x| = 2$

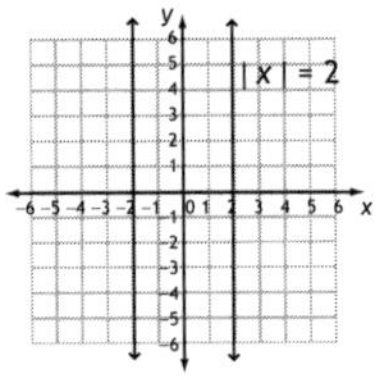

b $|y| = 4$

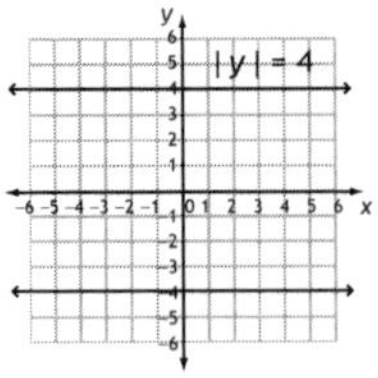

c $y = |x|$

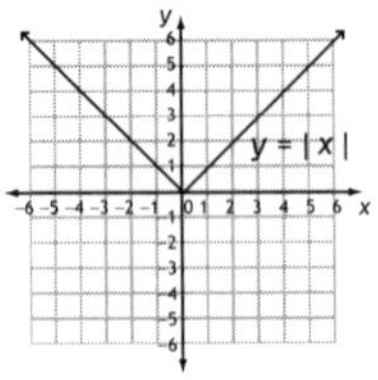

91 **a** $|x| = 4$

$x = -4$ or $x = 4$

b $|x - 1| = 5$

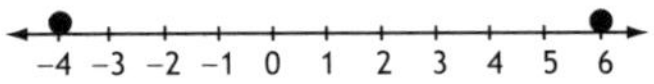

$x = -4$ or $x = 6$

c $|3x - 2| = 1$

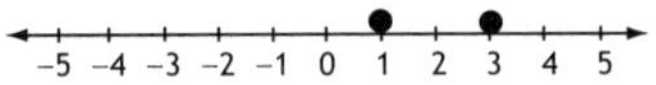

$3x = 1$ or $3x = 3$

$x = \frac{1}{3}$ $\quad x = 1$

92 **a** $|x| \leq 3$

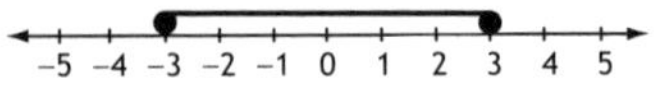

$-3 \leq x \leq 3$

b $|x - 2| > 2$

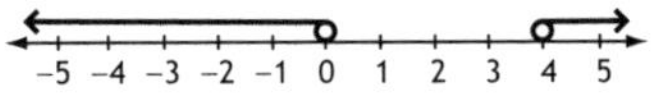

$x < 0$ or $x > 4$

c $|x + 1| < 3$

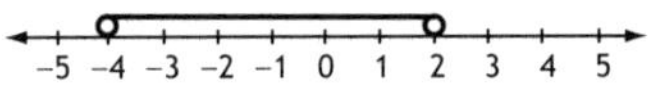

$-4 < x < 2$

d $|4x - 3| \geq 1$

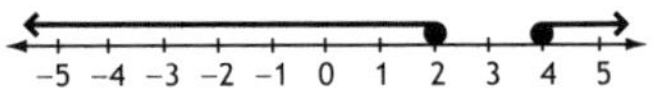

$4x \leq 2$ or $4x \geq 4$

$x \leq \frac{1}{2}$ $\quad x \geq 1$

93 **a** $x^2 - 10x + 16 = 0$

$(x - 8)(x - 2) = 0$

$x - 8 = 0$ or $x - 2 = 0$

$x = 8$ $\quad x = 2$

b $u^2 + 13u + 40 = 0$

$(u + 8)(u + 5) = 0$

$u + 8 = 0$ or $u + 5 = 0$

$u = -8$ $\quad u = -5$

c $2n^2 + 7n - 15 = 0$

$(2n - 3)(n + 5) = 0$

$2n - 3 = 0$ or $n + 5 = 0$

$2n = 3$ $\quad n = -5$

$n = 1\frac{1}{2}$ $\quad n = -5$

d $4a^2 - 24a + 35 = 0$

$(2a - 7)(2a - 5) = 0$

$2a - 7 = 0$ or $2a - 5 = 0$

$2a = 7$ $\quad 2a = 5$

$a = 3\frac{1}{2}$ $\quad a = 2\frac{1}{2}$

94 **a** $x^2 = 7x$

$x^2 - 7x = 0$

$x(x - 7) = 0$

$x = 0$ or $x - 7 = 0$

$x = 0$ $\quad x = 7$

b $g^2 = 12g - 32$

$g^2 - 12g + 32 = 0$

$(g - 4)(g - 8) = 0$

$g - 4 = 0$ or $g - 8 = 0$

$g = 4$ $\quad g = 8$

c $(k + 9)(k + 1) = 33$

$k^2 + 10k + 9 = 33$

$k^2 + 10k - 24 = 0$

$(k + 12)(k - 2) = 0$

$k + 12 = 0$ or $k - 2 = 0$

$k = -12$ $\quad k = 2$

d $7x^2 = 25x + 12$

$7x^2 - 25x - 12 = 0$

$(7x + 3)(x - 4) = 0$

$7x + 3 = 0$ or $x - 4 = 0$

$7x = -3$ $\quad x = 4$

$x = -\frac{3}{7}$ $\quad x = 4$

95 **a** $(m + 5)^2 = 25$

$m + 5 = -5$ or $m + 5 = 5$

$m = -10$ $\quad m = 0$

b $(3e - 4)^2 = 2$

$3e - 4 = \pm\sqrt{2}$

$3e = 4 \pm \sqrt{2}$

$e = \frac{4 \pm \sqrt{2}}{3}$

96 **a** $x^2 - 9x + 11 = 0$

$a = 1, b = -9, c = 11$

$$x = \frac{-b \pm \sqrt{b^2 - 4ac}}{2a}$$

$$= \frac{-(-9) \pm \sqrt{(-9)^2 - 4 \times 1 \times 11}}{2 \times 1}$$

$$= \frac{9 \pm \sqrt{37}}{2}$$

$x = \frac{9 + \sqrt{37}}{2}$ or $x = \frac{9 - \sqrt{37}}{2}$

$x = 7.541\,381\,265\ldots$ $\quad$ $x = 1.458\,618\,735\ldots$

$x = 7.5414$ $\quad$ $x = 1.4586$

[correct to 4 decimal places]

b $5x^2 + 8x - 6 = 0$

$a = 5, b = 8, c = -6$

$$x = \frac{-b \pm \sqrt{b^2 - 4ac}}{2a}$$

$$= \frac{-8 \pm \sqrt{8^2 - 4 \times 5 \times -6}}{2 \times 5}$$

$$= \frac{-8 \pm \sqrt{184}}{10}$$

$x = \frac{-8 + \sqrt{184}}{10}$ or $x = \frac{-8 - \sqrt{184}}{10}$

$x = 0.556\,465\,996\ldots$ $\quad$ $x = -2.156\,465\,997\ldots$

$x = 0.5565$ $\quad$ $x = -2.1565$

[correct to 4 decimal places]

97 **a** $x^2 + 11x + 12 = 0$

$a = 1, b = 11, c = 12$

$$x = \frac{-b \pm \sqrt{b^2 - 4ac}}{2a}$$

$$= \frac{-11 \pm \sqrt{11^2 - 4 \times 1 \times 12}}{2 \times 1}$$

$$= \frac{-11 \pm \sqrt{73}}{2}$$

b $2x^2 - 8x - 3 = 0$

$a = 2, b = -8, c = -3$

$$x = \frac{-b \pm \sqrt{b^2 - 4ac}}{2a}$$

$$= \frac{-(-8) \pm \sqrt{(-8)^2 - 4 \times 2 \times -3}}{2 \times 2}$$

$$= \frac{8 \pm \sqrt{88}}{4}$$

$$= \frac{8 \pm 2\sqrt{22}}{4}$$

$$= \frac{2(4 \pm \sqrt{22})}{4}$$

$$= \frac{4 \pm \sqrt{22}}{2}$$

98 **a** $y = 2x + 7$ **i**

$y = 4x + 13$ **ii**

$4x + 13 = 2x + 7$

$2x = -6$

$x = -3$

Substitute in **i**

$y = 2 \times -3 + 7$

$y = 1$

$\therefore x = -3$ and $y = 1$

[Check: $1 = 4 \times -3 + 13$]

b $4x - 7y = -1$ **i**

$3x + y = 18$ **ii**

From **ii**, $y = 18 - 3x$ **iii**

Substitute **iii** into **i**

$4x - 7(18 - 3x) = -1$

$4x - 126 + 21x = -1$

$25x = 125$

$x = 5$

Substitute in **iii**

$y = 18 - 3 \times 5$

$y = 3$

$\therefore x = 5$ and $y = 3$

[Check: $4 \times 5 - 7 \times 3 = -1$]

99 **a** $5p - q = 13$ **i**

$2p - q = 7$ **ii**

i – **iii**, $3p = 6$

$p = 2$

Substitute in **i**

$5 \times 2 - q = 13$

$10 - q = 13$

$q = -3$

$\therefore p = 2$ and $q = -3$

[Check: $2 \times 2 - (-3) = 7$]

b $11a + 9b = 34$ **i**

$5a - 9b = -50$ **ii**

i + **ii**, $16a = -16$

$a = -1$

Substitute in **i**

$11 \times -1 + 9b = 34$

$9b = 45$

$b = 5$

$\therefore a = -1$ and $b = 5$

[Check: $5 \times -1 - 9 \times 5 = -50$]

100 **a** $12y + 7z - 13 = 0$ **i**

$6y + z + 11 = 0$ **ii**

ii $\times 2$ $\quad 12y + 2z + 22 = 0$ **iii**

i – **iii** $\quad 5z - 35 = 0$

$5z = 35$

$z = 7$

continued ...

Substitute in **ii**

$$6y + 7 + 11 = 0$$
$$6y = -18$$
$$y = -3$$

$\therefore y = -3$ and $z = 7$

[Check: $12 \times -3 + 7 \times 7 - 13 = 0$]

b $7g - 3h = 9$ **i**

$5g + 2h = 23$ **ii**

i $\times 2$, $14g - 6h = 18$ **iii**

ii $\times 3$, $15g + 6h = 69$ **iv**

iii + **iv**, $29g = 87$

$g = 3$

Substitute in **i**

$$7 \times 3 - 3h = 9$$
$$-3h = -12$$
$$h = 4$$

$\therefore g = 3$ and $h = 4$

[Check: $5 \times 3 + 2 \times 4 = 23$]

Plane Geometry

1 **a** $x + 56 = 90$ [angles in a right angle]

$x = 34$

2 **a** $x + 49 = 180$ [angles on a straight line]

$x = 131$

b $x + 90 + 57 = 180$ [angles on a straight line]

$x = 33$

3 $\angle ABC = 138°$ [given]

$\angle ABE = 180° - 138°$ [angles on a straight line]

$= 42°$

$\angle ABD = 90°$ [given]

$\therefore \angle EBD = 90° - 42°$

$= 48°$

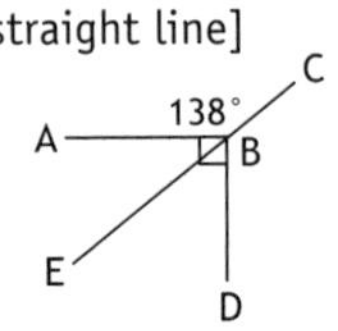

4 Let the angles be $2x°$, $3x°$ and $4x°$.

$2x + 3x + 4x = 180$ [angles on a straight line]

$9x = 180$

$x = 20$

$\therefore \quad 2x = 2 \times 20$

$= 40$

$\therefore \quad 3x = 3 \times 20$

$= 60$

$\therefore \quad 4x = 4 \times 20$

$= 80$

The angles measure 40°, 60° and 80°

5 **a** $x = 52$ [vertically opposite]

b $8x - 31 = 3x + 84$ [vertically opposite]

$5x = 115$

$x = 23$

6

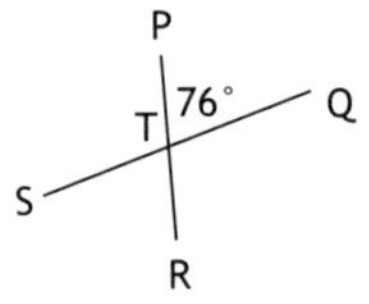

$\angle QTR = 180° - 76°$ [angles on a straight line]

$= 104°$

$\angle RTS = 76°$ [vertically opposite $\angle PTQ$]

$\angle STP = 104°$ [vertically opposite $\angle QTR$]

7 **a** $x + 36 = 360$ [angles at a point]

$x = 324$

b $x + 215 = 360$ [angles at a point]

$x = 145$

c $x + 90 = 360$ [angles at a point]

$x = 270$

d $x + 48 + 21 + 35 + 86 = 360$ [angles at a point]

$x + 190 = 360$

$x = 170$

8

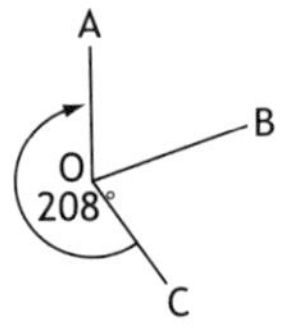

$\angle AOC + 208° = 360°$ [angles at a point]

$\angle AOC = 152°$

$\angle AOB = 152° \div 2$ [OB bisects $\angle AOC$]

$= 76°$

9 **a** $x = 118$ [alternate angles, parallel lines]

b $x = 138$ [corresponding angles, parallel lines]

c $x + 69 = 180$ [co-interior angles, parallel lines]

$x = 111$

10

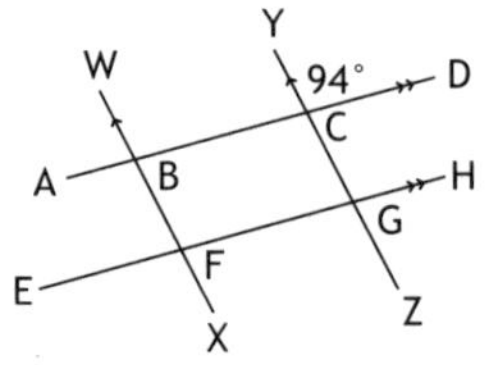

$\angle YCD = 94°$ [given]

$\angle CGH = 94°$ [corresponding to $\angle YCD$, AD || EH]

$\angle BFG = 94°$ [corresponding to $\angle CGH$, WX || YZ]

$\angle BFE + \angle BFG = 180°$ [angles on a straight line]

$\angle BFE + 94° = 180°$

$\angle BFE = 86°$

11

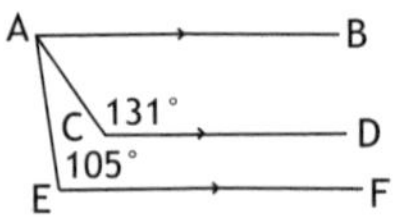

$\angle BAC + \angle ACD = 180°$ [co-interior, AB || CD]

$\angle BAC + 131° = 180°$

$\angle BAC = 49°$

continued ...

$\angle BAE + \angle AEF = 180°$ [co-interior, AB || EF]

$\angle BAE + 105° = 180°$

$\angle BAE = 75°$

$\angle EAC = \angle BAE - \angle BAC$

$= 75° - 49°$

$= 26°$

12 Construct FC parallel to AB.

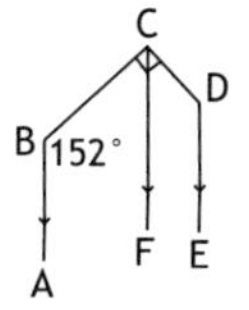

$\angle FCB + \angle ABC = 180°$ [co-interior, parallel lines]

$\angle FCB + 152° = 180°$

$\angle FCB = 28°$

$\angle BCD = 90°$ [given]

$\therefore \angle FCD = 90° - 28°$

$= 62°$

FC || DE [AB || DE, FC || AB]

$\angle CDE + \angle FCD = 180°$ [co-interior, parallel lines]

$\angle CDE + 62° = 180°$

$\therefore \angle CDE = 118°$

13 **a**

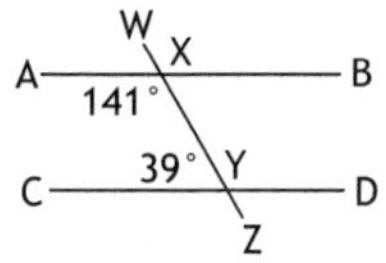

$\angle AXY + \angle CYX = 141° + 39°$

$= 180°$

$\therefore$ AB || CD [co-interior angles are supplementary]

b

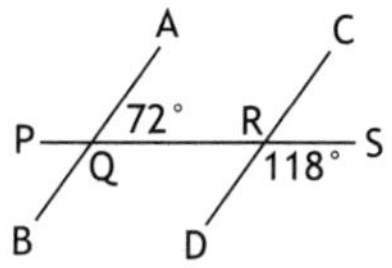

$\angle BQR + \angle RQA = 180°$ [angles on a straight line]

$\angle BQR + 72° = 180°$

$\angle BQR = 108°$

$\therefore \angle BQR \neq \angle DRS$

$\therefore$ AB is not parallel to CD

[corresponding angles are not equal]

c

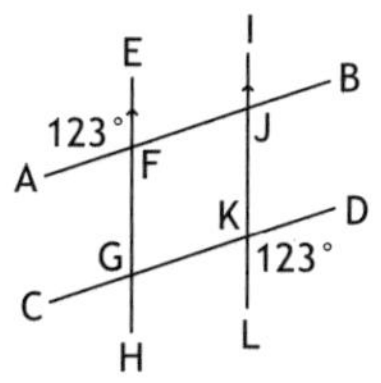

$\angle AFE = \angle FJI$ [corresponding, EH || IL]

$\therefore \angle FJI = 123°$

$\angle BJK = 123°$ [vertically opposite $\angle FJI$]

$\therefore \angle BJK = \angle DKL$

$\therefore$ AB || CD [corresponding angles are equal]

14 **a** $x° + 82° + 43° = 180°$ [angles in a triangle]

$x° + 125° = 180°$

$x° = 55°$

b $x° + 90° + 53° = 180°$ [angles in a triangle]

$x° + 143° = 180°$

$x° = 37°$

c $x° + 131° + 19° = 180°$ [angles in a triangle]

$x° + 150° = 180°$

$x° = 30°$

15 Let the angles measure $x°$, $2x°$ and $3x°$.

$x + 2x + 3x = 180$ [angles in a triangle]

$6x = 180$

$x = 30$

$\therefore 2x = 2 \times 30$

$= 60$

$\therefore 3x = 3 \times 30$

$= 90$

The angles of the triangle measure 30°, 60° and 90°.

16 **a** $x = 43 + 57$ [exterior angle of a triangle]

$x = 100$

b $x + 39 = 81$ [exterior angle of a triangle]

$x = 42$

c $x + 90 = 137$ [exterior angle of a triangle]

$x = 47$

d $x = 52 + 52$ [exterior angle of a triangle]

$x = 104$

17

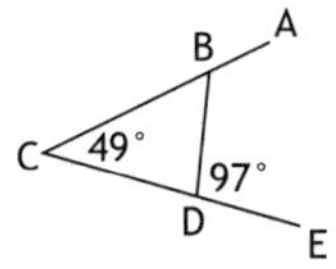

$\angle CDB + \angle BDE = 180°$ [angles on a straight line]

$\angle CDB + 97° = 180°$

$\angle CDB = 83°$

$\angle ABD = \angle BCD + \angle CDB$

[exterior angle of a triangle]

$= 49° + 83°$

$= 132°$

18 **a** $x + 134 + 73 + 87 = 360$ [angles in a quadrilateral]

$x + 294 = 360$

$x = 66$

b $x + 117 + 78 + 81 = 360$ [angles in a quadrilateral]

$x + 276 = 360$

$x = 84$

c $x + 90 + 56 + 90 = 360$ [angles in a quadrilateral]

$x + 236 = 360$

$x = 124$

d $x + 201 + 21 + 90 = 360$ [angles in a quadrilateral]

$x + 312 = 360$

$x = 48$

19 Let the angles measure $2x°$, $3x°$, $4x°$ and $6x°$.

$2x + 3x + 4x + 6x = 360$ [angles in a quadrilateral]

$15x = 360$

$x = 24$

Smallest angle $= 2 \times 24°$

$= 48°$

20 **a** An octagon has 8 sides.

Angle sum $= (2n - 4)$ right angles

$= (2 \times 8 - 4) \times 90°$

$= 1080°$

b An dodecagon has 12 sides.

Angle sum $= (2n - 4)$ right angles

$= (2 \times 12 - 4) \times 90°$

$= 1800°$

21 Angle sum $= (2n - 4)$ right angles

$3780° = (2n - 4) \times 90°$

$\therefore\ 2n - 4 = 3780° \div 90°$

$2n - 4 = 42$

$2n = 46$

$n = 23$

$\therefore$ the polygon has 23 sides

22 The polygon has 6 sides (hexagon).

Angle sum $= (2n - 4)$ right angles

$= (2 \times 6 - 4) \times 90°$

$= 720°$

$x + 129 + 141 + 93 + 134 + 88 = 720$

$x + 585 = 720$

$x = 135$

23 **a** A pentagon has 5 sides.

Angle sum $= (2n - 4)$ right angles

$= (2 \times 5 - 4) \times 90°$

$= 540°$

Each angle $= 540° \div 5$

$= 108°$

b A decagon has 10 sides.

Angle sum $= (2n - 4)$ right angles

$= (2 \times 10 - 4) \times 90°$

$= 1440°$

Each angle $= 1440° \div 10$

$= 144°$

24 Angle sum $= (2n - 4)$ right angles

$= (2 \times 24 - 4) \times 90°$

$= 3960°$

continued ...

Each angle $= 3960° \div 24$

$= 165°$

25 Let the number of sides be n.

Each angle $= 160°$

$\therefore$ angle sum $= 160n°$

but angle sum $= (2n - 4)$ right angles

$\therefore (2n - 4) \times 90° = 160n°$

$180n° - 360° = 160n°$

$20n° = 360°$

$n = 18$

$\therefore$ the polygon has 18 sides

26 $x + 58 + 47 + 87 + 68 = 360$

[angle sum of exterior angles]

$x + 260 = 360$

$x = 100$

27 Angle sum of the exterior angles $= 360°$

Each exterior angle $= 360° \div 5$

$= 72°$

28 **a** Angle sum of the exterior angles $= 360°$

Each exterior angle $= 360° \div 6$

$= 60°$

b Each interior angle $= 180° - 60°$

$= 120°$

29 **a**

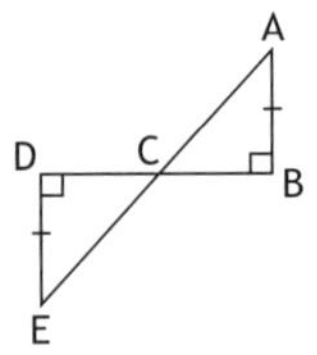

In ΔABC, ΔEDC,

$\angle ABC = \angle EDC$	[both 90°, given]
$\angle ACB = \angle ECD$	[vertically opposite]
$AB = ED$	[given]
$\therefore \Delta ABC \equiv \Delta EDC$	[AAS]

b

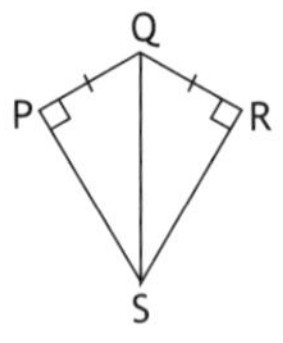

In ΔPQS, ΔRQS,

$\angle QPS = \angle QRS$	[both 90°, given]
$QS = QS$	[common side]
$PQ = RQ$	[given]
$\therefore \Delta PQS \equiv \Delta RQS$	[RHS]

c

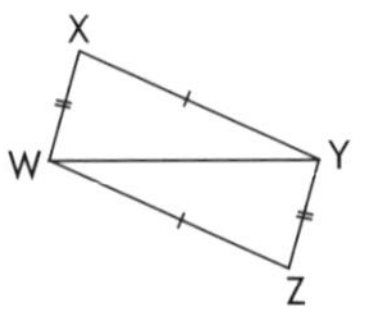

In ΔWXY, ΔYZW,

XY = ZW	[given]
WX = YZ	[given]
WY = YW	[common side]
$\therefore$ ΔWXY $\equiv$ ΔYZW	[SSS]

d

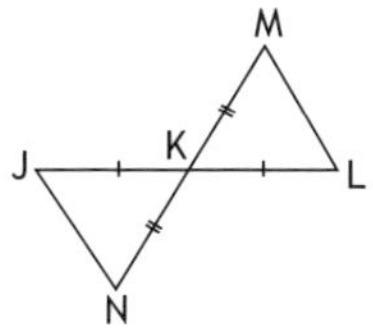

In ΔJKN, ΔLKM,

JK = LK	[given]
$\angle$JKN = $\angle$LKM	[vertically opposite]
NK = MK	[given]
$\therefore$ ΔJKN $\equiv$ ΔLKM	[SAS]

30

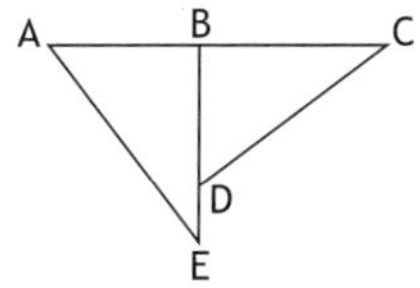

In ΔABE, ΔDBC,

AE = DC	[given]
AB = DB	[given]
BE = BC	[given]
$\therefore$ ΔABE $\equiv$ ΔDBC	[SSS]

$\therefore$ $\angle$ABE = $\angle$DBC

[corresponding angles of congruent triangles]

but $\angle$ABE + $\angle$DBC = 180° [angles on a straight line]

$\therefore$ $\angle$ABE = 90°

31

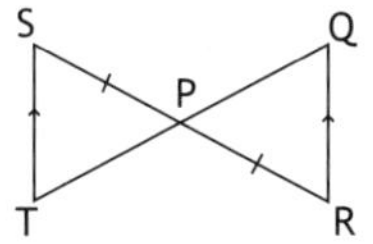

In ΔTSP, ΔQRP,

$\angle$TSP = $\angle$QRP	[alternate, ST || QR]
$\angle$SPT = $\angle$RPQ	[vertically opposite]
SP = RP	[P is the midpoint of SR]
$\therefore$ ΔTSP $\equiv$ ΔQRP	[AAS]

$\therefore$ TP = QP

[corresponding sides of congruent triangles]

$\therefore$ P is the midpoint of TQ

32

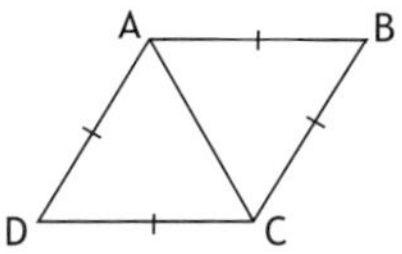

In ΔABC, ΔADC,

AB = AD	[given]
BC = DC	[given]
AC = AC	[common side]
$\therefore$ ΔABC $\equiv$ ΔADC	[SSS]

continued ...

$\therefore$ $\angle$BAC = $\angle$DAC

[corresponding angles of congruent triangles]

$\therefore$ CA bisects $\angle$DAB

33 **a** $x = 72$ [base angles of isosceles triangle]

b $x + 63 + 63 = 180$ [angle sum of isosceles triangle]

$x + 126 = 180$

$x = 54$

c $x + x + 18 = 180$ [angle sum of isosceles triangle]

$2x + 18 = 180$

$2x = 162$

$x = 81$

d $x = 60$ [equilateral triangle]

34

$\angle$BAC = $\angle$BCA [base angles of isosceles triangle]

$\angle$BAC + $\angle$BCA + $\angle$ABC = 180° [angle sum of ΔABC]

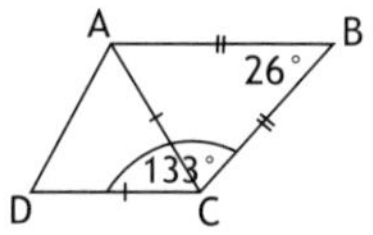

2$\angle$BCA + 26° = 180°

2$\angle$BCA = 154°

$\angle$BCA = 77°

but $\angle$BCD = 133°

$\angle$ACD = 133° − 77°

= 56°

$\angle$DAC + $\angle$ADC + $\angle$ACD = 180° [angle sum of Δ]

but $\angle$DAC = $\angle$ADC [base angles of isosceles triangle]

2$\angle$ADC + 56° = 180°

2$\angle$ADC = 124°

$\angle$ADC = 62°

35 $a + 79 = 180$ [co-interior angles, parallel lines]

$a = 101$

$b = 79$ [opposite angles of a parallelogram]

36

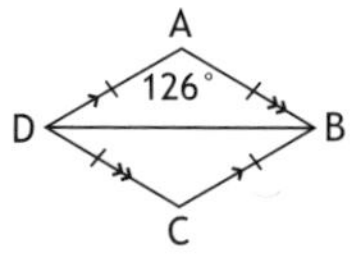

$\angle$DAB = 126°

$\angle$DAB + $\angle$ABC = 180° [co-interior angles, AD || BC]

$\therefore$ $\angle$ABC = 54°

$\therefore$ $\angle$DBC = 54° ÷ 2 [diagonals of a rhombus bisect the angles]

= 27°

37 **a** The diagonals of a rectangle are equal.

$\therefore 5x + 27 = 2x + 45$

$3x = 18$

$x = 6$

b When $x = 6$,

$5x + 27 = 5 \times 6 + 27$

$= 57$

$\therefore$ both diagonals are 57 cm long

38 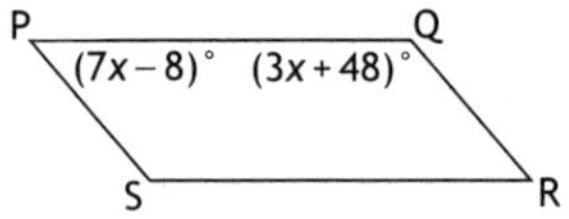

a $\angle SPQ + \angle PQR = 180°$
[co-interior angles, PS || QR]
$\therefore 7x - 8 + 3x + 48 = 180$
$10x + 40 = 180$
$10x = 140$
$x = 14$

b When $x = 14$,
$3x + 48 = 3 \times 14 + 48$
$= 90$
$\therefore \angle PQR = 90°$

c PQRS is a rectangle because it is a parallelogram with one angle 90°.

39 **a** A parallelogram because the diagonals bisect each other.

b A rhombus. A parallelogram because one pair of opposite sides are equal and parallel. A rhombus because it is a parallelogram with a pair of adjacent sides equal.

c A rhombus because the diagonals bisect each other at right angles.

d A rectangle. A parallelogram because both pairs of opposite sides are parallel.
$x + x = 180$ [co-interior angles, parallel lines]
$\therefore \quad x = 90$
A rectangle because it is a parallelogram with one angle 90°.

40 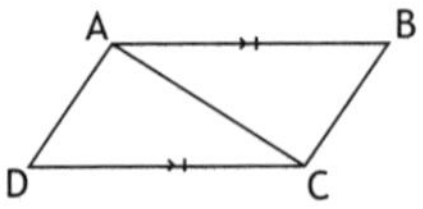

a In ΔBAC, ΔDCA,

$AB = DC$	[given]
$\angle BAC = \angle DCA$	[alternate, AB || DC]
$AC = CA$	[common side]
$\therefore \Delta BAC \equiv \Delta DCA$	[SAS]

b $\angle BCA = \angle DAC$
[corresponding angles of congruent triangles]
$\therefore BC \parallel AD$ [alternate angles are equal]

41 **a** 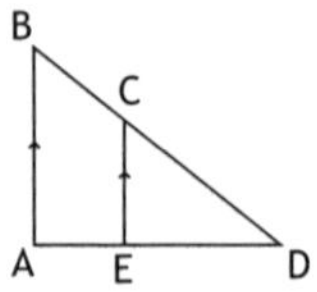

In ΔABD, ΔECD,

$\angle ADB = \angle EDC$	[common angle]
$\angle ABD = \angle ECD$	[corresponding, AB || EC]
$\therefore \Delta ABD \ \vert\vert\vert \ \Delta ECD$	

b 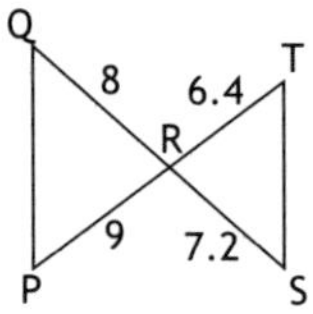

In ΔPQR, ΔSTR,
$\angle PRQ = \angle SRT$ [vertically opposite]
$\frac{QR}{TR} = \frac{8}{6.4}$
$= 1.25$
$\frac{PR}{SR} = \frac{9}{7.2}$
$= 1.25$
$\therefore \frac{QR}{TR} = \frac{PR}{SR}$
$\therefore \Delta PQR \ |||\ \Delta STR$

c 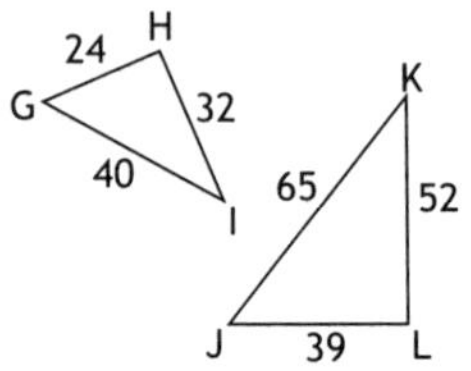

In ΔGHI, ΔJLK,
$\frac{GH}{JL} = \frac{24}{39} = \frac{8}{13}$ $\quad \frac{HI}{LK} = \frac{32}{52} = \frac{8}{13}$ $\quad \frac{IG}{KJ} = \frac{40}{65} = \frac{8}{13}$
$\therefore \frac{GH}{JL} = \frac{HI}{LK} = \frac{IG}{KJ}$
$\therefore \Delta GHI \ |||\ \Delta JLK$

42 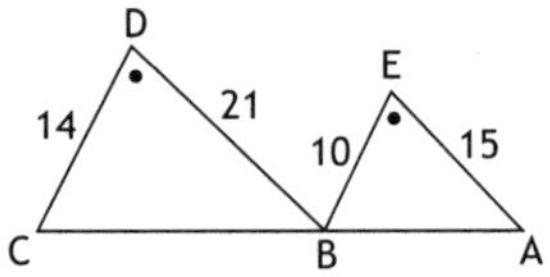

a In ΔAEB, ΔBDC,
$\angle AEB = \angle BDC$ [given]
$\frac{AE}{BD} = \frac{15}{21} = \frac{5}{7}$ $\quad \frac{EB}{DC} = \frac{10}{14} = \frac{5}{7}$
$\therefore \frac{AE}{BD} = \frac{EB}{DC}$
$\therefore \Delta AEB \ |||\ \Delta BDC$

b $\frac{AB}{BC} = \frac{5}{7}$
[corresponding sides of similar triangles]
Let $AB = x$
$\therefore BC = 43.2 - x$
$\frac{x}{43.2 - x} = \frac{5}{7}$
$7x = 5(43.2 - x)$

continued ...

$$7x = 216 - 5x$$
$$12x = 216$$
$$x = 18$$
$\therefore$ AB = 18 units

43

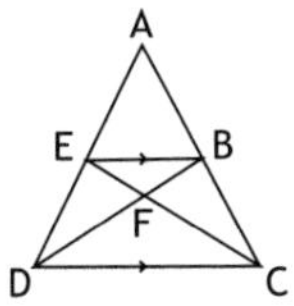

a In ΔABE, ΔACD,

$\angle$EAB = $\angle$DAC [common angle]

$\angle$ABE = $\angle$ACD [corresponding, EB || DC]

$\therefore$ ΔABE ||| ΔACD

b In ΔEBF, ΔCDF,

$\angle$EBF = $\angle$CDF [alternate, EB || DC]

$\angle$EFB = $\angle$CFD [vertically opposite]

$\therefore$ ΔEBF ||| ΔCDF

c $\frac{CF}{EF} = \frac{CD}{EB}$

[corresponding sides of similar triangles, EBF, CDF]

$\frac{AC}{AB} = \frac{CD}{EB}$

[corresponding sides of similar triangles, ABE, ACD]

$\therefore \frac{CF}{EF} = \frac{AC}{AB}$

Let CF = x

$$\frac{x}{2} = \frac{10}{4}$$
$$4x = 20$$
$$x = 5$$

$\therefore$ CF = 5 cm

$\therefore$ EC = 7 cm

44

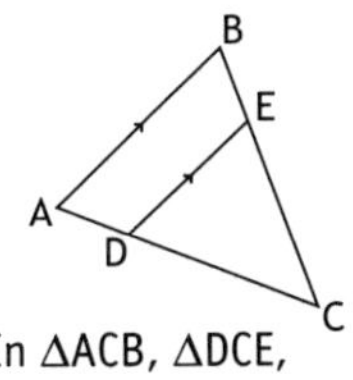

In ΔACB, ΔDCE,

$\angle$ACB = $\angle$DCE [common angle]

$\angle$ABC = $\angle$DEC [corresponding, AB || DE]

$\therefore$ ΔACB ||| ΔDCE

$\therefore \frac{CD}{CA} = \frac{CE}{CB}$

[corresponding sides of similar triangles]

45

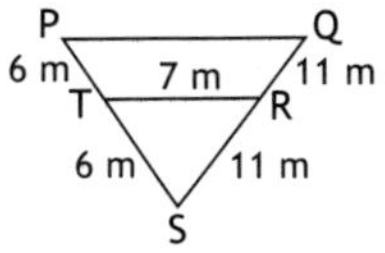

a In ΔPQS, ΔTRS,

$\angle$PSQ = $\angle$TSR [common]

$\frac{PS}{TS} = \frac{12}{6} = 2$ $\qquad$ $\frac{QS}{RS} = \frac{22}{11} = 2$

$\therefore \frac{PS}{TS} = \frac{QS}{RS}$

$\therefore$ ΔPQS ||| ΔTRS

b $\angle$PQS = $\angle$TRS [corresponding angles of similar triangles]

$\therefore$ PQ || TR [corresponding angles are equal]

c $\frac{PQ}{TR} = \frac{QS}{RS}$

[corresponding sides of similar triangles]

$\frac{PQ}{7} = 2$

PQ = 14 m

46 **a** Parallel lines preserve ratios.

$$\therefore \frac{x}{9} = \frac{35}{15}$$
$$15x = 315$$
$$x = 21$$

b Parallel lines cut equal intercepts.

$\therefore x = 19$

47 Parallel lines preserve ratios.

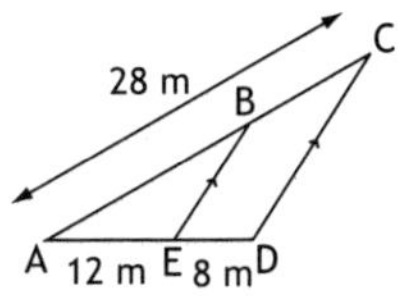

$\therefore \frac{BC}{AB} = \frac{ED}{AE}$

Let BC = x

$\therefore$ AB = 28 − x

$$\frac{x}{28-x} = \frac{8}{12} = \frac{2}{3}$$
$$3x = 2(28-x)$$
$$3x = 56 - 2x$$
$$5x = 56$$
$$x = 11.2$$

$\therefore$ BC = 11.2 m

48 **a** $x^2 = 7^2 + 24^2$

$= 625$

$x = \sqrt{625}$ $[x > 0]$

$= 25$

b $x^2 = 14^2 + 9^2$

$= 277$

$x = \sqrt{277}$ $[x > 0]$

$= 16.64331698\ldots$

$= 16.6$ [1 d.p.]

49 **a** $x^2 = 73^2 - 55^2$

$= 2304$

$x = \sqrt{2304}$ $[x > 0]$

$= 48$

b $x^2 = 23^2 - 11^2$

$= 408$

$x = \sqrt{408}$ $[x > 0]$

$= 20.19900988\ldots$

$= 20.2$ [1 d.p.]

50 **a** $x^2 = 12.5^2 - 7.5^2$

$= 100$

$x = \sqrt{100}$ $[x > 0]$

$= 10$

b $x^2 = 91^2 + 60^2$

$= 11881$

$x = \sqrt{11881}$ $[x > 0]$

$= 109$

c $x^2 = 42^2 - 13^2$
$= 1595$
$x = \sqrt{1595}$ $[x > 0]$
$= 39.9374511\ldots$
$= 39.9$ [1 d.p.]

d $x^2 = 33^2 + 19^2$
$= 1450$
$x = \sqrt{1450}$ $[x > 0]$
$= 38.07886553\ldots$
$= 38.1$ [1 d.p.]

51 **a** $x^2 = 4^2 + 1^2$
$= 17$
$x = \sqrt{17}$ $[x > 0]$

b $x^2 = 3^2 + 3^2$
$= 18$
$x = \sqrt{18}$ $[x > 0]$
$= \sqrt{9} \times \sqrt{2}$
$= 3\sqrt{2}$

c $x^2 = 8^2 - 4^2$
$= 48$
$x = \sqrt{48}$ $[x > 0]$
$= \sqrt{16} \times \sqrt{3}$
$= 4\sqrt{3}$

52 **a** $187^2 + 84^2 = 42\,025$
$205^2 = 42\,025$
$\therefore 187^2 + 84^2 = 205^2$
$\therefore$ the triangle is right-angled

b $57^2 + 44^2 = 5185$
$71^2 = 5041$
$\therefore 57^2 + 44^2 \neq 71^2$
$\therefore$ the triangle is not right-angled

c $16^2 + 23.1^2 = 789.61$
$28.1^2 = 789.61$
$\therefore 16^2 + 23.1^2 = 28.1^2$
$\therefore$ the triangle is right-angled

d $31.2^2 + 53.3^2 = 3814.33$
$61.9^2 = 3831.61$
$\therefore 31.2^2 + 53.3^2 \neq 61.9^2$
$\therefore$ the triangle is not right-angled

53 **a** $A = \frac{1}{2}bh$
$= \frac{1}{2} \times 15 \times 8$
$\therefore$ area $= 60$ m^2

b $A = bh$
$= 8 \times 9$
$\therefore$ area $= 72$ m^2

c $A = \dfrac{h}{2}(a + b)$
$= \dfrac{7}{2} \times (11 + 17)$
$\therefore$ area $= 98$ cm^2

54 **a** $A = bh$
$= 18 \times 12$
$\therefore$ area $= 216$ m^2

b $A = \frac{1}{2}bh$
$= \frac{1}{2} \times 20 \times 21$
$\therefore$ area $= 210$ m^2

55 **a** $A = bh$
$= 8 \times 6$
$\therefore$ area $= 48$ cm^2

b $A = \frac{1}{2}xy$
$= \frac{1}{2} \times 8 \times 6$
$\therefore$ area $= 24$ m^2

56 **a** $A = bh - \frac{1}{2}xy$
$= 9 \times 7 - \frac{1}{2} \times 9 \times 7$
$\therefore$ area $= 31.5$ m^2

b $A = \frac{1}{2}BH - \frac{1}{2}bh$
$= \frac{1}{2} \times 73 \times 37 - \frac{1}{2} \times 48 \times 19$
$\therefore$ area $= 894.5$ mm^2

57 **a** $A = \frac{1}{2}bh + \frac{1}{2}bH$
$= \frac{1}{2} \times 14 \times 5 + \frac{1}{2} \times 14 \times 11$
$\therefore$ area $= 112$ cm^2

b

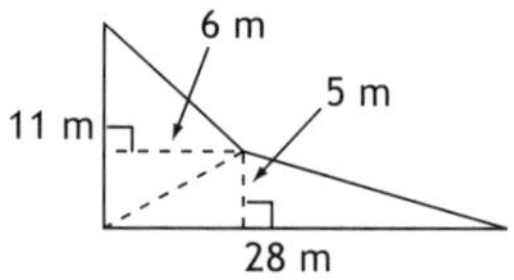

$A = \frac{1}{2}BH + \frac{1}{2}bh$
$= \frac{1}{2} \times 28 \times 5 + \frac{1}{2} \times 11 \times 6$
$\therefore$ area $= 103$ m^2

58 $\angle BCD + \angle CDB + \angle DBC = 180°$
[angle sum of a triangle]

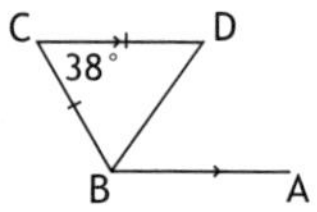

$\angle BCD = 38°$
$\therefore \angle CDB + \angle DBC = 142°$
but $\angle CDB = \angle DBC$
[base angles of isosceles triangle]
$\therefore \angle CDB = 71°$
$\therefore \angle DBA = 71°$ [alternate, CD || BA]

59

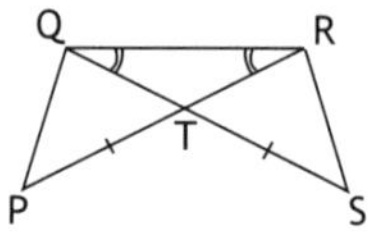

a In ΔQTP, ΔRTS,
$PT = ST$ [given]
$\angle PTQ = \angle STR$ [vertically opposite]
$QT = RT$ [equal sides of isosceles ΔQTR]
$\therefore \Delta QTP \equiv \Delta RTS$ [SAS]

b In ΔPQR, ΔSRQ,
$\angle PRQ = \angle SQR$ [given]
$\angle QPR = \angle RSQ$ [corresponding angles of congruent triangles]
$PQ = SR$ [corresponding sides of congruent triangles]
$\therefore \Delta PQR \equiv \Delta SRQ$ [AAS]

60

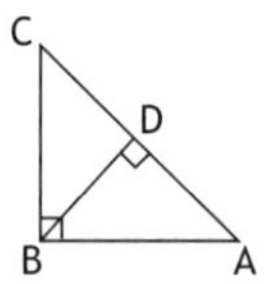

a In ΔABD, ΔACB
$\angle BAD = \angle CAB$ [common]
$\angle ADB = \angle ABC$ [both 90°, given]
$\therefore \Delta ABD \;|||\; \Delta ACB$

b AB = 15 m, AC = 25 m

i $BC^2 = AC^2 - AB^2$
$= 25^2 - 15^2$
$= 400$
$BC = \sqrt{400}$ [BC > 0]
$= 20$ m

ii $\frac{BD}{BC} = \frac{AB}{AC}$ [corresponding sides of similar triangles]
$\frac{BD}{20} = \frac{15}{25}$
$= \frac{3}{5}$
$\therefore$ BD = 12 m

c $AD^2 = AB^2 - BD^2$
$= 15^2 - 12^2$
$= 81$
AD = 9 m [AD > 0]
$A = \frac{1}{2}bh$
$= \frac{1}{2} \times 9 \times 12$
$\therefore$ area = 54 m^2

Linear Functions and Lines

1 **a** $y = x - 5$

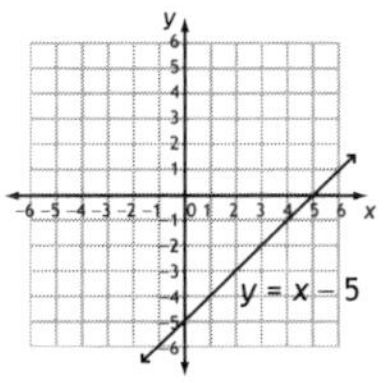

b $y = 2x + 1$

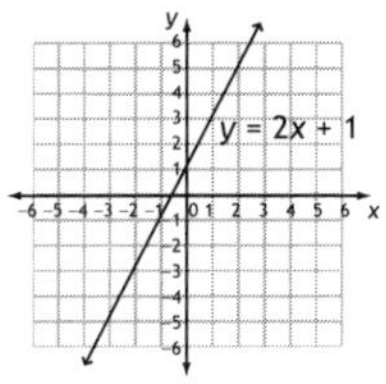

c $y = 2 - 3x$

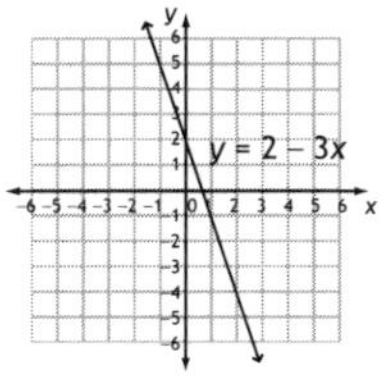

d $y = \frac{3}{4}x - \frac{1}{4}$

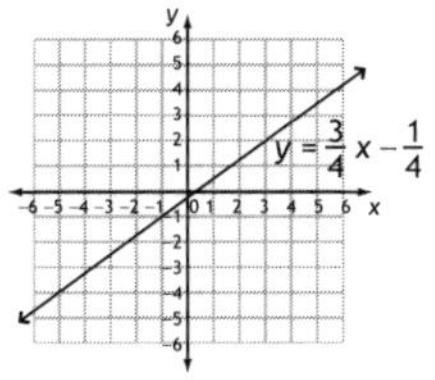

e $x = 3$

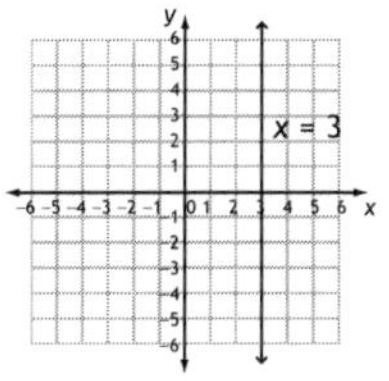

f $y = -4$

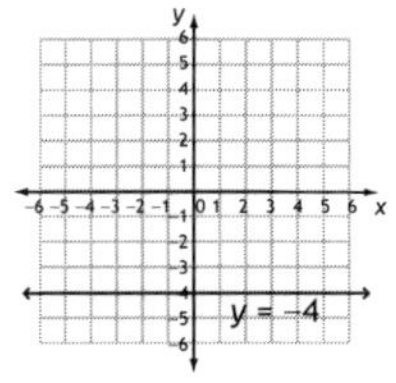

2 **a** $y = 7x + 3$
gradient $m = 7$
y-intercept = 3

b $y = -4x - 2$
gradient $m = -4$
y-intercept = −2

c $y = 6 - 5x$
gradient $m = -5$
y-intercept = 6

d $y = \frac{2}{3}x - \frac{3}{5}$
gradient $m = \frac{2}{3}$
y-intercept = $-\frac{3}{5}$

e $y = -2$
gradient $m = 0$
y-intercept = −2

f $y = -x$
gradient $m = -1$
y-intercept = 0

3 **a** $m = 8$, y-intercept = −1
$y = 8x - 1$

b $m = 1$, y-intercept = 0
$y = x$

c $m = \frac{1}{4}$, y-intercept = 9
$y = \frac{1}{4}x + 9$

4 **a** $y = x + 2$
$m = 1$
y-intercept = 2

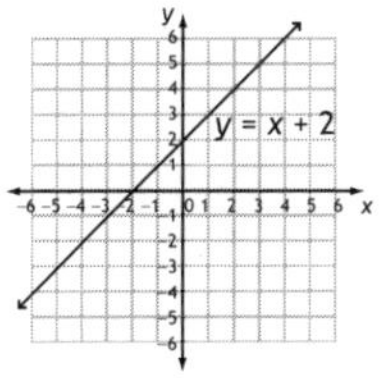

b $y = -2x - 1$
$m = -2$
y-intercept = −1

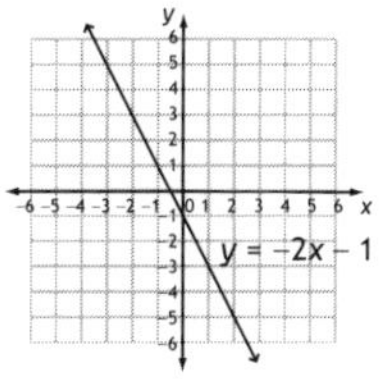

5 $y = 3x - 11$
$m = 3$
$\therefore \tan\theta = 3$
$\theta = 71.565\,051\,18\ldots°$
$= 72°$ [nearest degree]

6 $m = \tan 135°$
$= -1$
y-intercept = 7
$\therefore$ the equation is $y = -x + 7$

7 **a** $(3, 7)$, $(4, 11)$
$m = \frac{y_2 - y_1}{x_2 - x_1}$
$= \frac{11 - 7}{4 - 3}$
$= 4$

b $(-2, 5)$, $(7, -1)$
$m = \frac{y_2 - y_1}{x_2 - x_1}$
$= \frac{-1 - 5}{7 - (-2)}$
$= -\frac{2}{3}$

8 $P(x, -3)$, $Q(6, 9)$, $m = 3$
$m = \frac{y_2 - y_1}{x_2 - x_1}$
$3 = \frac{9 - (-3)}{6 - x}$
$3 = \frac{12}{6 - x}$
$3(6 - x) = 12$

continued ...

$$18 - 3x = 12$$
$$3x = 6$$
$$x = 2$$

9 **a** $(2, 5),\ m = 3$
$$y - y_1 = m(x - x_1)$$
$$y - 5 = 3(x - 2)$$
$$y - 5 = 3x - 6$$
$$y = 3x - 1$$

b $(-3, -1),\ m = 2$
$$y - y_1 = m(x - x_1)$$
$$y - (-1) = 2(x - (-3))$$
$$y + 1 = 2x + 6$$
$$y = 2x + 5$$

c $(4, 0),\ m = -5$
$$y - y_1 = m(x - x_1)$$
$$y - 0 = -5(x - 4)$$
$$y = -5x + 20$$

d $(-1, 2),\ m = \frac{3}{2}$
$$y - y_1 = m(x - x_1)$$
$$y - 2 = \frac{3}{2}(x - (-1))$$
$$y - 2 = \frac{3}{2}x + \frac{3}{2}$$
$$y = \frac{3}{2}x + 3\frac{1}{2}$$

10 $(7, 0),\ m = -2$
$$y - y_1 = m(x - x_1)$$
$$y - 0 = -2(x - 7)$$
$$y = -2x + 14$$
y-intercept $= 14$

The line cuts the y-axis at $(0, 14)$

11 **a**
$$y = 3x + 2$$
$$3x - y + 2 = 0$$

b
$$y = -2x - 5$$
$$2x + y + 5 = 0$$

c
$$y = \frac{2}{5}x - \frac{1}{5}$$
$$5y = 2x - 1$$
$$2x - 5y - 1 = 0$$

12 **a**
$$2x + y - 7 = 0$$
$$y = -2x + 7$$

b
$$3x - 2y + 6 = 0$$
$$2y = 3x + 6$$
$$y = \frac{3}{2}x + 3$$

c
$$x + 4y - 2 = 0$$
$$4y = -x + 2$$
$$y = -\frac{1}{4}x + \frac{1}{2}$$

13 **a** $(1, 8),\ m = -4$
$$y - y_1 = m(x - x_1)$$
$$y - 8 = -4(x - 1)$$
$$y - 8 = -4x + 4$$
$$4x + y - 12 = 0$$

b $(-2, -5),\ m = \frac{4}{3}$
$$y - y_1 = m(x - x_1)$$
$$y - (-5) = \frac{4}{3}(x - (-2))$$
$$y + 5 = \frac{4}{3}(x + 2)$$
$$3(y + 5) = 4(x + 2)$$
$$3y + 15 = 4x + 8$$
$$4x - 3y - 7 = 0$$

14
$$3x + 4y - 4 = 0$$
$$4y = -3x + 4$$
$$y = -\frac{3}{4}x + 1$$
gradient $m = -\frac{3}{4}$

y - intercept $= 1$

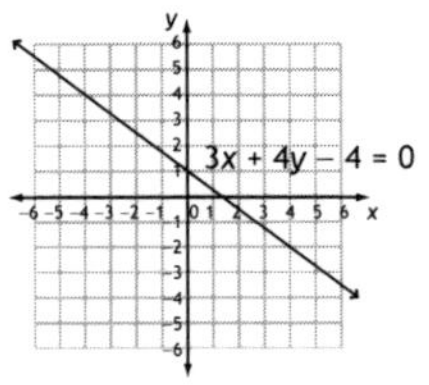

15 **a** $(3, 1),\ (5, 2)$
$$\frac{y - y_1}{x - x_1} = \frac{y_2 - y_1}{x_2 - x_1}$$
$$\frac{y - 1}{x - 3} = \frac{2 - 1}{5 - 3}$$
$$\frac{y - 1}{x - 3} = \frac{1}{2}$$
$$2(y - 1) = x - 3$$
$$2y - 2 = x - 3$$
$$x - 2y - 1 = 0$$

b $(-2, 4),\ (2, 10)$
$$\frac{y - y_1}{x - x_1} = \frac{y_2 - y_1}{x_2 - x_1}$$
$$\frac{y - 4}{x - (-2)} = \frac{10 - 4}{2 - (-2)}$$
$$\frac{y - 4}{x + 2} = \frac{3}{2}$$
$$2(y - 4) = 3(x + 2)$$
$$2y - 8 = 3x + 6$$
$$3x - 2y + 14 = 0$$

c $(-6, -7),\ (-3, 8)$
$$\frac{y - y_1}{x - x_1} = \frac{y_2 - y_1}{x_2 - x_1}$$
$$\frac{y - (-7)}{x - (-6)} = \frac{8 - (-7)}{-3 - (-6)}$$
$$\frac{y + 7}{x + 6} = \frac{15}{3}$$
$$\frac{y + 7}{x + 6} = 5$$
$$y + 7 = 5(x + 6)$$
$$y + 7 = 5x + 30$$
$$y = 5x + 23 \quad [\text{or } 5x - y + 23 = 0]$$

16 **a** $3x - 2y + 8 = 0$

gradient $= -\frac{a}{b}$
$$= -\frac{3}{-2}$$
$$= \frac{3}{2}$$

y - intercept $= -\frac{c}{b}$
$$= -\frac{8}{-2}$$
$$= 4$$

b $x + 5y + 2 = 0$

$$\text{gradient} = -\frac{a}{b} = -\frac{1}{5} \qquad y\text{-intercept} = -\frac{c}{b} = -\frac{2}{5}$$

c $4x + 3y = 0$

$$\text{gradient} = -\frac{a}{b} = -\frac{4}{3} \qquad y\text{-intercept} = -\frac{c}{b} = -\frac{0}{3} = 0$$

17 $7x - 3y + 5 = 0$

$$\begin{aligned}\text{gradient} &= -\frac{a}{b}\\ &= -\frac{7}{-3}\\ &= \frac{7}{3}\end{aligned}$$

$$\begin{aligned}\therefore\ \tan\theta &= \frac{7}{3}\\ \theta &= 66.801\,409\,49\ldots^\circ\\ &= 67^\circ\ \text{[nearest degree]}\end{aligned}$$

18 $(5, 1), (-3, 4)$ $\qquad$ $3x + 8y = 1$

$$m_1 = \frac{y_2 - y_1}{x_2 - x_1} = \frac{4-1}{-3-5} = -\frac{3}{8} \qquad m_2 = -\frac{a}{b} = -\frac{3}{8}$$

$\therefore m_1 = m_2$

$\therefore$ the lines are parallel

19 $2x + 4y - 7 = 0$

Parallel line has form $2x + 4y + k = 0$

This line passes through $(7, 1)$

$$\begin{aligned}2\times 7 + 4\times 1 + k &= 0\\ 18 + k &= 0\\ k &= -18\end{aligned}$$

$$\begin{aligned}\therefore\ 2x + 4y - 18 &= 0\\ x + 2y - 9 &= 0\end{aligned}$$

Required equation is $x + 2y - 9 = 0$

20 $2x + 5y - 5 = 0$

$$\begin{aligned}\text{gradient } m_1 &= -\frac{a}{b}\\ &= -\frac{2}{5}\end{aligned}$$

Perpendicular line has gradient $m_2 = \frac{5}{2}$

21 $y = 2 - 3x$

gradient $m_1 = -3$

continued ...

$3x - 9y + 5 = 0$

$$\begin{aligned}\text{gradient } m_2 &= -\frac{a}{b}\\ &= -\frac{3}{-9}\\ &= \frac{1}{3}\end{aligned}$$

$m_1 m_2 = -1$

$\therefore$ the lines are perpendicular

22 $6x + 5y + 1 = 0$

Perpendicular line has equation $5x - 6y + k = 0$

This line passes through $(4, -2)$

$$\begin{aligned}5\times 4 - 6\times -2 + k &= 0\\ 32 + k &= 0\\ k &= -32\end{aligned}$$

$5x - 6y - 32 = 0$ is the required equation

23

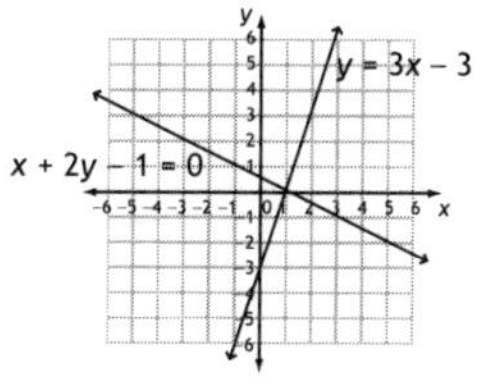

Point of intersection $(1, 0)$

24 **a**

$$\begin{aligned}y &= 5x - 1 \qquad \textbf{i}\\ y &= -x + 5 \qquad \textbf{ii}\end{aligned}$$

$$\begin{aligned}5x - 1 &= -x + 5\\ 6x &= 6\\ x &= 1\end{aligned}$$

Substitute in **ii**, $y = -1 + 5$

$y = 4$

$\therefore$ the point of intersection is $(1, 4)$

b

$$\begin{aligned}x + y - 6 &= 0 \qquad \textbf{i}\\ 2x - y + 12 &= 0 \qquad \textbf{ii}\end{aligned}$$

i + **ii** $\quad 3x + 6 = 0$

$$\begin{aligned}3x &= -6\\ x &= -2\end{aligned}$$

Substitute in **i**, $-2 + y - 6 = 0$

$$\begin{aligned}y - 8 &= 0\\ y &= 8\end{aligned}$$

$\therefore$ the point of intersection is $(-2, 8)$

25

$$\begin{aligned}5x - 3y - 19 &= 0 \qquad \textbf{i}\\ 7x + 2y - 8 &= 0 \qquad \textbf{ii}\end{aligned}$$

i $\times 2$ $\quad 10x - 6y - 38 = 0 \quad$ **iii**

ii $\times 3$ $\quad 21x + 6y - 24 = 0 \quad$ **iv**

iii + **iv** $\quad 31x - 62 = 0$

$$\begin{aligned}31x &= 62\\ x &= 2\end{aligned}$$

Substitute in **ii**, $7\times 2 + 2y - 8 = 0$

$$\begin{aligned}2y + 6 &= 0\\ 2y &= -6\\ y &= -3\end{aligned}$$

$\therefore$ the point of intersection is $(2, -3)$

26 $2x - y + 6 = 0$ **i**

$3x + y - 11 = 0$ **ii**

i + ii $5x - 5 = 0$

$5x = 5$

$x = 1$

Substitute in **ii**, $3 \times 1 + y - 11 = 0$

$y = 8$

$\therefore$ the point of intersection is $(1, 8)$

$x + 3y - 25 = 0$

$1 + 3 \times 8 - 25 = 0$

$0 = 0$

$\therefore$ the line $x + 3y - 25 = 0$ passes through the point of intersection

27 Required equation is in the form:

$6x + 5y - 8 + k(4x + 7y + 2) = 0$

This line passes through $(-1, 6)$

$6 \times -1 + 5 \times 6 - 8 + k(4 \times -1 + 7 \times 6 + 2) = 0$

$16 + 40k = 0$

$40k = -16$

$k = -\frac{16}{40}$

$= -\frac{2}{5}$

$6x + 5y - 8 - \frac{2}{5}(4x + 7y + 2) = 0$

$5(6x + 5y - 8) - 2(4x + 7y + 2) = 0$

$30x + 25y - 40 - 8x - 14y - 4 = 0$

$22x + 11y - 44 = 0$

$2x + y - 4 = 0$

28 **a** $y < 2x + 2$

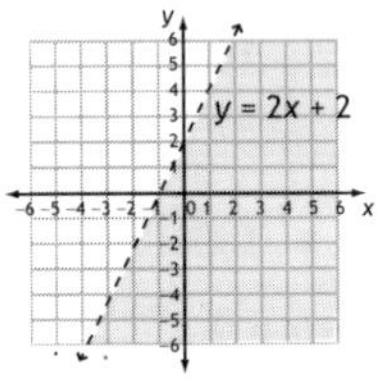

b $5x + 2y - 4 \geq 0$

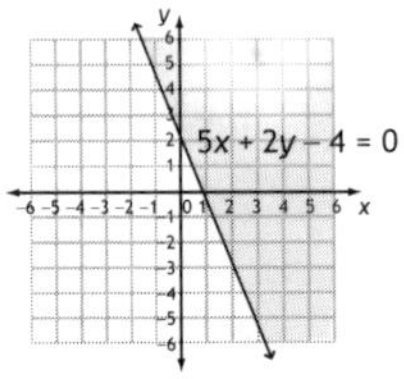

29 **a** $y \geq x$ and $y \leq 3x - 1$

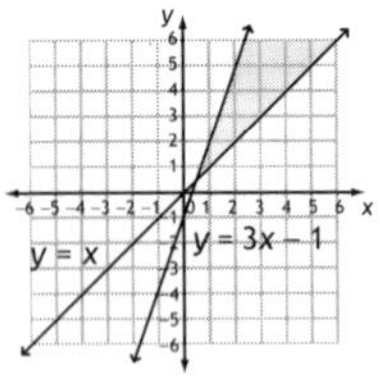

b $5x + y > 0$ and $3x - 4y - 5 > 0$

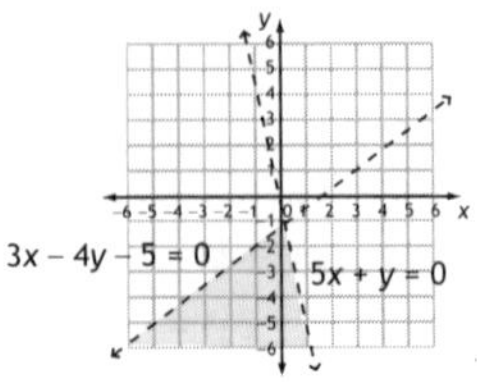

30

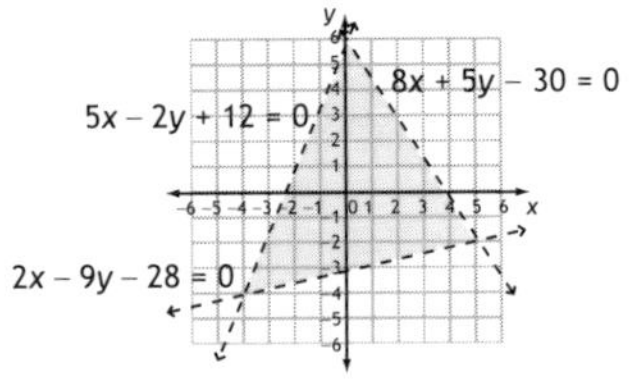

$(0, 0)$ is inside the triangle

Test in $5x - 2y + 12$,

$5 \times 0 - 2 \times 0 + 12 = 12$ $[> 0]$

$\therefore$ $5x - 2y + 12 > 0$

Test in $2x - 9y - 28$

$2 \times 0 - 9 \times 0 - 28 = -28$ $[< 0]$

$\therefore$ $2x - 9y - 28 < 0$

Test in $8x + 5y - 30$

$8 \times 0 + 5 \times 0 - 30 = -30$ $[< 0]$

$\therefore$ $8x + 5y - 30 < 0$

The region is defined by:

$5x - 2y + 12 > 0$, $2x - 9y - 28 < 0$ and $8x + 5y - 30 < 0$

31 **a** $(4, 7)$ $(-3, 7)$

Both points lie on the line $y = 7$

distance $= 4 - (-3)$

$= 7$ units

b $(3, 12)$ $(8, 0)$

$d = \sqrt{(x_2 - x_1)^2 + (y_2 - y_1)^2}$

$= \sqrt{(8 - 3)^2 + (0 - 12)^2}$

$= \sqrt{169}$

$\therefore$ distance $= 13$ units

c $(-4, 8)$ $(5, -2)$

$d = \sqrt{(x_2 - x_1)^2 + (y_2 - y_1)^2}$

$= \sqrt{(5 - (-4))^2 + (-2 - 8)^2}$

$\therefore$ distance $= \sqrt{181}$ units

32 $P(1, -7)$ $Q(9, -1)$

$d = \sqrt{(x_2 - x_1)^2 + (y_2 - y_1)^2}$

$= \sqrt{(9 - 1)^2 + (-1 - (-7))^2}$

$= \sqrt{100}$

PQ $= 10$ units

$P(1, -7)$ $R(-5, 1)$

$d = \sqrt{(x_2 - x_1)^2 + (y_2 - y_1)^2}$

$= \sqrt{(-5 - 1)^2 + (1 - (-7))^2}$

$= \sqrt{100}$

PR $= 10$ units

PQ $=$ PR

$\therefore$ P is equidistant from Q and R

33 **a** $(6, 2)$, $8x - 6y + 3 = 0$

$$a = 8, b = -6, c = 3$$

$$\begin{aligned} d &= \left| \frac{ax_1 + by_1 + c}{\sqrt{a^2 + b^2}} \right| \\ &= \left| \frac{8 \times 6 + (-6) \times 2 + 3}{\sqrt{8^2 + (-6)^2}} \right| \\ &= \frac{39}{10} \end{aligned}$$

$\therefore$ distance = 3.9 units

b $(-3, -2)$, $2x - 3y - 9 = 0$

$$a = 2, b = -3, c = -9$$

$$\begin{aligned} d &= \left| \frac{ax_1 + by_1 + c}{\sqrt{a^2 + b^2}} \right| \\ &= \left| \frac{2 \times (-3) + (-3) \times (-2) + (-9)}{\sqrt{2^2 + (-3)^2}} \right| \\ &= \left| \frac{-9}{\sqrt{13}} \right| \\ &= \frac{9}{\sqrt{13}} \times \frac{\sqrt{13}}{\sqrt{13}} \end{aligned}$$

$\therefore$ distance $= \dfrac{9\sqrt{13}}{13}$ units

34

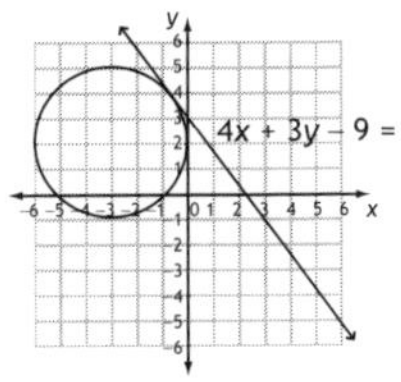

The length of the radius is equal to the perpendicular distance from the centre to the line.

$(-3, 2)$, $4x + 3y - 9 = 0$

$$a = 4, b = 3, c = -9$$

$$\begin{aligned} d &= \left| \frac{ax_1 + by_1 + c}{\sqrt{a^2 + b^2}} \right| \\ &= \left| \frac{4 \times -3 + 3 \times 2 + (-9)}{\sqrt{4^2 + 3^2}} \right| \\ &= \frac{15}{5} \\ &= 3 \end{aligned}$$

$\therefore$ the length of the radius is 3 units

35 **a** $(9, 1)$, $(3, 7)$

$$\begin{aligned} M(x, y) &= \left(\frac{x_1 + x_2}{2}, \frac{y_1 + y_2}{2} \right) \\ &= \left(\frac{9 + 3}{2}, \frac{1 + 7}{2} \right) \\ &= (6, 4) \end{aligned}$$

b $(-4, -6)$, $(-1, 0)$

$$\begin{aligned} M(x, y) &= \left(\frac{x_1 + x_2}{2}, \frac{y_1 + y_2}{2} \right) \\ &= \left(\frac{-4 + (-1)}{2}, \frac{-6 + 0}{2} \right) \\ &= \left(-2\tfrac{1}{2}, -3\right) \end{aligned}$$

36 $P(8, -2)$, $Q(x_2, y_2)$

$$M(x, y) = \left(\frac{x_1 + x_2}{2}, \frac{y_1 + y_2}{2} \right)$$

$$(-2, 5) = \left(\frac{8 + x_2}{2}, \frac{-2 + y_2}{2} \right)$$

$$-2 = \frac{8 + x_2}{2} \quad \text{and} \quad 5 = \frac{-2 + y_2}{2}$$

$$-4 = 8 + x_2 \qquad 10 = -2 + y_2$$

$$x_2 = -12 \qquad y_2 = 12$$

$\therefore$ Q is the point $(-12, 12)$

Real Functions of a Real Variable

1 **a**

$$\begin{aligned} y &= 9 - 2x \\ \text{When } x &= 4, \\ y &= 9 - 2 \times 4 \\ &= 1 \end{aligned}$$

b

$$\begin{aligned} y &= x^2 - 5x \\ \text{When } x &= 3, \\ y &= 3^2 - 5 \times 3 \\ &= -6 \end{aligned}$$

2 $f(x) = x^3 - x^2 + x - 4$

a $f(1) = 1^3 - 1^2 + 1 - 4$
$= -3$

b $f(2) = 2^3 - 2^2 + 2 - 4$
$= 2$

c $f(0) = 0^3 - 0^2 + 0 - 4$
$= -4$

d $f(-3) = (-3)^3 - (-3)^2 + (-3) - 4$
$= -43$

e $f\left(\tfrac{1}{2}\right) = \left(\tfrac{1}{2}\right)^3 - \left(\tfrac{1}{2}\right)^2 + \left(\tfrac{1}{2}\right) - 4$
$= -3\tfrac{5}{8}$

3

$$f(x) = \begin{cases} 3x - 4 & \text{for } x < 2 \\ x & \text{for } 2 \le x \le 3 \\ x^2 - 6 & \text{for } x > 3 \end{cases}$$

a $f(5) = 5^2 - 6$
$= 19$

b $f(-1) = 3 \times -1 - 4$
$= -7$

c $f(2.5) = 2.5$

4

$$\begin{aligned} f(x) &= x^3 + x \\ f(x) + f(-x) &= x^3 + x + (-x)^3 + (-x) \\ &= x^3 + x - x^3 - x \\ &= 0 \end{aligned}$$

5 $$f(x) = x^2 + 4x$$

$$\begin{aligned}\frac{f(x+h) - f(x)}{h} &= \frac{(x+h)^2 + 4(x+h) - (x^2 + 4x)}{h} \\ &= \frac{x^2 + 2xh + h^2 + 4x + 4h - x^2 - 4x}{h} \\ &= \frac{2xh + h^2 + 4h}{h} \\ &= \frac{h(2x + h + 4)}{h} \\ &= 2x + h + 4\end{aligned}$$

6 $p(x) = 3x^2 - 5x$

a $$\begin{aligned}p(2) &= 3 \times 2^2 - 5 \times 2 \\ &= 2\end{aligned}$$

b $$\begin{aligned}p(-2) &= 3 \times (-2)^2 - 5 \times (-2) \\ &= 22\end{aligned}$$

7 $$\begin{aligned}h(z) &= \frac{z+2}{z+7} \\ h(3) &= \frac{3+2}{3+7} \\ &= \frac{5}{10} \\ &= \frac{1}{2}\end{aligned}$$

8 $$\begin{aligned}g(n) &= n^2 + \frac{1}{n^2} \\ g(4) &= 4^2 + \frac{1}{4^2} \\ &= 16\tfrac{1}{16} \\ g\left(\tfrac{1}{4}\right) &= \left(\tfrac{1}{4}\right)^2 + \frac{1}{\left(\frac{1}{4}\right)^2} \\ &= \frac{1}{16} + \frac{1}{\frac{1}{16}} \\ &= \frac{1}{16} + 16 \\ &= g(4)\end{aligned}$$

9 a $y = 3x^2$

Domain: all real x

b $y = \dfrac{x+3}{x+4}$

Domain: $x \neq -4$

All real x except $x = -4$

c $y = \sqrt{x^2 - 16}$

Domain: $x^2 - 16 \geq 0$

$x \leq -4$ or $x \geq 4$

d $y = \dfrac{1}{x^3 + 1}$

Domain: $x^3 + 1 \neq 0$

$x^3 \neq -1$

$x \neq -1$

All real x except $x = -1$

10 a $y = 2x + 7, -2 \leq x \leq 3$

When $x = -2$, $y = 2 \times -2 + 7 = 3$

When $x = 3$, $y = 2 \times 3 + 7 = 13$

$\therefore 3 \leq y \leq 13$

b $y = x^2, -4 \leq x \leq 4$

When $x = 4$, $y = 4^2 = 16$

When $x = -4$, $y = (-4)^2 = 16$

Now $x^2 \geq 0$ for all real x

$x^2 = 0$ when $x = 0$

Range: $0 \leq y \leq 16$

11 a $y = x^2 + 3$

Domain: all real x

$x^2 \geq 0$ for all real x

$x^2 + 3 \geq 3$

Range: $y \geq 3$

b $y = \dfrac{1}{x}$

$x \neq 0$

Domain: all real x except $x = 0$

$$\begin{aligned}y &= \frac{1}{x} \\ xy &= 1 \\ x &= \frac{1}{y}\end{aligned}$$

Range: $y \neq 0$

12 a $y = 2x + 1$

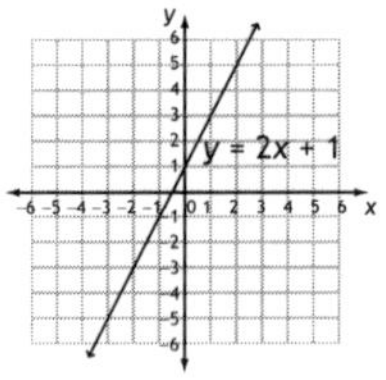

b $y = 3 - x^2$

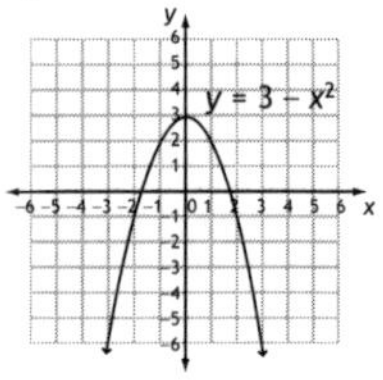

c $y = \dfrac{4}{x}$

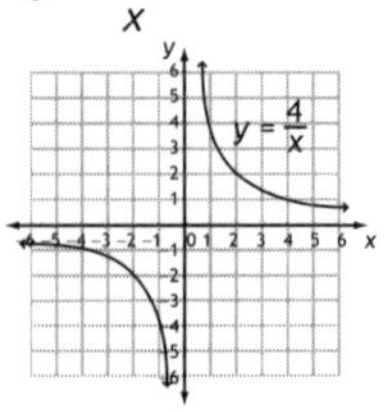

d $y = |x| + 1$

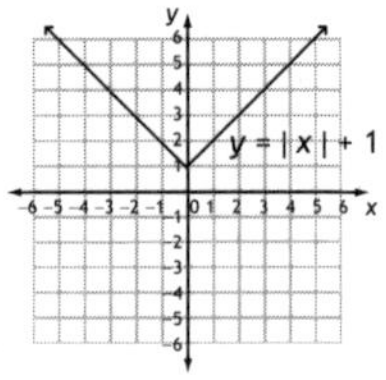

e $y = \sqrt{25 - x^2}$

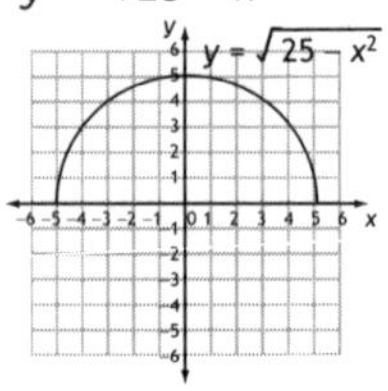

f $y = 3^x$

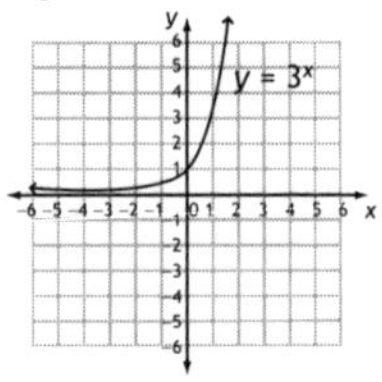

13 **a** $y=-x^3,\ -2\le x\le 2$

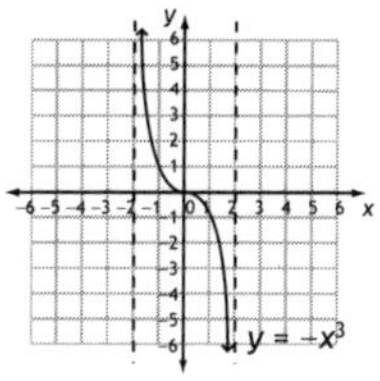

b $f(x)=\begin{cases}x^2-2 & \text{for} \quad x\le 2\\ x & \text{for} \quad x>2\end{cases}$

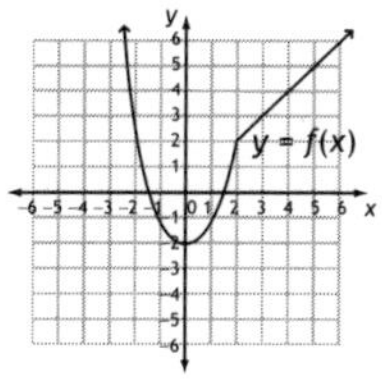

14 **a**

$$y=-x^2$$
$$f(x)=-x^2$$
$$f(-x)=-(-x)^2$$
$$=-x^2$$
$$=f(x)$$

$\therefore$ the function is even

b

$$y=x^3+2$$
$$f(x)=x^3+2$$
$$f(-x)=(-x)^3+2$$
$$=-x^3+2$$

$\therefore$ the function is neither even nor odd

c

$$f(x)=x+\frac{1}{x}$$
$$f(-x)=-x+\frac{1}{-x}$$
$$=-\left(x+\frac{1}{x}\right)$$
$$=-f(x)$$

$\therefore$ the function is odd

d

$$f(x)=x^4-2x^2$$
$$f(-x)=(-x)^4-2(-x)^2$$
$$=x^4-2x^2$$
$$=f(x)$$

$\therefore$ the function is even

15 **a** $y=|x|$

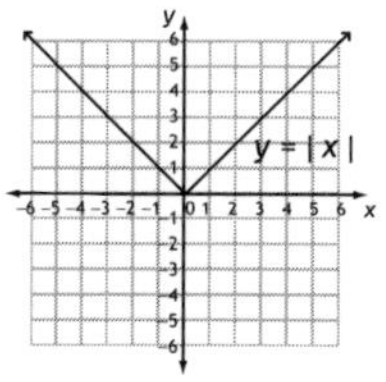

The function is even.

b $y=1-2x$

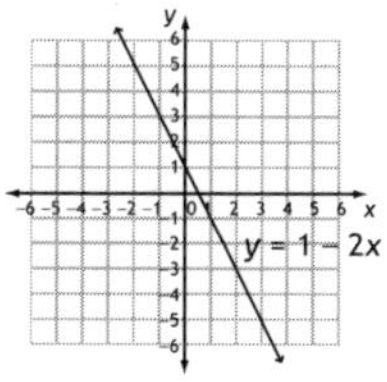

The function is neither odd nor even.

c $xy=-2$

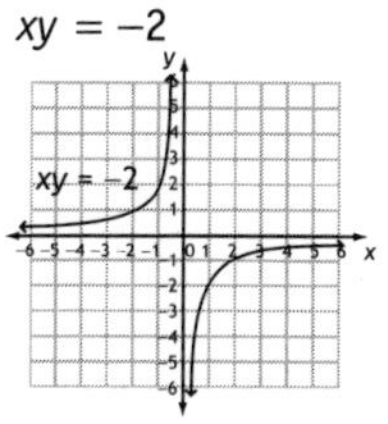

The function is odd.

16 **a** $y=10^x$

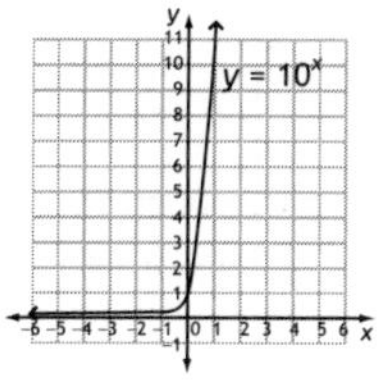

b $y=\dfrac{3}{x}$

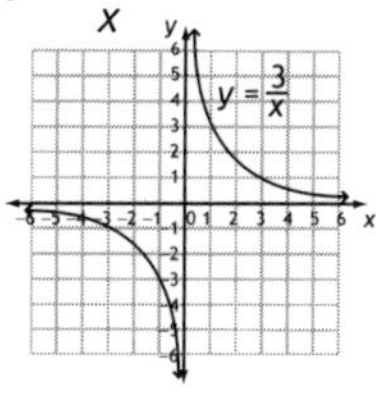

17 $y=\dfrac{1}{x+1}$

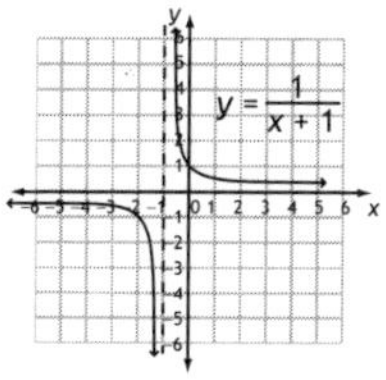

Domain: $x+1\ne 0$

$x\ne -1$

If $x<-1,\ y<0$

If $x>-1,\ y>0$

Range: $y\ne 0$

If $x=0,\ y=1$

18 **a** Centre $(0,0)$, radius 7 units

$$x^2+y^2=7^2$$
$$x^2+y^2=49$$

b Centre $(-2,-5)$, radius 1 unit

$$(x-(-2))^2+(y-(-5))^2=1^2$$
$$(x+2)^2+(y+5)^2=1$$

19 **a** $(x-2)^2+(y+4)^2=16$

Centre $(2,-4)$, radius 4 units

b $(x+3)^2+(y-1)^2=12$

Centre $(-3,1)$, radius $=\sqrt{12}$ units

$=2\sqrt{3}$ units

20 **a**

$$x^2+y^2-16x-8y-20=0$$
$$x^2-16x+y^2-8y=20$$
$$x^2-16x+64+y^2-8y+16=100$$
$$(x-8)^2+(y-4)^2=10^2$$

Centre $(8,4)$, radius 10 units

b

$$x^2+y^2+22x-2y+41=0$$
$$x^2+22x+y^2-2y=-41$$
$$x^2+22x+121+y^2-2y+1=81$$
$$(x+11)^2+(y-1)^2=9^2$$

Centre $(-11,1)$, radius 9 units

21 Centre $(-2,4)$

$(x+2)^2+(y-4)^2=r^2$ passes through $(13,12)$

When $x=13,\ y=12$

$$(13+2)^2+(12-4)^2=r^2$$
$$289=r^2$$
$$\therefore\ r=17\quad [r>0]$$

Equation is $(x+2)^2+(y-4)^2=17^2$

22 **a** $y=\sqrt{36-x^2}$

Centre $(0,0)$, radius 6 units

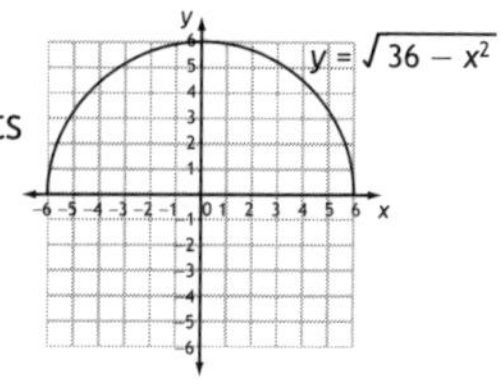

b $y = -\sqrt{25 - x^2}$

Centre $(0, 0)$, radius 5 units

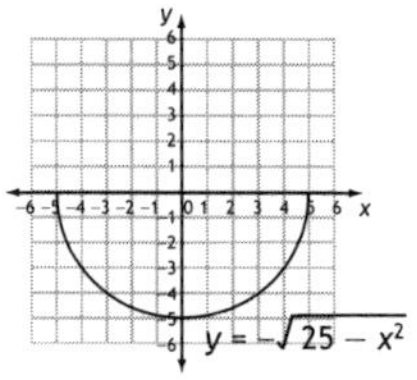

23 **a** $f(x) = 7 + \sqrt{4 - (x+1)^2}$

Centre: $(-1, 7)$

Radius 2 units

Domain: $-3 \le x \le 1$

Range: $7 \le y \le 9$

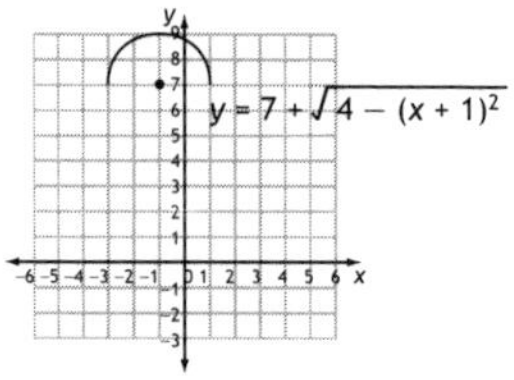

b $f(x) = 2 - \sqrt{16 - (x-3)^2}$

Centre: $(3, 2)$

Radius 4 units

Domain: $-1 \le x \le 7$

Range: $-2 \le y \le 2$

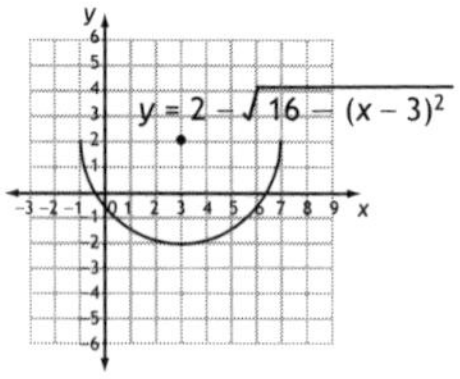

24 **a** The locus is a circle, centre (1, −5), radius 4 units.

b $P(x, y),\ Q(1, -5)$

$$PQ = 4$$
$$PQ^2 = 16$$
$$(x-1)^2 + (y+5)^2 = 16$$

25
$$x^2 = 4 - y^2$$
$$x^2 + y^2 = 4$$

The locus is a circle, centre the origin and radius 2 units.

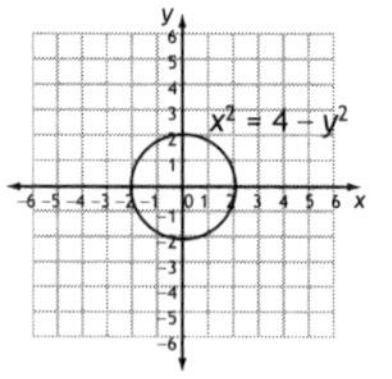

26 $P(x, y),\ Q(3, 8),\ R(7, -2)$

$$PQ = PR$$
$$PQ^2 = PR^2$$
$$(x-3)^2 + (y-8)^2 = (x-7)^2 + (y+2)^2$$
$$x^2 - 6x + 9 + y^2 - 16y + 64$$
$$= x^2 - 14x + 49 + y^2 + 4y + 4$$
$$8x - 20y + 20 = 0$$
$$2x - 5y + 5 = 0$$

27 **a** $P(x, y),\ Q(1, 5)$

$$m = \frac{y_2 - y_1}{x_2 - x_1} = \frac{5 - y}{1 - x}$$

b $P(x, y),\ R(9, -1)$

$$m = \frac{y_2 - y_1}{x_2 - x_1} = \frac{-1 - y}{9 - x}$$

c PQ is perpendicular to PR.

$$\therefore\ \frac{5-y}{1-x} = -\frac{9-x}{-1-y}$$
$$\frac{5-y}{1-x} = \frac{9-x}{1+y}$$
$$(5-y)(1+y) = (9-x)(1-x)$$
$$5 + 4y - y^2 = 9 - 10x + x^2$$
$$x^2 - 10x + y^2 - 4y + 4 = 0$$

d
$$x^2 - 10x + y^2 - 4y + 4 = 0$$
$$x^2 - 10x + 25 + y^2 - 4y + 4 = 25$$
$$(x-5)^2 + (y-2)^2 = 5^2$$

The locus is a circle centre (5, 2) and radius 5 units.

28 $P(x, y),\ S(5, 0)$

$$PS^2 = (x-5)^2 + (y-0)^2$$
$$= (x-5)^2 + y^2$$

$P(x, y),\quad x + 5 = 0$

$$x = -5$$
$$d = |x + 5| \text{ units}$$
$$d^2 = (x+5)^2$$
$$\therefore\ (x-5)^2 + y^2 = (x+5)^2$$
$$x^2 - 10x + 25 + y^2 = x^2 + 10x + 25$$
$$y^2 = 20x$$

29 $P(x, y),\ S(1, 4)$

$$PS^2 = (x-1)^2 + (y-4)^2$$

$P(x, y)$, x-axis

$$d = |y| \text{ units}$$
$$d^2 = y^2$$
$$\therefore\ (x-1)^2 + (y-4)^2 = y^2$$
$$x^2 - 2x + 1 + y^2 - 8y + 16 = y^2$$
$$x^2 - 2x + 17 = 8y$$
$$y = \frac{1}{8}(x^2 - 2x + 17)$$

30 **a** $y \ge 4 - 3x$

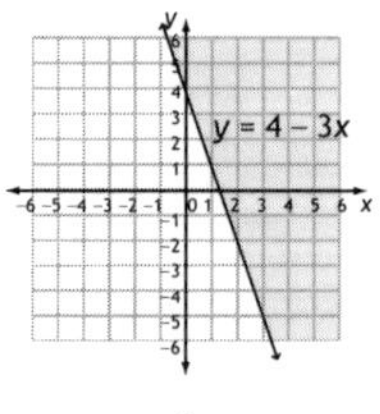

b $y < 3 - x^2$

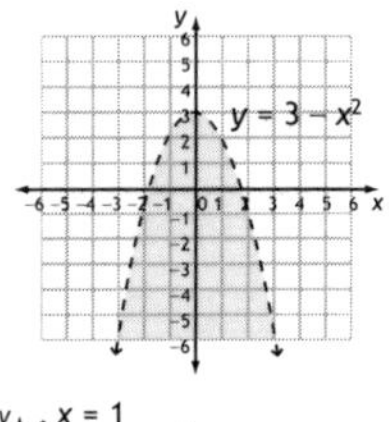

31
$$x^2 + (y-1)^2 \le 16$$
$$y \ge x$$
$$x < 1$$

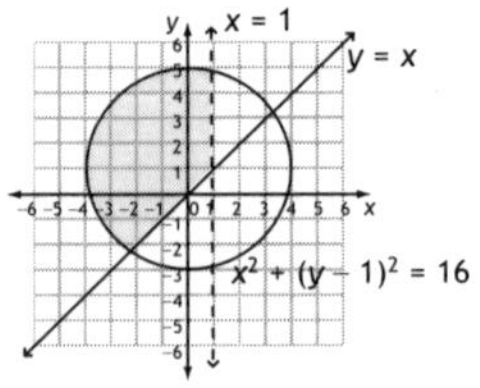

32 $x^2 + y^2 \le 12\frac{1}{4},\ x > 0,\ y < 2$

The region lies inside, and on the boundary, of a circle of radius 3.5 units, to the right of the y-axis and below the line $y = 2$.

33
$$x^2 + y^2 < 4$$
$$y > 0$$
$$x > -1$$

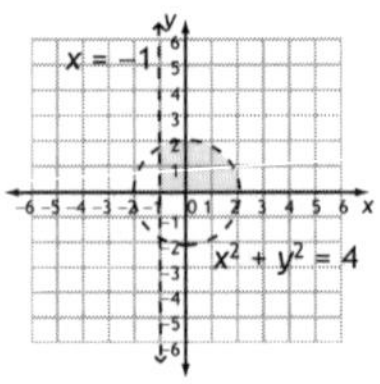

Trigonometric Ratios

1 **a** $\sin 36° = \dfrac{x}{5}$

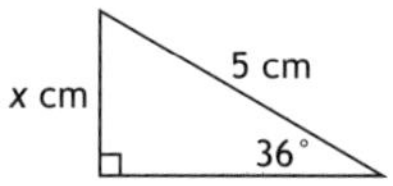

$x = 5 \times \sin 36°$
$= 2.938926261\ldots$
$= 2.94$ [2 decimal places]

b $\tan 51° = \dfrac{x}{4.4}$

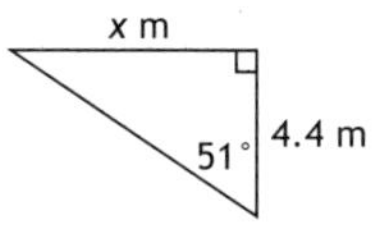

$x = 4.4 \times \tan 51°$
$= 5.433547489\ldots$
$= 5.43$ [2 decimal places]

c $\cos 73° = \dfrac{x}{19.75}$

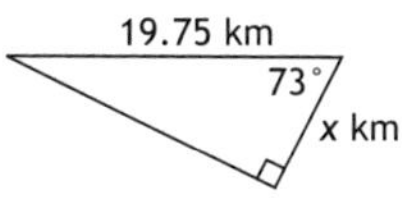

$x = 19.75 \times \cos 73°$
$= 5.774341168\ldots$
$= 5.77$ [2 decimal places]

2 **a** $\tan 66° = \dfrac{694}{QR}$

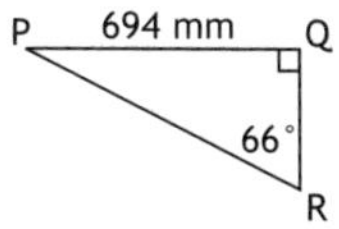

$QR = \dfrac{694}{\tan 66°}$
$= 308.9887076\ldots$
$= 309.0$ mm [1 decimal place]

or: $\angle QPR = 90° - 66°$
$= 24°$

$\tan 24° = \dfrac{QR}{694}$
$QR = 694 \times \tan 24°$
$= 308.9887076\ldots$
$= 309.0$ mm [1 decimal place]

b $\cos 24° = \dfrac{13}{QR}$

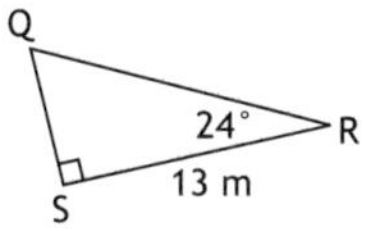

$QR = \dfrac{13}{\cos 24°}$
$= 14.23027162\ldots$
$= 14.2$ m [1 decimal place]

3 **a** $\tan \theta = \dfrac{6}{5}$

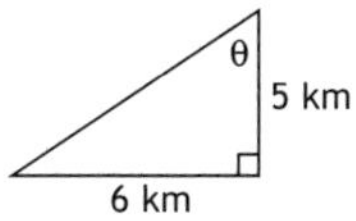

$\therefore\ \theta = 50.19442891\ldots°$
$= 50°12'$ [nearest minute]

b $\sin \theta = \dfrac{3.1}{10.4}$

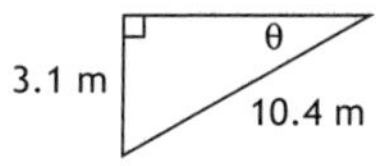

$\therefore\ \theta = 17.34213522\ldots°$
$= 17°21'$ [nearest minute]

c $\cos \theta = \dfrac{8}{9.8}$

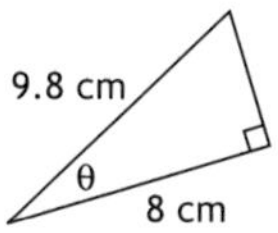

$\therefore\ \theta = 35.28126183\ldots°$
$= 35°17'$ [nearest minute]

4 **a** $\operatorname{cosec} 25° = \dfrac{1}{\sin 25°}$
$= 2.366201583\ldots$
$= 2.3662$ [4 decimal places]

b $\sec 13° = \dfrac{1}{\cos 13°}$
$= 1.026304108\ldots$
$= 1.0263$ [4 decimal places]

c $\cot 20° = \dfrac{1}{\tan 20°}$
$= 2.747477419\ldots$
$= 2.7475$ [4 decimal places]

d $\sec 28°15' = \dfrac{1}{\cos 28°15'}$
$= 1.135214569\ldots$
$= 1.1352$ [4 decimal places]

e $\operatorname{cosec} 48°45' = \dfrac{1}{\sin 48°45'}$
$= 1.330070568\ldots$
$= 1.3301$ [4 decimal places]

f $\cot 87°26' = \dfrac{1}{\tan 87°26'}$
$= 0.044826773\ldots$
$= 0.0448$ [4 decimal places]

5 **a** $\sec \theta = 4.5976$
$\cos \theta = 0.217504785\ldots$
$\theta = 77.43748084\ldots°$
$= 77°26'$ [nearest minute]

b $\cot \theta = 0.2376$
$\tan \theta = 4.208754209\ldots$
$\theta = 76.63435803\ldots°$
$= 76°38'$ [nearest minute]

c $\operatorname{cosec} \theta = 10.4334$
$\sin \theta = 0.095846032\ldots$
$\theta = 5.500016141\ldots°$
$= 5°30'$ [nearest minute]

6 **a** $\cos \theta = 0.6 \quad 0° \le \theta \le 90°$
$\therefore\ x = 0.6$
Now $x^2 + y^2 = 1$
$(0.6)^2 + y^2 = 1$
$0.36 + y^2 = 1$
$y^2 = 0.64$
$\therefore\ y = 0.8 \quad [0° \le \theta \le 90°,\ y \ge 0]$
$\therefore\ \sin \theta = 0.8$

b $\tan \theta = \dfrac{\sin \theta}{\cos \theta}$
$= \dfrac{0.8}{0.6}$
$= 1.\dot{3}$

c $\operatorname{cosec} \theta = \dfrac{1}{\sin \theta}$
$= \dfrac{1}{0.8}$
$= 1.25$

7 **a** sin 97° positive [2nd quadrant]
b tan 176° negative [2nd quadrant]
c cos 321° positive [4th quadrant]
d sec 205° negative [3rd quadrant]
e cosec 289° negative [4th quadrant]

8 **a** $\sin(180° - \theta) = \sin\theta = 0.549$ **b** $\sin(180° + \theta) = -\sin\theta = -0.549$

c $\sin(-\theta) = -\sin\theta = -0.549$ **d** $\sin(360° - \theta) = -\sin\theta = -0.549$

9 **a** $\tan 315° = \tan(360 - 45)° = -\tan 45° = -1$

b $\tan(-45°) = \tan(360 - 45)° = -\tan 45° = -1$

c $\tan 225° = \tan(180 + 45)° = \tan 45° = 1$

d $\tan 135° = \tan(180 - 45)° = -\tan 45° = -1$

e $\tan 405° = \tan(360 + 45)° = \tan 45° = 1$

10 $0° \le \theta \le 360°$

a $\sin\theta = 0.8953$
$\theta = 63°33'$ or $\theta = 180° - 63°33'$
$\theta = 63°33'$ $\theta = 116°27'$

b $\cos\theta = -0.2126$
Now $\cos 77°44' = 0.2126$
cos is negative in the 2nd and 3rd quadrants
$\therefore$ $\theta = 180° - 77°44'$ or $\theta = 180° + 77°44'$
$\theta = 102°16'$ $\theta = 257°44'$

c $\tan\theta = -2.1357$
Now $\tan 64°55' = 2.1357$
tan is negative in the 2nd and 4th quadrants
$\therefore$ $\theta = 180° - 64°55'$ or $\theta = 360° - 64°55'$
$\theta = 115°5'$ $\theta = 295°5'$

11 **a** $\sin 30° = \cos(90 - 30)° = \cos 60° = 0.5$

b $\cos 240° = \cos(180 + 60)° = -\cos 60° = -0.5$

c $\sin 330° = \sin(360 - 30)° = -\sin 30° = -0.5$

12 **a** $y = \cos x°$ for $0° \le x° \le 360°$

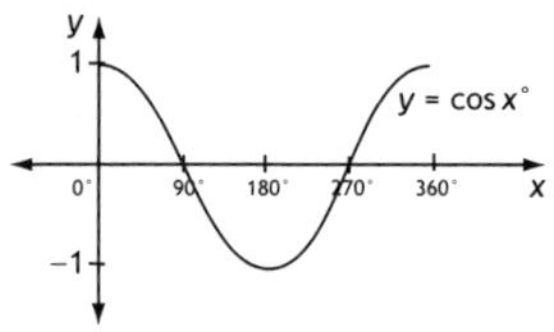

b $y = \sin x°$ for $-180° \le x° \le 180°$

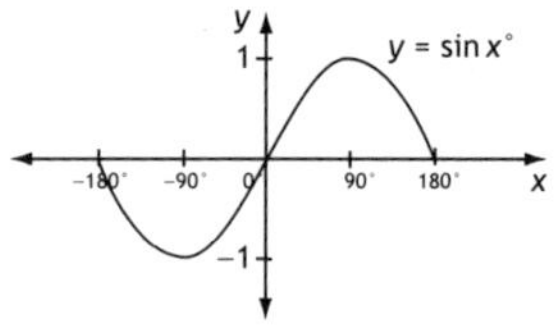

c $y = \tan x°$ for $-90° \le x° \le 90°$

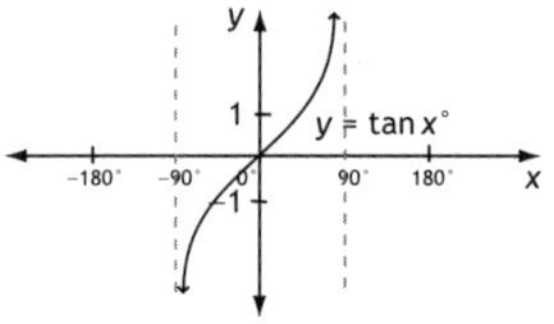

13 $$\cot^2\theta - \cos^2\theta = \frac{\cos^2\theta}{\sin^2\theta} - \cos^2\theta = \cos^2\theta\left(\frac{1}{\sin^2\theta} - 1\right) = \cos^2\theta\left(\frac{1 - \sin^2\theta}{\sin^2\theta}\right) = \cos^2\theta\left(\frac{\cos^2\theta}{\sin^2\theta}\right) = \cos^2\theta\cot^2\theta$$

14 $$\tan\theta + \cot\theta = \frac{\sin\theta}{\cos\theta} + \frac{\cos\theta}{\sin\theta} = \frac{\sin^2\theta + \cos^2\theta}{\sin\theta\cos\theta} = \frac{1}{\sin\theta\cos\theta}$$

15 **a** $\sin 30° = \frac{1}{2}$ **b** $\tan 45° = 1$

c $\cos 120° = \cos(180 - 60)° = -\cos 60° = -\frac{1}{2}$

d $\tan 315° = \tan(360 - 45)° = -\tan 45° = -1$

e $\sin 180° = \sin(180 - 0)° = \sin 0° = 0$

f $\tan 150° = \tan(180 - 30)° = -\tan 30° = -\frac{1}{\sqrt{3}}$

g $\cos 330° = \cos(360 - 30)°$
$= \cos 30°$
$= \frac{\sqrt{3}}{2}$

h $\tan(-60°) = \tan(360 - 60)°$
$= -\tan 60°$
$= -\sqrt{3}$

i $\sin 270° = \sin(180 + 90)°$
$= -\sin 90°$
$= -1$

j $\cot 30° = \tan(90 - 30)°$
$= \tan 60°$
$= \sqrt{3}$

k $\operatorname{cosec} 300° = \frac{1}{\sin 300°}$
$\sin 300° = \sin(360 - 60)°$
$= -\sin 60°$
$= -\frac{\sqrt{3}}{2}$
$\therefore \operatorname{cosec} 300° = -\frac{2}{\sqrt{3}}$

16 $\angle DBC = 30°$

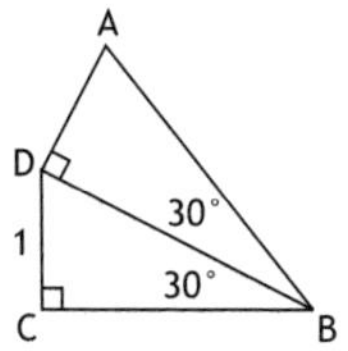

In ΔDBC, $\sin 30° = \frac{DC}{DB}$
$\frac{1}{2} = \frac{1}{DB}$
$\therefore DB = 2$ units
$\angle ABD = 30°$
In ΔABD, $\cos 30° = \frac{DB}{AB}$
$\frac{\sqrt{3}}{2} = \frac{2}{AB}$
$\therefore AB = \frac{4}{\sqrt{3}}$
$AB = \frac{4\sqrt{3}}{3}$ units

17 **a**

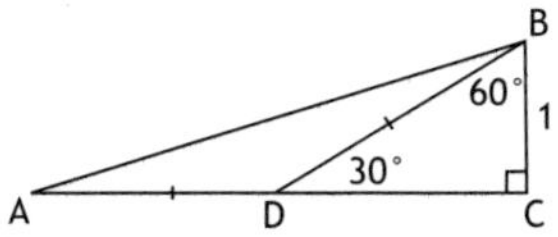

In ΔDBC, $\tan 30° = \frac{BC}{DC}$
$\frac{1}{\sqrt{3}} = \frac{1}{DC}$
$\therefore DC = \sqrt{3}$ units
In ΔDBC, $\sin 30° = \frac{BC}{BD}$
$\frac{1}{2} = \frac{1}{BD}$
$\therefore BD = 2$ units

continued ...

$BD = AD$
$\therefore AD = 2$ units
$AC = AD + DC$
$= (2 + \sqrt{3})$ units

b $\angle ABD = \angle BAD$ [base angles of isosceles triangle]
but $\angle ABD + \angle BAD = \angle BDC$ [exterior angle]
$2\angle BAD = 30°$
$\angle BAD = 15°$
In ΔBAC,
$\tan 15° = \frac{BC}{AC}$
$= \frac{1}{2 + \sqrt{3}}$
$= \frac{1}{2 + \sqrt{3}} \times \frac{2 - \sqrt{3}}{2 - \sqrt{3}}$
$= \frac{2 - \sqrt{3}}{4 - 3}$
$= 2 - \sqrt{3}$

18 $8 \cos 3\theta = 5 - 2\cos 75°$
$\cos 3\theta = \frac{5 - 2\cos 75°}{8}$
$= 0.560295238\ldots$
$3\theta = 55.92378207\ldots°$
$\theta = 18.64126069\ldots°$
$= 18°38'$ [nearest minute]

19 **a** $9 \sin x = 4 \sin x + 3$
$5 \sin x = 3$
$\sin x = 0.6$
$x = 36°52'$ or $x = 180° - 36°52'$
$x = 36°52'$ $\quad x = 143°8'$

b $\sin x - \tan x = 0$
$\sin x - \frac{\sin x}{\cos x} = 0$
$\sin x\left(1 - \frac{1}{\cos x}\right) = 0$
$\sin x = 0$ or $1 - \frac{1}{\cos x} = 0$
$\sin x = 0$ $\quad \cos x = 1$
$x = 0°, 180°$ or $360°$

c $2\cos^2 x - 1 = 0$
$2\cos^2 x = 1$
$\cos^2 x = \frac{1}{2}$
$\cos x = \pm\sqrt{\frac{1}{2}}$
$\cos x = \pm\frac{1}{\sqrt{2}}$
$x = 45°, 180° - 45°, 180° + 45°$ or $360° - 45°$
$x = 45°, 135°, 225°$ or $315°$

20 $\cot^2 x = 3$

$\cot x = \pm\sqrt{3}$

$\tan x = \pm\dfrac{1}{\sqrt{3}}$

$x = 30°, 180° - 30°, -30° \text{ or } -(180 - 30)°$

$x = -150°, -30°, 30° \text{ or } 150°$

21 Let P be a point due north of K.

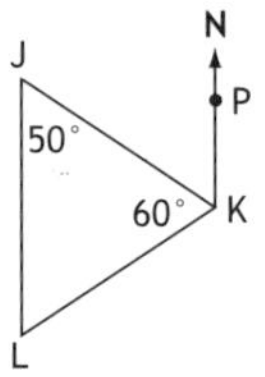

$\angle JKP = 50°$ [alternate to $\angle LJK$]

Exterior angle PKL $= 360° - (50° + 60°)$

$= 250°$

$\therefore$ the bearing of L from K is 250°

22 $\angle TSU = 108° - 90°$

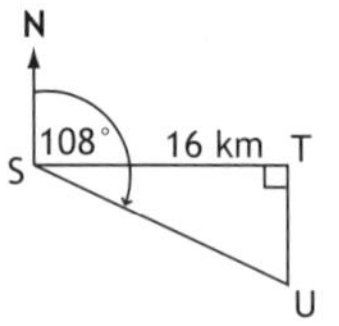

$= 18°$

In ΔTSU

$\cos 18° = \dfrac{16}{SU}$

$\therefore SU = \dfrac{16}{\cos 18°}$

$= 16.82339559\ldots$

$= 16.8$ [1 decimal place]

$\therefore$ the distance from Upton to Saxby is 16.8 kilometres

23 Let P be a point due north of Kendall and due east of Jackson.

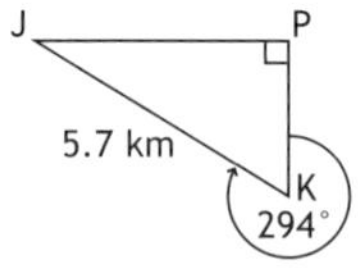

$\angle PKJ = 360° - 294°$

$= 66°$

$\cos 66° = \dfrac{PK}{5.7}$

$PK = 5.7 \times \cos 66°$

$= 2.318398866\ldots$

$= 2.3$ [1 decimal place]

$\therefore$ Jackson is 2.3 kilometres north of Kendall

24 Let h m be the height of the cliff.

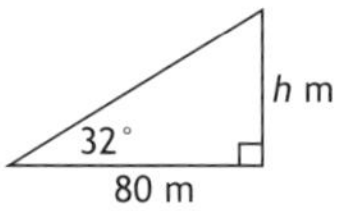

$\tan 32° = \dfrac{h}{80}$

$h = 80 \times \tan 32°$

$= 49.98954815\ldots$

$= 50$ [nearest whole number]

$\therefore$ the height of the cliff is 50 metres to the nearest metre

25 Let the angle of elevation be θ.

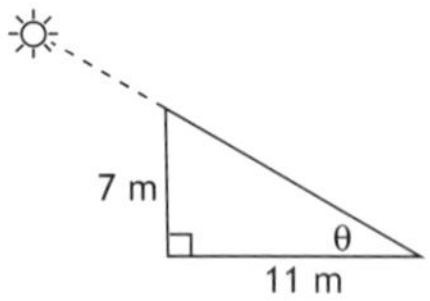

$\tan\theta = \dfrac{7}{11}$

$\theta = 32.47119229\ldots°$

$= 32°$ [nearest degree]

$\therefore$ the angle of elevation of the sun is 32°

26

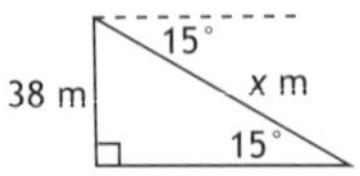

continued ...

Let the distance between the brothers be x m.

$\sin 15° = \dfrac{38}{x}$

$x = \dfrac{38}{\sin 15°}$

$= 146.8207256\ldots$

$= 147$ [nearest whole number]

$\therefore$ the brothers are 147 metres apart to the nearest metre

27 **a** $\dfrac{x}{\sin X} = \dfrac{y}{\sin Y}$

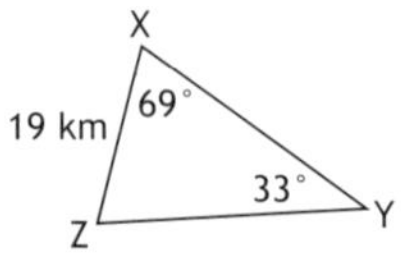

$\dfrac{x}{\sin 69°} = \dfrac{19}{\sin 33°}$

$x = \dfrac{19\sin 69°}{\sin 33°}$

$= 32.5684113\ldots$

$\therefore YZ = 32.6$ km [1 decimal place]

b $\angle X = 180° - (140° + 18°)$

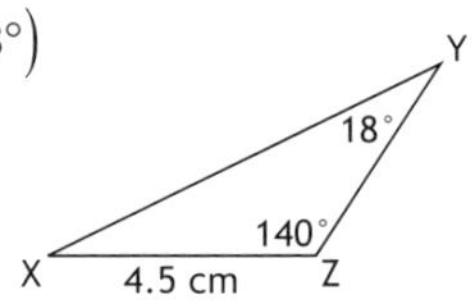

$= 22°$

$\dfrac{x}{\sin X} = \dfrac{y}{\sin Y}$

$\dfrac{x}{\sin 22°} = \dfrac{4.5}{\sin 18°}$

$x = \dfrac{4.5\sin 22°}{\sin 18°}$

$= 5.455135805\ldots$

$\therefore YZ = 5.5$ cm [1 decimal place]

28 $\angle X = 180° - (95° + 29°)$

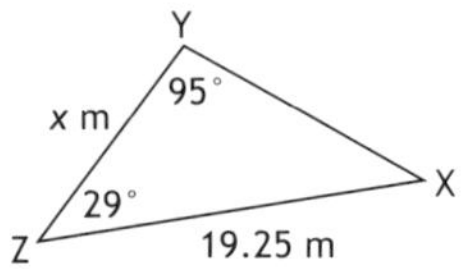

$= 56°$

$\dfrac{x}{\sin X} = \dfrac{y}{\sin Y}$

$\dfrac{x}{\sin 56°} = \dfrac{19.25}{\sin 95°}$

$x = \dfrac{19.25\sin 56°}{\sin 95°}$

$= 16.01993396\ldots$

$\therefore YZ = 16$ m [nearest metre]

29 $\dfrac{\sin P}{p} = \dfrac{\sin Q}{q}$

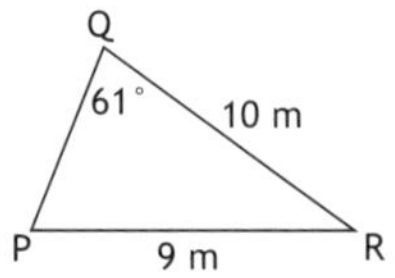

$\dfrac{\sin P}{10} = \dfrac{\sin 61°}{9}$

$\sin P = \dfrac{10\sin 61°}{9}$

$= 0.971799674\ldots$

$\angle P = 76°$ or $180° - 76°$

$\angle P = 76°$ or $104°$ [nearest degree]

30 $\dfrac{\sin H}{h} = \dfrac{\sin I}{i}$

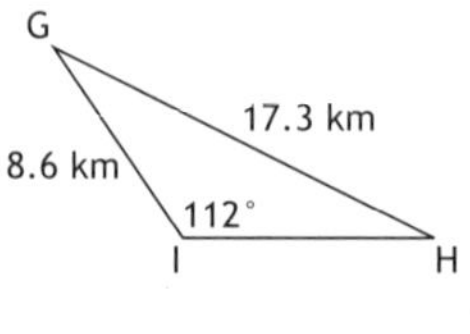

$\dfrac{\sin H}{8.6} = \dfrac{\sin 112°}{17.3}$

continued ...

$$\sin H = \frac{8.6 \sin 112°}{17.3}$$
$= 0.460912205\ldots$

$\angle H = 27°27'$ [nearest minute]

31 $c^2 = a^2 + b^2 - 2ab\cos C$

$= 67^2 + 93^2 - 2 \times 67 \times 93 \times \cos 36°$

$= 3056.030216\ldots$

$c = 55.28137314\ldots$ $[c > 0]$

AB = 55.3 m [1 decimal place]

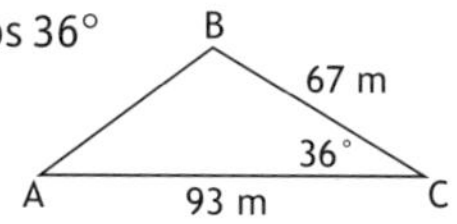

32 $n^2 = l^2 + m^2 - 2lm\cos N$

$= 170^2 + 250^2 - 2 \times 170 \times 250 \times \cos 25°$

$= 14363.8381\ldots$

$n = 119.8492307\ldots$ $[n > 0]$

LM = 120 m [nearest metre]

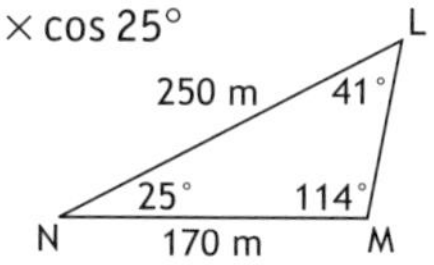

33 $$\cos A = \frac{b^2 + c^2 - a^2}{2bc}$$
$$= \frac{7^2 + 10^2 - 14^2}{2 \times 7 \times 10}$$
$= -0.335714285\ldots$

A = 110° [nearest degree]

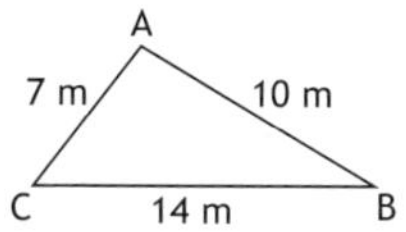

34 $$\cos A = \frac{b^2 + c^2 - a^2}{2bc}$$
$$\cos\theta = \frac{5.1^2 + 8.1^2 - 11.7^2}{2 \times 5.1 \times 8.1}$$
$= -0.547930283\ldots$

$\theta = 123°14'$ [nearest minute]

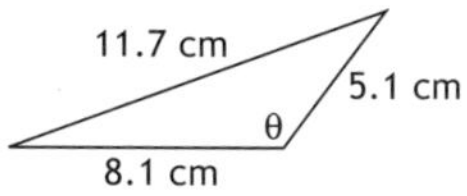

35 **a** $A = \frac{1}{2}bc\sin A$

$= \frac{1}{2} \times 9 \times 8 \times \sin 65°$

$= 32.62708033\ldots$

$\therefore$ area $= 32.6\text{ m}^2$ [1 decimal place]

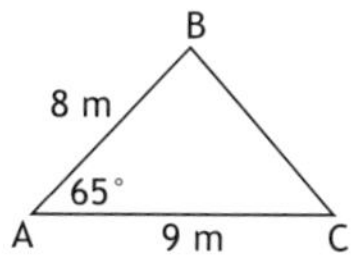

b $A = \frac{1}{2}pq\sin R$

$= \frac{1}{2} \times 8.8 \times 6.1 \times \sin 100°$

$= 26.43224009\ldots$

$\therefore$ area $= 26.4\text{ m}^2$ [1 decimal place]

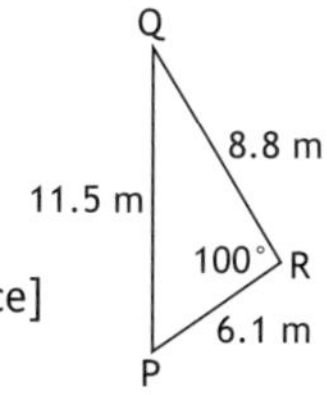

36 $A = 2 \times \frac{1}{2}ab\sin C$

$= 9.7 \times 5.1 \times \sin 119°$

$= 43.26743691\ldots$

$\therefore$ area $= 43.3\text{ cm}^2$ [1 decimal place]

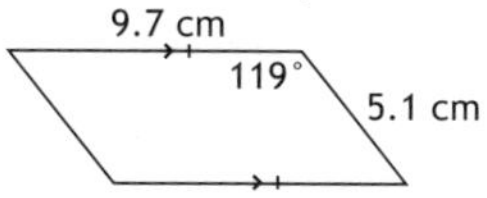

37 **a** In ΔADC,

$$\cos 64° = \frac{18}{AC}$$
$$AC = \frac{18}{\cos 64°}$$
$= 41.06109659\ldots$

$= 41.1$ m [1 decimal place]

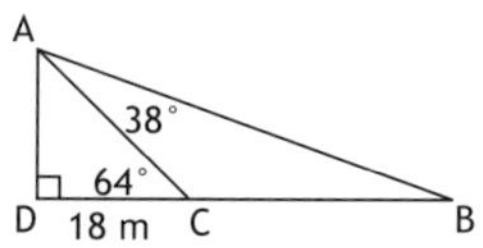

b $\angle ACB = 180° - 64$ [angles on a straight line]

$= 116°$

$\angle ABC = 180° - (38° + 116°)$

[angle sum of a triangle]

$= 26°$

In ΔABC,

$$\frac{c}{\sin C} = \frac{b}{\sin B}$$
$$\frac{c}{\sin 116°} = \frac{AC}{\sin 26°}$$
$$c = \frac{AC\sin 116°}{\sin 26°}$$
$= 84.18772408\ldots$

AB = 84.2 m [1 decimal place]

38

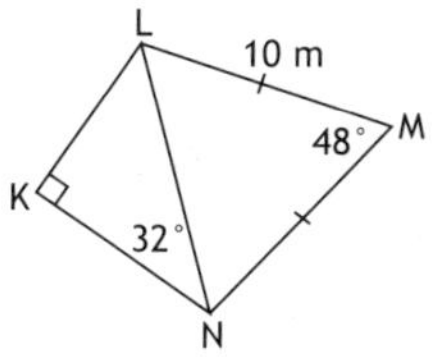

a In ΔLMN,

$m^2 = l^2 + n^2 - 2ln\cos M$

$= 10^2 + 10^2 - 2 \times 10 \times 10 \times \cos 48°$

$= 66.17387873\ldots$

$m = 8.134732862\ldots$ $[m > 0]$

$\therefore$ LN = 8.1 m [1 decimal place]

b In ΔLKN,

$$\cos 32° = \frac{KN}{LN}$$
KN = LN cos 32°

$= 6.898644716\ldots$

$= 6.9$ m [1 decimal place]

39 **a** In ΔBCD,

$$\frac{c}{\sin C} = \frac{d}{\sin D}$$
$$\frac{BD}{\sin 43°} = \frac{9.4}{\sin 70°}$$
$$BD = \frac{9.4\sin 43°}{\sin 70°}$$

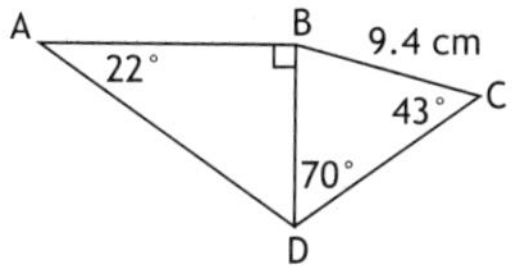

b In ΔABD,

$$\tan 22° = \frac{BD}{AB}$$
$$AB = \frac{BD}{\tan 22°}$$
$= 16.88557332\ldots$

$= 16.9$ cm [1 decimal place]

40 **a** In ΔPQR,

$$\cos P = \frac{q^2 + r^2 - p^2}{2qr}$$
$$\cos\theta = \frac{15^2 + 7^2 - 13^2}{2 \times 15 \times 7}$$

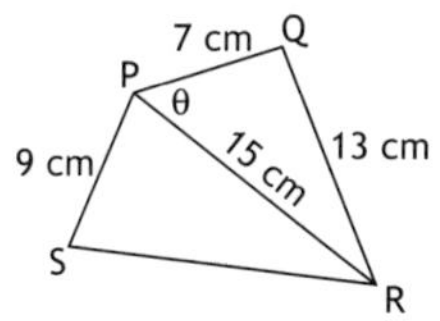

continued ...

$$= \frac{105}{210}$$
$$= \frac{1}{2}$$

b $\cos\theta = \frac{1}{2}$

$\therefore \theta = 60°$

$\angle SPQ = 147°$

$\angle SPR = 147° - 60°$

$= 87°$

$A = \frac{1}{2} rs \sin P$

$= \frac{1}{2} \times 9 \times 15 \times \sin 87°$

$= 67.4074936\ldots$

$\therefore$ area $= 67.4\ \text{cm}^2$ [1 decimal place]

The Quadratic Polynomial and the Parabola

1 a $x^2 - 11x + 30 = 0$

$(x-6)(x-5) = 0$

$x - 6 = 0$ or $x - 5 = 0$

$x = 6$ $\quad$ $x = 5$

b $y^2 + 7y + 10 = 0$

$(y+5)(y+2) = 0$

$y + 5 = 0$ or $y + 2 = 0$

$y = -5$ $\quad$ $y = -2$

c $h^2 - 6h - 16 = 0$

$(h-8)(h+2) = 0$

$h - 8 = 0$ or $h + 2 = 0$

$h = 8$ $\quad$ $h = -2$

d $6 - 5a - a^2 = 0$

$(6+a)(1-a) = 0$

$6 + a = 0$ or $1 - a = 0$

$a = -6$ $\quad$ $a = 1$

e $2w^2 + 20w - 48 = 0$

$2(w^2 + 10w - 24) = 0$

$2(w+12)(w-2) = 0$

$w + 12 = 0$ or $w - 2 = 0$

$w = -12$ $\quad$ $w = 2$

2 a $3x^2 - 17x - 6 = 0$

$(3x+1)(x-6) = 0$

$3x + 1 = 0$ or $x - 6 = 0$

$3x = -1$ $\quad$ $x = 6$

$x = -\frac{1}{3}$

b $6z^2 + 13z - 28 = 0$

$(3z-4)(2z+7) = 0$

$3z - 4 = 0$ or $2z + 7 = 0$

continued ...

$3z = 4$ or $2z = -7$

$z = 1\frac{1}{3}$ $\quad$ $z = -3\frac{1}{2}$

3 a $x^2 + 10x = 24$

$x^2 + 10x + 25 = 24 + 25$

$(x+5)^2 = 49$

$x + 5 = -7$ or $x + 5 = 7$

$x = -12$ $\quad$ $x = 2$

b $x^2 - 24x + 137 = 0$

$x^2 - 24x + 144 = 7$

$(x-12)^2 = 7$

$x - 12 = \pm\sqrt{7}$

$x = 12 \pm \sqrt{7}$

c $25x^2 - 20x = 12$

$25x^2 - 20x + 4 = 16$

$(5x-2)^2 = 16$

$5x - 2 = -4$ or $5x - 2 = 4$

$5x = -2$ $\quad$ $5x = 6$

$x = -0.4$ $\quad$ $x = 1.2$

d $4x^2 + 28x + 47 = 0$

$4x^2 + 28x + 49 = 2$

$(2x+7)^2 = 2$

$2x + 7 = \pm\sqrt{2}$

$2x = -7 \pm \sqrt{2}$

$$x = \frac{-7 \pm \sqrt{2}}{2}$$

4 $x^2 + 8x + 25 = 0$

$x^2 + 8x + 16 + 9 = 0$

$(x+4)^2 + 9 = 0$

Now $(x+4)^2 \geq 0$ for all real values of x.

$\therefore (x+4)^2 + 9 \geq 9$ for all real values of x.

$\therefore$ the minimum value of $y = x^2 + 8x + 25$ is 9

5 a $45 + 2x - 8x^2 = 0$

$a = -8, b = 2, c = 45$

$$x = \frac{-b \pm \sqrt{b^2 - 4ac}}{2a}$$
$$= \frac{-2 \pm \sqrt{2^2 - 4 \times -8 \times 45}}{2 \times -8}$$
$$= \frac{-2 \pm \sqrt{1444}}{-16}$$

$x = \frac{-2+38}{-16}$ or $x = \frac{-2-38}{-16}$

$= -2.25$ $\quad$ $= 2.5$

b $3x^2 + 11x + 7 = 0$

$a = 3, b = 11, c = 7$

continued ...

$$x = \frac{-b \pm \sqrt{b^2 - 4ac}}{2a}$$
$$= \frac{-11 \pm \sqrt{11^2 - 4 \times 3 \times 7}}{2 \times 3}$$
$$= \frac{-11 \pm \sqrt{37}}{6}$$

c $x^2 - 6x + 2 = 0$

$a = 1, b = -6, c = 2$

$$x = \frac{-b \pm \sqrt{b^2 - 4ac}}{2a}$$
$$= \frac{-(-6) \pm \sqrt{(-6)^2 - 4 \times 1 \times 2}}{2 \times 1}$$
$$= \frac{6 \pm \sqrt{28}}{2}$$
$$= \frac{6 \pm 2\sqrt{7}}{2}$$
$$= 3 \pm \sqrt{7}$$

6 $y = 6x^2 - 31x - 60$

When $x = -1.5$,

$$y = 6(-1.5)^2 - 31(-1.5) - 60$$
$$= 0$$

$\therefore x = -1.5$ is a root of the equation $6x^2 - 31x - 60 = 0$

7 **a** $2x^2 - 11x + 5 = 0$

$(2x - 1)(x - 5) = 0$

$2x - 1 = 0$ or $x - 5 = 0$

$2x = 1$ $\quad x = 5$

$x = 0.5$ $\quad x = 5$

b $x^2 + 7x + 2 = 0$

$a = 1, b = 7, c = 2$

$$x = \frac{-b \pm \sqrt{b^2 - 4ac}}{2a}$$
$$= \frac{-7 \pm \sqrt{7^2 - 4 \times 1 \times 2}}{2 \times 1}$$
$$= \frac{-7 \pm \sqrt{41}}{2}$$

8 **a** $x^2 + 8x + 17 = 0$

$x^2 + 8x = -17$

$x^2 + 8x + 16 = -1$

$(x + 4)^2 = -1$

but $(x + 4)^2 \geq 0$ for all real values of x

$\therefore x^2 + 8x + 17 = 0$ has no real roots

b $9x^2 + 12x + 4 = 0$

$(3x + 2)^2 = 0$

$3x + 2 = 0$

$3x = -2$

continued ...

$3x = -2$

$x = -\frac{2}{3}$

$\therefore 9x^2 + 12x + 4 = 0$ has only one root

9 **a**

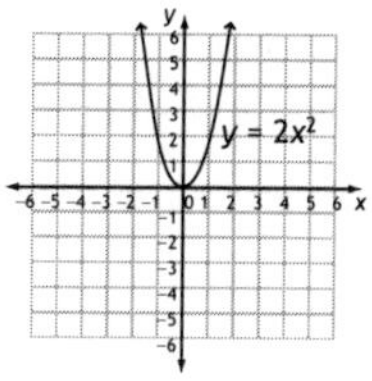

b

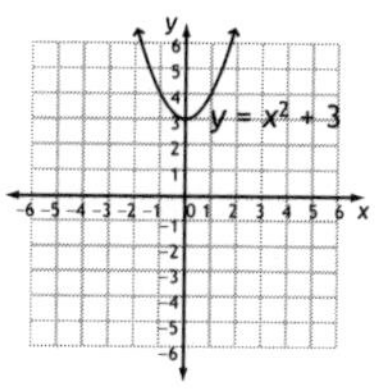

c

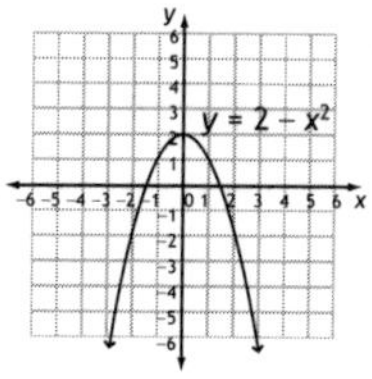

d

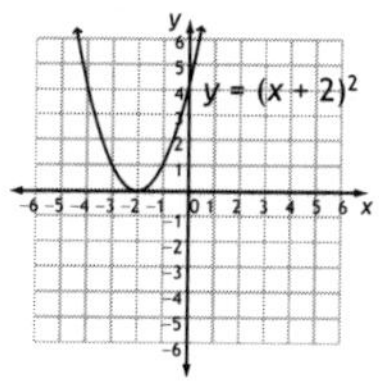

10 **a**

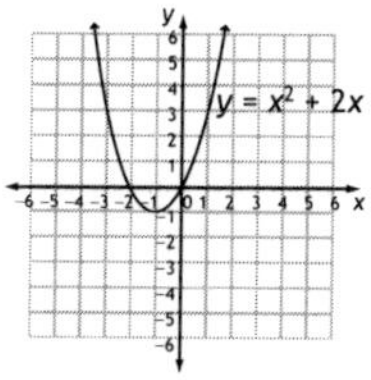

b

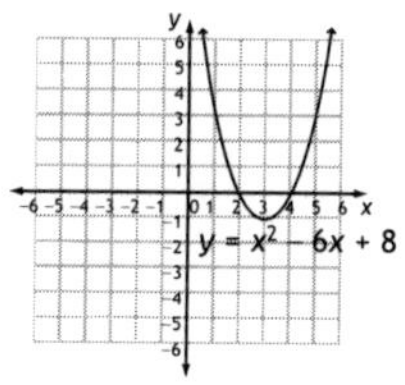

c

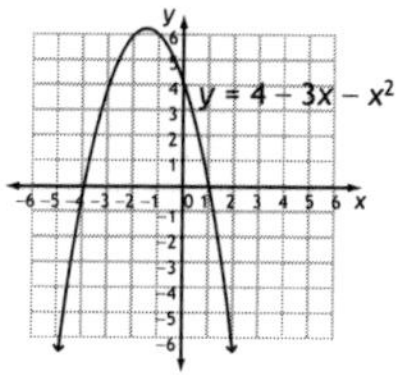

d

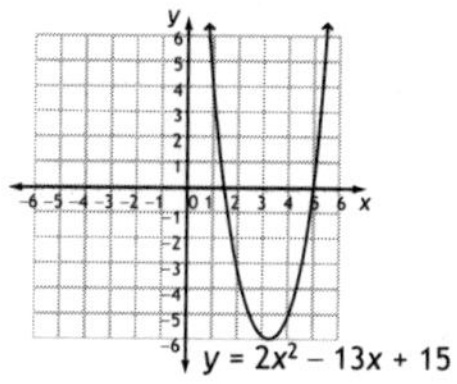

11 **a** $x^2 - 3x \leq 0$

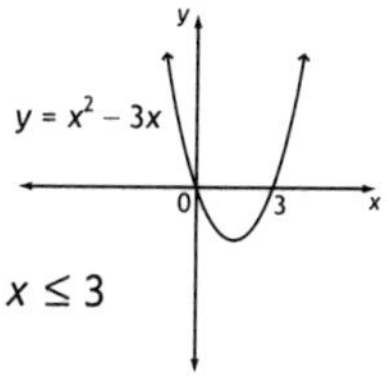

Let $y = x^2 - 3x$

$= x(x - 3)$

From the graph, $y \leq 0$ when $0 \leq x \leq 3$

$\therefore x^2 - 3x \leq 0$ when $0 \leq x \leq 3$

b $x^2 + 2x - 8 > 0$

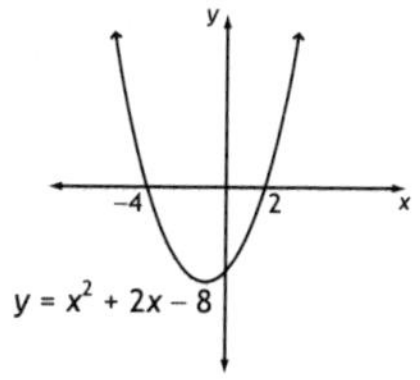

Let $y = x^2 + 2x - 8$

$= (x + 4)(x - 2)$

From the graph, $y > 0$ when $x < -4$ or $x > 2$

$\therefore x^2 + 2x - 8 > 0$ when $x < -4$ or $x > 2$

c $3 + 2x - x^2 < 0$

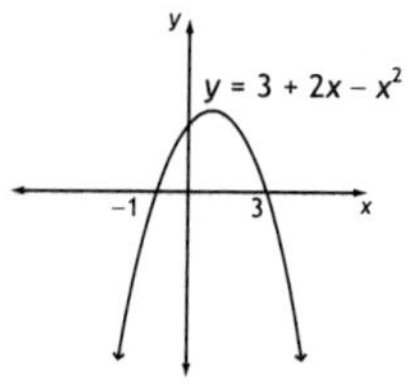

Let $y = 3 + 2x - x^2$

$= (3 - x)(1 + x)$

From the graph, $y < 0$ when $x < -1$ or $x > 3$

$\therefore 3 + 2x - x^2 < 0$ when $x < -1$ or $x > 3$

d $3x^2 + 11x + 6 \geq 0$

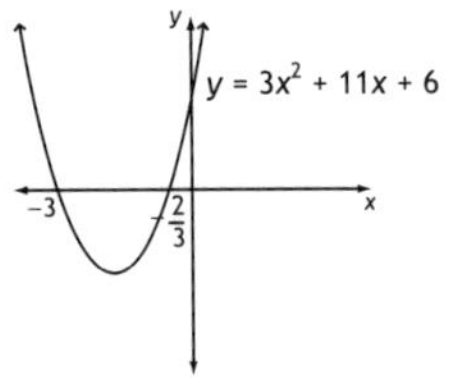

Let $y = 3x^2 + 11x + 6$

$= (3x+2)(x+3)$

From the graph, $y \geq 0$ when $x \leq -3$ or $x \geq -\frac{2}{3}$

$\therefore 3x^2 + 11x + 6 \geq 0$ when $x \leq -3$ or $x \geq -\frac{2}{3}$

12 $2x^2 + 11x + 6 = 0$

a $\alpha + \beta = -\frac{b}{a}$

$= -\frac{11}{2}$

$= -5.5$

b $\alpha\beta = \frac{c}{a}$

$= \frac{6}{2}$

$= 3$

c $\alpha^2 + \beta^2 = (\alpha+\beta)^2 - 2\alpha\beta$

$= (-5.5)^2 - 2 \times 3$

$= 24.25$

d $\frac{1}{\alpha} + \frac{1}{\beta} = \frac{\alpha+\beta}{\alpha\beta}$

$= \frac{-5.5}{3}$

$= -1\frac{5}{6}$

e $\alpha^2\beta + \alpha\beta^2 = \alpha\beta(\alpha+\beta)$

$= 3 \times -5.5$

$= -16.5$

13 $3x^2 + kx + 4 = 0$

Let the roots be α and 3α.

$\alpha + 3\alpha = -\frac{b}{a}$

$4\alpha = -\frac{k}{3}$

$\alpha = -\frac{k}{12}$ **i**

$\alpha \times 3\alpha = \frac{c}{a}$

$3\alpha^2 = \frac{4}{3}$

$\alpha^2 = \frac{4}{9}$

$\left(-\frac{k}{12}\right)^2 = \frac{4}{9}$ from **i**

$\frac{k^2}{144} = \frac{4}{9}$

$k^2 = 64$

$k = -8$ or $k = 8$

14 **a** $y = x^2 - 10x + 9$

Axis: $x = -\frac{b}{2a}$

continued ...

$x = -\frac{-10}{2 \times 1}$

$x = 5$

Least value $= \frac{4ac - b^2}{4a}$

$= \frac{4 \times 1 \times 9 - (-10)^2}{4 \times 1}$

$= -16$

$\therefore$ the parabola has axis $x = 5$ and the least value of y is -16

b $y = -x^2 + 2x - 9$

Axis: $x = -\frac{b}{2a}$

$x = -\frac{2}{2 \times -1}$

$x = 1$

Greatest value $= \frac{4ac - b^2}{4a}$

$= \frac{4 \times -1 \times -9 - 2^2}{4 \times -1}$

$= -8$

$\therefore$ the parabola has axis $x = 1$ and the greatest value of y is -8

c $y = 5x^2 - 4x + 11$

Axis: $x = -\frac{b}{2a}$

$x = -\frac{-4}{2 \times 5}$

$x = 0.4$

Least value $= \frac{4ac - b^2}{4a}$

$= \frac{4 \times 5 \times 11 - (-4)^2}{4 \times 5}$

$= 10.2$

$\therefore$ the parabola has axis $x = 0.4$ and the least value of y is 10.2

15 **a** $y = 2x^2 + 8x - 5$

Axis: $x = -\frac{b}{2a}$

$x = -\frac{8}{2 \times 2}$

$x = -2$

Least value $= \frac{4ac - b^2}{4a}$

$= \frac{4 \times 2 \times -5 - 8^2}{4 \times 2}$

$= -13$

$\therefore$ the vertex is at $(-2, -13)$

b $y = 10 - 2x - 3x^2$

Axis: $x = -\dfrac{b}{2a}$

$x = -\dfrac{-2}{2 \times -3}$

$x = -\dfrac{1}{3}$

Greatest value $= \dfrac{4ac - b^2}{4a}$

$= \dfrac{4 \times -3 \times 10 - (-2)^2}{4 \times -3}$

$= 10\frac{1}{3}$

$\therefore$ the vertex is at $\left(-\frac{1}{3}, 10\frac{1}{3}\right)$

16 **a** $4x^2 - 3x - 2 = 0$

$a = 4, b = -3, c = -2$

$\Delta = b^2 - 4ac$

$= (-3)^2 - 4 \times 4 \times -2$

$= 41$

$\therefore$ the roots are real, irrational and unequal

b $2x^2 + x + 7 = 0$

$a = 2, b = 1, c = 7$

$\Delta = b^2 - 4ac$

$= 1^2 - 4 \times 2 \times 7$

$= -55$

$\therefore$ the roots are not real

c $16x^2 - 8x + 1 = 0$

$a = 16, b = -8, c = 1$

$\Delta = b^2 - 4ac$

$= (-8)^2 - 4 \times 16 \times 1$

$= 0$

$\therefore$ the roots are real, rational and equal

d $9x^2 - 36x + 20 = 0$

$a = 9, b = -36, c = 20$

$\Delta = b^2 - 4ac$

$= (-36)^2 - 4 \times 9 \times 20$

$= 576$

$= 24^2$

$\therefore$ the roots are real, rational and unequal

17 **a** $x^2 - 6x + m = 0$

$a = 1, b = -6, c = m$

$\Delta = b^2 - 4ac$

$= (-6)^2 - 4 \times 1 \times m$

$= 36 - 4m$

The roots are real when $\Delta \geq 0$

$36 - 4m \geq 0$

$-4m \geq -36$

$m \leq 9$

$\therefore$ the roots are real when $m \leq 9$

b $3x^2 + mx + 12 = 0$

$a = 3, b = m, c = 12$

$\Delta = b^2 - 4ac$

$= m^2 - 4 \times 3 \times 12$

$= m^2 - 144$

The roots are equal when $\Delta = 0$

$m^2 - 144 = 0$

$m^2 = 144$

$m = \pm 12$

$\therefore$ the roots are equal when $m = \pm 12$

18 **a** $2x^2 + x - 5$

$a = 2, b = 1, c = -5$

$\Delta = b^2 - 4ac$

$= 1^2 - 4 \times 2 \times -5$

$= 41$

$\Delta > 0$

$\therefore$ the expression is indefinite

b $-x^2 + 5x - 8$

$a = -1, b = 5, c = -8$

$\Delta = b^2 - 4ac$

$= 5^2 - 4 \times -1 \times -8$

$= -7$

$\Delta < 0, \ a < 0$

$\therefore$ the expression is negative definite

c $-3x^2 + 6x + 8$

$a = -3, b = 6, c = 8$

$\Delta = b^2 - 4ac$

$= 6^2 - 4 \times -3 \times 8$

$= 132$

$\Delta > 0$

$\therefore$ the expression is indefinite

d $7x^2 + 4x + 1$

$a = 7, b = 4, c = 1$

$\Delta = b^2 - 4ac$

$= 4^2 - 4 \times 7 \times 1$

$= -12$

$\Delta < 0, \ a > 0$

$\therefore$ the expression is positive definite

19 **a** $9x^2 + kx + 4$

$a = 9, b = k, c = 4$

$\Delta = b^2 - 4ac$

$= k^2 - 4 \times 9 \times 4$

$= k^2 - 144$

Now $a > 0$, the expression will always be positive if $\Delta < 0$.

$k^2 - 144 < 0$

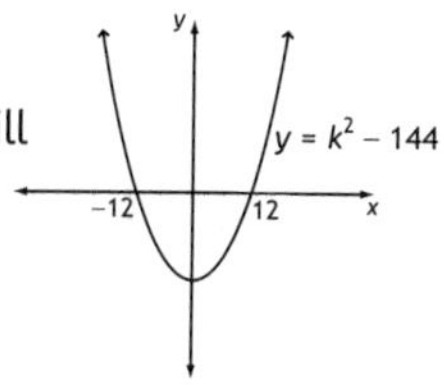

Let $y = k^2 - 144$

$= (k + 12)(k - 12)$

continued ...

From the graph, $y < 0$ when $-12 < k < 12$.
$\therefore$ the expression will always be positive when $-12 < k < 12$

20 **a** $(x+3)(x+2) = 20$

$x^2 + 5x + 6 = 20$

$x^2 + 5x - 14 = 0$

$(x+7)(x-2) = 0$

$x + 7 = 0$ or $x - 2 = 0$

$x = -7$ $\quad x = 2$

b $16x^2 = (x+6)^2$

$16x^2 = x^2 + 12x + 36$

$15x^2 - 12x - 36 = 0$

$3(5x^2 - 4x - 12) = 0$

$3(5x+6)(x-2) = 0$

$5x + 6 = 0$ or $x - 2 = 0$

$5x = -6$ $\quad x = 2$

$x = -1.2$ $\quad x = 2$

21 **a** $x^4 - 26x^2 + 25 = 0$

Let $u = x^2$

$u^2 - 26u + 25 = 0$

$(u-25)(u-1) = 0$

$u - 25 = 0$ or $u - 1 = 0$

$u = 25$ $\quad u = 1$

$\therefore$ $x^2 = 25$ $\quad x^2 = 1$

$x = \pm 5$ $\quad x = \pm 1$

b $3x^4 - 10x^2 - 8 = 0$

Let $u = x^2$

$3u^2 - 10u - 8 = 0$

$(3u+2)(u-4) = 0$

$3u + 2 = 0$ or $u - 4 = 0$

$3u = -2$ $\quad u = 4$

$u = -\frac{2}{3}$ $\quad u = 4$

$\therefore$ $x^2 = -\frac{2}{3}$ $\quad x^2 = 4$

no solution $\quad x = \pm 2$

$\therefore x = 2$ or $x = -2$

c $4^x - 10(2^x) + 16 = 0$

$(2^2)^x - 10(2^x) + 16 = 0$

$(2^x)^2 - 10(2^x) + 16 = 0$

Let $u = 2^x$

d $u^2 - 10u + 16 = 0$

$(u-2)(u-8) = 0$

$u - 2 = 0$ or $u - 8 = 0$

$u = 2$ $\quad u = 8$

$\therefore$ $2^x = 2$ $\quad 2^x = 8$

$x = 1$ $\quad x = 3$

$(x^2 - 8x)^2 + 3(x^2 - 8x) - 108 = 0$

Let $u = x^2 - 8x$

$u^2 + 3u - 108 = 0$

$(u+12)(u-9) = 0$

$u + 12 = 0$ or $u - 9 = 0$

$x^2 - 8x + 12 = 0$ $\quad x^2 - 8x - 9 = 0$

$(x-2)(x-6) = 0$ $\quad (x+1)(x-9) = 0$

$x - 2 = 0$ or $x - 6 = 0$ $\quad x + 1 = 0$ or $x - 9 = 0$

$x = 2$ $\quad x = 6$ $\quad x = -1$ $\quad x = 9$

22 **a** $3x^2 - 2x + 3 \equiv Ax(x+1) + Bx + C$

$\equiv Ax^2 + Ax + Bx + C$

$\equiv Ax^2 + (A+B)x + C$

$\therefore A = 3,$ $\quad A + B = -2,$ $\quad C = 3$

$3 + B = -2$

$B = -5$

$\therefore 3x^2 - 2x + 3 \equiv 3x(x+1) - 5x + 3$

23 $5x^2 - 4x - 7 \equiv Ax(x-1) + B(x-1) + C$

Let $x = 1$

$5 \times 1^2 - 4 \times 1 - 7 = A \times 1 \times (1-1) + B(1-1) + C$

$C = -6$

Let $x = 0$

$5 \times 0^2 - 4 \times 0 - 7 = A \times 0 \times (0-1) + B(0-1) + C$

$-7 = -B - 6$

$-1 = -B$

$B = 1$

Let $x = 2$

$5 \times 2^2 - 4 \times 2 - 7 = A \times 2 \times (2-1) + B(2-1) + C$

$5 = 2A - 5$

$2A = 10$

$A = 5$

$\therefore A = 5, B = 1, C = -6$

$\therefore 5x^2 - 4x - 7 \equiv 5x(x-1) + (x-1) - 6$

24 $Q(x) = ax^2 + bx + c$

$Q(0) = 5,$ $\quad 5 = a \times 0^2 + b \times 0 + c$

$c = 5$

$Q(1) = 3,$ $\quad 3 = a \times 1^2 + b \times 1 + 5$

$3 = a + b + 5$

$-2 = a + b$ **i**

$Q(-1) = 13,$ $\quad 13 = a \times (-1)^2 + b \times -1 + 5$

$13 = a - b + 5$

$8 = a - b$ **ii**

i + ii $\quad 6 = 2a$

$a = 3$

Substitute in **i**

$-2 = 3 + b$

$b = -5$

$\therefore Q(x) = 3x^2 - 5x + 5$

25 a
$$x^2 = 16y$$
$$\therefore 4A = 16$$
$$A = 4$$
Vertex $(0, 0)$
Focus $(0, 4)$
Directrix $y = -4$

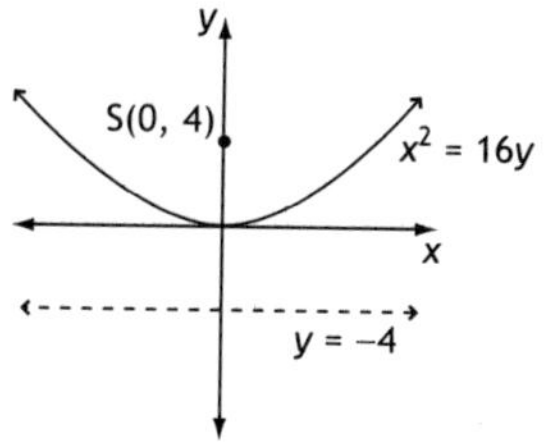

b
$$y^2 = 20x$$
$$\therefore 4A = 20$$
$$A = 5$$
Vertex $(0, 0)$
Focus $(5, 0)$
Directrix $x = -5$

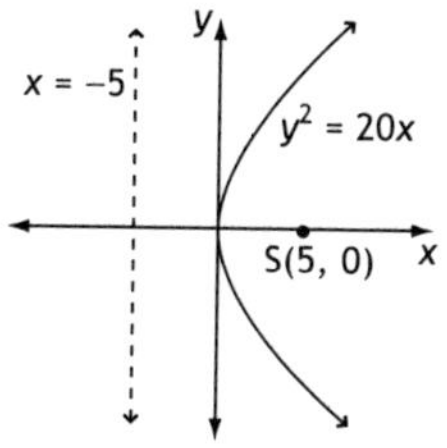

c
$$x^2 = -8y$$
$$\therefore 4A = 8$$
$$A = 2$$
Vertex $(0, 0)$
Focus $(0, -2)$
Directrix $y = 2$

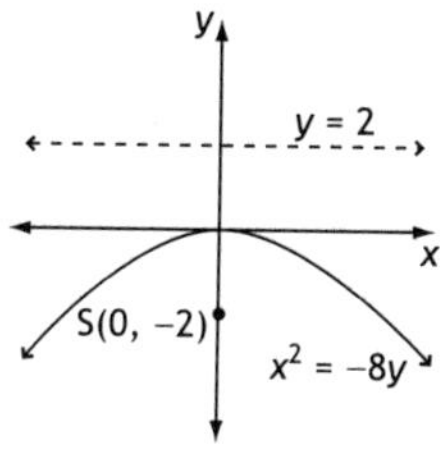

d
$$y^2 = -2x$$
$$\therefore 4A = 2$$
$$A = 0.5$$
Vertex $(0, 0)$
Focus $(-0.5, 0)$
Directrix $x = 0.5$

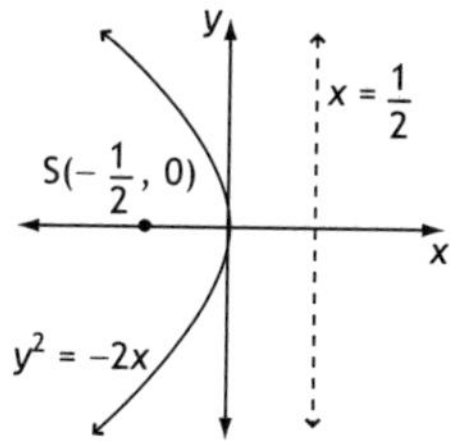

26 a $(x-4)^2 = 12(y-2)$
Vertex $(4, 2)$, axis: $x = 4$
$$4A = 12$$
$$\therefore \ A = 3$$
Focus $(4, 5)$
Directrix $y = -1$

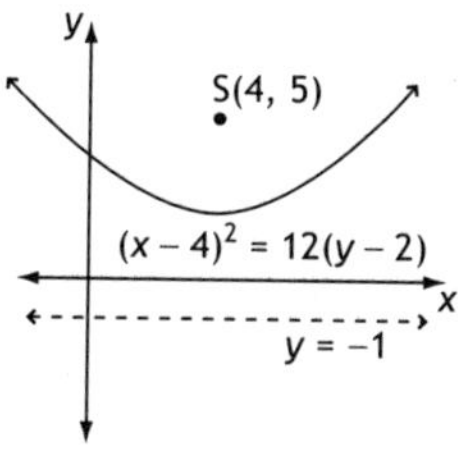

b $(y+6)^2 = -4(x-4)$
Vertex $(4, -6)$
axis: $y = -6$
$$4A = 4$$
$$\therefore \ A = 1$$
Focus $(3, -6)$
Directrix $x = 5$

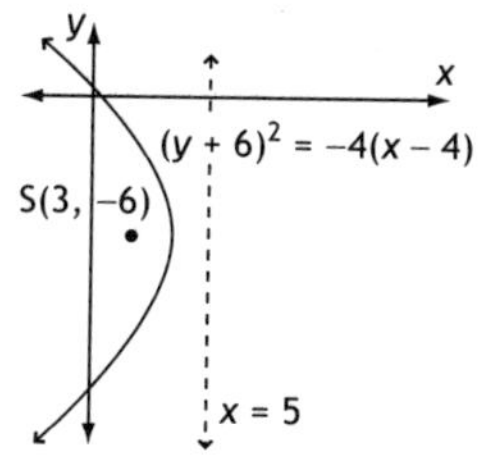

c $y^2 = 16(x-1)$
Vertex $(1, 0)$, axis: $y = 0$
$$4A = 16$$
$$\therefore \ A = 4$$
Focus $(5, 0)$
Directrix $x = -3$

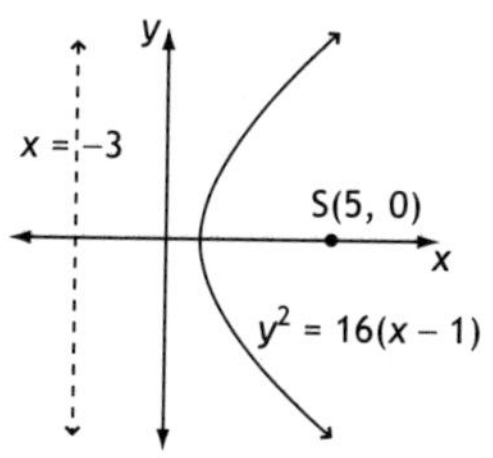

d $(x+3)^2 = -8(y+3)$
Vertex $(-3, -3)$,
axis: $x = -3$
$$4A = 8$$
$$\therefore \ A = 2$$
Focus $(-3, -5)$
Directrix $y = -1$

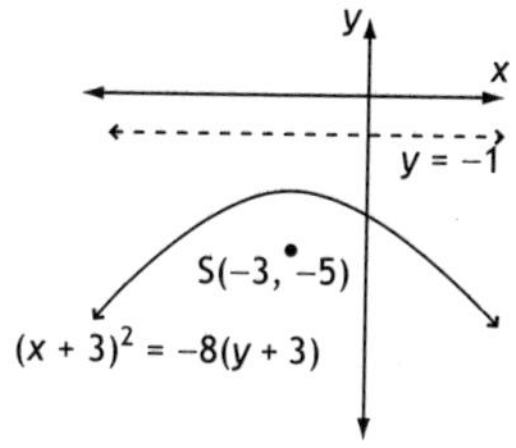

27 a
$$y = x^2 - 4x + 7$$
$$x^2 - 4x = y - 7$$
$$x^2 - 4x + 4 = y - 7 + 4$$
$$(x-2)^2 = y - 3$$

b
$$y = -\tfrac{1}{2}x^2 - x + \tfrac{1}{2}$$
$$2y = -x^2 - 2x + 1$$
$$x^2 + 2x = -2y + 1$$
$$x^2 + 2x + 1 = -2y + 2$$
$$(x+1)^2 = -2(y-1)$$

c
$$y = 4x^2 - 40x + 97$$
$$4x^2 - 40x = y - 97$$
$$x^2 - 10x = \tfrac{1}{4}y - 24\tfrac{1}{4}$$
$$x^2 - 10x + 25 = \tfrac{1}{4}y - 24\tfrac{1}{4} + 25$$
$$(x-5)^2 = \tfrac{1}{4}y + \tfrac{3}{4}$$
$$(x-5)^2 = \tfrac{1}{4}(y+3)$$

d
$$y = 9 - 8x - 2x^2$$
$$2x^2 + 8x = -y + 9$$
$$x^2 + 4x = -\tfrac{1}{2}y + 4\tfrac{1}{2}$$
$$x^2 + 4x + 4 = -\tfrac{1}{2}y + 8\tfrac{1}{2}$$
$$(x+2)^2 = -\tfrac{1}{2}y + \tfrac{17}{2}$$
$$(x+2)^2 = -\tfrac{1}{2}(y-17)$$

28 a
$$y = x^2 + 10x + 25$$
$$x^2 + 10x + 25 = y$$
$$(x+5)^2 = y$$
Vertex $(-5, 0)$
$$4A = 1$$
$$\therefore \ A = \tfrac{1}{4}$$
Focus $(-5, \tfrac{1}{4})$
Directrix $y = -\tfrac{1}{4}$

b
$$x = \tfrac{1}{2}y^2 - 3y + 5$$
$$2x = y^2 - 6y + 10$$
$$y^2 - 6y = 2x - 10$$
$$y^2 - 6y + 9 = 2x - 1$$
$$(y-3)^2 = 2(x - \tfrac{1}{2})$$

continued ...

Vertex $\left(\frac{1}{2}, 3\right)$

$$4A = 2$$

$$\therefore \quad A = \tfrac{1}{2}$$

Focus $\left(1, 3\right)$

Directrix $x = 0$

29 **a** Vertex $\left(2, 5\right)$, focus $\left(2, 9\right)$, axis: $x = 2$

Focal length $= 9 - 5$

$= 4$ units

$\therefore \quad A = 4$

$$\left(x - x_0\right)^2 = 4A\left(y - y_0\right)$$

$$\left(x - 2\right)^2 = 4 \times 4 \times \left(y - 5\right)$$

$$\left(x - 2\right)^2 = 16\left(y - 5\right)$$

b Vertex $\left(6, 4\right)$, focus $\left(6, -3\right)$, axis: $x = 6$

Focal length $= 4 - \left(-3\right)$

$= 7$ units

$\therefore \quad A = 7$

$$\left(x - x_0\right)^2 = -4A\left(y - y_0\right)$$

$$\left(x - 6\right)^2 = -4 \times 7 \times \left(y - 4\right)$$

$$\left(x - 6\right)^2 = -28\left(y - 4\right)$$

c Vertex $\left(1, -2\right)$, directrix $x = 3$, axis: $y = -2$

Focal length $= 3 - 1$

$= 2$ units

$\therefore \quad A = 2$

$$\left(y - y_0\right)^2 = -4A\left(x - x_0\right)$$

$$\left(y - \left(-2\right)\right)^2 = -4 \times 2 \times \left(x - 1\right)$$

$$\left(y + 2\right)^2 = -8\left(x - 1\right)$$

d Focus $\left(1, 5\right)$, directrix: $y = -5$, axis: $x = 1$

Focal length $= \frac{1}{2}\left(5 - \left(-5\right)\right)$

$= 5$ units

$\therefore \quad A = 5$

Vertex $\left(1, 0\right)$

$$\left(x - x_0\right)^2 = 4A\left(y - y_0\right)$$

$$\left(x - 1\right)^2 = 4 \times 5 \times \left(y - 0\right)$$

$$\left(x - 1\right)^2 = 20y$$

30 **a** Vertex $\left(-1, 3\right)$, axis: $x = -1$

Focal length $= 2.25$ units

$\therefore \quad A = 2.25$

$$\left(x - x_0\right)^2 = \pm 4A\left(y - y_0\right)$$

$$\left(x - \left(-1\right)\right)^2 = \pm 4 \times 2.25 \times \left(y - 3\right)$$

$$\left(x + 1\right)^2 = \pm 9\left(y - 3\right)$$

b Focus $\left(3, 0\right)$, axis: x-axis $\left(y = 0\right)$

Focal length $= 3$ units

$\therefore \quad A = 3$

Either: vertex $\left(0, 0\right)$

$$y^2 = 4Ax$$

$$y^2 = 4 \times 3 \times x$$

$$y^2 = 12x$$

or: vertex $\left(6, 0\right)$

$$\left(y - y_0\right)^2 = -4A\left(x - x_0\right)$$

$$\left(y - 0\right)^2 = -4 \times 3 \times \left(x - 6\right)$$

$$y^2 = -12\left(x - 6\right)$$

The Tangent to a Curve and the Derivative of a Function

1 **a** $\lim\limits_{x \to 2}\left(4x - 1\right) = 4 \times 2 - 1$

$= 7$

b $\lim\limits_{x \to 3}\left(1 - x^2\right) = 1 - 3^2$

$= -8$

c $\lim\limits_{x \to -1}\left(3 + 5x\right) = 3 + 5 \times -1$

$= -2$

2 **a**

$$\lim_{x \to 4} \frac{x^2 - 16}{x - 4} = \lim_{x \to 4} \frac{\left(x - 4\right)\left(x + 4\right)}{x - 4}$$

$$= \lim_{x \to 4}\left(x + 4\right)$$

$$= 4 + 4$$

$$= 8$$

b

$$\lim_{h \to 0} \frac{h^2 - 16h}{h} = \lim_{h \to 0} \frac{h\left(h - 16\right)}{h}$$

$$= \lim_{h \to 0}\left(h - 16\right)$$

$$= 0 - 16$$

$$= -16$$

c

$$\lim_{x \to 10} \frac{x^2 - 16x + 60}{x^2 - 6x - 40} = \lim_{x \to 10} \frac{\left(x - 6\right)\left(x - 10\right)}{\left(x + 4\right)\left(x - 10\right)}$$

$$= \lim_{x \to 10} \frac{\left(x - 6\right)}{\left(x + 4\right)}$$

$$= \frac{10 - 6}{10 + 4}$$

$$= \frac{2}{7}$$

3 **a** $\lim\limits_{x \to -\infty} \dfrac{3}{x} = 0$

b

$$\lim_{x \to \infty} \frac{1 - x^2}{x^2} = \lim_{x \to \infty}\left(\frac{1}{x^2} - 1\right)$$

$$= -1$$

4 **a** continuous **b** discontinuous
c continuous **d** discontinuous

5 **a** $f(x) = \dfrac{x^2 - 9}{x - 3}$

$f(3) = \dfrac{3^2 - 9}{3 - 3}$

$= \dfrac{0}{0}$

$\therefore f(3)$ is undefined

$\therefore$ the curve is not continuous at $x = 3$

b $f(x) = 2x^2 + 7$

$f(3) = 2 \times 3^2 + 7$

$= 25$

$\lim\limits_{x \to 3}(2x^2 + 7) = 2 \times 3^2 + 7$

$= 25$

$\therefore f(3) = \lim\limits_{x \to 3} f(x)$

$\therefore$ the curve is continuous at $x = 3$

c $f(x) = \begin{cases} x^2 - 8 & \text{if } x > 3 \\ 1 & \text{if } x = 3 \\ 2x - 5 & \text{if } x < 3 \end{cases}$

$f(3) = 1$

For $x > 3$, $\lim\limits_{x \to 3}(x^2 - 8) = 3^2 - 8$

$= 1$

For $x < 3$, $\lim\limits_{x \to 3}(2x - 5) = 2 \times 3 - 5$

$= 1$

$\therefore f(3) = \lim\limits_{x \to 3} f(x)$

$\therefore$ the curve is continuous at $x = 3$

d $f(x) = \dfrac{x^2 + 2x - 15}{x + 5}$

$f(3) = \dfrac{3^2 + 2 \times 3 - 15}{3 + 5}$

$= 0$

$\lim\limits_{x \to 3} \dfrac{x^2 + 2x - 15}{x + 5} = \lim\limits_{x \to 3} \dfrac{(x - 3)(x + 5)}{x + 5}$

$= \lim\limits_{x \to 3}(x - 3)$

$= 3 - 3$

$= 0$

$\therefore f(3) = \lim\limits_{x \to 3} f(x)$

$\therefore$ the curve is continuous at $x = 3$

6 **a** $y = f(x)$, $(2, 5)$, $(5, 11)$

$m = \dfrac{f(x) - f(c)}{x - c}$

$= \dfrac{11 - 5}{5 - 2}$

$= 2$

$\therefore$ the gradient of the secant is 2

b $y = x^3$, $x = 1$, $x = 2$

$m = \dfrac{f(x) - f(c)}{x - c}$

$= \dfrac{2^3 - 1^3}{2 - 1}$

$= 7$

$\therefore$ the gradient of the secant is 7

c $y = x^2 - x$, $x = -1$, $x = 3$

$m = \dfrac{f(x) - f(c)}{x - c}$

$= \dfrac{(3^2 - 3) - \left[(-1)^2 - (-1)\right]}{3 - (-1)}$

$= 1$

$\therefore$ the gradient of the secant is 1

7 $y = x^2$, $x = -1$

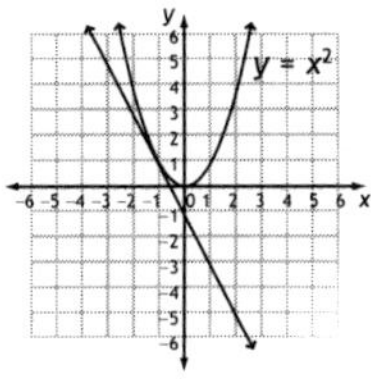

$f'(c) = \lim\limits_{x \to c} \dfrac{f(x) - f(c)}{x - c}$

$f'(-1) = \lim\limits_{x \to -1} \dfrac{f(x) - f(-1)}{x - (-1)}$

$= \lim\limits_{x \to -1} \dfrac{x^2 - 1}{x + 1}$

$= \lim\limits_{x \to -1} \dfrac{(x - 1)(x + 1)}{x + 1}$

$= \lim\limits_{x \to -1}(x - 1)$

$= -1 - 1$

$= -2$

8 $y = 3 - x^2$, $x = 1$

$f'(c) = \lim\limits_{x \to c} \dfrac{f(x) - f(c)}{x - c}$

$f'(1) = \lim\limits_{x \to 1} \dfrac{f(x) - f(1)}{x - 1}$

$= \lim\limits_{x \to 1} \dfrac{(3 - x^2) - (3 - 1^2)}{x - 1}$

$= \lim\limits_{x \to 1} \dfrac{1 - x^2}{x - 1}$

$= \lim\limits_{x \to 1} \dfrac{(1 + x)(1 - x)}{x - 1}$

$= \lim\limits_{x \to 1}[-(1 + x)]$

$= -(1 + 1)$

$= -2$

9 **a** $y = x^3$, $(-1, -1)$

$f'(c) = \lim\limits_{x \to c} \dfrac{f(x) - f(c)}{x - c}$

$f'(-1) = \lim\limits_{x \to -1} \dfrac{f(x) - f(-1)}{x + 1}$

$= \lim\limits_{x \to -1} \dfrac{x^3 - (-1)^3}{x + 1}$

continued ...

$$= \lim_{x \to -1} \frac{x^3 + 1}{x + 1}$$
$$= \lim_{x \to -1} \frac{(x+1)(x^2 - x + 1)}{x + 1}$$
$$= \lim_{x \to -1} (x^2 - x + 1)$$
$$= (-1)^2 - (-1) + 1$$
$$= 3$$

$$m = 3,\ (-1, -1)$$
$$y - y_1 = m(x - x_1)$$
$$y - (-1) = 3(x - (-1))$$
$$y + 1 = 3x + 3$$
$$y = 3x + 2$$

$\therefore$ the equation of the tangent is $y = 3x + 2$

b $y = 2x^2,\ x = 1$

$$f'(c) = \lim_{x \to c} \frac{f(x) - f(c)}{x - c}$$
$$f'(1) = \lim_{x \to 1} \frac{f(x) - f(1)}{x - 1}$$
$$= \lim_{x \to 1} \frac{2x^2 - (2 \times 1^2)}{x - 1}$$
$$= \lim_{x \to 1} \frac{2x^2 - 2}{x - 1}$$
$$= \lim_{x \to 1} \frac{2(x^2 - 1)}{x - 1}$$
$$= \lim_{x \to 1} \frac{2(x+1)(x-1)}{x - 1}$$
$$= \lim_{x \to 1} [2(x + 1)]$$
$$= 2(1 + 1)$$
$$= 4$$

$$m = 4,\ (1, 2)$$
$$y - y_1 = m(x - x_1)$$
$$y - 2 = 4(x - 1)$$
$$y - 2 = 4x - 4$$
$$y = 4x - 2$$

$\therefore$ the equation of the tangent is $y = 4x - 2$

10 a

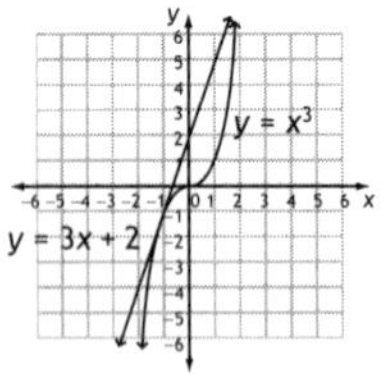

b

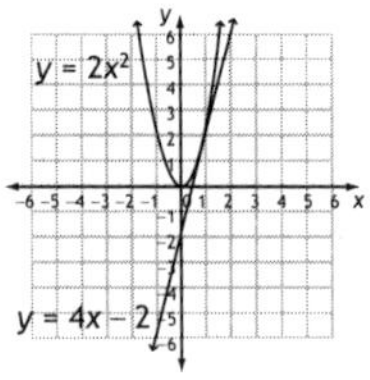

11 a $f(x) = 4x^2,\ x = 2$

$$f'(c) = \lim_{h \to 0} \frac{f(c + h) - f(c)}{h}$$
$$f'(2) = \lim_{h \to 0} \frac{f(2 + h) - f(2)}{h}$$

continued ...

$$= \lim_{h \to 0} \frac{4(2 + h)^2 - 4 \times 2^2}{h}$$
$$= \lim_{h \to 0} \frac{4(4 + 4h + h^2) - 16}{h}$$
$$= \lim_{h \to 0} \frac{16 + 16h + 4h^2 - 16}{h}$$
$$= \lim_{h \to 0} \frac{4h(4 + h)}{h}$$
$$= \lim_{h \to 0} [4(4 + h)]$$
$$= 16$$

b $f(x) = x^2 + 2x,\ x = 5$

$$f'(c) = \lim_{h \to 0} \frac{f(c + h) - f(c)}{h}$$
$$f'(5) = \lim_{h \to 0} \frac{f(5 + h) - f(5)}{h}$$
$$= \lim_{h \to 0} \frac{(5 + h)^2 + 2(5 + h) - (5^2 + 2 \times 5)}{h}$$
$$= \lim_{h \to 0} \frac{25 + 10h + h^2 + 10 + 2h - 35}{h}$$
$$= \lim_{h \to 0} \frac{12h + h^2}{h}$$
$$= \lim_{h \to 0} \frac{h(12 + h)}{h}$$
$$= \lim_{h \to 0} (12 + h)$$
$$= 12$$

c $f(x) = 1 - x^3,\ x = 0$

$$f'(c) = \lim_{h \to 0} \frac{f(c + h) - f(c)}{h}$$
$$f'(0) = \lim_{h \to 0} \frac{f(0 + h) - f(0)}{h}$$
$$= \lim_{h \to 0} \frac{1 - h^3 - (1 - 0^3)}{h}$$
$$= \lim_{h \to 0} \frac{-h^3}{h}$$
$$= \lim_{h \to 0} (-h^2)$$
$$= 0$$

12 a $f(x) = 7 - 2x,\ x = 1$

$$f'(c) = \lim_{h \to 0} \frac{f(c + h) - f(c)}{h}$$
$$f'(1) = \lim_{h \to 0} \frac{f(1 + h) - f(1)}{h}$$
$$= \lim_{h \to 0} \frac{7 - 2(1 + h) - (7 - 2 \times 1)}{h}$$
$$= \lim_{h \to 0} \frac{7 - 2 - 2h - 5}{h}$$
$$= \lim_{h \to 0} \frac{-2h}{h}$$

continued ...

$$= \lim_{h\to 0}(-2)$$
$$= -2$$

b $f(x) = 7 - 2x, \; x = 4$

$$f'(c) = \lim_{h\to 0} \frac{f(c+h) - f(c)}{h}$$
$$f'(4) = \lim_{h\to 0} \frac{f(4+h) - f(4)}{h}$$
$$= \lim_{h\to 0} \frac{7 - 2(4+h) - (7 - 2\times 4)}{h}$$
$$= \lim_{h\to 0} \frac{7 - 8 - 2h + 1}{h}$$
$$= \lim_{h\to 0} \frac{-2h}{h}$$
$$= \lim_{h\to 0}(-2)$$
$$= -2$$

c $f(x) = 7 - 2x, \; x = -2$

$$f'(c) = \lim_{h\to 0} \frac{f(c+h) - f(c)}{h}$$
$$f'(-2) = \lim_{h\to 0} \frac{f(-2+h) - f(-2)}{h}$$
$$= \lim_{h\to 0} \frac{7 - 2(-2+h) - (7 - 2\times -2)}{h}$$
$$= \lim_{h\to 0} \frac{7 + 4 - 2h - 11}{h}$$
$$= \lim_{h\to 0} \frac{-2h}{h}$$
$$= \lim_{h\to 0}(-2)$$
$$= -2$$

13 a $f(x) = x^2$

$$f'(c) = \lim_{x\to c} \frac{f(x) - f(c)}{x - c}$$
$$= \lim_{x\to c} \frac{x^2 - c^2}{x - c}$$
$$= \lim_{x\to c} \frac{(x+c)(x-c)}{x - c}$$
$$= \lim_{x\to c}(x + c)$$
$$= c + c$$
$$= 2c$$
$$\therefore f'(x) = 2x$$

b $f(x) = x - x^2$

$$f'(c) = \lim_{x\to c} \frac{f(x) - f(c)}{x - c}$$
$$= \lim_{x\to c} \frac{x - x^2 - (c - c^2)}{x - c}$$
$$= \lim_{x\to c} \frac{x - x^2 - c + c^2}{x - c}$$

continued ...

$$= \lim_{x\to c} \frac{x - c - (x^2 - c^2)}{x - c}$$
$$= \lim_{x\to c} \frac{x - c - (x-c)(x+c)}{x - c}$$
$$= \lim_{x\to c} \frac{(x-c)[1 - (x+c)]}{x - c}$$
$$= \lim_{x\to c}(1 - x - c)$$
$$= 1 - c - c$$
$$= 1 - 2c$$
$$\therefore f'(x) = 1 - 2x$$

c $f(x) = x^3 + x$

$$f'(c) = \lim_{x\to c} \frac{f(x) - f(c)}{x - c}$$
$$= \lim_{x\to c} \frac{x^3 + x - (c^3 + c)}{x - c}$$
$$= \lim_{x\to c} \frac{x^3 - c^3 + x - c}{x - c}$$
$$= \lim_{x\to c} \frac{(x-c)(x^2 + cx + c^2) + x - c}{x - c}$$
$$= \lim_{x\to c} \frac{(x-c)(x^2 + cx + c^2 + 1)}{x - c}$$
$$= \lim_{x\to c}(x^2 + cx + c^2 + 1)$$
$$= c^2 + c^2 + c^2 + 1$$
$$= 3c^2 + 1$$
$$\therefore f'(x) = 3x^2 + 1$$

14 a $y = x^2 + 3x$

$$f'(c) = \lim_{x\to c} \frac{f(x) - f(c)}{x - c}$$
$$= \lim_{x\to c} \frac{x^2 + 3x - (c^2 + 3c)}{x - c}$$
$$= \lim_{x\to c} \frac{x^2 - c^2 + 3x - 3c}{x - c}$$
$$= \lim_{x\to c} \frac{(x+c)(x-c) + 3(x-c)}{x - c}$$
$$= \lim_{x\to c} \frac{(x-c)(x+c+3)}{x - c}$$
$$= \lim_{x\to c}(x + c + 3)$$
$$= c + c + 3$$
$$= 2c + 3$$
$$\therefore \frac{dy}{dx} = 2x + 3$$

b $\frac{dy}{dx} = 2x + 3$

When $x = 3$, $\frac{dy}{dx} = 2\times 3 + 3$
$$= 9$$

At the point where $x = 3$ the gradient of the tangent to the curve is 9.

15 $f(x) = 2 - \frac{1}{2}x^2$

a $$f'(c) = \lim_{x \to c} \frac{f(x) - f(c)}{x - c}$$
$$= \lim_{x \to c} \frac{2 - \frac{1}{2}x^2 - \left(2 - \frac{1}{2}c^2\right)}{x - c}$$
$$= \lim_{x \to c} \frac{2 - \frac{1}{2}x^2 - 2 + \frac{1}{2}c^2}{x - c}$$
$$= \lim_{x \to c} \frac{-\frac{1}{2}\left(x^2 - c^2\right)}{x - c}$$
$$= \lim_{x \to c} \frac{-\frac{1}{2}(x - c)(x + c)}{x - c}$$
$$= \lim_{x \to c} -\frac{1}{2}(x + c)$$
$$= -\frac{1}{2}(2c)$$
$$= -c$$
$$\therefore f'(x) = -x$$

b

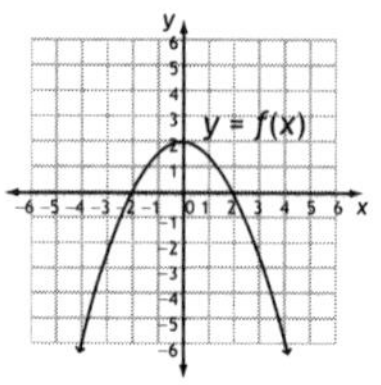

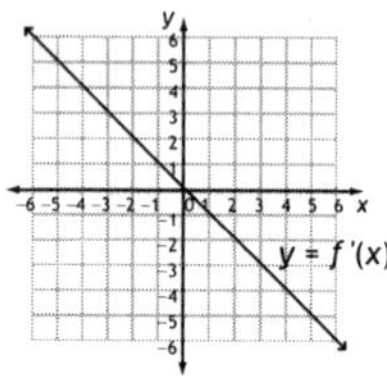

c The gradient of the tangent decreases as x increases. It is positive when the curve is increasing and negative when the curve is decreasing. When the curve neither increases nor decreases, the gradient of the tangent is zero.

16 **a** $3x - 7$

$$f'(c) = \lim_{h \to 0} \frac{f(c + h) - f(c)}{h}$$
$$= \lim_{h \to 0} \frac{3(c + h) - 7 - (3c - 7)}{h}$$
$$= \lim_{h \to 0} \frac{3c + 3h - 7 - 3c + 7}{h}$$
$$= \lim_{h \to 0} \frac{3h}{h}$$
$$= \lim_{h \to 0} (3)$$
$$= 3$$
$$\therefore f'(x) = 3$$

b $7x^2 + 1$

$$f'(c) = \lim_{h \to 0} \frac{f(c + h) - f(c)}{h}$$
$$= \lim_{h \to 0} \frac{7(c + h)^2 + 1 - (7c^2 + 1)}{h}$$
$$= \lim_{h \to 0} \frac{7c^2 + 14ch + 7h^2 + 1 - 7c^2 - 1}{h}$$
$$= \lim_{h \to 0} \frac{7h(2c + h)}{h}$$
$$= \lim_{h \to 0} 7(2c + h)$$
$$= 14c$$
$$\therefore f'(x) = 14x$$

17 **a** $y = x^4$, $\frac{dy}{dx} = 4x^3$ **b** $y = x^8$, $\frac{dy}{dx} = 8x^7$

c $y = x^{11}$, $\frac{dy}{dx} = 11x^{10}$ **d** $y = x^{47}$, $\frac{dy}{dx} = 47x^{46}$

18 $y = x^5$

$\frac{dy}{dx} = 5x^4$

When $x = 3$, $\frac{dy}{dx} = 5 \times 3^4$

$= 405$

19 **a** $y = x^2$

$\frac{dy}{dx} = 2x$

When $x = 1$, $\frac{dy}{dx} = 2 \times 1$

$= 2$

$m = 2,\ (1, 1)$

$y - y_1 = m(x - x_1)$

$y - 1 = 2(x - 1)$

$y - 1 = 2x - 2$

$y = 2x - 1$

b

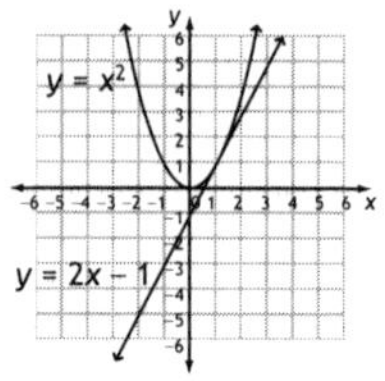

20 **a** $y = 5$, $\frac{dy}{dx} = 0$ **b** $y = 12$, $\frac{dy}{dx} = 0$

c $f(x) = -7$, $f'(x) = 0$ **d** $f(x) = 0$, $f'(x) = 0$

21 **a** $y = x^6 + x^4$, $\frac{dy}{dx} = 6x^5 + 4x^3$ **b** $y = x^7 - x^5$, $\frac{dy}{dx} = 7x^6 - 5x^4$

c $f(x) = x^3 + 8$, $f'(x) = 3x^2$ **d** $f(x) = x^8 - x^2 + x - 4$, $f'(x) = 8x^7 - 2x + 1$

e $f(x) = x^4 - x^3 + 6$, $f'(x) = 4x^3 - 3x^2$

22 **a** $y = 3x$, $\frac{dy}{dx} = 3$ **b** $f(x) = 2x^2$, $f'(x) = 4x$

c $y = -3x^4$, $\frac{dy}{dx} = -12x^3$ **d** $y = -x^6$, $\frac{dy}{dx} = -6x^5$

e $f(x) = 12x^9$, $f'(x) = 108x^8$

23 a $y = 4x^2 + 5x$

$\frac{dy}{dx} = 8x + 5$

b $y = 3x^3 - 2x^2 + x + 1$

$\frac{dy}{dx} = 9x^2 - 4x + 1$

c $f(x) = -x^5 + 7x^4 - 2x^3$

$f'(x) = -5x^4 + 28x^3 - 6x^2$

d $f(x) = 2x^8 - 3x^{10}$

$f'(x) = 16x^7 - 30x^9$

e $y = 3x^6 - 2x^5 - 3x^4 + 5x^3 - 9x^2 - 3$

$\frac{dy}{dx} = 18x^5 - 10x^4 - 12x^3 + 15x^2 - 18x$

24 a $y = x^2$

$\frac{dy}{dx} = 2x$

When $x = \frac{1}{2}$, $\frac{dy}{dx} = 2 \times \frac{1}{2} = 1$

∴ the gradient of the tangent is 1

∴ the gradient of the normal is $m = -1$

When $x = \frac{1}{2}$, $y = \left(\frac{1}{2}\right)^2 = \frac{1}{4}$

$m = -1, \left(\frac{1}{2}, \frac{1}{4}\right)$

$$\begin{aligned} y - y_1 &= m(x - x_1) \\ y - \tfrac{1}{4} &= -1\left(x - \tfrac{1}{2}\right) \\ y - \tfrac{1}{4} &= -x + \tfrac{1}{2} \\ y &= -x + \tfrac{3}{4} \end{aligned}$$

∴ the equation of the normal is $y = -x + \frac{3}{4}$

[or $4x + 4y - 3 = 0$]

b $y = x - x^2$

$\frac{dy}{dx} = 1 - 2x$

When $x = 1$, $\frac{dy}{dx} = 1 - 2 \times 1 = -1$

∴ the gradient of the tangent is - 1

∴ the gradient of the normal is $m = 1$

$m = 1, (1, 0)$

$$\begin{aligned} y - y_1 &= m(x - x_1) \\ y - 0 &= 1(x - 1) \\ y &= x - 1 \end{aligned}$$

∴ the equation of the normal is $y = x - 1$

25 a $y = 2x^{10} - 3x$

$y' = 20x^9 - 3$

b $f(x) = 1 - 3x - 2x^2$

$f'(x) = -3 - 4x$

c $\frac{d}{dx}\left(3x^9 - 2x^8 + 7x^7\right) = 27x^8 - 16x^7 + 49x^6$

26 a $y = 3t^4 - 5t^2$

$\frac{dy}{dt} = 12t^3 - 10t$

b $s = 9t^3 + 6t^2 - t$

$\frac{ds}{dt} = 27t^2 + 12t - 1$

27 a $p = 4q^2 - 9$

$\frac{dp}{dq} = 8q$

b $u = 3v^2 + 8v - 7$

$\frac{du}{dv} = 6v + 8$

c $h = -m^4 + 5m^3 - 2m - 3$

$\frac{dh}{dm} = -4m^3 + 15m^2 - 2$

28 a $\frac{d}{dx}\left(7x^2 - x\right) = 14x - 1$

b $\frac{d}{dt}\left(t - 6t^2\right) = 1 - 12t$

c $\frac{d}{du}\left(u^3 + 5u^2 - 7u\right) = 3u^2 + 10u - 7$

29 a $f(y) = y^3 + y^2$

$f'(y) = 3y^2 + 2y$

b $p(x) = 2x^4 - x^3 + 5x^2 + 5x - 11$

$p'(x) = 8x^3 - 3x^2 + 10x + 5$

c $g(a) = -4a^5 - 7a^3 + 9a - 1$

$g'(a) = -20a^4 - 21a^2 + 9$

30 a $y = x^{-3}$

$\frac{dy}{dx} = -3x^{-4}$

b $y = x^2 + x^{-2}$

$\frac{dy}{dx} = 2x - 2x^{-3}$

c $y = -3x^{-4}$

$\frac{dy}{dx} = 12x^{-5}$

d $y = x^{-8} - 7x + 3$

$\frac{dy}{dx} = -8x^{-9} - 7$

31 a $y = \frac{1}{x^7} = x^{-7}$

$\frac{dy}{dx} = -7x^{-8} = -\frac{7}{x^8}$

b $y = \frac{2}{x^6} = 2x^{-6}$

$\frac{dy}{dx} = -12x^{-7} = -\frac{12}{x^7}$

c $y = \frac{1}{x} - \frac{3}{x^2} = x^{-1} - 3x^{-2}$

$\frac{dy}{dx} = -x^{-2} + 6x^{-3} = -\frac{1}{x^2} + \frac{6}{x^3}$

$\left[= \frac{6 - x}{x^3}\right]$

32 **a** $y = x^{1.3}$

$\frac{dy}{dx} = 1.3x^{0.3}$

b $y = 2x^{2.5}$

$\frac{dy}{dx} = 5x^{1.5}$

c $y = 4\sqrt{x}$

$= 4x^{\frac{1}{2}}$

$\frac{dy}{dx} = 2x^{-\frac{1}{2}}$

$= \frac{2}{\sqrt{x}}$

d $y = \sqrt[4]{x}$

$= x^{\frac{1}{4}}$

$\frac{dy}{dx} = \frac{1}{4}x^{-\frac{3}{4}}$

$= \frac{1}{4\sqrt[4]{x^3}}$

e $y = \sqrt{x^7}$

$= x^{\frac{7}{2}}$

$\frac{dy}{dx} = \frac{7}{2}x^{\frac{5}{2}}$

$= \frac{7}{2}\sqrt{x^5}$

33 **a** $y = x^{-0.7}$

$\frac{dy}{dx} = -0.7x^{-1.7}$

b $f(x) = \frac{1}{\sqrt{x}}$

$= x^{-\frac{1}{2}}$

$f'(x) = -\frac{1}{2}x^{-\frac{3}{2}}$

$= -\frac{1}{2\sqrt{x^3}}$

$\left[= -\frac{1}{2x\sqrt{x}}\right]$

c $y = \frac{4}{\sqrt[3]{x}}$

$= 4x^{-\frac{1}{3}}$

$\frac{dy}{dx} = -\frac{4}{3}x^{-\frac{4}{3}}$

$= -\frac{4}{3\sqrt[3]{x^4}}$

d $f(x) = x^2\sqrt{x}$

$= x^2 \times x^{\frac{1}{2}}$

$= x^{\frac{5}{2}}$

$f'(x) = \frac{5}{2}x^{\frac{3}{2}}$

$= \frac{5}{2}x\sqrt{x}$

34 $y = u^3$ $\quad$ $u = 5x - 1$

$\frac{dy}{du} = 3u^2$ $\quad$ $\frac{du}{dx} = 5$

$\frac{dy}{dx} = 3u^2 \times 5$

$= 15u^2$

$= 15(5x-1)^2$

35 **a** $y = (x^2+5)^2$

$= x^4 + 10x^2 + 25$

$\frac{dy}{dx} = 4x^3 + 20x$

b $y = (x^2+5)^2$

$\frac{dy}{dx} = 2(x^2+5) \times \frac{d}{dx}(x^2+5)$

$= 2(x^2+5) \times 2x$

$= 4x(x^2+5)$

36 **a** $y = (4x+3)^3$

$\frac{dy}{dx} = 3(4x+3)^2 \times \frac{d}{dx}(4x+3)$

$= 3(4x+3)^2 \times 4$

$= 12(4x+3)^2$

b $f(x) = (x^3-5)^7$

$f'(x) = 7(x^3-5)^6 \times \frac{d}{dx}(x^3-5)$

$= 7(x^3-5)^6 \times 3x^2$

$= 21x^2(x^3-5)^6$

c $y = (x^2+7x-6)^4$

$\frac{dy}{dx} = 4(x^2+7x-6)^3 \times \frac{d}{dx}(x^2+7x-6)$

$= 4(x^2+7x-6)^3 \times (2x+7)$

$= 4(2x+7)(x^2+7x-6)^3$

37 **a** $y = \sqrt{16-x^2}$

$= (16-x^2)^{\frac{1}{2}}$

$\frac{dy}{dx} = \frac{1}{2}(16-x^2)^{-\frac{1}{2}} \times \frac{d}{dx}(16-x^2)$

$= \frac{1}{2\sqrt{16-x^2}} \times -2x$

$= -\frac{x}{\sqrt{16-x^2}}$

b $y = \frac{1}{4x}$

$= (4x)^{-1}$

$\frac{dy}{dx} = -(4x)^{-2} \times \frac{d}{dx}(4x)$

$= -\frac{1}{16x^2} \times 4$

$= -\frac{1}{4x^2}$

c $y = \frac{1}{(2x+3)^5}$

$= (2x+3)^{-5}$

$\frac{dy}{dx} = -5(2x+3)^{-6} \times \frac{d}{dx}(2x+3)$

$= -\frac{5}{(2x+3)^6} \times 2$

$= -\frac{10}{(2x+3)^6}$

38 **a** $y = x(x^2 - 3x + 4)$
$= x^3 - 3x^2 + 4x$
$\frac{dy}{dx} = 3x^2 - 6x + 4$

b $y = (x-2)(x+7)$
$= x^2 + 5x - 14$
$\frac{dy}{dx} = 2x + 5$

39 **a** $y = x(x^2 - 3x + 4)$

$$\frac{dy}{dx} = u\frac{dv}{dx} + v\frac{du}{dx}$$
$$= x \times \frac{d}{dx}(x^2 - 3x + 4) + (x^2 - 3x + 4) \times \frac{d}{dx}(x)$$
$$= x \times (2x - 3) + (x^2 - 3x + 4) \times 1$$
$$= 2x^2 - 3x + x^2 - 3x + 4$$
$$= 3x^2 - 6x + 4$$

b $y = (x-2)(x+7)$

$$\frac{dy}{dx} = u\frac{dv}{dx} + v\frac{du}{dx}$$
$$= (x-2) \times \frac{d}{dx}(x+7) + (x+7) \times \frac{d}{dx}(x-2)$$
$$= (x-2) \times 1 + (x+7) \times 1$$
$$= x - 2 + x + 7$$
$$= 2x + 5$$

40 **a** $y = (x-3)(x^2 + x - 3)$

$$\frac{dy}{dx} = u\frac{dv}{dx} + v\frac{du}{dx}$$
$$= (x-3) \times \frac{d}{dx}(x^2 + x - 3) + (x^2 + x - 3) \times \frac{d}{dx}(x-3)$$
$$= (x-3) \times (2x+1) + (x^2 + x - 3) \times 1$$
$$= 2x^2 - 5x - 3 + x^2 + x - 3$$
$$= 3x^2 - 4x - 6$$

b $y = (x^4 - 2)(5 - 3x - x^2)$

$$\frac{dy}{dx} = u\frac{dv}{dx} + v\frac{du}{dx}$$
$$= (x^4 - 2) \times \frac{d}{dx}(5 - 3x - x^2)$$
$$+ (5 - 3x - x^2) \times \frac{d}{dx}(x^4 - 2)$$
$$= (x^4 - 2) \times (-3 - 2x) + (5 - 3x - x^2) \times 4x^3$$
$$= -3x^4 - 2x^5 + 6 + 4x + 20x^3 - 12x^4 - 4x^5$$
$$= -6x^5 - 15x^4 + 20x^3 + 4x + 6$$

41 **a** $y = x(x^2 - 1)^5$

$$\frac{dy}{dx} = u\frac{dv}{dx} + v\frac{du}{dx}$$
$$= x \times \frac{d}{dx}(x^2 - 1)^5 + (x^2 - 1)^5 \times \frac{d}{dx}(x)$$
$$= x \times 5(x^2 - 1)^4 \times 2x + (x^2 - 1)^5 \times 1$$
$$= 10x^2(x^2 - 1)^4 + (x^2 - 1)^5$$

continued ...

$$= (x^2 - 1)^4(10x^2 + x^2 - 1)$$
$$= (x^2 - 1)^4(11x^2 - 1)$$

b $y = x^3(5 - 4x)^4$

$$\frac{dy}{dx} = u\frac{dv}{dx} + v\frac{du}{dx}$$
$$= x^3 \times \frac{d}{dx}(5 - 4x)^4 + (5 - 4x)^4 \times \frac{d}{dx}(x^3)$$
$$= x^3 \times 4(5 - 4x)^3 \times -4 + (5 - 4x)^4 \times 3x^2$$
$$= -16x^3(5 - 4x)^3 + 3x^2(5 - 4x)^4$$
$$= x^2(5 - 4x)^3[-16x + 3(5 - 4x)]$$
$$= x^2(5 - 4x)^3(-28x + 15)$$

c $y = (x-1)^2(x+2)^3$

$$\frac{dy}{dx} = u\frac{dv}{dx} + v\frac{du}{dx}$$
$$= (x-1)^2 \times \frac{d}{dx}(x+2)^3 + (x+2)^3 \times \frac{d}{dx}(x-1)^2$$
$$= (x-1)^2 \times 3(x+2)^2 \times 1 + (x+2)^3 \times 2(x-1) \times 1$$
$$= 3(x-1)^2(x+2)^2 + 2(x+2)^3(x-1)$$
$$= (x-1)(x+2)^2[3(x-1) + 2(x+2)]$$
$$= (x-1)(x+2)^2(3x - 3 + 2x + 4)$$
$$= (x-1)(x+2)^2(5x+1)$$

d $y = \sqrt{x}(4x-1)^6$
$= x^{\frac{1}{2}}(4x-1)^6$

$$\frac{dy}{dx} = u\frac{dv}{dx} + v\frac{du}{dx}$$
$$= x^{\frac{1}{2}} \times \frac{d}{dx}(4x-1)^6 + (4x-1)^6 \times \frac{d}{dx}\left(x^{\frac{1}{2}}\right)$$
$$= x^{\frac{1}{2}} \times 6(4x-1)^5 \times 4 + (4x-1)^6 \times \tfrac{1}{2}x^{-\frac{1}{2}}$$
$$= 24x^{\frac{1}{2}}(4x-1)^5 + \tfrac{1}{2}x^{-\frac{1}{2}}(4x-1)^6$$
$$= (4x-1)^5\left[24x^{\frac{1}{2}} + \tfrac{1}{2}x^{-\frac{1}{2}}(4x-1)\right]$$
$$= (4x-1)^5\left(24x^{\frac{1}{2}} + 2x^{\frac{1}{2}} - \tfrac{1}{2}x^{-\frac{1}{2}}\right)$$
$$= (4x-1)^5\left(26\sqrt{x} + \frac{1}{2\sqrt{x}}\right)$$

e $y = x\sqrt{1-x}$
$= x(1-x)^{\frac{1}{2}}$

$$\frac{dy}{dx} = u\frac{dv}{dx} + v\frac{du}{dx}$$
$$= x \times \frac{d}{dx}(1-x)^{\frac{1}{2}} + (1-x)^{\frac{1}{2}} \times \frac{d}{dx}(x)$$
$$= x \times \tfrac{1}{2}(1-x)^{-\frac{1}{2}} \times -1 + (1-x)^{\frac{1}{2}} \times 1$$

continued ...

$$= -\frac{x}{2\sqrt{1-x}} + \sqrt{1-x}$$

$$\left[= -\frac{x}{2\sqrt{1-x}} + \frac{2(1-x)}{2\sqrt{1-x}} = \frac{2-3x}{2\sqrt{1-x}}\right]$$

42 a $y = \frac{1}{3x}$

$$\frac{dy}{dx} = \frac{v\frac{du}{dx} - u\frac{dv}{dx}}{v^2}$$

$$= \frac{3x \times 0 - 1 \times 3}{(3x)^2}$$

$$= \frac{-3}{9x^2}$$

$$= -\frac{1}{3x^2}$$

b $y = \frac{x-1}{x+3}$

$$\frac{dy}{dx} = \frac{v\frac{du}{dx} - u\frac{dv}{dx}}{v^2}$$

$$= \frac{(x+3) \times 1 - (x-1) \times 1}{(x+3)^2}$$

$$= \frac{x+3-x+1}{(x+3)^2}$$

$$= \frac{4}{(x+3)^2}$$

43 a $y = \frac{2x}{x^3 - 5}$

$$\frac{dy}{dx} = \frac{v\frac{du}{dx} - u\frac{dv}{dx}}{v^2}$$

$$= \frac{(x^3-5) \times 2 - 2x \times 3x^2}{(x^3-5)^2}$$

$$= \frac{2x^3 - 10 - 6x^3}{(x^3-5)^2}$$

$$= \frac{-4x^3 - 10}{(x^3-5)^2}$$

b $y = \frac{x^2 - 3x - 1}{x}$

$$\frac{dy}{dx} = \frac{v\frac{du}{dx} - u\frac{dv}{dx}}{v^2}$$

$$= \frac{x \times (2x-3) - (x^2 - 3x - 1) \times 1}{x^2}$$

continued ...

$$= \frac{2x^2 - 3x - x^2 + 3x + 1}{x^2}$$

$$= \frac{x^2 + 1}{x^2}$$

44 a $y = \frac{(5x+3)^5}{x}$

$$\frac{dy}{dx} = \frac{v\frac{du}{dx} - u\frac{dv}{dx}}{v^2}$$

$$= \frac{x \times 5(5x+3)^4 \times 5 - (5x+3)^5 \times 1}{x^2}$$

$$= \frac{25x(5x+3)^4 - (5x+3)^5}{x^2}$$

$$= \frac{(5x+3)^4[25x - (5x+3)]}{x^2}$$

$$= \frac{(5x+3)^4(20x-3)}{x^2}$$

b $f(x) = \frac{2x-1}{(x+1)^3}$

$$f'(x) = \frac{v\frac{du}{dx} - u\frac{dv}{dx}}{v^2}$$

$$= \frac{(x+1)^3 \times 2 - (2x-1) \times 3(x+1)^2 \times 1}{\left[(x+1)^3\right]^2}$$

$$= \frac{2(x+1)^3 - 3(2x-1)(x+1)^2}{(x+1)^6}$$

$$= \frac{(x+1)^2[2(x+1) - 3(2x-1)]}{(x+1)^6}$$

$$= \frac{(2x+2-6x+3)}{(x+1)^4}$$

$$= \frac{-4x+5}{(x+1)^4}$$

Topic Test 1 – Basic Arithmetic and Algebra

1 $|-6|-2|-5| = 6-2\times5$
$= -4$

2 $\dfrac{3.6+4.25}{\sqrt{5.1^2+2.3^2}} = 1.403128636\ldots$
$= 1.4$ [1 decimal place]

3 $1-4(2m-1) = 1-8m+4$
$= 5-8m$

4 Decrease $= \$21\,400 - \$17\,120$
$= \$4280$

% decrease $= \dfrac{\$4280}{\$21\,400}\times100\%$
$= 20\%$

5 $0.91\dot{6} = 0.916\,666\,666\,666\ldots$
Let $x = 0.916\,666\,666\,666\ldots$
$10x = 9.166\,666\,666\,666\ldots$
$9x = 8.25$
$x = \dfrac{8.25}{9}$
$= \dfrac{825}{900}$
$= \dfrac{11}{12}$
$\therefore 0.91\dot{6} = \dfrac{11}{12}$

6 $\dfrac{15}{4-\sqrt{11}} = \dfrac{15}{4-\sqrt{11}}\times\dfrac{4+\sqrt{11}}{4+\sqrt{11}}$
$= \dfrac{15(4+\sqrt{11})}{16-11}$
$= \dfrac{15(4+\sqrt{11})}{5}$
$= 3(4+\sqrt{11})$
$= 12+3\sqrt{11}$

7 $\dfrac{3a-1}{3} - \dfrac{2a-3}{4} = 7$
$12\times\left(\dfrac{3a-1}{3}\right) - 12\times\left(\dfrac{2a-3}{4}\right) = 12\times7$
$4(3a-1)-3(2a-3) = 84$
$12a-4-6a+9 = 84$
$6a+5 = 84$
$6a = 79$
$a = 13\frac{1}{6}$

8 $\dfrac{(a^2b^3)^4 \div ab^2}{(a^3b)^2\times a^2b^3} = \dfrac{a^8b^{12}\div ab^2}{a^6b^2\times a^2b^3}$
$= \dfrac{a^7b^{10}}{a^8b^5}$
$= \dfrac{b^5}{a}$

9 $r = \sqrt{\dfrac{3V}{\pi h}}$
When $V = 10\,000$ and $h = 2.5$,
$r = \sqrt{\dfrac{3\times10\,000}{\pi\times2.5}}$
$= 61.80387232\ldots$
$= 62$ [2 sig. figs.]

10 $\dfrac{m^2-25}{m^2-7m+10} \div \dfrac{m^2+9m+20}{m^2+m-6}$
$= \dfrac{(m-5)(m+5)}{(m-5)(m-2)} \div \dfrac{(m+5)(m+4)}{(m+3)(m-2)}$
$= \dfrac{(m-5)(m+5)}{(m-5)(m-2)} \times \dfrac{(m+3)(m-2)}{(m+5)(m+4)}$
$= \dfrac{m+3}{m+4}$

11 $9-\dfrac{x}{3} \ge 12$
$-\dfrac{x}{3} \ge 3$
$x \le -9$

12 $2x^2-6x+1 = 0$
$a = 2, b = -6, c = 1$
$x = \dfrac{-b\pm\sqrt{b^2-4ac}}{2a}$
$= \dfrac{-(-6)\pm\sqrt{(-6)^2-4\times2\times1}}{2\times2}$
$= \dfrac{6\pm\sqrt{28}}{4}$
$= \dfrac{6\pm2\sqrt{7}}{4}$
$= \dfrac{2(3\pm\sqrt{7})}{4}$
$= \dfrac{3\pm\sqrt{7}}{2}$

Topic Test 2 – Basic Arithmetic and Algebra

1 $\sqrt{2\frac{7}{9}} = \sqrt{\frac{25}{9}}$

$= \frac{5}{3}$

$= 1\frac{2}{3}$

2 $(2x-1)^2 - (x+1)(x-1) = 4x^2 - 4x + 1 - (x^2 - 1)$

$= 4x^2 - 4x + 1 - x^2 + 1$

$= 3x^2 - 4x + 2$

3 $(0.0535)^3 \div 45\,500 = 3.365502747\ldots \times 10^{-9}$

$= 3.37 \times 10^{-9}$ [3 sig. figs.]

4 Land plus commission = \$91 000

∴ 104% of land price = \$91 000

1% = \$875

4% = \$3500

∴ the commission is \$3500

5 $x^3 - x^2 - 9x + 9 = x^2(x-1) - 9(x-1)$

$= (x^2 - 9)(x-1)$

$= (x+3)(x-3)(x-1)$

6 $5(3x-2) = 7 - 2(3-x)$

$15x - 10 = 7 - 6 + 2x$

$15x - 10 = 1 + 2x$

$13x = 11$

$x = \frac{11}{13}$

7 $s = ut + \frac{1}{2}at^2$

When $s = 130$, $u = 1$ and $t = 5$

$130 = 1 \times 5 + \frac{1}{2} \times a \times 5^2$

$130 = 5 + \frac{25a}{2}$

$125 = \frac{25a}{2}$

$25a = 250$

$a = 10$

8 $\frac{1}{11} = 0.09090909\ldots$

$= 0.\dot{0}\dot{9}$

9 $(6 - \sqrt{3})^2 = x + y\sqrt{3}$

$(6 - \sqrt{3})^2 = 36 - 12\sqrt{3} + 3$

$= 39 - 12\sqrt{3}$

∴ $x = 39$ and $y = -12$

10

	$5p - 2q = 20$	**i**
	$3p + 4q = 38$	**ii**
i × 2	$10p - 4q = 40$	**iii**

continued ...

ii + iii $13p = 78$

$p = 6$

Substitute in **i**

$5 \times 6 - 2q = 20$

$2q = 10$

$q = 5$

∴ $p = 6$ and $q = 5$

11 $\frac{x-4}{5} \le 1 + \frac{x}{3}$

$15 \times \left(\frac{x-4}{5}\right) \le 15 \times 1 + 15 \times \frac{x}{3}$

$3(x-4) \le 15 + 5x$

$3x - 12 \le 15 + 5x$

$-2x \le 27$

$x \ge -13.5$

12 $\frac{2}{e^2 + 2e} - \frac{3}{e^2 + 3e} = \frac{2}{e(e+2)} - \frac{3}{e(e+3)}$

$= \frac{2(e+3)}{e(e+2)(e+3)} - \frac{3(e+2)}{e(e+2)(e+3)}$

$= \frac{2e + 6 - 3e - 6}{e(e+2)(e+3)}$

$= \frac{-e}{e(e+2)(e+3)}$

$= \frac{-1}{(e+2)(e+3)}$

Topic Test 3 – Plane Geometry

1 **a** $(x+2)^2 = x^2 + (x-7)^2$

$x^2 + 4x + 4 = x^2 + x^2 - 14x + 49$

$x^2 - 18x + 45 = 0$

$(x-15)(x-3) = 0$

$x - 15 = 0$ or $x - 3 = 0$

$x = 15$ $\qquad x = 3$

But if $x = 3$,

BC = 3 − 7

= −4 m

∴ $x \ne 3$

∴ $x = 15$ is the only value of x

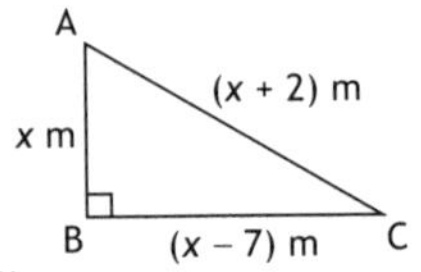

b AB = 15 m

BC = 15 − 7 m

= 8 m

Area $= \frac{1}{2}bh$

$= \frac{1}{2} \times 8\text{ m} \times 15\text{ m}$

$= 60\text{ m}^2$

2 Let ∠DAC = x

∴ ∠CAB = x [AC bisects ∠DAB]

and ∠DAB = $2x$

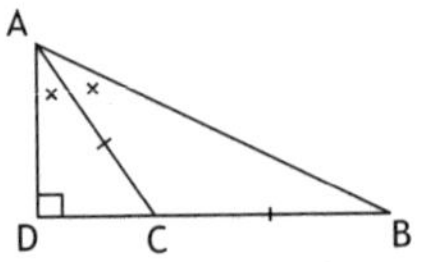

continued ...

$\angle ABC = \angle CAB$ [base angles of isosceles triangle]

$= x$

$\angle DAB + \angle ABD + \angle ADB = 180^\circ$ [angle sum of ΔADB]

$2x + x + 90^\circ = 180^\circ$

$3x = 90^\circ$

$x = 30^\circ$

$\therefore \angle DAC = 30^\circ$

$\angle ACB = 90^\circ + 30^\circ$ [exterior angle of ΔACD]

$= 120^\circ$

3 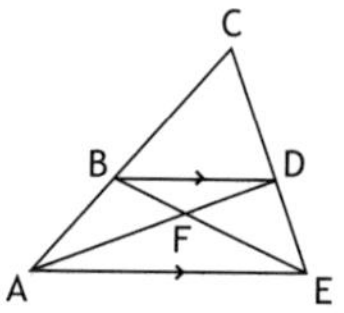

a In ΔBCD, ΔACE,

$\angle BCD = \angle ACE$ [common angle]

$\angle CBD = \angle CAE$ [corresponding angles, BD || AE]

$\therefore \Delta BCD\ |||\ \Delta ACE$

b In ΔBFD, ΔEFA,

$\angle BFD = \angle EFA$ [vertically opposite]

$\angle FBD = \angle FEA$ [alternate angles, BD || AE]

$\therefore \Delta BFD\ |||\ \Delta EFA$

c $\dfrac{AC}{BC} = \dfrac{AE}{BD}$ [corresponding sides of similar triangles, ACE and BCD]

$\dfrac{AF}{FD} = \dfrac{AE}{BD}$ [corresponding sides of similar triangles, EFA and BFD]

$\therefore \dfrac{AF}{FD} = \dfrac{AC}{BC}$

$\dfrac{AF}{8} = \dfrac{40}{16}$

AF = 20 cm

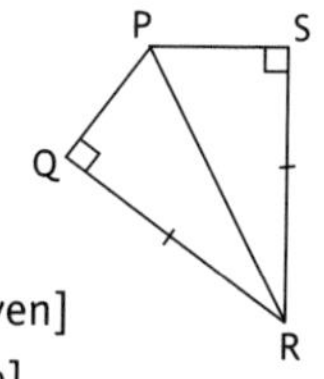

4 a In ΔPQR, ΔPSR,

$\angle PQR = \angle PSR$ [both 90°, given]

PR = PR [common side]

QR = SR [given]

$\therefore \Delta PQR \equiv \Delta PSR$ [RHS]

$\therefore \angle PRQ = \angle PRS$ [corresponding angles of congruent triangles]

b In ΔQTR, ΔSTR,

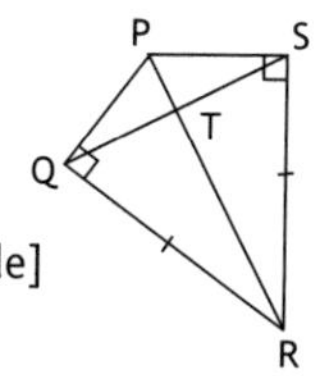

QR = SR [given]

$\angle TRQ = \angle TRS$ [proven]

TR = TR [common side]

$\therefore \Delta QTR \equiv \Delta STR$ [SAS]

$\therefore \angle QTR = \angle STR$ [corresponding angles of congruent triangles]

but $\angle QTR + \angle STR = 180^\circ$ [angles on a straight line]

$\therefore \angle QTR = 90^\circ$

Topic Test 4 – Plane Geometry

1 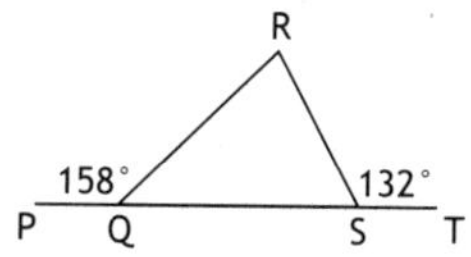

$\angle RQS = 180^\circ - 158^\circ$ [angles on a straight line]

$\therefore \angle RQS = 22^\circ$

$\angle RST = \angle QRS + \angle RQS$ [exterior angle]

$\therefore \angle QRS = 132^\circ - 22^\circ$

$= 110^\circ$

2 a An octagon has 8 sides.

Angle sum = $(2n - 4)$ right angles

$= (2 \times 8 - 4) \times 90^\circ$

$= 1080^\circ$

b A regular octagon has 8 equal angles.

Each angle = $1080^\circ \div 8$

$= 135^\circ$

3 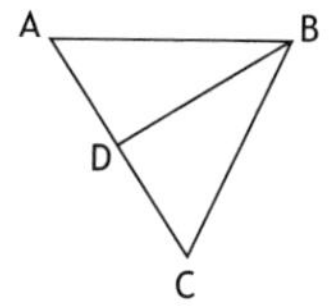

a Let $\angle ABD = x^\circ$

$\therefore \angle DBC = x^\circ$ [DB bisects $\angle ABC$]

$\angle BAC = \angle ABC$ [base angles of isosceles triangle, AC = BC]

$\therefore \angle BAC = 2x^\circ$

b $\angle BCD = \angle DBC$

[base angles of isosceles triangle, BD = DC]

$\therefore \angle BCD = x^\circ$

$\angle BCD + \angle ABC + \angle BAC = 180^\circ$

[angle sum of ΔABC]

$x^\circ + 2x^\circ + 2x^\circ = 180^\circ$

$5x^\circ = 180^\circ$

$x^\circ = 36^\circ$

$\therefore \angle ACB = 36^\circ$

4 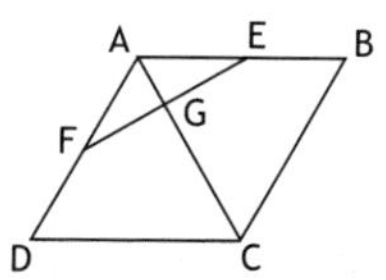

a In ΔAEG, ΔAFG,

AE = AF [AB = AD, sides of rhombus, E and F are midpoints]

$\angle EAG = \angle FAG$ [diagonals of rhombus bisect angles]

AG = AG [common side]

$\therefore \Delta AEG \equiv \Delta AFG$ [SAS]

b $\angle AGE = \angle AGF$

[corresponding angles of congruent triangles]

but $\angle AGE + \angle AGF = 180°$

[angles on a straight line]

$\therefore \quad \angle AGE = 90°$

$\therefore EF \perp AC$

5

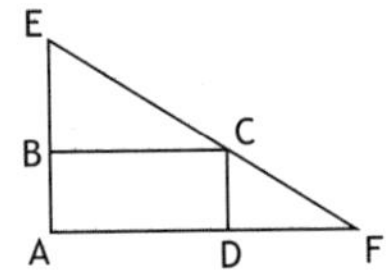

a In $\Delta EBC, \Delta CDF$,

$\angle BEC = \angle DCF$ [corresponding, $AE \parallel DC$]

$\angle EBC = \angle CDF$ [corresponding, $BC \parallel AF$]

$\therefore \Delta EBC \parallel\!| \Delta CDF$

b ABCD is a rectangle

$\therefore \quad CD = AB = 8$ cm

and $AD = BC = 18$ cm

$DF = 24 - 18$ cm

$= 6$ cm

$\frac{EB}{CD} = \frac{BC}{DF}$ [corresponding sides of similar triangles]

$\frac{EB}{8} = \frac{18}{6}$

$EB = 3 \times 8$

$= 24$ cm

c $AE = 8 + 24$

$= 32$ cm

$EF^2 = AE^2 + AF^2$

$= 32^2 + 24^2$

$= 1600$

$EF = 40$ cm $[EF > 0]$

Topic Test 5 – Linear Functions and Lines

1 **a** $2x - 5y + 15 = 0$

This line cuts the y-axis when $x = 0$

$2 \times 0 - 5y + 15 = 0$

$-5y + 15 = 0$

$-5y = -15$

$y = 3$

$\therefore$ P is the point $(0, 3)$

b Parallel line is of the form $2x - 5y + k = 0$

$Q(0, -2)$ lies on this line

$\therefore 2 \times 0 - 5 \times -2 + k = 0$

$10 + k = 0$

$k = -10$

$\therefore l_2 : 2x - 5y - 10 = 0$

c $2x - 5y - 10 = 0$

This line cuts the x-axis when $y = 0$

$2x - 5 \times 0 - 10 = 0$

$2x - 10 = 0$

$2x = 10$

$x = 5$

$\therefore$ The line cuts the x-axis at $R(5, 0)$

d

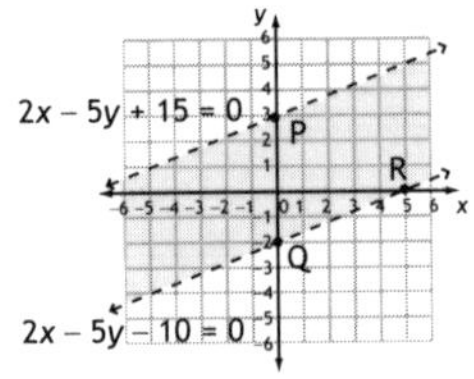

e $2x - 5y + 15 > 0$

$2x - 5y - 10 < 0$

2 **a** $k: 2x - 3y + 39 = 0$ has gradient $m_1 = -\frac{a}{b}$

$= \frac{2}{3}$

$l: ax + 2y + 13 = 0$ has gradient $m_2 = -\frac{a}{b}$

$= -\frac{a}{2}$

The lines are perpendicular

$\therefore \quad m_1 m_2 = -1$

$\frac{2}{3} \times -\frac{a}{2} = -1$

$-\frac{a}{3} = -1$

$a = 3$

b

	$2x - 3y + 39 = 0$	**i**
	$3x + 2y + 13 = 0$	**ii**
i $\times 2$	$4x - 6y + 78 = 0$	**iii**
ii $\times 3$	$9x + 6y + 39 = 0$	**iv**
iii + **iv**	$13x + 117 = 0$	
	$13x = -117$	
	$x = -9$	

Substitute in **i**

$2 \times -9 - 3y + 39 = 0$

$-3y = -21$

$y = 7$

$\therefore$ P is the point $(-9, 7)$

c Line parallel to k has $m = \frac{2}{3}$

$Q(5, -1), \quad m = \frac{2}{3}$

$y - y_1 = m(x - x_1)$

$y - (-1) = \frac{2}{3}(x - 5)$

$3(y + 1) = 2(x - 5)$

$3y + 3 = 2x - 10$

$2x - 3y - 13 = 0$

d $2x - 3y - 13 = 0$ **i**

$3x + 2y + 13 = 0$ **ii**

continued ...

$$\begin{array}{lll} \mathbf{i} \times 2 & 4x - 6y - 26 = 0 & \mathbf{iii} \\ \mathbf{ii} \times 3 & 9x + 6y + 39 = 0 & \mathbf{iv} \\ \mathbf{iii} + \mathbf{iv} & 13x + 13 = 0 & \\ & 13x = -13 & \\ & x = -1 & \end{array}$$

Substitute in **i**

$$2 \times -1 - 3y - 13 = 0$$
$$-3y = 15$$
$$y = -5$$

$\therefore$ R is the point $(-1, -5)$

e $P(-9, 7)$, $Q(5, -1)$

$$M(x, y) = \left(\frac{x_1 + x_2}{2}, \frac{y_1 + y_2}{2}\right) = \left(\frac{-9 + 5}{2}, \frac{7 + (-1)}{2}\right) = (-2, 3)$$

$\therefore$ M is the point $(-2, 3)$

f $M(-2, 3)$, $R(-1, -5)$, $S(x_2, y_2)$

$$M(x, y) = \left(\frac{x_1 + x_2}{2}, \frac{y_1 + y_2}{2}\right)$$
$$(-2, 3) = \left(\frac{-1 + x_2}{2}, \frac{-5 + y_2}{2}\right)$$

$\therefore \frac{-1 + x_2}{2} = -2$ and $\frac{-5 + y_2}{2} = 3$

$-1 + x_2 = -4$ $\quad -5 + y_2 = 6$

$x_2 = -3$ $\quad y_2 = 11$

$\therefore$ S is the point $(-3, 11)$

g $k: 2x - 3y + 39 = 0$, $S(-3, 11)$

$$2 \times -3 - 3 \times 11 + 39 = 0$$
$$0 = 0$$

$\therefore$ S lies on the line $2x - 3y + 39 = 0$

h $Q(5, -1)$, $S(-3, 11)$

$$m_1 = \frac{y_2 - y_1}{x_2 - x_1} = \frac{11 - (-1)}{-3 - 5} = \frac{12}{-8} = -\frac{3}{2}$$

R and P both lie on line l

l has gradient $m_2 = -\frac{3}{2}$

$\therefore m_1 = m_2$

$\therefore$ QS is parallel to RP

Topic Test 6 – Linear Functions and Lines

1 a $Q(10, -1)$, $R(1, -3)$

$$m = \frac{y_2 - y_1}{x_2 - x_1} = \frac{-3 - (-1)}{1 - 10} = \frac{2}{9}$$

$\therefore$ parallel line has $m = \frac{2}{9}$

$m = \frac{2}{9}$, $(3, 5)$

$$y - y_1 = m(x - x_1)$$
$$y - 5 = \tfrac{2}{9}(x - 3)$$
$$9y - 45 = 2x - 6$$
$$2x - 9y + 39 = 0$$

b $P(3, 5)$, $R(1, -3)$

$$M(x, y) = \left(\frac{x_1 + x_2}{2}, \frac{y_1 + y_2}{2}\right) = \left(\frac{3 + 1}{2}, \frac{5 + (-3)}{2}\right) = (2, 1)$$

$\therefore$ M is the point $(2,1)$

c $Q(10, -1)$, $M(2, 1)$

$$\frac{y - y_1}{x - x_1} = \frac{y_2 - y_1}{x_2 - x_1}$$
$$\frac{y - (-1)}{x - 10} = \frac{1 - (-1)}{2 - 10}$$
$$\frac{y + 1}{x - 10} = -\frac{1}{4}$$
$$4y + 4 = -x + 10$$
$$x + 4y - 6 = 0$$

d

$$\begin{array}{lll} & 2x - 9y + 39 = 0 & \mathbf{i} \\ & x + 4y - 6 = 0 & \mathbf{ii} \\ \mathbf{ii} \times 2 & 2x + 8y - 12 = 0 & \mathbf{iii} \\ \mathbf{iii} - \mathbf{i} & 17y - 51 = 0 & \\ & 17y = 51 & \\ & y = 3 & \end{array}$$

Substitute in **ii** $\quad x + 4 \times 3 - 6 = 0$

$$x + 6 = 0$$
$$x = -6$$

$\therefore$ S is the point $(-6, 3)$

e $S(-6, 3)$, $R(1, -3)$ $\qquad$ $P(3, 5)$, $Q(10, -1)$

$$m_1 = \frac{y_2 - y_1}{x_2 - x_1} = \frac{-3 - 3}{1 - (-6)} = -\frac{6}{7} \qquad m_2 = \frac{y_2 - y_1}{x_2 - x_1} = \frac{-1 - 5}{10 - 3} = -\frac{6}{7}$$

continued ...

$\therefore m_1 = m_2$

$\therefore$ SR is parallel to PQ

f $P(3, 5),\ Q(10, -1)$

$$d = \sqrt{(x_2 - x_1)^2 + (y_2 - y_1)^2}$$
$$= \sqrt{(10-3)^2 + (-1-5)^2}$$

$\therefore\ PQ = \sqrt{85}$ units

$P(3, 5),\ S(-6, 3)$

$$d = \sqrt{(x_2 - x_1)^2 + (y_2 - y_1)^2}$$
$$= \sqrt{(-6-3)^2 + (3-5)^2}$$

$\therefore\ PS = \sqrt{85}$ units

$\therefore PQ = PS$

2 a $l_1 : 2x - y - 4 = 0$

Perpendicular line is of the form $x + 2y + k = 0$

$(-2, 2)$ lies on the line.

$$-2 + 2 \times 2 + k = 0$$
$$2 + k = 0$$
$$k = -2$$

$\therefore$ the equation is $x + 2y - 2 = 0$

b

$2x - y - 4 = 0$ **i**

$x + 2y - 2 = 0$ **ii**

i $\times 2$ $\quad 4x - 2y - 8 = 0$ **iii**

ii + **iii** $\quad 5x - 10 = 0$

$x = 2$

Substitute in **i**

$$2 \times 2 - y - 4 = 0$$
$$y = 0$$

$\therefore$ Point of intersection is $(2, 0)$

$\therefore$ the lines intersect on the x-axis

c $l_1 : 2x - y - 4 = 0$

On the y-axis, $x = 0$

$$2 \times 0 - y - 4 = 0$$
$$y = -4$$

$(0, -4),\ (-2, 2)$

$$\frac{y - y_1}{x - x_1} = \frac{y_2 - y_1}{x_2 - x_1}$$
$$\frac{y - (-4)}{x - 0} = \frac{2 - (-4)}{-2 - 0}$$
$$\frac{y + 4}{x} = -3$$
$$y + 4 = -3x$$
$$3x + y + 4 = 0$$

d The origin (0, 0), lies inside the triangle so must satisfy each inequality.

continued ...

The region is defined by:

$2x - y - 4 < 0$

$x + 2y - 2 < 0$

$3x + y + 4 > 0$

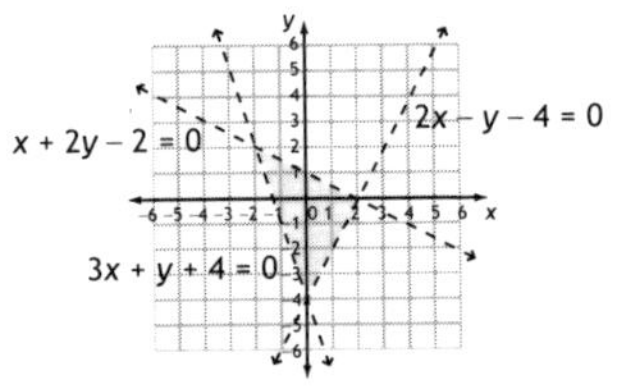

Topic Test 7 – Real Functions of a Real Variable

1 a $y = \dfrac{1}{2x - 1}$

$$2x - 1 \neq 0$$
$$2x \neq 1$$
$$x \neq \tfrac{1}{2}$$

Domain: all real x, except $x = \frac{1}{2}$

b Range: all real y except $y = 0$

2 $f(x) = \begin{cases} 1 - x & \text{if} \quad x < -1 \\ 2 & \text{if} \quad -1 \le x \le 1 \\ x + 1 & \text{if} \quad x > 1 \end{cases}$

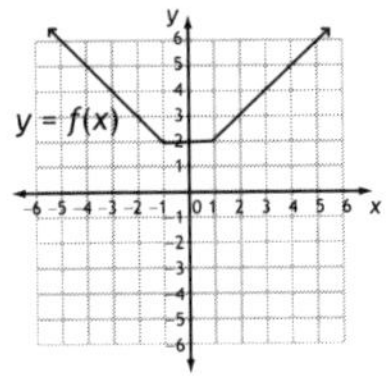

3 a

$$f(x) = x^2 + x$$
$$f(x+h) - f(x) = (x+h)^2 + (x+h) - (x^2 + x)$$
$$= x^2 + 2xh + h^2 + x + h - x^2 - x$$
$$= 2xh + h^2 + h$$

b

$$\frac{f(x+h) - f(x)}{h} = \frac{2xh + h^2 + h}{h}$$
$$= \frac{h(2x + h + 1)}{h}$$
$$= 2x + h + 1$$

4 a

$$f(x) = a + bx - cx^2$$
$$f(-x) = a + b(-x) - c(-x)^2$$
$$= a - bx - cx^2$$
$$f(x) + f(-x) = a + bx - cx^2 + a - bx - cx^2$$
$$= 2a - 2cx^2$$

b $f(x) + f(-x)$ is an even function.

$2a - 2c(-x)^2 = 2a - 2cx^2$

5 a

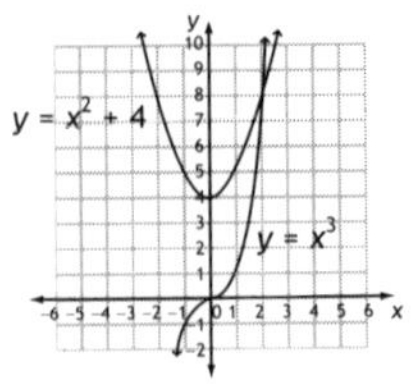

b $x^3 = x^2 + 4$ when $x = 2$

6 $P(x, y),\ y = 4x$

$4x - y = 0$

$a = 4, b = -1, c = 0$

$d = \left|\dfrac{ax_1 + by_1 + c}{\sqrt{a^2 + b^2}}\right|$

$d = \left|\dfrac{4 \times x - 1 \times y + 0}{\sqrt{4^2 + (-1)^2}}\right|$

$d = \left|\dfrac{4x - y}{\sqrt{17}}\right|$

$P(x, y),\ x - 4y = 0$

$a = 1, b = -4, c = 0$

$d = \left|\dfrac{ax_1 + by_1 + c}{\sqrt{a^2 + b^2}}\right|$

$d = \left|\dfrac{1 \times x - 4 \times y + 0}{\sqrt{1^2 + (-4)^2}}\right|$

$d = \left|\dfrac{x - 4y}{\sqrt{17}}\right|$

If P is equidistant from these lines

$$\left|\frac{4x - y}{\sqrt{17}}\right| = \left|\frac{x - 4y}{\sqrt{17}}\right|$$

$$(4x - y)^2 = (x - 4y)^2$$

$$16x^2 - 8xy + y^2 = x^2 - 8xy + 16y^2$$

$$15x^2 - 15y^2 = 0$$

$$x^2 - y^2 = 0$$

$$y^2 = x^2$$

$$y = x \text{ or } y = -x$$

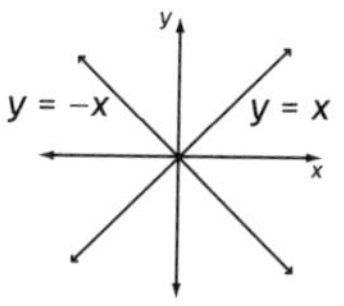

Topic Test 8 – Real Functions of a Real Variable

1 a $f(x) = x^2 - 6x + 11$

Domain: all real x

$$x^2 - 6x + 11 = x^2 - 6x + 9 + 2$$

$$= (x - 3)^2 + 2$$

Now $(x - 3)^2 \geq 0$ for all real x

$\therefore (x - 3)^2 + 2 \geq 2$

Range: $y \geq 2$

b $f(x) = x^2 - 6x + 11$

$$f(x - 2) = (x - 2)^2 - 6(x - 2) + 11$$

$$= x^2 - 4x + 4 - 6x + 12 + 11$$

$$= x^2 - 10x + 27$$

2 a

$$f(x) = \begin{cases} x + 1 & \text{for} \quad x < 0 \\ 1 & \text{for} \quad 0 \leq x < 1 \\ x & \text{for} \quad x \geq 1 \end{cases}$$

$$f(-2) + f(2) = (-2 + 1) + 2$$

$$= 1$$

b

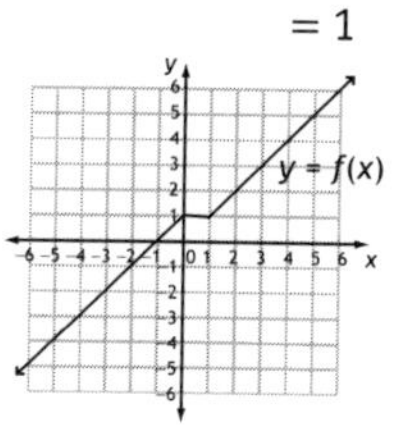

3 $x^2 + y^2 \leq 16,\ y > |x|$

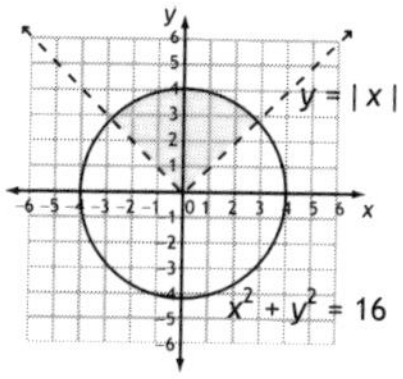

4 a $A(0, 2),\ P(x, y)$

$$PA = \sqrt{(x_2 - x_1)^2 + (y_2 - y_1)^2}$$

$$= \sqrt{(x - 0)^2 + (y - 2)^2}$$

$$= \sqrt{x^2 + (y - 2)^2}$$

b $P(x, y),\ l: x + 1 = 0$

$a = 1, b = 0, c = 1$

$$d = \left|\frac{ax_1 + by_1 + c}{\sqrt{a^2 + b^2}}\right|$$

$$= \left|\frac{1 \times x + 0 \times y + 1}{\sqrt{1^2 + 0^2}}\right|$$

$$= |x + 1|$$

c

$$PA = 2d$$

$$PA^2 = 4d^2$$

$$x^2 + (y - 2)^2 = 4(x + 1)^2$$

$$x^2 + y^2 - 4y + 4 = 4(x^2 + 2x + 1)$$

$$x^2 + y^2 - 4y + 4 = 4x^2 + 8x + 4$$

$$3x^2 + 8x - y^2 + 4y = 0$$

5 a

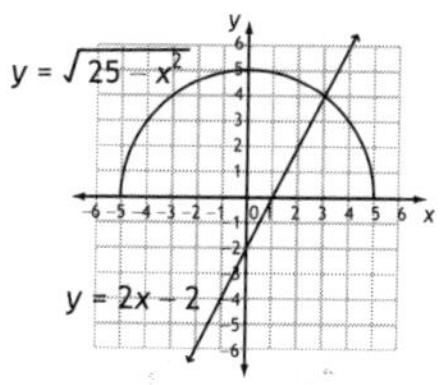

b From the graph, the point of intersection of the functions is (3, 4).

$\therefore 2x - 2 = \sqrt{25 - x^2}$ when $x = 3$

Topic Test 9 – Trigonometric Ratios

1 Let h m be the height of the kite.

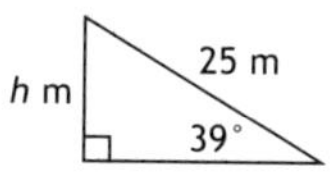

$$\sin 39° = \frac{h}{25}$$

$$h = 25 \sin 39°$$

$$= 15.73300978\ldots$$

$$= 15.7 \quad \text{[1 decimal place]}$$

$\therefore$ the kite is 15.7 metres above the ground

2 Let θ be the size of the largest angle.

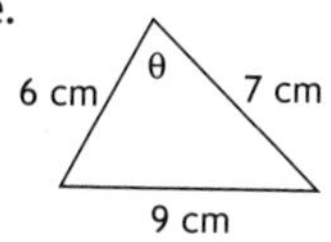

By the cosine rule,

$$\cos C = \frac{a^2 + b^2 - c^2}{2ab}$$

continued ...

$$\cos\theta = \frac{6^2 + 7^2 - 9^2}{2 \times 6 \times 7}$$
$$= 0.047619047\ldots$$
$$\theta = 87.27059736\ldots^\circ$$
$$= 87^\circ \quad \text{[nearest degree]}$$
$\therefore$ the largest angle measures 87°

3 **a** $\operatorname{cosec}\theta = \dfrac{1}{\sin\theta}$

$$\cot\theta = \frac{1}{\tan\theta} = \frac{\cos\theta}{\sin\theta}$$

b $$\operatorname{cosec}^2\theta - \cot^2\theta = \left(\frac{1}{\sin\theta}\right)^2 - \left(\frac{\cos\theta}{\sin\theta}\right)^2$$
$$= \frac{1}{\sin^2\theta} - \frac{\cos^2\theta}{\sin^2\theta}$$
$$= \frac{1 - \cos^2\theta}{\sin^2\theta}$$
$$= \frac{\sin^2\theta}{\sin^2\theta}$$
$$= 1$$

4 **a** $\angle DAB = 180^\circ - 60^\circ$

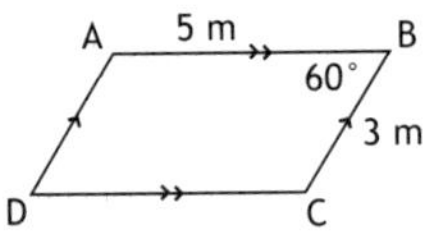

$$= 120^\circ$$
$AD = BC = 3$ m

In ΔDAB,
$$a^2 = b^2 + d^2 - 2bd\cos A$$
$$= 3^2 + 5^2 - 2 \times 3 \times 5 \times \cos 120^\circ$$
$$= 49$$
$$a = 7 \quad [a > 0]$$
$\therefore BD = 7$ m

b $$\text{Area} = 2 \times \tfrac{1}{2} bd \sin A$$
$$= 3 \times 5 \times \sin 120^\circ$$
$$= 15 \times \frac{\sqrt{3}}{2}$$
$$= \frac{15\sqrt{3}}{2}\ \text{m}^2$$

5 **a** $\angle AMB = 180^\circ - (64 + 71)^\circ$

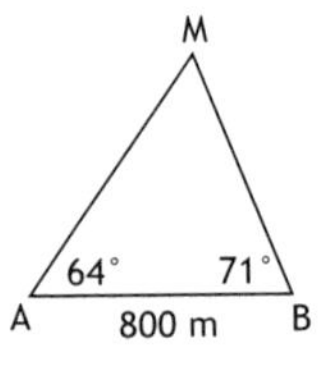

$$= 45^\circ$$
$$\frac{a}{\sin A} = \frac{m}{\sin M}$$
$$\frac{MB}{\sin 64^\circ} = \frac{800}{\sin 45^\circ}$$
$$MB = \frac{800\sin 64^\circ}{\sin 45^\circ}$$

b Let x m be the distance of the monument from the road.

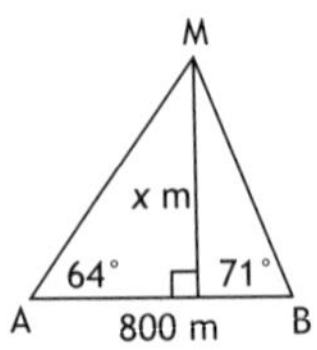

$$\sin 71^\circ = \frac{x}{MB}$$

continued ...

$$x = MB\sin 71^\circ$$
$$= \frac{800\sin 64^\circ \sin 71^\circ}{\sin 45^\circ}$$
$$= 961.4688916\ldots$$
$$= 960 \quad \text{[nearest 10]}$$
$\therefore$ the monument is 960 m from the road

6 $$2\sin^2\theta + \sin\theta - 1 = 0$$
$$(2\sin\theta - 1)(\sin\theta + 1) = 0$$
$2\sin\theta - 1 = 0$ or $\sin\theta + 1 = 0$

$2\sin\theta = 1$ $\qquad$ $\sin\theta = -1$

$\sin\theta = \frac{1}{2}$ $\qquad$ $\sin\theta = -1$

$\sin 30^\circ = \frac{1}{2}$

sin is positive in the 1st and 2nd quadrants

$\theta = 30^\circ$ or $\theta = (180 - 30)^\circ$

$\theta = 30^\circ$ $\qquad$ $\theta = 150^\circ$

$\sin 90^\circ = 1$

sin is negative in the 3rd and 4th quadrants

$\theta = (180 + 90)^\circ$ or $\theta = (360 - 90)^\circ$

$\theta = 270^\circ$ $\qquad$ $\theta = 270^\circ$

$\therefore \theta = 30^\circ, 150^\circ$ or 270°

Topic Test 10 – Trigonometric Ratios

1 Let x m be the width of the verandah.

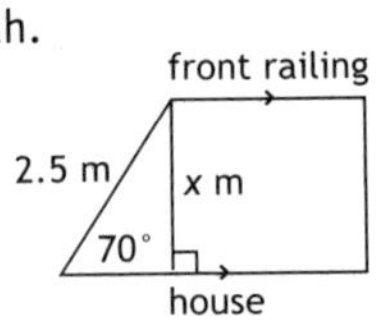

$$\sin 70^\circ = \frac{x}{2.5}$$
$$x = 2.5\sin 70^\circ$$
$$= 2.349231552\ldots$$
$$= 2.35 \quad \text{[2 decimal places]}$$
$\therefore$ the verandah is 2.35 metres wide

2 $$\tan\alpha + \cot\alpha = \frac{\sin\alpha}{\cos\alpha} + \frac{\cos\alpha}{\sin\alpha}$$
$$= \frac{\sin^2\alpha + \cos^2\alpha}{\sin\alpha\cos\alpha}$$
$$= \frac{1}{\sin\alpha\cos\alpha}$$

3 $\angle ACB = 312^\circ - 286^\circ$

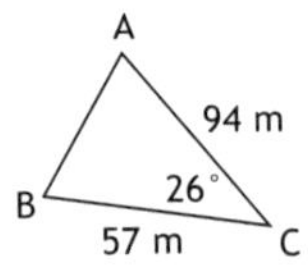

$$= 26^\circ$$
$$c^2 = a^2 + b^2 - 2ab\cos C$$
$$= 57^2 + 94^2 - 2 \times 57 \times 94 \times \cos 26^\circ$$
$$= 2453.523\ldots$$
$$c = 49.53304957\ldots \quad [c > 0]$$
$$= 49.5 \quad \text{[1 decimal place]}$$
$\therefore AB = 49.5$ m

4 $\angle ABC = 180^\circ - (75 + 45)^\circ$

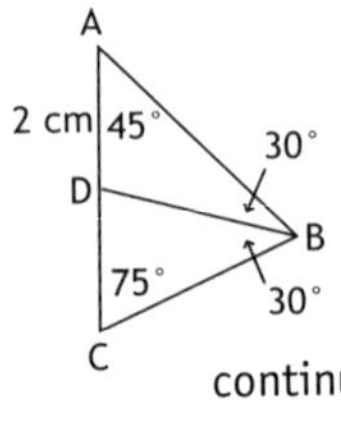

$$= 60^\circ$$
but DB bisects $\angle ABC$

$\therefore \angle ABD = 30^\circ$

continued ...

In ΔABD

$$\frac{a}{\sin A} = \frac{b}{\sin B}$$

$$\frac{BD}{\sin 45°} = \frac{2}{\sin 30°}$$

$$BD = \frac{2\sin 45°}{\sin 30°}$$

$$= \frac{2 \times \frac{1}{\sqrt{2}}}{\frac{1}{2}}$$

$$= \frac{4}{\sqrt{2}}$$

$$= 2\sqrt{2} \text{ cm}$$

5 $\tan\theta = -1$

$\tan 45° = 1$

tan is negative in the 2nd and 4th quadrants

but $0° \leq \theta \leq 180°$

$\therefore \theta$ lies in the 2nd quadrant

$$\therefore \theta = (180 - 45)°$$
$$= 135°$$

6 $\cos\theta = -0.6$

$\cos^2\theta + \sin^2\theta = 1$

$$\sin^2\theta = 1 - \cos^2\theta$$
$$= 1 - (0.6)^2$$
$$= 0.64$$

Now $\sin\theta < 0$

$\therefore \sin\theta = -0.8$

$$\tan\theta = \frac{\sin\theta}{\cos\theta}$$
$$= \frac{-0.8}{-0.6}$$
$$= \frac{4}{3}$$

7 **a** $\angle ADB = 29° - 22°$
$= 7°$

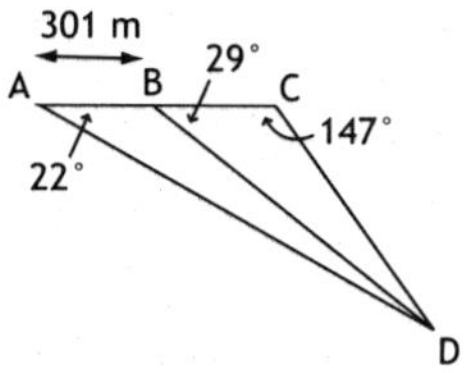

In ΔABD, $\dfrac{a}{\sin A} = \dfrac{d}{\sin D}$

$$\frac{BD}{\sin 22°} = \frac{301}{\sin 7°}$$

$$BD = \frac{301\sin 22°}{\sin 7°}$$

b $\angle BDC = 180° - (147 + 29)°$
$= 4°$

In ΔBCD, $\dfrac{d}{\sin D} = \dfrac{c}{\sin C}$

$$\frac{BC}{\sin 4°} = \frac{BD}{\sin 147°}$$

$$BC = \frac{BD\sin 4°}{\sin 147°}$$
$$= 118.501322\ldots$$
$$= 118.5 \text{ m} \quad \text{[1 decimal place]}$$

Topic Test 11 – The Quadratic Polynomial and the Parabola

1 Let $y = 3x^2 - 7x + 4$

$$\text{Least value} = \frac{4ac - b^2}{4a}$$
$$= \frac{4 \times 3 \times 4 - (-7)^2}{4 \times 3}$$
$$= -\frac{1}{12}$$

$\therefore$ the minimum value of $3x^2 - 7x + 4$ is $-\dfrac{1}{12}$

2 $x^2 = 4Ay$

This parabola passes through $(-12, 6)$

$$\therefore (-12)^2 = 4A \times 6$$
$$144 = 24A$$
$$A = 6$$

$\therefore$ the focal length of the parabola is 6 units

3 $9x^2 + 6x + m^2$

$a = 9, b = 6, c = m^2$

$$\Delta = b^2 - 4ac$$
$$= 6^2 - 4 \times 9 \times m^2$$
$$= 36 - 36m^2$$

$a > 0$, the expression will be positive definite when $\Delta < 0$

$$36 - 36m^2 < 0$$
$$1 - m^2 < 0$$

Let $y = 1 - m^2$

$$= (1 - m)(1 + m)$$

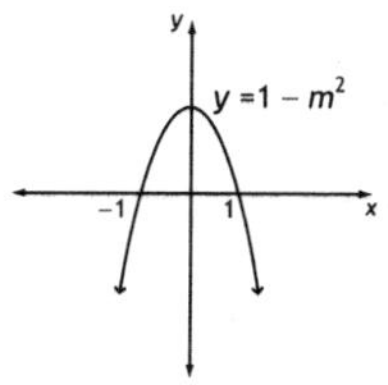

From the graph, $y < 0$ when $m < -1$ and $m > 1$.

$\therefore$ the expression will always be positive when $m < -1$ and $m > 1$

4 $x^2 - x = ax(x + 1) + bx$

$$= ax^2 + ax + bx$$
$$= ax^2 + (a + b)x$$

$\therefore a = 1$ and $a + b = -1$

$$1 + b = -1$$
$$b = -2$$

$a = 1$ and $b = -2$

5 $(m - 2)x^2 + (m + 1)x + 3 = 0$

$a = m - 2, b = m + 1, c = 3$

$$\Delta = b^2 - 4ac$$
$$= (m + 1)^2 - 4(m - 2) \times 3$$
$$= (m + 1)^2 - 12(m - 2)$$
$$= m^2 + 2m + 1 - 12m + 24$$
$$= m^2 - 10m + 25$$
$$= (m - 5)^2$$

continued ...

The roots are real when $\Delta \geq 0$

But $(m-5)^2 \geq 0$ for all real values of m

$\therefore$ the equation will have real roots for all values of m

6 **a** $S(2, 0)$, $P(x, y)$, $l: y = 4$

The locus is a parabola, focus (2, 0) and directrix $y = 4$

Axis: $x = 2$

$$\text{Focal length} = \tfrac{1}{2}(4-0) = 2 \text{ units}$$

$$A = 2$$

Vertex (2, 2)

Equation: $(x-2)^2 = -4 \times 2(y-2)$

$$(x-2)^2 = -8(y-2)$$

b

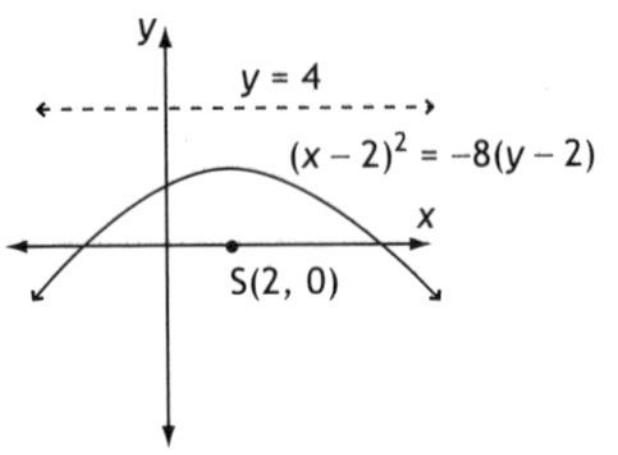

7 $kx^2 - (3k+1)x - 15 = 0$

$a = k, b = -(3k+1), c = -15$

Let the roots be 5 and α.

$$5 + \alpha = -\frac{b}{a} \quad \textbf{i}$$

and $$5\alpha = \frac{c}{a} \quad \textbf{ii}$$

From **ii** $$5\alpha = \frac{-15}{k}$$

$$\alpha = -\frac{3}{k}$$

From **i** $$5 + \alpha = \frac{3k+1}{k}$$

$$\therefore 5 - \frac{3}{k} = \frac{3k+1}{k}$$

$$5k - 3 = 3k + 1$$

$$2k = 4$$

$$k = 2$$

$$\therefore \alpha = -\frac{3}{2}$$

$\therefore$ the other root is -1.5

Topic Test 12 – The Quadratic Polynomial and the Parabola

1 **a** $(x-1)^2 = 12y$

Vertex $(1, 0)$

b $4A = 12$

$\therefore A = 3$

Focal length = 3 units

Focus $(1, 3)$

2 $(x^2+7x)^2 + 2(x^2+7x) = 80$

Let $u = x^2 + 7x$

$$u^2 + 2u = 80$$

$$u^2 + 2u - 80 = 0$$

$$(u+10)(u-8) = 0$$

$u + 10 = 0$ or $u - 8 = 0$

$x^2 + 7x + 10 = 0$ $x^2 + 7x - 8 = 0$

$(x+5)(x+2) = 0$ $(x+8)(x-1) = 0$

$x + 5 = 0$ or $x + 2 = 0$ $x + 8 = 0$ or $x - 1 = 0$

$x = -5$ $x = -2$ $x = -8$ $x = 1$

$\therefore x = -8, -5, -2$ or 1

3 $y = 3x^2 - 8x + 5$

$3x^2 - 8x + 5 = 0$

$a = 3, b = -8, c = 5$

$$\Delta = b^2 - 4ac$$

$$= (-8)^2 - 4 \times 3 \times 5$$

$$= 4$$

As $\Delta > 0$, the equation has real roots.

$\therefore y = 3x^2 - 8x + 5$ will cross the x-axis

4 $x^2 + qx + r = 0$

The roots are in the ratio 3 : 2

Let the roots be 3α and 2α

$$3\alpha + 2\alpha = -\frac{b}{a}$$

$$5\alpha = -q$$

$$\alpha = -\frac{q}{5} \quad \textbf{i}$$

$$3\alpha \times 2\alpha = \frac{c}{a}$$

$$6a^2 = r$$

$$6\left(-\frac{q}{5}\right)^2 = r \quad \text{from } \textbf{i}$$

$$6\frac{q^2}{25} = r$$

$$6q^2 = 25r$$

5 $y = 2x + 3$ **i**

$x^2 = -4y$ **ii**

Substitute **i** into **ii**

$$x^2 = -4(2x+3)$$

$$x^2 = -8x - 12$$

$$x^2 + 8x + 12 = 0$$

$$(x+6)(x+2) = 0$$

continued ...

$$x + 6 = 0 \quad \text{or} \quad x + 2 = 0$$
$$x = -6 \qquad\qquad x = -2$$

Substitute into **i**

When $x = -6$, $\quad y = 2 \times -6 + 3$
$= -9$

When $x = -2$, $\quad y = 2 \times -2 + 3$
$= -1$

$\therefore$ the points of intersection are $(-6, -9)$ and $(-2, -1)$

6 **a** $x^2 = 16y$
$4A = 16$
$A = 4$
Focus $S(0, 4)$

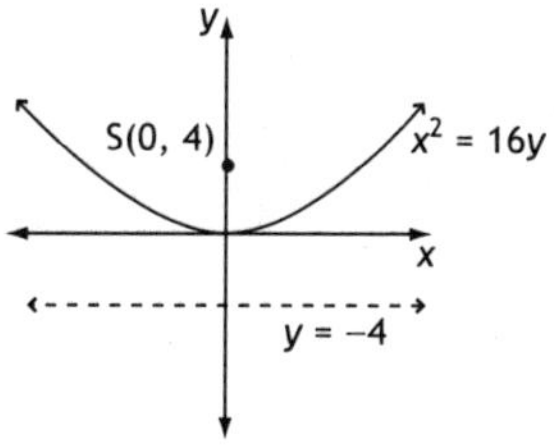

b Vertex $(-2, 4)$, focus $S(0, 4)$, axis: $y = 4$

Focal length $= 0 - (-2)$
$= 2$ units
$\therefore\ A = 2$

The equation is given by :
$$(y - y_0)^2 = 4A(x - x_0)$$
$$(y - 4)^2 = 4 \times 2 \times (x - (-2))$$
$$(y - 4)^2 = 8(x + 2)$$

c $x^2 = 16y$
Directrix: $y = -4$
$(y - 4)^2 = 8(x + 2)$
Directrix: $x = -4$
$\therefore$ P is the point $(-4, -4)$

Topic Test 13 – The Tangent to a Curve and the Derivative of a Function

1 $f(x) = x^6 - 2x^3 + 7x$
$f'(x) = 6x^5 - 6x^2 + 7$
$f'(2) = 6(2)^5 - 6(2)^2 + 7$
$= 175$

2
$$\lim_{x \to -2} \frac{4 - x^2}{x + 2} = \lim_{x \to -2} \frac{(2 - x)(2 + x)}{x + 2}$$
$$= \lim_{x \to -2} (2 - x)$$
$$= 2 - (-2)$$
$$= 4$$

3 **a** $f(x) = x^2 - 6x + 5$
$f'(x) = 2x - 6$

b The gradient is zero when $f'(x) = 0$
$2x - 6 = 0$
$2x = 6$
$x = 3$
$f(3) = 3^2 - 6 \times 3 + 5$
$= -4$

$\therefore$ the gradient of the tangent is zero at the point $(3, -4)$

4 $y = 3x - 2x^2$
$\dfrac{dy}{dx} = 3 - 4x$

When $x = 1$, $\dfrac{dy}{dx} = 3 - 4 \times 1$
$= -1$

$\therefore$ the gradient of the tangent is -1
$\therefore$ the gradient of the normal is $m = 1$

When $x = 1$, $\quad y = 3 \times 1 - 2 \times 1^2$
$= 1$

$m = 1,\ (1, 1)$
$y - y_1 = m(x - x_1)$
$y - 1 = 1(x - 1)$
$y - 1 = x - 1$
$y = x$

$\therefore$ the equation of the normal is $y = x$

5
$$y = \frac{5x}{x^2 - 2}$$
$$\frac{dy}{dx} = \frac{v\dfrac{du}{dx} - u\dfrac{dv}{dx}}{v^2}$$
$$= \frac{(x^2 - 2) \times 5 - 5x \times 2x}{(x^2 - 2)^2}$$
$$= \frac{5x^2 - 10 - 10x^2}{(x^2 - 2)^2}$$
$$= \frac{-5x^2 - 10}{(x^2 - 2)^2}$$
$$= \frac{-5(x^2 + 2)}{(x^2 - 2)^2}$$

6 **a**
$$\frac{1}{1 - x} = (1 - x)^{-1}$$

b
$$\frac{d}{dx}\left(\frac{1}{1 - x}\right) = \frac{d}{dx}(1 - x)^{-1}$$
$$= -1(1 - x)^{-2} \times -1$$
$$= (1 - x)^{-2}$$
$$= \frac{1}{(1 - x)^2}$$

7 $f(x)=2x^3$

$$
\begin{aligned}
f'(c) &= \lim_{x\to c}\frac{f(x)-f(c)}{x-c}\\
&= \lim_{x\to c}\frac{2x^3-2c^3}{x-c}\\
&= \lim_{x\to c}\frac{2(x^3-c^3)}{x-c}\\
&= \lim_{x\to c}\frac{2(x-c)(x^2+cx+c^2)}{x-c}\\
&= \lim_{x\to c}2(x^2+cx+c^2)\\
&= 2(c^2+c^2+c^2)\\
&= 6c^2
\end{aligned}
$$

$f'(x)=6x^2$

Topic Test 14 — The Tangent to a Curve and the Derivative of a Function

1 a

$$
\begin{aligned}
y &= \frac{3}{x^5}\\
&= 3x^{-5}\\
y' &= -15x^{-6}\\
&= -\frac{15}{x^6}
\end{aligned}
$$

b $y=x(7-4x)^9$

$$
\begin{aligned}
\frac{dy}{dx} &= u\frac{dv}{dx}+v\frac{du}{dx}\\
&= x\times 9(7-4x)^8\times -4+(7-4x)^9\times 1\\
&= -36x(7-4x)^8+(7-4x)^9\\
&= (7-4x)^8(-36x+7-4x)\\
&= (7-4x)^8(7-40x)
\end{aligned}
$$

c $y=\dfrac{2x+1}{2x-1}$

$$
\begin{aligned}
\frac{dy}{dx} &= \frac{v\frac{du}{dx}-u\frac{dv}{dx}}{v^2}\\
&= \frac{(2x-1)\times 2-(2x+1)\times 2}{(2x-1)^2}\\
&= \frac{4x-2-4x-2}{(2x-1)^2}\\
&= \frac{-4}{(2x-1)^2}
\end{aligned}
$$

2 $y=x^2+1,\ x=-1$ and $x=3$

$$
m=\frac{f(x)-f(c)}{x-c}
$$

continued ...

$$
\begin{aligned}
&= \frac{3^2+1-\left((-1)^2+1\right)}{3-(-1)}\\
&= \frac{8}{4}\\
&= 2
\end{aligned}
$$

$\therefore$ the gradient of the secant is 2

3 $f(x)=\begin{cases}\dfrac{x^2-3x+2}{x-2} & \text{for } x\neq 2\\ 1 & \text{for } x=2\end{cases}$

$f(2)=1$

$$
\begin{aligned}
\lim_{x\to 2}\frac{x^2-3x+2}{x-2} &= \lim_{x\to 2}\frac{(x-2)(x-1)}{x-2}\\
&= \lim_{x\to 2}(x-1)\\
&= 2-1\\
&= 1
\end{aligned}
$$

$\therefore \lim_{x\to 2} f(x)=f(2)$

$\therefore f(x)$ is continuous at $x=2$

4 a

$$
\begin{aligned}
y &= (x-2)^2\\
&= x^2-4x+4\\
\frac{dy}{dx} &= 2x-4
\end{aligned}
$$

When $x=3$, $\dfrac{dy}{dx}=2\times 3-4 = 2$

$\therefore$ the gradient of the tangent is $m=2$

When $x=3$, $y=(3-2)^2 = 1$

$m=2,\ (3,\ 1)$

$$
\begin{aligned}
y-y_1 &= m(x-x_1)\\
y-1 &= 2(x-3)\\
y-1 &= 2x-6\\
y &= 2x-5
\end{aligned}
$$

b

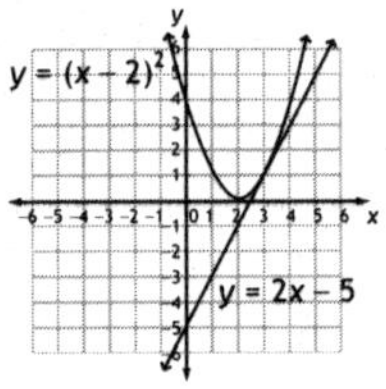

5 a

$$
\begin{aligned}
y &= x^2+8x\\
\frac{dy}{dx} &= 2x+8
\end{aligned}
$$

b $f(x)=x^2+8x$

$$
\begin{aligned}
f'(c) &= \lim_{x\to c}\frac{f(x)-f(c)}{x-c}\\
&= \lim_{x\to c}\frac{x^2+8x-(c^2+8c)}{x-c}\\
&= \lim_{x\to c}\frac{x^2-c^2+8x-8c}{x-c}\\
&= \lim_{x\to c}\frac{(x+c)(x-c)+8(x-c)}{x-c}\\
&= \lim_{x\to c}\frac{(x-c)(x+c+8)}{x-c}
\end{aligned}
$$

continued ...

$$= \lim_{x \to c} (x + c + 8)$$
$$= c + c + 8$$
$$= 2c + 8$$
$$\therefore f'(x) = 2x + 8$$

Sample Examination Paper One

1 **a** $275\,596\,240 = 275\,600\,000$ correct to 4 significant figures
$$= 2.756 \times 10^8$$

b $|x + 1| = 3$

$x + 1 = -3$ or $x + 1 = 3$

$x = -4$ $\quad\quad$ $x = 2$

c
$$7m^2 - 28 = 7(m^2 - 4)$$
$$= 7(m - 2)(m + 2)$$

d **i**
$$\frac{x-5}{3} - \frac{2x+1}{4} = \frac{4(x-5) - 3(2x+1)}{12}$$
$$= \frac{4x - 20 - 6x - 3}{12}$$
$$= \frac{-2x - 23}{12}$$

ii
$$\frac{x-5}{3} - \frac{2x+1}{4} < 1$$
$$\frac{-2x - 23}{12} < 1$$
$$-2x - 23 < 12$$
$$-2x < 35$$
$$x > -17.5$$

e
$$a - \sqrt{b} = \frac{8}{1 - \sqrt{5}}$$
$$= \frac{8}{1 - \sqrt{5}} \times \frac{1 + \sqrt{5}}{1 + \sqrt{5}}$$
$$= \frac{8(1 + \sqrt{5})}{1 - 5}$$
$$= \frac{8(1 + \sqrt{5})}{-4}$$
$$= -2(1 + \sqrt{5})$$
$$= -2 - 2\sqrt{5}$$
$$= -2 - \sqrt{4} \times \sqrt{5}$$
$$= -2 - \sqrt{20}$$
$\therefore a = -2$ and $b = 20$

f $0.\dot{6}\dot{3} = 0.636\,363\,636\,363\ldots$

Let $x = 0.636\,363\,636\,363$

$100x = 63.636\,363\,636\,363$

$99x = 63$
$$x = \frac{63}{99}$$
$$= \frac{7}{11}$$

2 **a** $l\colon y = 2x + 2$ has gradient $m_1 = 2$

$k\colon x + 2y - 14 = 0$ has gradient $m_2 = -\frac{1}{2}$

$m_1 m_2 = -1$

$\therefore k$ and l are perpendicular

b $l\colon y = 2x + 2$

$k\colon x + 2y - 14 = 0$

Substitute l into k
$$x + 2(2x + 2) - 14 = 0$$
$$x + 4x + 4 - 14 = 0$$
$$5x = 10$$
$$x = 2$$
Substitute into l
$$y = 2 \times 2 + 2$$
$$= 6$$
$\therefore$ P is the point $(2, 6)$

c $l\colon y = 2x + 2$ cuts the x-axis when $y = 0$

i.e. $2x + 2 = 0$
$$2x = -2$$
$$x = -1$$
$\therefore$ Q is the point $(-1, 0)$

$k\colon x + 2y - 14 = 0$ cuts the x-axis when $y = 0$

i.e. $x + 2 \times 0 - 14 = 0$
$$x - 14 = 0$$
$$x = 14$$
$\therefore$ R is the point $(14, 0)$

d

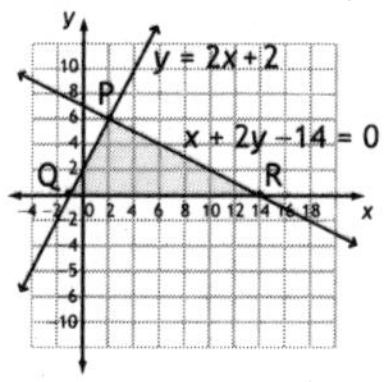

e $y < 2x + 2,\ x + 2y - 14 < 0,\ y > 0$

[Although the lines are solid in the diagram, this question asks for the region inside the diagram.]

f
$$A = \tfrac{1}{2}bh$$
$$= \tfrac{1}{2} \times 15 \times 6$$
$\therefore$ area $= 45$ units^2

3 **a**
$$5(2x - 3) - 4(2 - x) = 19$$
$$10x - 15 - 8 + 4x = 19$$
$$14x - 23 = 19$$
$$14x = 42$$
$$x = 3$$

b

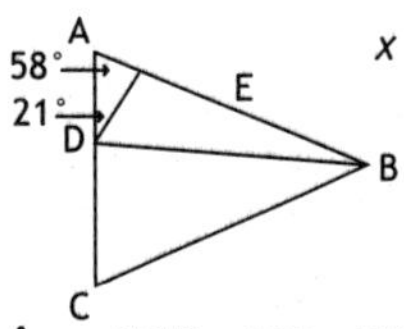

i $\angle DEB = 21° + 58°$ [exterior angle of ΔDEA]
$$= 79°$$
$\angle BDE = \angle DEB$ [base angles of isosceles ΔBDE]

$\therefore \angle BDE = 79°$

ii $\angle ADB = 21° + 79°$
$= 100°$
$\angle ACB = \angle CAB$ [base angles of isosceles ΔABC]
$\therefore \angle ACB = 58°$
$\angle ADB = \angle ACB + \angle CBD$ [exterior angle of ΔCBD]
$\therefore \angle CBD = 100° - 58°$
$= 42°$

c i $x^2 = -12y$
$4A = 12$
$A = 3$
$\therefore$ the focal length is 3 units

ii Vertex (0, 0)
iii The focus is 3 units below the vertex.
Focus: (0, −3)
iv The directrix is 3 units above the vertex.
Directrix: $y = 3$

d i $g(t) = t^2 - 4t - 2$
$g(1) = 1^2 - 4 \times 1 - 2$
$= -5$

ii $g(t) = 3$
$t^2 - 4t - 2 = 3$
$t^2 - 4t - 5 = 0$
$(t+1)(t-5) = 0$
$t + 1 = 0$ or $t - 5 = 0$
$t = -1$ $\quad t = 5$

4 a i Discount = 6% of \$21 600
= \$1296

ii Discounted price = \$21 600 − \$1296
= \$20 304

iii Increase = \$22 800 − \$21 600
= \$1200
Percentage increase = $\frac{\$1200}{\$21\,600} \times 100\%$
$= 5.55555\ldots\%$
$= 5.6\%$ [1 decimal place]

b i $f(x) = 6x - x^2$

$$\frac{f(x+h) - f(x)}{h} = \frac{6(x+h) - (x+h)^2 - (6x - x^2)}{h}$$
$$= \frac{6x + 6h - (x^2 + 2xh + h^2) - 6x + x^2}{h}$$
$$= \frac{6h - 2xh - h^2}{h}$$
$$= \frac{h(6 - 2x - h)}{h}$$
$$= 6 - 2x - h$$

ii $f'(x) = \lim_{h\to 0} \frac{f(x+h) - f(x)}{h}$
$= \lim_{h\to 0}(6 - 2x - h)$
$= 6 - 2x$

iii $f'(x) = 6 - 2x$
$f'(3) = 6 - 2 \times 3$
$= 0$
$\therefore$ when $x = 3$ the gradient of the curve is 0

c i $x^2 + 12x = p$
$x^2 + 12x + 36 = p + 36$
$(x+6)^2 = p + 36$
$x + 6 = \pm\sqrt{p+36}$
$x = -6 \pm \sqrt{p+36}$

ii $x = -6 \pm \sqrt{p+36}$
When $p = 253$
$x = -6 \pm \sqrt{253+36}$
$= -6 \pm 17$
$x = -23$ or $x = 11$

d $A = \frac{1}{2}ac \sin B$
$= \frac{1}{2} \times 12 \times 8 \times \sin 60°$
$= 48 \times \frac{\sqrt{3}}{2}$
$\therefore$ area $= 24\sqrt{3}$ m^2

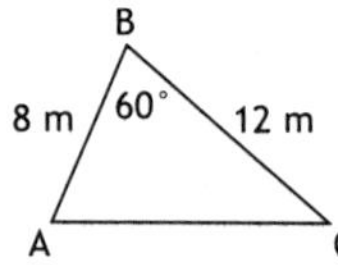

5 a i $f(x) = (x^2 - 2)^5$
$f'(x) = 5(x^2 - 2)^4 \times 2x$
$= 10x(x^2 - 2)^4$

ii $y = \frac{2x - 3}{3x + 4}$

$$\frac{dy}{dx} = \frac{v\frac{du}{dx} - u\frac{dv}{dx}}{v^2}$$
$$= \frac{(3x+4) \times 2 - (2x-3) \times 3}{(3x+4)^2}$$
$$= \frac{6x + 8 - 6x + 9}{(3x+4)^2}$$
$$= \frac{17}{(3x+4)^2}$$

iii $y = x(3x+1)^8$

$$\frac{dy}{dx} = u\frac{dv}{dx} + v\frac{du}{dx}$$
$$= x \times 8(3x+1)^7 \times 3 + (3x+1)^8 \times 1$$
$$= 24x(3x+1)^7 + (3x+1)^8$$
$$= (3x+1)^7(27x+1)$$

b $4\cos^2 x - 3 = 0$

$$4\cos^2 x = 3$$

$$\cos^2 x = \frac{3}{4}$$

$$\cos x = \pm\sqrt{\frac{3}{4}}$$

$$= \pm\frac{\sqrt{3}}{2}$$

Now $\cos 30° = \dfrac{\sqrt{3}}{2}$

$\therefore x = 30°, (180-30)°, (180+30)° \text{ or } (360-30)°$

$= 30°, 150°, 210° \text{ or } 330°$

c $x^2 + y^2 \le 9,\ \ y > x,\ \ x < -1$

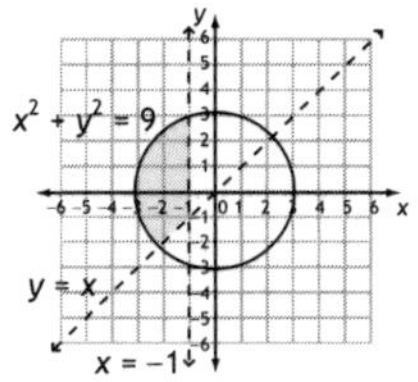

6 **a** **i** Perimeter = 8.4 *m*

$\therefore x + h + 3.5 = 8.4$

$x + h = 4.9$

$x = 4.9 - h$

ii

$$x^2 = 3.5^2 + h^2$$

$$(4.9 - h)^2 = 3.5^2 + h^2$$

$$24.01 - 9.8h + h^2 = 12.25 + h^2$$

$$24.01 - 9.8h = 12.25$$

$$-9.8h = -11.76$$

$$h = 1.2$$

iii $x = 4.9 - h$

$= 4.9 - 1.2$

$= 3.7$

$\therefore$ the hypotenuse is 3.7 m long

b $f(x) = \begin{cases} \dfrac{x^2 + x}{x+1} & \text{if } x \ne -1 \\ 1 & \text{if } x = -1 \end{cases}$

$f(-1) = 1$

$$\lim_{x\to -1} \frac{x^2 + x}{x+1} = \lim_{x\to -1} \frac{x(x+1)}{x+1}$$

$$= \lim_{x\to -1} (x)$$

$$= -1$$

$\therefore f(-1) \ne \lim\limits_{x\to -1} \dfrac{x^2 + x}{x+1}$

$\therefore f(x)$ is not continuous at $x = -1$

c PQRS is a rhombus of side 2 m.

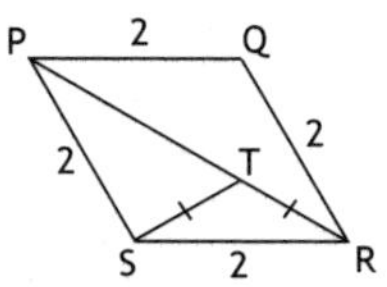

i In ΔTRS, ΔSPR,

∠TRS = ∠SPR	[ΔSPR is isosceles]
∠TSR = ∠SRP	[ΔTSR is isosceles]

$\therefore$ ΔTRS ||| ΔSPR

ii $\dfrac{PR}{RS} = \dfrac{SP}{TR}$ [corresponding sides of similar triangles]

$$\frac{PR}{2} = \frac{2}{\sqrt{5} - 1}$$

$$PR = \frac{4}{\sqrt{5} - 1}$$

$$= \frac{4}{\sqrt{5} - 1} \times \frac{\sqrt{5} + 1}{\sqrt{5} + 1}$$

$$= \frac{4(\sqrt{5} + 1)}{5 - 1}$$

$$= (\sqrt{5} + 1)\text{ m}$$

iii $PT = PR - TR$

$= \sqrt{5} + 1 - (\sqrt{5} - 1)$

$= 2$ m

$\therefore PT = PS$

7 **a** $h(t) = -t^5 + 4t^4 + 5t^2 - 9t + 7$

$h'(t) = -5t^4 + 16t^3 + 10t - 9$

$h'(4) = -5 \times 4^4 + 16 \times 4^3 + 10 \times 4 - 9$

$= -225$

b $f(x) = \begin{cases} x + a & \text{if } x < 0 \\ a - bx & \text{if } x \ge 0 \end{cases}$

i $f(-3) = 7$

$-3 + a = 7$

$a = 10$

$f(3) = 4$

$a - 3b = 4$

$10 - 3b = 4$

$3b = 6$

$b = 2$

$\therefore a = 10$ and $b = 2$

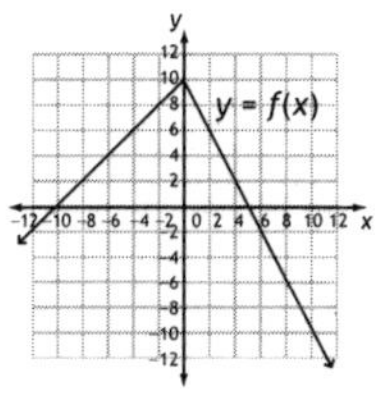

ii $f(x) = \begin{cases} x + 10 & \text{if } x < 0 \\ 10 - 2x & \text{if } x \ge 0 \end{cases}$

iii Domain: all real x

Range: $y \le 10$

c

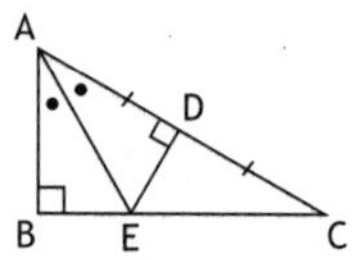

i In ΔAED, ΔCED,

AD = CD	[given]
∠ADE = ∠CDE	[both 90°, given]
DE = DE	[common side]
∴ ΔAED ≡ ΔCED	[SAS]

ii Let ∠ECD = $x°$

∠EAD = ∠ECD

[corresponding angles of congruent triangles]

continued ...

$\therefore\ \angle EAD = x°$

$\angle BAC = 2\angle EAD$ [EA bisects $\angle BAC$]

$= 2x°$

$\angle BAC + \angle ACB + \angle CBA = 180°$

[angle sum of a triangle]

$2x° + x° + 90° = 180°$

$3x° = 90°$

$x° = 30°$

$\therefore\ \angle ECD = 30°$

8 **a** $9x^2 - 42x + 49 = 0$

$a = 9, b = -42, c = 49$

$\Delta = b^2 - 4ac$

$= (-42)^2 - 4 \times 9 \times 49$

$= 0$

$\therefore$ the roots are real, rational and equal

b **i** In ΔPSR,

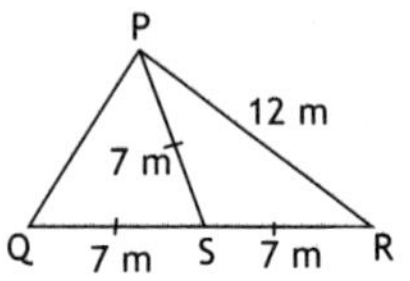

$$\cos R = \frac{p^2 + s^2 - r^2}{2ps}$$

$$= \frac{7^2 + 12^2 - 7^2}{2 \times 7 \times 12}$$

$$= \frac{6}{7}$$

ii In ΔPQR,

$r^2 = p^2 + q^2 - 2pq \cos R$

$= 14^2 + 12^2 - 2 \times 14 \times 12 \times \frac{6}{7}$

$= 52$

$r = \sqrt{52}$ $[r > 0]$

$= 2\sqrt{13}$

$\therefore PQ = 2\sqrt{13}$ m

iii In ΔPQR,

$$\cos P = \frac{r^2 + q^2 - p^2}{2rq}$$

$$= \frac{52 + 12^2 - 14^2}{2 \times \sqrt{52} \times 12}$$

$= 0$

$\therefore \angle P = 90°$

c **i** $A(-2, 3)$, $P(x, y)$

$$m_1 = \frac{y_2 - y_1}{x_2 - x_1}$$

$$= \frac{y - 3}{x + 2}$$

$B(6, -3)$, $P(x, y)$

$$m_2 = \frac{y_2 - y_1}{x_2 - x_1}$$

$$= \frac{y + 3}{x - 6}$$

ii If $PA \perp PB$, $m_1 m_2 = -1$

$$\frac{y - 3}{x + 2} \times \frac{y + 3}{x - 6} = -1$$

$(y - 3)(y + 3) = -(x + 2)(x - 6)$

$y^2 - 9 = -(x^2 - 4x - 12)$

$y^2 - 9 = -x^2 + 4x + 12$

$x^2 - 4x + y^2 - 21 = 0$

iii $x^2 - 4x + y^2 = 21$

$x^2 - 4x + 4 + y^2 = 25$

$(x - 2)^2 + y^2 = 5^2$

The locus is a circle,
centre $(2, 0)$, radius 5 units

9 **a**

$3a + 4b - 5 = 0$ **i**

$5a - b - 16 = 0$ **ii**

ii $\times 4$ $20a - 4b - 64 = 0$ **iii**

i + **iii** $23a - 69 = 0$

$23a = 69$

$a = 3$

Substitute in **ii**

$5 \times 3 - b = 16$

$15 - b = 16$

$b = -1$

$\therefore a = 3$ and $b = -1$

b $y = \sqrt{x}$

$= x^{\frac{1}{2}}$

$$\frac{dy}{dx} = \tfrac{1}{2} x^{-\frac{1}{2}}$$

$$= \frac{1}{2\sqrt{x}}$$

When $x = 1$, $\dfrac{dy}{dx} = \dfrac{1}{2}$

$\therefore$ the gradient of the tangent is $\frac{1}{2}$

$\therefore$ the gradient of the normal is -2

$m = -2$, $(1, 1)$

$y - y_1 = m(x - x_1)$

$y - 1 = -2(x - 1)$

$y - 1 = -2x + 2$

$y = -2x + 3$

c **i** $B(4, 1)$, $C(0, 3)$

$$M(x, y) = \left(\frac{x_1 + x_2}{2}, \frac{y_1 + y_2}{2}\right)$$

$$= \left(\frac{4 + 0}{2}, \frac{1 + 3}{2}\right)$$

$= (2, 2)$

$\therefore$ D is the point $(2, 2)$

ii $A(5, 8)$, $D(2, 2)$

$$\frac{y - y_1}{x - x_1} = \frac{y_2 - y_1}{x_2 - x_1}$$

$$\frac{y - 8}{x - 5} = \frac{2 - 8}{2 - 5}$$

$$\frac{y - 8}{x - 5} = 2$$

$y - 8 = 2(x - 5)$

$y - 8 = 2x - 10$

$2x - y - 2 = 0$

iii $2x - y - 2 = 0$

At E, $x = 0$

$2 \times 0 - y - 2 = 0$

$y = -2$

$\therefore$ E is the point $(0, -2)$

$C(0, 3),\ E(0, -2)$

$\therefore$ CE = 5 units

$B(4, 1),\ E(0, -2)$

$$d = \sqrt{(x_2 - x_1)^2 + (y_2 - y_1)^2}$$
$$= \sqrt{(0 - 4)^2 + (-2 - 1)^2}$$
$$= \sqrt{25}$$

$\therefore$ BE = 5 units

$\therefore$ CE = BE

10 **a** $5 - 5\cos^2\theta - 4\sin^2\theta = 5(1 - \cos^2\theta) - 4\sin^2\theta$
$$= 5\sin^2\theta - 4\sin^2\theta$$
$$= \sin^2\theta$$

b **i** $x^2 = 4y$

$4A = 4$

$A = 1$

Focus $(0, 1)$

ii $x^2 = 4y$ **i**

$y = 13 - 3x^2$ **ii**

Substitute **ii** into **i**

$x^2 = 4(13 - 3x^2)$

$x^2 = 52 - 12x^2$

$13x^2 = 52$

$x^2 = 4$

$x = -2$ or $x = 2$

Substitute into **ii**

When $x = -2$: $y = 13 - 3(-2)^2 = 1$

When $x = 2$: $y = 13 - 3(2)^2 = 1$

$\therefore$ the points of intersection are $(-2, 1)$ and $(2, 1)$

iii The straight line passing through both (−2, 1) and (2, 1) is $y = 1$. As S is the point (0, 1), this line also passes through S.

c **i** In ΔBCD, $\cos\theta = \dfrac{CD}{BC}$

$\therefore\ \cos\theta = CD$

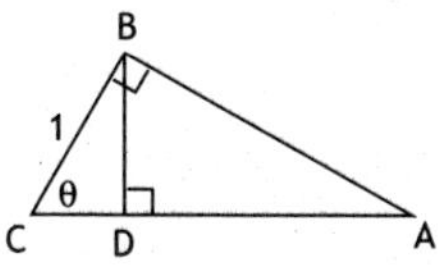

In ΔABC, $\sec\theta = \dfrac{AC}{BC}$

$\therefore\ \sec\theta = AC$

$AC = CD + DA$

but $DA = CD + 1$

$\therefore\ AC = 2CD + 1$

$\therefore\ \sec\theta = 2\cos\theta + 1$

ii
$$\frac{1}{\cos\theta} = 2\cos\theta + 1$$
$$1 = 2\cos^2\theta + \cos\theta$$
$$2\cos^2\theta + \cos\theta - 1 = 0$$

iii
$$2\cos^2\theta + \cos\theta - 1 = 0$$
$$(2\cos\theta - 1)(\cos\theta + 1) = 0$$

$2\cos\theta - 1 = 0$ or $\cos\theta + 1 = 0$

$\cos\theta = \frac{1}{2}$ $\cos\theta = -1$

But θ is an acute angle

$\therefore \cos\theta = \frac{1}{2}$

$\theta = 60°$

Sample Examination Paper Two

1 **a** $115\% = 345$

$1\% = 3$

$100\% = 300$

$\therefore$ 300 tiles were needed

b $S = \dfrac{a(1 - r^n)}{1 - r}$

When $a = 64$, $n = 5$ and $r = \frac{1}{2}$

$$S = \frac{64\left[1 - \left(\frac{1}{2}\right)^5\right]}{1 - \frac{1}{2}}$$
$$= 124$$

c $|x - 3| \geq 4$

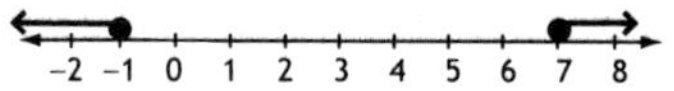

d $\dfrac{3.2 + 4.7}{3.2 \times 4.7} = 0.525265957\ldots$

$= 0.53$ [2 decimal places]

e $(2a^2b^3)^3 \div (ab^2)^4 = 8a^6b^9 \div a^4b^8$
$$= 8a^2b$$

f
$$\frac{\sqrt{75} - \sqrt{3}}{\sqrt{12}} = \frac{5\sqrt{3} - \sqrt{3}}{2\sqrt{3}}$$
$$= \frac{4\sqrt{3}}{2\sqrt{3}}$$
$$= 2$$

2 **a** Let TV = x cm

$\therefore$ QT = $(18 - x)$ cm

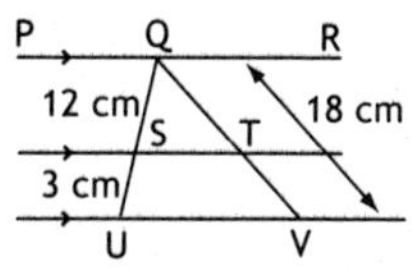

Parallel lines preserve ratios

$$\therefore\ \frac{TV}{QT} = \frac{SU}{QS}$$
$$\frac{x}{18 - x} = \frac{3}{12}$$
$$= \frac{1}{4}$$

continued ...

$$4x = 18 - x$$
$$5x = 18$$
$$x = 3.6$$
$\therefore$ TV = 3.6 cm

b Centre (2, −5), radius 13 units

Equation: $(x-2)^2 + (y+5)^2 = 13^2$

Circle cuts x-axis when $y = 0$

$$(x-2)^2 + (0+5)^2 = 13^2$$
$$(x-2)^2 + 25 = 169$$
$$(x-2)^2 = 144$$

$x - 2 = -12$ or $x - 2 = 12$

$x = -10$ $\qquad$ $x = 14$

The circle cuts the x-axis at (−10, 0) and (14, 0)

c i $y = 2x - 2$

This line has gradient $m = 2$

$$m = \tan\theta$$
$$\tan\theta = 2$$
$$\theta = 63.43494882\ldots^\circ$$
$$= 63^\circ \quad \text{[nearest degree]}$$

ii A(4, 6), $l: y = 2x - 2$

$$6 = 2 \times 4 - 2$$
$$6 = 6$$

$\therefore$ A lies on the line $y = 2x - 2$

iii B(−3, 2), $l: y = 2x - 2$

A line parallel to l has gradient $m = 2$

$$y - y_1 = m(x - x_1)$$
$$y - 2 = 2(x - (-3))$$
$$y - 2 = 2x + 6$$
$$2x - y + 8 = 0$$

iv The shortest distance is the perpendicular distance.

A(4, 6), $2x - y + 8 = 0$

$a = 2, b = -1, c = 8$

$$d = \left|\frac{ax_1 + bx_1 + c}{\sqrt{a^2 + b^2}}\right|$$
$$= \left|\frac{2 \times 4 + -1 \times 6 + 8}{\sqrt{2^2 + (-1)^2}}\right|$$
$$= \left|\frac{10}{\sqrt{5}}\right|$$
$$= \frac{10}{\sqrt{5}} \times \frac{\sqrt{5}}{\sqrt{5}}$$
$$= \frac{10\sqrt{5}}{5}$$

$\therefore$ distance $= 2\sqrt{5}$ units

3 a $y = x(2-3x)^4$

$$\frac{dy}{dx} = u\frac{dv}{dx} + v\frac{du}{dx}$$
$$= x \times 4(2-3x)^3 \times -3 + (2-3x)^4 \times 1$$
$$= -12x(2-3x)^3 + (2-3x)^4$$
$$= (2-3x)^3(-12x + 2 - 3x)$$
$$= (2-3x)^3(2-15x)$$

b
$$9 - 4x > 3$$
$$-4x > -6$$
$$x < 1.5$$

c
$$5x^2 - x + 4 = A + B(1+x) + Cx(1+x)$$
$$= A + B + Bx + Cx + Cx^2$$
$$= (A+B) + (B+C)x + Cx^2$$

$\therefore C = 5,$ $\quad B + C = -1$ and $A + B = 4$

$B + 5 = -1$

$B = -6$ $\qquad$ $A - 6 = 4$

$A = 10$

$$\therefore 5x^2 - x + 4 = 10 - 6(1+x) + 5x(1+x)$$

d i $y = x^2 - 2x$ for $0 \le x \le 4$

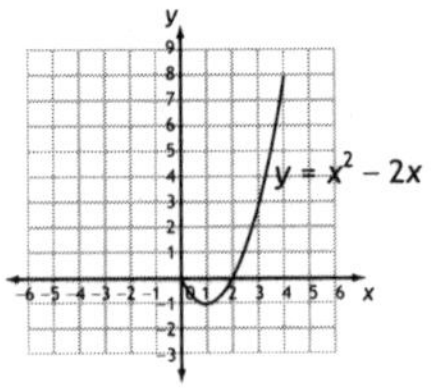

Range: $-1 \le y \le 8$

ii

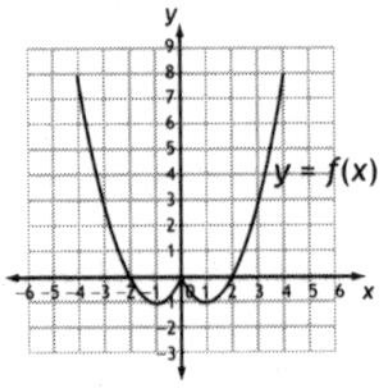

iii

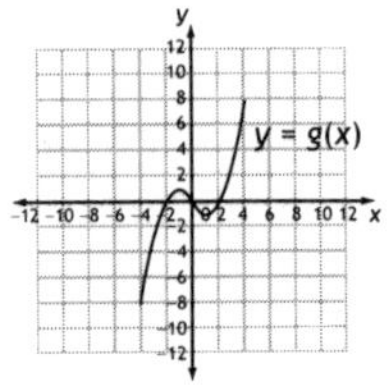

4 a
$$\frac{x^2 - 4x - 12}{x^2 - 4} = \frac{(x-6)(x+2)}{(x+2)(x-2)}$$
$$= \frac{x-6}{x-2}$$

b
$$q^7 = 1.2765$$
$$q = 1.035489814$$
$$= 1.035 \quad \text{[4 sig. figs.]}$$

c $y = x^5 - 2x^4$

$$\frac{dy}{dx} = 5x^4 - 8x^3$$

When $x = 2$, $\dfrac{dy}{dx} = 5 \times 2^4 - 8 \times 2^3$

$= 16$

When $x = 2$, $y = 2^5 - 2 \times 2^4$

$= 0$

continued ...

$m = 16, \ (2, 0)$

$$y - y_1 = m(x - x_1)$$
$$y - 0 = 16(x - 2)$$
$$y = 16x - 32$$

d $\angle SPQ = 180° - 74°$

$= 106°$

$\angle PSQ = 180° - (106 + 47)°$

$= 27°$

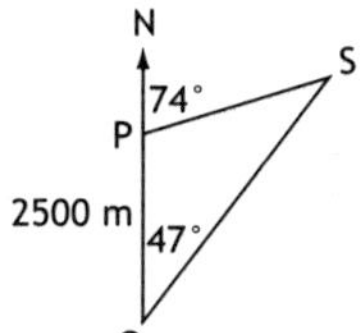

$$\frac{p}{\sin P} = \frac{s}{\sin S}$$
$$\frac{SQ}{\sin 106°} = \frac{2500}{\sin 27°}$$
$$SQ = \frac{2500 \sin 106°}{\sin 27°}$$
$$= 5293.402045$$
$$= 5300 \text{ m} \quad \text{[nearest 100 m]}$$

5 **a** $y = \dfrac{x+4}{x+1}$

$$\frac{dy}{dx} = \frac{v\dfrac{du}{dx} - u\dfrac{dv}{dx}}{v^2}$$
$$= \frac{(x+1)\times 1 - (x+4)\times 1}{(x+1)^2}$$
$$= \frac{x+1-x-4}{(x+1)^2}$$
$$= \frac{-3}{(x+1)^2}$$

When $x = 2$, $\dfrac{dy}{dx} = \dfrac{-3}{(2+1)^2}$

$$= -\frac{1}{3}$$

b

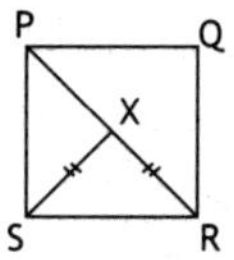

$\angle QRS = 90°$ [angle of a square]

$\angle XRS = 45°$ [diagonals bisect angles]

$\angle XSR = \angle XRS$ [ΔXRS is isosceles]

$\therefore \angle XSR = 45°$

$\angle PXS = \angle XSR + \angle XRS$ [exterior angle of ΔXRS]

$= 45° + 45°$

$= 90°$

c **i** $P(x, y)$, $A(1, -3)$

$$PA^2 = (x_2 - x_1)^2 + (y_2 - y_1)^2$$
$$= (1 - x)^2 + (-3 - y)^2$$

$P(x, y)$, $B(7, 5)$

$$PB^2 = (x_2 - x_1)^2 + (y_2 - y_1)^2$$
$$= (7 - x)^2 + (5 - y)^2$$

ii

$$PA^2 + PB^2 = 100$$
$$(1-x)^2 + (-3-y)^2 + (7-x)^2 + (5-y)^2 = 100$$
$$1 - 2x + x^2 + 9 + 6y + y^2$$
$$+ 49 - 14x + x^2 + 25 - 10y + y^2 = 100$$
$$2x^2 - 16x + 2y^2 - 4y = 16$$
$$x^2 - 8x + y^2 - 2y = 8$$
$$x^2 - 8x + 16 + y^2 - 2y + 1 = 25$$
$$(x-4)^2 + (y-1)^2 = 5^2$$

$\therefore$ the locus is a circle, centre $(4, 1)$ and radius 5 units

6 **a** $\dfrac{1}{u} - \dfrac{2}{u(3-u)} = \dfrac{3-u}{u(3-u)} - \dfrac{2}{u(3-u)}$

$$= \frac{1-u}{u(3-u)}$$

b Let x m be the length of the third side of the paddock.

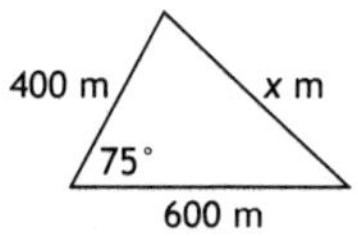

By the cosine rule

$$c^2 = a^2 + b^2 - 2ab\cos C$$
$$x^2 = 400^2 + 600^2 - 2 \times 400 \times 600 \times \cos 75°$$
$$= 395766.8584\ldots$$
$$x = 629.1000384\ldots \quad [x > 0]$$

$\therefore$ side $= 629$ m [nearest metre]

Perimeter $= (400 + 600 + 629)$ m

$= 1629$ m

c **i** $x^2 - 4x - 4 = 8y$

$$x^2 - 4x = 8y + 4$$
$$x^2 - 4x + 4 = 8y + 8$$
$$(x-2)^2 = 8(y+1)$$

Vertex $(2, -1)$

ii $4A = 8$

$A = 2$

Focal length $= 2$ units

d **i** $x^2 + (m+7)x + (m+6) = 0$

$a = 1, b = m + 7, c = m + 6$

$$\Delta = b^2 - 4ac$$
$$= (m+7)^2 - 4 \times 1 \times (m+6)$$
$$= m^2 + 14m + 49 - 4m - 24$$
$$= m^2 + 10m + 25$$

The equation has equal roots when $\Delta = 0$

i.e. $m^2 + 10m + 25 = 0$

$$(m+5)^2 = 0$$
$$m = -5$$

ii Yes, the roots are rational because Δ is a perfect square. $\left[\Delta = (m+5)^2\right]$

7 **a** **i**

$$f(x) = x^2 - x^3$$

$$\begin{aligned} f(x) - f(c) &= x^2 - x^3 - (c^2 - c^3) \\ &= x^2 - x^3 - c^2 + c^3 \\ &= x^2 - c^2 - x^3 + c^3 \\ &= x^2 - c^2 - (x^3 - c^3) \\ &= (x+c)(x-c) - (x-c)(x^2 + cx + c^2) \\ &= (x-c)[(x+c) - (x^2 + cx + c^2)] \end{aligned}$$

ii

$$\begin{aligned} f'(c) &= \lim_{x \to c} \frac{f(x) - f(c)}{x - c} \\ &= \lim_{x \to c} \frac{(x-c)[(x+c) - (x^2 + cx + c^2)]}{x - c} \\ &= \lim_{x \to c}[(x+c) - (x^2 + cx + c^2)] \\ &= c + c - (c^2 + c^2 + c^2) \\ &= 2c - 3c^2 \end{aligned}$$

$\therefore f'(x) = 2x - 3x^2$

b **i** A(2, 3), C(−6, 1)

$$\begin{aligned} M(x, y) &= \left(\frac{x_1 + x_2}{2}, \frac{y_1 + y_2}{2}\right) \\ &= \left(\frac{2 + (-6)}{2}, \frac{3 + 1}{2}\right) \\ &= (-2, 2) \end{aligned}$$

∴ P is the point (−2, 2)

B(4, −1), C(−6, 1)

$$\begin{aligned} M(x, y) &= \left(\frac{x_1 + x_2}{2}, \frac{y_1 + y_2}{2}\right) \\ &= \left(\frac{4 + (-6)}{2}, \frac{-1 + 1}{2}\right) \\ &= (-1, 0) \end{aligned}$$

∴ Q is the point (−1, 0)

ii A(2,3), B(4,−1)

$$\begin{aligned} m_1 &= \frac{y_2 - y_1}{x_2 - x_1} \\ &= \frac{-1 - 3}{4 - 2} \\ &= -2 \end{aligned}$$

P(−2,2), Q(−1,0)

$$\begin{aligned} m_2 &= \frac{y_2 - y_1}{x_2 - x_1} \\ &= \frac{0 - 2}{-1 - (-2)} \\ &= -2 \end{aligned}$$

$\therefore m_1 = m_2$

∴ AB is parallel to PQ

iii A(2, 3), B(4, −1)

$$\begin{aligned} d &= \sqrt{(x_2 - x_1)^2 + (y_2 - y_1)^2} \\ &= \sqrt{(4-2)^2 + (-1-3)^2} \\ &= \sqrt{20} \\ &= \sqrt{4} \times \sqrt{5} \end{aligned}$$

∴ AB = $2\sqrt{5}$ units

iv P(−2, 2), Q(−1, 0)

$$\begin{aligned} d &= \sqrt{(x_2 - x_1)^2 + (y_2 - y_1)^2} \\ &= \sqrt{(-1-(-2))^2 + (0-2)^2} \end{aligned}$$

∴ PQ = $\sqrt{5}$ units

∴ AB is twice the length of PQ

8 **a**

$$\begin{aligned} \lim_{x \to 3} \frac{x^2 - 9}{x^2 - 7x + 12} &= \lim_{x \to 3} \frac{(x-3)(x+3)}{(x-4)(x-3)} \\ &= \lim_{x \to 3} \frac{x+3}{x-4} \\ &= \frac{3+3}{3-4} \\ &= -6 \end{aligned}$$

b **i** $y = 2x^2 - 8x + 11$

Axis of symmetry: $x = -\frac{b}{2a}$

$$x = -\frac{-8}{2 \times 2}$$

$$x = 2$$

ii When $x = 2$, $y = 2 \times 2^2 - 8 \times 2 + 11$
$= 3$

∴ the vertex is at (2,3)

iii The equation has no real roots. The least value of the parabola is 3.

c

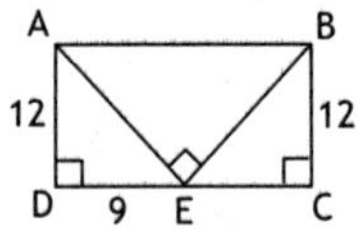

i In △ADE, △ECB,

∠ADE = ∠ECB = 90° [ABCD is a rectangle]

∠EBC + 90° + ∠BEC = 180° [angle sum of △BEC]

∠DEA + 90° + ∠BEC = 180° [angles on a straight line]

∴ ∠DEA = ∠EBC

∴ △ADE ||| △ECB

ii AD = BC = 12 cm, DE = 9 cm

$\frac{EC}{AD} = \frac{BC}{DE}$ [corresponding sides of similar triangles]

$$\begin{aligned} \frac{EC}{12} &= \frac{12}{9} \\ EC &= \frac{12}{9} \times 12 \\ &= 16 \text{ cm} \\ DC &= 9 + 16 \\ &= 25 \text{ cm} \\ A &= lb \\ &= 25 \times 12 \end{aligned}$$

∴ area = 300 cm^2

9 **a** **i**

$$x^2 + y^2 = 1$$
$$x^2 + \left(\frac{1}{2}\right)^2 = 1$$
$$x^2 + \frac{1}{4} = 1$$
$$x^2 = \frac{3}{4}$$
$$x = \pm\sqrt{\frac{3}{4}}$$
$$= \pm\frac{\sqrt{3}}{2}$$

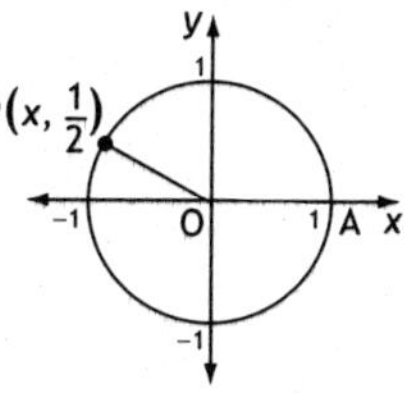

But P lies in the 2nd quadrant, so x is negative.

$$x = -\frac{\sqrt{3}}{2}$$

ii $\tan\angle POA = \frac{y}{x}$

$$= \frac{\frac{1}{2}}{-\frac{\sqrt{3}}{2}}$$
$$= \frac{1}{2} \times -\frac{2}{\sqrt{3}}$$
$$= -\frac{1}{\sqrt{3}}$$

b

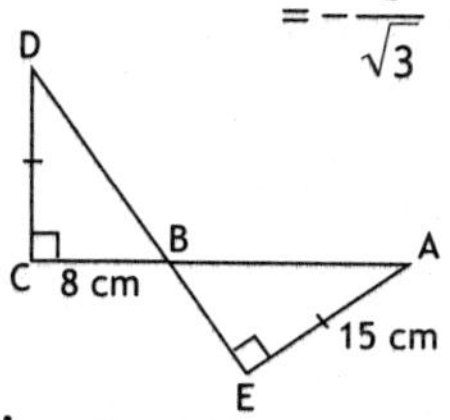

i In ΔDCB, ΔAEB,

$\angle DCB = \angle AEB$	[both 90°, given]
$\angle DBC = \angle ABE$	[vertically opposite]
$DC = AE$	[given]
$\therefore \Delta DCB \equiv \Delta AEB$	[AAS]

ii $BE = BC$

[corresponding sides of congruent triangles]

$\therefore BE = 8$ cm

$$DB^2 = DC^2 + BC^2$$
$$= 15^2 + 8^2$$
$$= 289$$

$DB = 17$ cm $[DB > 0]$

$DE = 17$ cm $+ 8$ cm

$= 25$ cm

c $f(x) = \begin{cases} ax + b & \text{for } x < 2 \\ bx - a & \text{for } 2 \le x \le 4 \\ x^2 - 4x & \text{for } x > 4 \end{cases}$

i $f(-3) = f(2) = f(5)$

$$f(5) = 5^2 - 4 \times 5$$
$$= 5$$

continued ...

$$f(-3) = a \times -3 + b$$
$$= -3a + b$$

but $f(-3) = f(5)$

$\therefore -3a + b = 5$

$b = 5 + 3a$ **i**

$$f(2) = b \times 2 - a$$
$$= 2b - a$$

but $f(2) = f(5)$

$\therefore 2b - a = 5$ **ii**

Substitute **i** into **ii**

$$2(5 + 3a) - a = 5$$
$$10 + 5a = 5$$
$$5a = -5$$
$$a = -1$$

Substitute into **i**

$$b = 5 + 3 \times -1$$
$$= 2$$

$\therefore a = -1$ and $b = 2$

ii $f(x) = \begin{cases} -x + 2 & \text{for } x < 2 \\ 2x + 1 & \text{for } 2 \le x \le 4 \\ x^2 - 4x & \text{for } x > 4 \end{cases}$

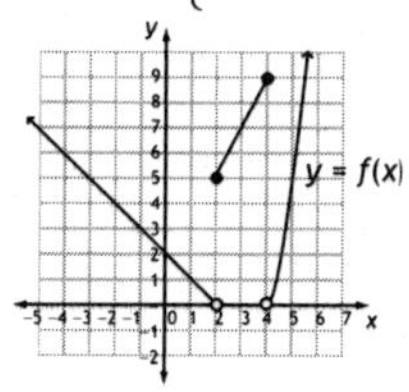

10 **a**

$$(x + 6)^2 = (x - 3)^2 + (x + 4)^2$$
$$x^2 + 12x + 36 = x^2 - 6x + 9 + x^2 + 8x + 16$$
$$x^2 + 12x + 36 = 2x^2 + 2x + 25$$
$$x^2 - 10x - 11 = 0$$
$$(x - 11)(x + 1) = 0$$

$x - 11 = 0$ or $x + 1 = 0$

$x = 11$ $\quad x = -1$

But if $x = -1$, a side measures -4 units.

$\therefore x = 11$ is the only solution

b

$$x(x + 3) \le 4$$
$$x^2 + 3x \le 4$$
$$x^2 + 3x - 4 \le 0$$

Let $y = x^2 + 3x - 4$

$= (x + 4)(x - 1)$

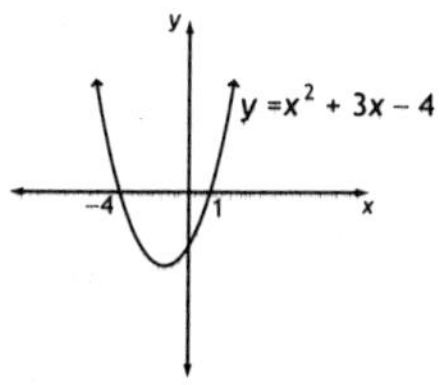

From the graph, $y \le 0$ when $-4 \le x \le 1$

$\therefore x(x + 3) \le 4$ when $-4 \le x \le 1$

c **i** $\cos^2\theta - \sin^2\theta = (1 - \sin^2\theta) - \sin^2\theta$

$= 1 - 2\sin^2\theta$

ii $\cos^2\theta - \sin^2\theta = \frac{1}{2}$

$1 - 2\sin^2\theta = \frac{1}{2}$

continued ...

$$2\sin^2\theta = \tfrac{1}{2}$$
$$\sin^2\theta = \tfrac{1}{4}$$
$$\sin\theta = \pm\tfrac{1}{2}$$

Now $\sin 30° = \tfrac{1}{2}$

$\therefore \theta = 30°, (180-30)°, (180+30)°$ or $(360-30)°$

$= 30°, 150°, 210°$ or $330°$

Sample Examination Paper Three

1 **a** $780 \text{ million} = 780\,000\,000$

$= 7.8 \times 10^8$

b $(7x-1)-(3x-8) = 7x-1-3x+8$

$= 4x+7$

c $100\% - 12.5\% = 87.5\%$

$87.5\% = \$1484$

$1\% = \$16.96$

$100\% = \$1696$

$\therefore$ the full price is \$1696

d $m = \dfrac{2k}{3-t}$

When $m = 9$ and $t = 2\tfrac{3}{4}$

$9 = \dfrac{2k}{3-2\frac{3}{4}}$

$9 = \dfrac{2k}{\frac{1}{4}}$

$9 = 8k$

$k = \dfrac{9}{8}$

$= 1\tfrac{1}{8}$

e $2|-2|-4|7| = 2\times 2 - 4\times 7$

$= -24$

f $\dfrac{1}{\sqrt{3}-2} = \dfrac{1}{\sqrt{3}-2}\times\dfrac{\sqrt{3}+2}{\sqrt{3}+2}$

$= \dfrac{\sqrt{3}+2}{3-4}$

$= -(\sqrt{3}+2)$

$= -\sqrt{3}-2$

$\sqrt{3}-2+\dfrac{1}{\sqrt{3}-2} = \sqrt{3}-2-\sqrt{3}-2$

$= -4$

$\therefore \sqrt{3}-2+\dfrac{1}{\sqrt{3}-2}$ is rational

2 **a** $p = 3q^7 - q^9$

$\dfrac{dp}{dq} = 21q^6 - 9q^8$

b $ax^2+bx+c=0$ has solutions for $x=0$, $x=1$ and $x=2$

$\therefore a = b = c = 0$

[A quadratic equation has solutions for at most two values of x.]

c $\dfrac{7x-21}{x^2-9}\times\dfrac{x^2-9x}{x^2-7x-18}$

$= \dfrac{7(x-3)}{(x-3)(x+3)}\times\dfrac{x(x-9)}{(x-9)(x+2)}$

$= \dfrac{7x}{(x+3)(x+2)}$

d **i** $\theta = 135°$, y-intercept $= 5$

$m = \tan\theta$

$= \tan 135°$

$= -1$

$\therefore$ the equation is $y = -x+5$

$l_1: x+y-5=0$

ii $7x+y+8=0$

Parallel lines are of the form $7x+y+k=0$

$(15,2)$ lies on this line

$7\times 15+2+k=0$

$107+k=0$

$k=-107$

$\therefore 7x+y-107=0$ is the required equation

iii $P(7,8)$, $l_1: x+y-5=0$

$a=1, b=1, c=-5$

$d = \left|\dfrac{ax_1+by_1+c}{\sqrt{a^2+b^2}}\right|$

$= \left|\dfrac{1\times 7+1\times 8+(-5)}{\sqrt{1^2+1^2}}\right|$

$= \left|\dfrac{10}{\sqrt{2}}\right|$

$= \dfrac{10}{\sqrt{2}}\times\dfrac{\sqrt{2}}{\sqrt{2}}$

$\therefore$ distance $= 5\sqrt{2}$ units

$P(7,8)$, $l_2: 7x+y-107=0$

$a=7, b=1, c=-107$

$d = \left|\dfrac{ax_1+by_1+c}{\sqrt{a^2+b^2}}\right|$

$= \left|\dfrac{7\times 7+1\times 8+(-107)}{\sqrt{7^2+1^2}}\right|$

$= \left|\dfrac{-50}{\sqrt{50}}\right|$

$= \dfrac{50}{5\sqrt{2}}$

$= \dfrac{10}{\sqrt{2}}$

$\therefore$ distance $= 5\sqrt{2}$ units

$\therefore$ P is equidistant from l_1 and l_2

3 **a** 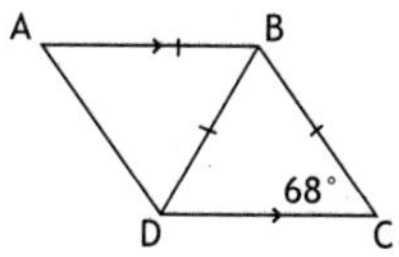

ΔBDC is isosceles [BC = BD, given]

$\therefore \angle BDC = 68°$

$\angle ABD = 68°$ [alternate, AB || DC]

$\angle BAD + \angle ADB + \angle ABD = 180°$

[angle sum of a triangle]

$\therefore \angle BAD + \angle ADB = 180° - 68°$

$= 112°$

but $\angle BAD = \angle ADB$

[base angles of isosceles triangle]

$\therefore \angle BAD = 112° \div 2$

$= 56°$

b **i** 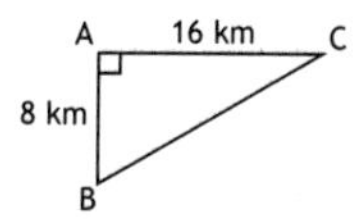

ii $\tan C = \dfrac{8}{16}$

$C = 26.56505118\ldots°$

$= 27°$ [nearest degree]

A is due west of C

$\therefore$ the bearing of A from C is 270°

$\therefore$ the bearing of B from C is $270° - 27° = 243°$

c **i** 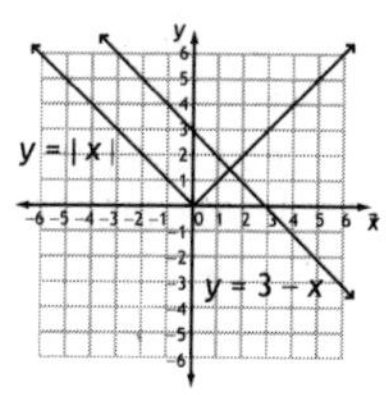

ii Point of intersection is (1.5, 1.5)

d Focus $(-4, 3)$, vertex $(-1, 3)$, axis: $y = 3$

Focal length $= -1 - (-4)$

$= 3$ units

$\therefore A = 3$

The focus is 3 units left of the vertex.

$\therefore$ the equation is of the form:

$(y - y_0)^2 = -4A(x - x_0)$

$\therefore\ (y - 3)^2 = -12(x + 1)$ is the equation of the parabola

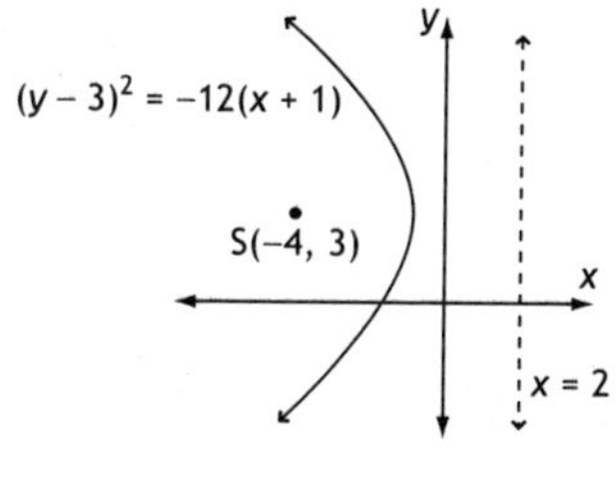

4 **a** $0.2\dot{1}\dot{3} = 0.213\,131\,313\,131\ldots$

Let $x = 0.213\,131\,313\,131\ldots$

$100x = 21.313\,131\,313\,131\ldots$

$99x = 21.1$

$x = \dfrac{21.1}{99}$

$x = \dfrac{211}{990}$

$\therefore 0.2\dot{1}\dot{3} = \dfrac{211}{990}$

b $9x^2 - 6x + 2 = 0$

$a = 9, b = -6, c = 2$

$\alpha + \beta = -\dfrac{b}{a}$ $\qquad \alpha\beta = \dfrac{c}{a}$

$= -\dfrac{-6}{9}$ $\qquad = \dfrac{2}{9}$

$= \dfrac{2}{3}$

$\alpha^2 + \beta^2 = (\alpha + \beta)^2 - 2\alpha\beta$

$= \left(\dfrac{2}{3}\right)^2 - 2\left(\dfrac{2}{9}\right)$

$= 0$

c 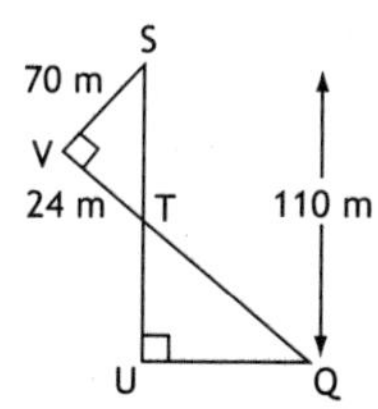

i In ΔSTV, ΔQTU,

$\angle SVT = \angle QUT$ [both 90°, given]

$\angle STV = \angle QTU$ [vertically opposite]

$\therefore \Delta STV \,|||\, \Delta QTU$

ii In ΔSVT,

$ST^2 = SV^2 + VT^2$

$= 70^2 + 24^2$

$= 5476$

$ST = 74$ m [ST > 0]

$TU = 110 - 74$

$= 36$ m

$\dfrac{TQ}{ST} = \dfrac{TU}{VT}$ [corresponding sides of similar triangles]

$\dfrac{TQ}{74} = \dfrac{36}{24}$

$TQ = \dfrac{36 \times 74}{24}$

$= 111$ m

$VQ = 24 + 111$

$= 135$ m

5 **a** $f(x) = \dfrac{x^2+1}{x}$

$$f\left(\frac{1}{x}\right) = \frac{\left(\frac{1}{x}\right)^2 + 1}{\frac{1}{x}}$$

$$= \left(\frac{1}{x^2} + 1\right) \times \frac{x}{1}$$

$$= \frac{1}{x} + x$$

$$= \frac{1+x^2}{x}$$

$$= f(x)$$

b **i** $\angle CAB = 180° - (90+45)°$

$= 45°$

$\therefore \Delta ACB$ is isosceles

$\therefore \quad CB = 1$ m

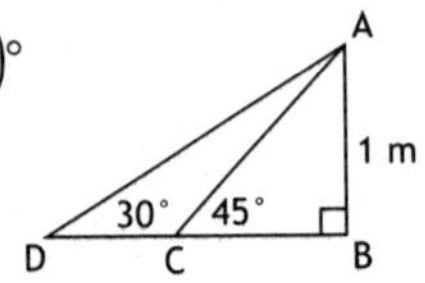

$\angle DAB = 180° - (90+30)°$

$= 60°$

$\tan 60° = \dfrac{DB}{AB}$

$DB = \tan 60°$

$= \sqrt{3}$

$DC = DB - CB$

$= \left(\sqrt{3} - 1\right)$ m

ii $\sin 45° = \dfrac{1}{\sqrt{2}}$

$\therefore \; AC = \sqrt{2}$ m

$\angle DAC = 60° - 45°$

$= 15°$

In ΔADC,

$$\frac{\sin A}{a} = \frac{\sin D}{d}$$

$$\frac{\sin 15°}{\sqrt{3}-1} = \frac{\sin 30°}{\sqrt{2}}$$

$$= \frac{\frac{1}{2}}{\sqrt{2}}$$

$$= \frac{1}{2\sqrt{2}}$$

$$\sin 15° = \frac{\sqrt{3}-1}{2\sqrt{2}}$$

c **i** $f(x) = x^4$

$$f(x) - f(c) = x^4 - c^4$$

$$= \left(x^2+c^2\right)\left(x^2-c^2\right)$$

$$= \left(x^2+c^2\right)(x+c)(x-c)$$

ii $f'(c) = \lim\limits_{x \to c} \dfrac{f(x) - f(c)}{x - c}$

$$= \lim_{x \to c} \frac{x^4 - c^4}{x - c}$$

$$= \lim_{x \to c} \frac{\left(x^2+c^2\right)(x+c)(x-c)}{x-c}$$

$$= \lim_{x \to c}\left[\left(x^2+c^2\right)(x+c)\right]$$

$$= \left(c^2+c^2\right)(c+c)$$

$$= \left(2c^2\right)(2c)$$

$$= 4c^3$$

$$\therefore f'(x) = 4x^3$$

6 **a** $13^{-1.5} = 0.021334622\ldots$

$= 0.021$ [3 decimal places]

b **i** $f(x) = x^3$

$f'(x) = 3x^2$

ii

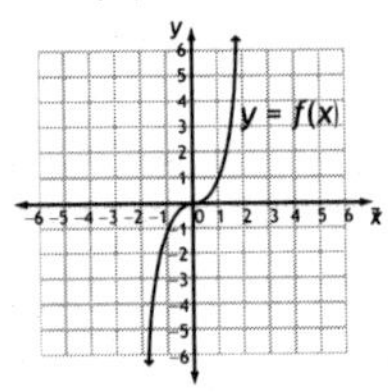

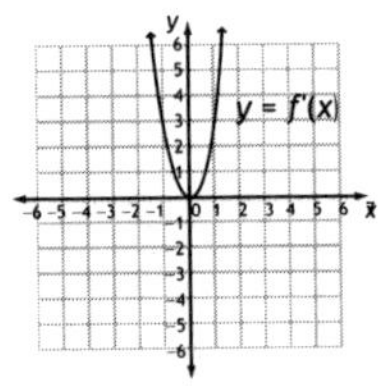

iii The graph of $y = f'(x)$ shows the gradient of the curve $y = f(x)$ at each point. When the curve is negative $f'(x)$ is decreasing and when the curve is positive $f'(x)$ is increasing. The curve increases except when $x = 0$. The gradient is always positive except when $x = 0$, when it is zero.

c **i**

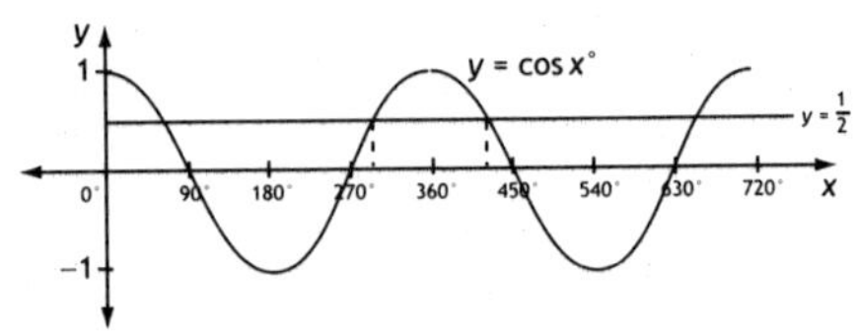

ii From the graph, $\cos x° = \frac{1}{2}$ when $x = 60°$, $300°$, $420°$ and $660°$.

7 **a**

$$5x^2 = 2x + 3$$

$$5x^2 - 2x - 3 = 0$$

$$5x^2 - 5x + 3x - 3 = 0$$

$$5x(x-1) + 3(x-1) = 0$$

$$(x-1)(5x+3) = 0$$

$x - 1 = 0$ or $5x + 3 = 0$

$x = 1$ $\quad 5x = -3$

$x = 1$ $\quad x = -0.6$

b **i** $f(x) = \sqrt{4 - x^2}$

Domain: $-2 \le x \le 2$

Range: $0 \le y \le 2$

ii

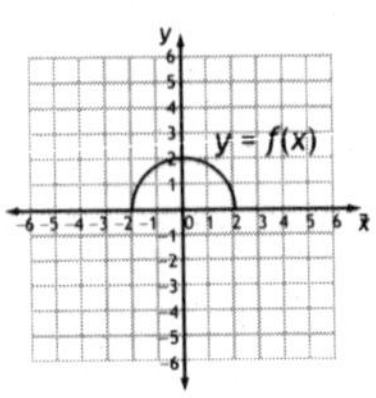

c $x^2 + (p+2)x + p = 0$

$a = 1, b = p+2, c = p$

$\Delta = b^2 - 4ac$

$= (p+2)^2 - 4 \times 1 \times p$

$= p^2 + 4p + 4 - 4p$

$= p^2 + 4$

Now $p^2 \geq 0$ for all real values of p

$\therefore p^2 + 4 \geq 4$ for all real values of p

i.e. $\Delta > 0$ for all real p

$\therefore$ the equation has real roots for all real values of p

d $y = x^2 - 5x$

$\frac{dy}{dx} = 2x - 5$

but $m = -3$

$\therefore$ at the point of contact $2x - 5 = -3$

$2x = 2$

$x = 1$

When $x = 1$, $y = 1^2 - 5 \times 1$

$= -4$

$\therefore$ the point of contact is $(1, -4)$

8 **a** **i** $y = \frac{1}{2}x^2 - 2x - 1$

$2y = x^2 - 4x - 2$

$x^2 - 4x = 2y + 2$

$x^2 - 4x + 4 = 2y + 6$

$(x-2)^2 = 2(y+3)$

The locus is a parabola, vertex $(2, -3)$

Axis: $x = 2$

$4A = 2$

$A = \frac{1}{2}$

The focal length is $\frac{1}{2}$ unit

$\therefore$ the fixed point, the focus, is at $\left(2, -2\frac{1}{2}\right)$

ii The fixed line is the directrix: $y = -3\frac{1}{2}$

b **i** $\angle ABC = \angle BCD = 90°$

[angles of a square]

$\angle EBC = \angle BCE = 60°$

[angles of equilateral Δ]

$\therefore \angle ABE = \angle DCE = 30°$

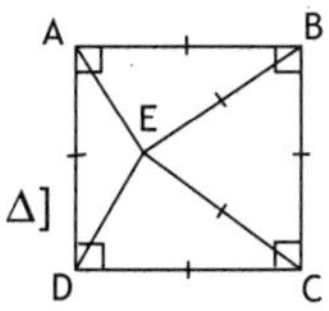

ii In ΔABE, ΔDCE,

$AB = DC$	[sides of a square]
$\angle ABE = \angle DCE$	[both 30°]
$BE = CE$	[sides of equilateral Δ]
$\therefore \Delta ABE \equiv \Delta DCE$	[SAS]

iii $AE = ED$

[corresponding sides of congruent triangles]

$\therefore \Delta AED$ is isosceles

iv $AB = BC$ [sides of a square]

$BE = BC$ [sides of equilateral Δ]

$\therefore AB = BE$

$\therefore \angle BAE = \angle BEA$

$\angle BAE + \angle BEA + \angle ABE = 180°$

[angle sum of ΔABE]

$2\angle BAE + 30° = 180°$

$\angle BAE = 75°$

$\angle BAD = 90°$ [angle of square]

$\angle EAD = 90° - 75°$

$= 15°$

$\therefore \angle EDA = 15°$

[base angles of isosceles Δ]

$\angle AED = 180° - 2 \times 15°$

[angle sum of ΔAED]

$= 150°$

9 **a** $\tan x + \sqrt{3} = 0$

$\tan x = -\sqrt{3}$

Now $\tan 60° = \sqrt{3}$

tan is negative in the 2nd and 4th quadrants

$\therefore x = (180 - 60)°$ or $(360 - 60)°$

$= 120°$ or $300°$

b

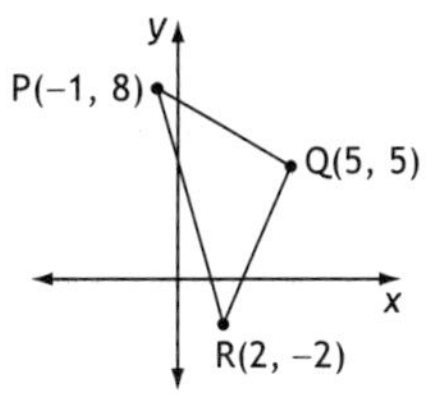

i $Q(5, 5)$, $R(2, -2)$

$d = \sqrt{(x_2 - x_1)^2 + (y_2 - y_1)^2}$

$= \sqrt{(2-5)^2 + (-2-5)^2}$

$\therefore QR = \sqrt{58}$ units

ii $Q(5, 5)$, $R(2, -2)$

$\frac{y - y_1}{x - x_1} = \frac{y_2 - y_1}{x_2 - x_1}$

$\frac{y - 5}{x - 5} = \frac{-2 - 5}{2 - 5}$

$\frac{y - 5}{x - 5} = \frac{7}{3}$

$3(y - 5) = 7(x - 5)$

$3y - 15 = 7x - 35$

$7x - 3y - 20 = 0$

iii $P(-1, 8)$, $7x - 3y - 20 = 0$

$a = 7, b = -3, c = -20$

$d = \left|\frac{ax_1 + by_1 + c}{\sqrt{a^2 + b^2}}\right|$

$= \left|\frac{7 \times -1 + -3 \times 8 + (-20)}{\sqrt{7^2 + (-3)^2}}\right|$

continued ...

$$= \left|\frac{-51}{\sqrt{58}}\right|$$

$$= \frac{51}{\sqrt{58}} \times \frac{\sqrt{58}}{\sqrt{58}}$$

$$\therefore \text{distance} = \frac{51\sqrt{58}}{58} \text{ units}$$

iv

$$A = \tfrac{1}{2}bh$$

$$= \tfrac{1}{2} \times \sqrt{58} \times \frac{51}{\sqrt{58}}$$

$$\therefore \text{area} = 25.5 \text{ units}^2$$

10 a i

$$y = \frac{1}{x}$$

$$= x^{-1}$$

$$\frac{dy}{dx} = -x^{-2}$$

$$= -\frac{1}{x^2}$$

ii

$$y = x\sqrt{x}$$

$$= x \times x^{\frac{1}{2}}$$

$$= x^{\frac{3}{2}}$$

$$\frac{dy}{dx} = \frac{3}{2}x^{\frac{1}{2}}$$

$$= \frac{3\sqrt{x}}{2}$$

b i $P(x, y)$, $Q(1, -2)$

$$PQ^2 = (x_2 - x_1)^2 + (y_2 - y_1)^2$$

$$= (1 - x)^2 + (-2 - y)^2$$

$P(x, y)$, $R(7, 4)$

$$PR^2 = (x_2 - x_1)^2 + (y_2 - y_1)^2$$

$$= (7 - x)^2 + (4 - y)^2$$

ii

$$PQ^2 = PR^2$$

$$(1 - x)^2 + (-2 - y)^2 = (7 - x)^2 + (4 - y)^2$$

$$1 - 2x + x^2 + 4 + 4y + y^2$$

$$= 49 - 14x + x^2 + 16 - 8y + y^2$$

$$12x + 12y - 60 = 0$$

$$x + y - 5 = 0$$

The locus is a straight line.

It is the perpendicular bisector of QR.

iii

$$PQ = 2PR$$

$$PQ^2 = 4PR^2$$

$$(1 - x)^2 + (-2 - y)^2 = 4\left[(7 - x)^2 + (4 - y)^2\right]$$

$$1 - 2x + x^2 + 4 + 4y + y^2$$

$$= 4\left(49 - 14x + x^2 + 16 - 8y + y^2\right)$$

$$x^2 - 2x + y^2 + 4y + 5$$

$$= 4x^2 - 56x + 4y^2 - 32y + 260$$

$$3x^2 - 54x + 3y^2 - 36y + 255 = 0$$

$$x^2 - 18x + y^2 - 12y + 85 = 0$$

$$x^2 - 18x + 81 + y^2 - 12y + 36 = 32$$

$$(x - 9)^2 + (y - 6)^2 = \left(4\sqrt{2}\right)^2$$

This is the equation of a circle, centre $(9, 6)$, radius $4\sqrt{2}$ units

Quick Answers to Exercises

Basic Arithmetic and Algebra

1 a $\frac{3}{7}$ b $\frac{4}{9}$

2 a $\frac{7}{9}$ b $\frac{3}{4}$ c $\frac{2}{5}$ d $\frac{1}{2}$

3 a $\frac{5}{32}$ b $\frac{6}{11}$ c $\frac{1}{6}$

4 a $1\frac{2}{5}$ b $\frac{3}{13}$

5 a $\frac{8}{9}$ b $1\frac{1}{4}$ c $7\frac{1}{2}$

6 a 1.1 b 5.36 c 0.0006 d 100

7 a $\frac{12}{25}$ b $\frac{107}{500}$ c $\frac{1}{1250}$ d $5\frac{9}{20}$

8 a 0.875 b $0.91\dot{6}$ c $0.8\dot{3}$ d $0.\dot{0}\dot{9}$

9 a $\frac{8}{9}$ b $\frac{14}{33}$ c $7\frac{79}{333}$ d $\frac{23}{450}$

10 a $\frac{63}{100}$ b $\frac{1}{5}$ c $\frac{2}{25}$ d $\frac{7}{8}$

11 a 0.16 b 0.04 c 9 d 0.0375

12 a 76% b 37.5% c $16\frac{2}{3}$%

13 a 56% b 107% c 1.25%

14 $202.50

15 25%

16 17 890 000

17 a 390 625 b 0.000 729
c 0.0625 d 0.015 625

18 a 8.76 b 11

19 a 0.0025 b $5\frac{19}{25}$ c $5\frac{1}{16}$ d 1.2
e $3\frac{1}{3}$

20 a 5×10^4 b 4.67×10^7 c 3.12×10^3
d 7×10^{-6} e 6.1839×10^{-5}

21 a 30 000 b 5 180 000 000
c 0.000 062 5 d 0.001

22 4.94×10^{11}

23 a 5.24 b 19.22 c 0.68

24 a 2.418 b 345.219 c 10.000

25 a 251 600 000 b 13.24
c 0.030 85 d 0.009 818

26 a 8.57×10^9 b 1.48×10^{-4}

27 126.1442

28 a 1.8 b 14.3 c 3.8

29 $\frac{1}{6}$

30 a $8p^2 - 3p$ b $7k^2 - 8k^3 + 2k - 2$

31 a $120abc$ b $27x^4$ c $32t^{12}$ d $6x^6y^7$

32 a 5 b $3t^4$ c $7a^2b$ d $\frac{2m^3}{3n^3}$

33 a $16a^{10}$ b x^9y^{12} c $7c^6d^{14}$ d $81a^8b^{12}c^{16}$

34 a $24x - 3y$ b $3e^3 - 5e^2 + 7e$
c $-10x + 55y - 5z$ d $4x^3 - 12x$
e $2p^5q^{10} + 10p^6q^6$ f $-7 + 8u$

35 a $6m - 4$ b $53e^2 - 49e - 16$
c $12n^2 + 19n - 3$

36 a $a^2 - a - 20$ b $b^2 - 7b + 6$
c $16p^2 + 46pq + 15q^2$ d $7xy + 14xz - y^2 - 2yz$

37 a $6t^2 + 17t + 56$ b $8 - 3n - 8n^2$

38 $2p^2 + 19p + 67$

39 a $2k^3 + 21k^2 + 29k + 3$ b $a^2 + 8a - b^2 + 2b + 15$

40 a $e^2 - 16e + 64$ b $25m^2 + 20mn + 4n^2$
c $a^4 - 14a^2b + 49b^2$

41 a $a^2 + 10a + 25$ b $b^2 - 16b + 64$
c $25c^2 + 20c + 4$ d $16d^2 - 24de + 9e^2$

42 a $y^2 - 49$ b $9k^2 - 64$
c $x^4 - 25y^2$

43 a $2u^2 + 8u + 7$ b $5k^2 + 12k - 34$

44 a $y = -2$ b $y = 2$ c $y = -4$

45 $r = 950$

46 $y = 4$

47 $A = 361.283$

48 −29

49 $a = 27$

50 a $7(k + 4)$ b $h(h - 8)$
c $4(4x + 3y - 9z)$ d $5n(n + 5m)$
e $a^3b^6(b - a)$

51 a $(e - 10)(e + 10)$ b $(1 - r)(1 + r)$
c $(8p - 11q)(8p + 11q)$ d $(g^2 - 3hk)(g^2 + 3hk)$

52 a $(q + 6)(p + r)$ b $(z + 7)(z + y)$
c $(m - 3)(m + 2n)$ d $(x + y)(x + 1)$

53 a $(b - 9)(a - 7)$ b $(p + q)(p - m)$

54 a $(x + 4)(x + 3)$ b $(g + 11)(g - 8)$
c $(k - 5)(k - 4)$ d $(c - 7d)(c + 5d)$

55 a $(x+2)(2x+5)$ b $(x+8)(3x-1)$
c $(a-5)(4a-3)$ d $(2n-3)(3n+2)$

56 a $(a-3)(a^2+3a+9)$ b $(h+10)(h^2-10h+100)$
c $(2-5k)(4+10k+25k^2)$
d $(4p+7q)(16p^2-28pq+49q^2)$

57 a $(x-3)(x+3)$ b $x(x-9)$
c $(x+9)(x-1)$ d $x^2(x+8)$
e $(x-2)(x^2+2x+4)$ f $(x+1)(x^2+1)$

58 a $3(c-10)(c+10)$ b $7(y+1)(y^2-y+1)$
c $5(h-5)(h+1)$ d $(m-2)(m+2)(m^2+4)$
e $(k-3)(k+3+7m)$ f $p(q+3)(r-5)$

59 a $7\sqrt{6}$ b $5\sqrt{3}-8\sqrt{2}$ c $7\sqrt{11}$
d 0 e $6-2\sqrt{7}+7\sqrt{2}$

60 a $\sqrt{30}$ b $8\sqrt{30}$ c 7 d 50
e 126 f $\sqrt{3}$ g 3 h $3\sqrt{2}$

61 a $2\sqrt{7}$ b $3\sqrt{5}$ c $10\sqrt{3}$ d $5\sqrt{3}$
e $6\sqrt{10}$

62 a $\sqrt{175}$ b $\sqrt{486}$

63 a 6 b $5\sqrt{6}$ c $12\sqrt{3}$

64 a $13\sqrt{2}$ b $3\sqrt{6}-2\sqrt{5}$ c $16\sqrt{2}$

65 a $\sqrt{21}+\sqrt{14}+\sqrt{15}+\sqrt{10}$
b $\sqrt{22}-7\sqrt{11}-9\sqrt{2}+63$
c $9\sqrt{3}-6\sqrt{15}+24-16\sqrt{5}$
d $72+8\sqrt{6}-45\sqrt{2}-10\sqrt{3}$

66 a $13+2\sqrt{30}$ b $29-8\sqrt{13}$ c $42+24\sqrt{3}$

67 a 1 b −4 c 222 d 47

68 $8+6\sqrt{7}$

70 a $\frac{\sqrt{2}}{2}$ b $\sqrt{11}$ c $\frac{\sqrt{6}}{3}$ d $\frac{3\sqrt{5}}{10}$

71 a $\sqrt{3}+\sqrt{2}$ b $\frac{5-\sqrt{21}}{2}$
c $7(\sqrt{5}-2)$ d $\frac{3\sqrt{30}+\sqrt{10}+3\sqrt{6}+\sqrt{2}}{52}$

73 a $a=-3$ and $b=6$

74 a $a-2b$ b $\frac{5}{1-2m}$ c $\frac{2}{3}$ d $h-5$
e $\frac{n+1}{n}$ f $\frac{1}{d-8}$ g $\frac{e-3}{e+3}$ h $\frac{x+1}{x-7}$

75 a $\frac{9e}{11}$ b $\frac{h}{2}$ c $\frac{62d}{63}$ d $\frac{3u+4}{v}$
e $\frac{19m-27}{15}$

76 a $\frac{z}{12}$ b $\frac{a-b}{a}$
c $\frac{11k+101}{63}$ d $\frac{7m-35}{30}$

77 a $\frac{2}{(x+3)(x+4)(x+5)}$ b $\frac{3(a^2-a-1)}{a(a-1)(a+1)}$

78 a $\frac{5x}{3x+7}$ b 1

79 a $\frac{u}{u+8}$ b $\frac{(z+4)^2}{(z-3)(z+9)}$

80 a $m=7$ b $k=320$
c $j=-3\frac{2}{3}$ d $e=-22$

81 a $w=1.5$ b $n=3\frac{1}{3}$
c $b=-7\frac{3}{14}$ d $v=-1.5$

82 a $k=14\frac{2}{3}$ b $a=5$
c $u=-1\frac{13}{70}$ d $n=32.5$

83 a $a>-2$ b $m\geq 25$ c $k<10\frac{1}{3}$ d $p\leq -2$

84 a $x<1$ b $w\geq 114$ c $x>17$ d $e\leq -3$

85 a
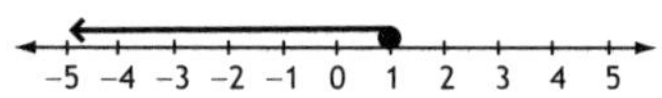
b
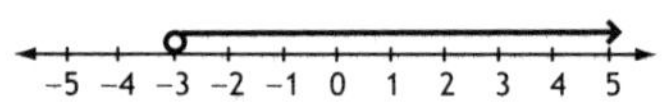

86 a $x\leq -1$
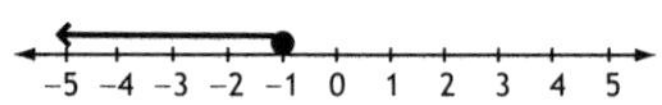
b $x<4$
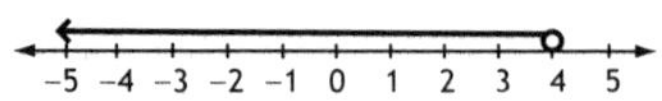

87 a 12 b 12 c 10 d 10
e 5 f 5 g 16 h 2

88 a 5 b 5 c −5 d 24
e −1

89 a
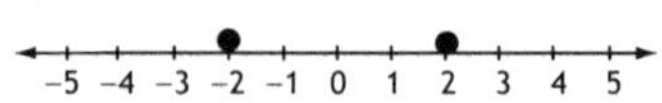
b
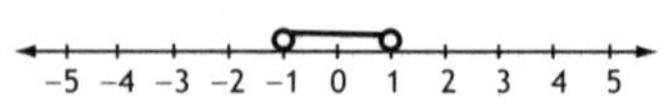
c
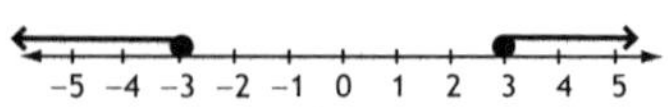
d
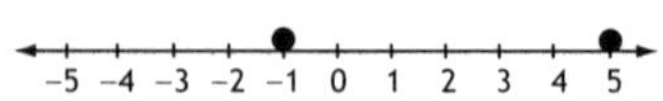
e
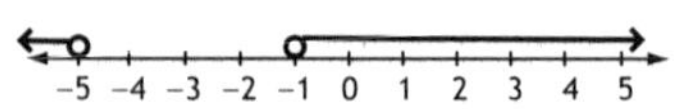

90 a 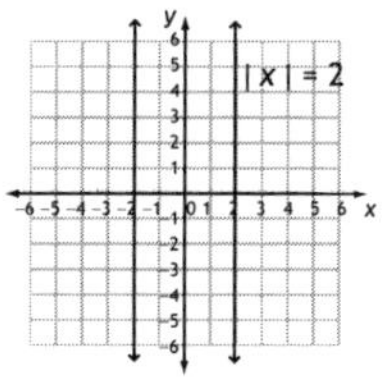

b 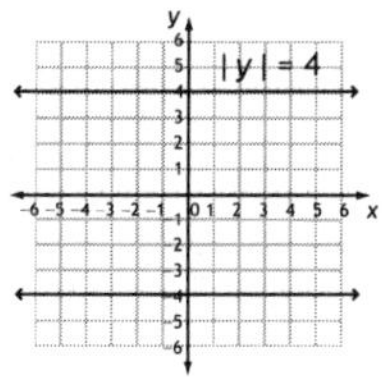

c 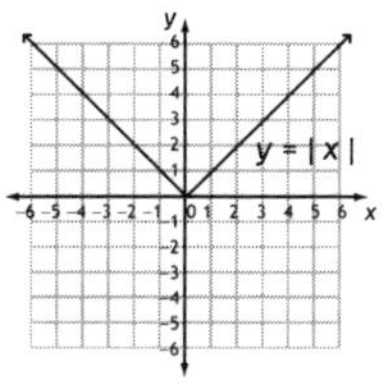

91 a $x = -4$ or $x = 4$ b $x = -4$ or $x = 6$
c $x = \frac{1}{3}$ or $x = 1$

92 a $-3 \le x \le 3$ b $x < 0$ or $x > 4$
c $-4 < x < 2$ d $x \le \frac{1}{2}$ or $x \ge 1$

93 a $x = 8$ or $x = 2$ b $u = -8$ or $u = -5$
c $n = 1\frac{1}{2}$ or $n = -5$ d $a = 3\frac{1}{2}$ or $a = 2\frac{1}{2}$

94 a $x = 0$ or $x = 7$ b $g = 4$ or $g = 8$
c $k = -12$ or $k = 2$ d $x = -\frac{3}{7}$ or $x = 4$

95 a $m = -10$ or $m = 0$ b $e = \frac{4 \pm \sqrt{2}}{3}$

96 a $x = 7.5414$ or $x = 1.4586$
b $x = 0.5565$ or $x = -2.1565$

97 a $x = \frac{-11 \pm \sqrt{73}}{2}$ b $x = \frac{4 \pm \sqrt{22}}{2}$

98 a $x = -3$ and $y = 1$ b $x = 5$ and $y = 3$

99 a $p = 2$ and $q = -3$ b $a = -1$ and $b = 5$

100 a $y = -3$ and $z = 7$ b $g = 3$ and $h = 4$

Plane Geometry

1 a $x = 34$
2 a $x = 131$ b $x = 33$
3 48°
4 40°, 60° and 80°
5 a $x = 52$ b $x = 23$
6 ∠QTR = 104°, ∠RTS = 76°, ∠STP = 104°
7 a $x = 324$ b $x = 145$ c $x = 270$ d $x = 170$
8 76°
9 a $x = 118$ b $x = 138$ c $x = 111$
10 86°
11 26°
12 118°
13 a parallel b not parallel c parallel
14 a $x = 55$ b $x = 37$ c $x = 30$
15 30°, 60° and 90°
16 a $x = 100$ b $x = 42$ c $x = 47$ d $x = 104$
17 132°
18 a $x = 66$ b $x = 84$ c $x = 124$ d $x = 48$
19 48°
20 a 1080° b 1800°
21 23
22 $x = 135$
23 a 108° b 144°
24 165°
25 18
26 $x = 100$
27 72°
28 a 60° b 120°
30 90°
33 a $x = 72$ b $x = 54$ c $x = 81$ d $x = 60$
34 62°
35 $a = 101$, $b = 79$
36 27°
37 a $x = 6$ b 57 cm
38 a $x = 14$ b 90° c rectangle
39 a parallelogram b rhombus
c rhombus d rectangle
42 b 18 units
43 c 7 cm
45 c 14 m
46 a $x = 21$ b $x = 19$
47 11.2 m
48 a 25 m b 16.6 cm
49 a 48 m b 20.2 cm
50 a 10 m b 109 cm c 39.9 km d 38.1 m
51 a $\sqrt{17}$ m b $3\sqrt{2}$ units c $4\sqrt{3}$ cm
52 a right-angled b non right-angled
c right-angled d non right-angled
53 a 60 m^2 b 72 m^2 c 98 cm^2
54 a 216 m^2 b 210 m^2
55 a 48 cm^2 b 24 m^2
56 a 31.5 m^2 b 894.5 mm^2
57 a 112 cm^2 b 103 m^2
58 71°
60 b i 20 m ii 12 m iii 54 m^2

Linear Functions and Lines

1 a 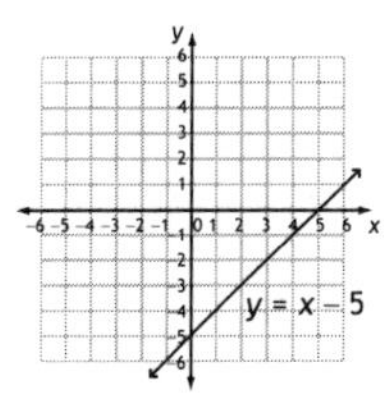

b 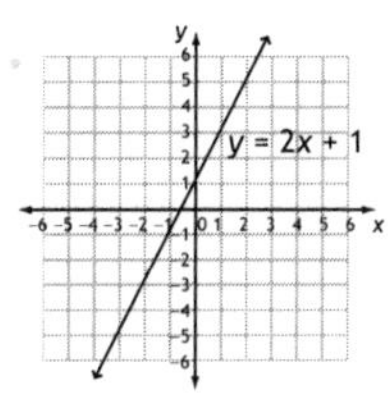

c 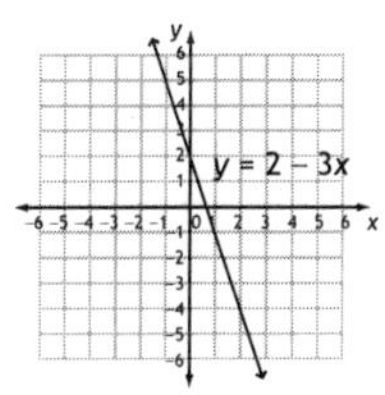

d 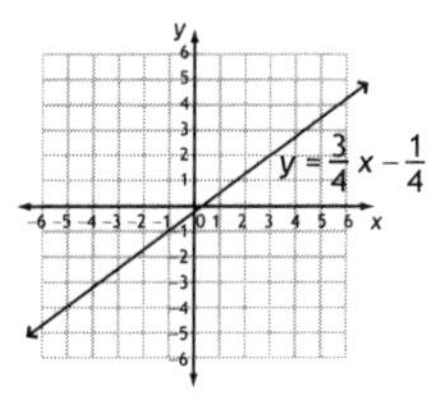

e
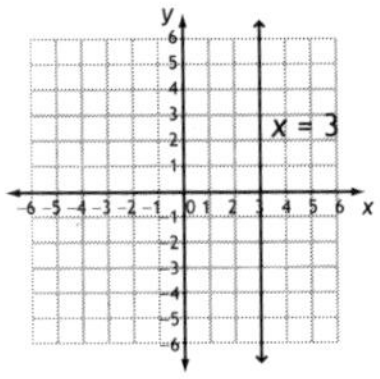

f
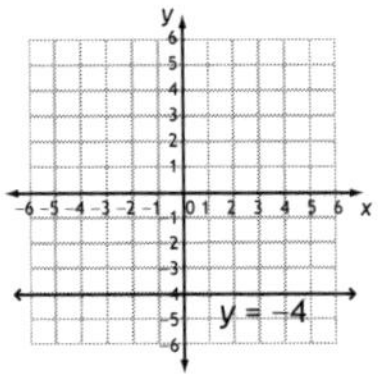

2 **a** gradient 7, y-intercept 3
b gradient −4, y-intercept −2
c gradient −5, y-intercept 6
d gradient $\frac{2}{3}$, y-intercept $-\frac{3}{5}$
e gradient 0, y-intercept −2
f gradient −1, y-intercept 0

3 **a** $y = 8x - 1$ **b** $y = x$ **c** $y = \frac{1}{4}x + 9$

4 **a** gradient 1, y-intercept 2
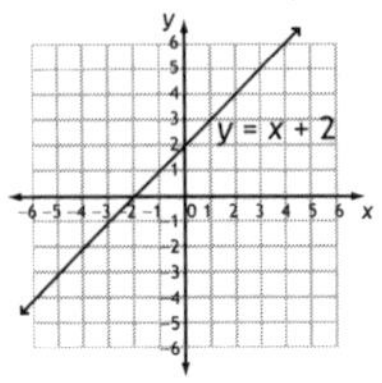

b gradient −2, y-intercept −1
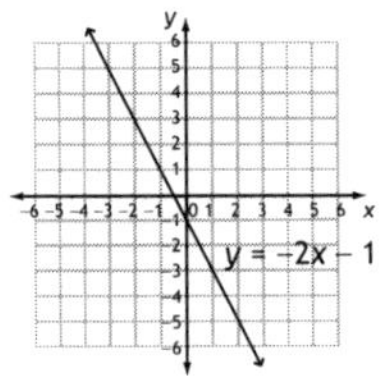

5 72°
6 $y = -x + 7$
7 **a** 4 **b** $-\frac{2}{3}$
8 2
9 **a** $y = 3x - 1$ **b** $y = 2x + 5$
c $y = -5x + 20$ **d** $y = \frac{3}{2}x + 3\frac{1}{2}$
10 (0, 14)
11 **a** $3x - y + 2 = 0$ **b** $2x + y + 5 = 0$
c $2x - 5y - 1 = 0$
12 **a** $y = -2x + 7$ **b** $y = \frac{3}{2}x + 3$
c $y = -\frac{1}{4}x + \frac{1}{2}$
13 **a** $4x + y - 12 = 0$ **b** $4x - 3y - 7 = 0$
14 **a** gradient $-\frac{3}{4}$, y-intercept 1
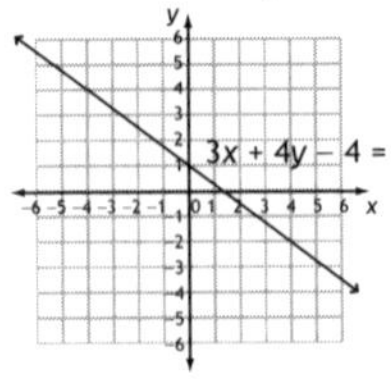

15 **a** $x - 2y - 1 = 0$ **b** $3x - 2y + 14 = 0$
c $y = 5x + 23$

16 **a** gradient $\frac{3}{2}$, y-intercept 4
b gradient $-\frac{1}{5}$, y-intercept $-\frac{2}{5}$
c gradient $-\frac{4}{3}$, y-intercept 0
17 67°
19 $x + 2y - 9 = 0$
20 $\frac{5}{2}$
22 $5x - 6y - 32 = 0$
23 (1, 0)
24 **a** (1, 4) **b** (−2, 8)
25 (2, −3)
27 $2x + y - 4 = 0$
28 **a**
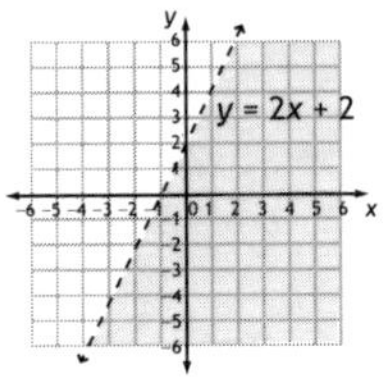

b
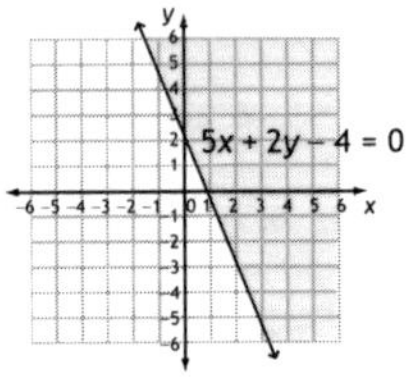

29 **a**
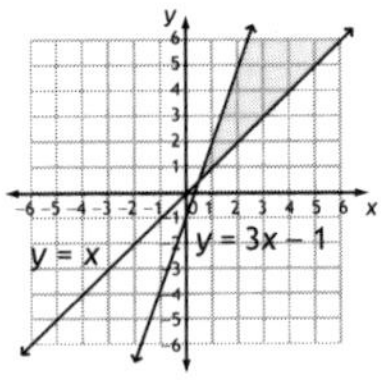

b
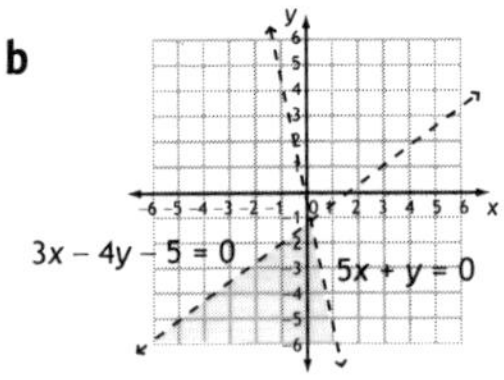

30 $5x - 2y + 12 > 0$, $2x - 9y - 28 < 0$, $8x + 5y - 30 < 0$
31 **a** 7 units **b** 13 units **c** $\sqrt{181}$ units
33 **a** 3.9 units **b** $\frac{9\sqrt{13}}{13}$ units
34 3 units
35 **a** (6, 4) **b** $\left(-2\frac{1}{2}, -3\right)$
35 (−12, 12)

Real Functions of a Real Variable

1 **a** 1 **b** −6
2 **a** −3 **b** 2 **c** −4 **d** −43
e $-3\frac{5}{8}$
3 **a** 19 **b** −7 **c** 2.5
4 0
5 $2x + h + 4$
6 **a** 2 **b** 22
7 $\frac{1}{2}$

9 **a** all real x **b** $x \neq -4$
c $x \leq -4$ or $x \geq 4$ **d** $x \neq -1$

10 **a** $3 \leq y \leq 13$ **b** $0 \leq y \leq 16$

11 **a** domain: all real x, range: $y \geq 3$
b domain: $x \neq 0$, range: $y \neq 0$

12 **a**

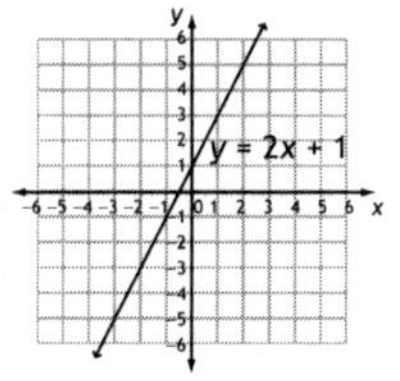

b

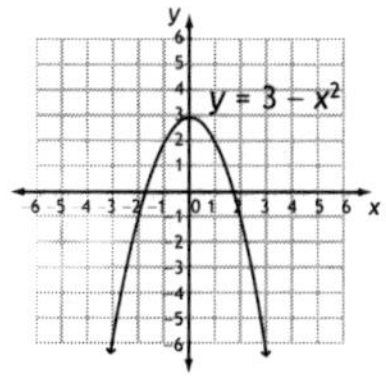

c

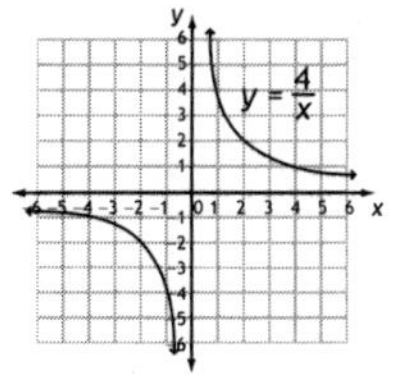

d

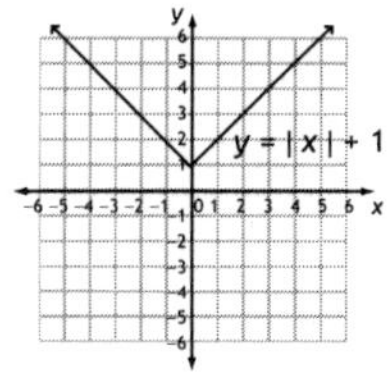

e

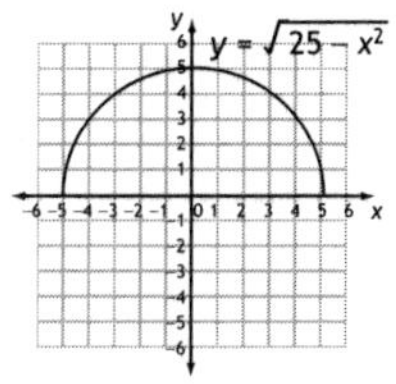

f

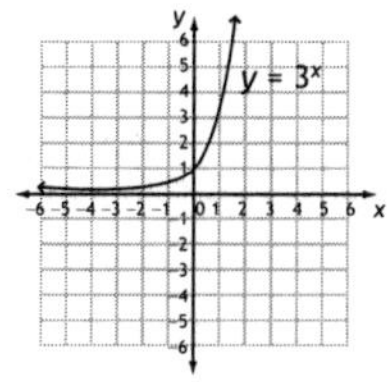

13 **a**

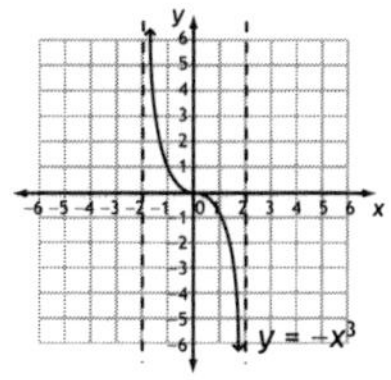

b

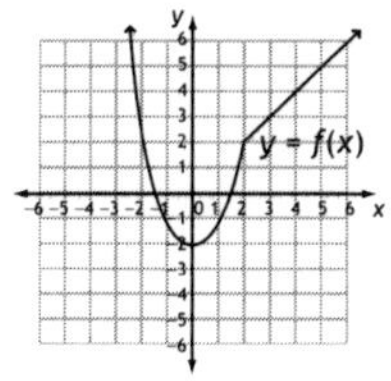

14 **a** even **b** neither **c** odd **d** even

15 **a** even

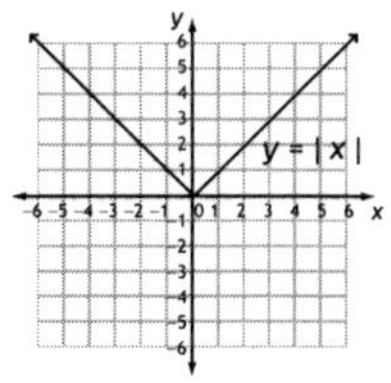

b neither

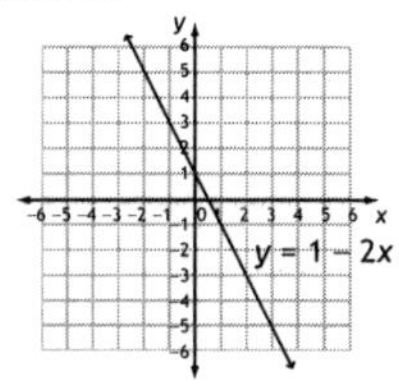

c odd

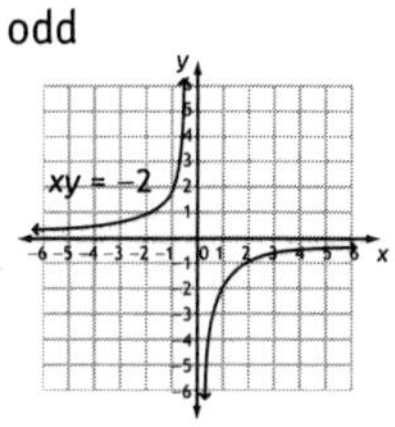

16 **a**

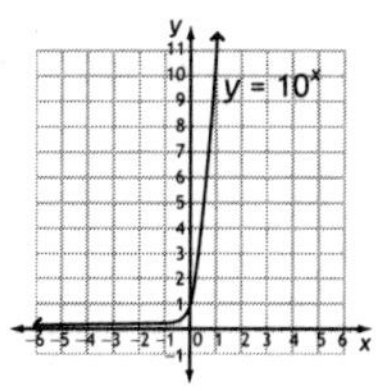

b

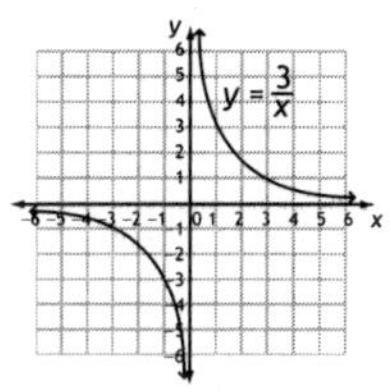

17 **a**

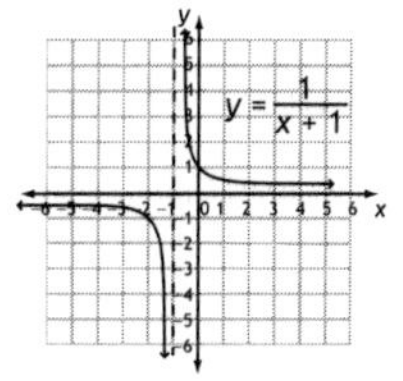

18 **a** $x^2 + y^2 = 49$ **b** $(x+2)^2 + (y+5)^2 = 1$

19 **a** centre (2, –4), radius 4 units
b centre (–3, 1), radius $2\sqrt{3}$ units

20 **a** centre (8, 4), radius 10 units
b centre (–11, 1), radius 9 units

21 $(x+2)^2 + (y-4)^2 = 17^2$

22 **a** centre (0, 0), radius 6 units

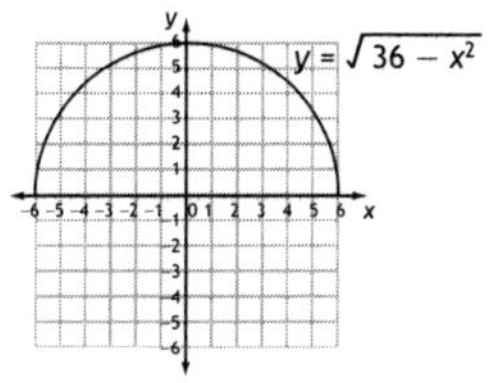

b centre (0, 0), radius 5 units

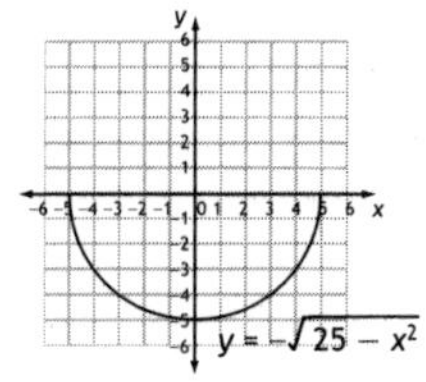

23 **a** centre (–1, 7), radius 2 units, domain: $-3 \leq x \leq 1$, range: $7 \leq y \leq 9$

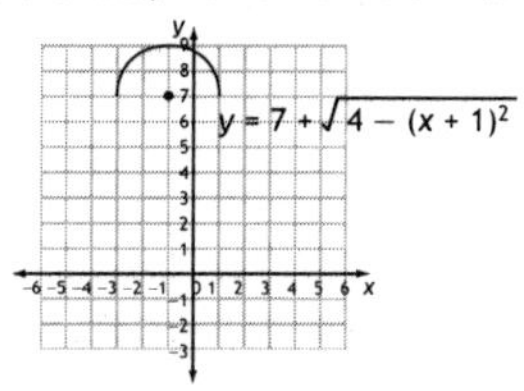

b centre (3, 2), radius 4 units, domain: $-1 \leq x \leq 7$, range: $-2 \leq y \leq 2$

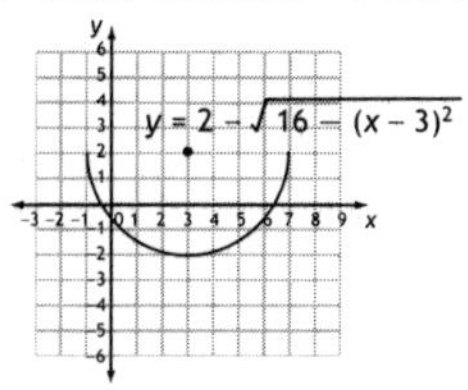

24 **a** circle, centre (1, –5), radius 4 units
b $(x-1)^2 + (y+5)^2 = 16$

25 **a** circle, centre (0, 0), radius 2 units

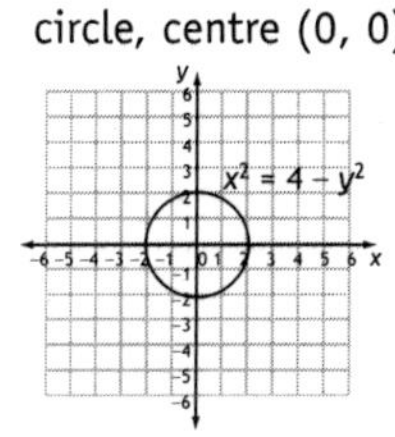

26 $2x - 5y + 5 = 0$

27 **a** $\dfrac{5-y}{1-x}$ **b** $\dfrac{-1-y}{9-x}$

c $x^2 - 10x + y^2 - 4y + 4 = 0$

d circle, centre (5, 2), radius 5 units

28 $y^2 = 20x$

29 $y = \dfrac{1}{8}\left(x^2 - 2x + 17\right)$

30 **a**

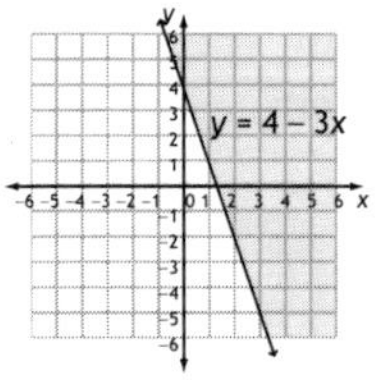

b

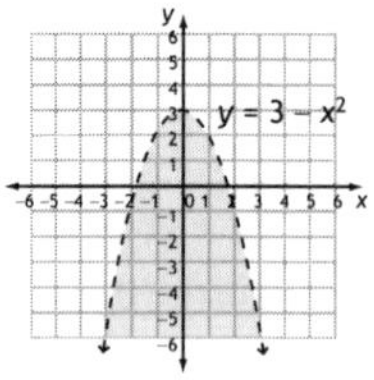

31

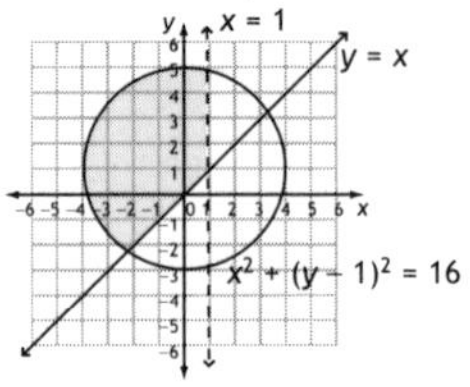

32 Boundary and interior of a circle of radius 3.5 units, to the right of the y-axis and below the line $y = 2$.

33 $x^2 + y^2 < 4,\ y > 0,\ x > 1$

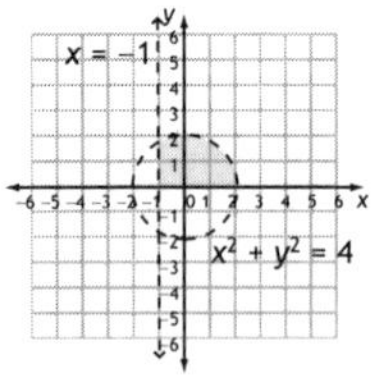

Trigonometric Ratios

1 **a** 2.94 **b** 5.43 **c** 5.77

2 **a** 309.0 mm **b** 14.2 m

3 **a** 50°12′ **b** 17°21′ **c** 35°17′

4 **a** 2.3662 **b** 1.0263 **c** 2.7475 **d** 1.1352
e 1.3301 **f** 0.0448

5 **a** 77°26′ **b** 76°38′ **c** 5°30′

6 **a** 0.8 **b** $1.\dot{3}$ **c** 1.25

7 **a** positive **b** negative **c** positive **d** negative
e negative

8 **a** 0.549 **b** −0.549 **c** −0.549 **d** −0.549

9 **a** −1 **b** −1 **c** 1 **d** −1
e 1

10 **a** 63°33′ or 116°27′ **b** 102°16′ or 257°44′
c 115°5′ or 295°5′

11 **a** 0.5 **b** −0.5 **c** −0.5

12 **a**

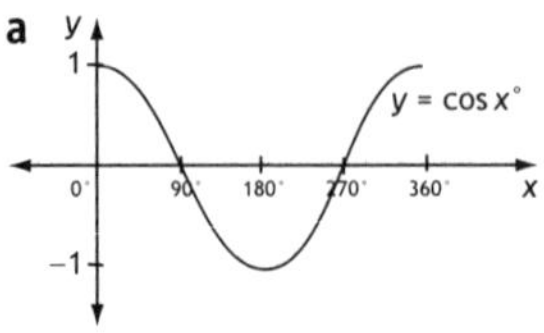

b

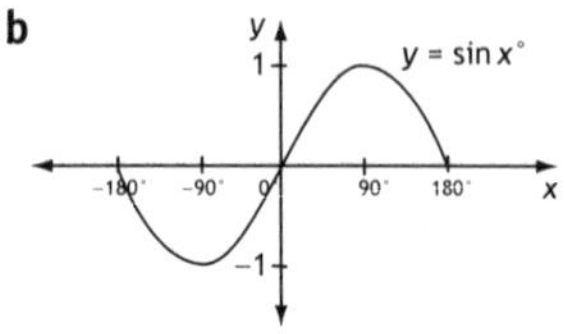

c

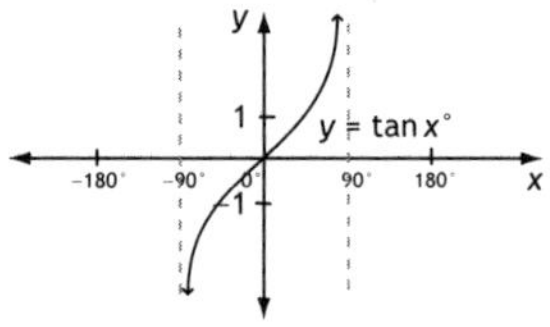

15 **a** $\dfrac{1}{2}$ **b** 1 **c** $-\dfrac{1}{2}$ **d** −1

e 0 **f** $-\dfrac{1}{\sqrt{3}}$ **g** $\dfrac{\sqrt{3}}{2}$ **h** $-\sqrt{3}$

i −1 **j** $\sqrt{3}$ **k** $-\dfrac{2}{\sqrt{3}}$

16 $\dfrac{4\sqrt{3}}{3}$ units

17 **a** $\left(2+\sqrt{3}\right)$ units

18 18°38′

19 **a** 36°52′ or 143°8′ **b** 0°, 180° or 360°
c 45°, 135°, 225° or 315°

20 **a** −150°, −30°, 30° or 150°

21 250°

22 16.8 km

23 2.3 km

24 50 m

25 32°

26 147 m

27 **a** 32.6 km **b** 5.5 cm

28 16 m

29 76° or 104°

30 27°27′

31 55.3 m

32 120 m

33 110°

34 123°14′

35 **a** 32.6 m² **b** 26.4 m²

36 43.3 cm²

37 **a** 41.1 m **b** 84.2 m

38 **a** 8.1 m **b** 6.9 m

39 **b** 16.9 cm

40 **b** 67.4 cm²

Quadratic Polynomial and the Parabola

1 **a** $x = 6$ or $x = 5$ **b** $y = -5$ or $y = -2$
c $h = 8$ or $h = -2$ **d** $a = -6$ or $a = 1$
e $w = -12$ or $w = 2$

2 **a** $x = -\dfrac{1}{3}$ or $x = 6$ **b** $z = 1\dfrac{1}{3}$ or $z = -3\dfrac{1}{2}$

3 **a** $x = -12$ or $x = 2$ **b** $x = 12 \pm \sqrt{7}$

c $x = -0.4$ or $x = 1.2$ **d** $x = \dfrac{-7 \pm \sqrt{2}}{2}$

4 $\left(x+4\right)^2+9=0,\ 9$

5 **a** $x = -2.25$ or $x = 2.5$ **b** $x=\dfrac{-11\pm\sqrt{37}}{6}$

c $x=3\pm\sqrt{7}$

7 **a** $x = 0.5$ or $x = 5$ **b** $x=\dfrac{-7\pm\sqrt{41}}{2}$

9 **a**

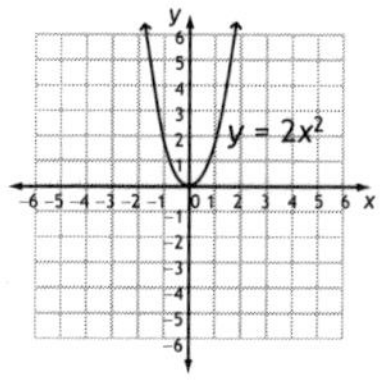

b

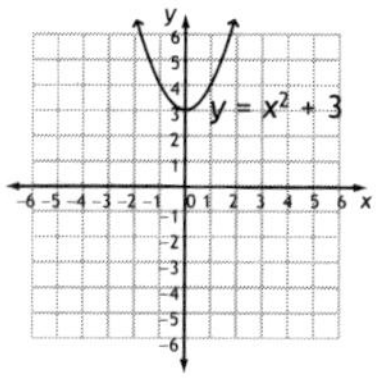

c

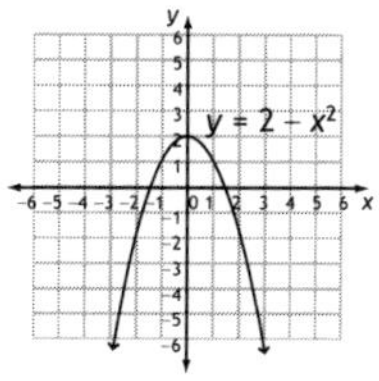

d

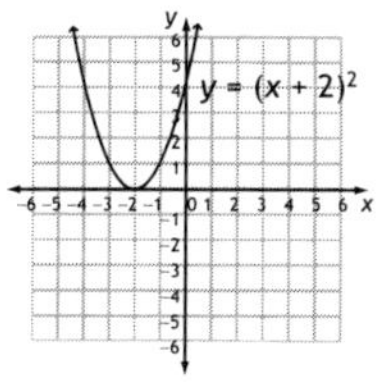

10 **a**

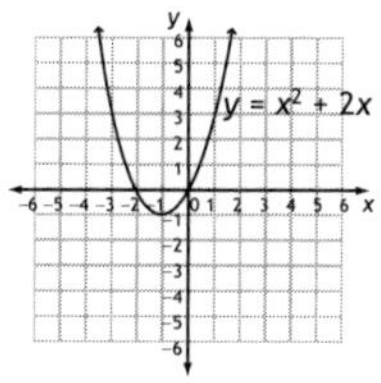

b

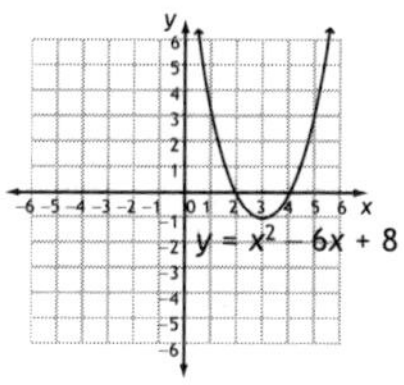

c

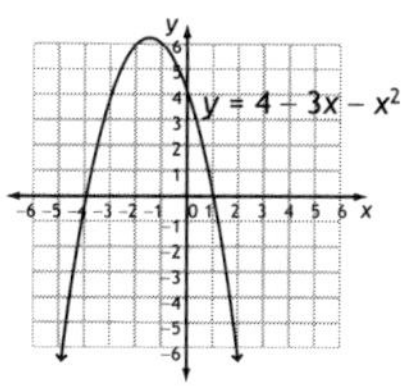

d

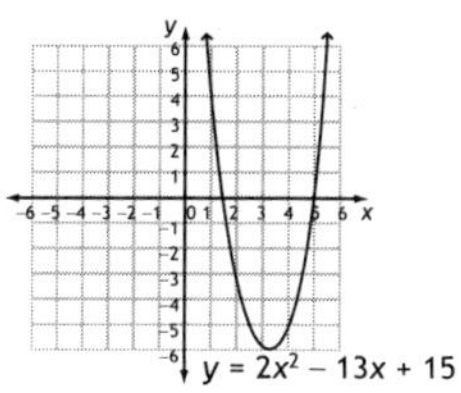

11 **a** $0 \le x \le 3$ **b** $x < -4$ or $x > 2$

c $x < -1$ or $x > 3$ **d** $x \le -3$ or $x \ge -\dfrac{2}{3}$

12 **a** -5.5 **b** 3 **c** 24.25 **d** $-1\dfrac{5}{6}$

e -16.5

13 $k = -8$ or $k = 8$

14 **a** axis: $x = 5$, least value: -16

b axis: $x = 1$, greatest value: -8

c axis: $x = 0.4$, least value: 10.2

15 **a** $(-2, -13)$ **b** $\left(-\dfrac{1}{3}, 10\dfrac{1}{3}\right)$

16 **a** $\Delta = 41$; roots are real, irrational and unequal

b $\Delta = -55$; roots are not real

c $\Delta = 0$; roots are real, rational and equal

d $\Delta = 576$; roots are real, rational and unequal

17 **a** $m \le 9$ **b** $m = \pm 12$

18 **a** indefinite **b** negative definite

c indefinite **d** positive definite

19 $-12 < k < 12$

20 **a** $x = -7$ or $x = 2$ **b** $x = -1.2$ or $x = 2$

21 **a** $x = \pm 5$ or $x = \pm 1$ **b** $x = 2$ or $x = -2$

c $x = 1$ or $x = 3$

d $x = 2$ or $x = 6$ or $x = -1$ or $x = 9$

22 $3x(x + 1) - 5x + 3$

23 $5x(x - 1) + (x - 1) - 6$

24 $Q\left(x\right)=3x^2-5x+5$

25 **a**

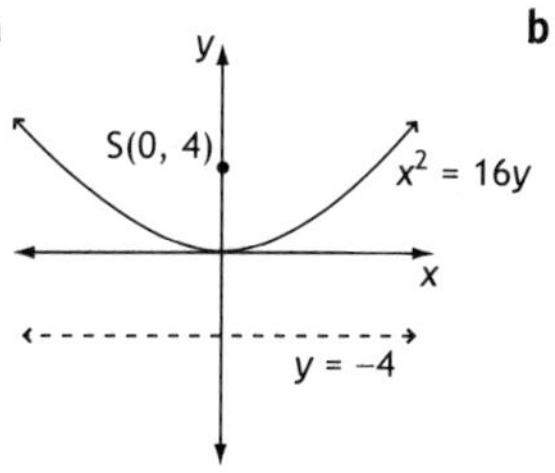

b

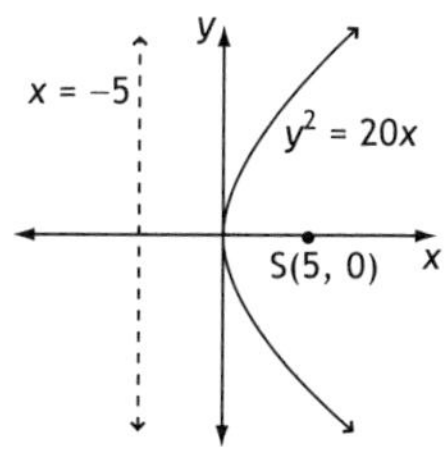

c

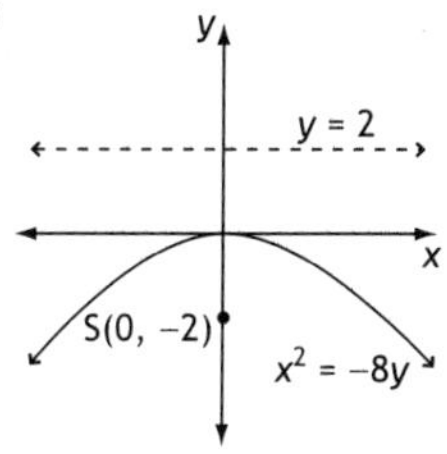

d

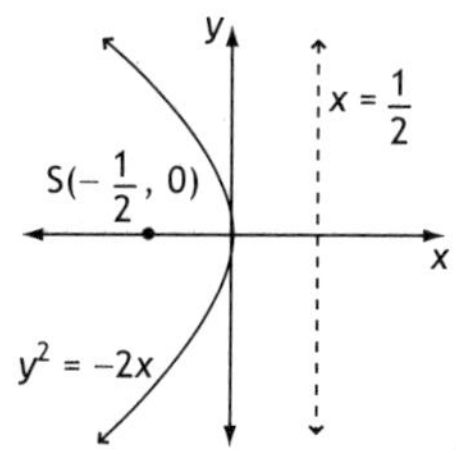

26 **a** vertex $(4, 2)$
axis: $x = 4$
focus $(4, 5)$
directrix: $y = -1$

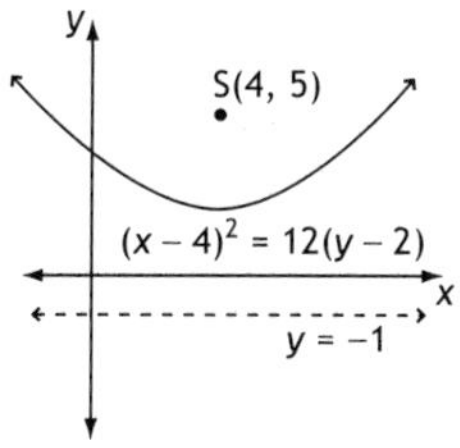

b vertex $(4, -6)$
axis: $y = -6$
focus $(3, -6)$
directrix: $x = 5$

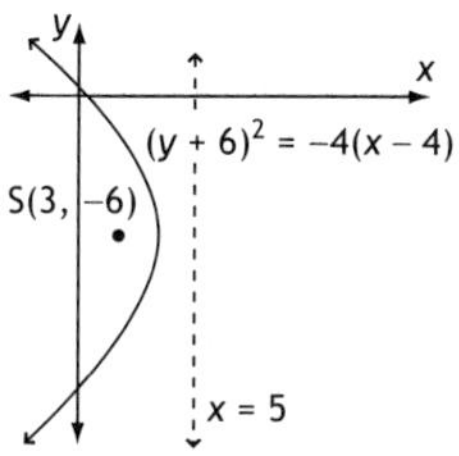

c vertex $(1, 0)$
axis: $y = 0$
focus $(5, 0)$
directrix: $x = -3$

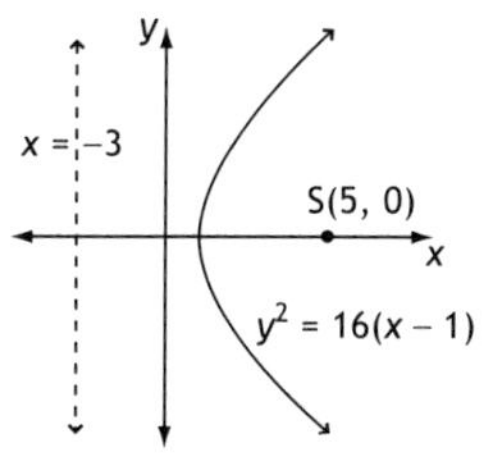

d vertex $(-3, -3)$
axis: $x = -3$
focus $(-3, -5)$
directrix: $y = -1$

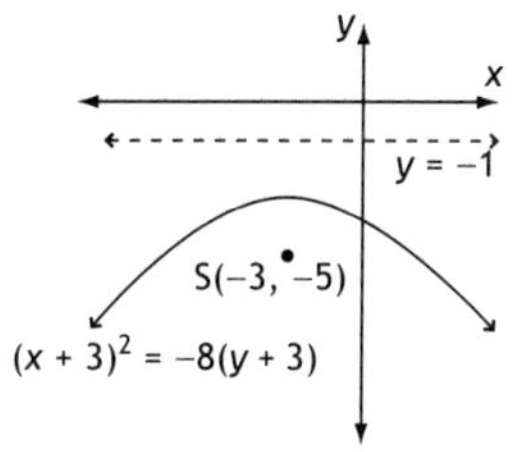

27 a $(x-2)^2 = y-3$ b $(x+1)^2 = -2(y-1)$

c $(x-5)^2 = \frac{1}{4}(y+3)$ d $(x+2)^2 = -\frac{1}{2}(y-17)$

28 a focus $\left(-5, \frac{1}{4}\right)$, directrix: $y = -\frac{1}{4}$

b focus (1, 3), directrix: $x = 0$

29 a $(x-2)^2 = 16(y-5)$ b $(x-6)^2 = -28(y-4)$

c $(y+2)^2 = -8(x-1)$ d $(x-1)^2 = 20y$

30 a $(x+1)^2 = \pm 9(y-3)$

b $y^2 = 12x$ or $y^2 = -12(x-6)$

Tangent to a Curve and the Derivative of a Function

1 a 7 b −8 c −2

2 a 8 b −16 c $\frac{2}{7}$

3 a 0 b −1

4 a continuous b discontinuous
c continuous d discontinuous

5 a not continuous b continuous
c continuous d continuous

6 a 2 b 7 c 1

7 −2

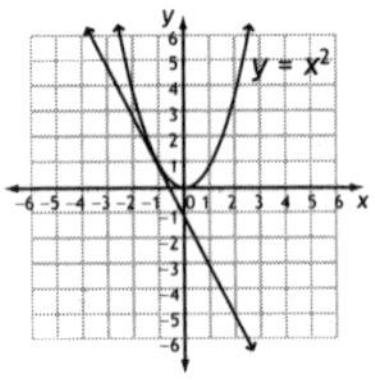

8 −2

9 a $y = 3x + 2$ b $y = 4x - 2$

10 a

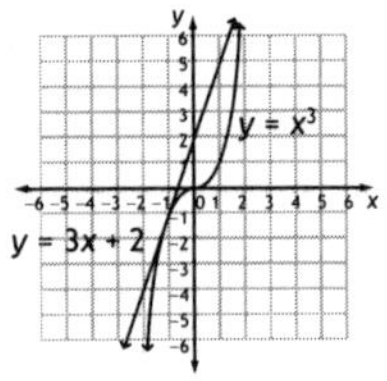

b

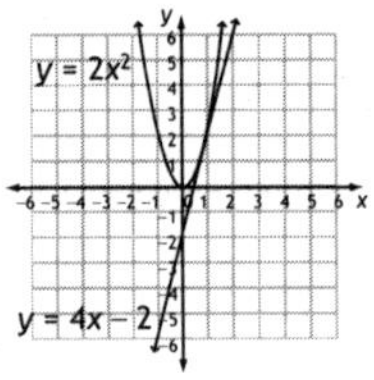

11 a 16 b 12 c 0

12 a −2 b −2 c −2

13 a 2x b $1 - 2x$ c $3x^2 + 1$

14 a $2x + 3$ b 9

15 a $-x$ b
c see solutions

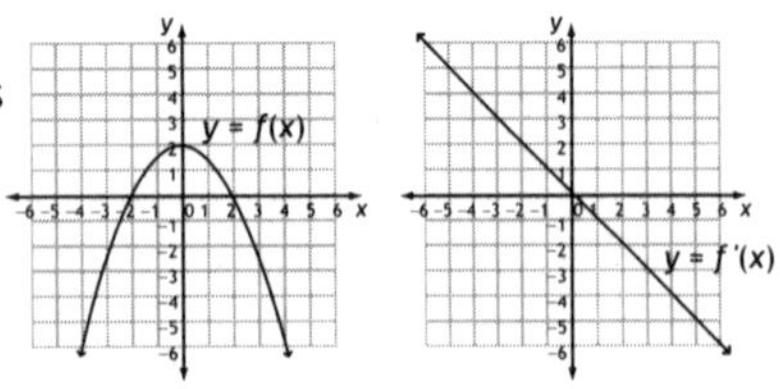

16 a 3 b $14x$

17 a $4x^3$ b $8x^7$ c $11x^{10}$ d $47x^{46}$

18 405

19 a $y = 2x - 1$ b

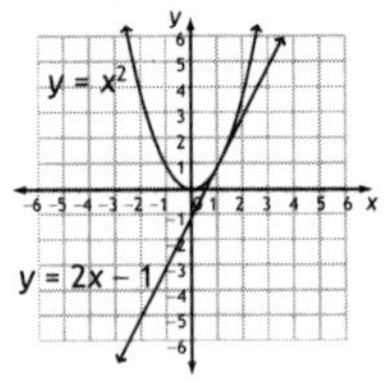

20 a 0 b 0 c 0 d 0

21 a $6x^5 + 4x^3$ b $7x^6 - 5x^4$
c $3x^2$ d $8x^7 - 2x + 1$
e $4x^3 - 3x^2$

22 a 3 b $4x$ c $-12x^3$ d $-6x^5$
e $108x^8$

23 a $8x + 5$ b $9x^2 - 4x + 1$
c $-5x^4 + 28x^3 - 6x^2$ d $16x^7 - 30x^9$
e $18x^5 - 10x^4 - 12x^3 + 15x^2 - 18x$

24 a $y = -x + \frac{3}{4}$ b $y = x - 1$

25 a $20x^9 - 3$ b $-3 - 4x$
c $27x^8 - 16x^7 + 49x^6$

26 a $12t^3 - 10t$ b $27t^2 + 12t - 1$

27 a $8q$ b $6v + 8$
c $-4m^3 + 15m^2 - 2$

28 a $14x - 1$ b $1 - 12t$
c $3u^2 + 10u - 7$

29 a $3y^2 + 2y$ b $8x^3 - 3x^2 + 10x + 5$
c $-20a^4 - 21a^2 + 9$

30 a $-3x^{-4}$ b $2x - 2x^{-3}$
c $12x^{-5}$ d $-8x^{-9} - 7$

31 a $-\frac{7}{x^8}$ b $-\frac{12}{x^7}$ c $-\frac{1}{x^2} + \frac{6}{x^3}$

32 a $1.3x^{0.3}$ b $5x^{1.5}$ c $\frac{2}{\sqrt{x}}$ d $\frac{1}{4\sqrt[4]{x^3}}$
e $\frac{7}{2}\sqrt{x^5}$

33 a $-0.7x^{-1.7}$ b $-\frac{1}{2\sqrt{x^3}} \left[= -\frac{1}{2x\sqrt{x}}\right]$
c $-\frac{4}{3\sqrt[3]{x^4}}$ d $\frac{5}{2}x\sqrt{x}$

34 $15(5x-1)^2$

35 a $4x^3 + 20x$ b $4x(x^2 + 5)$

36 **a** $12(4x+3)^2$ **b** $21x^2(x^3-5)^6$

c $4(2x+7)(x^2+7x-6)^3$

37 **a** $-\dfrac{x}{\sqrt{16-x^2}}$ **b** $-\dfrac{1}{4x^2}$

c $-\dfrac{10}{(2x+3)^6}$

38 **a** $3x^2-6x+4$ **b** $2x+5$

39 **a** $3x^2-6x+4$ **b** $2x+5$

40 **a** $3x^2-4x-6$

b $-6x^5-15x^4+20x^3+4x+6$

41 **a** $(x^2-1)^4(11x^2-1)$ **b** $x^2(5-4x)^3(-28x+15)$

c $(x-1)(x+2)^2(5x+1)$ **d** $(4x-1)^5\left(26\sqrt{x}-\dfrac{1}{2\sqrt{x}}\right)$

$-\dfrac{x}{2\sqrt{1-x}}+\sqrt{1-x}\ \left[=\dfrac{2-3x}{2\sqrt{1-x}}\right]$ **e**

42 **a** $-\dfrac{1}{3x^2}$ **b** $\dfrac{4}{(x+3)^2}$

43 **a** $\dfrac{-4x^3-10}{(x^3-5)^2}$ **b** $\dfrac{x^2+1}{x^2}$

44 **a** $\dfrac{(5x+3)^4(20x-3)}{x^2}$ **b** $\dfrac{-4x+5}{(x+1)^4}$

Quick Answers to Topic Tests & Sample Examination Papers

Topic Test 1 – Basic Arithmetic and Algebra

1 −4 **2** 1.4

3 5 − 8m **4** 20%

5 $\dfrac{11}{12}$ **6** $12+3\sqrt{11}$

7 $a=13\dfrac{1}{6}$ **8** $\dfrac{b^5}{a}$

9 62 **10** $\dfrac{m+3}{m+4}$

11 $x\le -9$ **12** $\dfrac{3\pm\sqrt{7}}{2}$

Topic Test 2 – Basic Arithmetic and Algebra

1 $1\dfrac{2}{3}$ **2** $3x^2-4x+2$

3 3.37×10^{-9} **4** \$3500

5 $(x+3)(x-3)(x-1)$ **6** $x=\dfrac{11}{13}$

7 $a=10$ **8** $0.\dot{0}\dot{9}$

9 $x=39,\ y=-12$ **10** $p=6,\ q=5$

11 $x\ge -13.5$ **12** $\dfrac{-1}{(e+2)(e+3)}$

Topic Test 3 – Plane Geometry

1 **a** $x=15$ **b** 60 m^2

2 **a** 120°

3 **c** 20 cm

Topic Test 4 – Plane Geometry

1 110° **2** **a** 1080° **b** 135°

3 **b** 36° **5** **b** 24 cm **c** 40 cm

Topic Test 5 – Linear Functions and Lines

1 **a** (0, 3) **b** $2x-5y-10=0$

c (5, 0) **d**

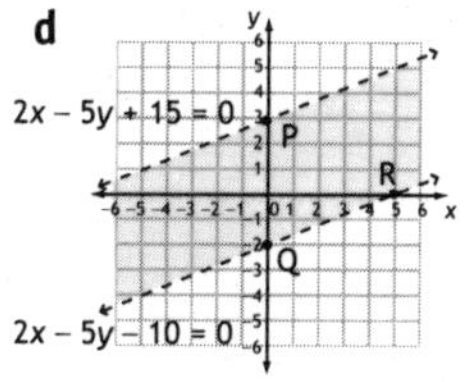

e $2x-5y+15>0$
$2x-5y-10<0$

2 **a** $a=3$ **b** (−9, 7) **c** $2x-3y-13=0$

d (−1, −5) **e** (−2, 3) **f** S(−3, 11)

Topic Test 6 – Linear Functions and Lines

1 **a** $2x-9y+39=0$ **b** (2, 1)

c $x+4y-6=0$ **d** (−6, 3)

2 **a** $x+2y-2=0$ **c** $3x+y+4=0$

d $2x-y-4<0$
$x+2y-2<0$
$3x+y+4>0$

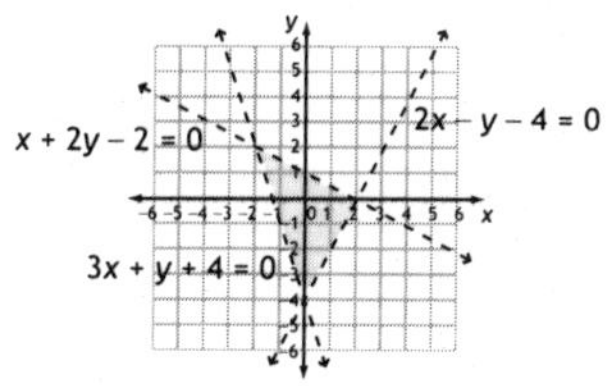

Topic Test 7 – Real Functions of a Real Variable

1 **a** $x \neq \frac{1}{2}$ **b** $y \neq 0$

2

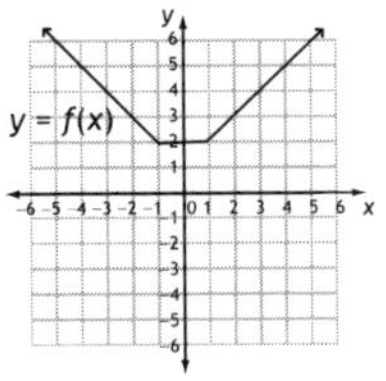

3 **a** $2hx + h^2 + h$ **b** $2x + h + 1$

4 **a** $2a - 2cx^2$ **b** even

5 **a**

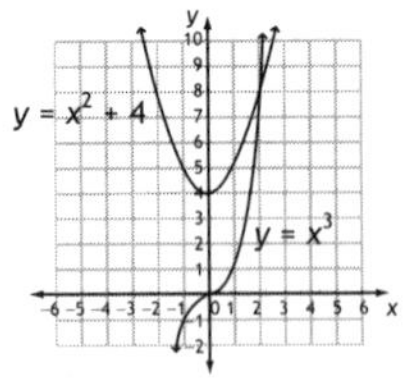

b $x = 2$

Topic Test 8 – Real Functions of a Real Variable

1 **a** domain: all real x, range: $y \geq 2$

b $x^2 - 10x + 27$

2 **a** 1 **b**

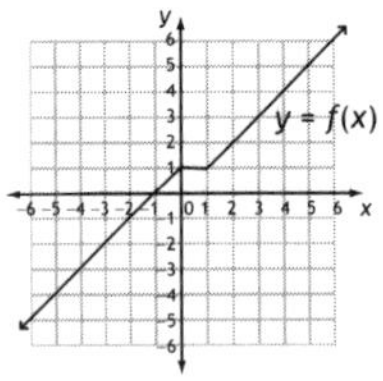

3

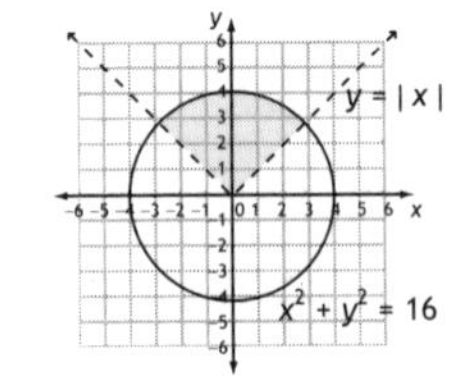

4 **a** $\sqrt{x^2 + (y-2)^2}$ **b** $|x+1|$

c $3x^2 + 8x - y^2 + 4y = 0$

5 **a**

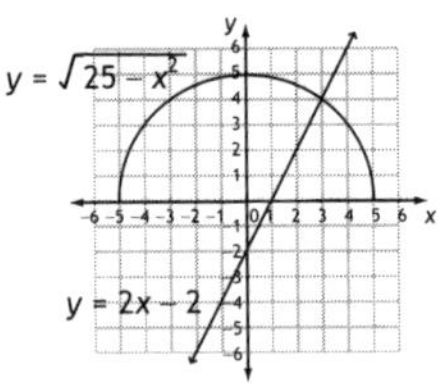

b $x = 3$

Topic Test 9 – Trigonometric Ratios

1 15.7 m

2 87°

3 $\frac{1}{\sin\theta}, \frac{\cos\theta}{\sin\theta}$

4 **a** 7 m **b** $\frac{15\sqrt{3}}{2}$ m^2

5 **a** $\frac{800\sin 64°}{\sin 45°}$ **b** 960 m

6 $\theta = 30°, 150°$ or $270°$

Topic Test 10 – Trigonometric Ratios

1 2.35 m **3** 49.5 m

4 $2\sqrt{2}$ cm **5** 135°

6 $\frac{4}{3}$ **7** **a** $\frac{301\sin 22°}{\sin 7°}$

b 118.5 m

Topic Test 11 – The Quadratic Polynomial and the Parabola

1 $-\frac{1}{12}$ **2** 6 units

3 $m < -1$ and $m > 1$ **4** $a = 1, b = -2$

5 all real m

6 **a** $(x-2)^2 = -8(y-2)$ **b**

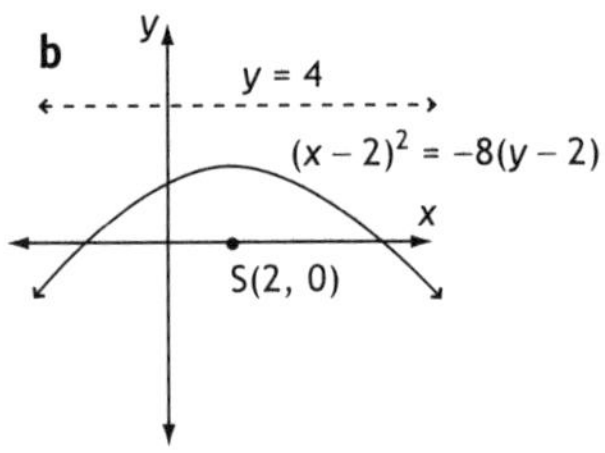

7 −1.5

Topic Test 12 – The Quadratic Polynomial and the Parabola

1 **a** (1, 0) **b** (1, 3) **2** $x = -8, -5, -2$ or 1

3 Crosses the x-axis **5** (−6, −9), (−2, −1)

6 **a**

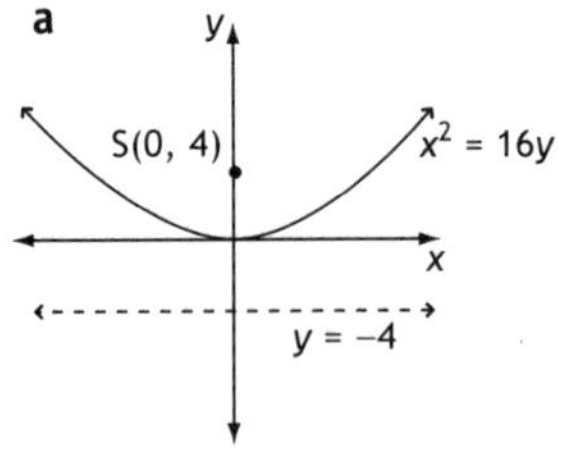

b $(y-4)^2 = 8(x+2)$

c (−4, −4)

Topic Test 13 – The Tangent to a Curve and the Derivative of a Function

1 175 **2** 4

3 **a** $2x - 6$ **b** (3, −4) **4** $y = x$

5 $-\frac{5(x^2+2)}{(x^2-2)^2}$

6 **a** $(1-x)^{-1}$ **b** $\frac{1}{(1-x)^2}$

7 $6x^2$

Topic Test 14 – The Tangent to a Curve and the Derivative of a Function

1 a $-\dfrac{15}{x^6}$ b $(7-4x)^8(7-40x)$

c $\dfrac{-4}{(2x-1)^2}$

2 2

3 continuous

4 a $y = 2x - 5$ b 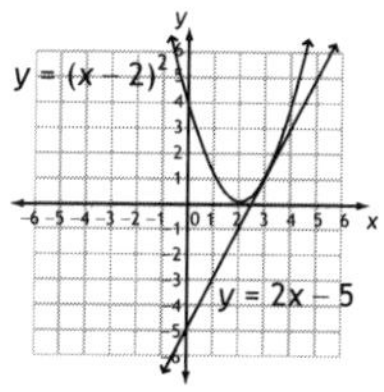

5 $2x + 8$

Sample Examination Paper One

1 a 2.756×10^8 b $x = -4$ or $x = 2$

c $7(m - 2)(m + 2)$

d i $\dfrac{-2x-23}{12}$ ii $x > -17.5$

e $a = -2$, $b = 20$ f $\dfrac{7}{11}$

2 b $(2, 6)$ c Q(−1, 0), R(14, 0)

d 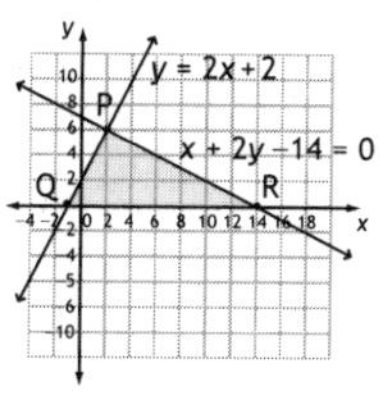

e $y < 2x + 2$, $x + 2y - 14 < 0$, $y > 0$

f 45 units^2

3 a $x = 3$

b i 79° ii 42°

c i 3 units ii (0, 0) iii (0, −3) iv $y = 3$

d i −5 ii $t = -1$ or $t = 5$

4 a i \$1296 ii \$20 304 iii 5.6%

b i $6 - 2x - h$ ii $6 - 2x$ iii 0

c i $x = -6 \pm \sqrt{p+36}$ ii $x = -23$ or $x = 11$

d $24\sqrt{3}$ m^2

5 a i $10x(x^2-2)^4$ ii $\dfrac{17}{(3x+4)^2}$

iii $(3x+1)^7(27x+1)$

b $x = 30°, 150°, 210°$ or $330°$

c 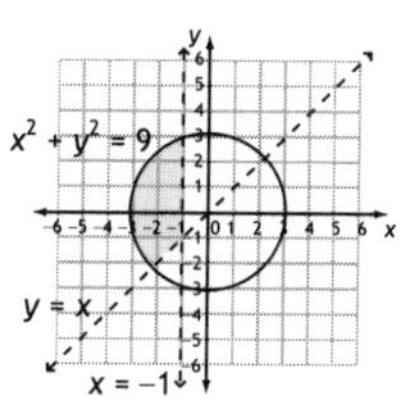

6 a i $x = 4.9 - h$ ii $h = 1.2$ iii 3.7 m

b not continuous

c ii $(\sqrt{5}+1)$ m

7 a −225

b i $a = 10$, $b = 2$ ii 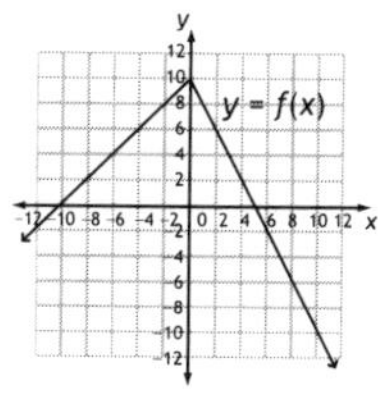

iii domain: all real x, range: $y \le 10$

c ii 30°

8 a 0, real, rational, equal

b ii $2\sqrt{13}$ m iii 90°

c i PA : $\dfrac{y-3}{x+2}$, PB : $\dfrac{y+3}{x-6}$

iii circle, centre (2, 0), radius 5 units

9 a $a = 3$, $b = -1$

b $y = -2x + 3$

c i (2, 2) ii $2x - y - 2 = 0$

10 a $\sin^2\theta$

b i (0, 1) ii (−2, 1), (2, 1)

c iii 60°

Sample Examination Paper Two

1 a 300 b $S = 124$

c 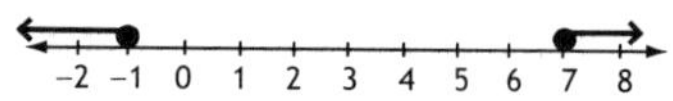 d 0.53

e $8a^2b$ f 2

2 a 3.6 cm b (−10, 0), (14, 0)

c i 63° iii $2x - y + 8 = 0$ iv $2\sqrt{5}$ units

3 a $(2-3x)^3(2-15x)$ b $x < 1.5$

c $10 - 6(1 + x) + 5x(1 + x)$

d i range: $-1 \le y \le 8$ 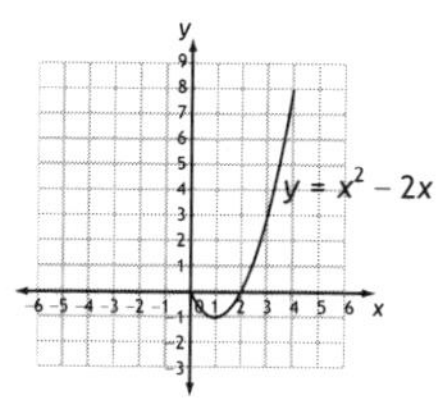

ii 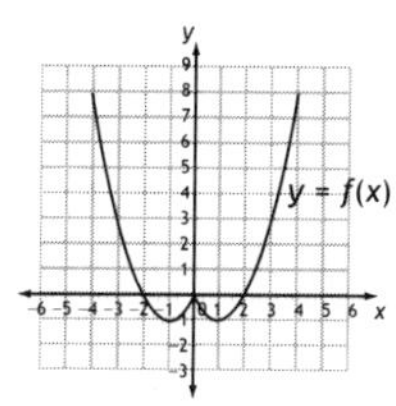

iii 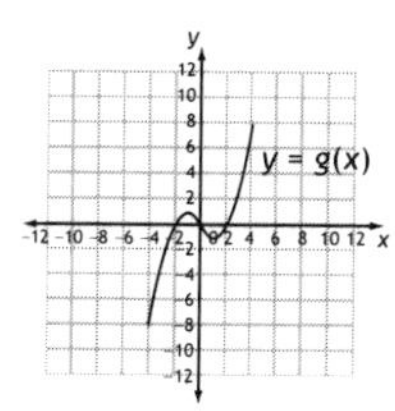

4 a $\dfrac{x-6}{x-2}$ b 1.035

c $y = 16x - 32$ d 5300 m

5 a $-\dfrac{1}{3}$ b 90°

c i PA^2: $(1-x)^2 + (-3-y)^2$, PB^2: $(7-x)^2 + (5-y)^2$

ii centre (4, 1), radius 5 units

6 **a** $\dfrac{1-u}{u(3-u)}$ **b** 1629 m

c **i** (2, −1) **ii** 2 units

d **i** $m = -5$ **ii** Yes, Δ is a perfect square.

7 **a** **ii** $2x - 3x^2$

b **i** P(−2, 2), Q(−1, 0) **iii** $2\sqrt{5}$ units

8 **a** −6

b **i** $x = 2$ **ii** (2, 3) **iii** no real roots

c **ii** 300 cm²

9 **a** **i** $x = -\dfrac{\sqrt{3}}{2}$ **ii** $-\dfrac{1}{\sqrt{3}}$

b **ii** 25 cm

c **i** $a = -1$, $b = 2$ **ii**

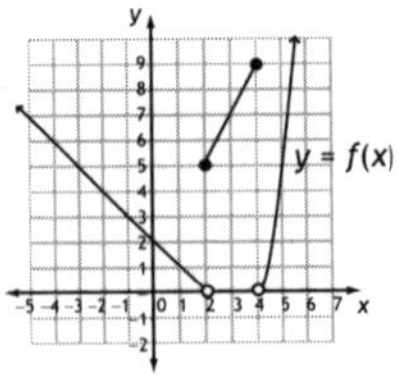

10 **a** $x = 11$

b $-4 \le x \le 1$

c **ii** θ = 30°, 150°, 210° or 330°

Sample Examination Paper Three

1 **a** 7.8×10^8 **b** $4x + 7$ **c** $1696

d $k = 1\frac{1}{8}$ **e** −24

2 **a** $21q^6 - 9q^8$ **b** $a = b = c = 0$ **c** $\dfrac{7x}{(x+3)(x+2)}$

d **i** $x + y - 5 = 0$ **ii** $7x + y - 107 = 0$

3 **a** 56° **b** **i**

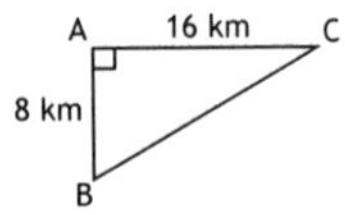

ii 243°

c **i**

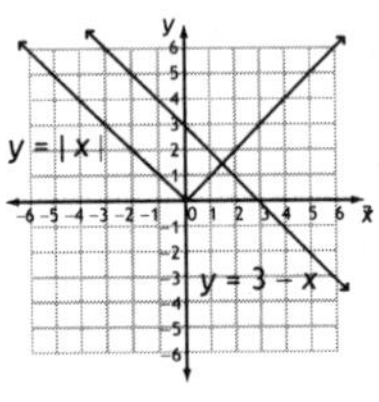

ii (1.5, 1.5)

d $(y-3)^2 = -12(x+1)$

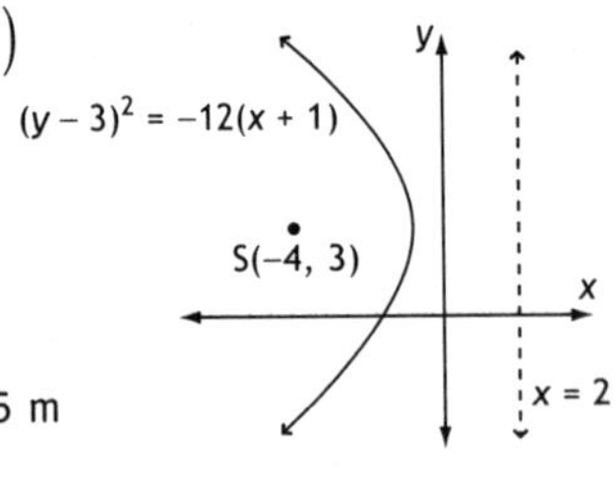

4 **a** $\dfrac{211}{990}$ **c** **ii** 135 m

5 **c** **ii** $4x^3$

6 **a** 0.021

b **i** $3x^2$

ii

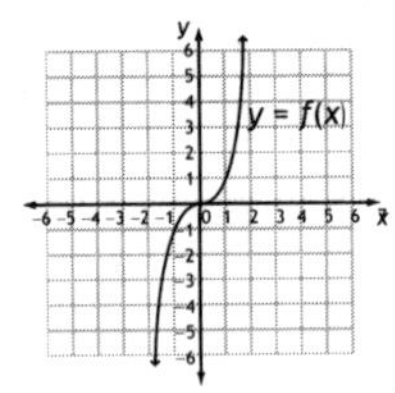

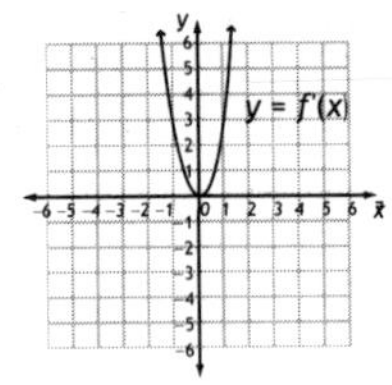

iii see worked solutions

c **i**

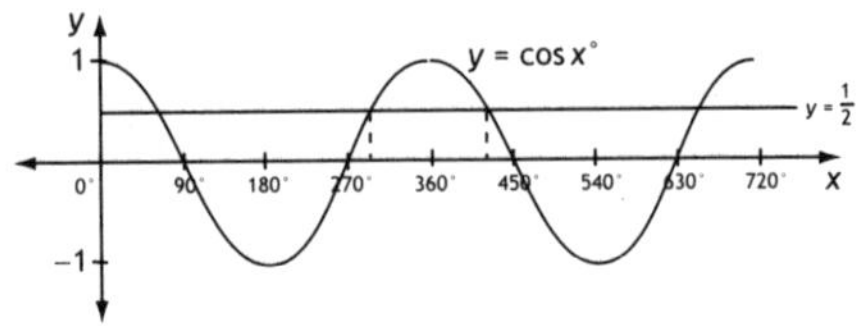

ii $x = 60°, 300°, 420°, 660°$

7 **a** $x = 1$ or $x = -0.6$

b **i** domain: $-2 \le x \le 2$, range: $0 \le y \le 2$

ii

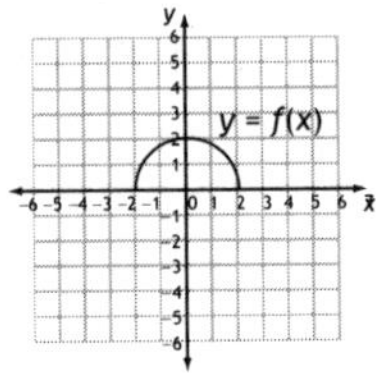

d (1, −4)

8 **a** **i** (2, −2.5) **ii** $y = -3.5$

b **iv** 150°

9 **a** $x = 120°$ or $300°$

b **i** $\sqrt{58}$ units **ii** $7x - 3y - 20 = 0$

iii $\dfrac{51\sqrt{58}}{58}$ units **iv** 25.5 units²

10 **a** **i** $-\dfrac{1}{x^2}$ **ii** $\dfrac{3\sqrt{x}}{2}$

b **i** $PQ^2: (1-x)^2 + (-2-y)^2$, $PR^2: (7-x)^2 + (4-y)^2$

ii $x + y - 5 = 0$, straight line

iii centre (9, 6), radius $4\sqrt{2}$ units

Index